D1226761

YESHUA

THE LIFE OF MESSIAH
FROM A MESSIANIC JEWISH
PERSPECTIVE

THE ABRIDGED VERSION

Other Books by Dr. Arnold G. Fruchtenbaum

The Sabbath

Jesus Was a Jew

A Passover Haggadah for Jewish Believers

Israelology: The Missing Link in Systematic Theology

Ha-Mashiach: The Messiah of the Hebrew Scriptures

*An Historical and Geographical Study Guide of Israel:
With a Supplement on Jordan*

The Historical and Geographical Maps of Israel and Surrounding Territories

God's Will & Man's Will: Predestination, Election, and Free Will

The Footsteps of the Messiah: A Study of the Sequence of Prophetic Events

*The Remnant of Israel: The History, Theology, and Philosophy of the Messianic Jewish
Community*

*Faith Alone: The Condition of our Salvation (An Exposition of the Book of Galatians
and Other Relevant Topics)*

Ariel's Harmony of the Gospels

Yeshua: The Life of Messiah from a Messianic Jewish Perspective, Volumes 1-4

Ariel's Bible Commentary Series:

The Messianic Jewish Epistles (Hebrews, James, I & II Peter, Jude)

Judges and Ruth

The Book of Genesis

Biblical Lovemaking: A Study of the Song of Solomon

Ariel's Come and See Series:

The Word of God: Its Nature and Content

What We Know About God: Theology Proper

Messiah Yeshua, Divine Redeemer: Christology from a Messianic Jewish Perspective

YESHUA

The Life of Messiah
from a Messianic Jewish
Perspective

The Abridged Version

Arnold G. Fruchtenbaum, Th.M., Ph.D.

Yeshua: The Life of Messiah from a Messianic Jewish Perspective,
The Abridged Version
Author: Arnold G. Fruchtenbaum, Th.M., Ph.D.
© 2017 by Ariel Ministries

ISBN 978-1-935174-72-1

Library of Congress Control Number:
2017948790

REL101000 RELIGION / Messianic Judaism / Yeshua / Jesus / Gospels

All rights reserved. No part of this publication may be reproduced, distributed, or transmitted in any form or by any means, including photocopying, recording, or other electronic or mechanical methods, without the prior written permission of the publisher, except in the case of brief quotations embodied in critical reviews and certain other noncommercial uses permitted by copyright law. For permission requests, write to the publisher at the address below.

All Scripture quotations, unless otherwise noted, are from the 1901 *American Standard Version* (Oak Harbor, WA: Logos Research Systems, Inc., 1994). However, the archaic language has been changed with one exception: The archaic *ye* has been retained in order to distinguish the second person plural from the singular *you*. The word "Christ" has been replaced with "Messiah," and all names have been transliterated from the Hebrew (see list on page xxvii).

Edited and formatted by Christiane Jurik, M.A.
Printed in the United States of America
Cover illustration by Jesse and Josh Gonzales (*http://www.vipgraphics.net*)

Published by Ariel Ministries
P.O. Box 792507
San Antonio, TX 78279-2507
www.ariel.org

THIS
VOLUME IS
DEDICATED
TO THE MESSIANIC COMMUNITY
AROUND THE WORLD, WHO IS
ALWAYS DESIRING TO LEARN MORE
ABOUT THE JEWISH
BACKGROUND OF NEW
TESTAMENT STUDIES. MANY
KNOW AND UNDERSTAND HOW
AND WHERE TO FIND IT, BUT MANY DO
NOT. MAY THE VOLUME BE A HELP AND
BENEFIT TO
ALL.

Contents

I. THE INTRODUCTION OF THE KING
— §§ 3–27 —

II. THE AUTHENTICATION OF THE KING
— §§ 28–57 —

III. THE CONTROVERSY OVER THE KING
— §§ 58–73 —

V. THE OPPOSITION TO THE KING
— §§ 99–112 —

VI. THE PREPARATION OF THE DISCIPLES BY THE KING
— §§ 113–131 —

VIII. THE PREPARATION FOR THE DEATH OF THE KING
— §§ 145–164 —

IX. THE TRIAL OF THE KING
— §§ 165–175 —

X. THE DEATH OF THE KING
— §§ 176–181 —

Foreword and Acknowledgements

It has taken about four decades of research and work for this account of the life and ministry of Yeshua the Messiah to come into its present form, published by Ariel Ministries in four volumes and the abridged version you hold in your hands now. This abridgment contains essentially the same material, but excludes many quotes by other authors as well as the rabbinic source texts of this teaching. It is geared to those who, for a variety of reasons, cannot take time to study, but are satisfied with the basic and essential content, which has been my teaching for many, many years. Those desiring the sources after reading the abridged volume will find them in the four-volume set.

Many different people were involved in putting all the information together that makes up this book. The ones mentioned below were those involved with the project from its inception, or specifically contributed to the publication of the final volume. Three women require special mention.

The first is Charmaine O'Neill, Ariel Ministries' first secretary during its initial Texas days, who typed up the rough draft of this work using a manual typewriter. The manuscript she produced became the foundation for the whole endeavor.

The second is Roxanne Tretheway, who served as my secretary while Ariel Ministries was based in California. She literally copied thousands of pages of my many sources and filed them away until my research period was over and it was time to put all the pieces together. She also oversaw our transition from typewriters to computers.

The third is Christiane Jurik, who became the ministry's editor-in-chief after its move back to Texas. She applied her editorial expertise to every page of this work and oversaw the final publication. Thanks to her German work ethic and her ability to encourage the team of copy-editors and proofreaders to finish their excellent work and meet their deadlines, she finally brought the volume(s) to completion.

The author also wishes to express his deep sense of gratitude and indebtedness to the following people who contributed to the successful publication of *Yeshua: The Life of Messiah from a Messianic Jewish Perspective*:

✿ Joni Bohannon and Nanette Keao, for coming alongside Christiane and superbly copyediting the text.

✿ The following proofreaders, who sacrificed their time and talent to find the last missing comma: first and foremost, Pauline Ilsen, our master-proofreader, the lady with the keen eye for punctuation and grammar; second, Laurie Combs, whose enthusiasm for the work inspired us to finish strong; third, Udaya Thangasamy, who meticulously checked each and every Scripture reference; and last but most certainly not least, Sue Kennedy, Eric and Mary Vear, Helen Mackie, Nigel Bates, Raye Lynn Snyder, and those who opted to stay unnamed.

✿ Jesse and Josh Gonzales, for designing the cover art and some of the graphs.

✿ Debra Riley, for providing the maps found in this book.

Without the contributions and support of these people, this book would not have been published.

Arnold G. Fruchtenbaum

Summer of 2017
San Antonio, TX

INDEX OF NAMES

Aharon = Aaron

Andrei = Andrew

Avraham = Abraham

Bar Abba = Barabbas

Bar Talmai = Bartholomew

Bartimai = Bartimaeus

Beit Anyah = Bethany

Beit Chesda = Bethesda

Beit Lechem = Bethlehem

Beit Pagei = Bethphage

Beit Tzaida = Bethsaida

Berechyah = Barachiah

Bnei Regesh = Boanerges

Chakeil D'ma = Akeldama

Chalphi = Alphaeus

Chanan = Annas

Kirenyah = Cyrene

Korazin = Chorazin

Dalmanuta = Dalmanutha

Didymos = Didymus

Einon = Aenon

Elazar = Lazarus

Elisheva = Elizabeth

Eliyahu = Elijah

Gavriel = Gabriel

Galil = Galilee

Gat Shemen = Gethsemane

Ginosar = Gennesaret

Golgota = Calvary

Hevel = Abel

Ish Kriyot = Iscariot

Kayapha = Caiaphas

Keipha = Cephas

Kfar Nachum = Capernaum

Kliyopas = Cleopas

Magdalit = Magdalene

Marta = Martha

Mattai = Matthew

Melech = Malchus

Miriam = Mary

Mosheh = Moses

Nakdimon = Nicodemus

Natzeret = Nazareth

Netanel = Nathanael

Noach = Noah

Ramatayim = Arimathaea

Sedom = Sodom

Shaleim = Salim

Shiloach = Siloam

Shimon = Simon

Shlomoh = Solomon

Shomron = Samaria

Shoshanah = Susanna

Taddai = Thaddaeus

Talyeta = Talitha

Timai = Timaeus

Toma = Thomas

Tverya = Tiberias

Tzarfat = Zarephath

Tzidon = Sidon

Tzion = Zion

Tzor = Tyre

Yaakov = Jacob, James

Yair = Jairus

Yarden = Jordan

Yehudah = Judea, Judah, Judas

Yericho = Jericho

Yerushalayim = Jerusalem

Yeshayahu = Isaiah

Yeshua = Jesus

Yirmeyahu = Jeremiah

Yishai = Jesse

Yisrael = Israel

Yitzchak = Isaac

Yochanah = Joanna

Yochanan = John

Yonah = Jonah

Yosei = Joses

Yoseph = Joseph

Zakkai = Zacchaeus

Zavdi = Zebedee

Zecharyah = Zechariah

Zvulun = Zebulun

PREFACE

A. Purpose and Importance

The purpose of this book is to trace the life of Yeshua the Messiah based on a harmonization of the four Gospels. The harmony used in this work is that of A. T. Robertson,[1] though there are changes to his order for reasons explained below. However, there is a more specific purpose of this work: to present the life of the Messiah from a Jewish perspective. More than a century ago, Alfred Edersheim wrote his classic, *The Life and Times of Jesus the Messiah*,[2] with the same purpose in mind. It is still in print but, unfortunately, seldom read. This work follows Edersheim's goal of putting the life of the Messiah into its Jewish frame of reference, though it will not always be along the same lines.[3]

---

[1] A. T. Robertson, *A Harmony of the Gospels* (New York: Harper & Row, Publishers, 1920).

[2] Alfred Edersheim, *The Life and Times of Jesus the Messiah* (Peabody, MA: Hendrickson Publishers, 1997).

[3] Edersheim wrote in the style of the 19th century, which was more circuitous, sentimental, and wordy than what will be presented here. Furthermore, this work

Generally speaking, in most Christian colleges and seminaries, only the Greek and Roman historical and cultural backgrounds of the New Testament are addressed in the courses of study. These backgrounds are valuable and necessary for the study of certain books of the Bible, such as the latter half of the book of Acts, Galatians, Colossians, I and II Corinthians, etc., because much of what is presented in those particular books is written from this frame of reference. However, it is very important to note that the life of Yeshua does not play itself out within the framework of Greek or Roman culture, but within Jewish culture—and a specific type of Jewish culture: that of first-century Israel. As a result, throughout the Gospels, words are said the way they are said, events happen the way they happen, and things are written the way they are written because of this specific Jewish frame of reference. Many of the situations, statements, and issues presented in these first four books of the *Brit Chadashah* (New Testament) were commonplace in the Jewish world of Yeshua's day.

Although knowledge of that Jewish frame of reference was always available, starting at around the fourth century (and in some cases earlier) the larger church chose to ignore it, resulting in a lot of theological confusion. In the course of history, church wars were fought, denominations were split, and new denominations developed over little phrases, such as "to be born of water." As this work will show, the phrase "to be born of water" has a specific Jewish meaning, but ignorance of this fact led to the false concept of baptismal regeneration and to a new denomination. This illustrates that a full understanding of the Gospels is not attainable without knowledge of the Jewish frame of reference. When the Gospel writers wrote their accounts, they used Jewish backgrounds, Jewish phraseology, and Jewish terms. They did not bother to explain what those terms meant because at the time the Gospels were written, they were commonly understood. However, much of that knowledge is not available to the general Christian public

---

uses the thematic approach to studying the Gospels, while Edersheim used the geographical approach (see pp. 5-6).

today. While many secular universities do provide a Jewish Studies department, they are virtually non-existent in Christian schools.[4]

Hence, this study is very important, not only for Jewish believers but also for Gentile believers. Many of the divisions in church history could have been avoided if the Jewish frame of reference had not been ignored.

B. Methodology

There are two basic ways of approaching a study of the life of the Messiah. The most common is the **geographical** approach, where Yeshua's life and ministry are categorized by geographic locations. A study based on this approach would first address the narratives of His birth and early life, then move on to His early Judean ministry, followed by the early Galilean, middle Judean, middle Galilean, Perean, and later Galilean ministry, hence categorizing the events by where He was when they occurred. The geographical approach would then end with the events of the final week of His life. In his *A Harmony of the Gospels*, A. T. Robertson uses the geographical approach,[5] as do most "Life of Christ" books. Though this is a legitimate approach to use in studying His life, there is one major drawback: It fails to show the correlation between events. This approach takes Yeshua's teachings, His actions, His miracles, etc., as a series of isolated, independent events until the last week of His life, when the atonement was made. There is no real correlation made between an event or teaching and the following event or teaching.

---

[4] Some notable exceptions are Moody Bible Institute and Cairn University on the collegiate level and Tyndale Seminary and Chafer Seminary on the seminary level. It would seem that dispensational seminaries would have a vested interest in establishing such departments, but, thus far, they have shown a lack of interest, though a dispensational theology lends itself to such a department of study. See this author's *Israelology: The Missing Link in Systematic Theology* (San Antonio, TX: Ariel Ministries, 1994).

[5] Robertson, *A Harmony of the Gospels*, pp. xi-xii.

The second way to study the life of the Messiah is to approach it **thematically**. The advantage of a thematic approach is that correlations can be seen between a teaching and an event, and vice versa. Therefore, this approach provides a better overall picture as to how things in the life of the Messiah were related to each other. The significance of details which may have seemed to be casually mentioned becomes clear.

This study follows a thematic approach. The basic theme being developed is Yeshua, the Messianic King. The Gospels record the coming of the King, the reactions to the King, the subsequent rejection of the King, the death and resurrection of the King, the departure of the King, and the promise of the return of the King. In this study, the issue of the kingship of Yeshua, His Messianic declarations, and His subsequent rejection will be very heavily interrelated with Pharisaic Judaism. While the harmony used in this study is based on that of A. T. Robertson, it will not use his outline. The outline used will follow a thematic approach.[6]

Based on the theme, Yeshua, the Messianic King, the life of the Messiah will be studied in eleven major divisions:

✿ **Part I. The Coming of the King:** This section concerns the birth narratives, infancy, baptism, and temptation. It marks God's official presentation of Yeshua as the Messianic King.

✿ **Part II. The Authentication of the King:** Yeshua begins to present Himself to Israel as the promised Messiah and authenticates Himself with miracles, signs, and wonders. This is the time when He goes from city to city and synagogue to synagogue, offering the messianic kingdom to Israel. To receive the messianic kingdom, Israel must accept Him as the Messianic King. During this period, He receives opposition from the Pharisees.

---

[6] This outline is largely based on one developed by J. Dwight Pentecost and handed out to his students at Dallas Theological Seminary in his "Life of Christ" course. The same outline, with some adjustments and changes, was later incorporated into his book, *The Words and Works of Jesus* (Grand Rapids, MI: The Zondervan Corporation, 1981). This study uses the same basic outline, but there will be a number of modifications.

✣ **Part III. The Controversy over the King:** In this section, the leadership of Israel officially rejects Him, largely due to His repudiation of Pharisaic Judaism. In response to this rejection, there is a radical change in the nature of His ministry.

✣ **Part IV. The Training of the Twelve by the King:** Following His rejection, He works primarily with His disciples, training them for their mission—a mission they will perform later in the book of Acts.

✣ **Part V. The Opposition to the King:** Whereas earlier the opposition came only from the leaders, now it also comes from the common people. In this section, the people begin to follow the leaders, rejecting His Messiahship and the authenticating miracles, signs, and wonders.

✣ **Part VI. The Preparation of the Disciples by the King:** This section covers the final period of His public ministry, and there is a special focus on preparing the disciples for their future work, described in the book of Acts.

✣ **Part VII. The Official Presentation of the King:** This section actually closes His public ministry. It begins with His triumphant ride into Jerusalem and final conflict with the Pharisees and closes with His lengthy denunciation of the spiritual leaders of Israel for leading the nation to reject Him. He also lays down the precondition for His return and the setting up of the messianic kingdom.

✣ **Part VIII. The Preparation for the Death of the King:** This section begins with the Olivet Discourse, which contains prophecies of the coming destruction of Jerusalem and the Temple and His second coming. This is followed by His last Passover and the Upper Room Discourse and concludes with the agony of Gethsemane.

✣ **Part IX. The Trial of the Messiah:** Here the rejection of the Messiah is carried out.

✣ **Part X. The Death of the King:** The events surrounding the death of the Messiah are detailed here in chronological sequence.

✡ **Part XI. The Resurrection and the Ascension of the King:** This marks the period of the final training of the apostles and the ascension of the Messiah to heaven. It concludes with a promise of His return.

✡ **Part XII. The Sequels:** The remainder of the New Testament records occurrences in Jerusalem, Judea, Samaria, and the surrounding Gentile world in the immediate decades after Yeshua's ascension. This concluding section will look at the New Testament development of several issues that originated in the Gospels.

C. Translation

The basic translation used in this work is the American Standard Version of 1901. However, the archaic language (e.g., *thee, thou, hast, wast,* etc.) has been modernized. One exception is the pronoun *you.* In modern English, the word is used as both the singular and plural second person pronoun. Therefore, to more accurately translate the original Greek text, the archaic second person plural pronoun *ye* has been retained in the Scripture quotations.

The reader will find the names of persons and places transliterated in accordance with Hebrew pronunciation. In the commentary, the English names will appear, but certain names will also be transliterated: Jesus will appear as *Yeshua,* John as *Yochanan,* and Mary as *Miriam.*[7]

---

[7] While the name *Yochanan* will be used for both the apostle and the baptizer, the books the apostle wrote will still be referred to by their English titles.

INTRODUCTORY MATERIAL
— §§ 1-2 —

[§ 1] — A. Luke's Prologue:
The Sources of Knowledge

Luke 1:1-4

If the life of the Messiah could be encompassed by a circle, the circle would contain everything Yeshua ever said and did, from individual incidents and teachings to every aspect of His entire life. When each one of the four Gospel writers was inspired by the Holy Spirit to write an account of the life of the Messiah, none was able to include everything Yeshua said and did. Yochanan the apostle admitted this at the end of his Gospel (Jn. 21:25). He wrote that what he had recorded was only a small part of that to which he was an eyewitness; otherwise, his task would have been impossible, for no one would be able to record everything that Yeshua said and did. Each of the Gospel writers had to be selective about what he recorded and what he chose not to record. The criterion each one used to decide what he would pull out of the circle and record was based on the specific theme he wanted to develop. For example, when Matthew chose to write his account of the life of the

Messiah, he knew that he could not write down everything that Yeshua had said and done. Therefore, he chose a specific theme and picked out incidents and teachings that illustrated that theme. Incidents not related to it he ignored. Mark also wanted to write an account of the life of the Messiah, but he chose a different theme, so he ignored some of the incidents that Matthew recorded. Other incidents were recorded by both Matthew and Mark, but were written from different perspectives because each had a different theme. The two other Gospel authors did the same. Some incidents and teachings, therefore, may not have been recorded by any of the evangelists. A few were recorded by all four, but when they did record the same event, the way they chose to word it differed, depending upon how the event was related to their own theme.

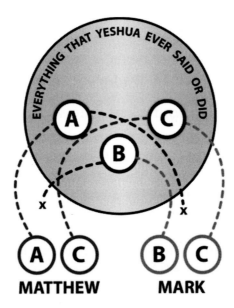

Therefore, the Gospels are in fact complementary to each other, not contradictory. The differences in how an event was recorded, the details that were given, were generally based upon the purpose of the author and the theme he chose to develop. If Matthew looked into the aforementioned circle and saw event A and it was an event that fit his theme, he chose to record it. When he looked at event B and it did nothing for his theme, he ignored it. When he looked at event C and it connected well with his theme, he recorded it. When Mark looked into the same circle, he also saw event A. However, because it did not illustrate his theme, he ignored it. Event B, on the other hand, worked for him, and so he chose to record it while Matthew left it out. Event C helped Matthew, and it also helped Mark, and therefore, in this instance, they both recorded the same event. However, if there are differences in the way Mark recorded an event as compared to the way Matthew chose to record it, it does not mean the Gospel writers contradicted each other. They merely had different themes in mind when they wrote their accounts, and what each chose to write down about any particular event had to fit into the theme of his Gospel.

1. The Gospel of Matthew:
Yeshua the Messiah, the King of the Jews

Each Gospel writer tried to meet a specific need. Naturally, since the first believers were Jews, the need would have originally arisen among them. Initially, Jewish believers stayed together under the direct authority of the apostles, who had been eyewitnesses to all that Yeshua said and taught. If a person had a question, such as, "What did the Messiah say about this" or "What did the Messiah say about that?", he could go to an apostle, ask the question, and get the answer. That all changed after the events described in Acts 7. As a result of the persecution that followed the stoning of Stephen, the messianic community of Jerusalem was scattered throughout the Middle East. There was no longer one central, unified body of believers under the direct authority of the apostles. While the apostles stayed in Jerusalem, many in the messianic community went to areas outside the land, such as Antioch. Now that the Jewish believers were dispersed and they were no longer under the direct influence of the apostles, they needed an authoritative source to which they could refer as they proclaimed Yeshua as the Messiah, the King of the Jews. To meet that need, Matthew wrote his Gospel and made heavy use of messianic prophecy to show that this man, Yeshua of Nazareth, fulfilled all those prophecies that predicted the coming of the Messiah.

The purpose of Matthew's Gospel was to show that this Yeshua really was the Messianic Davidic King. This raised the same question among the Jewish people then, as it does among Jewish unbelievers to this day: If He were the Messiah, where is the kingdom? Where is the world peace Messiah was supposed to inaugurate? In writing his Gospel, Matthew explained why, even though Yeshua was the Messianic King, He did not set up His kingdom. Matthew explained more about God's kingdom program than the other Gospel writers did because a key question for the Jewish mind is, "Where is that kingdom?" Matthew showed that although the messianic kingdom was not set up (for reasons he explains in chapters 12-13), this One was still that Messianic King.

Another important aspect of Matthew's Gospel is that it is written in light of impending judgment. Jeremiah, too, prophesied in light of impending judgment—the judgment of the coming Babylonian destruction of the city of Jerusalem and the First Temple. Matthew writes in light of the coming Roman destruction of Jerusalem and the Second Temple. Because the King had been rejected and the unpardonable sin had been committed, Jerusalem was now under the judgment of coming destruction. The Jewish believers would have to respond in a specific way when that judgment came, and this Gospel is written to prepare them to deal with that issue.

2. The Gospel of Mark:
Yeshua the Messiah, the Servant of Jehovah

While Matthew wrote for the Jews, Mark wrote for the Romans. In the culture of that day and in the context of the Roman Empire, their main interest was action; they were far more interested in action than in teaching. So, Mark was far more interested in recording the deeds of the Messiah than what He taught. The ideal Roman was someone who could receive a commission, carry it out, and come back as quickly as possible to report that the mission had been accomplished. Mark presents the Messiah as a man of action. He pictures Him as someone who has received a commission and who is eager to carry it out. In the Gospel of Mark, there is the rapidity of action, a sense of urgency, a sense of immediacy, a sense of getting the job done. Over forty times Mark uses the Greek word *eutheos* or *euthus*, translated three different ways in the English Bible as "immediately," "straightaway," or "forthwith." Since Mark wrote for Romans, he emphasized the immediacy of obedient action on the part of Yeshua.

Although Mark pictured the Messiah in a context that would communicate to his Roman audience, he did not forget his own Jewish frame of reference. He used a theme developed by Isaiah the prophet as the background to his Gospel. The prophet's favorite title for the Messiah was *the Servant of Jehovah*, who was sent by God to accomplish a certain mission. Mark portrays Yeshua as this ideal servant of the only true God. He had a commission to carry out, and He "straightaway," "forthwith," and "immediately" fulfilled His tasks. Mark's intention was to show that Yeshua of Nazareth fulfilled what Isaiah said about *the Servant of Jehovah*.

3. The Gospel of Luke:
Yeshua the Messiah, the Son of Man

Luke wrote his Gospel to emphasize the humanity of the Messiah. While Matthew wrote to the Jews and Mark to the Romans, Luke wrote to the Greeks. The Greeks had two major areas of interest. The first area was their concept of the ideal man. This would be someone who was self-disciplined, fit, and agile in both mind and body. The Greeks revered philosophy and philosophers such as Socrates and Aristotle, and they revered athletes and athletic pursuits such as the Olympian and Isthmian Games. Luke presents Yeshua as such a person, One who had full control over His thoughts and His body. As to the humanity of the Messiah, it is Luke who tells us how He developed from His youth. More so than the other Gospel writers, he notes that Yeshua was hungry, thirsty, tired, etc. It is man that needs to eat, drink, and sleep, not deity, for God never gets hungry, thirsty, or tired: *Behold, he that keeps Yisrael will neither slumber nor sleep* (Ps. 121:4).

The second major area of interest to the Greeks was historical accuracy. Many of the earliest histories come from Grecian records. For instance, much of what is known of ancient Egypt stems from these sources. It is this second area of Greek concern, historical accuracy, which explains why Luke chose to write his own Gospel the way he did. In the first two verses, he admits that other narratives were already available. And, indeed, the Gospels of Matthew and Mark were already in circulation. Like the Gospel of John, they were written by eyewitnesses of Messiah's life. Luke, on the other hand, became a believer through Paul's ministry after Yeshua had lived, died, risen from the dead, and ascended into heaven. So why did he feel the need to write an account of his own when he himself had not witnessed the life of the Messiah? The answer is in verse 3 of Luke 1: *it seemed good to me also, having traced the course of all things accurately from the first, to write unto you in order, most excellent Theophilus.* The Greek word for *in order* is *kathexeis,* which means "one after another," "successively," and "in order." The NASB correctly translates this term as *consecutive order.* This shows Luke's motivation. He wanted to communicate the Messiah's life in a way that would appeal to the Greek mindset. For the Greeks, an accurate, chronological history would verify a claim. Matthew, Mark, and Yochanan the apostle were not concerned with the strict chronological sequence, so they organized the events of the life of Yeshua according to their themes. Luke, on the other hand, was concerned with the chronological sequence of events, and thus, this study will always follow his order for one simple reason: He alone stated that he had put his material in chronological sequence.

Not having been an eyewitness of the Messiah's life himself, Luke needed access to people who had walked with Yeshua personally (Lk. 1:2). He was in the area of Jerusalem for two years while Paul was imprisoned in Caesarea, and this was the time when he would have had access to these eyewitnesses. Matthew and Mark would have been available to tell him of their experiences with Yeshua, and Luke obviously spoke with Miriam, the mother of Yeshua, as he revealed her actual thoughts, things she had kept *in her heart* (Lk. 2:19, 51). How would Luke have known her inward, secret thoughts, unless he had actually talked with her? Luke says the accounts of the eyewitnesses were "delivered to us," from the Greek word *paredosan,* referring to something that was "handed down." This was normally a Jewish term for something handed down by tradition.

As mentioned before, Luke wrote his Gospel for one specific person: Theophilus. Some take the name to refer to a group or body of believers, but there is no reason to take it as anything other than the name of an individual. Beyond his name, nothing more is known of Theophilus. It is not clear whether he was a Jew or a Gentile. It is also unclear whether he was an interested unbeliever, an unsure believer looking for verification of the facts he had heard about, or a strong believer looking for written verification of all that he had received orally.

Luke had three special concerns. His first concern was Jerusalem. He revealed what Yeshua said and did in this city, and he taught things about Jerusalem that the other three Gospel writers left out. While in the book of Acts, the movement is from Jerusalem to the uttermost parts of the world, in Luke, the story begins and ends in Jerusalem. Luke's second special concern was the Gentiles. He recorded details of Yeshua's ministry among them and His teachings and sayings about them that the other Gospel writers chose to omit. Luke's concern makes sense, because he was led to the Lord by Paul, the apostle to the Gentiles. According to the book of Acts and Paul's Epistles, Luke traveled frequently with Paul when he was engaged in Gentile evangelism. It is obvious that he shared the apostle's special concern for these people. Luke's third special concern was women. He records the ministries women had with, to, or from Yeshua that the other Gospel writers left out.

4. The Gospel of John:
Yeshua the Messiah, the Son of God

The Gospel of John had an evangelistic purpose, and therefore, the author's intention was to prove the Messiahship of Yeshua. This goal becomes evident in John 20:31: *but these are written, that ye may believe that Yeshua is the Messiah, the Son of God; and that believing ye may have life in his name.* Evidently, the apostle's goal in writing his Gospel was to reach the lost. Who the lost were cannot be determined with certainty; however, it seems that the Jews portrayed in his account were outsiders to the church, meaning unbelievers. However, there are other verses which portray certain Gentiles as if they were believers. If one takes these two rather distinct groups into consideration, a twofold goal of the Gospel comes into view. On one hand, he wanted to provide for the church a tool for evangelism. On the other hand, he wanted to strengthen the faith of those who already believed.

While Luke emphasized the humanity of the Messiah, Yochanan the apostle emphasized His deity. Luke was concerned with showing Yeshua to be fully human; the apostle's concern was to show that He was fully God. By the time he wrote his Gospel, Matthew, Mark, and Luke already had a wide circulation. While the three Gospels preceding his were written to specific ethnic audiences (Jews, Romans, and Greeks), his Gospel was written for the church at large and to unbelievers, so that they could be convinced that Yeshua was the Messiah (Jn. 20:30-31). He concentrated on adding those details the other three Gospel writers had left out. A large body of material in his Gospel is not found in Matthew, Mark, or Luke. While Mark was mostly interested in what Yeshua did, Yochanan was more interested in what the Messiah said and taught. There are sermons and discourses in his Gospel not found in the other narratives.

While the apostle's main theme was Yeshua the Messiah, the Son of God, he interwove two sub-themes with his Gospel. The first sub-theme is the conflict of light and darkness. Yochanan used those very terms, "light" and "darkness," as well as "night" and "day." He sometimes made statements that seem to be irrelevant unless this sub-theme is recognized. For example, he recorded that after the Messiah identified Judas as the betrayer at the last Passover, Judas left. The apostle added, *and it was night* (Jn. 13:30). Obviously, it was night; Passover is always observed at night, never in the daytime. It seems to be an irrelevant statement—except it is part of the apostle's sub-theme on the conflict of light and darkness. Yochanan was not just making a statement of fact, that it was night outside. That was obvious. The point is that Judas himself was "of the night" and "of the darkness." The deed he was about to do was not a deed "of the light" or "of the day."

The second sub-theme in the Gospel of John is that the Messiah came for the purpose of being the Father's revealer. That explains why the apostle spent much more time on what Yeshua said and taught rather than on what He did. In all of His sermons, discourses, and teachings, He revealed the nature of the Father to man.

Another aspect of the Gospel of John is that it records things in sevens, specifically, seven signs Yeshua performed, seven discourses He gave, and seven "I Am" statements He made. These "I Am" statements will be pointed out during the course of this study.

[§ 2] — B. The Prologue in the Gospel of John: The Preexistence of the Messiah

John 1:1-18

1. The *Logos* in the Gospel of John

John 1:1-18 comprise the introduction to Yochanan's Gospel. The opening words of verse 1 are: *In the beginning was the Word, and the Word was with God, and the Word was God.* The Greek term translated into English as "Word" is *Logos*. The apostle used this term as a title or a name, and he seemed to assume that the reader would understand the significance of it. Therefore, the usage of "Logos" in this way must have been a familiar concept in the first century. There are three possible sources for it: Greek philosophy, the writings of Philo, or rabbinic theology regarding the concept of the *Memra*.

a. Greek Philosophy

Because Yochanan the apostle used the word *Logos*, many commentaries on his Gospel begin with a discourse on what the term meant in Greek philosophy. In Greek philosophy, the Logos had two aspects: the aspect of reason and the aspect of speech. Having said this, the commentaries then try to show that the author revealed how the Messiah came to fulfill the goals of Greek philosophy in both of these areas: By reason, Yeshua was the very idea of God, and by speech, He was the very expression of God. What these commentators forget is that by profession Yochanan the apostle was not a Greek philosopher, but a Jewish fisherman.

b. Philonic Writings

The second possible source for the term *Logos* is in the writings of Philo. This Hellenistic Jewish philosopher lived in Alexandria, Egypt, and was a contemporary of both Yeshua and His apostle Yochanan. Philo was well versed in Greek philosophy and used it to interpret the Jewish Scriptures, employing an allegorical approach. The essence of the Logos in Philo's writings can be summarized in five points:

- ✡ The Logos is the *eikon*, the image of God.
- ✡ It is close to *Metatron*, the angel closest to God in rabbinic angelology.
- ✡ It is the high priest acting as a mediator.
- ✡ It is the paraclete.
- ✡ It is not a person, but something shadowy and unreal.

As can be seen from the above list, there are similarities between the writings of Yochanan and Philo, but there are also strong points of dissimilarity, and this indicates that the apostle, a Galilean fisherman, was not influenced by the writings of Philo, the Alexandrian philosopher. The source for the apostle's usage of the term *Logos* was not the writings of Philo. The Galilean fisherman simply did not travel in the same circles as the Alexandrian philosopher. To find the source of his Logos, we actually need look no further than the Judaism that he grew up with, the Judaism of the land of Israel. While this form of Judaism was varied, it was distinctive from the Hellenistic Judaism that Philo represented.

2. Six Theological Truths about the *Memra*

The apostle's concept of the Logos shows that he was very familiar with the Aramaic translation and interpretation of the Hebrew Scriptures called the Targumim. In the Targumim, the translators used the word *Memra*, and the Targumic usage of this term is where we find the source of Yochanan's Logos. The Hebrew equivalent of the word *Memra* is *Davar*. Based upon this term, as it is used in the Hebrew Scriptures, the rabbis derived six specific theological truths about the Memra. The introduction of the Gospel of John refers to all six of these in some form or another.

a. Distinct from God, but the Same as God

The first truth about the Memra is that it was sometimes distinct from God, but other times the same as God. In all of their writings, the rabbis never tried to explain this obvious paradox. How is it possible for the Memra to be distinct from God, and yet at the same time be God? They taught both statements as being true and left it there. Yochanan the apostle did the same thing in the first verse of his Gospel. When he stated that the Logos *was with God*, he made Him distinct from God. Then he stated that the Logos *was God*, making Him the same as God. Like the rabbis, he did not try to explain the paradox at this point, but simply stated this as being true. Later in his writings, he explained these seemingly contradictory statements in terms of the Trinity. The One he wrote about is distinct from God because He is not God the Father, nor is He God the Holy Spirit, yet He is the same as God in that He is the second member of the Trinity—God the Son. Only in terms of this triunity can the rabbinic paradox be explained.

b. The Agent of Creation

The second truth about the Memra is that it was the agent of creation. Whenever God created anything, He did so by means of His Memra, His Word. Everything that exists does so because of His Memra. Without the Memra, nothing that exists would exist. Therefore, the Memra was both there at and active in *the beginning*. This was derived from passages like Genesis 1, when God simply said, "Let there be", an expression which in English contains three words, but in Hebrew only one. Whatever followed "Let there be" would immediately come into existence. John 1:3 states: *All things were made through him; and without him was not anything made that has been made.* Here, Yochanan the apostle connected what is known about the Memra with his Logos.

Everything was made through Him (the Logos), and without Him nothing would exist. The Logos is the agent of creation, and this is stated both positively (*All things were made through him*) and negatively (*without him was not anything made that has been made*). The role of the Son in creation is also found in Colossians 1:16 and Hebrews 1:2.

c. The Agent of Salvation

The third theological truth about the Memra is that it was the agent of salvation. Throughout the history of the Hebrew Bible, God provided salvation by means of His Memra. Whether it was a physical salvation (such as the Exodus out of Egypt) or a spiritual salvation, He always saved by means of His Word. John 1:12 reads: *But as many as received him, to them gave he the right to become children of God, even to them that believe on his name.* The apostle's point is that the One who is the Logos, or the Memra, is the agent of salvation, because those who believe on Him, those who receive Him, are the ones who receive their salvation.

d. The Means by which God Became Visible

The fourth theological truth about the Memra is that it was the means by which God became visible. From time to time throughout the history of the Hebrew Bible, God took on some kind of a visible form. When He did so, it was by means of His Memra, by means of His Word. In Christian theology, these visible manifestations are referred to as "theophanies." The rabbis had a different term to describe the same thing. They called it *Shechinah*. The Shechinah was often connected with God's glory, so the two words were frequently used together: the Shechinah glory of God. By way of definition, the Shechinah glory is the visible manifestation of God's presence. Whenever the invisible God became visible, whenever the omnipresence of God was localized, this visible, localized presence was referred to as the Shechinah glory. Throughout Old Testament history, it came primarily in three forms: light, fire, or cloud, or some combination of the three. Another form by which God became visible was as the Angel of Jehovah. Whenever one of these visible manifestations occurred, it was by means of the Memra, by means of the Word.

John 1:14 states: *And the Word became flesh.* The *Word,* the Logos, that was in the beginning with God and who was God (Jn. 1:1) now, at a certain point of human history, took on visible form. However, what became visible was not intangible light, fire, or cloud. This time, God's visible manifestation became very tangible flesh. By means of the incarnation, He became human, a man of flesh and bone. Then the Gospel of John tells us that this manifestation *dwelled among us.* The Greek word translated as *dwelled* literally means "to tabernacle," and so the text literally reads, *and the Word became flesh, and tabernacled among us.* As mentioned above, the Jews used the word *Shechinah* to describe the visible manifestations of God's presence. In writing his Gospel, Yochanan the apostle did not use the regular Greek verb for "to dwell," but the term *skeinei,* which literally means "to tabernacle." The Hebrew *Shechinah* and the Greek *skeinei* are closely related. The origin of the word *Shechinah* goes back to Exodus 40, where the Shechinah glory, in the form of a cloud, took up residency within the Holy of Holies of the Tabernacle. The Hebrew word for "tabernacle" is *mishkan,* which comes from the same Hebrew root as Shechinah. It took up residence in the Holy of Holies of the *mishkan,* the Tabernacle. For the next several centuries, it "tabernacled" with the people of Israel until the Shechinah glory reluctantly departed from Israel in four stages in the days of Ezekiel, as recorded in chapters 8-11 of his book. Now, after about six centuries of absence, the Shechinah glory had returned, not in the form of light, fire, or cloud, but in the form of flesh, and once again *tabernacled among us,* "tabernacled" with the people of Israel.

Like the rabbis, the Gospel writer quickly connected this with God's glory: *(and we beheld his glory, glory as of the only begotten from the Father), full of grace and truth* (Jn. 1:14). Normally, the Shechinah glory exudes light, and thus has a brightness about it. However, the flesh of Yeshua's physical body served as a veil that covered the brightness of His glory. When people looked upon Him, He looked no different than any other Jewish male of first-century Israel. Only one time during His public ministry, at the transfiguration, did the Shechinah glory shine through. It penetrated through the veil of His flesh, affecting His clothing, making His garments exceedingly white, and His face began to shine with the brightness of the sun. Three of His apostles saw the brightness of His glory on that occasion. Among them was Yochanan, who wrote as an eyewitness: *we beheld his glory.* Just as in rabbinic theology, the Memra was the means by which God took on visible form, the same is now true of the Logos. Yeshua was the visible manifestation of God's presence.

e. The Means by which God Signed His Covenants

The fifth theological truth about the Memra is that it was the means by which God signed His covenants. In the Hebrew Bible, God made eight specific covenants. Three were made with humanity in general. These are the Edenic Covenant, the Adamic Covenant, and the Noahic Covenant. Five were made specifically with the Jewish people. These are the Abrahamic Covenant, the Mosaic Covenant, the Land Covenant, the Davidic Covenant, and the New Covenant. All eight covenants were signed and sealed by means of His Memra, by means of His Word.

The Gospel of John hints at this fact in verse 17: *For the law was given through Mosheh; grace and truth came through Yeshua the Messiah.* Biblically, human history can be described in terms of ages, or dispensations, and these dispensations correspond with God's covenants. The age, or dispensation, of the law was based upon the Mosaic Covenant, which was signed and sealed by the Shechinah glory, described in Exodus 24:1-18. The new age, or dispensation, of grace is based upon the New Covenant, which was signed and sealed by the shedding of Messiah's blood when He died on the cross. One of the many things He accomplished through His death was the signing and sealing of the New Covenant (Lk. 22:20; Heb. 8:1–10:18). In that sense, He is also a covenant-signer.

f. The Agent of Revelation

The sixth theological truth about the Memra is that it was the agent of revelation. Whenever God revealed Himself, He did so by means of the Memra, by means of the Word. Whatever we know about Him, we know because the Memra chose to reveal it. This is based upon many passages that say, "The *Word* of the Lord came to this or that prophet."

John 1:18 states: *No man has seen God at any time; the only begotten Son, who is in the bosom of the Father, he has declared <him>.* The fact that the Messiah came to reveal the Father to mankind is one of the Gospel's two sub-themes. It is through His teachings that the Messiah revealed the nature of God, and as previously mentioned, Yochanan the apostle focused his attention on this teaching rather than on Yeshua's actions. Because of that sub-theme, he is the only one who recorded the event where a disciple asked the Messiah, *show us the Father* (Jn. 14:8), to which Yeshua replied: *He that has seen me has seen the Father* (Jn. 14:9). Everything true about the divine nature of the Father is true of the divine nature of the Son. To know the Son is to know the Father. Hebrews 1:1-3 makes the same point: In the past, God had revealed Himself in many different ways; in these last days, He revealed Himself by means of the Son, the Logos, the agent of revelation.

3. Conclusion

The opening verses of the Gospel of John do not argue that Yeshua came to fulfill the goals of Greek philosophy, but that He came to fulfill the Jewish messianic hope. The six things the rabbis had been teaching about the Memra are true of Yeshua of Nazareth.

The origin of the rabbinic concept of the Memra is in the way the Old Testament used the noun *Davar*. This Hebrew noun, which in Aramaic is Memra, has dual meaning: It denotes what is spoken and what is done. God spoke and through words brought the universe into being. In Genesis 15:1, the Word of God is personified as a revealer. God revealed Himself to Abraham by means of His Word. Psalm 33:4-6 describes the Word of God as the agent of creation. In Psalm 147:15, the Word *runs very swiftly*, thus being personified, and it accomplishes things. In Isaiah 9:8, the Lord sent *a word into Yaakov*; the Word is something God can send, and therefore, it is distinct from God. Isaiah 55:10-11 pictures the Word coming and going. In Isaiah 45:23, the Word goes out *in righteousness*. According to Ezekiel 1:3, the Word *came expressly* to the prophet. These examples show that the Word is sometimes identified with God, but is distinct from God; it is the agent of creation and a revealer in some visible form, as in Genesis 15, etc. From such Old Testament passages, the rabbis developed their concept of the Memra.

With all this in mind, the first verses of the Gospel of John can be summarized in four simple points:

1. The Word—the Davar, the Memra, the Logos—came in visible form.

2. Sadly, the world in general failed to recognize Him.

3. Even more tragically, His own Jewish people failed to recognize Him as well.

4. Those individual Jews and Gentiles who did recognize Him are the ones who became the children of the Shechinah light and received their salvation from Him who is the agent of salvation.

4. Additional Aspects of the Prologue

Three additional things should be noted regarding the introduction of the Gospel of John. In verses 4-9, the apostle introduced one of his sub-themes: the conflict between light and darkness. In Yeshua, the Word *was life, and the life was the light of men* (Jn. 1:4). It is a light that *shines in the darkness, and the darkness apprehended it not* (Jn. 1:5). It was the *true light, even the light which lights every man* (Jn. 1:9). Thus, the Messiah is both the source of life and the source of light. In passages such as Isaiah 42:6 and 49:5-6, the Hebrew Bible connected the Messiah with salvation light.

A second phrase in the Gospel's introductory text which demands special attention is *only begotten* (Jn. 1:18). Certain cultic groups that deny the deity of the Son often use this verse to show that Yeshua has an origin. They claim that being called the *only begotten Son* means that He could not have eternally co-existed with God. This is an example of interpreting Jewish literature with a Gentile mindset. The term *only begotten* is translated from a single Greek word meaning "unique", "one of a kind", or "one and only". It does not necessarily emphasize origin; it can emphasize uniqueness. A good example is Genesis 22:2, where

God told Abraham to offer up Isaac: *Take now your son, your only son.* This was no idle request.[1] However, Isaac was not Abraham's only son. He had another son, Ishmael, and later on, he was blessed with six more sons. Therefore, in this case, the word *only* cannot mean origin. So in what way was Isaac Abraham's only son? In the sense of uniqueness, not origin. Isaac was the covenantal son, as the Abrahamic Covenant would be sustained only through him, not through Ishmael or any of his brothers. He was uniquely Abraham's only son in that he alone was his father's covenantal son. The Messiah is not the only one referred to as "son of God." Angels are called "sons of God" (e.g., Job 1:6, 38:7), Israel is called "the son of God" (e.g., Ex. 4:22; Hos. 11:1), and believers are called "sons of God" (e.g., Rom. 8:14; Gal. 4:6). However, Yeshua is *uniquely* the Son of God because of His eternal preexistence. As long as the Father existed, He existed. He was in the beginning with God, and God existed for eternity past.

Cultic groups also try to deny the deity of the Messiah on the basis of John 1:1: *and the Word was God.* In the Greek text, there is no definite article before "God," so they claim that it simply means "a god." Their point is that Yeshua is not *the* God, but was simply *a* god, in the same sense that all human beings can become a god. Therefore, Yeshua does not share the eternal deity of God the Father. However, in John 1:18, there is a clear reference to God the Father: *No man has seen God at any time; the only begotten Son, who is in the bosom of the Father, he has declared <him>.* Obviously, the word *God* in verse 18 is a reference to God the Father, because the Son is mentioned in the next phrase, and He is distinct from this God. In the Greek text, there is no article before *God* here, either. Yet those who translate verse 1 as "a god" do not translate verse 18 to read, "No man has seen a god." To be consistent with their view of Greek grammar, they would have needed to translate it this way, but it contradicts their argument. The lack of the definite article does not mean "a god." It simply emphasizes the nature of the thing described. The nature of the Father is that He is divine. The nature of the Son, or the Word, is that He is divine. The text reads correctly as all translations have rendered it: *the Word was God.* Therefore,

---

[1] John R. Cross, *The Stranger on the Road to Emmaus* (Ontario, Canada: GoodSeed International, 2000), p. 107.

all that is true of the divine nature of the Father is also true of the divine nature of the Son.

I. The Introduction
of the King
— §§ 3–27 —

The first division in this study of the life of the Messiah encompasses His genealogy, the birth narratives, His baptism, the temptations, and Yochanan's public identification of Yeshua to be the Messiah.

[§§ 3–19] — A. The Arrival of the King

[§ 3] — 1. The Genealogy of the King

Matthew 1:1-17, Luke 3:23d-38

Of the four Gospels, only Matthew and Luke give accounts of the birth and early life of Yeshua. For that reason, only these two have genealogies, since genealogies are concerned with origins. From the context alone, it should be evident that the genealogy in Matthew is that of the person who had the active role in that account, and the same logic would apply to Luke's genealogy. What we see in Matthew is that an angel appeared to Joseph, but there is no record of angels appearing to Miriam; the text reveals what Joseph was thinking and what was going on in his mind, but nothing of what Miriam was thinking. On the other hand, in Luke an angel appeared to Miriam, but there is no record of angels coming to Joseph; the text reveals what she was thinking, what was going on in her mind, but nothing about what Joseph was thinking. So, Matthew recorded the events surrounding the birth of Yeshua from Joseph's viewpoint, and Luke's focus was on Miriam; thus, the genealogy in Matthew is Joseph's, while the genealogy in Luke is Miriam's.

a. Why Two Genealogies?

It is, therefore, generally agreed that the genealogy in Matthew is Joseph's and the one in Luke Miriam's, but this raises a question: Why include Joseph's genealogy? As Yeshua was his adopted son, not his biological son, why does Matthew record Joseph's line of descent at all? In other words, why are there two genealogies? The answer usually posited is as follows: Matthew's genealogy shows that Joseph was of the *royal* line of the house of David; he was the heir apparent to David's throne. Since Yeshua was the adopted son of Joseph, He could claim the right to the throne by virtue of that adoption. However, Luke's genealogy gives the *real* line, that Yeshua Himself was a descendant of David through His mother, Miriam. So Yeshua received His Davidic descent through His mother, but His right to rule through His stepfather, and so the two genealogies are necessary to establish Yeshua's right to inherit David's throne.

However, Matthew's point is actually quite different from the answer given above. He was proving in his genealogy that Yeshua could not inherit His right to the throne of David through Joseph. This will be discussed in depth later, but this is an appropriate place in our study to introduce the topic of the two requirements in the Old Testament for acceding to the throne in Israel. One was applied to the southern kingdom of Judah, with its capital in Jerusalem, while the other was applied to the northern kingdom of Israel, with its capital in Samaria. As to the southern kingdom of Judah, only a descendant of David could become king. If a person was not a member of the house of David, he could not sit upon the throne in Jerusalem. In the seventh and eighth chapter of his book, Isaiah warned that any conspiracy to do away with the house of David for the purpose of setting up a new dynasty was doomed to failure because no one outside the house of David could sit upon the throne in Jerusalem. As to the northern kingdom of Israel, unless the king was appointed by God or had the sanctioning of a prophet, he could not sit upon the throne of Samaria. If anyone tried to do so, he would be assassinated. In II Kings 10:30, God told Jehu that his descendants would be allowed to sit upon the throne of Samaria for four generations, and it was so. When the fifth of his descendants tried to gain the throne, he was assassinated (II Kgs. 15:8-12) because he was neither divinely appointed nor sanctioned by a prophet.

The significance of these two requirements for kingship in Israel will become apparent in the Gospel accounts of the events surrounding the birth of Yeshua.

b. Matthew's Account

In his account of Joseph's line (Mt. 1:1-17), Matthew omitted some names and included four women, and this was not the traditional way a Jewish genealogy would be rendered. Yet by omitting some names, Matthew also employed a common midrashic method of mnemonics.[1] For example, the Talmudic tractate *Avot* 5:2-3 mentions ten generations from Adam to Noah and includes Adam in the count. Then it mentions ten generations from Noah to Abraham, but here Noah is not counted. Matthew chose to put his list together in three sets of fourteen (Mt. 1:17). The key person of his genealogy is David, and Matthew probably based his mnemonic on the numeric value of the king's Hebrew name, which is fourteen.

Matthew listed the names of four women in his genealogy: Tamar (Mt. 1:3); Rahab, whose Hebrew name was *Rachav* (Mt. 1:5); Ruth (Mt. 1:5); and the pronoun *her* (Mt. 1:6), which refers to Bathsheba. Normally, women would not be mentioned in Jewish genealogies, but in the Hebrew Bible there were some exceptions: Genesis 11:29, 25:1,

---

[1] Compare Ezra 7:1-5 with I Chronicles 6:11-14.

35:22-26, 36:10, 22, I Chronicles 2:4, 18-21, 24, 34, 46-49, 7:24. Further-more, the women he named were not the most significant in the messianic line. For example, he left out Sarah and Rebecca, who were far more important. Yet, there are several reasons for naming these four and not others. First, these four women were Gentiles. Tamar and Rahab were Canaanites, and Ruth was a Moabitess. Bathsheba was probably a Hittite.

By including the names of four Gentile women early in his Gospel, Matthew hinted at a point which he later amplified: While the primary purpose of the coming of Yeshua was for the lost sheep of the house of Israel, the Gentiles would also benefit.

The second noteworthy fact about these women is that three of them were involved in specific sexual sins: Bathsheba was guilty of adultery, Tamar was guilty of incest, and Rahab was guilty of prostitution. Ruth was not herself guilty of sexual sin, but she was a Moabitess. The Moab-ites originated from the commission of a sexual sin, as they were the product of an incestuous relationship Lot had with one of his daugh-ters. The point Matthew hinted at here was that Yeshua came for the purpose of saving sinners. However, women, Gentiles, and sinners are not the key points of Matthew's genealogy. The theme of his Gospel was Yeshua the Messiah, the King of the Jews. Since Jewish history began with Abraham, Matthew went back in time and, beginning with Abraham, traced the line forward to his own day. From Abraham, whose name in Hebrew was *Avraham* (Mt. 1:2), he traced the line to King David (Mt. 1:6). From David's many sons he chose one, Solomon, whose name in Hebrew was *Shlomoh* (Mt. 1:6), and traced the line to Jechoniah (Mt. 1:11): *and Yoshiyahu begat Yechanyahu and his brethren, at the time of the carrying away to Babylon.* In verse 12, Matthew picked up with Jechoniah and traced the line to Joseph, the stepfather of Yeshua, whose name in Hebrew was *Yoseph* (Mt. 1:16). According to Matthew, Joseph was a direct descendant of David through Solomon, but also through Jechoniah. This one fact means that Joseph could not have been the heir apparent to David's throne. The reason is found in Jeremiah 22:24-30:

> *[24] As I live, says Jehovah, though Coniah the son of Jehoiakim king of Yehudah were the signet upon my right hand, yet would I pluck you*

thence; 25 and I will give you into the hand of them that seek your life, and into the hand of them of whom you are afraid, even into the hand of Nebuchadnezzar king of Babylon, and into the hand of the Chaldeans. 26 And I will cast you out, and your mother that bare you, into another country, where ye were not born; and there shall ye die. 27 But to the land whereunto their soul longs to return, thither shall they not return. 28 Is this man Coniah a despised broken vessel? is he a vessel wherein none delights? wherefore are they cast out, he and his seed, and are cast into the land which they know not? 29 O earth, earth, earth, hear the word of Jehovah. 30 Thus says Jehovah, Write ye this man childless, a man that shall not prosper in his days; for no more shall a man of his seed prosper, sitting upon the throne of David, and ruling in Yehudah.

In the days of Jeremiah, God pronounced a curse upon King Jechoniah[2] because of the kind of man he was, and as the provisions of the curse were pronounced, they grew in intensity from mild to severe. Jeremiah began by pointing out that Jechoniah would be taken into Babylonian Captivity (Jer. 22:25). He would spend the rest of his life in Babylonia and would die there, never to see his homeland again. When the high point of the curse was reached, God called upon the whole earth three times over to hear it (Jer. 22:29). The culmination of the curse was that no descendant of Jechoniah would ever have the right to sit upon the throne of David (Jer. 22:30). Until Jeremiah, the only requirement for kingship in Judah had been membership in the house of David. With Jeremiah, that requirement was limited further: one still had to be a member of the house of David, but apart from Jechoniah.

Here we return to the issue of the requirement for acceding to the throne in Judah and to the question, "Why are there two genealogies?" Joseph was a descendant of David through Jechoniah, so he was under the curse of Jeremiah 22. Contrary to some explanations for the two genealogies, he could not have been the heir apparent to David's throne. Therefore, Matthew could not have included Joseph's genealogy in his Gospel to show that Yeshua claimed His legal right to the throne of David as Joseph's adopted son. He had a different purpose in mind. Unlike Luke, Matthew began his Gospel with the genealogy. He

---

[2] The ASV renders Jechoniah's name as *Coniah* which is the shortened form.

presented the "Jechoniah problem," but then immediately solved it with the account of the virgin conception and birth. Yeshua was not the real son of Joseph; there was no biological connection, so there was no "Jechoniah problem." Yet this answer raises another question: How did Matthew indicate that Yeshua was descended only from Miriam and was not Joseph's biological son? He told us that Joseph was *the husband of Miriam, of whom was born Yeshua, who is called Messiah* (Mt. 1:16). The pronoun *whom* in the Greek text is feminine, putting the emphasis on the mother alone—*of whom* [Miriam] *was born Yeshua.* Joseph was the husband of Miriam. He was Yeshua's legal father, but he was not His biological father. The child was hers alone. Luke entirely avoided this issue by beginning his Gospel with the events surrounding the virgin conception and birth, not providing a genealogy until chapter 3. As will be shown, he recorded the genealogy with an entirely different purpose in mind.

Turning to Luke's genealogy (Lk. 3:23-38), this Gospel writer strictly followed Jewish custom and procedure: He did not mention women and did not skip names. The rule against naming women in a Jewish genealogy would raise a question: If you wished to trace a woman's line, how would you do so without using her name? The answer is that under Jewish law you would use the name of her husband. However, this answer presents a problem: How then would you know if the genealogy is that of the wife or the husband? If someone like Luke was doing research and came across a genealogy, how could he tell by looking at the genealogy whether it was that of Miriam or that of Joseph, since Joseph's name would be found in both? The answer is quite simple if you are reading the genealogy from a first-century document written in Greek, yet it poses a problem when the New Testament is translated into English. It is not grammatically correct to use the definite article before a proper name in English, yet it was in Greek grammar. Therefore, it was quite allowable to speak of **the** Miriam or **the** Joseph. Every single name in Luke's genealogy is preceded by the definite article except one, the name of Joseph, and this allows for how it is rendered into English, *being the son (as was supposed) of Yoseph, the <son> of Eili* (Lk. 3:23). Someone reading the original language could tell by the missing article that this is not really Joseph's line; it is the line of his wife, Miriam. In the Old Testament, there were two cases where a woman's line was traced by the name of her husband: Ezra 2:61 and Nehemiah 7:63. It is no accident that the Talmud refers to Miriam as "the daughter of Heli," for the rabbis knew that when this genealogy referred to Joseph as "of Heli," it was not actually his genealogy but, instead, that of his wife. The missing definite article told them this, and so they referred to her as the daughter of Heli.

Unlike Matthew, Luke worked backward in time and began his genealogy with the name Joseph as a substitute for Miriam. Verse 31 then traces Miriam's line back to David, stating, *the <son> of Malah, the <son> of Manna, the <son> of Mattatah, the <son> of Natan, the <son> of David.* Like her husband, Miriam was a descendant of David. However, while her husband's lineage led back to Solomon, she was a descendant of one of David's other sons, Nathan. As a result, she did not have the blood of Jechoniah running through her veins. She was a descendant of David apart from Jechoniah. Since Yeshua was the real son of Miriam, He too was a descendant of David apart from Jechoniah. This means that He fulfilled the first Old Testament requirement for becoming king over Judah: He was a member of the house of David apart from Jechoniah. However, at this point in Jewish history, there were a great number of other Jews who were descendants of David apart from Jechoniah. Thus, Yeshua was not the only one who fulfilled the first requirement. Why was His the legitimate claim to the throne? The answer lies in the second Old Testament requirement: that of divine appointment. Yeshua also fulfilled this second requirement for the kingship of Israel, as will be seen in the birth narrative in Luke's Gospel.

Luke ended his genealogy with Adam, thus drawing attention to Yeshua's humanity.

Matthew's and Luke's genealogies contain four of the many titles of the Messiah. In Matthew 1:1, He is called *the son of David* and *the son of Avraham.* In Luke 3:38, He is called *the son of Adam* and *the son of God.* Each title emphasizes a different aspect of His person and His work: As the Son of David, Yeshua is a king; as the Son of Abraham, He is a Jew; as the Son of Adam, He is human; and as the Son of God, He is God. These four titles portray the Messianic Person as the Jewish God-Man King. Furthermore, by calling the Messiah the Son of David, Matthew connected His coming with one of the four eternal covenants

God made with Israel, namely, the Davidic Covenant. By calling Him the Son of Abraham, he connected Him with the Abrahamic Covenant.

[§§ 4–11] — 2. The Advent of the King

[§ 4] — a. The Annunciation of Yochanan's Birth to Zechariah[3]

Luke 1:5-25

(1) The Twenty-Four Courses

After the introduction to his Gospel, in which he explained the purpose for which he wrote and how he gathered his information, Luke provided some details regarding the political and religious rulers of his time. In verse 5, he stated, *There was in the days of Herod, king of Yehudah, a certain priest named Zecharyah, of the course of Aviyah.* In I Chronicles 24:1-19, King David divided the tribe of Levi into 24 courses. There was one high priest, and below him were 24 chief priests. Under them were the common priests, and they formed the 24 courses, called *mishmarot*, or "watches." The head of each priestly division was called *rosh hamishmar.* Each watch was to serve in the Temple twice a year for one week at a time, from Sabbath to Sabbath. Their times of service were determined by lot.

After the Babylonian Captivity, only four of the original 24 courses returned (Ezra 2:36-39; 10:18-22), so certain adjustments had to be made. These four courses were divided by lot into 24 divisions, and the original names were retained even though they were no longer accurate. Many centuries later, Zechariah, the father of Yochanan the Baptizer, really did not belong to the family of Abijah (I Chr. 24:10), but to the course of Abijah. Just as they did during the time of David, the priests functioned as officials and judges (I Chr. 23:4), as assistants (I Chr. 23:28), as worship leaders (I Chr. 25:6), and as doorkeepers and

---

[3] Zechariah's name is also spelled *Zacharias* or *Zachariah.*

guards (I Chr. 26:12-16). Each of the 24 courses served in rotation, performing the regular daily functions and rituals at the Temple for one week twice a year. By the first century, the estimated number of priests was 18,000. As the number of common priests had grown so large, a method was needed to select those who would perform the duties at the Temple. The solution was the casting of lots. It was quite possible that a priest would only be chosen once in his entire life to perform any of the priestly duties at the Temple.

Zechariah was a common priest of one of the 24 courses, the Course of Abijah. Luke 1:6 states that he and his wife Elizabeth were *both righteous before God, walking in all the commandments and ordinances of the Lord blameless.* They were members of the believing Jewish remnant of that day. The word *blameless* does not mean sinless; it means that when they did sin, they offered the necessary sacrifices to have their sins expiated and were, therefore, rendered blameless. They were *both righteous before God,* emphasizing their internal righteousness. They were regenerate, saved people who showed their faith externally by their works and by *walking in all the commandments and ordinances of the Lord.* Zechariah's name in Hebrew means "Jehovah remembers," and "Elizabeth" means "the oath of God." Later, there will be a bit of wordplay with the meaning of their names.

As Luke's Gospel opens, Zechariah is the common priest who had been chosen to burn the incense. He took hot coals from the altar of sacrifice outside the Temple building and brought them into the first room of the Temple, which was the Holy Place. He put the hot coals upon the altar of incense that stood in front of the thick curtain, separating the Holy of Holies from the holy place. Then he dropped some incense on the coals. This caused a sweet-smelling smoke to ascend and penetrate the thick veil into the Holy of Holies. This special incense was to be burned perpetually before the Lord upon the golden altar of incense (Ex. 30:8); thus, it was called "the perpetual offering." The offerings were made at sunrise and at dusk. Preparations for the evening service started at around 2:30 p.m. so that the incense could be taken to the altar an hour later. As this offering coincided with the evening prayer, it was often well attended, and it seems from what Luke says in 1:10 that Zechariah's encounter with the angel took place during the evening service as *the whole multitude of the people* were present.

The honor of being the priest who would enter the Holy Place and presented to God this symbol of intercession on the altar of incense was already great for Zechariah. That God would now speak to him through an angel is most certainly the climax of his career.

In Leviticus 10, Nadab and Abihu, the two sons of Aaron, improperly burned the special incense before the Lord and were smitten dead. This incident led the rabbis in Zechariah's day to teach that if any priest burned the incense improperly, he would also be struck dead. However, before death came, the Angel of Death would appear, standing on the right side of the altar of incense. Luke 1:10 states that while Zechariah burned the incense *the whole multitude of the people were praying without at the hour of incense*. While performing the ritual, Zechariah suddenly saw an angel standing on the right side of the altar of incense (Lk. 1:11), and Zechariah *was troubled when he saw <him>, and fear fell upon him* (Lk. 1:12). Naturally, he was troubled and fearful, as he had been taught he was about to die. However, the message of the angel was not one of judgment and death, but that of blessing and new life to come.

(2) The Message to Zechariah

Zechariah and Elizabeth had remained childless and had grown elderly (Lk. 1:7), which in rabbinic tradition meant they were over sixty years old. Instead of the dreaded judgment, the angel Gabriel (Lk. 1:19) announced that Zechariah's wife would conceive and bear him a son. He was to call him Yochanan (Lk. 1:13). In Hebrew, the root of this name is "grace," and so Yochanan means "Jehovah is gracious." With this name, God was announcing the coming of a new age (Jn. 1:17).

Gabriel then proclaimed six things about this son that Zechariah would sire.

(a) He Shall be Great in the Sight of the Lord

The first pronouncement the angel made was that Yochanan would *be great in the sight of the Lord* (Lk. 1:15a). His position before the Lord would be a state of greatness. In fact, the Messiah Himself later said, *Verily I say unto you, Among them that are born of women, there has not arisen a greater than Yochanan the Baptizer* (Mt. 11:11). Indeed, *he shall be great in the sight of the Lord.*

(b) A Nazirite from Birth

The second pronouncement the angel made was that Yochanan would *drink no wine nor strong drink* (Lk. 1:15b), meaning that he was to be a Nazirite from birth. The Nazirite vow, described in Numbers 6:2-8, was taken voluntarily, and both men and women were allowed to take this vow for an optional duration of time. There were specific restrictions placed upon the person taking the vow: They were to separate themselves *unto Jehovah* (Num. 6:2) and abstain *from wine or strong drink* (Num. 6:3). In fact, they were not to partake of anything of the grape, whether solid (grapes, raisins, the vine, the kernels, etc.) or liquid (wine, juice, or vinegar). No razor was to *come upon his head* (Num. 6:5); therefore, their hair was to be allowed to grow until the specific time of their vow had been fulfilled. Furthermore, the person who made the vow could not come near a corpse because this would render him ceremonially unclean.

As stated earlier, the Nazirite vow was usually taken on a voluntary basis, but three men in biblical history were appointed to be Nazirites from birth. Two of them, Samson and Samuel, are in the Hebrew Bible. Samson is characterized as one who was not faithful to the Nazirite vow, while Samuel is characterized as having been faithful. Yochanan is the third and last person in Scripture called upon to be a Nazirite from birth.

When the rabbis spoke about wine, they used two Hebrew words. The first one is *tirosh*, meaning "must," "fresh," or "new wine." This word is found 38 times in the Hebrew Scriptures. Tirosh is freshly extracted grape juice that, by implication, was rarely fermented. Once it was put in wineskins (Lk. 5:37-38), it was given time to age and turn into alcohol. This wine was associated with God's blessing of His people (found, for example, in Gen. 27:28, 37; Deut. 7:13; Jer. 31:12; Hos. 2:8; Joel 2:19, 24; and Zech. 9:17). The second Hebrew word is *yayin*, and it refers to intoxicating wine. It is used 141 times in the Hebrew Scriptures. One of the ways of disinfecting water at the time was to mix it with yayin, as the alcohol content therein would kill harmful micro-organisms. There is a third Hebrew word which was used to speak about a strong, intoxicating drink, and that was *shekar*, meaning "liquor." It refers to alcoholic beverages made from fruits other than grapes, grain, dates, honey, or barley. While this would have included beer, it is not the same as whiskey, gin, or vodka, as these are distilled alcoholic beverages and distillation was unknown at the time.

While abstention from tirosh, yayin, and shekar was a key element of the Nazirite vow, it does not imply anything inherently evil about drinking alcohol. Whether the baptizer was a Nazirite all his life or for a set amount of time is not clear from the Gospel accounts.

(c) Controlled by the Spirit

The third proclamation the angel made was that Yochanan would *be filled with the Holy Spirit, even from his mother's womb* (Lk. 1:15c). To be *filled* means to be "controlled." From the time he was in his mother's womb, the Holy Spirit would control him. An example of the exercise of that control will be seen later.

(d) He Would Begin a Repentance Movement

Gabriel's fourth proclamation was that through Yochanan *many of the children of Yisrael* shall be turned *unto the Lord their God* (Lk. 1:16). His basic task was to begin a repentance movement, the purpose of which was to have a group ready to accept the Messiah once He was identified. Yochanan's ministry would be to turn the children of Israel back to the Lord their God by telling them to repent, the same ministry as the Old Testament prophets.

(e) In the Spirit of Elijah

The fifth proclamation of the angel was that Yochanan would *go before his face in the spirit and power of Eliyahu* (Lk. 1:17a). The text does not say that Yochanan **was** *Eliyahu*, or Elijah, but that he would come *in the spirit and power of Eliyahu*.

Like Elijah, he was going to have a special ministry to the believing remnant of Israel. The correlation between Yochanan the Baptizer and Elijah the prophet will be developed further as this study continues through the Gospels. For now, the one thing to note is that the angel did not say that Yochanan was Elijah.

(f) Yochanan's Call

Gabriel's sixth and final proclamation about Yochanan was that his ministry would be *to make ready for the Lord a people prepared <for him>* (Lk. 1:17c). His calling was to have *a people prepared* to accept Yeshua as the Messiah, once He was so identified. Therefore, those baptized by Yochanan had made a commitment to believe on whomever he pointed out to be the Messiah. It will be seen that when those who were baptized by Yochanan were finally told who the Messiah was, they did believe. Those who rejected the baptism of Yochanan also ended up rejecting Yeshua. Yochanan's special calling was to be the forerunner of the Messiah and the herald of the King.

(3) Zechariah's Reaction to the Angels' Annunciation

Up to this point in the account, Zechariah had only been listening. When he finally spoke, he uttered a question of unbelief: *Whereby shall I know this? for I am an old man, and my wife well stricken in years* (Lk. 1:18). The question could be rephrased as, "How can I know that this is really true?" When Zechariah spoke, it was a word of doubt and unbelief. In response, the angel declared that the priest would speak no more until the promise was fulfilled. Verse 19 identifies the angel as Gabriel, whose name in Hebrew is *Gavriel*.

Generally, at the time for the burning of the incense, the priest would go into the Temple, drop some of the essence on the coals, and come out. The procedure did not take very long. However, having a conversation with an angel would mean it took a bit more time than normal. By now, the crowd had finished the evening prayers, and Luke says, *they marveled while he tarried in the temple* (Lk. 1:21). Perhaps they were wondering if he had been smitten dead. When Zechariah finally left the sanctuary, he stood on the steps with the other priests overlooking the crowd and was unable to tell them what had happened. He had not been smitten dead, but mute.

When *the days of his ministration were fulfilled*, Zechariah returned home (Lk. 1:23). In keeping with the angelic promise, *Elisheva his wife* *conceived; and she hid herself for five months, saying, Thus has the Lord done unto me in the days wherein he looked upon <me>, to take away my reproach among men* (Lk. 1:24-25). The *reproach* refers to a common attitude of that day, often seen in biblical history. Women who were unable to conceive and produce children were despised; they were reproached for endangering the continuity of the husband's line. For Elizabeth, that reproach had now been removed.

[§ 5] — b. The Annunciation of Yeshua's Birth to Miriam

Luke 1:26-38

Verse 26 states that *in the sixth month* (that is, six months after Elizabeth became pregnant with Yochanan), Gabriel, the same angel who had announced the birth of Yochanan the Baptizer to Zechariah, now announced the birth of Yeshua to Miriam. At this point, Miriam was living in the town of Nazareth in Galilee (Lk. 1:26).

The passage clearly emphasizes that Miriam was a virgin (Lk. 1:27b). She was *betrothed*, or engaged, to Joseph (Lk. 1:27a), and as the betrothed of Joseph, she had a specific legal status. Very similar language is used in Deuteronomy 22:23-24, and we can derive from these verses that the Jewish marriage process involved two stages. The first stage is the engagement or betrothal. Legally, the woman now belonged to her husband-to-be and was called his wife, though the second stage of the marriage process, the ceremony itself, took place about a year later when the groom took her home. Because of the legal aspects involved, Miriam's betrothal should not be thought of as equivalent to a modern engagement of marriage. It was a very different arrangement. In the first century, girls as young as age twelve could have been bound that way to a man. Neither Matthew nor Luke specify Miriam's exact age when she became engaged to Joseph. What is specified is the fact that she was a virgin. The Greek word for "virgin," *parthenos*, never refers to a married woman or one who has already engaged in sexual relations. To prove the bride's purity, a waiting period of one year before finalizing the marriage process was the norm. During this time, only death or divorce could sever the contract, and a girl whose groom died during this period of waiting was referred to as a widow. The marriage ceremony lasted for seven days, and only afterwards was the marriage consummated. From the Gospel of John and the book of Acts, we know that Miriam was still alive when Yeshua was crucified. She would have been in her late forties or early fifties.

(1) The Angel's Message

In verse 28, the angel greeted Miriam with the words, *Hail, you that are highly favored, the Lord <is> with you.* In Greek, *highly favored* is *kecharitomene*, which comes from the root *charitoó*, meaning "I bestow freely on," "I favor." The verb is used twice in the New Testament, here in Luke 1:28 and in Ephesians 1:6, and both times it speaks of God extending Himself to freely bestow grace (favor) upon someone. So, the angel greeted Miriam and referred to her as one who had received special grace from God. As she would soon be told (Lk. 1:31-33), the special grace was that she had been chosen to be the mother of the Messiah. She was being favored by God, she was receiving His grace; yet there is nothing in the text that even remotely implies that she herself was sinless. Miriam was a humble sinner, a truth she herself acknowledged when she said, *My spirit has rejoiced in God my Savior* (Lk. 1:47). Only a sinful person needs a redeemer, so clearly, Miriam was not sinless from her conception, as some teach. Therefore, when God called Miriam to become the mother of the Messiah, He enabled her to take on this role, and His choice of Miriam was rooted in His grace. God did not act because of her but on behalf of her.

According to verse 29, *Miriam was greatly troubled at the saying, and cast in her mind what manner of salutation this might be.* The angel calmed her fears by telling her again that she had *found favor with God.* Then he delivered God's message to her. It contained five specific points.

(a) Virgin Birth

The angel did not mention Joseph, nor did he mention marriage, and from Miriam's response in Luke 1:34, it is clear that she understood what he was declaring: She would conceive and bear a son in her virgin state (Lk. 1:30-33). The meaning of Genesis 3:15 and Isaiah's prophecy of the virgin conception and birth in Isaiah 7:14 now became clear. God would become incarnate; He was going to become a man in the person of Yeshua, the Son of Miriam.

(b) The Messiah's Name

The angel's second point pertained to her son's name: Miriam was to call Him Yeshua. His actual name comes from a Hebrew root that means "to save," "salvation," or "savior." It is akin to the Hebrew word for "salvation," *yeshuah*. As Joseph would also be told, the child was to have the name Yeshua, "salvation," because He would *yoshia, save His people from their sins* (Mt. 1:21). The same root is the origin of other names, such as Joshua, Isaiah, and Hosea. When the Greek New Testament was translated into Latin, *Iesous* became *Iesus,* but the pronunciation did not change. Many centuries later, when the New Testament was translated from Latin into German and English, *Iesus* became "Jesus," and the English pronunciation eventually changed to what it is today.

(c) *He Shall Be Great*

The third point of the angel's message was that, as to His essential nature, Miriam's son *shall be great.*

(d) His Deity

Gabriel's fourth point was that the Messiah would *be called the Son of the Most High* (Lk. 1:32a). Miriam's son, Yeshua, will not be merely a man, He will be the God-Man. At the moment of conception, the second Person of the Trinity will add to His divine nature a human nature, thus becoming the biological descendant of Adam, Abraham, and David.

(e) Fulfiller of the Davidic Covenant

The angel's fifth point pertained to the Davidic Covenant (I Chr. 17:11-14). In this covenant, God promised David four specific things: an eternal throne, an eternal house or dynasty, an eternal kingdom, and an eternal descendant. He would settle this descendant in His house and His kingdom forever, and He would call Him His son. According to

Gabriel's message, Miriam's son is the one who will fulfill all four aspects of the Davidic Covenant. He would be this promised seed of David, and *he shall be called the Son of the Most High*. He will be given David's throne, He will rule *over the house of Yaakov for ever*, and His kingdom will have *no end*. Gabriel promised Miriam that *the Lord God shall give unto him the **throne** of his father David* (Lk. 1:32b, emphasis added). This means that her son would fulfill the two requirements given in the Hebrew Bible for kingship: He is a descendant of David (apart from Jechoniah), and He is being divinely appointed to be king over Israel. When Gabriel said, *the Lord God shall give unto him the throne*, Yeshua received this divine appointment. It should be mentioned that the Messiah is the only one who fulfills both of these requirements of the Hebrew Bible for kingship, and as He, by virtue of His resurrection, now lives forever, there will be no need for a successor. Concerning the house or dynasty, Gabriel stated that the Messiah would *reign over the **house** of Yaakov forever* (Lk. 1:33a, emphasis added); concerning the kingdom, it would have *no end* (Lk. 1:33b); and concerning the eternal descendant, Gabriel referred to Yeshua as the *Son of the Most High* (Lk. 1:32) and the *Son of God* (Lk. 1:35), declaring Him divine, and thus eternal. These four eternal aspects of the Davidic Covenant are here restated and promised to be fulfilled through Yeshua, the Messiah. The eternality of the house, throne, and kingdom is guaranteed because the seed of David culminates in a person who is Himself eternal: the God-Man.

(2) Miriam's Question

At this point, Miriam raised a question: *How shall this be, seeing I know not a man?* (Lk. 1:34). Zechariah's question was different: *Whereby shall I know this?* (Lk. 1:18). His question arose out of unbelief. Miriam, however, did not challenge the angel's word. Her question was not, "How will I know that this is true?" She asked, "How is this going to come to pass?" It is a logical question: How would this happen in light of the fact that she was a virgin?

(3) The Angel's Answer

In verse 35, Gabriel answered her question: *The Holy Spirit shall come upon you, and the power of the Most High shall overshadow you: wherefore also the holy thing which is begotten shall be called the Son of God* (Lk. 1:35). Because of what is said here, a common misconception has arisen which must be dispelled. Some teach that the virgin birth was necessary to keep the Messiah from inheriting the sin nature. This teaching is based upon the false assumption that the sin nature is transmitted only through the father. However, the sin nature is actually transmitted through both the father and the mother, and nowhere in the Bible does it ever say that the sin nature is transmitted through the male seed. Sometimes, the Bible even emphasizes the influence of the female side over the male side. For example, in Psalm 51:5b David said, *And in sin did my mother conceive me.* In reality, the sin nature is transmitted through both the father and the mother. So what protected the Messiah from inheriting the sin nature of Miriam? The overshadowing work of the Holy Spirit. This work protected Yeshua from inheriting the sin nature of man. God's omnipotence would have allowed Him to produce an absolutely sinless being by normal human conception, using both male sperm and a female egg. However, He chose to do it another way. The reason the Messiah was conceived in a virgin's womb was not that God had no other options. The reason was that this was the way He *chose* to take on human form. By choosing to do it this way, He would also fulfill His prophecies in the Hebrew Bible—hinted at in Genesis 3:15 and clearly stated in Isaiah 7:14. The Messiah would be conceived in the womb of a virgin, and His birth would provide Him with a unique credential.

Another false teaching is that Miriam's egg was not produced by her ovaries but implanted by the Holy Spirit. This would have made her a surrogate mother and is not the teaching of the text or the Bible as a whole. There had to be a biological connection between Adam, Abraham, Judah, David, and Yeshua for Him to be truly "the seed." So, Miriam's egg was generated by the Holy Spirit and what protected the conceived seed was the Spirit's overshadowing work.

The Greek verb which is translated into English as "shall overshadow" is *episkiasei*. It is used in the New Testament of God's overshadowing presence, which always brings His plan to pass. The word is used in those passages that describe Yeshua's transfiguration (Mt. 17:5; Mk. 9:7; Lk. 9:34). The angel went on to explain that because of the overshadowing work of the Holy Spirit, He who was conceived would be *holy*—that is, sinless. Furthermore, He would be called *the Son of God* (Lk. 1:35). This messianic title is based on Psalm 2:7-12 and Proverbs 30:4.

Gabriel further told Miriam that her cousin, Elizabeth, was also with child and already six months along (Lk. 1:36-37). This sets the stage for the next section, Miriam's departure to the hill country of Judah to see Elizabeth.

(4) Miriam's Response

Having received the prophecy and the answer to her subsequent question, the passage ends with Miriam's response: *Behold, the handmaid of the Lord; be it unto me according to your word* (Lk. 1:38). At this point, Miriam totally submits herself to the will and care of God. This was wise in light of three things. First, under the Mosaic Law, if a betrothed woman was found to be pregnant, the penalty she faced was execution by lapidation. Miriam would have to trust that God would protect her from such a horrible fate. Second, she had to trust God concerning the reaction of the community, for when it was known that she was pregnant, she would have been in danger of being expelled from the community and of being ostracized for the rest of her life. Third, she had to trust the Lord concerning her relationship to Joseph. Matthew tells us that Joseph was a righteous man and that he did contemplate divorcing her when it was found out that she was pregnant (Mt. 1:19). She gave herself over to the Lord completely and trusted Him to work out all of these important details.

[§ 6] — c. The Visit of Miriam to Elizabeth

Luke 1:39-45

Gabriel had told Miriam that her cousin, Elizabeth, was six months pregnant (Lk. 1:36) and that *no word from God shall be void of power*

(Lk. 1:37). His point was that since God had produced a child in a barren woman, who was already well past menopause, He could produce a child in the womb of a virgin. Having heard this, Miriam went to visit Elizabeth (Lk. 1:39-45), and she went *with haste* (Lk. 1:39), showing that a sense of urgency had been engendered in her by the divine revelation she had just received. This journey from Galilee to an unknown town in the hill country of Judah would require at least three days.

The angel had also said to Zechariah that his child would be controlled by the Spirit from the womb. Verse 41 says, *And it came to pass, when Elisheva heard the salutation of Miriam, the babe leaped in her womb.* Even before Yochanan was born, the Holy Spirit had inspired him to begin his work as the forerunner and herald of the King.

Luke then stated that Elizabeth's response to Yochanan's leap of joy (Lk. 1:44) was not the result of human logic, but because she, too, was *filled with the Holy Spirit* (Lk. 1:41). Hence, her utterance was divine. Controlled by the Spirit, she referred to her cousin as *the mother of my Lord* (Lk. 1:43). Through the filling of the Spirit, it was revealed to her that Yochanan, still as a babe in the womb, had begun his work as the herald and forerunner of the Messiah by identifying Miriam as His mother.

Still being controlled by the Holy Spirit, Elizabeth gave a prophetic utterance. There are six points to be considered. First, she exclaimed, *Blessed <are> you among women* (Lk. 1:42), essentially paraphrasing the words of Gabriel in verse 28, *Hail, you that are highly favored, the Lord <is> with you.* Because God specially favored her, she was blessed among women, in fact, the most blessed of all women because she would bear the greatest of all children. While Gabriel had informed her husband, Zechariah, that their son would be the forerunner of the Messiah and thus great, Miriam's son would be the Messiah Himself and thus greater. This portrays Elizabeth as a very humble woman who was herself excited about the fact that God's promises to Israel were about to be fulfilled.

Second, Elizabeth proclaimed a blessing on the child by stating, *blessed <is> the fruit of your womb* (Lk. 1:42b), the *fruit* being the babe Miriam was now carrying in her womb. It had been revealed to Elizabeth by the Holy Spirit who that baby was because, third, she said,

And whence is this to me, that the mother of my Lord should come unto me? (Lk. 1:43). Elizabeth referred to Miriam as *the mother of my Lord.* Because of this statement, in certain segments of the visible church, Miriam is sometimes referred to as "the mother of God." However, she is not the mother of God, because she is not the mother of the divine nature of Yeshua. That is something He had for all eternity past. She is only the mother of the humanity of Yeshua. The term *Lord* here is "Lord" in the sense of Messiah, which means she recognized Miriam to be the mother of the Messiah.

Fourth, in her prophetic utterance, Elizabeth pointed out that as soon as the voice of Miriam reached her ears, the babe in her womb, Yochanan, *leaped for joy*—not just leaped, but *leaped for joy.* This movement was not random, but the deliberate expression of a human emotion. That which is in the womb of the mother is treated in Scripture as being a person. In the leaping, Yochanan again was doing the work of the forerunner.

Fifth, Elizabeth continued her prophetic utterance with a special blessing upon Miriam: *And blessed <is> she that believed.* While Elizabeth's husband, Zechariah, did not believe, Miriam did believe the message of the angel, and the Holy Spirit had revealed this to Elizabeth.

Sixth, the prophecy ends with the statement that there would be a fulfillment of those things which were spoken to Miriam from the Lord. Elizabeth greatly praised the extent of her cousin's faith.

[§ 7] — d. The Song of Miriam

Luke 1:46-56

This song of Miriam reveals two things: First, it shows the extent of her personal spirituality, and second, it shows her knowledge of Scripture, because her song is very similar to Hannah's song in I Samuel 2:1-10.

Miriam's song can be divided into two sections, each section being devoted to one of the two main points of the song. The first section (Lk. 1:46-50) describes what God did for her. Verses 46-47 state: *And Miriam said, My soul does magnify the Lord, And my spirit has rejoiced in God my Savior.* She called God her *Savior.* The kind of people who need a savior are sinners. This statement clearly shows that Miriam was a sinner and proves false the teaching of a certain segment of Christendom that she was perpetually sinless. By calling God her *Savior*, she revealed that He saved her from her sins.

Then she used the word "for" three times, emphasizing that she was praising God because of what He had done for her. In verse 48a, she said, *For he has looked upon the low estate of his handmaid.* The *handmaid* was Miriam herself. She was of low estate economically because she lived in poverty. She was of low estate socially because she was from Nazareth, a town that had a poor reputation. In spite of all of this, God had looked upon her in grace. In verse 48b, Miriam continues, *For behold, from henceforth all generations shall call me blessed.* In spite of her low beginnings, all future generations would call Miriam *blessed* because it would always be recognized that she was the Messiah's mother. In verse 49a, she declared, *For he that is mighty has done to me great things.* The greatest thing was that she was going to be the mother of the Messiah. Miriam concluded this section of what God did for her by praising Him: *And holy is his name. And his mercy is unto generations and generations on them that fear him* (Lk. 1:49b-50).

In the second part of her song, verses 51-55, she declared what God will do for Israel, yet she expressed this in the past tense. Seven different times she used the term *He has*:

1. *He has showed strength with his arm.*
2. *He has scattered the proud in the imagination of their heart.*
3. *He has put down princes from <their> thrones.*
4. *and has exalted them of low degree.*
5. *The hungry He has filled with good things.*
6. *And the rich He has sent empty away.*
7. *He has given help to Yisrael his servant.*

The use of the Greek aorist in these verses has created some discussion. The term "aorist" defines a set of verb forms. In Ancient Greek, it is a tense which expresses an action that happened in the past, without clearly stating if the action was completed in past time or if it is still going on. Although Luke put the verses in the past tense, they describe that which is still to be accomplished in the future by the babe in Miriam's womb.

The birth narratives once again connect the coming of Yeshua with the various Jewish covenants. Here, in verses 54-55, the focus is on the Abrahamic Covenant: *He has given help to Yisrael his servant, That he might remember mercy (As he spoke unto our fathers) Toward Avraham and his seed forever.* Miriam will give birth to the One who will fulfill the Abrahamic Covenant.

The section ends in verse 56 with the statement that Miriam stayed with Elizabeth a total of three months. These three months were the seventh, eighth, and ninth months of Elizabeth's pregnancy. Miriam left her cousin's home just before Yochanan was born. By this time, she was herself three months pregnant and still in an unmarried state, though betrothed to Joseph. The birth of Yochanan created great attention in the town, perhaps attention Miriam did not wish to attract to herself.

[§ 8] — e. The Birth of Yochanan

Luke 1:57-80

(1) Yochanan's Birth

When Elizabeth gave birth to her son (Lk. 1:57), and when her neighbors and kinsfolk heard of it, they rejoiced with her (Lk. 1:58). It created a great stir in town because Elizabeth had been barren for so many years.

Verse 59 records the eighth day of Yochanan's life, the day of his circumcision. The biblical significance of this event will be discussed later, in connection with Yeshua's circumcision. Here it should be pointed out that this ritual was of high significance in Jewish circles and is highly regarded in rabbinic writings. Very few laws are permitted to override the Sabbath, and one of these is the law of circumcision. To this day, in Jewish tradition, practice, and custom, a male child is not named upon birth, but on the eighth day, which is the day of his circumcision. The Ashkenazi Jewish custom today is to name one's child after a relative who has passed away and not after a living relative.[4] However, the custom in Yeshua's day was slightly different. The Jews did name a child after a relative, but the relative did not have to be dead. The people who came to the circumcision of Yochanan assumed that the parents would name the child Zechariah, after his father. Since her husband was unable to speak, Elizabeth took the initiative and declared that he would not be named Zechariah, but Yochanan (Lk. 1:60). This went contrary to Jewish custom because, as the neighbors pointed out (Lk. 1:61), *There is none of your kindred that is called by this name.* In other words, there was no one, either in Zechariah's or Elizabeth's family, who had this name, and therefore, they were going against Jewish tradition and practice. In obedience to Gabriel's command, Elizabeth insisted that her son would be called Yochanan. The neighbors, however, assuming that Zechariah would certainly follow Jewish tradition and overrule his wife, tried to go over Elizabeth's head: *And they made signs unto his father* (Lk. 1:62). The fact that they had to make signs implies that Gabriel had actually struck Zechariah mute and deaf; otherwise, there would have been no need to make signs to him. They could have simply spoken to him, and Zechariah would have heard. Since he could not speak, he "asked" for a writing tablet and wrote, *His name is Yochanan* (Lk. 1:63), confirming what Elizabeth had told these neighbors. Although it was contrary to Jewish custom, they were naming the child Yochanan in obedience to the command of God. Because Zechariah obeyed, his tongue was loosed and he was able to speak and bless God.

Due to the peculiarity of these events, they *were noised abroad throughout all the hill country of Yehudah* (Lk. 1:65). There was general recognition that something supernatural had taken place, that Yochanan was somehow unique, and that he was going to play a special role in God's plan and program, though the people did not know what this was (Lk. 1:66).

Thus, Yochanan was given a name that did not appear in either family line. Throughout this study, it will be pointed out that what happens to the herald will happen to the King.

---

[4] Ashkenazi Jews are from northern and eastern Europe.

(2) Zechariah's Prophecy

Verse 67 states that *Zecharyah was filled with the Holy Spirit and prophesied.* Zechariah was now controlled by the Holy Spirit, and as a result, in verses 68-79, he issued a prophetic utterance. It can be divided into two sections: In verses 68-75, he spoke of the Messiah; in verses 76-79, he dealt with his son, Yochanan.

In his prophetic utterance (Lk. 1:72), Zechariah blessed God for remembering *his holy covenant.* In total, he connected the coming of the Messiah with three of the Jewish covenants, the first being the Davidic: *And has raised up a horn of salvation for us In the house of his servant David* (Lk. 1:69). In verse 73, Zechariah made the connection to the Abrahamic Covenant: *The oath which he spoke unto Avraham our father.* In verse 77, he made the connection to the New Covenant: *To give knowledge of salvation unto his people in the remission of their sins.* The *remission of their sins* was to be a product of the New Covenant.

(3) God Remembers His Oath

Earlier, it was pointed out that the meaning of the name Zechariah is "Jehovah remembers" and that the meaning of the name Elizabeth is "the oath of God." Here is the word play that uses the meaning of both names. The last line of verse 72 states, *And to remember his holy covenant.* The first line of verse 73 states, *The oath which he spoke unto Avraham our father.* So the two names together teach that "God remembers His oath." God will fulfill all His covenantal promises to Israel.

(4) Yochanan's Ministry

In verse 76, Zechariah spelled out exactly what Yochanan's task was going to be: He was going to be a prophet of God. A prophet was one who received direct revelation from God, and Yochanan received it. He was the last of the Old Testament-style prophets.[5]

---

[5] New Testament prophets begin with the new age following the death, resurrection, and ascension of the Messiah. The birth of the *ekklesia*, meaning the church, is recorded in Acts 2:1-4.

Furthermore, Yochanan was to *go before the face of the Lord.* In fulfillment of Malachi 3:1, he was Messiah's forerunner and the herald of the King.

In verse 78, Zechariah continued his prophetic utterance about his offspring and the Messiah: *Because of the tender mercy of our God, Whereby the dayspring from on high shall visit us.* The term *dayspring* means "the rising sun." It is a reference to *the sun of righteousness* of Malachi 4:2. The picture is that just as the morning star signals the coming of day, even so, Yochanan will be like the morning star who will precede the coming of the "Sun of Righteousness." When the "Sun of Righteousness" arrived (Lk. 1:79), He was to benefit two different groups of people, as evidenced by the change of pronouns: *To shine upon* **them** *that sit in darkness and the shadow of death; To guide* **our** *feet into the way of peace. Them* refers to the Gentiles, who, because they were not the recipients of divine revelation, were viewed as sitting *in darkness and the shadow of death.* The Messiah will benefit the Gentiles because it was prophesied that He would be their light (Is. 42:6; 49:6; Lk. 2:32). Furthermore, the Messiah will *guide our feet. Our* refers to the Jewish people; He will bring peace to Israel.

The passage ends in verse 80, which summarizes Yochanan's development in three areas. First, he *grew* physically. Second, *he waxed strong in spirit*; there was spiritual development. Third, he was *in the deserts.* Early in his life, Yochanan took off into the desert, the wilderness of Judah, where he spent a great part of his life. He remained there until his public *showing unto Yisrael.* Growing up in the desert meant that he was separated from the Rabbinic Judaism of his day, so when he began to proclaim his message to Israel, it was different from the rabbinic teachings of his day.

The whole section of Luke 1:5-80 shows the author's special concern for women and Gentiles.

[§ 9] — f. The Annunciation of Yeshua's Birth to Joseph

Matthew 1:18-25

The emphasis of this section is clearly on the virgin birth, which is mentioned three different times. Matthew, writing from Joseph's perspective, noted the following: *before they came together she was found with child of the Holy Spirit* (Mt. 1:18). This verse makes it very clear that Miriam was pregnant before there had been any sexual relations between her and her husband. The second time the virgin birth is emphasized is in verses 22-23. The fact that Isaiah 7:14 is quoted here clearly shows that at least some in first-century Judaism understood Isaiah's prophecy to speak of a virgin birth. For Matthew, of course, this solves the problem of the Jechoniah curse, which we discussed on pages 28-31. The virgin birth is emphasized for the third time in verse 25, where it says that Joseph *knew her not till she had brought forth a son.* Even after the wedding ceremony, they had no sexual relations whatsoever until after the birth of Yeshua. Conversely, the very word *till* points out that after the Messiah was born, they did have sexual relations. This statement refutes the claim of one segment of Christendom that teaches the perpetual virginity of Miriam. According to the Bible, it is not true. In fact, Miriam produced at least six more children: four sons and at least two daughters (Mt. 13:55-56).

Earlier in this study it was also pointed out that in the end, Miriam submitted herself totally to the will and care of God, because she had to be concerned about three things, one of which was her relationship with Joseph. Joseph would naturally assume the obvious: that Miriam had been unfaithful. Indeed, verse 19 states that Joseph had privately already begun to write out a bill of divorcement, concluding that in light of her pregnancy, she had been unfaithful. As *a righteous man*, he could not marry a woman he assumed was immoral. However, he chose to keep it private because he was *not willing to make her a public example* and shame her.

It was at this point that an angel appeared to Joseph with a message containing three essential elements (Mt. 1:20-23). First, he was to fulfill the marriage vow; although Miriam was pregnant, he was to proceed with the wedding ceremony. Second, the child was conceived of the

Holy Spirit, not through an immoral relationship. Third, it was pointed out to Joseph that everything was happening according to plan and that this pregnancy was the fulfillment of the divine prophecy of Isaiah 7:14, which states, *Therefore the Lord himself will give you a sign: behold, a virgin shall conceive, and bear a son, and shall call his name Immanuel.*

In verse 21, the angel instructed Joseph to call the baby to be born Yeshua. In that way, the naming of the Messiah was like the naming of Yochanan: No other family member on either side carried this name. The reason the angel told Joseph to call the child Yeshua was because *it is he that shall save his people from their sins.* The angel was speaking in Hebrew and used a Hebrew word-play: "You shall call his name **Yeshua**, for it is he that shall **yoshia** his people from their sins."

In keeping with the angel's command, Joseph did marry Miriam, but they had no sexual relations until after the birth of Yeshua.

[§ 10] — g. The Birth of the King

Luke 2:1-7

(1) The Timing of His Birth

A decree issued in the days of Caesar Augustus commanded all to be enrolled for tax purposes in their own city. This was not an income tax, but a property tax, and it shows the reason for the sojourn to Bethlehem. Since both Miriam and Joseph were originally from this town, it was mandatory for them to return to Bethlehem, despite her advanced state of pregnancy. This was in keeping with Bible prophecy for it was only in Bethlehem that the Messiah was to be born (Mic. 5:2). Assuming that they bypassed Samaria, this trip of ninety miles took them at least three days.

By correlating Luke's account with Matthew's and other historical sources from this period, especially Josephus, it is possible to pinpoint with a fair amount of accuracy the actual year Messiah was born. Four basic clues will be considered. The first clue concerns the year Herod died, which was the year 4 B.C. The Gospel accounts clearly state that when Yeshua was born, Herod the Great was alive. This means the

Messiah was born before the year 4 B.C. The second clue pertains to the decree that was issued in the days of Caesar Augustus, or more precisely the year 8 B.C. Luke's point is that the Messiah was born after Rome ordered the census. The first two clues combined give a four-year time frame, indicating that Yeshua was born somewhere between 8 and 4 B.C. The date can be narrowed down even further.

According to Josephus, Herod left Jerusalem for Jericho in the year 5 B.C., which is where he spent the last year of his life. He died in Jericho, never again to return to Jerusalem. Matthew stated that when the wise men met with the king, he was still in Jerusalem (Mt. 2:7, 16). We can therefore deduce from Josephus' writings and the Gospel account that they would have arrived in Jerusalem in or before the year 5 B.C. This serves as the third clue. The last clue concerns Yeshua's age. When the wise men met King Herod, the Messiah was already about two years old (Mt. 2:16). Putting all these clues together, we can conclude that Yeshua was born sometime between the years of 7 and 6 B.C.

(2) The Place of His Birth

Upon arrival in Bethlehem, a small village of a few hundred residents, Joseph and Miriam were unable to find accommodation in the public inn. Today, these places of lodgment would probably be called caravansaries or khans. Usually, they were built along travel roads in close proximity to water and pasture. They were large, square buildings with a court in the middle for the animals. The rooms in the inn were unfurnished and were available to the wayfarers for free. The inn in Bethlehem most likely only had one room. This meant that men, women, children, families, and single travelers had to share whatever was available. When Miriam and Joseph were told that they could not stay in the inn, they had to look for another place to sleep, and what they found was a stable. This was not like a modern-day barn, but, as was common in the hill country of Judah, it was a cave used for sheltering animals. Miriam gave birth to Yeshua in this stable-cave and then, according to verse 7, did two things: first, *she wrapped him in swaddling clothes*; and second, *she laid him in a manger*. The significance of these two actions will be discussed in the next section.

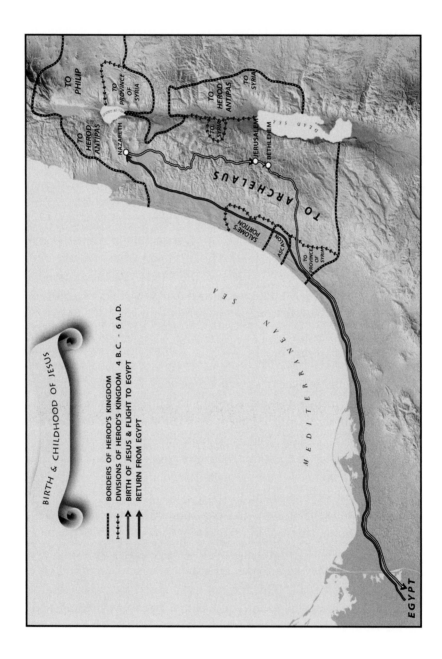

ABOVE: Like all other maps in this book, this map was created by Debra Riley and published by Ariel Ministries in Dr. Fruchtenbaum's *The Historical and Geographical Maps of Israel and Surrounding Territories* (2014). It shows Yeshua's birthplace and the journey His family had to embark on in order to flee from Herod's madness.

[§ 11] — h. The Announcement to the Shepherds

Luke 2:8-20

As pointed out earlier, Miriam gave birth to her first son sometime between the years 7 and 6 B.C., but there is not enough information available to reveal when during that year the Messiah was born. Verse 8 of the passage above is often used to argue against a December 25th date for His birth on the basis that there would not be shepherds and sheep out in the field in the month of December. However, Israel's rainy season is from mid-October to mid-April. In all other months, no rain falls, except on extremely rare occasions. As a result, by the time the first of October arrives, the hills and valleys are burned dry by the sun. By December, though, a lush green carpet covers the country. Even the Negev Desert has grass. It is a great time for sheep to be out in the fields. This is not to argue in favor of a December 25th date. Insofar as the biblical record is concerned, there are no details given that make it possible to determine with any certainty the season of the year in which Yeshua was born, let alone the exact month and day.

The early church itself was divided as to the exact date of Yeshua's birth. By the time of Augustine (A.D. 354-430), the Western church had agreed on the December date, which had been introduced a few decades earlier by Constantine and which corresponded to the ancient Roman festival of Saturnalia. The Eastern church fixed both the birthday and the arrival of the magi on January 6th. Especially in Messianic Jewish circles, there have been attempts to prove that Yeshua was born on a Jewish holy day, with *Sukkot*, the Feast of Tabernacles, being the most popular option. These attempts tend to be emotional reactions to the concept of Christmas Day, and often the arguments used are spurious, as the one mentioned above. The Gospel writers are quick to connect Yeshua with the Jewish festivals. Whatever Yeshua may have said or done on a Jewish festival is freely reported, as this study will show. However, the birth narratives by Matthew and Luke do not mention or even imply that the birth occurred during a feast day. Certainly Matthew, who wrote to a Jewish audience, would have made such a connection if it actually happened. The very fact that neither he nor Luke make such a reference shows that the Messiah was born on an ordinary day, somewhere between 7 and 6 B.C., but the exact date cannot be known.

On the day of Yeshua's birth, whatever day that may have been, something significant occurred in that two things became visible: the Shechinah glory and an angel. The Shechinah glory materialized in one of its more familiar Old Testament manifestations, that of light. This was the first time it appeared since its departure from Israel in the days of Ezekiel, about six centuries earlier (Ez. 8-11). Now, God used the Shechinah glory to announce the birth of the Messiah to Jewish shepherds. While shepherds were held in high respect in the pages of the Old Testament, by New Testament times, they were viewed quite negatively. They were considered untrustworthy and generally could not serve as witnesses. Their work rendered them unclean and excluded them from mainstream society.

Along with the Shechinah glory, an angel appeared to interpret the revelation (Lk. 2:10-12). The angel's message to the shepherds was threefold: first, *Be not afraid*; second, *a Savior* is born; and third, He is not just any savior, He is the Messiah Himself. The shepherds were instructed to go and find this child. However, there were many babies in Bethlehem, so how would they know which baby it was? The angel declared: *And this <is> the sign unto you* (Lk. 2:12). The term *sign* by itself does not require the miraculous, but minimally it does require the unusual, something out of the ordinary. This sign contained two elements: First, *a babe* was *wrapped in swaddling clothes*; and second, He was *lying in a manger*. The fact that the baby was *lying in a manger* told these shepherds not to look in the private homes of Bethlehem, but to look inside a cave that was used as a stable. Professional shepherds would know where these stable-caves were located.

The second clue the shepherds received was that the baby was wrapped in *swaddling clothes*. These could not be merely baby clothes because that would not be a sign. It was not unusual for a newborn to be wrapped in baby clothes. Being strips of cloth, the swaddling clothes gave the appearance of burial cloth. The symbolism should not be missed. On the very first day of His life, He was wrapped with the same type of cloth He would again be wrapped with on the last day of His life, showing the purpose of His birth. We were all born to live, but this

One was born to die, as signified by His being wrapped in what appeared to be burial cloth.

At this point, a host of angels became visible and proclaimed a two-fold message (Lk. 2:13), one about God and one about man. Concerning God, they exclaimed, *Glory to God in the highest.* Concerning man, they said, *And on earth peace among men in whom he is well pleased* (Lk. 2:14). Many of our popular Christmas carols, though pleasant sounding, are not always biblically accurate. One carol begins, "Hark the herald angels sing." The text does not say they sang. It simply says they were *praising God, and saying*; it was a verbal proclamation, but it was not put to music (Lk. 2:13).

Because of the two signs the shepherds had received from the angel, they were able to find the right child (Lk. 2:15-20). The first Jewish worship of the Messianic King is recorded here, initiated by means of the Shechinah glory.

But Miriam kept all these sayings, pondering them in her heart (Lk. 2:19). Much later, she would reveal these things to the writer, Luke, who would record these events from her perspective.

[§§ 12–19] — 3. His Infancy and Childhood

[§ 12] — a. The Circumcision

Luke 2:21

As it had been with Yochanan, Yeshua's name was chosen by God and revealed before His conception by an angel, but the official naming took place on the day of circumcision, or the eighth day of life.

Circumcision was commanded under two of the five Jewish covenants: the Abrahamic Covenant and the Mosaic Covenant. However, in each case, the meaning was a bit different. Under the Abrahamic Covenant, circumcision was a sign of the covenant and a sign of Jewishness. Under the Mosaic Covenant, circumcision was the means of submitting to the law. Under the Abrahamic Covenant, it was mandatory for all Jews and for those who were permanent residents within a Jewish household. Under the Mosaic Covenant, it was mandatory for Jews and for those Gentiles who wished to become part of the commonwealth of Israel. Because it was the means of submitting to the law, Paul warned the Gentile Galatians that if they submitted to circumcision, it would obligate them to keep the whole law, not just that one commandment of the law.

When Messiah died, He rendered the Mosaic Covenant and the Mosaic Law inoperative. So, today, there is no basis for circumcising either Jews or Gentiles under the Mosaic Law, which was also Paul's point in Galatians. The Abrahamic Covenant, on the other hand, is an eternal covenant, which makes circumcision still mandatory for Jews. Jewish believers are still obligated to circumcise their sons on the eighth day. In light of this, how do we explain Paul's actions in Acts 15 and 16? In Acts 15, the apostle would not permit Titus to be circumcised.[6] In the very next chapter, however, he initiates the circumcision of Timothy. Titus was a Gentile; he had no Jewish origins. Timothy, on the other hand, did. His mother was Jewish, and this put him under different covenantal obligations.

Circumcision shows the faith and obedience of the parents, not the child. If, at the age of eight days, the child had the option, he would probably choose to forego the experience. That is one of several reasons why baptism is not the anti-type to circumcision. Baptism shows the faith and obedience of the one being baptized. There is no passage in the New Testament which teaches that baptism is the anti-type to circumcision. There is an anti-type, but it is not baptism. In Scripture, the anti-type to circumcision of the flesh is circumcision of the heart, not baptism.

[§ 13] — b. The Presentation

Luke 2:22-38

The next recorded event in the life of the Messiah is the presentation that occurred when Yeshua was forty days old. Here, again, Luke shows two of his main concerns: Gentiles and women. And once again, the

---

[6] See also Galatians 2:3.

parents of Yeshua proved faithful and obedient to the Mosaic Law (Lk. 2:22-23). According to that law, a mother who gave birth to a girl was reckoned ceremonially unclean for a period of eighty days (Lev. 12:1-8). If she gave birth to a boy, she was reckoned ceremonially unclean for forty days. After this interval, the mother needed to undergo a purification ritual. Miriam had given birth to a boy. Therefore, the event described in the verses above occurred when Yeshua was forty days old.

(1) The Presentation

According to Jewish records, the events surrounding the presentation of Yeshua would have taken place at the east gate of the court, which is known as Nicanor Gate. The first purpose of the presentation was the aforementioned purification of the mother so that she would be no longer ceremonially unclean. After *the days of her purifying* (Lev. 12:6) were fulfilled, the mother had to bring to the priest at the door of the sanctuary a lamb, a young pigeon, or a dove. If she could not afford a lamb, two young pigeons or doves could be offered instead (Lev. 12:8).

The second purpose of the presentation was the consecration or redemption of the firstborn males to the Lord (Ex. 13:1-2, 11-16). Any male animal or human being that *opened the womb* was to be *set apart unto Jehovah* (Ex. 13:12). While the Scriptures related this commandment to the tenth plague during which God spared the life of the Jewish firstborns, the tradition became that the firstborn male was to serve Him in a special way. Eventually, this special duty of the firstborn was handed over to the tribe of Levi which meant that the parents could now "redeem" their son *for the money of five shekels* (Num. 18:15-16). Since Yeshua was Miriam's firstborn son, she would have paid the redemption price on this occasion.

In order to achieve purification for Miriam, she and her husband had to offer *a pair of turtledoves, or two young pigeons* (Lk. 2:24). This reveals the economic status of these two members of the house of David: On an economic scale, they were poor. The law only allowed the offering of two birds if one could not afford anything better (Lev. 12:8). Hence, Miriam and Joseph were poor, and this confirmed what was predicted in two Old Testament prophecies. Isaiah 11:1 predicted that the Messiah would appear only when the mighty house of David had been reduced to what it was in Jesse's day: a poor family in Bethlehem. Likewise, Amos 9:11 predicted that the Messiah would appear only when the mighty house of David had been reduced to ruins. And so it was. By the first century, the royal line of David had fallen on such hard times that Joseph and Miriam could not afford to offer an expensive animal, such as a lamb. Instead, they brought two birds: one for a sin offering, and the other for a burnt offering.

(2) Two Encounters

On this occasion, Luke records that Miriam and Joseph encountered two specific people. These encounters would have happened either in the Court of the Gentiles or the Court of the Women, because as a woman, Miriam could not go beyond the Nicanor Gate.

The first encounter was with a man named Simeon (Lk. 2:25-35), a man who *was righteous and devout, looking for the consolation of Yisrael: and the Holy Spirit was upon him* (Lk. 2:25). The term *righteous* means "just." Hence, he was Simeon the Just or Simeon the Righteous. In Jewish writings, there was a famous rabbi by this name who was a president of the Sanhedrin.[7] However, the Simeon described in these rabbinic writings was not the same as the one Luke is speaking of because he lived at an earlier period of time. Luke's Simeon was a *devout* man, a member of the believing Jewish remnant of that day. He was *looking for the consolation of Yisrael*, for the coming of the Messiah, with expectation.

Verse 25 goes on to say that *the Holy Spirit was upon him*; this is an instance in the New Testament of the Old Testament type ministry of the Holy Spirit. According to verse 26, the Holy Spirit had revealed to Simeon that he would not die before he had seen the *Lord's Messiah*,

---

[7] The Sanhedrin was an assembly of 23 to 71 men, appointed from every city of the land of Israel. During the first century, preceding the fall of the Second Temple, the Great Sanhedrin consisted of 71 members and was presided over by the high priest. This was the Supreme Court. Any minor court consisted of 23 men and was called a "Small Sanhedrin." In the Second Temple period, the Great Sanhedrin met in the Hall of Hewn Stones in the Temple in Jerusalem. The court convened every day, except during the feasts and on the Sabbath. The Sanhedrin is mentioned in the Gospels in relation to the trial of Yeshua and several times in the book of Acts (for example, in chapter 7, in connection with the stoning death of Stephen).

the Messianic Person. When Simeon, who at this time was elderly, came into the Temple compound, *he came in the Spirit* (Lk. 2:27). In other words, the Spirit led him into the Temple compound at this very point of time. When his eyes saw Yeshua, he recognized in this forty-day-old boy the fulfillment of that promise. Simeon's eyes had finally seen the Messiah. At that point, he spoke a prophetic utterance (Lk. 2:29-32) in which he said several things.

Simeon was now ready to die because the promise which had been made to him was fulfilled. He had seen the Messianic Person (Lk. 2:29). He declared, *For mine eyes have seen your salvation* (Lk. 2:30). This is a play upon words, for Simeon was not speaking English, but Hebrew. The Hebrew word for "salvation" is *yeshuah*. The Hebrew word for "Jesus" is almost the same: *Yeshua*. As mentioned before, both come from the same Hebrew root *yasha*, which means "to save." The only difference is the Hebrew letter *he*, "h," which itself is silent. So, in Hebrew, the word "salvation" and the word "Yeshua" sound virtually the same. In a real way, what he said was not only, *mine eyes have seen your salvation*, but, "mine eyes have seen your Yeshua." Indeed, he had recognized this forty-day-old child to be the Messianic Person.

Simeon pointed out that two groups would benefit from Messiah's coming (Lk. 2:31-32). Thus, he saw the same thing that Zechariah, the father of Yochanan the Baptizer, saw. The first group is the Gentiles: The Messiah will be a *light for revelation to the Gentiles*. Zachariah declared that it was the Gentiles who sat in darkness and the shadow of death, and upon them the light must shine. As previously mentioned, Isaiah prophesied that the Messiah would be the light to the Gentiles (Is. 42:6; 49:6). The second group who would benefit from the Messiah's coming was the Jewish people: *And the glory of your people Yisrael* (Lk. 2:32). In this short statement, Simeon summarized what a great many of the Old Testament prophets had said regarding Israel's final restoration and the messianic kingdom. One of them, Isaiah, proclaimed in 60:1-3:

> *¹ Arise, shine; for your light is come, and the glory of Jehovah is risen upon you. ² For, behold, darkness shall cover the earth, and gross darkness the peoples; but Jehovah will arise upon you, and his glory shall be*

seen upon you. ³ And nations shall come to your light, and kings to the brightness of your rising.

Israel's hope was that once God's glory would be seen upon her, the nations would recognize her special calling—for *salvation is from the Jews* (Jn. 4:22).

Having said these things about Yeshua, Simeon now had some strong words for the mother (Lk. 2:33-35). First, the coming of this child would mean a division within the Jewish world, a division between the believing remnant and the non-remnant, as prophesied by Isaiah (Is. 8:14-15). For some, He would mean *the falling* and for some *the rising*. Those who failed to believe on Him would fall. For the Jewish unbeliever, He would be the stone of stumbling and the rock of offense. For the Jewish believer, He was going to be the rising, because those who believed were going to receive the salvation that He offers. Second, He would be *spoken against* throughout the Jewish world and throughout Jewish history. Third, because of His coming, *a sword shall pierce* the soul of Miriam, and it did. She was present when the Jewish leaders rejected Him and called Him demon possessed. She observed the people turning against Him. The sword pierced its deepest when she saw her Son hanging upon the cross. Finally, Simeon pointed out that all this agony was necessary so that *thoughts out of many hearts may be revealed.*

The second person Miriam and Joseph encountered in the Temple compound was a woman (another topic which was of special interest to Luke). She was a *prophetess* by the name of *Hannah*, which is the Hebraic form for the Hellenized "Anna" (Lk. 2:36-38). She was of *the tribe of Asher.* Asher is one of the so-called "ten lost tribes," but Anna was not lost. In fact, there is no such thing as "the ten lost tribes of Israel." This is a myth. The Bible reveals exactly where the ten tribes settled. When the Jews returned from the Babylonian Captivity, members of all twelve tribes came back, not just members of the tribes of Judah and Benjamin. Anna is an example of this; she was of the tribe of Asher.

Anna was *of a great age*. In a footnote, A. T. Robertson explains that this phrase literally reads, "advanced in many years."[8] So Anna, advanced in many years, had been a widow for 84 years[9] and previously married for seven years. By the time she met Miriam and Joseph, she was over one hundred years old. The expression *"she was of a great age"* is a more emphatic form of what was said about Zechariah and Elizabeth: *and they both were now well stricken in years* (Lk. 1:7).

Anna, too, recognized the Messianic Person in this forty-day-old child. As a result, she went to announce to other members of the believing remnant of that day that the Messiah had been born and that she had seen Him.

Both Simeon and Anna passed away before Yeshua began His public ministry.

[§§ 14–16] — c. His Infancy

[§ 14] — (1) In Bethlehem
Matthew 2:1-12

In the United States, around Christmas time, nativity sets are displayed on church lawns, in church sanctuaries, and in front of private homes. They tend to look alike. There is a three-sided structure that represents a barn, though no Jewish person living in first-century Israel would have recognized it as such. In front of this "barn," or perhaps inside of it, are three people: Yeshua, Miriam, and Joseph. Yeshua is either still in the manger or on Miriam's lap. Facing them, to one side, are a group of shepherds (the actual number varies), and on the other side are three

---

[8] Robertson, *A Harmony of the Gospels*, p. 11.

[9] A. T. Robertson, the foremost Greek scholar of his day, used the English Revised Version of 1881 as the basis of his Harmony. The ERV translates Luke 2:37 as, *and she had been a widow even for four-score and four years.* The Greek New Testament allows for this rendering, though the ASV of 1901, which is based on the ERV, translates the phrase as, *and she had been a widow even unto eighty and four years.* This author bases his calculations of Anna's age on Robertson's work. If the prophetess got married at age 12, was married for seven years, and a widow for 84 years, this would make her 103 years old when she met Yeshua.

kings. However, the biblical birth narratives contradict these nativity sets. The shepherds and the so-called three kings never even met, as their arrivals in Bethlehem were separated by approximately two years.

(a) The Magi

The first line of a common English hymn sung during the Christmas season says, "We three kings of Orient are." There are two biblical errors in the first line of this song. First is the number "three." How many wise men actually travelled to Bethlehem? The Bible never states that there were three. In fact, it is only certain that there were at least two because the word *Wise-men* is in the plural. So there were at least two, but maybe there were twenty or two hundred or two thousand. There were enough to cause the whole city of Jerusalem to be tremendously stirred up (Mt. 2:3), and this implies that, perhaps, there were considerably more than just three of them. The second error is to call these men kings. The Bible never refers to them as kings, but refers to them as *magoi,* or *magi,* or wise men, a term that means "astrologers." These were experts in astrology and astronomy, and their studies of the stars included both science and superstition. It is very likely that the Greek term *magoi* is a translation of the Hebrew *chakkim,* also meaning "wise men." Chakkim occurs most frequently in the Hebrew Scriptures in the book of Daniel. These men came from the East, which in Scripture is the area of Mesopotamia. In this passage, an unknown number of Gentile astrologers from Babylonia arrived in Jerusalem and asked: *Where is he that is born King of the Jews?* (Mt. 2:2).

(b) How Did the Wise Men Know?

Matthew 2 raises a number of questions, such as, how did these Gentile astrologers from Babylonia know that a Jewish king had been born? And, even if they knew about it, why would they choose to come and worship him? There had been astrologers in Babylonia since at least the time of Nebuchadnezzar and kings in Israel for a millennium, yet there is no record of a Babylonian astrologer going to Jerusalem to worship a Jewish king until the birth of Yeshua. What was different about this infant Jewish king? Furthermore, does this passage authenticate a form of or the practice of "Christian astrology," even though the Bible clearly forbids any kind of contact with any form of astrology? These questions will be answered one by one.

i. The Harbinger

How did the magi know that a Jewish king had been born? How they knew is somehow connected with the star they saw in the east (Mt. 2:2). In antiquity, that a star would appear as the harbinger of a crucial point in history was not an unusual concept. But exactly what was this star? Many have tried to explain it astronomically, but all such explanations fail since nothing celestial can do what this star did. The basic rule of interpreting Scripture is to always take the Bible literally unless there is something in the context that will not allow it to be taken that way. There are five things about this star in this context that show it is some-thing other than a literal star. First, it is referred to by the possessive pronoun *his*. It was the Messiah's personal star. It belonged to Him in a way that was not true of any other star. Of course, all the stars are God's because He created them; but there was something unique about this one that made it the Messiah's personal star. Second, it appeared and disappeared on at least two occasions. Third, it moved from east to west. Fourth, it moved from north to south. Fifth, it literally came down and hovered over one particular house in the town of Bethlehem (Mt. 2:9). Any literal star coming down to hover over one house in Bethle-hem would have destroyed the entire planet. That is the nature of stars; they are a mass of burning gases, like our sun. If the sun came down to hover over one house in Bethlehem, it would obviously burn up this planet. Being so huge, stars, like the sun, are not able to simply confine their hovering over one small house in Bethlehem. This one fact makes what Matthew describes unusual.

If this was not a literal star, then what was it? As mentioned, there have been all kinds of attempts to explain this astronomically; however, all such explanations fail. Neither comets nor conglomerations of plan-ets nor constellations can do what this star did. The explanation lies in the word "heavenly," referring to the spiritual, not the physical realm. In Greek, the root of the word star means "radiance" or "brilliance." This "brilliance" is the Shechinah glory. Just as the Shechinah glory was used to announce the birth of the Messiah to Jewish shepherds, it was also used to announce the birth of the King of the Jews to Gentile astrologers. Just as the shepherds knew where to find the stable-caves, by virtue of their profession, the wise men would be the first to notice a new light in the heavens. In those days, astronomy and astrology were not separate disciplines; to study one was to study the other. When these Gentile astrologers saw the unusual brilliance in the sky, it somehow signaled to them that the Messiah, the King of the Jews, was born.

ii. The Announcement by the Star

The next question is how these Gentile astrologers from Babylonia would have known that the appearance of a star in the heavens was announcing the birth of the coming Jewish Messiah-King. Jews would have known from the Scriptures, but how would Gentile astrologers know? There is a Babylonian connection, and it is recorded in Scripture, specifically in the book of Numbers. In chapters 22-24, there is a record of God's dealings with a man named Balaam. Balaam was a Gentile astrologer, a seer, who came from the region of Babylon. He had established a considerable reputation for himself throughout the ancient world. It was widely believed that he whom Balaam cursed was cursed, and he whom Balaam blessed was blessed (Num. 22:6). At this point in the exodus from Egypt, the Israelites had arrived on the border of Moab and were about to enter the Promised Land. The king of Moab, one of the earliest anti-Semites in history, took objection to the prospect of new neighbors and decided to take action. Because of Balaam's reputation, the king called for the seer and commissioned him (for a considerable amount of money) to come and curse the Jews. Four different times the king of Moab took the seer to a high mountain where he could look down upon the Jewish encampment. Four different times Balaam tried to open his mouth to curse the Jews; four different times God took over his tongue, and Balaam blessed the Jews instead. In these blessings, he issued several messianic prophecies, one of which is found in Numbers 24:17:

> *I see him, but not now; I behold him, but not nigh:*
> *There shall come forth a star out of Yaakov,*
> *And a sceptre shall rise out of Yisrael,*

And shall smite through the corners of Moab,
And break down all the sons of tumult.

The word *sceptre* is a symbol of kingship. It was this Babylonian astrologer, Balaam, who connected the coming of the Messianic Person with kingship and with a star. Archaeologists have discovered that the Babylonians kept many historical records; much of our knowledge of the Genesis-Exodus period comes from Babylonian sources. Archaeologists have also found an inscription containing a prophecy of Balaam now housed at the Jordanian Museum of Archaeology in Amman.

Just as God interacted with Balaam in the Hebrew Scriptures, He made sure that these Babylonian astrologers would have had knowledge of the star and its import, but Balaam's prophecy says nothing about *when* the star would appear. Therefore, how would they have known when to look for the star, or, how would they have known that when a star appeared in the heavens it was the star that signaled the birth of the Messiah-King? Of all the Old Testament prophecies of the first coming of the Messiah, only one passage pinpointed how many years would pass before the Messiah would come, and that was Daniel 9:24-27. This passage contains the messianic timetable.

Unlike many of the other books of the Old Testament, the book of Daniel was not written in Israel, but in Babylon. In fact, half of the book is not written in Hebrew, the Jewish tongue, but in Aramaic, the language of the Babylonians. When Daniel was taken to Babylon, he and his three friends were chosen to be instructed at the school of the wise men. Then a day came when Daniel was able to save the lives of all the Babylonian wise men. These astrologers were unable to interpret one of Nebuchadnezzar's dreams. Therefore, the king sentenced every one of them to death. Daniel and his three friends were among those arrested because, from the Babylonian frame of reference, he was considered to be one of the incompetent astrologers. However, Daniel requested and received an audience with the king. He interpreted the dream and, by so doing, saved his life and the lives of all the Babylonian astrologers. No doubt, because of that experience, many of these astrologers turned away from the worship of the stars and became believers in the God of Israel, Daniel's God, the God of Abraham, Isaac, and Jacob.

According to the book of Daniel, Nebuchadnezzar, the king, must not have been a man with great spiritual insight. When he saw that Daniel had some unique abilities, he assumed that he must be a superior astrologer. As a result, Nebuchadnezzar appointed him as head of the Babylonian school of astrology. However, Daniel never received his information and revelation from the stars, but from the Creator of those stars, the God of Israel. Generations later, the Babylonians still had in their possession a book written by one of the former presidents of their school of astrology, the book of Daniel, which pinpointed how many years would pass before the Messiah would appear; therefore, they knew *when* to look. However, Daniel had not implied anywhere in his book that the Messiah's arrival would be connected with the appearance of a star or some brilliance in the sky. This they knew from the prophecies of the Gentile astrologer Balaam, and, knowing Daniel's timetable, when they saw this unusual brilliance in the sky, they took it to be the signal that the Messiah was born. Again, the source was divine revelation, the written record, the book of Daniel, and *not* astrology. In no way can this passage be used to support any practice of "Christian astrology."

In summary, we can say that Balaam connected the star with the kingship of the Messiah, while Daniel provided the messianic time table. As a result, the Gentile astrologers of Matthew 2 knew about the coming of the Messiah-King. Having a timetable from Daniel, the unusual brilliance in the sky told them that the prophecy had been fulfilled. That is why they came to Jerusalem asking the question, *Where is he that is born King of the Jews?* (Mt. 2:2).

But why Jerusalem? Although the wise men had the book of Daniel, they did not have the book of Micah. It was Micah who prophesied in 5:2 that the Messiah would be born in Bethlehem. The magi did not know that. Neither did Herod the Great. So when the wise men came to Jerusalem and asked for the King of the Jews, he gathered together *all the chief priests and scribes* (Mt. 2:4) and inquired of them where the Messiah should be born. Their answer was, *Beit Lechem of Yehudah* (Mt. 2:5). From the perspective of the Gentile astrologers, the logical place for the King of the Jews to be born would be the capital of Israel, Jerusalem. Their question about the Messiah created such a great stir in the city that Herod called these men into his own palace. Matthew

2:7 points out that he did so *privately* and *learned of them exactly what time the star appeared.* Herod wanted to know how long it had been since that star first appeared. This was crucial in determining what age Yeshua was when these events occurred. From his later decree to kill all boys two years of age and younger, the astrologers' answer can be deduced: The star first appeared two years before they arrived in Jerusalem. After having learned this, Herod sent the wise men to Bethlehem (Mt. 2:8). He instructed them to report back to him after they had found the One they were looking for.

Having heard what Herod had to say, the wise men headed for Bethlehem. Because there were many houses and many two-year-old boys, it would be very difficult to find this child. Do they go house to house and door to door? And how would they know which two-year-old it was? At this point, the star they had seen earlier reappeared. It came down and hovered over *where the young child was* (Mt. 2:9). According to verse 11, the family was no longer in the cave-stable where the shepherds had found them, but in a private house. Therefore, the shepherds and the wise men never saw each other; the two events were separated by two years in time. The wise men came into the house and worshipped *the young child*, and this was the first Gentile worship of the Messianic Person. The first Jewish worship and the first Gentile worship were initiated in the same way: by means of the Shechinah glory.

(c) The Gifts

The wise men left behind three gifts: *gold and frankincense and myrrh* (Mt. 2:11). In the Hebrew Scriptures, all of these elements have symbolic significance. Gold is the symbol of kingship (e.g. I Kgs. 10:10); Yeshua is the King. Frankincense is the symbol of deity (e.g. Lev. 2:2); Yeshua is God. Myrrh is the symbol of death and sacrifice (e.g. Ex. 30:23); Yeshua is the final sacrifice for sin. While the first line of the popular Christmas song, "We three kings of Orient are," is not biblical, the last line is correct: "God and King and Sacrifice." It is the mention of three gifts that led to the assumption that there were three wise men. However, more than one person can give the same gift.

Although the wise men were told by Herod to come back to Jerusalem and let him know who the child was, God warned them in a dream not to do so (Mt. 2:12). They returned to Babylonia by a different route, bypassing Jerusalem, and they did not report to Herod the Great.

[§ 15] — (2) In Egypt

Matthew 2:13-18

After the wise men left Bethlehem, the angel again appeared to Joseph in a dream. As mentioned before, Matthew relates the events from Joseph's perspective, reporting that the angel appeared to him, warning him to flee to Egypt and to live there until they received word to return to the land. Since they were a poverty-stricken family, where did they get the money to make such a journey? The wise men gave them three types of gifts: gold, frankincense, and myrrh. These were expensive gifts which provided what they needed to pay for the journey to Egypt and the sojourn in that land. But why Egypt? The land of Egypt became a Roman province in 30 B.C. Thus, it was beyond the jurisdiction of Herod. According to some estimations, there were about one million Jews living in Egypt at the time of Yeshua's birth, some of whom might have well been relatives or friends of Miriam and Joseph. Furthermore, it would have taken the family only three days to cover the sixty miles to reach the border. Even during Old Testament times, Egypt was a classic land of refuge for people who needed to flee from their enemies in Israel (see I Kgs. 11:40; Jer. 26:21).

Matthew's theme is "Yeshua the Messiah, the King of the Jews." That very theme was Herod's fear. He was constantly in fear of someone plotting to usurp his throne. Herod is known in history as Herod the Great, but perhaps a more proper title would be Herod the Paranoid. Because of his paranoia, he was always looking out for conspiracies. During the course of his career, he killed his favorite wife, Mariamne, and three of his own sons, because he thought they were conspiring against him. The emperor of that day was Augustus who once said that it was better to be Herod's pig than Herod's son. Because Herod was a nominal convert to Judaism, he did not eat pork, and so Herod's pigs were safe. However, to be one of Herod's sons was an "occupational hazard." If Herod even suspected a conspiracy, executions followed.

This paranoia told Herod that there was a two-year-old in Bethlehem conspiring to take away his throne. When he realized the wise men had no intention of coming back to inform him where this child was, he took matters into his own hands. He ordered his soldiers to go to Bethlehem and to kill every male child of two years and under (Mt. 2:16). Because of God's intervention, Joseph had taken Miriam and Yeshua and fled to Egypt (Mt. 2:14). While many were killed, the Messianic Child was spared. The family remained in Egypt for one or two years.

[§ 16] — (3) In Nazareth
Matthew 2:19-23, Luke 2:39

When Herod finally died, in the year 4 B.C., an angel again appeared to Joseph. He told him to go back *into the land of Yisrael: for they are dead that sought the young child's life* (Mt. 2:20) When the family returned to Israel, the first area they came to was Judea.

When Herod died, his massive kingdom was divided among three of his sons. Archelaus, the firstborn, was called "ethnarch," not king, while his brothers, Antipas and Philip, were made tetrarchs. Having received the authority over Judea and Samaria, Archelaus, in some ways, was even worse than his father. In fact, when he succeeded to the throne, he killed three thousand Jews in the Temple compound during the Passover season. Even Herod never went to the extreme of killing people on the premises of the Temple. Because of the new ruler's reputation, Joseph decided against resettlement in the town of Bethlehem.

The settlement of the family in the Galilean town of Nazareth stigmatized Yeshua for the rest of His life, and He was frequently referred to as *a Nazarene* (Mt. 2:23). The Jews of Judea disdained Galilee. Galileans were considered materialistic and ignorant in spiritual matters. If one was only interested in getting rich, then he should go north, to Galilee. Anyone interested in obtaining divine, spiritual wisdom should go south, because that is where the rabbinic schools and academies were located. In John 7, when Nicodemus tried to make a defense on behalf of Yeshua, the other Pharisees blurted out mistakenly, *Search, and see that out of Galilee arises no prophet* (Jn. 7:52). They ignored the fact that there were prophets who had arisen out of Galilee, such as Hosea, Jonah, and Elisha.

While Judeans looked down on Galileans in general, Galileans looked down on those among them who came from Nazareth. Nazareth was a town of ill repute. Since it was the base of a Roman garrison, Jews who lived there were viewed as traitors. In John 1, when one of His future disciples was told, *We have found him* [the Messiah] ... *Yeshua of Natzeret* (Jn. 1:45), the response was, *Can any good thing come out of Natzeret?* (Jn. 1:46). Settling in Nazareth made Yeshua a despised and rejected individual, but that, too, was in keeping with the words of the prophets.

[§§ 17–19] — d. His Boyhood

[§ 17] — (1) His Growth

Luke 2:40

Luke's account describes Yeshua's human development because it is Luke who emphasized the humanity of Yeshua. In only one verse, he summarized the development of Yeshua from the age of about four to the age of twelve: He grew and became strong and was filled with wisdom, and God's favor was on Him. Luke gave no more details than that. Whatever else can be known about Yeshua's human development must come from other sources, and two such sources are available.

First, from rabbinic writings, we know quite a bit as to the nature of Jewish upbringing in first-century Israel. In the case of Yeshua, He grew up in a spiritual home, since both His mother and stepfather (or foster father) were members of the believing remnant of that day. The basic program of learning for a male child would have begun at the age of five with the study of the Written Law, the Torah. At the age of ten, he began his study of the Oral Law (to be discussed later). At the age of twelve, a son would be apprenticed to a specific profession. If it were to his father's profession, he would stay at home. However, sometimes the father would send his son or sons to another place to be apprenticed to a profession other than his own. Yeshua underwent some of this basic

Jewish education at home and at synagogue, and He was apprenticed to His stepfather's profession.

Although Yeshua was brought up in a spiritual Jewish home, this alone cannot explain His tremendous knowledge—knowledge which allowed Him to carry on an intelligent, theological discussion with the experts of the Mosaic Law by the age of twelve. This brings us to the second source of information—and one example of things that can be learned about the Messianic Person from the Hebrew Bible, things which are never actually detailed in the New Testament. As previously mentioned, Isaiah's favorite title for the Messiah was *Servant of Jehovah*. There are a number of "Servant of Jehovah" passages throughout his book. One of these is Isaiah 50:4-9:

> *⁴ The Lord Jehovah has given me the tongue of them that are taught, that I may know how to sustain with words him that is weary: he wakens morning by morning, he wakens mine ear to hear as they that are taught. ⁵ The Lord Jehovah has opened mine ear, and I was not rebellious, neither turned away backward. ⁶ I gave my back to the smiters, and my cheeks to them that plucked off the hair; I hid not my face from shame and spitting. ⁷ For the Lord Jehovah will help me; therefore have I not been confounded: therefore have I set my face like a flint, and I know that I shall not be put to shame. ⁸ He is near that justifies me; who will contend with me? let us stand up together: who is mine adversary? let him come near to me. ⁹ Behold, the Lord Jehovah will help me; who is he that shall condemn me? behold, they all shall wax old as a garment; the moth shall eat them up.*

Morning by morning, God the Father awakened His Son and took Him aside to disciple Him, to train Him, to teach Him who He is and what His mission was to be (Is. 50:4). Yeshua is a unique individual; He is the God-Man. Thus, theologically, He is referred to as the Theanthropic Person. He is only one person, but He has two distinct natures: a divine nature and a human nature. These two natures exist side by side; they never mixed. While in His deity, He is omniscient; in His humanity, He had to undergo the same type of learning experience that all humans have to undergo. In His humanity, He simply did not know everything. He needed to grow up and to be trained. God the Father did that by waking Him up *morning by morning* to train Him in matters concerning His person, His message, and His work. Even when He realized that His mission included suffering and death, He was not rebellious (Is. 50:5). He kept His ear open and did not try to *turn away backward* or escape His call. When the time finally came for Him to fulfill His mission, He gave His *back to the smiters*; He did not try to turn His back away from the pain (Is. 50:6). Furthermore, He gave His *cheeks to them that plucked off the hair*; He did not try to turn His head away to keep His tormentors from pulling out the hairs from His beard. Finally, He did not try to cover His face from the spittle that was being spat upon Him. He set His *face like a flint* to fulfill His mission (Is. 50:7-9). In fact, Luke used that same basic expression later: *He stedfastly* [like a flint] *set his face to go to Yerushalayim* (Lk. 9:51).

As a result of this training by God the Father, at the age of twelve Yeshua knew exactly who He was: the Son of God. He also knew the Scriptures so well that He was able to debate them with the scholars in the Temple compound.

[§ 18] — (2) The Visit to Jerusalem

Luke 2:41-50

Scripture records only one incident during Yeshua's development as a boy, and that was a visit to Jerusalem when He was twelve years old. This passage proves an observation made before: His mother and step-father were members of the believing remnant of that day, who obeyed the Mosaic Law (Lk. 2:41). Year after year, they went to Jerusalem for the Feast of Passover, as was commanded in the Mosaic Law (Ex. 23:14-17; Deut. 16:1-8). Under rabbinic law, only the adult males were required to go, but Miriam applied the Mosaic Law to herself.

When Yeshua was twelve years old, His parents took Him with them (Lk. 2:42). The location is specified to be Jerusalem, a city of about 80,000 residents at this point of history. However, during the festivals the population was considerably higher, especially during Passover. Sometimes verse 42 of the Luke passage is misconstrued to be Yeshua's *Bar Mitzvah*. Bar Mitzvah means "the son of the commandment." It refers to a form of confirmation, or coming of age ritual, that a Jewish boy undergoes at the age of 13. The term "Bar Mitzvah" was not used in the first century, but there was at that time a coming of age ritual that would later become known by this title. Yeshua was only twelve when the incident described in the passage above occurred, and since a Bar Mitzvah takes place at age 13, this was not the reason why His parents took Him to Jerusalem. There was another rabbinic tradition in the first century which comes into play here. After the son's twelfth birthday, in preparation for his Bar Mitzvah at the age of 13, he was to be taken to Jerusalem for the observance of the Passover. So this trip was not Yeshua's Bar Mitzvah, but it was in preparation for it.

As mentioned in § 17, at the age of twelve, young men were apprenticed to a profession. In Yeshua's case, He was apprenticed to His stepfather's profession, that of a carpenter. The word means more than just working with wood; it also has the meaning of "stone cutter." Since Israel is a land with a limited number of trees but a lot of rocks, this would make sense. In addition, He was to be apprenticed to His heavenly Father's profession.

The passage studied in this section records seven days of Yeshua's life, starting with two holy days: *and when they had fulfilled the days* (Lk. 2:43). The *days* referred to here are the day of the Passover and the first day of Unleavened Bread, on which travel was not permitted. On the third day, the family traveled back towards Nazareth. In those days, people usually traveled to the festivals in groups of various sizes, and so Miriam and Joseph assumed that Yeshua was somewhere in the party. It was a three-day walk from Jerusalem to Nazareth. Upon arriving at the first night's lodging, they realized that He was not among the group (Lk. 2:43-44). They traveled a whole day's journey back to Jerusalem: *and when they found him not they returned* (Lk. 2:45), which marks the fourth day. *And it came to pass, after three days* (Lk. 2:46); it took them three days of searching around Jerusalem before they found their son in the Temple area, which accounts for the fifth, sixth, and seventh days. There are not many events in the life of the Messiah recorded in the Gospels that provide that much daily detail.

When Miriam and Joseph finally found Yeshua, He was in the Temple, sitting in the midst of the doctors, those who were experts in the law. He was doing two things: *hearing them* (meaning He was hearing their deep theological discussions with understanding) *and asking them questions* (Lk. 2:46). They recognized that the questions He was asking were not the normal questions of a twelve-year-old, and so *all that heard him were amazed at his understanding and his answers* (Lk. 2:47). In other words, not only could He ask intelligent questions, He was also able to answer their questions. They were *amazed* at this because He was only twelve years old, and they knew He could not have learned all this from the Nazareth school system. This shows the results of His individual training by God the Father.

Joseph and Miriam had spent three days frantically searching for Him: *And when they saw him, they were astonished; and his mother said unto him, Son, why have you thus dealt with us?* (Lk. 2:48a). Miriam used an approach that is somewhat typical for Jewish mothers. She tried to give Yeshua a guilt trip: "Son, why have you done this to us?" One has to be sympathetic with her: She was the only Jewish mother who ever really did have a perfect child! Now and then, she forgot who He was, as she did here, and scolded Him. Part of the scolding was, *Behold, your father and I sought you sorrowing* (Lk. 2:48b). In the first recorded statement of Yeshua, His response was: *How is it that ye sought me? Knew ye not that I must be in my Father's house?* (Lk. 2:49). While Miriam was referring to His stepfather, He reminded her that Joseph is not His father, but that the God of Heaven is His Father. She should have known to look immediately in His true Father's house. The Greek for *in my Father's house* can also be translated as "I must be about My Father's business," or "about My Father's occupation." His point was that, at age twelve, He was not only going to be apprenticed to His stepfather's profession of carpentry, He was also going to be apprenticed to His heavenly Father's occupation. In His humanity, He clearly understood the kind of relationship He had with God. It was the relationship of a son to his father.

[§ 19] — (3) His Development

Luke 2:51-52

In these verses, Luke summarized Yeshua's development from the age of twelve until approximately the age of thirty. Three things should be noted here. First, Yeshua was *subject unto them* (Lk. 2:51a), meaning

His parents. This is the best verse to show that subjection is not an issue of superiority and inferiority. It is merely a matter of subordination, a matter of divine order. Here is a superior, the sinless God-Man, subjecting Himself to two inferiors, two sinful human beings. This was a matter of subordination and divine order. When the wife is asked to be in subjection to her husband, this, too, is not a matter of status, of superiority and inferiority, but a matter of one co-equal subjecting herself to another co-equal because of divine order.

Second, *and his mother kept all <these> sayings in her heart* (Lk. 2:51b). Luke, focusing on Miriam's perspective, explained that she took Yeshua's response, *I must be in my Father's house*, and contemplated what this meant, ultimately coming to the understanding that her son was the Messianic God-Man. While for a long time she kept these things *in her heart*, she later revealed them to Luke.

Third, Luke pointed out that Yeshua, in His humanity, developed in four specific areas, the same four areas in which we all have to develop. While in verse 16, Luke referred to Yeshua as *brephos* (baby), in verse 40, he called Him *paidion* (child) and in verse 43, *pais* (boy). In verse 52, Luke summarized Yeshua's human development one more time, explaining that He *advanced* or continued to grow until, at the approximate age of thirty, His life's story is picked up again by the Gospel narratives. The four areas in which Yeshua developed were:

1. *Wisdom*, meaning He developed mentally.

2. *Stature*, meaning He developed physically.

3. In *favor with God*, meaning He developed spiritually.

4. In favor with *men*; He developed socially.

[§§ 20–23] —
B. The Forerunner and Herald of the King

[§ 20] — 1. The Message to Yochanan

Mark 1:1, Luke 3:1-2

The first verse in Mark introduces his account of the life of Yeshua in three points. First, this is the beginning. For Mark, this does not hark back to Yeshua's genealogy or birth as was the case with Matthew. As in Luke, Mark's beginning starts with Yochanan, the forerunner of the Messiah and the herald of the King (Mk. 1:2). Second, this is *the gospel of Yeshua Messiah*. The term *gospel* means "good news," but its content can only be determined by the context. Thus, the good news in the four Gospels will not always have the same content as found in I Corinthians 15:1-4. Third, this Yeshua is the *Son of God*, a messianic title.

In the last mention of Yochanan, he had departed into the wilderness of Judah. He lived there separated from society, and now, in a specific year, he was called to begin the mission for which he was born. Luke added historical details to Mark's introduction. First, he mentioned the specific year: *Now in the fifteenth year of the reign of Tiberius Caesar* (Lk. 3:1). Tiberius ruled from A.D. 14 to 37. Then Luke mentioned some others who were involved in authority. In fact, he listed the names of the rulers of territories where Yeshua would sojourn over the course of His ministry. The first ruler mentioned is *Pontius Pilate*, who was procurator from A.D. 26 to 36 or 37. Then comes *Herod, tetrarch of Galil*. This is Herod Antipas, who began his rule of Galilee and Perea in 4 B.C., but was deposed in the year A.D. 39. The next ruler on the list is Antipas' brother, Philip, who ruled from 4 B.C. to A.D. 34. *Lysanias tetrarch of Abilene* (A.D. 25-30) is the next in line. Beyond that which is written in Luke's Gospel, nothing more is known of him except that he was probably also of the house of Herod the Great. Then comes *Chanan*, who served as high priest in the years A.D. 6 or 7 to 14 or 15, and *Kayapha*, who was the high priest in the years A.D. 18-36. Luke's list covers a period that stretches from A.D. 14 to 39. The most specific year Luke gives, though, is *the fifteenth year of the reign of Tiberius Caesar*. The question is whether he begins his count when Tiberius was co-regent with Caesar Augustus or when he was the sole ruler, or emperor of Rome. If it were the former, then the specific year would be A.D. 26 and the crucifixion would fall in the year A.D. 30. If it is the latter, then the year is A.D. 28/29, with the crucifixion being in A.D. 33. This author prefers the former, and this work will be based on A.D. 30 being the year of the crucifixion. Various reasons for this will be presented in the course of this work.

In the fifteenth year of Tiberius' reign, *the word of God came unto Yochanan the son of Zecharyah in the wilderness* (Lk. 3:2). The Greek term for *word* here is not Logos, but *rhema*, meaning "the spoken word." Yochanan heard the audible voice of God calling him to his mission. The term *Logos*, discussed previously, is the wider term and includes the written, spoken, and incarnate word, but *rhema* emphasizes the spoken word. This was the means God used to call Yochanan into his prophetic office. Such a direct revelation from God fulfills the promise made to his father, Zechariah, that his son would be a prophet.

[§ 21] — 2. The Message by Yochanan

Matthew 3:1-6, Mark 1:2-6, Luke 3:3-6

Matthew, Mark, and Luke are referred to as the *synoptics*, or synoptic Gospels, because their accounts of Yeshua's life are very similar; they include many of the same events and describe them in a similar fashion. They stand in contrast to the Gospel of John, which, by comparison, is quite different. The message by Yochanan is the first actual account found in all three synoptic Gospels.

Mark stated that the one who was to come, meaning Yochanan, fulfilled prophecy (Mk. 1:2-4), and indeed, two prophets predicted the coming of a forerunner of the Messiah: Isaiah (40:3) and Malachi (3:1). Mark quoted both passages because Yochanan's coming fulfilled both, examples of a literal prophecy with a literal fulfillment.[10] The basic content of Yochanan's message was threefold. First, *Repent ye* (Mt. 3:2). The term *repent* does not mean "to feel sorry for one's sins," but to change one's mind. It was a change of mind from one thing to another—from untruth to truth.

Second, Yochanan's message was kingdom-centered. The people who came to him were to repent *for the kingdom of heaven is at hand* (Mt. 3:2). Their repentance was to prepare them for the coming of that kingdom. Yochanan did not try to explain the nature of the kingdom he was proclaiming, so it is obvious he expected his audience to know what he was talking about. The Jewish audience of his day would automatically have understood him to be speaking of the messianic kingdom, described in great detail in their Scriptures by the prophets. If Yochanan had proclaimed any other kingdom, it would have been contrary to the Jewish context and the mind-set of that day. Neither he nor Yeshua ever explained that the kingdom they were talking about was anything other than what was already known from the Hebrew Scriptures. The Old Testament background and the Jewish kingdom concepts of the first century require this kingdom to be earthly and messianic, not some nebulous "spiritual kingdom of God's rule in one's heart." Such a rule is individual, not national.

Third, Yochanan proclaimed a *baptism of repentance unto remission of sins* (Lk. 3:3). Exactly what baptism means in the Jewish context will be discussed later, at the baptism of Yeshua. The main detail to note

---

[10] Every Old Testament quotation found within the New Testament will always fit into one of four categories of quotations. The first category is called "Literal Prophecy plus Literal Fulfillment." Any New Testament passage that records the literal fulfillment of a literal Old Testament prophecy falls into this category. The second category is called "Literal plus Typical." The meaning of the Old Testament text is taken literally, but it is applied as a type of the New Testament anti-type, hence "Literal plus Typical." The third category is called "Literal plus Application." Based upon one small point of similarity, an Old Testament verse is quoted and applied to what was a current situation for the New Testament writer. The fourth and last category is called "Summation." This category does not contain actual quotations of Old Testament Scriptures, but summaries. Instead of directly quoting Hebrew Scriptures, the New Testament authors summarized what these Scriptures teach about a specific person, situation, or future event.

here is that those who were baptized by Yochanan made a commitment: They would accept whomever Yochanan identified as the Messiah. By believing the baptizer's messianic message and repenting, they received *remission of sins*. Later in the Gospels, when those who were baptized by Yochanan encountered Yeshua, they did believe on Him.

Yochanan had been proclaiming his message for at least six months before he declared Yeshua to be the Messiah, so a great number of Jews from outside the country were baptized by him and then returned to wherever they lived. Many years later, in fact decades later (Acts 19:1-7), the Apostle Paul ran into a body of Jews who had been baptized by Yochanan, but had never heard who the Messiah was because they lived outside the land. Paul had to tell them that it was Yeshua of Nazareth. In keeping with their baptismal commitment to Yochanan, these people then accepted Yeshua as the Messiah and were baptized again into the believer's baptism.

Matthew stated in his Gospel that Yochanan's apparel was quite similar to that of Elijah the prophet (II Kgs. 1:8; Mt. 3:4). His basic diet was locust and wild honey, which were common to the area where Yochanan was ministering. Under the Law of Moses, no insects were allowed to be eaten, except for one kind of locust, the kind commonly found in the wilderness. That was part of Yochanan's sustenance. The second part of his diet was wild honey, a food staple also found in the wilderness of Judah.

Initially, Yochanan's ministry experienced a tremendous response. Mark 1:5 declares that people came from all over the country of Judea, from all around Jerusalem, and they went all the way down to the Jordan River, confessing their sins and being baptized by him. For the time being, these were the common people.

[§ 22] — 3. The Explanation by Yochanan

Matthew 3:7-10, Luke 3:7-14

a. Pharisees, Sadducees, and Herodians

When one has finished reading the Hebrew Bible, he will not have read anything about Pharisees, Sadducees, or Herodians. When one opens up the *Brit Chadashah* (New Testament), these groups appear without introduction. Obviously, some major changes had occurred in Judaism between the close of the Old Testament and the opening of the New. The first mention of any of these groups is by Yochanan here in Matthew 3:7, and his characterization of them is not flattering.

The Pharisees were religious leaders who played a major role in the various forms of first-century Judaism. They held to the belief that the Oral Law was equal in authority to the Written Law given to Moses by God, and they believed in passive resistance to Roman rule.[11]

On the other side were the Sadducees, who tended to come from rich, aristocratic families. They did not acknowledge "the tradition of the elders," as the Oral Law is called in the New Testament (Mt. 15:2). This difference in doctrine was a major area of conflict between the Pharisees and the Sadducees. Annas, the high priest, was a Sadducee, as were most of the priests. In the first century, the high priests were appointed by Rome, and since this is how they received their power, they were quite pleased to accept the status quo. In fact, they opposed anyone who tried to "rock the boat."

A third group mentioned in the Gospels is the Herodians. The name implies that they were willing to accept Roman rule over Israel as long as it came through the house of Herod. They were not a religious group.

The differing religious and political views of each of these groups not only put them in opposition to each other, they also put them in opposition to Yochanan and the Messiah. We see the beginning of this here in Matthew 3.

---

[11] See § 49 for more information on the Oral Law and on Pharisaic teaching.

b. The Sanhedrin's Investigation of Messianic Movements

Yochanan was proclaiming the coming of a king and a kingdom, and his preaching had obvious messianic overtones. According to Matthew 3:5-7, it caused quite a stir, drawing the attention of even the Pharisees and the Sadducees. It is this author's conclusion, deduced from the Gospel accounts, that there was a certain policy in place by which the Sanhedrin investigated any kind of messianic movement, and this is what is here recorded in Matthew and Mark. When such a movement was detected, the Sanhedrin conducted its investigation in two stages, the first being the stage of observation. A delegation was sent out to do nothing but observe what was being said, taught, and done. At this point, the representatives of the Sanhedrin did not ask questions or raise objections; they did not verbalize anything. All they did was observe. After a period of observation, they were to return to Jerusalem to give a report and issue a verdict. The verdict was to be that the movement was either significant or insignificant. If they declared the movement insignificant, the whole matter would be dropped. However, if they said the movement was significant, the second stage—the stage of interrogation—was put into motion. A second delegation was sent out, but this time they would ask questions, raise objections, and look for a basis to either accept or reject a person's messianic claims.

When the Sanhedrin became aware of Yochanan's ministry, they started their two-stage investigation, and *Yochanan saw many of the Pharisees and Sadducees coming to his baptism* (Mt. 3:7). This was the first stage of the investigation, the stage of observation. As this context shows, and as § 58 will show, the Pharisees and Sadducees did not come to be baptized by Yochanan, but they came *to his baptism* to observe. There is a distinction in terminology. Concerning the multitudes, they *went out to be baptized* (Lk. 3:7), but the Pharisees and the Sadducees merely came *to his baptism*. His response to them was: *Ye offspring of vipers, who warned you to flee from the wrath to come? Bring forth therefore fruits worthy of repentance* (Mt. 3:7-8). This shows there was no repentance on the part of the Pharisees and Sadducees, a prerequisite for being baptized by Yochanan. The *wrath to come* refers to the common teaching on the Day of Jehovah, also called the Day of the Lord in the Hebrew Bible. The phrase was always a reference to the period of the outpouring of divine judgment preceding the establishment of the messianic kingdom.

Yochanan warned the Pharisees and Sadducees against claiming, *We have Avraham to our father* (Mt. 3:9). The exact meaning of this will be dealt with in § 33. For now, the following should be noted. In Pharisaic theology, there was a concept referred to as *zekhut avot*, "the merits of the fathers." It taught that any descendant of the patriarchs, Abraham, Isaac, and Jacob, was protected from divine punishment simply on the merits of the fathers.

c. The Observations

The Pharisees and Sadducees who came to his baptism observed that Yochanan told people to do what was contrary to their nature and/or the office they held. Yochanan told the multitudes, *He that has two coats, let him impart to him that has none; and he that has food, let him do likewise* (Lk. 3:11). It is the nature of mankind to hoard wealth, not to merely take what is needed and give away the rest. What Yochanan was asking the people to do went contrary to their nature.

Among the crowd of people who came to be baptized by Yochanan were also publicans, or tax collectors. They said, *Teacher, what must we do?* (Lk. 3:12). The reason someone became a tax collector was not because the job paid well, but because of what Rome allowed them to get away with. If the Roman authorities decided that a person owed the government five *shekels* in taxes, the publican could collect ten, give five to Rome, and keep five for himself. Publicans became wealthy by extorting from their own people. Now they were told, *Extort no more than that which is appointed you* (Lk. 3:13). This was contrary to why they even took the office. The tax collectors were called *gabaim* in Hebrew and *telōnai* in Greek. Most of them were Jews. When they became head tax collectors by farming out "the territory to the *telōnai*, who, in order to make a profit, inflated the amount to be collected,"[12] they were called *mokhsim* (Hebrew for "tax farmers"), or *architelōnēs* (Lk. 19:2).

---

[12] Samuel Tobias Lachs, *A Rabbinic Commentary on the New Testament: The Gospels of Matthew, Mark and Luke* (Hoboken, Ny. KTAV Publishing House, Inc. and New York: Anti-Defamation League of B'nai B'rith, 1987), pp. 43-44.

Those whose business forced them to travel had to pay taxes every time they entered a new region or territory. This and the fact that Rome did not prevent arbitrariness and abuse of power led to the great contempt which the people had towards tax collectors.

Another group of people who came to be baptized by Yochanan were soldiers. They asked a similar question as the publicans: *And we, what must we do?* (Lk. 3:14). In this context, the soldiers would be Jews who worked as mercenaries in the Roman army. Why would they do so? If they had occupying authority, meaning they were assigned to an occupied people, then they could do what was forbidden under the Mosaic Law: they could exact things from the occupied people and commit acts of violence, forcing their victims to do things they wished not to do. Thus, these Jewish soldiers could supplement their income. When they asked Yochanan what he would have them do, he answered: *Extort from no man by violence, neither accuse <anyone> wrongfully; and be content with your wages.* In other words, he admonished them to do the exact opposite of what had driven them to become mercenaries.

At this point, what the delegation of Pharisees and Sadducees had observed was that Yochanan was telling the people to prepare for the coming of the king and the kingdom by doing that which went contrary to either their nature or their office. It will be obvious later that when this delegation returned to Jerusalem, they decreed that the movement of Yochanan the Baptizer was significant.

This first stage of investigation, the stage of observation, is the first recorded event of Yochanan's ministry in the Gospels. What happens to the herald will happen to the King.

[§ 23] — 4. The Promise by Yochanan

Matthew 3:11-12, Mark 1:7-8, Luke 3:15-18

In Matthew 3:11, Yochanan distinguished himself from the One who would come after him. Not only did he say he was unworthy to even *bear*, or carry, the sandals of the Messiah, he also points out a difference in the baptisms. While he, Yochanan, baptized with water, Yeshua would baptize *in the Holy Spirit and <in> fire* (Mt. 3:11). In the Greek, this verse features a common grammatical construction: a sentence contains two parts, and each part is individually explained. The One coming after Yochanan will also baptize. However, He will not do so by water, but by means of the Holy Spirit and fire. Matthew defined the difference between the two by stating, *whose fan is in his hand, and he will thoroughly cleanse his threshing-floor; and he will gather his wheat into the garner, but the chaff he will burn with unquenchable fire* (Mt. 3:12). In the context of Matthew's Gospel, *wheat* represents those who will believe in the Messiah and are therefore baptized by the Holy Spirit. They are the ones He will gather into His *garner*, or barn. In the context of Yochanan's preaching, the garner is the messianic kingdom. The people gathered into Messiah's barn are the ones who will enter the messianic kingdom. The *chaff*, on the other hand, represents unbelievers, those who reject Him and are therefore baptized *in fire*. The kind of fire with which they will be baptized is *unquenchable*. It is the fire of the Lake of Fire (Rev. 20:11-15).

According to Yochanan's explanation, everyone undergoes either one baptism or the other; there is no middle ground. The believers will be baptized by the Holy Spirit, but the unbelievers will be baptized by fire. That is why Paul writes in I Corinthians 12:13, *in one Spirit were we all baptized into one body.* Every believer is baptized by the Spirit into the body of the Messiah, the *kehillah* (Hebrew for "congregation"), or *ekklesia* (Greek for "church"). Those who reject the message are destined to have another kind of baptism, the baptism of *unquenchable fire.* In this immediate context, the fire is a judgment and not a blessing. Hence, the fire here is not the *tongues, parting asunder, like as of fire* of Acts 2:1-4, but the Lake of Fire.

Luke 3:18 summarized Yochanan's continuing influence: *With many other exhortations therefore preached he good tidings unto the people.*

[§§ 24–27] — C. The Approval of the King

After the Gospels report on the arrival of the Messiah and introduce His herald, they record three events that confirmed He was approved by God: His immersion (§ 24), His temptation (§ 25), and the testimony of His herald (§§ 26-27).

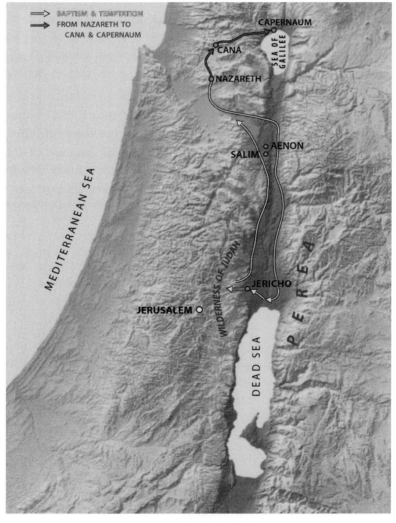

ABOVE: The map shows several important locations, such as where Yeshua was baptized, where He was tempted by Satan, and where He performed His first miracle.

[§ 24] — 1. At His Baptism

Matthew 3:13-17, Mark 1:9-11, Luke 3:21-23c

The baptism of Yeshua was the last act of His private life and the first act of His public life, and this was the first approval He received from the Father.

a. Baptism — A Jewish Ritual

Immersion was a very common Jewish practice long before baptism became a church ordinance. As a ritual, it did not begin with Yochanan or Yeshua. The Hebrew word which describes the act of immersion is *tvilah*. These ritual immersions took place in a *mikvah*. In the Hebrew Scriptures, ritual immersions largely had to do with the purification from ceremonial uncleanness. This was also the basic meaning of immersion within the Jewish community of the first century. Jewish baptism always required total immersion. Such immersions were mandatory for converts to Judaism, and the immersion required of proselytes had the added connotation of *identification*.

b. The English Term "Baptism"

As for the Greek, the initial root for the word translated into English as "baptism" is *bapto*, meaning "to dip" or "to dye." The term was used to describe the act of dipping a piece of cloth into dye to change its color, thereby changing its identification. It would no longer be identified as a white piece of cloth, but now was changed into (for example) a red piece of cloth. Its identity was permanently changed. Hence, the basic meaning of the act of baptism is identification with a person and/or a message and/or a group. From the Greek word *bapto,* there developed an intensified and more familiar word, *baptizo*, meaning "to immerse." This is the regular Greek verb used to describe the act of immersion, and it is equivalent to the Hebrew term *tvilah*. In Hebrew, Yochanan is called *Yochanan Ha-Matbil*, meaning "Yochanan the Immerser." The Greek *baptizo* is not necessarily limited to ritualistic use, but it was the common, everyday word for immersion. While *bapto* emphasizes the basic meaning of identification, *baptizo* emphasizes the mode, which is immersion.

While the English word "baptism" comes from the Greek word *baptizo*, it is not per se a natural English term. When the Bible was translated into English, the majority of the church was practicing sprinkling as the means of "baptism," and a smaller minority was practicing pouring. Almost no one was practicing immersion anymore. It would have been embarrassing to translate the Greek word literally as "immersion." To avoid having to change the church's way of performing the ordinance, the translators chose to transliterate rather than translate the word, and so the word "baptism" was "born." However, the Greek word simply means "immersion." Even as a ritual, baptism began with the Jewish community, and among the Jews, even to this day, the only way of "baptizing" is by immersion. Jews do not sprinkle or pour, so they would not consider either of those a valid baptism.

The basic idea behind baptism, then, is identification, and the one who is being baptized identifies himself with a person and/or a message and/or a group. By doing so, he disassociates himself from an old identification. Those who were baptized by Yochanan identified themselves with his message and prepared themselves to accept the Messiah. Whomsoever he would point out to be that Messiah, upon Him they would believe. It should be noted here that Yochanan's baptism was not the same as believer's baptism. That is why those who were baptized by Yochanan but had left the country before he could point them to Messiah had to be re-baptized into believer's baptism by Paul (Acts 19:1-7). In believer's baptism, one identifies with the death, burial, and resurrection of Yeshua (Rom. 6:3-4).

c. Yeshua's Baptism

The baptism which Yeshua underwent was neither proselyte baptism nor believer's baptism. It was Yochanan's baptism, a baptism of repentance and the return to God. When He came to be immersed in the Jordan River, *Yochanan would have hindered him, saying, I have need to be baptized of you, and you come to me?* (Mt. 3:14). The Baptizer recognized that Yeshua was the Messiah, and thus there was nothing for which He needed to repent. He would also have had no need to come back to God; He is God. So why would Yeshua bother to subject Himself to Yochanan's baptism in light of the fact that He had no need for repentance? As will be shown in this work, every major event in Yeshua's life (birth, baptism, transfiguration, death, burial, resurrection, ascension, etc.) carries theological implications.

There are six theologically relevant reasons for Yeshua's baptism, four of which come directly from the context of the three Gospel accounts of the immersion:

1. Yeshua's baptism was *to fulfill all righteousness* (Mt. 3:15). Righteousness, by definition, is consistently living with and perfectly conforming to an absolute standard, and the standard at this point was the Mosaic Law. By being baptized, the Messiah identified Himself with the righteousness of the law, showing that He would fulfill all of its righteous demands.

2. Yeshua was baptized to identify Himself with what Yochanan was preaching—that the people needed to prepare for the coming of the kingdom. Therefore, Yeshua identified Himself with this message.

3. His baptism publicly identified Him to Israel; He was publicly authenticated as the Messiah both verbally and visibly.

4. He was baptized to be identified with believers. Those who were the believing remnant of Israel in that day were responding to Yochanan's message and being baptized. Thus, Yeshua identified Himself with this group.

5. His baptism identified Him with sinners, as it says in II Corinthians 5:21: *Him who knew no sin he made to be sin on our behalf; that we might become the righteousness of God in him.* He took upon Himself the likeness of sinful flesh to be identified with sinners.

6. At His baptism, He would receive a special anointing by the Holy Spirit: *even Yeshua of Nazareth, how God anointed him with the Holy Spirit and with power: who went about doing good,*

and healing all that were oppressed of the devil; for God was with him (Acts 10:38).

d. The Presence of the Triune God

At the baptism of Yeshua, the Triune God made His appearance, both visibly and audibly. Matthew described this appearance with the following words:

> *3:16 And* Yeshua *when he was baptized, went up straightway from the water: and lo, the heavens were opened unto him, and he saw the Spirit of God descending as a dove, and coming upon him; 17 and lo, a voice out of the heavens, saying, This is my beloved Son, in whom I am well pleased.*

God the Son was present in the person of Yeshua, as He visibly *went up straightway from the water*. Note that Yeshua had to go *into* the water to come up out of it. This proves that He was immersed.

The second member of the Trinity, the Holy Spirit, was physically present, appearing in the form of *a dove* and came *upon* Yeshua. That this was not an actual dove nor some ghostly form is seen in Luke's Gospel, where it says that He *descended in a bodily form, as a dove* (Lk. 3:22). In all the various ways the Holy Spirit could have made His appearance, why did He choose a bird? And why specifically a dove? The first time the Holy Spirit appeared in the Scriptures was in Genesis 1:2, where it says that He *moved upon the face of the waters*. The Hebrew verb for *moved* is *merachephet*, a word used of a mother bird hovering over her eggs just before they hatch. Thus, the Hebrew wording of Genesis 1:2 relates this appearance of the Holy Spirit to the actions of a mother bird: He was brooding over the waters like a mother bird. The rabbis specified the bird of Genesis 1:2 to be a dove, and this was still the mindset of the Jewish community of Yeshua's day. To communicate this clearly in the passages that describe His baptism, the Holy Spirit did come down in the bodily form of a dove. The Son and the Spirit were now visible.

The final member of the Trinity, God the Father, made His presence known audibly: *Lo, a voice out of heaven, saying, This is my beloved Son, in whom I am well pleased* (Mt. 3:17). The account of the *voice out of heaven* also has a rabbinic background. In Hebrew, this voice is called *Bat Kol*, which literally means, "daughter of a voice." In rabbinic theology, the voice of the prophets ceased with Malachi. However, while the prophetic voice ended, the voice of God did not, and periodically God spoke a short sentence out of heaven: This was the Bat Kol. While the Shechinah glory is a visible manifestation of God, the Bat Kol is audible. What God the Father spoke audibly out of heaven at the baptism of Yeshua was: *This is my beloved Son, in whom I am well pleased* (Mt. 3:17), thus identifying Yeshua as the son mentioned in Psalm 2:12: *Kiss the son, lest he be angry, and ye perish in the way, For his wrath will soon be kindled. Blessed are all they that take refuge in him.* This son is the Messianic Son, God the Son. There were three times during Yeshua's public ministry when God the Father spoke audibly out of heaven. This was the first of those three times.

At the baptism, two things happened: first, God the Father verbally identified Yeshua as the Messianic Son; and second, the Holy Spirit anointed Him for service. Luke 3:23 states that He was *about thirty years of age* when these things happened. It does not say He was exactly thirty, but *about thirty*. As His baptism occurred around A.D. 27 and based upon the fact that He was born between 7-6 B.C., He was actually closer to 33 or 34 at this point of His life. The focus on the age of thirty may connect the calling of Yeshua to the prophetic ministry of Ezekiel (Ez. 1:1), who became a prophet at that age and whom God consistently referred to as *son of man* (i.e. Ez. 2:1). This became a messianic title of Yeshua, which emphasizes His humanity. His prophetic calling through the Holy Spirit was part of His humanity.

[§ 25] — 2. Through the Temptation

Matthew 4:1-11, Mark 1:12-13, Luke 4:1-13

The temptation is the second event that confirmed Yeshua was approved by God. The clear relationship between His baptism and His temptation should not be missed. This connection is seen in two ways. First, at His baptism, Yeshua said that He had come *to fulfil all righteousness* (Mt. 3:15); at His temptation, this righteousness was tested.

Second, at His baptism, God the Father declared Him to be the *beloved Son* (Mt. 3:17); at His temptation, He was challenged to prove this.

All three Gospel accounts make the point that the temptation of Yeshua was very much part of the divine plan, as it was the Holy Spirit who played the active role. Matthew stated, *Then was Yeshua led up of the Spirit* (Mt. 4:1). Mark added urgency to the same event: *And straightway the Spirit drives him forth* (Mk. 1:12). Luke mentioned the work of the Spirit twice: *And* Yeshua, *full of the Holy Spirit, returned from the Yarden, and was led in the Spirit* (Lk. 4:1). All this shows that the temptation was very much part of God's plan.

Mark's account simply states that Yeshua was in the wilderness for forty days and that He was tempted of Satan. It does not provide any details other than the following basic facts:

✿   The Spirit drove Yeshua into the wilderness.

✿   Yeshua was there for forty days.

✿   During the forty days, He was tempted of Satan.

✿   He was with the wild beasts.

Matthew and Luke both give the details, but there is a difference in the order of the temptations in the two Gospels. Matthew arranged his order based upon his theme, the kingship of Yeshua. For him, the key temptation was that of the kingdoms of the world, so he "saved the best for last," so to speak. Luke, who was historically minded, gave the actual order in which the temptations occurred. Therefore, as previously mentioned, this study follows his account because he is the only Gospel writer who claimed to have put his material into a chronological sequence.

God's aim in allowing these temptations was to prove the sinlessness of His Messiah. Satan's aim in these temptations was to cause Messiah to sin. He simply tried to accomplish the impossible. Messiah is impeccable. He simply is not able to sin. However, that did not discourage the fallen one from attempting the impossible. Satan's subsidiary aim was to keep Yeshua from the cross by offering Him a shortcut to His Messianic goal. If Yeshua had succumbed to this temptation, it would have been a good example of the attainment of a legitimate end by illegitimate means.

In His temptation, Yeshua played two representative roles, one for Israel and one for all believers. While many commentators and theologians recognize the second role, they fail to see the importance of His role for Israel. In His temptations, Yeshua was representing Israel. There are five ways in which this can be seen. The first way is that Yeshua was addressed as the Son of God, a title which relates Him to God's Chosen People. Israel, as a nation, is called "the son of God" in Exodus 4:22-23 and Hosea 11:1. Yeshua is called "the Son of God" in Matthew 2:15, which cites the Hosea account. In Matthew 4:3 and 4:6, Satan addresses Him in this way. So, the very title, "the Son of God," relates Messiah to Israel.

The second similarity which attests to Yeshua's representative role for Israel is that His temptation took place in the wilderness. Just as Israel was tested in the wilderness (I Cor. 10:1-13), Messiah's temptation also took place in the wilderness (Lk. 4:1).

The third similarity which shows this relationship between Israel and her Messiah is in the use of the figure forty. Israel spent forty years in the wilderness (Num. 32:13); Messiah spent forty days in the wilderness (Lk. 4:2). Though forty is a common figure in the Bible, here it relates the Messiah to His people.

The fourth way this relationship can be seen is that in both of the above cases, the Holy Spirit was present. The Holy Spirit was present with Israel during the wilderness wandering (Is. 63:7-14). Just so, the Spirit was present with Messiah (Lk. 4:1).

The fifth point which demonstrates Messiah as representative of the nation is that He responded to all three of Satan's temptations by citing Scripture from one book, the book of Deuteronomy, which is God's covenant book with the people of Israel.

Now, the point of all this is to show that where Israel as a nation has failed, the ideal Israelite, Yeshua the Messiah, succeeded. He became Israel's substitute, not only in these temptations, but also as the final substitute, the final sacrifice for sin.

Not only did Messiah play a representative role for Israel, He also represented all believers. Hebrews 4:15 says that He *was tempted in all points like as we are, yet without sin.* This, then, becomes the basis for

His priesthood. Because He was tempted as believers are, He could become their sympathetic High Priest. This does not mean that Yeshua suffered every type of temptation believers experience, just as they do not suffer every type of temptation He did. For example, they are never going to be tempted to turn stones into bread. On the other hand, having never married, Yeshua was never tempted to commit adultery.

Hebrews 4:15 can be explained by I John 2:16, which reads, *For all that is in the world, the lust of the flesh and the lust of the eyes and the vain glory of life, is not of the Father, but is of the world.* This verse points out that there are three areas of temptation: the lust of the flesh, the lust of the eyes, and the pride of life. Every specific type of temptation will fit into one of these categories. When Yeshua was tempted to change stones into bread, it was after He had fasted for forty days. He was extremely hungry, and His flesh cried out to be satisfied with food. This was a temptation in the area of the lust of the flesh. Of course, it was God's will for Yeshua to satisfy His own hunger, but it was not God's will for Him to use His Messianic power to achieve this.

In the second temptation, Yeshua was given a satanic vision whereby He was able to literally see all the kingdoms of the world in a moment of time. Satan then said, *To you will I give all this authority* (Lk. 4:6). As the prince of this world, Satan has authority over all kingdoms. The offer to transfer this authority to Yeshua was really an offer of a shortcut to His messianic goal. It is the will of God the Father for the Son to rule over the kingdoms of this world; but the means of attaining that authority was to be by the cross, not by worshipping Satan. Jesus could see what could be His for one act of worship. This was a temptation in the area of the lust of the eyes.

During the third temptation, Satan asked the Messiah to throw Himself off the pinnacle of the Temple to prove He was the Son of God. This was a temptation in the area of the pride of life, because He was asked to prove that He was the Messiah. The pinnacle of the Temple was the southeast corner of both the city wall and the Temple compound wall, the highest point from top to bottom. When Satan challenged Yeshua to throw Himself off the pinnacle of the Temple, he basically said, "If you are the Son of God, prove it to me by jumping off the pinnacle, because Psalm 91 says that if the Messiah stumbles, the angels will catch

Him, so He could not be hurt before His time. So if you are really the Son of God, prove it to me by jumping off, and let me see Psalm 91 fulfilled." Satan was right. If Yeshua had thrown Himself down, Psalm 91:11-12 would have applied. Angels would have rushed to His rescue because He was not allowed to die before His time. The angels would have let Him down gently from where He had jumped. The Temple compound was always full of people. If they had seen Yeshua jump from the pinnacle and float gently to the ground, they would have instantaneously proclaimed Him the Messiah. However, this was not the way God wanted to prove His Messiahship, and He had nothing to prove to Satan anyway.

The fact that Yeshua was tempted in all three areas of I John 2:16 proves that He indeed *has been in all points tempted like as we are, yet without sin* (Heb. 4 :15). The three temptations may be summarized as follows. The temptation to change stones into bread was a challenge that related to the will of God. Yeshua had to decide that while it was very much God's will to satisfy His hunger, was it God's will for Him to do it in this way, using His miraculous power? The answer was "no." When He was shown all the kingdoms of the world, it was a test of His submission. Would Yeshua consistently submit Himself to God the Father, or would He, on this one occasion, submit Himself to the authority of Satan in order to gain the power over the kingdoms of the world and bypass the suffering on the cross? It is God's will for Yeshua to rule over the kingdoms of the world one day, but this was not the manner in which He wanted His Son to achieve this messianic goal. The temptation at the pinnacle of the Temple was a test of His dependence upon God. There is a right way and a wrong way of depending upon God. The wrong way tests God, tempting Him to fulfill His promises. Indeed, if Yeshua had jumped off the pinnacle of the Temple merely on His own will, defying the will of the Father, He would have been testing God's promises. One must never test God's promises. One must simply believe that He will fulfill them in due time. While it was God's will for Yeshua to be proven the Son of God, this was not the means of achieving it.

Messiah resisted all the temptations Satan offered. It is noteworthy that He did so by citing Scripture, even when Satan misused verses by quoting them clearly out of context. This is the way all believers should resist Satan as well. The result was that *when the devil had completed every temptation,* meaning in all three points, *he departed from him* (Lk. 4:13). Yeshua's temptation proves a biblical principal found in James 4:7: If one resists Satan, he will flee, and resisting always comes by Scripture (Eph. 6:10-18). Luke added one last phrase and said that the victory was *for a season.* Every spiritual triumph is temporary. There will be more spiritual battles later, and the spiritual warfare must be fought until the day of death.

Both Matthew and Mark ended their accounts of the temptation of Yeshua by stating that angels came and ministered unto Him (Mt. 4:11; Mk. 1:13).

[§§ 26–27] — 3. By His Herald

The third approval of the King comes from Yeshua's herald, Yochanan the Baptizer.

[§ 26] — a. Yochanan's Testimony before Leaders

John 1:19-28

This section records the second stage of investigation by the Sanhedrin: the stage of interrogation. This time, the Pharisees and Sadducees were to ask questions. Three times it is stated that this was an official delegation. First, *And this is the witness of Yochanan, when the Jews sent unto him from Yerushalayim priests and Levites* (Jn. 1:19). This was an official delegation sent by the Sanhedrin, and priests and Levites were generally Sadducees. Second, when they asked, *Who are you? That we may give an answer to them that sent us* (Jn. 1:22), it again proves that this is a sent delegation. This reveals that following the first stage of observation the Sanhedrin considered Yochanan's ministry to be significant. Third, *And they had been sent from the Pharisees* (Jn. 1:24). The Pharisees initiated this stage of interrogation.

In answer to the question who he was, Yochanan denied being three things. First, he denied being the Messiah: *I am not the Messiah* (Jn. 1:20). Second, he denied being Elijah the prophet. Though he had come in the spirit and power of Elijah, which was his first correlation to the prophet, he denied being Elijah himself, *I am not* (Jn. 1:21). The correlation between Yochanan and Elijah will be developed further as this study proceeds. Third, he denied being *the prophet* (Jn. 1:21), meaning the prophet "like unto Moses" of Deuteronomy 18:15-18. Rabbis view that prophet and Messiah as being two different personalities.

When the delegation persisted in asking for an answer—*Who are you? . . . What do you say of yourself?* (Jn. 1:22)—he answered by quoting Isaiah 40:3: *I am the voice of one crying in the wilderness, Make straight the way of the Lord* (Jn. 1:23). In other words, he was claiming to be the Messiah's forerunner, the herald of the King. But he pointed out, *I baptize in water: in the midst of you stands one whom ye know not, <even> he that comes after me, the latchet of whose shoe I am not worthy to unloose* (Jn. 1:26-27). This statement shows that the Messiah was already present, but not yet identified by the baptizer.

Just as Yochanan underwent the second stage of investigation by the Sanhedrin, so, too, would the Messiah. What happens to the herald will happen to the King.

[§ 27] — b. Yochanan's Testimony to Yeshua

John 1:29-34

Verse 29 states that only one day transpired between this and the preceding event. This was the day ordained by God the Father for the Messiah to be publicly identified by His herald. There are various ways that Yochanan could have identified Yeshua, but he simply said, *Behold, the Lamb of God, that takes away the sin of the world* (Jn. 1:29). By calling Him the Lamb of God, Yochanan identified Yeshua with two Old Testament concepts: first, he identified Him with the paschal lamb of Exodus 12, and second, the messianic lamb of Isaiah 53. Of this He said: *After me comes a man who is become before me: for he was before me* (Jn. 1:30). Yochanan declared that Yeshua was both *after* him and *before* him. As to His humanity, Yeshua was after Yochanan, for He was six months younger. As to His deity, He was eternal. Therefore, He preceded Yochanan.

In verse 32, the baptizer went on to show how he could be certain that this was the Messianic Person. Initially, he *knew him not* (Jn. 1:33). However, it had been revealed to him that, *Upon whomsoever you shall see the Spirit descending, and abiding upon him, the same is he that baptizes in the Holy Spirit.* So then, at the baptism, when the Spirit descended in the form of a dove upon Yeshua, this certified once and for all to Yochanan that He was the Messianic King.

II. The Authentication
of the King
— §§ 28–57 —

The second main division of the life of the Messiah is the authentication of the King, which has two subdivisions: the acceptance of His Person and His authority as Israel's Messianic King.

[§§ 28–37] — A. Acceptance of His Person

[§ 28] — 1. The Belief by the First Disciples

John 1:35-51

In § 28, Yeshua begins gathering His disciples, and one will prove to be unworthy. The section covers the two-day period of Yeshua's life during which He called His first five disciples. It began one day after the previous event (Jn. 1:35) when Yochanan the Baptizer fulfilled his commission to identify the Messiah. On that day, he had identified Him publicly, and now, on this day, he identified Him to two of his disciples: *Behold the Lamb of God!* (Jn. 1:36). Upon hearing this, these two followers of the baptizer—Yochanan, the son of Zebedee, and Andrew— turned to follow Yeshua. Without understanding the Jewish frame of reference behind it, the conversation taking place here would seem a little strange. Yochanan and Andrew followed Yeshua from a distance (Jn. 1:37). After a while, the Messiah turned around and asked them a question: *What seek ye?* (Jn. 1:38a). They responded by asking a question of their own: *Rabbi, where do you live?* (Jn. 1:38b). His answer was: *Come, and ye shall see* (Jn. 1:39).

In the days of Yeshua, rabbis had disciples whom they would train and then ordain. A number of them had rabbinic schools around the Jerusalem area. Yochanan had introduced Yeshua as the Messiah, but his disciples addressed Him as "rabbi," the title of highest respect given by the Jews to those who were prepared to interpret the law to them. It seems they expected that the Messiah would be able to perfectly interpret the law for them, and so they revealed a desire to submit themselves to His teaching. When they asked, *Rabbi, where do you live?*, it was more than just idle curiosity. Yochanan and Andrew wanted to become Yeshua's disciples and subject themselves to His authority. In fact, it was such a major turning point in Yochanan's life that he specifically made note of the time, *about the tenth hour* (Jn. 1:39). If he was using Jewish time, it would have been 4:00 p.m. If he was using Roman time, it would have been 10:00 a.m. Yochanan became one of the apostles and authored the Gospel of John.

Andrew had a brother named Peter, who became the third member of the group (Jn. 1:40-42). When Andrew found his brother, Peter, he said, *We have found the Messiah*, and brought him to Yeshua. And Yeshua said to him: *You are Shimon the son of Yochanan: you shall be called Keipha* [Cephas] *– which is by interpretation, Peter. Shimon* was his Hebrew name, *Cephas* was his Aramaic name, and *Peter* was his Greek name. The day ended with three disciples gained.

Another day passed (Jn. 1:43). Before leaving Judea for Galilee, Yeshua Himself found Philip. When He called him to discipleship, Philip followed. Thus, the fourth disciple was gained.

Philip recruited the fifth disciple, Nathanael (Jn. 1:44-51).[1] Philip declared: *We have found Him, of whom Mosheh in the law, and the prophets, wrote, Yeshua of Natzeret, the son of Yoseph* (Jn. 1:45). Although Nathanael himself was a fellow Galilean, he held a low view of people from Nazareth: *Can any good thing come out of Natzeret?* (Jn. 1:46a). The whole idea of a Messiah coming from a place like Nazareth was a bit preposterous. However, Philip did not argue the case but simply said, *Come and see* (Jn. 1:46b).

Then another strange conversation took place—strange, that is, unless one understands the Jewish frame of reference behind it. Yeshua saw Nathanael coming, and before Nathanael could ask any questions, Yeshua referred to him not by name, but by description: *Behold, an Israelite indeed, in whom is no guile!* (Jn. 1:47) When He made that statement, Nathanael responded, *From where do you know me?* (Jn. 1:48a). In other words, "How can you know what I am really like?" From Nathanael's perspective, it was the first time the two had met. Yeshua answered: *Before Philip called you, when you were under the fig tree, I saw you* (Jn. 1:48b). Notice Nathanael's response: *Rabbi, you are the Son of God; you are the King of Yisrael* (Jn. 1:49). That would appear to be a strange conclusion. Just because of Yeshua's simple statement about seeing Nathanael under a fig tree, he declared Him to be the Messiah? Why would Nathanael come to such a strong conclusion based upon so little?

To understand the conversation, it must be taken in context. Yeshua did not call Nathanael by name, but by a title, *an Israelite indeed*, and then He added, *in whom is no guile*. Yeshua was making a contrast between this Israelite and Jacob, the first person to be called *Israel*. Church teaching has often portrayed the patriarch's life as one of guile, but this is not supported by the book of Genesis. Jacob was guilty of only one act of guile—deceiving his father—and that was done at his mother's insistence and over Jacob's personal objections. Because of this one act of guile, he had to flee from his father's household to the

---

[1] It is commonly believed that Nathanael and Bartholomew are the same person. A possible explanation for this is as follows: The Gospel of John mentions Nathanael twice, but never introduces the name of Bartholomew, while Matthew 10:3, Mark 3:18, and Luke 8:14 speak of Bartholomew, but not of Nathanael. Therefore, it is generally assumed that the two names identify the same person.

land of Haran, where he spent the next twenty years of his life. So in contrast to the first Israel, who committed one act of guile, this Israel, a descendant of the first one, is characterized as lacking guile. That is the first point which needs to be understood.

The next point concerns Yeshua's statement: *When you were under the fig tree, I saw you.* Yeshua is not merely talking about having seen Nathanael *under the fig tree;* that could have been incidental. The question is, what did Yeshua see Nathanael doing under the fig tree? In those days, when it was impossible for everyone to have a written copy of the Scriptures, the Jewish people spent a lot of their time memorizing them, and then they would meditate upon what they had learned. The rabbis said that the best place to meditate upon Scripture was under a fig tree.

Nathanael did not conclude that Yeshua was the Messiah based upon the fact that He happened to have seen him under a fig tree. Rather, Yeshua's comments (*an Israelite indeed; in whom is no guile!* and, *when you were under the fig tree, I saw you*) made Nathanael realize that this man knew the exact passage of Scripture upon which he had been meditating. Yeshua knew his very thoughts! This comes out clearly in the closing verse, in which Yeshua said to him, *Verily, verily, I say unto you, Ye[2] shall see the heaven opened, and the angels of God ascending and descending upon the Son of man* (Jn. 1:51). Genesis 28:12 is the only passage in the Hebrew Scriptures which speaks about angels ascending and descending. The passage records the content of a dream that Jacob had: *And behold, a ladder set up on the earth, and the top of it reached to heaven. And behold, the angels of God ascending and descending on it.* When did Jacob have this dream? On his first night away from home, after he had committed his one act of guile by deceiving his father. In other words, this shows that Nathanael's conclusion was correct: Yeshua had known the exact passage of Scripture he had been contemplating. Therefore, Yeshua had to be the Messianic King.

---

[2] Although Yeshua directly addressed Nathanael, He also included the other disciples who were with Him at the time by using the second person plural *ye.*

[§ 29] — 2. The Belief Through the First Miracle

John 2:1-11

The passage begins with, *And the third day* (Jn. 2:1). The mention of time is interesting because it indicates another set of seven consecutive days in Yeshua's ministry. This time, the days are recorded in the Gospel of John. The first day of this set is described in verse 1:19, when Yochanan the Baptizer was questioned. The second day is in verse 1:29, when Yochanan declared Yeshua to be the Lamb of God. The third day is recounted in verse 1:35, when Yeshua chose the first three disciples. The fourth day is covered in verse 1:45, when He gained two more disciples. Now, in verse 2:1, the author mentions *the third day*, meaning the third day of the three-day journey from Jerusalem to Galilee, which would include the fifth, sixth, and seventh days of this set. The town of Cana was located in Galilee.[3]

Another important point to mention about this passage is that it records the first of Yochanan's seven signs, the changing of the water into wine.

The Jewish wedding system of that day was comprised of two parts: After the wedding ceremony would come the wedding feast, which lasted for seven days. A smaller group would be invited to the wedding ceremony and a much larger group to the wedding feast. When Yeshua went to the wedding feast in Cana, He took with Him the five disciples He had gathered so far.

A terrible thing happened, something which must never happen at a Jewish wedding feast: The host ran out of wine![4] For some reason,

---

[3] In Israel today, there is a town marked as Cana of Galilee, about three miles east of Nazareth. Two churches are there, one built over the place where Yeshua changed the water into wine and the other marking the home of Bartholomew. Often churches like these are built on sites which are not authentic. The original Cana of Galilee was discovered seven miles north of Nazareth.

[4] It should be noted that the word "wine" in verses 3, 9, and 10 of this passage means wine. Both the Hebrew and the Greek languages have different terms for "juice." So this wine was made of fermented grapes. The Bible does not teach total abstention, but moderation. It is not the drinking of wine that is sin, it is drunkenness that is sin. It

Miriam, the mother of Yeshua, felt He must intervene in the situation: *And when the wine failed, the mother of* Yeshua *said unto him, They have no wine* (Jn. 2:3). Exactly why she felt He had to do something is not known. Perhaps the implication is that because He had brought five guests, they had run out of wine?

Yeshua responded to her by saying: *Woman, what have I to do with you? Mine hour is not yet come* (Jn. 2:4). Normally, the phrase, *Mine* (or My) *hour is not yet come* is a reference to His coming death. In this case and in this context, it means that He was not yet ready to go public with His miracles, because the place to go public would have been Jerusalem, not little Cana. Still, He did what Miriam asked Him to, but quietly, and for the most part, no one realized that a miracle had taken place. When Yeshua said to her, *Woman, what have I to do with you?* He was conveying that she no longer had parental authority over Him. At some point, a child must move from obeying the parents to honoring the parents. The point is that whatever He did would not be out of obedience, but rather out of honor.

Miriam instructed the servants to do whatever He requested: *Now there were six water pots of stone set there after the Jews' manner of purifying, containing two or three firkins apiece* (Jn. 2:6). Each of these pots could hold about twenty gallons of liquid, and they usually contained water used for purification purposes, such as the washing of hands prior to eating. Yeshua instructed the servants to fill all of these large pots with water. However, when they poured from them again, what came out was not water, but wine—in fact, high quality wine, which reversed the procedure of that day. Because the wedding feast lasted seven days, the host would serve the good wine at the beginning. Then after people had had some wine and their taste buds were not quite as attuned, the lesser quality wine would be served. The wine Yeshua made was of higher quality than that served at the beginning of the feast. In the Hebrew Bible, wine was the symbol of joy (Ps. 104:15), and the psalmist praised God for making *wine that makes glad the heart of man.*

---

is not the eating of food that is sin, it is gluttony that is sin. If to avoid drunkenness requires total abstention from alcohol, the same logic would require that to avoid gluttony requires total abstention from food.

By stating, *This beginning of his signs did Yeshua in Kana of Galil* (Jn. 2:11), the Gospel writer declared categorically that this was the first miracle actually performed by Yeshua. This disproves all the pseudo-gospels that record miracles He supposedly performed when He was a baby, a child, or a teenager. Yochanan makes it clear that this is the *beginning of his signs*; thus, this was His first miracle.

There were two results of this miracle (Jn. 2:11): first, He *manifested his glory,* because this showed His power to create; second, *his disciples believed on him.* What they had believed earlier about Yeshua had now been confirmed.

[§ 30] — 3. The Sojourn in Capernaum

John 2:12

From Cana, Yeshua, His mother, His half-brothers, and His disciples went on a family journey to Capernaum, where *they abode not many days.* Later, this city became His ministry headquarters.

[§ 31] — 4. The First Possession of the Temple

John 2:13-22

During the course of Yeshua's public ministry, four Passover feasts are mentioned, which shows that His ministry spanned a period of three years. Verse 13 records the events surrounding the first of these feasts. His baptism had happened anywhere from four to six months earlier.

At this first Passover, Yeshua came up to Jerusalem and went public by proclaiming His Messiahship and performing His first miracles. While the proclamation is studied in this section, the miracles will be detailed in § 32. It was a good time to go public because at Passover, hundreds of thousands of Jewish pilgrims came to Jerusalem from all over the country and from all parts of the world. In fact, sometimes the numbers were in the millions. Because there were so many people gathered in Jerusalem for the observance of the Passover, word would have spread rather quickly in Jewish communities both inside and outside the land, and inside and outside the Roman Empire, that a man named Yeshua of Nazareth was claiming to be the Messianic King.

The action in this passage primarily takes place in the Temple compound, parts of which were still under construction, but the Temple building itself had long been completed. Upon arrival in Jerusalem, Yeshua observed two groups of people in the Temple compound (Jn. 2:14). First were *those who sold oxen and sheep and doves*, which were sacrificial animals, and second were *the changers of money*. What Yeshua observed is also recorded in some detail in Pharisaic writings, and the Pharisees did not like what was going on either. All of this was the business venture of one man, the former high priest, Annas. Annas and his family essentially took firm control of the Temple compound and turned it into a private family business. The Pharisees referred to it as "the Bazaar of the Sons of Annas." Annas was a Sadducee. Josephus described him as being a hoarder of money, very rich, and despoiling the common priests by open violence. Rabbinic writings state that he made his sons the treasurers and his sons-in-law the assistant treasurers.

Yeshua cleansed the Temple twice, on the first and fourth Passovers of His public ministry. According to the Mosaic Law, a person had every right to bring his own sacrificial animal for the offering on the Passover or any other festival or Sabbath occasion. However, because the animal had to be *without spot, and without blemish* (Ex. 12:5; Lev. 22:18-20), a priest would have to inspect the sacrifice prior to the slaughter in order to ensure it met the standards of the law. The problem was that the whole procedure had become corrupt. It had been turned into a very profitable business for the high priest and his family. If a person brought his own sacrifice, the priests appointed to inspect the animals would invariably find some spot or blemish. So with his sacrifice disqualified, the owner had two options. The first option was to go home and get another animal, which was fine if he lived near Jerusalem, but not so fine if the journey home was long. The second option was more convenient. In the Temple compound, there was an area of stalls where the oxen, sheep, and doves which had passed inspection were sold. Of course, these were sold at highly inflated prices, and the money went into the private coffers of Annas and his family.

It was during Passover that everyone had to pay the annual half-*shekel* Temple tax. However, because Roman coinage was imprinted with an image of Caesar, it could not be used to pay the Temple tax. The money had to be exchanged by *the changers of money* (Jn. 2:14), and there was a service charge with each exchange. The service charge also went to the family of Annas. And so Yeshua's accusations against Annas were true. He had made His *Father's house a house of merchandise.* Verse 17 adds that when He said this, His disciples *remembered that it was written, Zeal for your house shall eat me up* (a reference to Ps. 69:9), meaning, "My zeal for your house will be the cause of my destruction." Overthrowing the moneychangers and driving out the animals and the vendors caused Annas and the other Sadducees to develop animosity against Yeshua. Three years later, at His trial, it was Annas who stood in front of Yeshua as His first judge, and Caiaphas, Annas' son-in-law, was His second judge.

When asked by what authority He cleansed the Temple compound, Yeshua gave a cryptic answer: *Destroy this temple, and in three days I will raise it up* (Jn. 2:19). The religious leaders misunderstood what He was saying. They assumed He was talking about the building, the Temple itself. However, as Yochanan pointed out, Yeshua was using the Temple as a symbol of His body. Three years later, the religious leaders took this statement out of context and used it against Yeshua, at the second stage of the religious trial.

This passage records the first time the leadership demanded Yeshua show them a sign to authenticate His actions and His words. It would not be the last. It seems the religious leaders had recognized that Yeshua's actions of cleansing the Temple, and thereby exercising authority over it, constituted a messianic work. This passage also recorded the first declaration of His coming death and resurrection, albeit in cryptic terminology.

By the time the cleansing of the Temple happened, the Temple compound had been under construction for 46 years. Later, in A.D. 67 (only three years before its total destruction by the Romans), the Bazaar of the Sons of Annas was destroyed by a mob, showing the depth of the Jewish indignation against this practice.

[§§ 32–33] — 5. Acceptance in Judea

[§ 32] — a. Faith in His Signs

John 2:23-25

After Yeshua had very publicly proclaimed Himself to be the Messiah by taking control of His *Father's house*, He began authenticating this by performing miracles. The one miracle He had performed up to this point was done rather quietly, and only a few people knew it had taken place. However, the next miracles were very public. For the first half of His ministry, the purpose of these public, authenticating miracles was to bring Israel to the point of decision: Would they accept Him as their Messiah, or would they reject Him? Later, the purpose for His miracles would change (see §63); but initially, they were to authenticate both His person and His message. As to His person, they were to prove that He was the Jewish Messiah. As to His message, they were to validate that He was offering to Israel the kingdom of the Jewish prophets. If Israel was willing to accept Him as the Messianic King, they would see the kingdom established in their day. Their acceptance of Yeshua as the long-awaited Messiah is the prerequisite for the establishment of the kingdom (see § 143; Mt. 23:39).

There was a positive response to the first public miracles: *many believed on his name, beholding his signs which he did* (Jn. 2:23). But while many put their trust in Him, Yeshua did not entrust Himself to them, for He recognized the nature of man. As the Apostle Yochanan developed the deity of the Son in his Gospel, he pointed out two things about Yeshua's omniscience. Negatively, *he needed not that anyone should bear witness concerning man*; and positively, *for he himself knew what was in man* (Jn. 2:25).

[§ 33] — b. The Explanation to Nicodemus

John 3:1-21

The Gospel of John records seven of Yeshua's discourses, this being the first, the discourse on the new birth. Among the many who heard what Yeshua proclaimed and saw what He did was *a man of the Pharisees named Nakdimon* (Jn. 3:1). The Hellenized form of his name is Nicodemus.

The Gospel of John also tells us that Nicodemus was a Pharisee, and this reveals his fundamental beliefs. Throughout history, one-word titles have been used to describe what people are theologically. If one identifies himself as a Baptist, it says that he is identifying himself with a particular set of theological doctrines. The same holds true for identifying oneself as a Presbyterian, Lutheran, Episcopalian, Calvinist, or Arminian. The same thing is true with the term "Pharisee." There were certain tenets to which a Pharisee held that distinguished him from a Sadducee, an Essene, a Zealot, or one of the other branches within Judaism of that day. An important tenet of Pharisaic Judaism was the belief that all Israel has a share in the age to come. This meant that anyone born a Jew automatically had the right to enter the kingdom of God. Those who were born as Gentiles either had to live consistently with the Noahic Covenant or convert to Judaism to qualify. A descendant of Abraham, Isaac, and Jacob would have automatic entry into the kingdom by virtue of God's election of Israel as a nation. That was the reason for the Pharisaic response to both Yochanan the Baptizer and Yeshua: When either of them pointed out the Pharisees were sinners, they responded that they were children of Abraham (Mt. 3:9; Lk. 3:8; Jn. 8:39). This answer reflects their belief that their genealogy was sufficient to inherit the kingdom of God.

Another teaching found in the rabbinic writings which supported this idea claimed that Abraham sits at the gates of Gehenna to snatch away any Israelite consigned thereto. In other words, if, by some heavenly bureaucratic mistake, a Jew was consigned to hell, he did not have to worry. Abraham, sitting at the very gates of hell, would catch him before he fell in, because all Israel has a share in the age to come.

A third teaching which expanded upon this theme claimed that anyone who was circumcised would not end up in Gehenna. By the second century, this teaching created a problem for the rabbis. They wanted to be able to say that Jewish believers in Yeshua ended up in Gehenna and would not inherit the kingdom of God. But Messianic Jews continued the practice of circumcision, and according to Pharisaic theology, anyone who was circumcised would be spared from hell. This dilemma led to a shift in rabbinic theology. The rabbis decreed that when a Jewish believer in Yeshua died, an angel would come down and put the foreskin back in place so that the person would end up in Gehenna after all. However, that was a second-century issue. In the first century, the belief was that all circumcised males born physically as Jews could not be consigned to Gehenna.

In Pharisaic writings, the phrase *to be born of water* was used to refer to physical birth. This was derived from passages such as Proverbs 5:15-23 where semen is symbolized as water. The expression simply meant that anyone who was born physically was born of water, and to be born physically as a Jew was sufficient to enter the kingdom of God.

It was a man with this particular theological frame of reference who came to Yeshua. He came because of what he had heard and what he had seen during the Passover in Jerusalem. Yochanan specified that Nicodemus came to Yeshua *by night* (Jn. 3:2). Many commentators see something sinister here, but this might be nothing more than a matter of convenience. Yeshua was quite busy during the day and was surrounded by crowds, making a private conversation impossible. On the other hand, in light of Yochanan's sub-theme of the conflict between light and darkness, the timing of his visit might indicate an element of secrecy, if not fear, on Nicodemus' part.

Before the conversation got very far, Yeshua declared, *Except one be born anew, he cannot see the kingdom of God* (Jn. 3:3). Unless Nicodemus experienced the new birth, he would not see the kingdom of God. Nicodemus was stumped: *How can a man be born when he is old? Can he enter a second time into his mother's womb, and be born?* (Jn. 3:4). Nicodemus' questions have frequently been misunderstood. They are invariably interpreted to mean that he did not know what Yeshua meant by that term, *Except one be born anew*. However, a closer look at his first question shows that this is not really the issue. His question was not: How is one born again? His question was: How is one born again *when he is old?* If his problem were only the new birth, what difference would age make? Why would it matter whether he was a child, a teenager, a young man, or an old man? He did know something about the term because it was commonly used in Pharisaic writings. What he did not understand is how one could experience this once he had reached a certain age in life and a certain status in Jewish society.

The reason for his lack of understanding is that in Pharisaic Judaism there were six different ways in which a person could be born anew. All six ways pertained to the realm of the physical, the realm of being born of water only. They involved certain rites of passage. As the biblical text will show, by the time Nicodemus met with Yeshua, he had experienced four of them; the other two would not have applied to him, for reasons which will become clear.

(a) Gentile Conversion

The first way to be born again in Pharisaic Judaism was for a Gentile to convert to Judaism. Conversion to Judaism was a process, and as a Gentile completed the process, he was declared born again. Nicodemus was born a Jew; he did not need to undergo the process of conversion. Therefore, he had not experienced this type of new birth.

(b) To Be Crowned King

The second way to be born again was to be crowned king. When a man was crowned king, he was declared born again. Nowhere in his Gospel does Yochanan imply that Nicodemus was a member of the house of David apart from Jechoniah, and one had to be a member of the house of David to be king in Israel. Even if he had been a descendant of David, at this point in history, the Jews were solidly under Roman domination. It would have been impossible for him to be crowned king. Therefore, Nicodemus would not have experienced this second kind of new birth.

(c) Bar Mitzvah

The third way to be born again was one's Bar Mitzvah. At the ceremony, several things changed for the thirteen-year-old lad. Jewish law then reckoned him as an adult. The common rabbinic teaching was that his parents were responsible for their son's sins until this moment, but from the time of his Bar Mitzvah, he was responsible for his own sins. The thirteen-year-old boy now took upon himself the obligations of the Mosaic Law. Also, according to rabbinic law, he could forthwith be legally counted among the ten adult males (the *minyan*) required to be present in order for a Jewish service to be conducted.

By the time Nicodemus met Yeshua, he was well past the age of 13, and thus, he had been born again for the first time at his own coming of age ceremony.

(d) Marriage

The fourth way to be born again in Pharisaic Judaism was to marry. When a Jewish man took a wife, he participated in a wedding ceremony with all of its various rituals, and then he was declared born again. Nowhere in this chapter of the Gospel of John is it stated in clear terms that Nicodemus was married. However, it can be deduced from the text that he indeed did have a wife. In John 3:1, Yochanan made two observations about Nicodemus. First, he mentioned that the man was a Pharisee. However, this says nothing specific about his marital status since Pharisees could be married or stay single. Second, Yochanan called Nicodemus *a ruler of the Jews.* That meant Nicodemus was one of the 71 members of the Sanhedrin. Among the prerequisites for membership in this Jewish council was marriage. A single man, no matter how old or how educated, would never qualify. The fact that Nicodemus was a member of the Sanhedrin meant he was also a married man.

Jewish males married between the ages of sixteen and twenty, so at that time of his life, Nicodemus had been born again for the second time. From a rabbinic viewpoint, the latest one should marry was the age of twenty. While being married was a prerequisite for membership in the Sanhedrin, other rabbis could stay single.

(e) Ordination

The fifth way to be born again was to be ordained a rabbi. When a man received his *smichut*, his rabbinic ordination, he was declared born again. Nicodemus, being a leading Pharisee and a member of the Sanhedrin, also had to be an ordained rabbi. Ordination occurred at the age of thirty in those days, so at that age, he was born again for the third time.

(f) Becoming the Head of a *Yeshiva*

The sixth way to be born again in Pharisaism was to become a *Rosh Yeshiva*, meaning, the head of a rabbinic academy or seminary, responsible for both training and ordaining future rabbis. When a man attained that status, he was declared born again. We know Nicodemus attained that level in Jewish society because of the way Yeshua addressed him: *Are you the teacher of Yisrael?* (Jn. 3:10). The American Standard Version translates this sentence correctly as *the* teacher. Other translations, such as the King James Version, read *a* teacher. However, the critical Greek text clearly has the definite article, *the,* in front of the word *teacher.* The New Testament has invariably been translated by Gentile committees who did not always understand Jewish nuances. They saw no difference between saying *a* teacher or *the* teacher and missed the point that Yochanan was making. Those who were common rabbis had the title of *Rav,* which means "a teacher;" but those who were Rosh Yeshiva had the title of *Rabban,* which means "the teacher." For example, Gamaliel, the teacher of the Apostle Paul, is always called "Rabban Gamliel" in Jewish writings, because he was the head of a yeshiva, an academy, and Paul happened to be one of his former students.

The fact that Yeshua called Nicodemus *the* teacher meant that he was a head of one of the rabbinic academies in the greater Jerusalem area. He attained this position around the age of fifty, so at that age, he was born again for the fourth and final time.

As a Jew, there were four ways Nicodemus could have been born again that were recognized by Pharisaic Judaism, and when he had experienced all four; there were no more options. That was the reason he asked the question the way he did: *How can a man be born when he is old?* (Jn. 3:4). His point was that he had used up all his options. As far as he could see, there was no other way of being born again except the way he suggested: to re-enter his mother's womb and become a fetus. He would have to be born physically, be born of water, once more and start the process all over.

When Yeshua responded to the question Nicodemus posed, He used a very common Jewish method of teaching—going from the known to the unknown. The known factor was the term *born again*. The unknown factor was its spiritual ramifications, because in Pharisaism, the term had nothing but a physical connotation. So Yeshua moved from the known to the unknown, from the physical to the spiritual: *Verily, verily, I say unto you, Except one be born of water and the Spirit, he cannot enter the kingdom of God!* (Jn. 3:5). When Yeshua declared that one must be born of both water and Spirit, He rejected the Pharisaic fundamental teaching that all Israel automatically have a share in the age to come. Merely being born of water was insufficient. One had to be born of both water **and** the Spirit. One must have two kinds of birth, a physical birth and a spiritual birth, to qualify for the kingdom. This verse is another example of a rather typical Greek construction where a sentence has two parts and each part is then elaborated upon separately. After stating that every person must have two kinds of birth, Yeshua defined the differences. To be born of water was to be born of the flesh: *That which is born of the flesh is flesh* (Jn. 3:6). However, this kind of birth alone is insufficient for entrance into the kingdom, and all human beings also have to undergo a spiritual birth because only *that which is born of the Spirit is spirit* (Jn. 3:6). To be born of the Spirit means the Holy Spirit regenerates the dead human spirit to become alive to God. That is the kind of new birth which is absolutely essential for the entry into the kingdom. Until Nicodemus experienced this kind of new birth, he would neither see nor enter God's kingdom.

The next question that would logically come to Nicodemus' mind was: *How can these things be?* (Jn. 3:9). How are you born again spiritually? Here, Yeshua further expounded upon His initial statement, pointing out that there were two steps involved. God must take the first step, but man must take the second: *And as Mosheh lifted up the serpent in the wilderness, even so must the Son of man be lifted up: that whosoever believes may in him have eternal life* (Jn. 3:14-15). The first step is the one God had to take, which was to send His Son. Through Him, God provided salvation for all; but the fact that salvation was provided for all, by itself, does not save anyone. Therefore, the second step is the necessary human responsibility, *that whosoever believes may in him have eternal life* (Jn. 3:15).

Probably the most famous verse in this Gospel is verse 16, which repeats the same two steps. First, *For God so loved the world, that he gave his only begotten Son* (Jn. 3:16a). The first step is finished. God has done all He needed to do to provide salvation for all. The provision of salvation for the whole world was based on the love of God. The fact that God provided salvation for all, by itself, will not save anyone. The second step is, *that whosoever believes on him shall not perish, but have eternal life* (Jn. 3:16b). Until Nicodemus came to believe that Yeshua is the Messianic Son of God, the Messianic King, he would neither see nor enter God's kingdom. For Nicodemus, this was not something he could accept right away. Those in Jewish ministries have long known it is a rare occasion when a Jewish person accepts the Gospel the first time he hears it. Jewish people undergo a tremendous struggle. It is a spiritual struggle, a religious struggle, a psychological struggle, a theological struggle, an ethnic struggle, and a mental struggle. They must begin to reprogram their whole way of thinking before they can begin to see the possibility of this One being the Messiah. Every Jewish believer has undergone this struggle for a short or a long period of time. For Nicodemus, the struggle began with this conversation with Yeshua and continued for three years. He is found two more times in Yochanan's Gospel. In John 7:50-51, he was not yet a believer, but willing to defend the Messiah's right to be heard before being condemned. In John 19:39, he openly identified himself as a believer when he took care of the Messiah's burial.

Because of his prominence in Jewish society, Nicodemus could not be ignored in rabbinic writings, nor was he, and so there are some things known about him from these sources. Today, rabbis receive salaries from synagogues, as pastors receive salaries from churches. However, in the first century, this was not the case, and rabbis did not make a living off the rabbinate. Every rabbi had to either pursue a trade or a side business from which he earned his living so that he could teach the Scriptures free of charge. That is why Paul, himself an ordained rabbi, was a tentmaker by profession. Nicodemus was a well-digger, and according to rabbinic writings, he became very wealthy. In fact, the Talmud declares that he was among the three wealthiest men of Jerusalem. The rabbinic writings proceed to record that when Nicodemus became a believer in Yeshua, he was reduced to poverty and died a pauper. His daughter had to go begging for bread. The rabbis record this story mainly to warn other Jews against believing in Yeshua, lest this bad luck should happen to them as well. It may very well be true that Nicodemus died physically poor, but he also died spiritually rich. He will someday have his place in the kingdom of God.

The conversation between Yeshua and Nicodemus represents the first real confrontation between the Messiah and a leading member of the Pharisaic party which dominated the Judaism of that day. It became evident early in His public ministry that He would challenge and deny some fundamental beliefs of Pharisaic Judaism.

The passage closes with a further example of Yochanan's sub-theme of the conflict between light and darkness (Jn. 3:19-21):

> *19 And this is the judgment, that the light has come into the world, and men loved the darkness rather than the light; for their works were evil. 20 For everyone that does evil hates the light, and comes not to the light, lest his works should be reproved. 21 But he that does the truth comes to the light, that his works may be made manifest, that they have been wrought in God.*

[§ 34] — 6. Yochanan's Witness

John 3:22-36

Generally, Yochanan the Baptizer ministered on the east bank of the Jordan River, at its southern end just before it emptied into the Dead Sea. During most of the year, the water was deep enough for immersion, but towards the end of the dry season, before the rains came, the river sometimes got too shallow for that purpose. Since all Jewish baptisms were by immersion, Yochanan had to go to *Einon near to Shaleim* (Jn. 3:23a), which was located further north towards the Sea of Galilee, *because there was much water there* (Jn. 3:23b). If Yochanan had practiced sprinkling or pouring, there would not have been any need for him to leave where he was, because there was always sufficient water for sprinkling or pouring. However, that was not the Jewish way of baptizing.

The disciples who were still with Yochanan observed that Yeshua was gathering more followers, and they became jealous for his sake. So they said, *he that was with you . . . baptizes, and all men come to him* (Jn. 3:26). They addressed Yochanan as "rabbi." At the time, "rabbi" did not have the full technical meaning it took on by the end of the first century. Part of the development involved the elevation of the status of a rabbi to the point of considering him to be the father of the world. Rabbis were also viewed as kings. The elevation of the rabbis' status went so far that they were considered to be equal to that of ministering angels. They were seen as the light and the eyes of the world.

Although his disciples were jealous for Yochanan's sake, the baptizer pointed out that this was the way it had to be (Jn. 3:27-30), because Yeshua was the Messiah. In his explanation, Yochanan mentioned three elements: the bride, the bridegroom, and the friend of the bridegroom. The motif here is the Jewish wedding system. It is developed later in the New Testament as the nature of the three elements is elaborated, and it becomes clear that the groom is the Messiah and the bride is the church. Yochanan, as an Old Testament saint, has nothing to do with the bride, the church, and therefore he cannot be the bridegroom, the Messiah. He identifies himself as *the friend of the bridegroom*, and this is the relationship of all Old Testament saints to the Messiah.[5]

In discussing the person of the Messiah (Jn. 3:31-36), Yochanan stated that Yeshua was not given *the Spirit by measure* (Jn. 3:34). As prophesied in Isaiah 11:1-5, the Messiah had the sevenfold fullness of the Holy Spirit. Believers receive the Spirit in measure (I Cor. 12), not based upon spirituality, but upon the tasks God has given them to perform and where He places them in the church. That is why all believers have spiritual gifts, but not all have the same spiritual gifts or the same

---

[5] For details, see Arnold G. Fruchtenbaum, *The Footsteps of the Messiah* (San Antonio, TX: Ariel Ministries, 2005).

number of gifts. Each one receives the gifts necessary for them to perform the specific task that God wants performed in the body. So each one receives a measure of the Spirit for that purpose, but the Messiah received the Spirit without measure.

[§ 35] — 7. Yochanan's Imprisonment

Matthew 4:12, Mark 1:14a, Luke 3:19-20, 4:14a, John 4:1-4

Yeshua departed for Galilee, and three reasons are given. First, Herod had imprisoned Yochanan (Lk. 3:19-20). The Herod of this passage is Herod Antipas, one of the sons of Herod the Great. His brother, Philip, ruled in the northeastern parts of the province, while Herod himself was the tetrarch of Galilee and Perea. During a visit to Rome, he had fallen in love with Philip's wife, Herodias, and seduced her into marrying him. This marriage was adulterous and, obviously, broke Mosaic Law. Because Yochanan preached against it, he was *delivered up*—and what happens to the herald will happen to the King. This incident caused Yeshua to leave Judea for Galilee.

The second reason for Yeshua's departure from Judea was that He *was making and baptizing more disciples than Yochanan* (Jn. 4:1) and the Pharisees were beginning to take note of Him. Although He Himself did not baptize (Jn. 4:2), He was officiating at the immersions, so they were credited to Him.

The third reason for Yeshua's departure was that it was part of the divine plan. Luke plainly stated this when he said Yeshua returned to Galilee *in the power of the Spirit* (Lk. 4:14). The Spirit led the Messiah from Judea through Samaria to Galilee, and He prompted Yeshua to *pass through Shomron* (Jn. 4:4). The unlikeliness of a Jew travelling through Samaria to Galilee will be discussed in § 36, but looking ahead, we can see that this route was necessary because the Messiah had a divine appointment with the Samaritan woman. Furthermore, the Spirit wanted Yeshua to perform His second miracle in Cana.

[§ 36] — 8. The Acceptance in Samaria

John 4:5-42

As Yeshua passed through Samaria, He came to Sychar, a town south of Shechem, located between the two mountains of Ebal and Gerizim. He sent His disciples into town to purchase food. In the meantime, He was sitting by the well of Sychar when a Samaritan woman came to draw water.

Two general observations should be noted before looking at the details of this encounter. The first observation pertains to one of the sub-themes of Yochanan's Gospel: Messiah came to reveal God the Father to humanity. Here, in His conversation with the Samaritan woman, He does just that, but the revelation came in five specific steps:

1. He revealed to the woman a new kind of life (Jn. 4:10-14).
2. He revealed to her something about herself (Jn. 4:15-19).
3. He revealed to her what constitutes true worship (Jn. 4:20-23).
4. He revealed to her the Father (Jn. 4:24).
5. He revealed to her His Messiahship (Jn. 4:25-26).

As their conversation progressed, Yeshua plainly stated to her that He was the long-awaited Messiah. She had been taught that when Messiah came, He would *tell us all things*, and one of the things He would reveal to man was the Father. In other words, the only way to the Father was through Him. This is true for all people, not just for the Samaritans.

The second observation is that during the course of their conversation, the woman's faith actually grew and developed. This can be seen by the four ways in which she addressed Yeshua. First, she referred to Him as *a Jew* (Jn. 4:9). Coming from a Samaritan, that was probably not a compliment. She then proceeded to a higher level of respect, calling Him *Sir* (Jn. 4:11, 15, 19). Then she called Him a *prophet* (Jn. 4:19). From the Samaritan perspective, the next prophet after Moses was to be the Messiah. Finally, she referred to Him as the Messiah (Jn. 4:25, 29).

When the Samaritan woman came to the well and Yeshua asked her for a drink (Jn. 4:7), she was a bit surprised and asked: *How is it that you, being a Jew, asks drink of me, who am a Samaritan woman?* (Jn. 4:9). As an explanation, Yochanan added, *For Jews have no dealings with Samaritans* (Jn. 4:9). His comment did not mean that they had no contact with them. Rather, Jewish law forbade Samaritans to benefit from Jews. *No dealings* meant there were to be no acts that would obligate a Jew to a Samaritan; therefore, Jews were forbidden to give anything (gratis) to a Samaritan. They were also forbidden to receive anything (gratis) from a Samaritan. Thus, the Samaritan woman was surprised by Yeshua's request for water without an immediate offer to pay for it, because this went contrary to Jewish practices of that day.

In rabbinic writings, there is a back-and-forth struggle with the issue of just how far Jews can have, or cannot have, dealings with the Samaritans. The conflict with the Samaritans began with the Jewish return from the Babylonian Captivity. When the Jews returned from the Babylonian Captivity and began rebuilding the Temple, the Samaritans, who were then living in the territory of what had been the Northern Kingdom of Israel, wished to help. However, they were not allowed because of their racial and religious heritage. Racially, they were descendants of Gentiles who had been forced by the Assyrian Empire to settle in the territory of Israel and who then intermarried with the local Jewish population that had been left behind. Furthermore, there was a religious issue which caused separation. The Samaritans had brought into the land of Israel the worship of the various gods of the countries from which they came. To solve a problem they were facing, they adopted Jehovah as the God of the land, but without repudiating the idolatry of the other gods. As a result, their religious system was syncretistic.

Although by the first century, the Samaritans were monotheistic, their origins could not be forgotten. Because their heritage, both racially and religiously, was not accepted by the Jews, they were not allowed to participate in the rebuilding of the Temple. As a result, the Samaritans changed two things. First, they made Mount Gerizim their holy mountain and no longer looked to Jerusalem as their place of worship. Mount Gerizim was one of the two mountains overshadowing Shechem and Sychar. Second, in reaction to the Jews' refusal to let them participate in the rebuilding of the Temple, the Samaritans went through the five books of Moses and eliminated all references to

Jerusalem. For example, the offering of Isaac (Gen. 22) took place on Mount Moriah, but in the Samaritan version of the book of Genesis, the location has been changed to Mount Gerizim.

Because the rabbis considered the Samaritans' faith to be a corruption of the true faith, they essentially excommunicated them and decreed there was to be limited contact with them. The extreme view was that a Jew could not eat even one mouthful of Samaritan food, while the more balanced view was that their food was *kosher*, as long as it was purchased. A Jew was not allowed to accept anything free of a Samaritan. Therefore, by not offering to pay the Samaritan woman when He asked her to bring Him water, Yeshua contradicted Jewish custom.

The Samaritans, of course, had equal animosity toward the Jews, if not more so. Frequently, they would stop Jews from passing through Samaria as they went toward Jerusalem. However, they never stopped any Jews coming from Jerusalem, as Yeshua was doing in the passage studied here. They liked to see Jews leaving Jerusalem, going by way of their holy mount, Mount Gerizim. Since Yeshua was passing through Samaria away from Jerusalem, they had no objections. Later, however, when He was heading towards the city and wanted to pass through their territory, the Samaritans stopped Him. In fact, there are records of Samaritans killing Jews who passed through Samaria to get to the city of Jerusalem.

The Samaritan woman's question shows she was obviously taken aback by Yeshua's request. He responded to her question with an answer meant to further pique her curiosity and to create in her a thirst for eternal life: *If you knew the gift of God, and who it is that says to you, Give me to drink; you would have asked of him, and he would have given you living water* (Jn. 4:10). What was this living water? Normally, living water is running water, water that is active, moving, the opposite of stagnant, but it will soon become apparent that this is not what Yeshua was offering her. The woman's response shows that she was puzzled by this statement: *Sir, you have nothing to draw with, and the well is deep: from where then have you that living water? Are you greater than our father Yaakov, who gave us the well, and drank thereof himself, and his sons, and his cattle?* (Jn. 4:11-12). She questioned Yeshua's ability to produce this water, but she also revealed some things about Samaritan theology. According to that theology, Jacob himself had provided this well for them. Was Yeshua claiming to be able to provide better water than Jacob had?

Yeshua then began to move from the physical to the spiritual, pointing out to her that anyone who drank of the water from that well would eventually be thirsty again. That was a simple fact of human life. However, Yeshua said, *whosoever drinks of the water that I shall give him shall never thirst; but the water that I shall give him shall become in him a well of water springing up unto eternal life* (Jn. 4:14). The water Yeshua offered would permanently quench one's thirst, not physically, but spiritually. The gift of this inner well of living water brought eternal life. However, the woman still did not quite understand the issue, as her response indicates: *Sir, give me this water, that I thirst not, neither come all the way hither to draw* (Jn. 4:15). She was not yet able to distinguish the spiritual from the physical and was still thinking materially; but Yeshua had already set the stage for the issue of her need for eternal life.

It is important to note that before anyone really understands the need for a savior, they must first see themselves as God sees them: as sinners. In the case of this woman, this had not yet happened. After kindling in her an interest in this living water and pointing out her need of it, but before showing her how this need could be met, He told her: *Go, call your husband, and come hither.* To that, the woman answered, *I have no husband* (Jn. 4:16-17a). Yeshua responded to her: *You said well, I have no husband: for you have had five husbands; and he whom you now have is not your husband: this have you said truly* (Jn. 4:17b-18). Here, He proceeded to point out the sin: She had been married five times and, apparently, had been divorced five times. Now she was living with a man to whom she was not married, and therefore, she lived in a state of immorality. By pointing out her sin, Yeshua proved to her that He was greater than Jacob after all.

At this point, the Samaritan woman wished to change the topic because she was not comfortable discussing her sin. So she reverted to a point of theology, saying: *Sir, I perceive that you are a prophet. Our fathers worshipped in this mountain; and ye say, that in Yerushalayim is the place where men ought to worship* (Jn. 4:19-20). This is rather typical of what unbelievers tend to do when confronted with their sin. They become uncomfortable and try to change the subject, challenging one's theology or asking deflective questions such as, "Where did Cain get his wife?" as if that has any relevance to their own spiritual needs.

The woman introduced her theological issue by stating, *I perceive that you are a prophet* (Jn. 4:19). That was a major step for her. As mentioned before, in Samaritan theology, the next prophet after Moses would be the Messiah. In other words, there was no prophet after Moses but the Messiah. That is why the Samaritans only had the five books of Moses as their Scriptures. They rejected the Prophets, and they rejected the Writings. They accepted only the five books of Moses, and even those had to be rewritten to avoid any reference to Jerusalem. So when she said, *I perceive that you are a prophet,* it meant that she already suspected that He might be the Messiah. Her theological issue was: *Our fathers worshipped in this mountain; and ye say, that in Yerushalayim is the place where men ought to worship* (Jn. 4:20). When she said *this mountain,* she meant a specific mountain: Mount Gerizim. Yeshua answered her question in John 4:21b-23:

> *21b Woman, believe me, the hour comes, when neither in this mountain, nor in Yerushalayim, shall you worship the Father. 22 Ye worship that which ye know not: we worship that which we know; for salvation is from the Jews. 23 But the hour comes, and now is, when the true worshippers shall worship the Father in spirit and truth: for such does the Father seek to be his worshippers.*

In answering her question, Yeshua stated that the Samaritan theology on Mount Gerizim was wrong, while the Jewish theology about Jerusalem was correct. Samaritans worshipped what they did not know, but Jews worshipped what they did know. Under the Mosaic Law, wherever the Tabernacle or Temple stood was the proper place of worship. When they first came into the land, the place of worship was at Shiloh. Later, it became the city of Jerusalem, which remained the center of worship right up to the time of Yeshua's coming. So on this issue, the Jews were correct, and the Samaritans were wrong. Jerusalem was the proper place for worship.

Yeshua then went back to the woman's real issue: her need for a savior, her need to have eternal life, her need to have the living waters, and her need to recognize true worship. Since *God is a Spirit,* He must be worshipped *in spirit and truth* (Jn. 4:24). The time was coming when, as a result of the Messiah's work, there would be no central place to worship. The proper place of worship was going to be *in spirit and truth.* Thus, Yeshua prophesied of this present age, the dispensation of grace, when one can worship God corporately anywhere in the world. That was not true under the Mosaic dispensation. It will also not be true in the kingdom dispensation, because there will again be a centralized area to worship, a millennial Temple. The city of Jerusalem will become the center of worldwide worship, and Gentiles will make pilgrimages to Jerusalem to worship in that city (Zech. 14:16-21). Many prophets emphasized that Jerusalem will be the center of worship in the kingdom, but for this present age, between Moses and the kingdom, there is no localized place of prayer or worship. *God is a Spirit: and they that worship him must worship in spirit and truth* (Jn. 4:24). Yeshua brought the woman right back to the issue of what constitutes proper worship.

She next stated, *I know that Messiah comes (he that is called Christ): and when he is come, he will declare unto us all things* (Jn. 4:25). In His response, Yeshua revealed the true content of faith: *I that speak unto you am <he>* (Jn. 4:26), clearly identifying Himself as the Messiah. This confirmed her suspicions that this person whom she perceived to be a prophet was indeed the Messiah.

It is at this point in the conversation that the disciples returned, and *they marveled that he was speaking with a woman* (Jn. 4:27). In rabbinic law, this just was not done. The risk a Jewish man took when he spoke to a Samaritan woman was even greater. Female Samaritans were viewed as being unclean from the cradle to the grave.

Leaving her water pot behind, the Samaritan woman returned to town and proclaimed to the inhabitants that she had met a man who had told her everything that she had ever done. He could read her mind! He could see exactly who and what she was. She concluded, *can this be the Messiah?* (Jn. 4:29).

Meanwhile, the disciples offered Yeshua some of the fresh food they had bought. In the conversation that ensued, Yeshua again moved from the physical to the spiritual, saying He had already eaten: My *meat is to do the will of him that sent me, and to accomplish His work* (Jn. 4:34). In His discussion with the Samaritan woman, which brought her to saving faith, He had indeed done the work of the Father, and that was His *meat*.

Yeshua now taught His disciples the principle of evangelism and salvation:

> *36 He that reaps receives wages, and gathers fruit unto life eternal, that he that sows and he that reaps may rejoice together. 37 For herein is the saying true, One sows and another reaps. 38 I sent you to reap that whereon ye have not labored: others have labored, and ye are entered into their labor.* (Jn. 4:36-38)

The principle of evangelism is that some sow and others reap. Both should rejoice together that the fruit of eternal life has been produced. Applying it to the disciples, Yeshua stated: *I sent you to reap that whereon ye not have labored* (Jn. 4:38). The apostles were already in the process of reaping (Jn. 4:1-4) because Yeshua was gaining more disciples than the baptizer, and the disciples were baptizing these new followers. Thus, they were reaping what others, such as Yochanan, had sown before them.

After Yeshua had taught His disciples the principle of sowing and reaping, they saw it in action: *And from that city many of the Samaritans believed on him because of the word of the woman, who testified* (Jn. 4:39). The Samaritan woman fit both categories: She did some sowing, and she did some reaping, and sometimes she did both. Many Samaritans believed because she had shared the gospel with them, and thus, she became the sower and the reaper. Others went out to see for themselves the One she was talking about: *So when the Samaritans came unto him, they besought him to abide with them: and he abode there two days* (Jn. 4:40). Many of them came to faith (Jn. 4:41-42). With them, she was the sower, while Yeshua did the actual reaping.

[§ 37] — 9. The Acceptance in Galilee

John 4:43-45

After spending two more days in Samaria, Yeshua finally arrived in Galilee. Upon His arrival, many of the Galileans believed on Him, because they had seen all the things He had done in Jerusalem at the first Passover of His public ministry. This was the result of His first public ministry in Judah.

[§§ 38–57] — B. The Authority of the King

[§ 38] — 1. Messiah's Authority to Preach

Matthew 4:17, Mark 1:14b-15, Luke 4:14-15

This records the first of several preaching tours around Israel. Having gone public in Jerusalem, Yeshua now began a very active ministry of proclaiming Himself as the Messianic King and offering the messianic kingdom. In this role, He fulfilled three functions: that of a rabbi, a teacher, and a prophet.[6] Mark 1:15 states that part of Yeshua's message was that *The time is fulfilled.* This was the time in God's program for the official offering of the messianic kingdom and of the Messiah as its king. Yeshua would now travel from city to city, and synagogue to synagogue.

Matthew provided the basic content of Yeshua's message, which was twofold. First, it was soteriological, or salvation-centered: *Repent ye*

---

[6] The word "teacher" is a generic term which describes any person who educates others about a certain subject. In first-century Israel, a teacher did not have disciples who travelled with him. Unlike the term "rabbi," the word "teacher" does not imply authority. A rabbi teaches, but his title is more official and it does carry authority. In first-century Israel, most rabbis had disciples who followed them wherever they went. The rabbis provided specialized training to their students and would also ordain others to become rabbis. The context of Yeshua's life indicates that He was a teacher of the Hebrew Scriptures and a rabbi, but the duty of ordaining others to become rabbis was not one of His goals.

(Mt. 4:17b). Mark added: *and believe in the gospel* (Mk. 1:15b). The word *gospel* means "good news." In I Corinthians 15:1-4, Paul defined the three points of the present gospel: First, the Messiah died for our sins; second, He was buried; and third, He rose again on the third day. However, that gospel could only be proclaimed after the Messiah had died. Since Yeshua had not yet died, this was obviously not the good news He and His disciples were proclaiming. The gospel they proclaimed at that point in history was that Yeshua was the Messianic King. So the content of the gospel was not always the same. In fact, later, when Yeshua began proclaiming His death and resurrection, it caught those same disciples by surprise.

Second, the content of Messiah's message was, *The time is fulfilled, for the kingdom of heaven is at hand* (Mt. 4:17). It was an eschatological message; it dealt with the end times in that the kingdom of God, the messianic kingdom, was the high point of all Old Testament prophecy. The Hebrew prophets were not given any revelation that went beyond the messianic kingdom, so the kingdom all Jews were waiting for was the kingdom prophesied by the Old Testament prophets, the kingdom of the Messiah. Yeshua did not elaborate on the nature of this coming kingdom. This shows that no explanation was needed.

Luke 4:14-15 reveals three characteristics of Yeshua's public ministry. First, it was Spirit-controlled: *in the power of the Spirit* (Lk. 4:14a). Second, He quickly became known throughout all the region of Galilee. His fame spread everywhere, and His message did not stay localized: *and a fame went out concerning him through all the region round about* (Lk. 4:14b). Third, the primary place of His teaching ministry was *in their synagogues* (Lk. 4:15).

[§ 39] — 2. The Messiah's Authority to Heal

John 4:46-54

This is the second of the seven signs Yeshua performed that Yochanan recorded in his Gospel. It is also Yeshua's second visit to Cana, the first being when He changed the water into wine. *And there was a certain nobleman, whose son was sick at Kfar Nachum* (Jn. 4:46). A nobleman was a king's officer, and by calling him so, Yochanan showed that he was a government official of Herod Antipas. This man had faith, for the distance from Capernaum to Cana was about twenty miles and virtually all uphill. Capernaum sits on the northern shore of the Sea of Galilee about six hundred feet below sea level, whereas Cana of Galilee sits about 1,500 feet above sea level. Upon arriving in Cana, the man *besought <him> that he would come down, and heal his son; for he was at the point of death* (Jn. 4:47). The phrase *come down* was geographically accurate, since Capernaum, as just discussed, sits much lower in altitude than Cana of Galilee. Yeshua responded to him by saying, *Except ye[7] see signs and wonders, ye will in no wise believe* (Jn. 4:48). He challenged the nobleman's motive for seeking Him out. Did he believe in Him? Did he have faith, or did he need convincing? Was he really just looking for a sign? The nobleman responded, *Sir, come down ere my child die* (Jn. 4:49). He was not asking for a sign. He did not need to be convinced. He already believed that Yeshua was who He claimed to be and therefore, could cure the child. He was only asking that Yeshua would go with him and heal his son before he died, perhaps assuming that His presence was necessary for the child to be healed. Yeshua answered: *Go your way; your son lives* (Jn. 4:50a). Yochanan added, *The man believed the word that Yeshua spoke unto him, and he went his way* (Jn. 4:50b). The man had true faith, evidenced by the fact that he trusted in Yeshua's promise.

As the nobleman headed back to Capernaum, his servants met and informed him that his son lived: *So he inquired of them the hour when he began to amend. They said therefore unto him, Yesterday at the seventh hour the fever left him* (Jn. 4:52). If Yochanan was using Roman time, the seventh hour would be 7:00 p.m. If he was using Jewish time, then the seventh hour was 1:00 p.m. The key word is "yesterday." It shows that the man stayed overnight in Cana. He did not rush home to see if what Yeshua said was true. Yeshua asked the man to believe in His words without the evidence of a sign or His personal appearance at the bedside of the sick child. The man did, and he received his son back. As a result, not only did he believe, but also his whole house (Jn. 4:53).

---

[7] Being a nobleman, he would not have traveled alone and would have had one or more servants with him, which explains the usage of the plural pronoun.

Yochanan concluded: *This is again the second sign that* Yeshua *did, having come out of Yehuda into Galil* (Jn. 4:54). Yochanan was not implying that this was only the second sign Yeshua had done up to this point in time, since he had already mentioned the many signs He had done in Jerusalem. Yochanan's point is that this was the second sign He had done in Cana.

[§ 40] — 3. The Initial Rejection in Nazareth

Luke 4:16-31

Nazareth was a microcosm of the nation as a whole, because what happened locally in Nazareth would ultimately happen nationally. This passage records the initial rejection of Jesus in Nazareth. The final rejection is in §71.

After His fame had begun to spread, Yeshua returned to His hometown of Nazareth (Lk. 4:16). As was His custom, He entered *into the synagogue on the Sabbath day, and stood up to read.* By the first century, synagogues had become an important facet of Jewish life. It was the structure of the synagogue service that gave rise to the weekly reading of the Law (*Torah*) and the Prophets (*Neviim*). A contrast was made between standing and sitting. Even today in the synagogue service, the person reading the scroll always stands, whether he is reading the Torah or the Prophets. While the reading of Scripture was done in a standing position, the rabbis always taught in a sitting position. It is stated many times throughout the Gospels that when Yeshua was teaching, He sat. In keeping with the Jewish frame of reference, Yeshua *stood up to read* (Lk. 4:16) and sat down to teach (Lk. 4:20). He may have read both the Torah portion and the prophetic portion, for each Torah portion has an accompanying portion from the Prophets (the *Haftarah*), and the person who read the last Torah portion also read the prophetic portion. Only the prophetic portion is actually mentioned in this passage, and it happened to be from Isaiah 61 (Lk. 4:17). The complete prophecy is Isaiah 61:1-3, and it is an example of a prophecy where aspects of the first and second comings are blended into one picture, there being no indication in the text itself that there is a gap of time between the events, or that the prophecy actually refers to two comings. Here we learn that this is the proper interpretation of this prophecy from Yeshua Himself. He read verse 1 and one clause of verse 2 and then stopped. He then said, *Today has this scripture been fulfilled in your ears* (Lk. 4:21). That day, Isaiah 61:1-2a had been fulfilled. The rest of verse 2 and all of verse 3 will be fulfilled in conjunction with the second coming. The purpose of His first coming was to bring the good news, to proclaim the gospel in all of its various facets. It is at His second coming that He will *proclaim the day of vengeance of our God.*

The rabbis had specific rules on how many verses should be read. At a normal Sabbath service, seven men were selected to read the Torah portion. The seventh reader, the *maftir*, would read a shorter part, but he must read at least three verses and then read from the Prophets. The rule was that this last reader, when reading from the Prophets, must not read less than 21 verses. However, if an interpreter was present or there was preaching on the Sabbath, the reader was not required to read all 21 verses. It was acceptable to read only three, five, or seven verses. This may mean that Yeshua read the short Torah portion, and then He was to read the appropriate passage from Isaiah 61, but He did not. He stopped in the middle of verse two (Lk. 4:18-19), *closed the book,* or, more correctly, the scroll, *and gave it back to the attendant* (the *chazzan*). Then He sat down (Lk. 4:20a) for the purpose of expounding upon the text, because, as previously stated, a rabbi would teach in a sitting position. This was a clear violation of the established rabbinic tradition, for He had read only half of the required minimum number of verses. This is one reason *the eyes of all in the synagogue were fastened on him* (Lk. 4:20b). This disregard for established tradition would have naturally drawn their attention. The entire prophecy would have included verses 1-3, but He would not read the entire prophecy because the remaining verses were not being fulfilled that very day. The second reason all eyes in the synagogue were fixed on Him was because He was getting ready to expound upon what He had read, and the rabbis were curious to see what He was going to say. Also, Isaiah 61 was recognized as a messianic prophecy even in rabbinic writings. Therefore, when Yeshua said, *Today has this scripture been fulfilled in your ears* (Lk. 4:21), the people clearly understood Him to say that He was fulfilling this part of the prophecy, thereby proclaiming Himself to be the Messiah.

Luke's account continues: *And all bore him witness, and wondered at the words of grace which proceeded out of his mouth* (Lk. 4:22a). Apparently, Yeshua must have said much more on this occasion, but Luke only recorded His main point. The congregation was impressed by what He had said, but they were also puzzled. They could not believe that He could speak so well or that He had said these things. Their response was, *Is not this Yoseph's son?* (Lk. 4:22b). They knew Him; they knew His parents; this was His hometown; these people had seen Him grow up. He could not be the Messiah! They had probably heard about His miracles, but they had not seen any.

Yeshua responded to the rejection by citing two events from the Old Testament that focused on special works God had done for Gentiles. Since Luke's sphere of interest included what Yeshua said about Gentiles, he recorded His words (Lk. 4:25-27). The first event happened during the days of Elijah. At the time, there were many Jewish widows in Israel; however, God sent Elijah to the home of a Gentile widow, a Phoenician woman (I Kgs. 17). The second event happened during the days of Elisha. At the time, there were many Jewish lepers in Israel; however, it was a Syrian (Aramean) leper that was healed (II Kgs. 5). The point of Yeshua's illustration is that the Jewish people would reject Him, just as Elijah and Elisha were rejected: *No prophet is acceptable in his own country* (Lk. 4:24). They would not accept Him as their Messiah; however, the Gentiles would.

He said these things in the synagogue where He was trained and in the town where He grew up, and it produced instantaneous anger in those who heard it (Lk. 4:28). The town of Nazareth is located in a little vale. South of the vale is a cliff that looks down upon the Jezreel Valley. That is where the enraged people now took Yeshua, *unto the brow of the hill . . . that they might throw him down headlong* (Lk. 4:29). Luke stated that *he passing through the midst of them went his way* (Lk. 4:30). The text simply notes that He walked away and went to Capernaum (Lk. 4:31), perhaps using His messianic power to escape. By Catholic tradition, He did not just walk away, He actually leapt from the cliff to Mount Tabor, which is a good three or four miles away. This tradition has actually been retained in the Hebrew name, for the cliff is called "The Mount of the Leap" to this day.

[§ 41] — 4. The Headquarters in Capernaum

Matthew 4:13-16

After being rejected in Nazareth, Yeshua set up His headquarters in Capernaum. Capernaum was located on the north shore of the Sea of Galilee. It was strategically positioned on a busy highway called the Via Maris, a major trade route that ran from Egypt through the land of Israel to Mesopotamia. The route traversed the coast of Israel, hence the name Via Maris, a Latin term meaning "Way of the Sea." This name comes from the Vulgate, the Latin translation of the Bible.[8]

The fact that Yeshua set up His headquarters along such an important trade route meant that news of what He was saying and doing would spread more quickly. His choice of Capernaum was significant. It was a very strategic location. Thus, it is no surprise that the majority of His ministry took place there. In verses 14-16, Matthew quoted Isaiah 9:1-2, a passage which predicted this choice of location:

> *[1] But there shall be no gloom to her that was in anguish. In the former time he brought into contempt the land of Zebulun and the land of Naphtali; but in the latter time hath he made it glorious, by the way of the sea [Latin: Via Maris], beyond the Jordan, Galilee of the nations. [2] The people that walked in darkness have seen a great light: they that dwelt in the land of the shadow of death, upon them hath the light shined.*

The focus is on the tribes of Zebulun and Naphtali. The city of Nazareth is in the tribal territory of Zebulun, which is where Yeshua grew up. Capernaum is in the territory of Naphtali, which is where His ministry was headquartered (see map on next page). Also in Naphtali's territory were the cities of Chorazin and Bethsaida, and it is in these two cities

---

[8] *Mesmin*, "The Way of the Sea."

where, along with Capernaum, Yeshua performed the majority of His miracles.

[§ 42] — 5. Messiah's Authority over Demons

Mark 1:21-28, Luke 4:31b-37

Mark specified that *on the Sabbath day he entered into the synagogue and taught* (Mk. 1:21). As Yeshua's reputation spread, it led to a debate. The question was: By what authority was He teaching? Both Mark 1:22a and Luke 4:32a state that the people *were astonished at his teaching*. The people who heard Yeshua were impressed with the content of His teaching and marveled at the authority with which He taught. Luke stated that *his word was with authority* (Lk. 4:32b), and Mark added: *For he taught them as having authority, and not as the scribes* (Mk. 1:22b). Rabbis received their authority from the academy they attended. Since Yeshua never studied in a rabbinic academy, what was the source of His authority? The people recognized that He was teaching something new and that He taught them as having authority in Himself. Unlike the scribes, He did not require previous rabbinic authorization. His teaching and authority came from above, from the Father (Is. 50:4-5).

While people were slow to recognize His authority, demons were not. Whenever demons confronted Yeshua, they immediately recognized Him and even cried out, *I know you who you are, the Holy One of God* (Mk. 1:24; Lk. 4:34). However, anytime a demon or a group of demons declared who He was, Yeshua always silenced and rebuked them, saying, *Hold your peace* (Mk. 1:25; Lk. 4:35). He accepted no testimony from demons, probably for the simple reason that they do not make good character witnesses. Here, in the synagogue in Capernaum, Yeshua ordered the demon to come out of the man, and it obeyed, but not without violently displaying its reluctance. Mark described him as coming out *with a loud voice* (Mk. 1:26), causing one last spasm of convulsions upon the victim. Luke added the fact that the demon threw the victim to the ground, but it did not cause any harm to the person (Lk. 4:35). As a trained doctor, Luke tended to provide more details concerning the medical aspects of the miracles of Yeshua.

When Yeshua cast out a demon by His own authority, by merely commanding it to come out, it created further astonishment: *And amazement came upon all* (Lk. 4:36). This is followed by the question: *What is this? A new teaching! With authority he commands even the unclean spirits, and they obey him* (Mk. 1:27). Not only did He teach authoritatively, but He also cast out demons with authority. Furthermore, He did it with a simple word and not with any of the formulas used by the exorcists of Judaism. What is of note here is the question raised by those in attendance in the synagogue: By what authority does He cast out demons?

This incident in the synagogue of Capernaum caused the word about Yeshua to spread quickly within the immediate area: *And the report of him went out straightway everywhere into all the region of Galil round about* (Mk. 1:28). The news set the stage for the next event.

[§ 43] — 6. Messiah's Authority over Disease

Matthew 8:14-17, Mark 1:29-34, Luke 4:38-41

a. The Healing of Peter's Mother-in-Law

Yeshua had just cast out a demon during a Sabbath service at the synagogue in Capernaum, and *the report of him went out straightway everywhere into all the region of Galil round about* (Mk. 1:28). Now, the service was over, and it was time to eat the Sabbath meal. To this day, the Jewish practice is to have a special meal after the morning synagogue service. In keeping with the tradition, Yeshua went to the home of Peter to partake of the Sabbath meal. Peter's mother-in-law was living in the house as well, and she was very ill. Both Matthew 8:14 and Mark 1:30 state she was laid up in bed due to being *sick of a fever*. Again, Luke the physician was more specific: *She was holden with a great fever* (Lk. 4:38), meaning a severe or high fever. Furthermore, the Greek tense indicates it was chronic; she had been ill for some time.

All three synoptic accounts report that Yeshua healed Peter's mother-in-law, but each states it differently based upon the author's particular theme. Matthew's theme was kingship, so he wrote in 8:15 that Yeshua *touched her hand.* The mere touch of the King was sufficient to bring about the necessary results. Mark, whose theme was the Messiah's perfect servanthood, stated in 1:31 that He *took her by the hand, and raised her up.* This is the action of a servant. Luke, whose theme was Messiah, the ideal man, recorded in 4:39 that *he stood over her, and rebuked the fever.*

So, each Gospel writer reported the healing differently, including only what would emphasize the theme of his Gospel. There are no discrepancies between the three accounts; the differences in the details are actually complementary information. Furthermore, all three accounts state that *the fever left her* (Mt. 8:15; Mk. 1:31; Lk. 4:39). All three accounts also state that the healed woman was able to serve the guests. Luke the doctor added the word *immediately* (Lk. 4:39), reflecting a prompt infusion of strength. She recovered immediately and began to serve the Sabbath meal. Mark and Luke both reported that she served *them,* focusing on the group in general. However, Matthew stated she served *him,* focusing on Yeshua. She was healed to serve the King.

b. The Evening after the Sabbath

Then evening came, and all three Gospel accounts make that point (Mt. 8:16; Mk. 1:32; Lk. 4:40). This is to emphasize that the Sabbath was ending, and the new day was beginning. According to the rabbis, the new day begins at sundown once three stars are visible in the sky. As soon as the Sabbath had ended, people started to arrive: *they brought unto him all that were sick, and them that were possessed with demons* (Mk. 1:32). Based upon what had happened that morning in the synagogue, the people were looking for healing. Why would they wait until evening? According to rabbinic teaching, no healing could occur on the Sabbath day unless a life was endangered. Therefore, those who wanted to be healed had to wait for the sun to set before they could arrive.

Mark 1:32 describes two categories of people who were brought to Him: the sick and the demon possessed. There is a clear distinction made between physical sickness and demonic possession. A common misconception is that every illness or sickness is caused by demons. It is also taught in some circles that just as medicine is specialized, demons specialize in certain illnesses. Therefore, if a person has more than one problem, he has more than one demon. Biblically, that is simply not true. Not all physical illnesses are caused by demons. Mark clearly distinguished between two categories: those who were physically ill because of human frailty and those who were demonically afflicted. Luke made that same distinction. In verse 4:40, he mentioned those who were physically ill and were healed. In verse 4:41, he mentioned those who were demonized and set free. As he had done previously, Luke repeated that the demons recognized who Yeshua was, saying: *You are the Son of God*, but Yeshua silenced their witness.

Matthew added two elements to his account that the other Gospel writers left out. First, he described the method that Yeshua used to cast out demons: *with a word* (Mt. 8:16). A simple command was sufficient, and He did not resort to the rituals of the rabbis. Second, Matthew quoted Isaiah 53:4 (Mt. 8:17), saying: *Himself took our infirmities, and bore our diseases.* This has led some to teach that physical healing is in the atonement, that Yeshua's death on the cross provided physical and spiritual healing, and if a believer has enough faith, they can be physically healed, that all who are saved can claim healing today. This teaching has caused undue agony, disappointment, and insecurity among many believers. What Matthew recorded happened well before Yeshua died and well before He made the atonement. Therefore, this passage cannot mean that all believers will automatically be healed because of the atonement. Rather, this quotation falls into the category of literal plus application. In the context of Isaiah 53, the prophet was describing the fact of spiritual healing from sin through atonement. In other words, he explained what the result of the Messiah's death would be. Because of one point of similarity, the passage is applied to the situation described by Matthew. Using the principle of application, Matthew applied what Isaiah said to the physical healing accomplished by Yeshua during His public ministry. This does not mean that atonement guarantees physical healing in this life. That will only come with the resurrection and the glorified body.

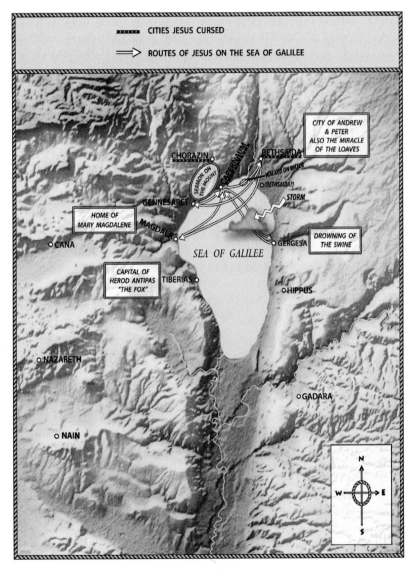

ABOVE: This map shows several important locations, such as where Yeshua set up His headquarters (Capernaum).

[§ 44] — 7. Messiah's Authority to Preach

Matthew 4:23-25, Mark 1:35-39, Luke 4:42-44

Early the next morning, Yeshua went off alone to pray. He sought a time of solitude, a time away from the crowds, yet a time with the Father to prepare for the next phase of His ministry (Mk. 1:35; Lk. 4:42). When the apostles found Him, He informed them that He would not remain in Capernaum, but would go from city to city, proclaiming the good news of the kingdom (Mk. 1:38; Lk. 4:43). This would be Yeshua's second major preaching tour. The Gospel accounts go on to describe the place, content, and authentication of His ministry. As to place, He primarily spent time teaching *in their synagogues* (Mt. 4:23; Lk. 4:44). As to the content, He preached *the gospel* [or the good news] *of the kingdom* (Mt. 4:23). At the time, the gospel He was proclaiming was not that He died for their sins, was buried, and rose again, because those events had not yet taken place. As mentioned before, the content of the good news was not always the same, but must be determined by the context, and the gospel in this context was the good news *of the kingdom* and the fact that He was the Messianic King. If they would accept Him as the Messiah, they could see the kingdom established in their day. As to authentication, He authenticated His message by *healing all manner of disease and all manner of sickness* (Mt. 4:23) and *casting out demons* (Mk. 1:39).

Because of this second preaching tour, Yeshua's reputation spread even further: *And the report of him went forth into all Syria* (Mt. 4:24). The term *Syria* refers to the larger Roman district of that name, which included the land of Israel. The more the reports of His ministry spread, the more people flocked to Him; the more people flocked to Him, the more miracles He performed. Matthew lists sickness, disease, torments, demonization, epilepsy, and paralysis. All of this was further authentication of His Messiahship. Matthew added: *And there followed him great multitudes from Galil and Decapolis and Yerushalayim and Yehudah and <from> beyond the Yarden* (Mt. 4:25). By now, His reputation had spread to both sides of the Jordan. *Decapolis* refers to a union of ten Greek cities, nine of which were in the Transjordan area, and all had minority Jewish populations. Even Greek Gentile cities had heard about Yeshua. It is simply not true that He was merely a local rabbi or "miracle worker" who was not very well known.

[§ 45] — 8. Messiah's Authority over Nature

Matthew 4:18-22, Mark 1:16-20, Luke 5:1-11

In this section, Peter, Andrew, and Yochanan are called again to follow Yeshua. James, the brother of Yochanan, is added, becoming the sixth disciple. Luke provides the historical background to the call. It opens with Yeshua teaching: *And he sat down and taught the multitudes* (Lk. 5:3). Because the masses had *pressed upon him* (Lk. 5:1), He decided to teach them from a boat. The location was the Sea of Galilee.

After teaching the masses, Yeshua told His disciples: *Put out into the deep, and let down your nets for a draught* (Lk. 5:4). This was contrary to the experience of these professional fishermen, and Peter responded: *Master, we toiled all night, and took nothing* (Lk. 5:5a). The implication was that Peter knew more about fishing than Yeshua, since he was the fisherman and Yeshua a carpenter. Peter's experience was that to put out the nets would be of no use. If they could not catch any fish at night, it was even less likely they would catch anything in the heat of the day. Nevertheless, after stating his objection, Peter obeyed. Note that in this instance obedience came before experience: *but at your word I will let down the nets* (Lk. 5:5b). Contrary to Peter's expectation, they caught a large multitude of fish (Lk. 5:6), so many that the nets began to tear apart and they had to call for others to help (Lk. 5:7). Both boats were so full that they actually began to sink!

When the boats *began to sink* (Lk. 5:7), Peter recognized the Messiah's authority over nature itself, and he responded: *Depart from me; for I am a sinful man, O Lord* (Lk. 5:8). The others were equally amazed (Lk. 5:9-10). Although they were experienced fishermen, they had never before seen anything like this. When they recognized the uniqueness of the Messianic Person, they could then see themselves for what they were: sinners. If we compare ourselves with others, we might come out pretty well, for there is always someone worse than we are. The proper comparison, however, is with the one absolute standard, the God-Man, Messiah Yeshua. When we compare ourselves with Him, our conclusion must be the same as Peter's: We are sinful indeed. In response to Peter's statement, Yeshua did not depart from them, but instead He called them to leave what they were doing and follow Him. This was a call to full-time discipleship: *Fear not; from henceforth you shall catch men* (Lk. 5:10). In the words of Matthew 4:19 and Mark 1:17, it says, *Come ye after me, and I will make you fishers of men.* And indeed, *they left all, and followed him* (Lk. 5:11). The result of this call was that Peter and the others left their fishing business (Mt. 4:20, 22; Mk. 1:18, 20). Following Yeshua meant a total commitment to full-time discipleship. It also meant trusting Him to provide for their needs, because they had left their main source of income.

[§ 46] — 9. Messiah's Authority over Defilement: The Healing of the Jewish Leper

Matthew 8:2-4, Mark 1:40-45, Luke 5:12-16

a. Hansen's Disease

In the Mosaic Law, the issue of leprosy received very special treatment. The key Hebrew word Moses used for leprosy is *tzaraat*, which literally means a "mark" or "stroke." The basic meaning of *tzaraat* is "infectious skin disease" or "to become diseased on the surface of the skin." It is a generic term which is used to describe all sorts of dermatological diseases of humans, but also applies to mildew on fabrics and mineral compositions on stone walls. Concerning human skin ailments, the meaning of the term includes the traditional understanding of leprosy, such as Hansen's disease and elephantiasis, as well as other dermatological problems. The leprosy mentioned in the Gospels would refer to Hansen's disease, which is caused by a bacterial infection. In the vast majority of cases, the initial symptom is numbness in the fingers and toes, and if left untreated, the disease slowly progresses to the next stages. Yellowish lesions develop deep in the skin on the genitalia, face, forehead, and joints. The hair growing in the affected areas assumes the same color as the lesions, and as the disease progresses so slowly, it can take up to ten years for the microorganisms to eventually penetrate through the cellular tissue and reach the muscles and bones. Hair begins to turn white, wooly, and eventually falls out. There is gelatinous swelling that forms in the cellular tissue. As time progresses, the skin becomes hard, rough, and seamy. Large scabs form which fall off from time to time, exposing running sores. The nails swell, curl up, and fall off. There is a loss of mucus membrane, resulting in constantly bleeding gums. The nose is stuffed, and there is a constant flow of saliva. Because the bacteria attack the nerves, the senses become dull. In the last stages of leprosy, the victim experiences extreme weight loss and becomes very weak, suffering from chronic diarrhea, chronic thirst, and a burning fever. Finally, there is an attack on the internal and vital organs, leading to death. The leper in this account has entered into the final stages of the disease, and we know this because Luke again records something the other Gospels do not, observing that the man was *full of leprosy.*

b. A Very Special Miracle

It is accepted by many theologians and historians alike that the Gospel accounts are valuable in understanding Second Temple Judaism and the messianic expectation during the time. Even secular scholars agree that they provide a credible transmission of the life and message of the historical Yeshua. Just as these scholars are willing to quote New Testament texts when discussing topics like messianic movements during the first century, this author, too, will attempt to prove his conclusions about certain topics from the Scriptures themselves. One of these topics he has titled "The Three Messianic Miracles," and an objective of this work is to show that certain key miracles recorded in the Gospels were different from anything else that had ever been performed in the Hebrew Scriptures. These miracles caused unique reactions among the people. The reactions, as well as the fact that these particular signs had never been performed before, constitute two primary criteria for determining that the miracles were messianic.

It should be stated that the general ability to perform signs and wonders is not unique to Yeshua. During the time of Moses and the days of Elijah and Elisha, God worked through miracles. Therefore, to heal someone or raise him from the dead was not unique to Yeshua. Elijah and Elisha both did this (I Kgs. 17:17-22; II Kgs. 4:32-35). However, the divine purpose of the signs and wonders Moses, Elijah, and Elisha performed was different. They were to authenticate the prophetic calling of these men, but when the prophets performed them, no one asked, "Can this be the Messiah?" Just so, when Yeshua performed the same miracles, the people *glorified God, saying, A great prophet is arisen among us: and, God has visited his people* (Lk. 7:11-17). They recognized His supernatural character and compared Him to Yochanan the Baptizer, Elijah, Jeremiah, or one of the other prophets (Mt. 16:14). However, the Scriptures show that He performed some miracles that were uniquely different, and their purpose was to authenticate His Messiahship: *If I had not done among them the works which none other did, they had not had sin: but now have they both seen and hated both me and my Father* (Jn. 15:24).

The first miracle that this author considers to be messianic is the healing of a Jewish leper, recorded in Matthew 8:2-4, Mark 1:40-45, and Luke 5:12-15. In Leviticus, there are 116 verses devoted to the topic (Lev. 13:1-14:57), and no other disease is treated so extensively by the law. Very specific instructions are given for determining if a person was afflicted with leprosy and also of how the priest was then to proceed. Only a priest had the authority to declare someone a leper. Once a priest did so, the lepers would have to immediately tear their garments and from then on walk around in torn clothing (Lev. 13:45). They had to keep their faces covered from the nose down (Lev. 13:45). They were ostracized from the Jewish community and would need to live in places reserved for lepers only (Lev. 13:46). They were also prohibited from entering the Tabernacle or Temple compound and could not receive the spiritual benefits of the Tabernacle or Temple service. Anyone touching a leper would become ceremonially unclean as well. Therefore, if lepers were traveling on a road from one location to another, they had to warn others by crying out, "Unclean, unclean!" (Lev. 13:45).

Moses also provided details of what the priesthood would need to do if a Jew were healed of leprosy. If someone declared himself a healed leper, a priest would need to meet and inspect him outside the camp (Lev. 14:3). If he declared the person healed, on that same day, he would need to make an offering of two birds (Lev. 14:4). One bird was killed by the shedding of blood, and the other bird was dipped into the blood of the first bird and then set free (Lev. 14:6-7). For the next seven days, the priests would need to thoroughly investigate the situation in order to be sure of the healing. As to the question of having been a leper, there would be a record of it since only a priest had the authority to declare someone a leper, and as to the question of the healing, every part of the body was carefully examined for a total of seven consecutive days. All hairs, including eyebrows, were shaved off to make sure the examination was thorough. If there were specific circumstances to the healing, then that too would come out in the investigation. If everything proved positive after seven days, the eighth day would be a lengthy day of ritual. On that day, there would be four specific offerings: a sin offering, a trespass offering, a burnt offering, and a meal offering. The blood of the sin offering would be applied to three parts of the leper's body: the right earlobe, right thumb, and right big toe (Lev. 14:14-17). The same procedure was followed with the blood of the trespass offering. The ceremony would conclude with the anointing, during which oil was poured on the same three parts of the body. Only then were the former lepers free to reenter Jewish society, and only then would they have access to the Tabernacle or the Temple. Furthermore, though rabbinic writings contained cures for many different diseases, leprosy was not one of them.

In the Hebrew Bible, three Jews were stricken with leprosy as a divine judgment: Miriam, the sister of Moses and Aaron (Num. 12:9-15); Gehazi, the servant of Elisha (II Kgs. 5:25-27); and Uzziah or Azariah, king of Judah (II Kgs. 15:5; II Chron. 26:16-21). As a result, leprosy was viewed as a divine judgment by God, and the feeling was that there would simply be no possibility of curing a Jewish person of leprosy. Interestingly, from the time of the completion of the Torah, meaning the completion of the Mosaic Law in Deuteronomy (Deut. 31:24-26), there is no record in the Hebrew Bible of a Jew ever having been healed of leprosy. In the case of Miriam, which is described in Numbers 12, the healing occurred before the completion of the law. Furthermore, her leprosy cannot be compared to the disease described in the Gospels— or any other non-biblical source for that matter—as it came and went quickly:

Num. 12:9 And the anger of Jehovah was kindled against them; and he de-parted. 10 And the cloud removed from over the Tent; and, behold, Miriam was leprous, as white as snow: . . . 13 And Moses cried unto Jehovah, say-ing, Heal her, O God, I beseech you. 14 And Jehovah said unto Moses, . . . let her be shut up without the camp seven days, and after that she shall be brought in again.

Clearly the result of divine punishment, Miriam's leprosy set in instantaneously (instead of over several years) and disappeared after seven days.

In the case of Naaman (II Kgs. 5), the nationality needs to be considered. Naaman was Aramean (Syrian), not Jewish. His healing would not have required the priests to perform all that was written in the law. Yeshua even stated that there were many Jewish lepers in the days of Elisha, but only Naaman the Syrian was healed of his leprosy (Lk. 4:27), and thus the proposition remains: There is no record in the Hebrew Scriptures of any Jew ever having been healed of this dreaded disease.

Then comes Yeshua, who, in the early days of His public ministry, healed a Jewish leper whose leprosy was fully developed (Lk. 5:12), meaning the disease would soon take the leper's life. The fact that this leper was coming to Yeshua for healing would also have meant that he already believed in Him. Mark 1:40 stated his request: *If you will, you can make me clean.* He did not ask, "Can you make me clean?" In other words, he did not doubt Yeshua's abilities. He believed that Yeshua could make him clean if He was so willing. He also did not say, "If you will, you can heal me," but, *you can make me clean.* The issue was not healing but that this was a special disease, unlike any other, that had rendered this man permanently unclean.

Indeed, it was His will. Mark revealed Yeshua's motivation to heal: *being moved with compassion* (Mk. 1:41). Luke described the method of healing: *And he stretched forth his hand, and touched him* (Lk. 5:13). All three Gospel writers took note of the fact that Yeshua touched the leper, even though this was not necessary for the miracle to occur. As the account of the nobleman's son showed (Jn. 4:46-50), Yeshua could easily heal from afar. Why the emphasis on touching? It was an act of love, a mark of Yeshua's compassion, because this would have been the first time this man had been touched by human hands since having been declared a leper. He had been rendered untouchable by a priest, and for this leper, it would have been many years of suffering, since at this point, the leprosy had fully developed. Yeshua's touch was sufficient to heal, and all three Gospels state that the healing was instantaneous (Mt. 8:3; Mk. 1:42; Lk. 5:13).

Yeshua healed him by touching him, and then instructed him not to engage in lengthy conversations, but to go directly to the priesthood and begin the process of cleansing as commanded in the Mosaic Law. All of the rituals and procedures discussed above would need to be performed. Then all three Gospel accounts (Mt. 8:4; Mk. 1:44; Lk. 5:14) tell us something Yeshua said that is very significant: When the man presented himself to the priests to perform all of the rituals Moses had commanded, it was to be *for a testimony unto them*, obviously meaning the priests. There was a purpose to this miracle beyond it being an act of compassion toward the man or more than an evidence of Yeshua's ability to perform great healing. The cleansing of this leper was to testify something to the priests. So Yeshua deliberately sent this cleansed leper to the priesthood in order to cause the leaders to start investigating His ministry and the message He was proclaiming. He wanted to force them to make a decision regarding His person (that He was the Messiah) and His message (that He was offering to Israel the kingdom predicted by the Jewish prophets). So, on the day the man appeared before the leadership and said, "I was a leper and have been healed of my disease," they would have to offer up the two birds. For the next seven days, they would then investigate the man, finding the answer to these three questions: Had he really been a leper? Was he really healed of his disease? What were the circumstances of the healing?

Since only a priest could have declared the man a leper, there would have been a record of it in the Temple. This would have answered question one. The seven-day inspection would prove that he had indeed been healed of the disease, an answer to question two. The investigation of the healing, finally, would have revealed that a man named Yeshua of Nazareth was the one who had healed the leper, shedding light on question three. In other words, the first recorded healing of a Jewish leper could not be ignored: A unique miracle had indeed occurred.

As a result of this, the report of Yeshua began to spread abroad even further (Lk. 5:15). It resulted in the fact that Yeshua *could no more openly enter into a city* (Mk. 1:45). No previous miracle caused the stir that this one had. Yeshua of Nazareth had done something never seen before, and the Jewish response was unique, as we will see next, in § 47. It was now known something very significant was happening in Israel.

Also, at this crucial point of His public ministry, Yeshua withdrew to the desert for a time of prayer (Lk. 5:16). Contextually, He was praying for what was about to happen next.

[§ 47] — 10. Messiah's Authority to Forgive Sin

Matthew 9:1-8, Mark 2:1-12, Luke 5:17-26

As mentioned in the introduction, studying the life of the Messiah thematically instead of geographically has the advantage that one can easily see the relationship between one event and another. This section will serve as a very good example. What happened here was a direct result of the healing of the Jewish leper.

a. The Investigation

The first point to observe is that the event described in these verses took place in Capernaum (Mk. 2:1), a three-day journey from Jerusalem—the center of Rabbinic Judaism. Capernaum is on the north shore of the Sea of Galilee, about sixty miles north of Jerusalem. In light of this, the statement in Luke 5:17 is striking: *And it came to pass on one of those days, that he was teaching; and there were Pharisees and doctors of the law sitting by, who were come out of every village of Galil and Yehudah and Yerushalayim.* The men who were listening to what Yeshua was saying were not just a few local Pharisees from Capernaum. Luke specifically stated that spiritual leaders from all over the country had traveled to Capernaum. He affirmed that they came from *every village* of Galilee and Judea, as well as Jerusalem itself. The question is, why? Why did religious leaders from all over the country come to Capernaum?

Only if one correctly understands the implications of the healing of the Jewish leper can he answer this question. This was the response of the religious leaders to a miracle that they knew was vastly different and had never been performed since the Mosaic Law had been established. This special miracle triggered an investigation by the Sanhedrin, and what can be seen here was the stage of observation, the first of the two investigative stages discussed earlier in connection with Yochanan's ministry. He was also investigated by the Sanhedrin, and now we have an instance of the principle that what happened to the herald would happen to the king. During the observation stage, the religious leaders only observed what was being said, taught, and done. At this point, they did not verbalize any questions or objections, and it was not necessary for all the leaders to go. A small delegation like the one previously sent to Yochanan the Baptizer would have been sufficient. However, this time, they were not responding to someone who they thought was merely claiming to be the Messiah; this one had also performed a unique miracle. Therefore, in place of a small delegation, religious leaders from all over the country chose to go. There were so many of them *that there was no longer room <for them>, no, not even about the door* (Mk. 2:2). It was no accident that when Yeshua had so many of Israel's spiritual leaders in front of Him, He made a claim that only God could make.

Luke the doctor mentioned that *the power of the Lord was with him to heal* (Lk. 5:17). While the leaders were observing what He was saying and teaching, four friends of a paralytic tried to deliver the man to Yeshua for healing; but they were unable to do so, because the religious leaders were blocking the doorway. In those days, roofs were flat, and many homes had outdoor stairwells leading to the housetop. In the heat of the summer, it was an enjoyable place to ascend as the late afternoon winds cooled down the land. The four friends managed to get the man up to the roof, which was quite an effort on their part, since the man was a paralytic and could be of no help to them. Once on top of the house, they proceeded to break the roof apart (Mk. 2:4) and lowered the man through the tiles of the roof. The paralytic was still lying on his litter when he was lowered to where Yeshua happened to be teaching (Lk. 5:19). All three Gospel writers made it clear that Yeshua responded to the faith of the four men (Mt. 9:2; Mk. 2:5; Lk. 5:20). Nothing was said about the faith of the paralytic.

b. The Source of Yeshua's Authority

On similar occasions, Yeshua simply proceeded to heal, but not this time. Rather, He chose to make an announcement. Matthew noted that Yeshua began by saying, *Son, be of good cheer* (Mt. 9:2). In the New Testament, this statement is used only by Yeshua. All three Gospels then quoted Him as saying, *your sins are forgiven.* He knew very well that claiming the authority to forgive sins in a salvation sense would raise some serious questions in the minds of the leaders, and so it did— and even more so, because He stated it in the passive voice, *your sins are forgiven.* One has to keep in mind that Yeshua was speaking in Hebrew. The Hebrew form of the passive, *your sins are forgiven,* is used only in one section of the entire Hebrew Bible, in Leviticus 4-6. The context of these chapters is atonement, as they detail the blood sacrifices necessary for the forgiveness of sins. The statement of forgiveness in a passive voice followed the sacrifice (e.g., Lev. 4:20, 26, 31, 35; 5:10, 13, 16, 18; 6:7). The Hebrew, *nislechu lecha chataecha,* means *your sins are forgiven you.* Furthermore, the Hebrew word for "forgiveness," *salach,* is used of God. The passive means that God is doing the forgiving. Being Pharisees, these people knew both the Torah and Hebrew, and they caught the connection He was making. He was claiming the authority that God asserted for Himself in Leviticus 4-6, that by means of blood atonement, God had forgiven their sins. In the New Testament, this phraseology was used only by Yeshua Himself. Yeshua was, therefore, speaking as if He were God.

Yeshua's challenge raised serious objections among the Pharisees, but because this was the observation stage, they could not verbalize their disapproval. Two of the Gospel writers pointed this out. Mark stated they were *reasoning in their hearts* (Mk. 2:6). Matthew specified that they *said within themselves* (Mt. 9:3). Once the Jewish frame of reference is understood, these short phrases begin to make sense. According to Luke, Yeshua was well aware of their thoughts (Lk. 5:22) and perceived that their unexpressed objection was: *Why does this man thus speak? He blasphemes: who can forgive sins but one, <even> God?*

(Mk. 2:7). Their theology was correct. No one can forgive sins in a salvation sense except God alone. This meant one of two things: Either Yeshua was a blasphemer or He was indeed the Messianic Person, the God-Man.

By exercising the authority to forgive sins and speaking as only God speaks, Yeshua had caught their attention. He proceeded to reveal to the religious leaders that He knew what they were thinking (Mk. 2:8). He answered their question by asking a question of His own: *Which is easier, to say to the sick of the palsy, your sins are forgiven; or to say, Arise, and take up your bed, and walk?* (Mk. 2:9). This is a typical method of Jewish education in rabbinic schools, to answer a question with a question. The purpose is to get the student to think through his own question and come up with the right answer on his own. The question Yeshua asked was, "What is the easier thing to say?" The easier thing to say is, *your sins are forgiven*, because that by itself requires no outward, visible evidence. The harder thing to say is, "Rise up and walk, because I am healing you." This does require outward, visible evidence. Yeshua used a form of rabbinic logic called *kal v'chomer*, or "from heavy to light," "from difficult to easy," "from a stronger proposition to a weaker proposition." In this case, the argumentation is reversed, and the point is: "I will prove to you that I can say the easier (*your sins are forgiven*) by doing the harder (healing the paralytic)." Yeshua proceeded to do the harder by healing the paralytic: *And he arose, and straightway took up the bed* (Mk. 2:12). Luke wrote: *And immediately he rose up before them* (Lk. 5:25). There was instantaneous evidence that Yeshua had indeed healed the paralytic. Performing the harder became the evidence that He could claim the easier and tell the paralytic, *your sins are forgiven*. If He could say the easier because He had just performed the harder, it meant He is the Messianic God-Man. All three Gospel writers brought out this God-Man concept (Mt. 9:6; Mk. 2:10; Lk. 5:24). When Yeshua called Himself *the Son of man*, He gave Himself the messianic title that emphasized His humanity. When He claimed authority to forgive sins, He emphasized His deity, and as the God-Man, He has the authority to forgive sins in a salvation sense.

It is evident that when these leaders returned to Jerusalem, their verdict was, "The movement of Yeshua of Nazareth is significant." Now the second stage, the stage of interrogation, would begin.

[§ 48] — 11. Messiah's Authority over Men

Matthew 9:9-13, Mark 2:13-17, Luke 5:27-32

This is the beginning of the second stage of the Sanhedrin-led investigation, the stage of interrogation, which would continue until a crucial turning point occurred in Matthew 12. From this point on, the Pharisees followed Yeshua everywhere He went. However, this time they asked questions and raised objections, looking for a basis to accept or reject His Messiahship.

The interrogation stage began in conjunction with the call of the seventh disciple, Matthew. Luke 5:27 gives his name as *Levi* and Mark 2:14 elaborates, calling him *Levi the <son> of Chalphi*; however, in Matthew 9:9, he calls himself *Mattai*, which is Hebrew for "Matthew." Levi was probably his birth name and Matthew his post-conversion name. *Mattai*, or *Mattatyahu*, means "gift of *YHWH*," which would be an appropriate name after his new birth.

Matthew was a publican, or tax collector, a profession forbidden to Jews by Jewish law. Nevertheless, some Jews chose to bid for the office, not because they were paid well, but because they were allowed to collect more taxes than were actually due. Publicans were hated for two reasons: First, they worked on behalf of the subjugating Gentile Roman authorities, and second, they became wealthy by extorting from their own Jewish people.

In rabbinic writings, publicans were contrasted with the *chaver*. A chaver was the most observant of the observant, while the publican was the exact opposite of the righteous man and was pictured as a gross sinner. Once a man, even a religious man, became a publican, he was officially ostracized from the Jewish community. By Jewish law, the only kinds of people allowed to associate with publicans were other publicans and prostitutes. The word *sinner* in the context of our passage is often a euphemism for a prostitute (Mt. 9:11; Mk. 2:16; Lk. 5:30). Pharisees declared that repentance was virtually impossible for a publican. He was so undependable that he could not be a judge nor even be a witness in a court of law and therefore, could not serve as one of the two witnesses for an indictment to be established.

According to Jewish writings, there were two types of publicans. Both were bad, but one was worse than the other. The lesser of the two evils was the income tax official. The other one was the customs official. All three Gospel accounts state that Matthew was *sitting at the place of toll* (Mt. 9:9a; Mk. 2:14a; Lk. 5:27a), which means he was a customs official, the worst kind of all. It was to this kind of publican that Yeshua said, *Follow me* (Mt. 9:9b; Mk. 2:14b; Lk. 5:27b).

Normally, a man in Matthew's position would not just leave without making prior arrangements. However, Matthew recognized that the authority of the Messiah superseded the authority of Rome, *And he forsook all, and rose up and followed him* (Lk. 5:28). This marked the point of Matthew's new birth. To celebrate his conversion, Matthew *made him a great feast in his house* (Lk. 5:29). Only other publicans and prostitutes would attend a feast in the house of a tax collector, and the text shows that they were indeed present. However, Yeshua and the other six disciples also attended, and that was a breach of Pharisaic Law and tradition. So the Pharisees broke their silence and verbalized their objections, noting that *he eats and drinks with publicans and sinners* (Mk. 2:16). The point of their objection was that if Yeshua really was the Messiah, He would never associate with this class of society.

Yeshua responded to their objection by stating three things. First, it is the sick who need a doctor, not those who are well (Mt. 9:12). The Pharisees saw themselves as being spiritually well, and they agreed that the publicans were spiritually sick; so, should He not go to them? Second, the Pharisees were characterized by much sacrifice but little mercy, meaning they were very careful to keep the external demands of the Mosaic Law, but not as careful to keep its internal demands. Their lack of mercy was demonstrated by their many rules and regulations against the publicans. Yeshua introduced the second response with the phrase, *Go ye and learn* (Mt. 9:13a). His third response to the Pharisees' objection was that it is not the righteous who need to be called to repentance, but sinners (Mt. 9:13b).

This set the stage for the crucial turning point of Matthew 12. From this point on, everywhere Yeshua went, the Pharisees followed and raised objections, either to things He said or to things He did.

[§ 49] — 12. Messiah's Authority over Tradition

Matthew 9:14-17, Mark 2:18-22, Luke 5:33-39

During the second stage of the Sanhedrin's investigation of Yeshua, the real point of conflict between Him and the Pharisees became evident. This specific issue was the reason for their ultimate rejection of His Messiahship. A common misconception is that they rejected Yeshua because He would not overthrow Rome. However, this is not the reason they themselves gave. The real reason was that He rejected Pharisaism. Over the preceding four centuries, the Pharisees had developed a whole body of traditions, rules, and regulations. By the time of the first century, these rules had become sacrosanct and of equal validity to Scripture. To fully understand the issues, it is necessary to do some background work in Jewish history to see how Pharisaic Judaism had developed.

In the four hundred years that followed the completion of the Hebrew Scriptures, a transition had occurred from Biblical Judaism to Rabbinic, or Pharisaic Judaism. A certain school of rabbis called the *Sopherim*[9] had built a fence of numerous new rules and regulations around the 613 commandments of the Mosaic Law. The thinking was that while the Jews might break the rabbinic laws, the fence would still keep them from breaking the Mosaic Law and thereby preventing divine judgment like the Babylonian Captivity. So, the purpose of the fence was to avoid violating Torah commandments. These new laws were not made haphazardly, and hundreds, sometimes thousands, of regulations were issued for each of the original 613 commandments.

The Sopherim used a form of rabbinic logic called *pilpul*, a term that means "peppery" or "sharp." The underlying thought process could be summarized in the following question: Given a specific statement or commandment, how many new regulations could be logically derived from that original statement or commandment?

The following is an example of how pilpulistic logic works: Among the commandments God gave to Moses was one that forbade seething

---

[9] Plural for *sopher*.

(boiling) a kid (baby goat) in the milk of its mother. In all probability, this law was given to avoid a Canaanite practice. When a goat gave birth to its firstborn kid, the Canaanites would take the kid away from its mother, milk the mother, and then boil the meat of the kid in the milk of its mother as a firstfruits offering to Baal. Jews were not to practice that kind of idolatry, and so they were not to seethe a kid in the milk of its mother. God gave that commandment to Moses around 1,400 B.C. A thousand years later, in 400 B.C., there were no Canaanites around anymore. No one was boiling kids in the milk of the mother goat anymore, and so the original intent of that commandment had long been forgotten. In the school of the Sopherim, the question arose: How do we make sure we never, never, never, ever, ever, ever boil a kid in the milk of its mother? That is when the pilpulistic logic began to work. Suppose you eat a piece of meat, and with the meat, you drink a glass of milk. It is possible that the meat is from the young of the animal that produced the milk you are drinking. As you swallow both the meat and the milk, it mixes in your stomach, and you seethe a kid in the milk of its mother. Thus, a new law came into being: A Jew cannot eat meat and dairy at the same meal; they must be separated by about four hours.

However, the pilpulistic logic went even further. Suppose at noon you choose to eat a dairy meal. You take a plate, and from this, you eat some cheese. After you eat the cheese, you may wash and scrub the plate thoroughly, but there might be a tiny speck of cheese still left on the plate that you did not see. In the evening, you choose to eat meat and you place the meat on the same plate from which you ate the cheese earlier in the day. The meat might pick up that tiny speck of cheese. No matter how remote, it just might be possible that the cheese you had at noon was made from the milk of the mother of the baby goat you are eating later in the day. As you swallow this tiny speck of cheese with the meat, you seethe the kid in the milk of its mother and again violate the Torah. Thus, another new law came into being: All Jews must have two sets of dishes; one is to be used for dairy products and one for meat products. If one accidently uses the wrong dish for the item eaten, the dish must either be destroyed or given to a Gentile, but no Jew may eat from that plate again! To each of the 613 commandments God gave to Moses, the Sopherim issued multiple new rules and regulations. This process began around 450 B.C. and finally ended in the year 30 B.C.

Normally, it was passed from rabbi to rabbi, and it is said to have lasted from Ezra the scribe to Hillel. With Hillel came the end of the period of the Sopherim.

Then came a second school of rabbis called the *Tannaim*.[10] The Tannaim looked upon the work of the Sopherim and decided that there were still too many holes in this fence. They continued the process of establishing new rules and regulations from 30 B.C. until A.D. 220, the period from Hillel to Rabbi Judah Ha-Nasi. However, the principle of operation changed. The principle of the Sopherim was, "A sopher may disagree with a sopher, but he cannot disagree with the Torah." The principle of the Tannaim was, "A tanna may disagree with a tanna, but he cannot disagree with a sopher." That meant that from 30 B.C., shortly before Yeshua arrived, all the thousands of rules and regulations passed down by the Sopherim became sacrosanct and of equal validity with Scripture. In order to validate to the Jewish audience why the laws of the Sopherim were equal to the laws of Moses, the rabbis came up with a teaching that all Orthodox Jews believe and teach to this very day: What really happened on Mount Sinai was that God gave Moses two laws. The first law is called the Written Law, which contains the 613 commandments that Moses actually penned in the Books of Exodus, Leviticus, Numbers, and Deuteronomy. However, God also gave Moses a second law, which is called the Oral Law because Moses did not write all of its commandments down; he merely memorized them. By memory, they were passed down to Joshua, who then passed them down to the judges, who then passed them down to the prophets, who then passed them down to the Sopherim. In fact, the Oral Law was not written down for about six centuries, and a great part of the work of a rabbi consisted of memorization. By the third century A.D., fewer and fewer people were around to memorize all these laws, so in A.D. 220, the rabbis finally wrote them down at the order of Judah Ha-Nasi, the patriarch in the land. This ended the period of the Tannaim.

Then came a third school of rabbis called the *Amoraim*, plural for *amora*, an Aramaic term meaning "teacher" or "interpreter." They looked upon the work of the Tannaim and declared, "There are still too many holes in this fence." They continued the process of establishing

---

[10] Plural for *tanna*.

new rules and regulations until about A.D. 500, but they changed their principle of operation. Their principle was, "An amora may disagree with an amora, but he cannot disagree with a tanna." Thus, all the rules and regulations of the Tannaim also became sacrosanct, having equal validity with Scripture.

The work of the Sopherim and the Tannaim together is now called the *Mishnah*. The work of the Amoraim is called the *Gemara*. The two works together (Mishnah plus Gemara) comprise the Talmud. The Mishnah was written in Hebrew, and it averages about 1,500 pages in small print. The Gemara was written in Aramaic and is the size of the *Encyclopedia Britannica*.

In the life of the Messiah, the primary concern was not with the Gemara, which was put together after the time of Yeshua. It was the Mishnah that became the bone of contention between Yeshua and the Pharisees. The Pharisaic concept was that the Messiah Himself would be a Pharisee. He would be in submission to the laws of the Mishnah, and in fact, He would join them in the work of making new laws to plug up the holes in the fence. Anyone who was not a Pharisee under Mishnaic authority could not possibly be the true Messiah.

It should also be pointed out that the tannaitic rabbis, who were active in Yeshua's day, claimed that what later became the Mishnah was also given by God to Moses. For the remainder of this study, the terms Mishnaic Law, Pharisaic Law, Rabbinic Law, and the Oral Law will all be used interchangeably to refer to the body of material now known as the Mishnah. In the New Testament, it is known as *the tradition of the elders* or *the tradition of the fathers*. Yeshua's rejection of this law was the essential cause of disagreement between Him and the Pharisees.

One of the Pharisaic traditions was that of frequent fasting. It was customary for Pharisees to fast twice a week, on Mondays and Thursdays. In Luke 18, Yeshua told the story of a publican and a Pharisee praying in the Temple. This Pharisee is quoted as saying, *I fast twice in the week* (Lk. 18:12), meaning he fasted on Mondays and Thursdays.

Yochanan's disciples followed the rabbinic tradition of fasting, but Yeshua and His disciples did not. The question raised by both the Pharisees (Lk. 5:33) and Yochanan's disciples (Mt. 9:14) was, why did He not? Yeshua responded by stating four things.

Yeshua's first response was that a person does not come to a wedding feast to fast, but to celebrate (Lk. 5:34-35). Messiah, the bridegroom, was physically present, and as long as He was present, there simply would not be any room for fasting. Indeed, from the time He went public with His ministry at that first Passover, there was no record of Yeshua ever fasting. He also mentioned that the *bridegroom shall be taken away from them*, a terminology that usually referred to death. Then there would be time for fasting.

Yeshua's second response was that no one tears off a patch from a new garment and uses the new patch to cover a hole in an old garment (Lk. 5:36). For one thing, it destroys the new garment, and the new patch will not match the old garment. Furthermore, an old garment that has been washed many times has shrunk as much as it is going to shrink. If a new piece of cloth is used to cover a hole in the old garment, the next time it is washed, the new patch will shrink and pull the garment together, ruining the shape. Yeshua's point was that He had not come to join them in the work of patching up Pharisaic Judaism or plugging up the holes in the fence around the Mosaic Law. He was presenting something quite different. What Messiah had to offer would not merely straighten out or "patch up" Pharisaic Judaism. Therefore, the old would not mix with the new.

Yeshua's third response was that no one ever puts new wine into an old wineskin (Lk. 5:37-38). An old wineskin has stretched as much as it is ever going to stretch. If an old wineskin is filled with new wine that is still expanding as it undergoes the fermentation process, it will cause a tear or rip, and both the wineskin and the wine will be lost. Hence, old wine is poured into old wineskins, and new wine into new wineskins. Yeshua said that He did not come to put His teachings into the skin, or the mold, of Pharisaism. He was presenting something that was new, and the old cannot be mixed with the new.

Yeshua's fourth and last response could be taken in one of two ways. He said, *And no man having drunk old <wine> desires new; for he said, The old is good* (Lk. 5:39). One interpretation is that He was prophesying: In the end, they would reject the new and stay with the old. Another interpretation, which was directed toward their theology, is this: The old wine is Mosaic Judaism, and the new wine is Pharisaic Judaism. The old wine, Mosaic Judaism, is better.

The point of this analogy is that, in the end, the religious leaders of Israel will reject Yeshua in favor of Mishnaic Judaism.

[§§ 50–52] — 13. Messiah's Authority over the Sabbath

The Sabbath became a major observance in Pharisaic Judaism, especially after the Temple had been destroyed in A.D. 70. Its importance was so elevated that it was personified as the bride of Israel and as God's queen. Today, at a certain point in the Friday-night synagogue service, the door is opened and the worshippers welcome the Sabbath in by singing *Lecha Dodi, Likrat Kallah Shabbat*, a song whose title can be translated as "Welcome my Beloved, Let us Greet Queen Sabbath." When the question was raised as to why God created Israel, the answer was that God made Israel to honor the Sabbath. Therefore, Israel was made for the Sabbath.

To the one commandment Moses gave, *Remember the Sabbath Day to keep it holy* (Ex. 20:8), the Pharisees added approximately 1,500 additional rules and regulations. While the Messiah and the Pharisees debated over the authority of the Mishnah in general, one special area of debate was the proper way of observing the Sabbath. What does and what does not constitute Sabbath rest? Yeshua had three such conflicts in a row, which will be discussed in §§ 50–52.

[§ 50] — a. Through the Healing of a Paralytic

The first conflict pertained to the healing of a paralytic on a Sabbath day. The healing itself is recorded in John 5:1-47. This section contains the second of Yochanan's seven discourses, the discourse on the works of God, and the third of his seven signs. Furthermore, it presents another example of the conflict between light and darkness: *He was the lamp that burns and shines; and you were willing to rejoice for a season in his light* (Jn. 5:35).

(1) The Physical Healing

John 5:1-9

The healing took place not only on a Sabbath (Jn. 5:9), but on a feast day (Jn. 5:1), and Yeshua had gone up to Jerusalem. Generally, if a feast is mentioned but not specifically named, it would be the Feast of the Passover. If this is the case, then this is the second Passover mentioned in Yeshua's public ministry, which would make the ministry about one-and-a-half years old.

Yeshua approached a man at the Pool of Bethesda. It is significant to note the procedure He used in this case. First, He sought the man out. The man did not come to Him because he could not do so on his own, nor was he taken to Yeshua. It was Yeshua who saw the paralytic and purposefully approached him. Second, the Messiah did not demand any faith on the part of the man. At that point in His public ministry, faith was not necessary for a miracle to be received because the purpose of His miracles was to authenticate His messianic claims and to get people to believe. Third, there was no revelation of Yeshua's Messiah-ship. Yeshua did not tell the man who He was, and so *he that was healed knew not who it was* (Jn. 5:13). The paralytic could not believe that Yeshua was the Messiah because he didn't even know who it was who had done the healing. After asking the man if he wanted to be healed (Jn. 5:6) and receiving a positive answer, Yeshua said: *Arise, take up your bed, and walk. And straightway the man was made whole, and took up his bed and walked* (Jn. 5:9). The paralytic was healed immediately. However, when he took up his bed as Yeshua had ordered him, he violated the Pharisaic interpretation of the Sabbath commandment: Nothing could be carried from a public to a private domain or from a private to a public domain.

(2) The Spiritual Healing

John 5:10-18

By obeying Yeshua and picking up his bed, the man violated Pharisaic Law, and he was quickly confronted: *So the Jews said unto him that was cured, It is the Sabbath, and it is not lawful for you to take up your bed*

(Jn. 5:10b). In defense, the man responded that he was simply obeying the One who had healed him (Jn. 5:11). When the religious leaders asked, *Who is the man that said unto you, Take up <your bed>, and walk?* (Jn. 5:12), he could not answer them. He still did not know (Jn. 5:13). Afterwards, Yeshua found the man again, this time in the Temple (Jn. 5:14a), where he was perhaps thanking God for his healing and participating in the rituals of the feast. Yeshua said, *Behold, you are made whole: sin no more, lest a worse thing befall you* (Jn. 5:14b). This indicates the spiritual healing of the man. At that point, he discovered who Yeshua was, and he informed the others (Jn. 5:15). There is no need to see anything sinister here. Although the response of the hearers was negative, the motivation of the former paralytic may have been nothing more than to give them the information they were seeking.

The incident led to two specific accusations against Yeshua (Jn. 5:16-18). The first accusation was that He had healed someone on the Sabbath. This did not violate the Mosaic Law, but it did break Pharisaic Law, which forbade healing on the Sabbath day, except if there was a danger to life. As long as the man's life was not endangered, he should not have been healed on this day. Yochanan stated that this was a key reason why the religious leaders persecuted Yeshua (Jn. 5:16). Rabbis were very specific about the healings that could or could not be done on the Sabbath.

When Yeshua answered, *My Father works even until now, and I work* (Jn. 5:17), the second accusation came: He was claiming equality with God! This was so offensive to the audience that they *sought the more to kill him* (Jn. 5:18). Cultic groups often tend to base their denial of the deity of Yeshua on the assumption that a son is less than his father. Therefore, if Yeshua is the Son of God, He must be less than God. That was not how the Jewish audience understood it, though. According to their reckoning, the firstborn son is equal to the father. So, this verse, like many others, has to be viewed against the backdrop of the Jewish mindset of the day. What did the people think Yeshua meant when they heard Him speak? When He said, *My Father works ... I work*, they clearly understood that He was claiming to be equal with God, hence their strong reaction. There was no ambiguity to the Jewish mind. While it is true that in many Jewish prayers God is addressed as

"Father," it is always in a plural sense ("our Father"), and never in a singular sense ("my Father").

(3) The Defense

John 5:19-29

Yeshua defended Himself against these accusations by making four points. In the first defense, He pointed out that He was doing the works of the Father as His equal (Jn. 5:19-21). Their relationship was characterized by this equality, and what one does, the other does (Jn. 5:19a). The works of the Father are also the works of the Son (Jn. 5:19b). If it is the work of the Son, it is also the work of the Father. There is also equal love between the Father and the Son; both give rise to equally mighty works (Jn. 5:20). Furthermore, there is equal power, and the Son shares the Father's power to give life (Jn. 5:21). The giving of life was a divine ability (II Kgs. 4:32-35; 13:20-21); therefore, Yeshua must be divine. Because He does the work of the Father, works that only God can do, it means that He must be God.

Yeshua's second defense was that He will judge all men (Jn. 5:22-23), for the Father *has given all judgment unto the Son* (Jn. 5:22). In the Hebrew Scriptures, the final judgment was the prerogative of God (Ps. 9:7, 8). If the Son is going to do the judging, He must also be God. This also means He has equal honor with the Father.

Yeshua's third defense was that He has the power to provide eternal life (Jn. 5:24). In the Hebrew Scriptures, the one who had the ability to provide eternal life was God (Dan. 12:1-3). Therefore, if the Son has the power to provide eternal life, then He, too, must be God.

Yeshua's fourth defense was that He will bring about the resurrection of the dead (Jn. 5:25-29). In the Hebrew Scriptures, only God brought about the resurrection of the dead (Is. 26:19; Dan. 12:2; Hos. 13:14). If the Son is raising the dead, it means He must also be God.

Therefore, Yeshua is the God-Man, and both facets are stated here in the form of titles. In verse 25, He is the *Son of God*, emphasizing deity; in verse 27, a *son of man*, emphasizing humanity.

Verse 29 points out that there will be two distinct kinds of resurrection. For the believer, it will be the resurrection of life (Jn. 5:29a), or the first resurrection (Rev. 20:5). For the unbelievers, it will be the resurrection of judgment (Jn. 5:29b), or the second resurrection, leading to the second death (Rev. 20:6).

(4) The Fourfold Witness

John 5:30-47

After bringing forward His defense and declaring Himself to be the God-Man, Yeshua showed that there was a fourfold witness to His messianic assertions. In the Law of Moses, two or three witnesses were sufficient to establish a case. Yeshua provided four, thereby going beyond the demands of the law.

The first witness was Yochanan the Baptizer: *Ye have sent unto Yochanan, and he has born witness unto the truth* (Jn. 5:33). It was Yochanan who identified Yeshua as *the Lamb of God, that takes away the sin of the world* (Jn. 1:29).

The second witness was His works: *the very works that I do, bear witness of me, that the Father has sent me* (Jn. 5:36). His works—His miracles—authenticated His claims.

The third witness was God the Father: *And the Father that sent me, he has borne witness of me* (Jn. 5:37-38). God the Father spoke audibly out of heaven at Yeshua's baptism and declared, *This is my beloved Son, in whom I am well pleased* (Mt. 3:17). It was the witness of the *Bat Kol*, the voice of God, a concept that was viewed as authoritative among the Jews of that day.

The fourth witness was the Scriptures (Jn. 5:39-47): *Ye search the scriptures, because ye think that in them ye have eternal life; and these are they which bear witness of me* (Jn. 5:39). They bore witness because He was fulfilling first-coming prophecies. However, because the religious leaders did not understand Scripture, they failed to understand Him (Jn. 5:40-44). For that reason, they did not have *the love of God* and sought the glory of men instead of the Father. Therefore, the very Law of Moses on which they had set their hope condemned them (Jn. 5:45).

The leaders' real problem was their failure to believe Moses: *For if ye believed Mosheh, ye would believe me; for he wrote of me. But if ye believe not his writings, how shall ye believe my words* (Jn. 5:46-47). Accusing the Pharisees of not believing in Moses seems to be a stretch. It would be like approaching an Ultra-Orthodox Jew and saying, "You do not believe in the Mosaic Law." Who could be more zealous for this law? Yet, it is a valid accusation. The Pharisees believed in Moses as he was reinterpreted through the Mishnah. They did not believe Moses *as it is written*. Had they accepted Moses as it is written, they would not have failed to recognize that this was the Messiah.

[§ 51] — b. Through the Controversy over Grain

Matthew 12:1-8, Mark 2:23-28, Luke 6:1-5

Luke 6:1 provides the historical background to this controversy: *Now it came to pass on a Sabbath, that he was going through the wheatfields; and his disciples plucked the ears, and did eat, rubbing them in their hands.* The Pharisees came attacking (Lk. 6:2) because the disciples had broken four of the 1,500 Mishnaic Sabbath rules and regulations: reaping, threshing, winnowing, and storing. When they took the wheat off the stalk, they were guilty of reaping on the Sabbath day. When they rubbed the wheat in their hands in order to separate it from the chaff, they were guilty of threshing the wheat on the Sabbath day. When they blew into their hands to blow the chaff away, they were guilty of winnowing on the Sabbath day. When they swallowed the wheat, they were guilty of storing the wheat on the Sabbath day. That is how extreme the "building of the fence" had become by this time.

For that reason, some Pharisees would not walk on grass on the Sabbath day. If someone asked such a rabbi, "What is wrong with walking on grass on the Sabbath day?" he would answer, "Nothing. It is permissible to walk on the grass on the Sabbath day." However, there is a problem. What looks only like a grassy field might have one wild stalk of wheat growing in it. A person walking through the field of grass might inadvertently step on that one wild stalk of wheat and separate the wheat from its stalk. Thus, he would become guilty of reaping on the Sabbath day. Furthermore, if his foot came down and twisted the wheat just enough to separate the wheat from the chaff, he would be guilty of threshing on the Sabbath day. If he continued to walk, the outer hem of his garment might cause just enough breeze to blow the chaff away, and he would be guilty of winnowing on the Sabbath day. Finally, once the person had gone, a bird or rodent might see the exposed piece of wheat and swallow it, causing him to be guilty of storing the wheat on the Sabbath day.

Yeshua responded by stating six things. First, He appealed to the account of David's actions in I Samuel 21, pointing out that the king also violated Pharisaic Law when he ate the shewbread (Mt. 12:3-4; Mk. 2:25-26; Lk. 6:3-4). Moses never said that a Levite could not give the shewbread to a non-Levite. Pharisaic Law, however, did say that. In the case of the Pharisees, they could not claim that David lived before the Oral Law, because, according to their theology, God gave this law to Moses; therefore, it preceded the time of David. So, David himself broke Pharisaic Law, yet the rabbis never condemned the king. If he could break Pharisaic Law, so could His greater Son.

Second, the Sabbath law of rest did not apply in every situation (Mt. 12:5). Those, for example, who worked in the Temple compound did not enjoy the Sabbath as a day of rest, but had a day of labor. In fact, they had to work harder on the Sabbath than on a normal day. There were daily sacrifices and rituals, but on the Sabbath, all sacrifices were doubled. Furthermore, there were special rituals performed only on that day. This shows that the Law of Moses allowed and even commanded certain works to be done on the Sabbath. The Pharisees, too, authorized certain works on the Sabbath, such as midwifery, circumcision, and the preparation of a corpse. The point was that the law of Sabbath rest did not apply to every specific situation, and it did not apply merely to walking through a grain field and picking ears of grain to eat.

Third, Yeshua noted that He is *greater than the temple* (Mt. 12:6). If the Temple allowed certain works to be done on the Sabbath without violating the Law of Moses, so could the Messiah, since He is greater than any temple.

Fourth, quoting parts of Hosea 6:6 (*I desire goodness, and not sacrifice)*, Yeshua pointed out that certain works were always allowed on the

Sabbath day, such as works of necessity and works of mercy (Mt. 12:7). Eating is a work of necessity. Healing is a work of mercy. Such works were always allowed on the Sabbath.

Fifth, as the Messiah, He was the *lord of the Sabbath* (Mt. 12:8; Mk. 2:28; Lk. 6:5), and as such, He could allow what the Pharisees disallowed, and He could disallow what they allowed.

Sixth, Yeshua declared that the rabbis had totally misconstrued the purpose of the Sabbath (Mk. 2:27). Pharisaic Judaism taught that the reason God made Israel was for honoring the Sabbath. Therefore, Israel was made for the Sabbath. Yeshua, however, taught that the exact opposite was true: Israel was not made for the Sabbath, the Sabbath was made for Israel. The purpose of the Sabbath was to give Israel a day of refreshment and rest, not to enslave the people. Yet these 1,500 additional Mishnaic rules and regulations had the effect of enslaving the Jew to the Sabbath.

[§ 52] — c. Through the Healing of a Man with a Withered Hand

Matthew 12:9-14, Mark 3:1-6, Luke 6:6-11

The third Sabbath controversy took place in the synagogue. On this occasion, Yeshua was expounding the Word (Lk. 6:6). A man was in the audience who happened to have a withered hand. This was a medical problem, but it was not life threatening. Again, Luke's profession becomes evident. Both Matthew and Mark simply state that the man's hand was withered (Mt. 12:10a; Mk. 3:1); however, Dr. Luke specifies it was his right hand that was deformed.

It appears that the man was a plant for the purpose of entrapment, because some in the audience asked, *Is it lawful to heal on the Sabbath day?* Their goal was *That they might accuse him* (Mt. 12:10b). Luke specifies: *And the scribes and the Pharisees watched him, whether he would heal on the Sabbath* (Lk. 6:7). Clearly, the man with the withered hand was a plant.

Since this occurred during the interrogation stage, the religious leaders were still looking for a basis to accuse and reject Him. Yeshua clearly understood what the circumstances were (Lk. 6:8). Nevertheless, He again showed that He would not accept their Pharisaic authority. He began by reminding them of their own particular practice: *What man shall there be of you, that shall have one sheep, and if this fall into a pit on the Sabbath day, will he not lay hold on it, and lift it out? How much then is a man of more value than a sheep! Wherefore it is lawful to do good on the Sabbath day* (Mt. 12:11-12). Even the Pharisees believed that it was permitted to do good on the Sabbath. However, when Yeshua challenged them by asking, *Is it lawful on the Sabbath to do good, or to do harm? To save a life, or to destroy it?* (Lk. 6:9), they chose to remain silent (Mk. 3:4). Again, using the *kal v'chomer* argument (from the lesser to the greater), He stated that if it was permissible to do good for an animal on the Sabbath (the lesser), how much more would it be right to do good for a man on the Sabbath (the greater)? He repeated two lessons: Works of necessity and mercy were allowed on the Sabbath. This included work that would benefit animals. Healing was an act of mercy, and therefore, it did not violate the law.

Having made His point, Yeshua proceeded to heal the man's hand. By doing so, He again negated Pharisaic authority. The wording of Mark 3:5 implies He did it to spite them: *And when he had looked round about on them with anger, being grieved at the hardening of their heart, he said unto the man, Stretch forth your hand.* Yeshua healed by simply giving an order, and the healing was immediate. The Messiah did not ask the man if he believed or had faith; at that point, faith was not essential. Although the man was a plant, Yeshua went ahead and healed him, because at this point in His career, the purpose of His miracles was to authenticate His messianic claims.

The Pharisaic response to this incident and to the Sabbath controversies in general was threefold. First, the religious leaders *were filled* [or controlled] *with madness* (Lk. 6:11). They allowed the emotion of anger to overtake them, and the result was that they could no longer think logically and rationally. Second, *the Pharisees went out, and took counsel against him, how they might destroy him* (Mt. 12:14). They conspired how to be rid of Yeshua in one way or another and how to reject His Messiahship in spite of His special abilities. Third, *the Pharisees went out, and straightway with the Herodians took counsel against him, how they might destroy him* (Mk. 3:6). The Pharisees joined with the Herodians in their conspiracy against Yeshua. This, indeed, made for strange bedfellows, because they were at the opposite ends of the political spectrum and bitter enemies towards each other. The Pharisees were opposed to Roman rule in any form, while the Herodians favored it if it came through the house of Herod. Yet, on the issue of Yeshua, they had a common cause.

[§ 53] — 14. Messiah's Authority to Heal

Matthew 12:15-21, Mark 3:7-12

Mark points out three things. First, interest in Yeshua's unique work continued to increase (Mk. 3:7-8). His reputation had spread, not only throughout the country, but also to areas outside, including Gentile territory such as Idumea (located south of Judah), Tyre, and Sidon (north of Galilee). Second, masses of people thronged about Him, seeking to benefit from His healing ministry (Mk. 3:9-10). Third, demons continued to recognize His authority; but when they declared who Yeshua was, He still would not accept their testimony and commanded them to keep silent (Mk. 3:11-12).

The Matthew passage quotes Isaiah 42:1-4, which includes a prophecy of the nature of Messiah's ministry during His first coming. Therefore, Matthew 12:18-21 falls under the category of literal prophecy plus literal fulfillment.

[§ 54] — 15. The Choosing of the Twelve

Mark 3:13-19a, Luke 6:12-16

It was at this point in His public ministry and career that Yeshua closed the apostolic group of twelve. Out of many curious would-be disciples, and after an all-night prayer vigil (Lk. 6:12), He chose twelve specific men for three reasons. First, *that they might be with him* (Mk. 3:14a). Yeshua would now have a closed group of twelve men who would be with Him at all times, while the other disciples, like the seventy mentioned in Luke 10, would be on call and come and go. Second, *that he might send them forth to preach* (Mk. 3:14b). Yeshua gave these men the special ministry of proclaiming Him as king and offering the kingdom. Third, *to have authority to cast out demons.* While this authority was not given to all believers at this point, but only to the apostolic group of twelve, it will be extended to others later.

Luke drew a distinction: *And when it was day, he called his disciples; and he chose from them twelve, whom also he named apostles* (Lk. 6:13). Out of many disciples, Yeshua selected only twelve, and only those He called apostles. The word *disciple* merely means "learner." It was used of a follower of a specific rabbi. By itself, the term carries no implication of authority. The word *apostle*, however, means "a sent one." While a disciple did not carry any authority, an apostle had the authority of the sender.

Both passages list the twelve apostles, some of whom had more than one name. Each will be discussed individually. The first apostle had three names originating from three different languages. His Hebrew name was *Shimon* ("Simon" in English), his Aramaic name was *Keifa* (Cephas), and his Greek name was *Petros* (Peter). All three of these names are associated with a stone or rock.

The second apostle was *Andrei* ("Andrew" in English).

The third apostle was *Yochanan* ("John" in English), which means "YHWH is gracious." He was the son of *Shulamit* (Salome) and *Zavdi* (Zebedee).

The fourth apostle was Yochanan's brother, *Yaakov,* meaning "heel-grabber." In Greek, his name was *Iacobos,* and this is what the original text reads. In English, this name was translated in two ways. When it designates the patriarch, it is rendered as Jacob. For the apostle, it is translated as James.

The fifth apostle was *Philipos.* This Greek name has been rendered as "Philip" in the English language. It means "lover of horses."

The sixth apostle was *Netanel* ("Nathanael" in English), meaning "gift of God" (Jn. 1:45). He also went by the name of Bartholomew (Mt. 10:3; Mk. 3:18; Lk. 6:14; Acts 1:13), which is not really a name, but a title. Bartholomew was a Hellenized version of two Aramaic words, *Bar* and *Talmai*, meaning "Son of Talmai." His full name and title in Hebrew was *Netanel Bar Talmai*, or in English, "Nathanael Bartholomew."

The seventh apostle was *Toma* ("Thomas" in English). In Greek, his name was *Didymus*, and both the Hebrew and Greek mean "twin." So Thomas was the twin brother of someone else.

The eighth apostle was *Mattai* ("Matthew" in English), also known as Levi the son of Alphaeus. The Hebrew form of his father's name was *Chalphai*. So Levi the son of *Chalphai* was his original name; but when he became a believer, he changed his name to *Mattai*, a short form of the name *Mattatyahu*, meaning "the gift of YHWH."

The ninth apostle was another *Yaakov* (or Jacob or James). He was the son of *Chalphai* (Alphaeus), but not the same *Chalphai* who was Matthew's father. Chalphai was a common Hebrew name at that time.

The tenth apostle was *Yehudah* ("Judas" in English), the brother of *Yaakov* (James), the son of *Chalphai* (Alphaeus). *Ioudas* or Judas is a hellenized form of *Yehuda*, and it is the same name as the fourth son of Jacob. This disciple also went by the name of *Taddai* ("Thaddaeus" in English). His actual name was *Yehudah ben Taddai*.

The eleventh apostle was another *Shimon* ("Simon" in English). He was known as Simon the Zealot, meaning he was of the Zealot party. Holding to an extreme position of Pharisaism, the Zealots believed in active resistance to Roman rule and ultimately brought the nation into war by instigating the First Jewish Revolt (A.D. 66-70). In some translations, Simon the Zealot is called a Canaanite, but that is a misreading of the Greek text. In Hebrew-Aramaic, the term "Zealot" is *Ha-Kanai*, which was transliterated into Greek and then misread as Canaanite. The correct rendering is Zealot.

The twelfth apostle was *Yehudah Ish Kiryot* ("Judas Iscariot" in English). *Ish Kiryot* means "a man of the town of Kiryot," which was located in southern Judah. This would make Judas the only non-Galilean among the apostles. However, there are other possibilities as to the meaning of this name. In Aramaic, it could indicate that Judas was a tanner. Furthermore, a different form of the same Aramaic root means "strangulation," and so this could indicate that he was given the name because he was killed by strangulation.

Among the references to Yeshua in the Talmud is one which mentions five disciples who were led out and killed. Some of the names given are similar to what is in the New Testament. The first name listed is *Mattai*, which would correspond to Matthew. The second name is *Nakai*, which corresponds to Nicodemus (or *Nakdimon* in Hebrew), who was not among the twelve. The third name is *Nezer*, which does not correspond to any known name and may simply be reflecting *Natzrat* or *Natzeret* ("Nazareth" in English), the town Yeshua came from. The fourth name is *Buni* or *Bonai*. Again, it does not correspond to any known name. However, another passage in the Talmud states that *Bonai* is the same as Nicodemus. The fifth name is *Todah,* which would correspond to Thaddeus.

Within the apostolic group of twelve were three sets of brothers. The first set was Simon and Andrew, who were both sons of Yochanan. The second set of brothers was James and Yochanan, the sons of Salome. She was the sister of Miriam, the mother of Yeshua, making her His aunt and James and Yochanan His cousins. Yeshua gave these two brothers the nickname "Sons of Thunder," which, in Hebrew, is *Bnei Regesh* or *Bnei Raam*. The third set was James and Judas, the sons of Alphaeus.

In addition to the three sets of brothers, there were two extremes: Matthew the Publican and Simon the Zealot. The Zealots actively assassinated Jews who worked for Rome, and publicans were among their targets. Only Yeshua could bring such a diverse group together and get them to work alongside each other.

Altogether, there are four listings of the twelve apostles, which can be charted as follows (see next page):

Mt. 10:2-4	Mk. 3:16-19	Lk. 6:14-16	Acts 1:13
Simon	Simon	Simon	Simon
Andrew	James	Andrew	James
James	Yochanan	James	Yochanan
Yochanan	Andrew	Yochanan	Andrew
Philip	Philip	Philip	Philip
Bartholomew (Nathanael)	Bartholomew (Nathanael)	Bartholomew (Nathanael)	Thomas
Thomas	Matthew	Matthew	Bartholomew (Nathanael)
Matthew	Thomas	Thomas	Matthew
James the son of Alphaeus	James the son of Alphaeus	James the son of Alphaeus	James the son of Alphaeus
Thaddaeus	Thaddaeus	Simon the Zealot	Simon the Zealot
Simon the Zealot	Simon the Zealot	Judas the son of James (Thaddaeus)	Judas the son of James (Thaddaeus)
Judas Iscariot	Judas Iscariot	Judas Iscariot	

The first name (Simon) is the same all the way across, while the second, third, and fourth names are mixed. The fifth name (Philip) is the same all the way across, while the sixth, seventh, and eighth names are mixed. The ninth name (James the son of Alphaeus) is the same all the way across, while the tenth and eleventh names are mixed. Judas Iscariot is always mentioned last and placed there because of his infamous deed of betrayal.

What all this may indicate is that within the apostolic group of twelve, there were three divisions. Each division had four disciples and a head. Simon was the head of the first division, with James, Yochanan, and Andrew under him. Philip was the head of the second division, with Bartholomew (Nathanael), Matthew, and Thomas under him. James, the son of Alphaeus, was head of the third division, with

Thaddaeus (Judas the son of James), Simon the Zealot, and Judas under him.

[§ 55] — 16. Messiah's Authority to Interpret the Law

The segment of Scripture we are going to study carefully in this section is generally referred to as the Sermon on the Mount. It is found in two Gospels: Matthew 5:1 – 8:1 and Luke 6:17-49. The problem with that title is that it only states the geographical locality of the event; Yeshua was on a mount when He spoke these words. The title does not say anything about the content of the sermon. So the heading used here emphasizes the content of the Sermon on the Mount, which is the correct interpretation of the Mosaic Law.

By way of introduction, we need to study the historical background that led to this lengthy treatise. Furthermore, we need to find the answer to the question: "Exactly what is the Sermon on the Mount as a unit?" By this time, the interest in Yeshua's messianic claims had increased tremendously both inside and outside the borders of the land. At this time in history, the Jewish people were looking for the messianic redemption. From the prophets of the Hebrew Bible, who revealed so much about the messianic kingdom, they knew that righteousness was the means of entry into the kingdom. Over the preceding four centuries, Pharisaism had developed, offering a form of righteousness; however, it was a very wide road to righteousness, so wide that the rabbis taught that all Israel would have a share in the age to come. Anyone born a Jew would make it into the kingdom. However, only those who were faithful to the Mosaic Law would have positions of honor in the kingdom. Yeshua challenged that fundamental teaching by saying that a person must experience a new birth to qualify for the kingdom. The means of experiencing this new birth was by accepting Him as the Messianic King. He proclaimed a very narrow way to righteousness, so narrow that one had to accept Him as the Messianic King. In light of these conflicts with the Pharisees, the common people started to wonder if Pharisaic righteousness was sufficient after all. If it was not, then what kind of righteousness is necessary? Given that historical background, the key verse of the Sermon on the Mount is Matthew 5:20: *For*

I say unto you, that except your righteousness shall exceed <the righteousness> of the scribes and Pharisees, ye shall in no wise enter into the kingdom of heaven. With that one statement, Yeshua repudiated Pharisaism on two counts: He declared that the teaching of the scribes and Pharisees did not offer sufficient righteousness for entering the kingdom and that it misinterpreted the true righteousness of the Mosaic Law.

In regard to the question what exactly the sermon is as a unit, we will start by stating three negatives: First, the sermon is not the constitution of the future messianic kingdom, a common interpretation in some circles. That would require the reinstitution of all 613 commandments of the Mosaic Law. This will not happen, because the Law of Moses was forever rendered inoperative when Messiah died.

Second, it is not a way of salvation. This has been a common interpretation in more liberal circles who, like the Pharisees, wish to avoid the narrow way that a person must believe in Yeshua to be saved. They, too, try to provide an alternative teaching and claim that keeping the high standards of the Sermon on the Mount, or more specifically the Golden Rule, ensures a person will make it to heaven. However, even if we were capable of keeping these standards consistently, we still would not make it to heaven because that would mean salvation is based on works, not by grace through faith. This sermon is a rule of life for those already saved, not a means of earning salvation.

Third, the sermon is not Christian or church ethics for this age. If that were its purpose, it would obligate believers to keep all 613 commandments of the Mosaic Law. Matthew stated that a person may not break even *one of these least commandments*, meaning the least commandments of the Mosaic Law (Mt. 5:19). If the sermon is church ethics for this age, it would require all believers to keep the dietary code and the clothing laws (such as the prohibition of mixed threads and the wearing of tassels), and men's beards would have to be cornered and not rounded. The church would have to obey many other *least commandments*, not to mention that the priesthood and the sacrificial system would have to be reinstated. So, as a unit, church ethics was not the intent of the Sermon on the Mount. However, some of the things mentioned in the sermon are repeated later, either in the Gospels or in the Epistles, and whatever was repeated by the apostles did indeed become church ethics for this age.

On the positive side, the sermon is the Messiah's interpretation of the true righteousness of the Law of Moses in contradistinction to the Pharisaic interpretation. The most significant difference is this: Yeshua set forth the righteousness of God as demanded by the Mosaic Law.[11] This law required more than external conformity. It required both external and internal righteousness.

a. The Occasion

Matthew 5:1-2, Luke 6:17-19

Matthew stated that Yeshua *went up into the mountain* (Mt. 5:1a), which is why this is called the Sermon on the Mount. Luke added that it was *a level place* (Lk. 6:17), indicating that this mountain had some kind of a plateau where a great number of people could gather together to hear Him. The exact location is unknown. In Catholic tradition, the site is located on a hill overlooking the northwest shoreline of the Sea of Galilee. The Protestant site is further to the west on the Horns of Hattin.

Matthew specified that *he had sat down* (Mt. 5:1b), which gives the scene a Jewish flavor. A rabbi always taught in a sitting position. Matthew only mentioned the presence of Yeshua's disciples, while Luke added that a great number of other people had also come. These were not just local people from around the Sea of Galilee. People were there from Judea, Jerusalem, and the coastal plain of Tyre and Sidon (Lk. 6:17a). They had come for three reasons: to hear Him teach, to be healed of their diseases, and to be freed from demons (Lk. 6:17b-18). While Yeshua healed all who came to Him, His primary focus was what He had to teach His disciples. By the time He proclaimed this message, three things had already taken place. First, a great deal of interest in Yeshua had already been stirred up, both inside and outside the land.

---

[11] The Mosaic Law did not end with the coming of the Messiah. It only ended with His death. As long as He was alive, all 613 commandments of the Mosaic Law had to be kept.

Second, He had already had some initial conflicts with the Pharisees over the authority of the Mishnah. Third, it happened after He had chosen the apostolic group of twelve.

b. The Characteristics of True Righteousness

(1) Characteristics of Those Who Attain
Matthew 5:3-12, Luke 6:20-23

This section is known as the Beatitudes. Each verse begins with the word, *Blessed*; however, that is not the normal translation of the Greek word. A better translation would be *happy*. Happy are those who develop the characteristics described here by Yeshua. It is true that the modern English word *happy* may not be equivalent to the Hebrew word behind the Greek, but it is still more appropriate than *blessed*.

As stated before, Matthew mentioned the presence of disciples (Mt. 5:1-2), so he put the Beatitudes in the third person (Mt. 5:3-10), except for the last one (Mt. 5:11-12). Luke mentioned a host of others (Lk. 6:17), so he specified that Yeshua addressed His disciples (Lk. 6:20) and put all the Beatitudes in the second person.

The Beatitudes fall into two categories: those in relation to God (Mt. 5:3-6; Lk. 6:20-21) and those in relation to man (Mt. 5:7-12; Lk. 6:22-23).

(i) Characteristics in Relationship to God

Blessed [happy] *are the poor in spirit: for theirs is the kingdom of heaven* (Mt. 5:3). To be poor in spirit is the opposite of being prideful. It means to have a right and proper evaluation of oneself toward God. It is to recognize that man has no righteousness of his own and is utterly dependent on the righteousness of God for mercy and salvation. These are the ones who will enter the messianic kingdom.

Blessed are they that mourn: for they shall be comforted (Mt. 5:4). To mourn in this context means to develop a sensitivity to sin. Those who possess this sensitivity will naturally confess their sins to God as soon as they become aware of them, and they will be comforted. Luke's version states: *Blessed <are> ye that weep now: for ye shall laugh* (Lk.

6:21b). They will experience the joy and happiness of the forgiveness of sin.

Blessed are the meek: for they shall inherit the earth [or the land] (Mt. 5:5). To be meek means to have a quiet confidence in God, in recognition of and in submission to His authority. Those who have this quality and live a life of submission to God's authority will someday be given authority in the messianic kingdom.

Blessed are they that hunger and thirst after righteousness: for they shall be filled (Mt. 5:6). Righteousness means to live in accordance with an absolute standard. In the context of the Sermon on the Mount, this standard was the Mosaic Law. Happy are those who live consistently with the absolute standard, for they shall have that righteousness.

(ii) Characteristics in Relationship to Man

Blessed are the merciful: for they shall obtain mercy (Mt. 5:7). To be merciful means to be compassionate, to respond to the needs of others and seek to meet those needs. Those who are compassionate to others will receive compassion themselves, as they need it.

Blessed are the pure in heart: for they shall see God (Mt. 5:8). To be pure in heart means to operate out of a proper motivation. The actions toward others as they were described in the previous Beatitude are to come from a proper motivation. These are to be honest dealings, and so the motivation for deeds of mercy is to be pleasing to the Lord.

Blessed are the peacemakers: for they shall be called sons of God (Mt. 5:9). Peacemaking here is not in the sense of making peace among nations, but peace among fellow believers. The goal is to bring about a state of unity among the brethren.

Blessed are they that have been persecuted for righteousness' sake: for theirs is the kingdom of heaven (Mt. 5:10). While the righteousness mentioned earlier was in connection with God, this righteousness is in connection with man. It means living consistently with the standard of the Law of Moses and results in loving one's neighbor as oneself, even if it brings on persecution.

Blessed are ye when <men> shall reproach you, and persecute you, and say all manner of evil against you falsely, for my sake. Rejoice, and be exceedingly glad: for great is your reward in heaven: for so persecuted *they the prophets that were before you* (Mt. 5:11-12). The previous Beatitudes related only to the Mosaic Law. Now, an additional issue is added. With the coming of the Messiah, anyone who wants to attain the righteousness which leads to the kingdom must believe Yeshua is the Messianic King. Salvation is granted to those who own Him as such, and this will lead to persecution. However, it will also mean greater reward in the kingdom.

(2) Characteristics of Those Who Fail
Luke 6:24-26

Those who fail to attain the righteousness of the Mosaic Law are characterized as seeking four things: wealth, for materialism is their focus; self-satisfaction; mirth or laughter; and a reputation.

The Pharisees did not recognize their spiritual depravity. They saw no need for righteousness beyond their own and no need for repentance. They demanded submission to their authority and withheld mercy from those who needed it, such as the publicans. Furthermore, they were concerned only with the external demands of the law and caused discord among Jews in the Jewish world. Having a position of authority, they were guilty of persecuting others, particularly those who chose to believe in Yeshua.

(3) Characteristics in Relation to the World
Matthew 5:13-16

Those who attain the characteristics described in the Beatitudes become two things in relation to the world: salt and light.

Ye are the salt of the earth (Mt. 5:13). In ancient times, salt was used as a preservative and as a seasoning. Those who attain the righteousness of the law become both those things. A common teaching of the Old Testament prophets was that God would not destroy Israel for all their sins because of the believing remnant that always existed within the nation. An example of this teaching is found in Isaiah 1:9: *Except Jehovah of hosts had left unto us a very small remnant, we should have been as Sodom, we should have been like unto Gomorrah.* The existence of the remnant of Israel meant the survival of that nation. Today, Messianic Jews make up the believing remnant; they are the preserving force. They also fulfill the seasoning aspect of salt, because they are the ones who make life worth living in this world. The fellowship of believers, the *koinonia*, provides a haven from the world. Furthermore, salt creates thirst. As believers associate with the world, they should create a spiritual thirst that will draw unbelievers to the Messiah.

Ye are the light of the world (Mt. 5:14). Yeshua declares that those who have the truth are the ones who can provide spiritual light for those in spiritual darkness. Since they are the light of the world, the admonition is: *Even so let your light shine before men; that they may see your good works, and glorify your Father who is in heaven* (Mt. 5:16). The light of verse 14 is the good works of verse 16. Good works will not save, but those who are saved should display their salvation by performing good deeds. When unbelievers see their works and respond to the light generated by those works, they will come to the light and become believers themselves and glorify God.

c. The Code of True Righteousness

(1) Introduction

Matthew 5:17-20

Verse 17 spells out Messiah's purpose in regard to the Mosaic Law: *Think not that I came to destroy the law or the prophets: I came not to destroy, but to fulfill.* This verse is often used to claim that the Mosaic Law is still in effect, and all the passages in the Epistles that teach that it ended with Messiah's death are ignored. When Yeshua spoke the words recorded in verse 17, the Mosaic Law was in full effect. It did not end with His coming, but with His death, which terminated the rule of the law. Until Yeshua died, all 613 commandments were obligatory. In the context of His conflict with the Judaism of His time, Yeshua made the point that the Pharisees had essentially destroyed the law by reinterpreting it in the Mishnah. His purpose, however, was to fulfill the law as it was written, not as it had been reinterpreted.

Those who use the statement in Matthew to teach that the law is still in effect are never consistent, because they also teach that the vast majority of the 613 commandments are not applicable. However, Yeshua was the only Jew who ever kept the Mosaic Law perfectly insofar as the 613 commandments applied to Him. Indeed, He intended to fulfill every detail of it, or, as He stated in verse 18, every *jot* and every *tittle*. The Hebrew alphabet has 22 letters. The tenth letter is *yod*, which in English translates as "jot." The letters of the Hebrew alphabet are all essentially the same size, but this particular letter, yod, is only about a quarter of the size of the other letters. By saying that He would fulfill every yod, Yeshua declared He intended to fulfill the law down to the smallest letter of the Hebrew alphabet.

The term *tittle*, or "stroke," which in Hebrew is called *tag*, refers to a small part of a single letter. Certain letters of the Hebrew alphabet are very much alike, except for one small distinction. For example, the letters *beth* and *kaph* are virtually the same, except for a small protrusion on the *beth*, which is the tag, or tittle. The Hebrew letters *daleth* and

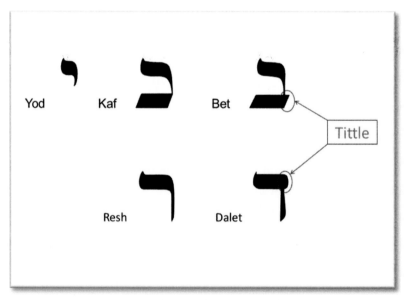

ABOVE: The term *yod* refers to the tenth letter of the Hebrew alphabet. The term *tittle* refers to a small part of a single letter that helps to distinguish between two similar-looking letters.

resh are differentiated by a similar protrusion—or tittle—on the *daleth*. Thus, Yeshua was saying He also intended to fulfill the law down to the smallest part of a single letter. The statement, *one jot or one tittle shall in no wise pass away from the law* (Mt. 5:18), meant He would fulfill the law to the smallest letter of the Hebrew alphabet and to the smallest portion of a single letter; and this He did. By perfectly keeping the law, He fulfilled every yod and tittle.

The fact that Yeshua mentioned specific parts of the Hebrew alphabet again directs the focus on the Written Law, not the Oral Law. With His death, Yeshua took upon Himself the curse of the law, died a penal substitutionary death, and rendered the law inoperative.

In verse 19, Yeshua then stated that as long as the Mosaic Law was in effect, even the *least commandments*—meaning even the most insignificant of the 613 commandments of the Mosaic Law—had to be kept. As previously stated, if Yeshua had intended this sermon to become church ethics, it would require the church to keep all 613 commandments of the Mosaic Law, including the least of them.

Having stated His own purpose for keeping the law, Yeshua went on to repudiate the Pharisaic interpretation of the law (Mt. 5:20). Although we discussed this verse before, His main message is worth repeating: He rejected Pharisaism on two counts, declaring that it did not offer sufficient righteousness for entering the messianic kingdom and that it misinterpreted the true righteousness of the Mosaic Law.

(2) The Examples

Yeshua then gave several examples in Matthew 5:21-48 and Luke 6:27-30, 32-38. Each section begins with, *You have heard that it was said* (Mt. 5:21, 27, 31, 33, 38, 43). This "formula" copied the common rabbinic phrase, "We have heard it said," and meant that the rules and regulations were "received by tradition." Each time Yeshua preceded His teaching with these words, it indicated that the issue discussed pertained to the Oral Law, which, at the time, was not available in written form. Because it could only be heard, not read, the issue clearly belonged to the Pharisaic, Oral Law. When the issue was a Mosaic commandment, the "formula" changed to *It is written.*

In this section of the sermon, Yeshua chose a Mosaic commandment of the Written Law and contrasted it with the Pharisaic interpretation of the commandment through the Oral Law, all the while focusing on the righteousness of the law. The righteousness of the commandments not only required external conformity, but also internal conformity. It was not only concerned with the mere act, but also with the intent of the heart—the spirit of the law, as well as the letter of the law.

i. The Law of Murder

Matthew 5:21-26

The first example is: *You shall not kill* (Mt. 5:21), a law against premeditated murder (Ex. 20:13). In the Pharisaic interpretation of the righteousness of the command, a person was not guilty of violating the righteousness of this command until he actually committed the act of murder. However, according to the Messiah, this was the wrong interpretation. It is true that a person does not violate the letter of the commandment until he commits the act. Therefore, he cannot be punished or executed until he commits the act. However, the issue here is the righteousness of the command, and the righteousness is broken even before the act is committed. Before anyone commits an act of premeditated murder, he first develops an internal animosity towards the victim. The moment animosity has taken root in the heart, the righteousness of this command has already been broken. In fact, as soon as name-calling begins in a tone of animosity rather than jesting between friends, the righteousness of the command has been broken. Yeshua stated, *whosoever shall say to his brother, Raca* (Mt. 5:22), he has already broken the command. *Raca* is both a Hebrew and an Aramaic term that means "empty" and carries the sense of "You empty head!". The internal violation can lead to the external violation of committing murder. Whether it does or does not lead to the act of murder, the righteousness of this command has already been broken.

If a person bringing a sacrifice to the altar remembers that there is bitterness with another, he should leave the sacrifice alone until he has reconciled with the other person (Mt. 5:23-24). It is better to settle things person to person than to wait and settle it in court (Mt. 5:25-26).

Because the sacrificial system is mentioned, this statement fits well in the context of the Law of Moses, but not in a church context.

ii. The Law of Adultery

Matthew 5:27-30

The second example concerns adultery (Ex. 20:14). According to the Pharisaic interpretation, a person was not guilty of violating the righteousness of this command until the act of adultery was committed. Again, Yeshua said that was the wrong interpretation. It is true that a person did not violate the letter of the law until he committed adultery, and he could not be stoned to death until he committed the act. However, the issue here is the righteousness of the command, and the righteousness is broken before the act is committed. Before any married man commits adultery, he first develops an internal lust for a woman who is not his wife. As soon as the lust is there internally, the righteousness of this command has been broken. The internal violation can lead to the external act. Again, whether it does or does not lead to the actual act of adultery, the righteousness of the law has already been broken. It is necessary to put away whatever may lead to the temptation.

iii. The Law of Divorce

Matthew 5:31-32

The third example concerns the law of divorce found in Deuteronomy 24:1. One school of Pharisees, the Hillel School, interpreted the commandment to mean that one may divorce his wife for any and every reason. Even the mere burning of soup became grounds for divorce. However, according to the Messiah, this was the wrong interpretation. God hates divorce, and that is the kind of righteousness that the law of divorce was perpetuating. Therefore, the grounds for divorce were to be extremely limited. In fact, according to Yeshua, there was only one proper ground for divorce, and that was fornication. To allow divorce for any and every cause went beyond what the Mosaic Law allowed, so the righteousness of the law was again violated. Yeshua's teaching was more in agreement with the Shammai School.

iv. The Law of Oaths

Matthew 5:33-37

In the Mosaic Law, the purpose of taking an oath was to emphasize that a person's word should be sufficient (Lev. 5:4-6; Num. 30:1-2). If a person's word should be good, then even more so, keeping an oath was mandatory. The Mishnah, however, provided all kinds of ways for a person to violate an oath. Affirmations became open to interpretation, especially if a person claimed he had mental reservations at the time.

To swear by heaven or by earth or by Jerusalem or even by one's life is empty (Mt. 5:34-35), since the person taking the oath has no control over any of these things. The righteousness of the law teaches that a person should develop a reputation for honesty, so that a *yea* could be taken as a trustworthy *yea* and a *nay* as a trustworthy *nay*.

v. The Law of Non-Resistance

Matthew 5:38-42

The context of the commandment, *An eye for an eye, and a tooth for a tooth* (Ex. 21:24; Mt. 5:38), was legal punishment by a court of law. The punishment had to fit the crime. The Pharisees took this law as a basis for personal vengeance, ignoring that the righteousness of the law taught the love of neighbor. Furthermore, according to God, vengeance was His (Deut. 32:35). There was no basis for personal vengeance; there were, however, legal ways of dealing with the lawbreaker. By using this commandment as a principle for personal vengeance, the righteousness of the law was violated. Rather than seeking redress in a court of civil law, it would be more characteristic of the law's righteousness to let go and not demand one's rights.

vi. The Law of Love

Matthew 5:43-48, Luke 6:27-30, 32-36

The last example concerns loving one's neighbor and hating one's enemy. The basis for this Pharisaic teaching is found in the Psalms: *Do not I hate them, O Jehovah, that hate you?* (Ps. 139:21). Some Pharisees defined *neighbor* as simply a fellow Jew. Other Pharisees did not include publicans or Sadducees under the definition of neighbor. However, the righteousness of the law defined a neighbor as anyone who had a need that could be met. True acts of love mean doing things for others, especially for those who have no means to repay.

d. The Conduct of True Righteousness

(1) Introduction

Matthew 6:1

As He did with the code of true righteousness, Yeshua began His teaching on the conduct of true righteousness with an introduction, stating the theme and then giving specific examples. The introductory principle is: *do not your righteousness before men, to be seen of them.* When doing external works of righteousness, the motivation should be to please God and not to receive commendation from men. Those who seek commendation from men will receive it, but that is all they will get; they will have no reward from the Lord.

(2) The Examples

i. The Giving of Alms

Matthew 6:2-4

The first example of what truly righteous conduct looks like is that of almsgiving. There were 13 large chests in the Temple compound used for gathering money. It was a common practice for the wealthy who were about to submit a major donation to let people know about it by announcing it through the sounding of a trumpet. It is obvious that this kind of practice was really to receive praise, approval, and honor from men. Segments of the church have often fallen into this kind of mentality. The Mosaic Law certainly encouraged the giving of alms, both to the poor and to the Tabernacle or the Temple; but the true practice of the law demanded that it be done for the honor of God, not for the honor of oneself. The principle was to do it in secret.

ii. Public Prayer

Matthew 6:5-15

The second example deals with prayer. Four lessons can be learned from Yeshua's teaching. The first lesson is that prayer should not be an opportunity to show off one's oratory skills (Mt. 6:5-6). In some areas of Pharisaic Judaism, prayer tended to be public, as with Pharisees congregating together in the open to pray three times a day. Frequently, the purpose of this was to advertise great spirituality and oratory skills. However, those who prayed this way publicly already received their reward and will receive no other reward from God. Yeshua is not teaching against public prayer, because public prayer and group prayer are encouraged elsewhere in Scripture (e.g,. Acts 2:42). However, the purpose of prayer is to communicate with God, not to exhibit one's skills.

Yeshua's second lesson is that prayer should not be prescribed: *And in praying use not vain repetitions, as the Gentiles do* (Mt. 6:7). What is common in most Gentile religions is the lack of extemporaneous prayers. The prayers are memorized or recited through prayer books. That is true with Buddhism, Islam, and most other Gentile religions. By Yeshua's day, it had also become true of Judaism, and to this day, Judaism does not practice extemporaneous prayer. There are daily prayer books, Sabbath prayer books, prayer books for special holy days such as *Yom Kippur* or *Rosh Hashanah*, and other prayer books for different occasions. Under Pharisaism, Judaism had become like a Gentile religion. Prayer, however, should come from the heart.

The third lesson is that prayer should not be haphazard, but should follow an organized format (Mt. 6:9-13). Yeshua outlined a model prayer with six parts. This has traditionally been called "the Lord's Prayer," but the real Lord's prayer is found in John 17. Yeshua introduced this section with the words: *After this manner therefore pray ye* (Mt. 6:9). He did not say, "Pray this prayer!" He said, "Pray in *this manner*," meaning, "Follow this basic outline." Yet, a segment of the church repeats this prayer every Sunday, turning it into vain repetition. That was not the intent. The intent was to teach how to organize one's prayer life. This does not rule out short, quick prayers throughout the day, of course; but for regular prayer time, believers are advised to follow a six-point outline.

The first part of the prayer is to address it to God the Father: *Our Father who is in heaven* (Mt. 6:9a). Believers are never told to address their prayers to the Son or to the Holy Spirit, and there are no examples of any such prayers in the Scriptures. Every prayer to the invisible God is addressed to the Father. This is not to imply that it is either sinful or wrong to pray to the Son or the Spirit, but it is clearly not the biblical pattern.

The second part of prayer should be to sanctify God: *Hallowed be your name* (Mt. 6:9b). This is the time to meditate on God as a person, His various attributes, how each of them reveals His uniqueness, and the practical ramifications they might have in the believer's life.

The third part of the prayer is for the kingdom program: *Your kingdom come. Your will be done, as in heaven, so on earth* (Mt. 6:10). This means more than just to pray for His return. It includes all facets of God's kingdom program, such as the work of evangelism and missions. This is the time to pray for the work of the church, the pastor, and the Sunday school teacher. It is also the time to pray for the various missionaries that the church or individual may be supporting. Finally, this is the time to pray for unsaved relatives, friends, and fellow workers. This is all part of God's kingdom program.

The fourth part of the prayer is for personal needs: *Give us this day our daily bread* (Mt. 6:11). This is the time to pray for one's daily needs, the ministry in which one is involved, and any crisis that one might be facing.

The fifth part of the prayer is forgiveness of sin: *And forgive us our debts, as we also have forgiven our debtors* (Mt. 6:12). In other translations this is rephrased as: *Forgive us our trespasses as we forgive those who trespass against us.* The tendency is to think that confession of sins should come first to wipe the slate clean before making any requests known to God. However, that not the order Yeshua gives in this outline. After addressing the Father, after sanctifying His name, after praying for the kingdom program, and after praying for our own daily needs, then it is time to wipe the slate clean. It is at this point that we may see that, in order to have these requests answered, we must confess every sin of which we are aware since the last confession. This is the time to ask the Lord's forgiveness, even for unknown sins and for the sin nature with which believers must contend, and it is the time to apply I John 1:9: *If we confess our sins, he is faithful and righteous to forgive us our sins, and to cleanse us from all unrighteousness.*

The sixth part of the prayer concerns spiritual warfare: *And bring us not into temptation, but deliver us from the evil <one>* (Mt. 6:13). This is the time to pray concerning the spiritual conflicts from the world, the flesh, and the devil.

Yeshua's fourth and final lesson about prayer concerns the condition for forgiveness (Mt. 6:14-15). In order for the Lord to hear the person praying, they need to have a forgiving spirit toward fellow saints. If they are not willing to forgive those who have offended them, then they should not expect to receive family forgiveness from the Lord.

iii. Fasting

Matthew 6:16-18

The third example of what truly righteous conduct looks like is fasting. Nowhere in the New Testament is fasting commanded. It is purely optional, but if one chooses to fast, they are not to make a show of it. Fasting will not make a person more holy or give greater victory in spiritual warfare. The principle is that once it becomes obvious that a person is fasting, it is time for them to eat again.

e. The Practice of True Righteousness

(1) Concerning Money

Matthew 6:19-24

The practice of true righteousness includes the proper attitude toward money (Mt. 6:19-21). Money is not something that should be hoarded for the sake of hoarding. Rather, money should be used in a proper way, for purchasing what is needed and to establish family security.

There is nothing wrong with having a savings account. However, when money becomes the all-consuming passion and the savings account becomes a person's security, then the believer is no longer serving the Lord in the manner he should. The principle concerning money is that a person cannot serve two masters. One either serves God or mammon. The term "mammon" is a loan word from Mishnaic Hebrew meaning "money," "wealth," "possessions," and possibly "that in which one trusts." It is a term referring to everything that this world has to offer materially. One is either a servant of God or a servant of materialism, but one cannot be a servant of both. If we are serving materialism and if material things are the basis for our security, then we are not God's servants. God is not the master; mammon is the master. On the other hand, if we are truly serving God and are finding our security in Him, we will have a proper balance concerning material goods. We will know how to use the money that is entrusted to us. We will maintain a proper balance between what God has provided for our families, present and future, and the accumulation of wealth.

(2) Concerning Anxiety

Matthew 6:25-34

The practice of true righteousness will also affect how the believer deals with anxiety. The principle is found in verse 25: *be not anxious for your life, what ye shall eat, or what ye shall drink; nor yet for your body, what ye shall put on.* If God provides what is needed for both the animal kingdom and for the vegetable kingdom, and if He cares for the inanimate as well as the animate world, then how much more will He certainly provide for the believer who seeks His righteousness? This is a *kal v'chomer* argument. Under normal circumstances, God promises to provide the basic necessities of food, clothing, and shelter. He does not promise to fulfill wants, but He does promise to provide the basic needs of life. The book of Hebrews makes it clear that in times of persecution, people may lose their homes or be deprived of food and clothing. In such circumstances, believers have died of exposure and starvation. So the Matthew passage describes what believers may anticipate under normal conditions, and the focus must be this: *But seek ye first his kingdom, and his righteousness; and all these things shall be added unto you* (Mt. 6:33). The believer's goal is to advance God's kingdom program and to live righteously. In this context, it means to live consistently with the standard of the Law of Moses. Those who fulfill this call will have food, clothing, and shelter provided. Therefore, Yeshua made the application: *Be not therefore anxious for the morrow* (Mt. 6:34). He concluded with the same admonition with which He began: Do not be anxious about the basic necessities of life. Such anxieties only show a lack of faith.

This does not rule out an individual's responsibility to work and earn a living. Elsewhere, the Scriptures teach that if a person does not work, he should not eat. Believers should not expect to live off other saints; individual responsibility remains. In fact, if we seek His kingdom and His righteousness, we will fulfill our personal responsibility in these areas and trust God to meet the needs accordingly.

(3) Concerning Judging
Matthew 7:1-6, Luke 6:37-42

The practice of true righteousness will manifest itself in how the believer judges others. The principle is found in Matthew 7:1: *Judge not, that ye be not judged.* The first three admonitions are all expressed in the negative (*lay not, be not, judge not*) which indicates three things believers should not be doing.

Matthew 7:1 has been taken out of context to teach that believers should never judge others under any circumstances; but that contradicts other places in Scripture where believers are told to exercise judgment in certain cases. Even Matthew's own Gospel, in chapter 18, teaches the principles of church discipline, which requires judging. One-on-one confrontation of a believer regarding a sin requires a measure of judging. Yeshua is not teaching that believers must never judge. Rather, the actual point made is: *For with what judgment ye judge, ye shall be judged: and with what measure ye mete, it shall be measured unto you* (Mt. 7:2). Believers are not to use man-made standards to judge others. The religious leaders of Yeshua's times used the Mishnah to judge other Jews whose spirituality they determined by measuring to what degree they conformed to these man-made standards. The church has fallen into the same trap by using church rules as the criteria for measuring one's spirituality. However, the only proper benchmark is the Scriptures, and the only proper basis for judging is God's standards, not man-made standards.

Yeshua notes the hypocrisy of those who wish to remove a splinter from another's eye, failing to recognize they have a log in their own eye (Mt. 7:3-5). Using man-made standards to judge others is like trying to clear a small piece of sawdust from a brother's eye, while having a plank in one's own eye. Both the sawdust and the plank are made of the same material, and they differ only in size. A piece of sawdust will only irritate the eye, but a whole plank will blind it. Therefore, when a person judges another person based on man-made standards, he is actually blind because he is using the wrong criteria, and eventually, he himself will fail to measure up to those very same standards.

Furthermore, Yeshua admonishes His disciples about giving truth to those already committed to rejecting it (Mt. 7:6). In the context of first-century Judaism, expecting the Pharisees to accept these truths is like casting pearls before swine.

(4) Concerning Prayer

Matthew 7:7-11

Yeshua had already taught four lessons on prayer, saying that prayer should not be a time to show off oratory skills; it should not be prescribed; it should not be haphazard, but organized; and one should pray with a spirit of forgiveness. Now comes a fifth lesson: Prayer should be persistent. The phrase *how much more* indicates that Yeshua again used a *kal v'chomer* argument.

Persistent prayer is defined by the key words *ask, seek,* and *knock* (Mt. 7:7). In the Greek, these verbs are in the present tense, emphasizing continuous action. The sense is: keep on asking, keep on seeking, and keep on knocking. In other words, there should be persistence in prayer life. A person should persist in prayer as long as the problem remains or as long as the burden for it is there. Since it is still coming from the heart, this is not vain repetition.

At this point, Yeshua said nothing about praying in His name, because He was dealing with the issue of righteousness under the Mosaic Law. Under this law, His name was not the basis of prayer. Later, when He taught further truth concerning prayer, linking it to the law of Messiah and the age of grace, He admonished His disciples to pray in His name (Jn. 14:13-14).

(5) The Core of Practice of True Righteousness
Matthew 7:12, Luke 6:31

Matthew 7:12 is the core of the righteousness which the law requires, and the verse has become known as the Golden Rule. It summarizes what *the law and the prophets* teach concerning human relationships. To do unto others *whatever ye would that men should do unto you* is the outworking of loving one's neighbor as oneself, and it shows that true righteousness is being practiced. It is not a way of earning salvation, as liberalism will often teach. Rather, it describes the conduct of a believer.

f. The Warnings Concerning True Righteousness

As Yeshua closes His teaching about true righteousness, He gives certain warnings organized in four sets of pairs.

(1) The Two Ways
Matthew 7:13-14

The first pair contrasts two ways: the broad way and the narrow way. The way of the Pharisees was the wide way, so wide that all Israel had a share in the age to come. In reality, it led to destruction. In contrast, the godly way leads through a very narrow gate: One must believe that Yeshua is the Messianic King in order to have God's righteousness imputed to them, which will then qualify them for the kingdom.

(2) The Two Trees

Matthew 7:15-20, Luke 6:43-45

The second pair contrasts two trees. The difference between true teachers or prophets and false teachers or prophets is the difference between fruitfulness and fruitlessness. The principle is: *Therefore by their fruits ye shall know them* (Mt. 7:20). The prophecies of a true prophet will be fulfilled. A true prophet is one who lives consistently with the demands of written Scripture. His teachings are in accordance with the written Word of God. With a false teacher or prophet, everything is reversed. The prophecies of a false prophet do not come true, and he does not live consistently with what he proclaims. In the Pharisaic context, a false teacher follows man-made rules and regulations. Yeshua will only go by the Written Law, which will produce the fruit of righteousness; the false teacher will follow another law and thus fail to produce the fruit of righteousness.

(3) The Two Professions

Matthew 7:21-23, Luke 6:46

The third pair contrasts two professions or testimonies. Yeshua warned that not everyone who calls Him "Lord" is necessarily a believer: *Not everyone that said unto me, Lord, Lord, shall enter into the kingdom of heaven* (Mt. 7:21). The Pharisees were false teachers who never used His name. However, other false teachers will have no problem using His name. In fact, these false teachers may even do great works in His name, and Yeshua mentioned three: They may proclaim prophecies that come to pass; they may cast out demons; they may perform *mighty works*, such as miracles of healing (Mt. 7:22). However, on the day of judgment, Yeshua will say to them, *I never knew you: depart from me, ye that work iniquity* (Mt. 7:23). In Scripture, the existence of outward manifestations never verifies godly righteousness. It is always conformity to the written Word of God which validates a person. The real question was always: Is what is being said, taught, and done consistent with what Scripture teaches? Satan can duplicate outward manifestations—even to the point of the creation of life. When *Aaron cast down his rod before Pharaoh*, it became a serpent (Ex. 7:10). The Egyptian magicians threw their staffs down, and they also became snakes (Ex. 7:12). Where did they get their power? Not from God. When Moses and Aaron brought up frogs from the earth, the Egyptian magicians did the same thing (Ex. 8:1-7). Where did they get their power? Not from God. Again, the determining factor is not external manifestations, even when they mimic biblical examples. By themselves, these manifestations are insufficient evidence. The reason many fall into deception is because they think external manifestations are proof that the person performing these mighty works is from God.

(4) The Two Builders
Matthew 7:24-27, Luke 6:47-49

The fourth pair contrasts two builders. Yeshua gave the Jewish masses a choice. They could continue building upon the Pharisaic interpretation of the righteousness of the law, which means building upon a foundation of sand, and any structure built on that foundation would collapse; or they could build upon His interpretation of the righteousness of the law, which means they would be building upon a solid rock, and any structure built upon that foundation would survive.

g. The Conclusion

Matthew 7:28-8:1

When Yeshua finished the sermon, the *multitudes were astonished at his teaching: for he taught them as <one> having authority, and not as their scribes* (Mt. 7:28-29). By examining a few pages of rabbinic literature of that time period, it is easy to see how the scribes taught. Over and over again, the formula was: "Rabbi so-and-so said in the name of Rabbi such-and-such this." Every rabbi taught on the basis of previous rabbinic authorization. Yeshua, however, quoted no rabbi, no Pharisee, and no scribe, but taught as one who had absolute authority to interpret the true meaning of the Law of Moses. As the Messiah, He had that authority, and there was a noticeable contrast in His method of teaching compared to that of the Pharisees, particularly the scribes, who were experts in the Scriptures. So, by the time Yeshua finished teaching, the people clearly understood what He was saying, and more significantly, they clearly knew where He differed from the scribes and Pharisees.

As a unit, the Sermon on the Mount was the Messiah's interpretation of the true righteousness of the Law of Moses in contradistinction with the Pharisaic interpretation of this righteousness. As a unit, it was also Yeshua's public rejection of Pharisaic Judaism as embodied in the Mishnah. It was His rejection of Mishnaic Judaism that led to their rejection of His messianic claims.

[§ 56] — 17. Recognition of Authority in Capernaum

Matthew 8:5-13, Luke 7:1-10

What makes this section unique is that this time a Gentile recognized Yeshua's authority. For Luke, this shows his special interest in Gentiles. For Matthew, it provides another opportunity to teach about the facets of the messianic kingdom.

Matthew stated that when Yeshua entered into Capernaum, *there came unto him a centurion* (Mt. 8:5). The word *centurion* refers specifically to the officer's position in the Roman army; he had authority over one hundred men. In the world of that day, servants were dispensable; but this centurion had a concern for his servant which shows that he was a unique individual. Luke's account mentions that the officer did not come personally, but that *he sent unto him elders of the Jews, asking him that he would come and save his servant* (v. 3). Those who see a contradiction here fail to recognize the Jewish context. The Talmud states, ". . . a man's agent [*shaliach*] is equivalent to himself."[12] If someone is sent with the sender's authority, it is the same as if the sender himself had gone. Luke noted that the centurion *sent* the elders of the Jews; the Jewish leaders did not take the initiative on their own. Because

---

[12] *b. Berakoth* 34b.

the centurion sent the elders to Yeshua, it is viewed as if he had gone himself.

The Jewish elders did not merely convey a personal request. They actually tried to convince Yeshua to heal the servant, even though the centurion was a Gentile. Luke noted, *And they, when they came to Yeshua, besought Him earnestly* (Lk. 7:4a). They did what they could to convince Yeshua to heal the man, saying, *He is worthy that you should do this for him* (Lk. 7:4b). Generally speaking, the Jews viewed the Romans as enemies; however, as far as the elders of this synagogue were concerned, this Gentile was worthy and the miracle should be done for him. They gave two reasons for his worthiness. First, *he loves our nation* (Lk. 7:5a). He was a Gentile lover of Israel and the Jewish people; therefore, he fell under the blessing aspect of the Abrahamic Covenant, *I will bless them that bless you* (Gen. 12:3). Second, he *built us our synagogue* (Lk. 7:5b). In other words, he financed the synagogue building in which Yeshua preached and taught.

In response, Yeshua began moving toward the home of the centurion. When the centurion heard that Yeshua was heading toward his house, he sent another message telling Him that He did not need to come all the way to his house. Matthew quotes him as saying, *Lord, I am not worthy that you should come under my roof* (Mt. 8:8). This was in sharp contrast to what the Jewish elders had said about him. In English, the religious leaders and the centurion use the same word, *worthy*, but in Greek, two different words are used. The Jewish leaders called the centurion *axios*, meaning "of weight," "of worth," "worthy." The centurion said that he was not *hikanos*, not "sufficient," meaning, "I am not deserving that you should even enter under my roof." Both Gospel writers clearly show the extent of this centurion's faith: *but only say the word, and my servant shall be healed* (Mt. 8:8b; Lk. 7:7b). The centurion recognized that all Yeshua had to do was speak the word and the servant would be healed. To support what he said, the centurion made a very specific comparison: *For I also am a man under authority, having under myself soldiers* (Mt. 8:9; Lk. 7:8). Note the word *also*. Because he himself was in a position of authority, he was able to recognize Yeshua's position of authority. As the leader of a legion of soldiers, a simple word would suffice to get the job done. The same was true of Yeshua. A mere commandment from Him was sufficient to heal the servant. This took a lot of faith on the part of a Gentile. In fact, Yeshua Himself said: *I have not found so great faith, no, not in Yisrael* (Mt. 8:10; Lk. 7:9).

This event foreshadowed something that would happen later on a national scale: The Gentiles would recognize what the Jewish leaders failed to see, with the result that *many shall come from the east and the west, and shall sit down with Avraham, and Yitzchak, and Yaakov, in the kingdom of heaven* (Mt. 8:11). When the messianic kingdom is established, many Gentiles will come to Israel from all over the world; from the east and the west they will come to the land, and will sit with Abraham, Isaac, and Jacob. The Greek word for *sit* means "to recline," a Jewish way of feasting, as at the Passover. Many Gentiles will be banqueting and feasting with Abraham, Isaac, and Jacob. Having recognized Messiah's authority, they will enter the kingdom. However, *the sons of the kingdom shall be cast forth into the outer darkness: there shall be the weeping and the gnashing of teeth* (Mt. 8:12). The Pharisees, in particular, considered themselves to be the *sons of the kingdom* and believed they would recline at Messiah's table, feasting off the leviathan. Yeshua, however, contradicted this thought and said that they will be excluded and will be put into the place of the *outer darkness* and the place of *weeping and gnashing of teeth*, two descriptive terms for the Lake of Fire.

Matthew's account records Yeshua's concluding statement to the centurion: *as you have believed, <so> be it done unto you* (Mt. 8:13). Because of the centurion's faith, his servant was healed from a distance.

[§ 57] — 18. Recognition of Authority Throughout the Land

Luke 7:11-17

While walking in Galilee, Yeshua went by a town called Nain[13], located on the northern slopes of the hill of Moreh. On the southern slope of the mountain was the town of Shunem, where, years earlier, Elisha had

---

[13] *Nayim* in Hebrew.

raised a woman's son back to life. Now, Yeshua also raised a woman's son back to life, making this the second time that, geographically speaking, the hill of Moreh became a witness of God's power in resurrection.

As Yeshua *drew near to the gate of the city, behold, there was carried out one that was dead, the only son of his mother* (Lk. 7:12). The tragedy of the situation was that the woman was already a widow. Under the Mosaic and Jewish laws, the son was responsible for the physical welfare of the mother once the husband died. However, because she had only one son and that son had now died, she had lost her only means of support and would soon be reduced to being a beggar. Yeshua had compassion on her (Lk. 7:13) and touched the coffin (Lk. 7:14), which, according to Numbers 19:11, would have rendered Him unclean. However, according to Leviticus 21:1, only the members of the tribe of Levi were forbidden to actually touch the dead. Yeshua then declared: *Young man, I say unto you, Arise* (Lk. 7:14), and the son was resurrected back from the dead; *And He gave him to his mother* (Lk. 7:15). The mother had her son back, and he would be able to sustain her for the rest of her life.

The resurrection of this son resulted in three things. First, *fear took hold on all; and they glorified God* (Lk. 7:16a). Those who observed this miracle developed an awesome and divine fear, and they glorified God. Second, they concluded, *A great prophet is arisen among us: and, God has visited his people* (Lk. 7:16b). Yes, He was a great prophet indeed, just as great as Elijah and Elisha, but that was still an insufficient conclusion. This One was more than a prophet; He was the Messianic King. Third, *And this report went forth concerning him in the whole of Yehudah, and all the region round about* (Lk. 7:17). His reputation began to spread even further. The event took place in Galilee, but news that Yeshua had raised someone from the dead spread to Judea and all the regions around the area.

It should be noted that Luke was the only one who recorded this event, showing again that he was concerned about the place of women in the life of Yeshua, either in their ministry to Him or His ministry to them.

ABOVE: This painting by Denise Hayden depicts the ruins of the synagogue at Capernaum. It is considered to have been built not long after Yeshua's time on the foundation of the synagogue that He taught in (Jn. 6:59).

III. The Controversy
over the King
— §§ 58–73 —

The third major division of Yeshua's life is crucial because this is when a major turning point of His career occurs. It begins with the rejection of the herald and ends with his death.

[§ 58] — A. The Rejection of the Herald

Matthew 11:2-19, Luke 7:18-35

By now, Yochanan had been in prison for some time. He still had his own disciples, and they were reporting Yeshua's activities to him. They were also reporting to Yochanan that Yeshua was not getting a very positive response from the Jewish leadership, and even the masses who did recognize His uniqueness had not proclaimed Him to be anything more than a prophet. Yochanan, like the apostles, did not understand that the Messiah was to come twice. Like the apostles, he had antici-pated that Yeshua had come to usher in the kingdom. In light of these negative circumstances (his own imprisonment, the negative response from the leaders, and the fact that the kingdom was not being set up), an element of doubt set in. Yochanan sent two of his disciples to Yeshua (perhaps to fulfill the Mosaic Law requirement of two witnesses) with the question: *Are you he that comes, or look we for another?* (Mt. 11:3; Lk. 7:19). The point of the question was: Did Yochanan make a mistake and accidentally point out the wrong Messiah? Is it possible that Yeshua was only another forerunner like himself?

At the moment when Yochanan's disciples arrived to raise the ques-tion, Yeshua happened to be curing diseases and plagues, casting out demons, and restoring sight to the blind (Lk. 7:21). Instead of a simple "yes" or "no," Yeshua said: *Go and tell Yochanan the things which ye hear and see* (Mt. 11:4; Lk. 7:22). He told them to report two things. First, they were to pass on to Yochanan what they had heard, and what they had heard was His proclamation to be the Messianic Person, that *the poor have good tidings* [Gospel] *preached to them* (Mt. 11:5; Lk. 7:22). The preaching included that the kingdom of heaven is at hand. Second, they were to pass on to Yochanan what they had seen, and what they had seen were His miracles. The purpose of these miracles was to authenticate His Messiahship: *the blind receive their sight, and the lame walk, the lepers are cleansed, and the deaf hear, and the dead are raised up* (Mt. 11:5; Lk. 7:22). Yeshua concluded that Yochanan need not stumble over His person (Mt. 11:6; Lk. 7:23).

After Yochanan's disciples left, the King gave an evaluation of His herald, and both Gospel writers took note of the five things He stated. First, Yochanan was not a *reed shaken with the wind* (Mt. 11:7; Lk. 7:24), meaning he was not wishy-washy. When Yochanan spoke, everyone knew exactly where he stood on any issue. When the Pharisees and Sadducees came, Yochanan called them a *brood of vipers* (Mt. 3:7; Lk. 3:7); he was not ambiguous. Second, he was not a *man clothed in soft <raiment>* (Mt. 11:8; Lk. 7:25). In other words, he was not accustomed to luxurious living. His clothes were made of camel skin, and his diet consisted of locusts and wild honey (Mt. 3:4). Third, he was a prophet (Mt. 11:9a; Lk. 7:26a). A prophet was one who re-ceived direct revelation from God, and Yochanan was a recipient of divine revelation (Jn. 1:31-34). Fourth, Yeshua declared: *Yea, I say unto you, and much more than a prophet* (Mt. 11:9b; Lk. 7:26b), and proceeded to quote Malachi 3:1: *Behold, I send my messenger, and he shall prepare the way before me.* Yes, he was a prophet; but more than that, he was the forerunner of the Messiah in fulfillment of Malachi's prophecy.[1] Fifth, and this may be the most amazing statement of all: *Among them that are born of women there has not arisen a greater than Yochanan the Baptist* (Mt. 11:11a; Lk. 7:28a). In other words, Yeshua proclaimed that Yochanan was the greatest of the Old Testament saints. On the surface, this may be hard to believe. How could Yochanan be greater than men like Abraham, Moses, and David? Yet, that is exactly what Yeshua said, and therefore, it must be true. The natural reluctance to accept this is due to the fact that a lot of detail is known about the lives of the above-mentioned saints, but not much is known about Yochanan's ministry. The Gospels correctly focused on the Messiah, not on His forerunner. However, there are clues that Yochanan had tremendous influence, not only within the land, but also outside the land. In Acts 19:1-7, Paul ran into a body of men in far-away Ephesus who were disciples of Yochanan the Baptizer, but had not yet heard that he had identified Yeshua as the Messiah. In fact, there are villages in present-day Syria where the Aramaic language is still spoken and Yochanan is considered the prophet of the people. The Mandaeans, a people living in the border area between Iraq and Iran, trace their origins to Yochanan. Therefore, Yochanan had a far wider influence than the Gospels alone indicate.

After evaluating His forerunner, Yeshua added: *yet he that is but little in the kingdom of heaven is greater than he* (Mt. 11:11b; Lk. 7:28b). While Yochanan is the greatest of the Old Testament saints, the least member of this new facet of God's kingdom program (to be revealed in Matthew 16 as the church) is greater than he: Being in the position of a New Testament believer—being "in the Messiah"—is greater than being in the position of an Old Testament saint. Yeshua implied here that Yochanan would die before the new facet of God's program would be established. Focusing a lot of his Gospel's attention on this program, Matthew added: *And from the days of Yochanan the Baptist until now*

---

[1] This prophecy fits into the category of literal prophecy plus literal fulfillment.

the kingdom of heaven suffers violence, and men of violence take it by force. For all the prophets and the law prophesied until Yochanan (Mt. 11:12-13). From the time Yochanan started proclaiming the kingdom, his preaching received violent opposition. The opposition primarily came from the Pharisees, and secondarily from the Sadducees, who tried to block the way into this kingdom. When Yeshua stated, *For all the prophets and the law prophesied until* Yochanan, He again declared the baptizer to be the last of the Old Testament prophets.

Matthew also recorded the next comment of Yeshua: *And if ye are willing to receive <it,> this is Eliyahu, that is to come* (Mt. 11:14). This is another correlating statement about Elijah and Yochanan the Baptizer. To summarize the two previous statements, Yochanan came in the spirit and power of Elijah (Lk. 1:17), and when he was asked, *Are you Eliyahu?* he answered, *I am not* (Jn. 1:21). Now the third element is this: If the Messiah was accepted as the Messianic King, and if the kingdom offer was received, then Yochanan would have fulfilled Elijah's function, which was to restore all things (Mal. 4:5-6). However, since the king and kingdom were rejected, Yochanan did not fulfill Elijah's function, and therefore, Elijah himself will someday return to fulfill it. This does not mean, however, that Yochanan's ministry was a failure. His calling was to prepare a people to accept the Messiah once He had been publicly identified. Luke makes it clear that Yochanan fulfilled his actual calling with great success: *And all the people when they heard, and the publicans, justified God, being baptized with the baptism of Yochanan* (Lk. 7:29). The common people who believed Yochanan's message and were baptized by him had no problem accepting Yeshua as their Messiah. However, the opposite was true of the Jewish leadership: *But the Pharisees and the lawyers rejected for themselves the counsel of God, being not baptized of him* (Lk. 7:30). These religious leaders became Yeshua's fierce opposition, and they were the source of the violence previously described by Matthew.

Both Gospels record the illustration Yeshua gave next: *But whereunto shall I liken this generation? It is like unto children sitting in the marketplaces, who call unto their fellows and say, We piped unto you, and ye did not dance; we wailed, and ye did not mourn* (Mt. 11:16-17; Lk. 7:31-32). Here, Yeshua used a phrase that will begin to appear frequently in the Gospels: *this generation*. This generation of religious leaders, what could He compare it to? He characterized the Pharisees who rejected Him as children who always insist on their own way with a tendency to rebel. Furthermore, He revealed that the real reason Yochanan was rejected was because he would not do it their way. He would not dance to the Pharisees' tune, and he would not support Pharisaic Judaism. While that was the real reason Yochanan was rejected, the reason given by the Pharisees was different: *For Yochanan came neither eating nor drinking, and they say, He has a demon. The Son of man came eating and drinking, and they say, Behold, a gluttonous man and a winebibber, a friend of publicans and sinners!* (Mt. 11:18-19; Lk. 7:33-34). Yochanan fasted and abstained from alcohol because he was a Nazirite from birth, and the religious leaders used that as a basis for rejecting him, claiming he was demon possessed. In contrast, Yeshua's life was not characterized by fasting, and He did not abstain from alcoholic beverages, but now they used this as grounds to reject Him. Either way, one could not win unless he was a Pharisee.

To summarize, although the given reason for rejecting Yochanan was that he was demon possessed, the real reason was that he would not uphold Pharisaism. Again, what happened to the herald would happen to the king. With this account, a transition to the rejection of Yeshua begins, and the seeds are sown. There is an emphasis on the rejection by the leaders, an emphasis on *this generation*. The next section continues with that transitional theme.

[§ 59] — B. Curses on Cities of Galilee

1. The Condemnation for Unbelief

Matthew 11:20-24

Yeshua cursed three key Galilean cities because the majority of the miracles He performed in His public ministry were performed in those cities. They were Chorazin, Bethsaida, and Capernaum, all on the north side of the Sea of Galilee (see map on next page).

The Gospels record miracles performed by Yeshua in Bethsaida and Capernaum, but not a single record exists of any miracle He performed in Chorazin. In fact, there is no account of His being there or even passing by as He did the town of Nain. Yet, it is obvious from what He said that He must have been there many times, since the majority of His miracles were done in this and the other two cities. This statement shows the truth of Yochanan's comment at the end of his Gospel that it would have been impossible for anyone to record all that Yeshua said and did, for the world could not contain the books that would have been written (Jn. 21:25). All four Gospel writers had to be selective in what they chose to record.

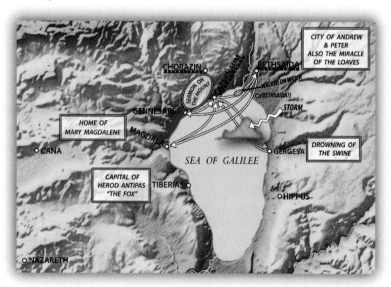

What Yeshua said also shows that while all unbelievers end up in the Lake of Fire, they will not suffer to the same degree. There will be degrees of punishment: *But I say unto you, it shall be more tolerable for Tzor and Tzidon in the day of judgment than for you . . . it shall be more tolerable for the land of Sedom in the day of judgment, than for you* (Mt. 11:22-24). Had these other Gentile cities seen the miracles Yeshua performed, they would have responded; but these Jewish cities had seen most of His signs and still did not accept Him as the Messiah. Yeshua's miracles were to serve as a sign to Israel to get them to make a decision, but they failed to make the correct decision, and it is clear from this passage that there will be degrees of punishment in the Lake of Fire. Those who deem themselves to be wise will be rejected.

2. The Explanation of Unbelief

Matthew 11:25-27

An explanation for the people's unbelief is revealed in Yeshua's prayer. On one hand is the providence of God, and on the other the sin of man. No man can come unto the Father unless the Spirit draws him. Therefore, those who thought of themselves as wise rejected, but the simple responded. The "wise" neither saw nor understood because of their own pride, but the light dawned upon those deemed to be simple-minded.

3. The Invitation to Belief and Discipleship

Matthew 11:28-30

This was a call by the Messiah for those who labor and are heavy laden to come to Him. They were heavy laden because they were wearing the heavy yoke of Pharisaism and Mishnaic Judaism. Yeshua admonished them: *Take my yoke* (Mt. 11:29). A. T. Robertson notes this is a rabbinic figure for going to school.[2] They should take Yeshua's yoke (go to school) and learn of Him because He is *meek and lowly in heart,* and only through Him would they find rest unto their souls (Mt. 11:29). In contrast to Pharisaism, His yoke is easy and His burden is light (Mt. 11:30).

---

[2] Robertson, *A Harmony of the Gospels*, p. 59.

[§ 60] — C. The Reception by a Sinner

Luke 7:36-50

Luke alone records the next incident, again showing his special interest in the role of women in the life of Yeshua: *And one of the Pharisees desired him that he would eat with him* (Lk. 7:36). On several occasions, Pharisees invited Yeshua to dine at their place, but always with an ulterior motive: to find a reason for rejecting Him. This event occurred in the private home of a Pharisee by the name of Simon. A woman described as a sinner entered and *began to wet his feet with her tears, and wiped them with the hair of her head, and kissed his feet, and anointed them with the ointment* (Lk. 7:38). In the Gospels, the term *sinner* is often a euphemism for a prostitute, and that is how it is used in this context.

There is a tradition that the sinner was Mary Magdalene, whose name in Hebrew was Miriam of Migdol or Magdala. However, there is no evidence in the Gospels that Miriam was ever a prostitute. The fact that the woman in this account was a prostitute and that she was touching Yeshua, weeping, anointing His feet, wetting them with her tears, wiping them with her hair, and even kissing them went against Pharisaic sensitivity. Furthermore, the ointment was not cheap olive oil, but expensive perfume.

Without verbalizing it (Lk. 7:39), the Pharisee said to himself, "If Yeshua really is the Messiah, he would not associate with this class of society. Furthermore, if he is merely a prophet, he would know what kind of woman this is and would not permit himself to be touched in these various ways." Yeshua responded by revealing Simon's thoughts, which proved He was indeed a prophet, the very thing that the Pharisee doubted at that moment. To make His point, Yeshua told him a story (Lk. 7:41-42): Two men were indebted to one lender, and the lender forgave both their debts. One was forgiven a very small amount, and the other was forgiven a large amount. The question was, which of them would love the lender the most. Simon answered: *He, I suppose, to whom he forgave the most*, and Yeshua said: *You have rightly judged*

(Lk. 7:43). In other words, the greater the debt that is forgiven, the greater the debtor feels indebted to and loves the one who forgave him.

In verses 44-47, Yeshua made the application by contrasting the way the woman treated Him with the way Simon had been treating Him. Simon failed to provide the Messiah with water to wash His feet; he did not greet Him with a kiss (which was the customary greeting in the Middle East), and he did not anoint His head with oil. In that day, these were the usual amenities that a host would generally extend to a guest, but this Pharisee failed to offer to Yeshua any of these common courtesies, casting doubt upon his true motives for inviting Yeshua to dine with him. The woman, on the other hand, washed His feet with tears and kissed and anointed them.

The point of the story was to convey to Simon why this woman had so lavished Him with her love: *Wherefore I say unto you, Her sins, which are many, are forgiven; for she loved much: but to whom little is forgiven, <the same> loves little* (Lk. 7:47). This explains why Simon showed so little concern towards Yeshua. He did not have the consciousness of sin that the woman had; therefore, he did not have the same sense of need for forgiveness. The woman, on the other hand, realized she had been forgiven much for her sins and lavished her courtesies and love upon Yeshua.

When Yeshua turned to the woman, saying, *Your sins are forgiven* (Lk. 7:48), He made a claim that only God can make. He claimed the prerogative of deity. The response was immediate, *And they that sat at meat with him began to say within themselves, Who is this that even forgives sins?* (Lk. 7:49). Their theology was correct. No one can forgive sins except God alone. So, either Yeshua was a blasphemer or He was who He claimed to be: the Messianic Person.

To make it clear exactly what caused Him to forgive her sins, Yeshua said to the woman: *Your faith has saved you; go in peace* (Lk. 7:50). It was her faith alone that saved her. The works that she performed were the evidence of her faith, but not the means of salvation.

[§ 61] — D. The Witness of the King to Women

Luke 8:1-3

In these verses, Luke summarized Yeshua's third major preaching tour around the country. The uniqueness of this occasion was that all twelve apostles were with Him, as He had closed the apostolic group after His second tour. He was *preaching and bringing the good tidings* [Gospel] *of the kingdom of God* (Lk. 8:1). The content of His message had not changed; He was still offering the kingdom.

Luke listed several women who also went on this tour after Yeshua had cast out demons from them or healed them of infirmities. There was *Miriam that was called Magdalit, from whom seven demons had gone out* (Lk. 8:2), and of whom more is revealed later. There was *Yochanah the wife of Kusa* (Lk. 8:3a), who worked as a steward for Herod Antipas. And there was *Shoshanah*, of whom nothing more is known. Luke specified there were also other unnamed women. In rabbinic writings, it is common to read of rabbis traveling with their disciples. However, women did not journey with such groups. This is unique to Yeshua's ministry. Luke also revealed exactly how the ministry of Yeshua and the twelve apostles was financed. Several wealthy women *ministered unto them of their substance* (Lk. 8:3b). Once again, it is Luke who was concerned with recording the women's roles in the ministry and life of the Messiah.

[§§ 62–63] —
E. The Rejection of the King by the Leaders

This is the major turning point in the public career of Yeshua the Messiah.

[§ 62] — 1. The Unpardonable Sin

Of the two accounts of this crucial event, Matthew's is the more detailed; therefore, this exposition will primarily focus on his account. However, two observations from Mark's Gospel which Mathew omitted are important to note. First, Yeshua's own friends recognized that something was about to happen, that some high point was about to be reached. They noticed Yeshua was acting differently, but they misinterpreted His actions. They thought He needed to be protected from Himself, because His zeal seemed to border on insanity: *He is beside himself* (Mk. 3:21). Second, while the event described took placed in Galilee, it was instigated by *scribes that came down from Yerushalayim* (Mk. 3:22). Both stages of investigation into a messianic movement were completed, and the religious leaders had reached a decision. Now, they were looking for an opportunity to make that decision public.

a. The Rejection

Matthew 12:22-24, Mark 3:19b-22

The incident began when Yeshua exorcised a demon that caused the possessed person to be both *blind and dumb*, meaning he could neither see nor speak (Mt. 12:22). Generally, exorcism was not all that unusual in the days of Yeshua's ministry. Even the Pharisees and their disciples practiced the casting out of demons, and Yeshua acknowledged it with His own challenging question: *by whom do your sons cast them out?* (Mt. 12:27). However, in rabbinic exorcisms, the exorcist would need to use a specific ritual that had distinctive steps. He would need to establish communication with the demon who was using the vocal cords of the person under his control. Then the exorcist had to discover the demon's name. This was an important facet of the exorcism. Once he knew the demon's name, he could use it to order the demon out of the possessed person. There were times when Yeshua Himself used that method (e.g., Mk. 5:9). However, He normally just ordered the demon out without any ritual at all, which is what made His exorcisms so different. From the study of the rabbinic method of exorcism, one can deduce that, within the framework of Pharisaic Judaism, there was one kind of demon an exorcist could not cast out: the kind of demon that caused the person controlled to be mute. There was no way to communicate with that kind of demon, no way of finding out its name.

Before the event described in the verses above, Yeshua had cast out many demons, and the people were astounded, *for with authority and power he commanded the unclean spirits, and they come out* (Lk. 4:36). They wondered by what authority He was able to do this. When Yeshua cast out this particular demon, the multitudes reacted differently. They raised the question: *Can this be the son of David?* (Mt. 12:23). This is a very different question than the one they had asked before. *Son of David* is a messianic title, so after witnessing this miracle, the multitudes were clearly asking if Yeshua could, indeed, be the Messiah. Something about this sign was so unique that they recognized that only Messiah could have performed it.

Their conclusion was correct; Yeshua had just performed the second messianic miracle. However, while the multitudes were willing to raise the question, they were not willing to answer it for themselves. From biblical times to the present, the Jewish people have labored under a "leadership complex," meaning, whichever way the leaders went, the people were sure to follow. This can be seen clearly in the Hebrew Scriptures. When a king did that which was right in the eyes of the Lord, the people followed. Conversely, when a king did that which was evil in the eyes of the Lord, they also followed. Even today, when believers speak to Jews about Yeshua's Messiahship, sooner or later, they will be confronted with the very same objection: "If Yeshua is the Messiah, why don't our rabbis believe in Him?" In New Testament times, the leadership complex was very strong because of the stranglehold Pharisaism had upon the masses through the Mishnah, and so, while the Jewish people in this account were willing to raise the question, they were not willing to answer it for themselves. They were looking to their leaders to give them direction.

In light of the question by the multitudes concerning Yeshua's Messiahship, the Pharisees had only two options. The first option was to officially recognize Yeshua as the long-awaited Messiah, and this they did not want to do because He rejected Pharisaic Judaism and the authority of the Oral Law. The second option was to reject His messianic claims. However, if they took that route, they would have to explain how Yeshua was able to perform miracles that had never before been done. In the end, the Pharisees took the second option and rejected Yeshua's messianic claims. To explain His special abilities, they came up with a rather radical solution. They declared that Yeshua was able to cast out the demon that caused muteness because He Himself was controlled by *the prince of the demons* (Mt. 12:24), Beelzebub. The original form of the name Beelzebub was Beelzebul, meaning, "the lord of the royal palace." He was the god of the Philistine city of Ekron. After the Jews had finally been cured of idolatry by the Babylonian Captivity, the rabbis liked to poke fun at various pagan gods and apply some of their names to different demons. Here, they changed the last letter so that the name became Beelzebub, meaning "the lord of the flies" or "the lord of the dung," the demon in charge of diseases.

This explanation became the official basis for the rejection of the Messiahship of Yeshua: Because He was demon possessed, Yeshua could not be the Messiah. However, being under the control of a demon gave Him the power to perform signs and wonders never seen before. This explanation is not only reflected in the Gospels, but also in rabbinic literature. One passage in the Talmud elaborates on why Yeshua was executed on Passover. Executions were not permitted on feast days. However, in the case of Yeshua, an exception could be made because of the nature of His crime: He had seduced Israel by the practice of sorcery, which is closely connected with demonism. Another passage in the Talmud states that when Yeshua was in Egypt, He made cuts in the skin of His flesh. He inserted the four-letter name of God, *YHVH*, into these cuts, which gave Him the power to perform His unique miracles. Neither in the Gospels nor in rabbinic literature did the religious leaders ever deny the fact of His miracles. There were too many eyewitnesses to those signs. However, they ascribed the power of the miracles to a demonic source.

Therefore, the official basis for rejecting the Messiahship of Yeshua was that He was demon possessed. That was the given reason, but the real reason was that He did not do it their way.

b. The Defense

Matthew 12:25-29, Mark 3:23-27

Yeshua defended Himself against the charge of being demon possessed by declaring four things:

1. This accusation could not be true because it would mean a division in Satan's kingdom (Mt. 12:25-26; Mk. 3:23-26).

2. The religious leaders themselves had long recognized that the gift of exorcism was a gift of God, so to accuse Him of this was inconsistent with their own theology (Mt. 12:27).

3. This miracle authenticated the claims and the message of the Messiah (Mt. 12:28).

4. This miracle showed that He was stronger than, not subservient to, Satan (Mt. 12:29; Mk. 3:27).

c. The Judgment

Matthew 12:30-37, Mark 3:28-30

After having defended Himself against the accusation of being demon possessed, Yeshua pronounced a special judgment upon that generation of Israel (Mt. 11:16-17) for being guilty of a very unique sin, which has become known as the unpardonable sin or the blasphemy of the Holy Spirit (Mt. 12:31). Because it was unpardonable, a judgment that could never be removed or alleviated was set against *this generation*. That judgment came forty years later, in the year A.D. 70, when Jerusalem and the Temple were destroyed.

It is very important to understand the unpardonable sin in its exact context, because this is the *only* context in which this sin is found.

Therefore, it must be interpreted accordingly. By definition, the unpardonable sin was the national rejection of the Messiahship of Yeshua on the grounds of demon possession while He was physically present on earth.

Let's further expound upon this definition. First, this was a national sin, not an individual sin. Individuals of that generation, like the Apostle Paul, could and did escape the judgment in ways that will be explained in the epilogue of this work. Furthermore, the sin cannot be committed today. The Bible makes one point very clear: The individual who will come to God through Messiah's blood will be forgiven regardless of what sin he has committed. The nature of the sin is irrelevant. The Messiah did not die on the cross only for certain kinds of sins. He died for every type of sin and rendered all of them forgivable to the individual who will come to God through His blood. The term *whosoever* in Matthew 12:32 can have either an individual or a corporate meaning, depending on the context. In this context, it is defined by the term *this generation* of verses 41 and 42, which state: *The men of Nineveh shall stand up in the judgment with this generation, and shall condemn it . . . The queen of the south shall rise up in the judgment with this generation, and shall condemn it . . .* (Mt. 12:41-42). This means that the word *whosoever* is corporate. The individual could be forgiven, but for the nation, it is now unpardonable.

Second, this sin is unique to the Jewish generation of Yeshua's day, and it cannot be applied to later Jewish generations, a fallacy the Catholic Church, for example, has taught. It was to this particular generation that the Messiah came both physically and visibly. He offered to establish the messianic kingdom for them, and He offered Himself as their Messianic King. It was also this specific generation that rejected Him. In carefully studying the Gospel accounts, it is quite evident that, from this point on, the phrase "this generation" is frequently used. This generation alone was guilty of *the blasphemy against the Spirit* (Mt. 12:31). The work of the Holy Spirit was the final testimony of the Messiahship of Yeshua. It was possible to reject Yeshua's messianic claims and still be convinced by the work of the Holy Spirit. However, to reject the witness of the Holy Spirit also meant rejecting the person of the Messiah. The sin, then, was the willful rejection of the person of the Messiah who had been authenticated by the signs of the Holy Spirit.

To ascribe those signs to Satan was to blaspheme the Holy Spirit, which, in turn, led to the rejection of Yeshua's Messiahship. The Messiah needed to be present to perform these signs, which is why this sin was limited to that generation and cannot be committed today.

Third, no other nation could commit this sin. Yeshua was never visibly and physically present with any other nation, offering Himself as that nation's Messiah. This was a unique relationship He had with Israel. There is only one covenant nation, Israel.

There were two consequences for the generation that committed the unpardonable sin: First, it meant that the offer of the messianic kingdom was rescinded, and that generation lost the opportunity, privilege, and benefit of seeing the kingdom established in their day. It is now destined to be reoffered to the future Jewish generation of the Great Tribulation who will accept it, as detailed in Matthew 24-25. Yeshua used the phrases *this world* and *that which is to come* (Mt. 12:32). In the Judaism of His day, the world or age to come was the messianic age. In other words, this generation was not going to see the kingdom established in their time, nor will they see it in an age to come. They will be long gone before it arrives.

Second, it meant that this generation was under a special divine judgment, a judgment of physical destruction, a judgment that was experienced forty years later, in A.D. 70, when Jerusalem and the Temple were destroyed. In rejecting Yeshua, this generation had reached the point of no return. In God's dealings with His covenant nation, once a generation reached the point of no return, nothing could be done to change the coming physical judgment. This was the third time a specific generation had reached such a point. The first time this happened was when Israel committed the sin of Kadesh-Barnea, as recorded in Numbers 13-14. After marching through the wilderness, the Israelites finally arrived at Kadesh-Barnea, an oasis located on the border of the Promised Land. From there, Moses sent out twelve spies, who came back forty days later. They all agreed that the land was everything God had described, *a land flowing with milk and honey* (Ex. 33:3). Then came a sharp point of disagreement. Only two of the spies, Joshua and Caleb, had faith in God and believed the Israelites could conquer the land. The other ten men gave a discouraging report, that due to the numerical superiority and military strength of the inhabitants, they could not take the land. The people made the faulty assumption that the majority must always be right. There was a massive rebellion against the authority of Moses and Aaron, and the two men almost lost their lives in a mob scene, until God intervened and rescued them. At that point, the Exodus generation had reached the point of no return, and God decreed the judgment of forty years of wandering and death in the wilderness outside Israel. The people could do nothing thereafter to change the judgment. Numbers 14 does say that they repented and that God forgave their sins (Num. 14:20). The sin did not affect anyone's individual salvation. However, the people still had to pay the physical consequences of going beyond the point of no return, which was death outside Israel. The offer of the land was rescinded from the Exodus generation, and it was reoffered to the wilderness generation, who accepted it and entered Israel under Joshua. Even Moses died outside the land because of a sin he had committed, but that did not affect his individual, personal salvation. The issue here is the physical, not the spiritual consequences of sin.

The second time the nation reached the point of no return was in the days of Manasseh, one of the cruelest kings of Jerusalem, who practiced extreme forms of idolatry, including human sacrifice. Much innocent blood was shed throughout his lengthy reign (II Kgs. 21:16). He turned the Temple, built by Solomon for the glory of the true God, into a major center of idolatry (II Kgs. 21:1-9; II Chron. 33:1-9). Finally, he reached the point of no return, and God decreed judgment. Jerusalem and the first Temple were destroyed by the Babylonians, and the people were led into captivity (II Kgs. 21:10-15). Nothing they did thereafter could change the course of judgment. Manasseh repented at the end of his life (II Chron. 33:10-13), and as an individual, he was a saved man. He was even followed by a good king, Josiah, who brought revival to Israel. The only thing God promised was that He would not bring the calamity during Josiah's day, but the judgment was still inevitable (II Chron. 34:22-28) because the people had reached the point of no return.

Now, for the third time, with the willful rejection of the person of the Messiah, Israel had reached the point of no return. Nothing they did thereafter could change the coming judgment. A study of the triumphal entry will show that a myriad of people proclaimed Yeshua to be the

Messiah when He rode into Jerusalem on a donkey (Mt. 21:1-17; Mk. 11:1-11; Lk. 19:29-40; Jn. 12:12-19). However, in the midst of their messianic acclamations, the words of the Messiah remained words of judgment, clearly stating that Jerusalem would be destroyed. This is the nature of the unpardonable sin. Physical consequences must be paid. It meant that no matter how many Jews came to believe—and myriads did come to believe—it would not change the fact of the coming physical judgment of A.D. 70.

[§ 63] — 2. The New Policy Concerning Signs

a. The Sign for that Generation

Matthew 12:38-40

After hearing Yeshua's words of rebuke and judgment, the Pharisees tried to retake the offensive by demanding yet another sign. In this context, the Pharisaic implication was that Yeshua had not done enough to authenticate His messianic claims. However, the fact is that He had performed numerous miracles since the Passover when He first went public with His ministry, including those that had never been done before and which the people viewed as messianic. In spite of this, the religious leaders based their rejection of Yeshua's Messiahship on demon possession.

As a result, Yeshua announced His new policy concerning the purpose of His signs. When He began His ministry, His miracles were to serve as signs to Israel in order to persuade the people to make a decision regarding His person. Since they had irrevocably rejected Him, He announced His new policy: There will be no more signs for the nation except one sign, the sign of Jonah, which is the sign of resurrection (Mt. 12:39). The purpose of performing miracles from that point on would be to train the twelve disciples for the new kind of work they would have to conduct because of this rejection, a work that is described in detail in the book of Acts.

The sign of Jonah will come to Israel on three occasions: the resurrection of Lazarus, the resurrection of Yeshua Himself, and the resurrection of the two witnesses in the tribulation (Rev. 11).[3] That is the only sign Yeshua will still give to the nation.

b. The Judgment of that Generation

Matthew 12:41-45

After announcing the new policy concerning the purpose of His signs, Yeshua returned to the theme of judgment, which the Pharisees had interrupted by their demand for another sign (Mt. 12:38). But now, notice the special emphasis on *this generation*: *The men of Nineveh shall stand up in the judgment with **this generation** and shall condemn it; The queen of the south shall rise up in the judgment with **this generation**, and shall condemn it* (Mt. 12:41-42, highlights added). Yeshua gave two examples from the Old Testament: the men of Nineveh and the Queen of Sheba. These were Gentiles who had received a lot less light, a lot less divine revelation, than *this generation* of the Jewish people, yet they responded to the light they were given. Therefore, at the judgment before the great white throne of Revelation 20:11, these Gentiles will stand and condemn this particular Jewish generation for being guilty of the unpardonable sin, a sin unique to them, because they rejected the greater light.

Yeshua concluded His words of judgment with the story of a demon that indwelled a person, resided in him, but then chose to leave him (Mt. 12:43). The demon was not cast out, but left of his own free will, looking for a better place to live. He searched for a while, but when he could find no vacancies, he decided to go back to the person he had indwelled previously. When the demon returned, he found the man swept and garnished, but still empty (Mt. 12:44). During the interim, the man was not indwelled by some other spirit, whether it be a demonic spirit or the Holy Spirit. Therefore, because he remained empty, the returning demon was able to reenter him. This time, the demon did not want to again live by himself, so he invited seven of his demon friends to join him (Mt. 12:45a). Yeshua concluded that *the last state of that man becomes worse than the first* (Mt. 12:45b). He started out with

---

[3] These will be discussed individually in their appropriate context.

only one demon; but because he stayed empty, he ended up with eight demons.

The point of this story is often missed, although Yeshua clearly gave the application: *Even so shall it be also unto this evil generation* (Mt. 12:45c). He again emphasized this particular generation which had begun with the preaching of Yochanan the Baptizer. Yochanan's calling was to prepare them to accept the Messiahship of Yeshua. This generation was swept and garnished by Yochanan's preaching and baptism. However, because they rejected Yeshua's Messiahship, they also remained empty, and their last state will be worse than the first. At the time when Yochanan started preaching, the Jews were under Roman domination and had to pay annual tribute to the emperor, but Rome still allowed them to retain their national identity. Jerusalem was standing, the Temple was functioning in all its Herodian glory, and the Jews had a semi-autonomous government in the Sanhedrin. However, forty years after Yeshua spoke these words, the Roman legions invaded the land. After a four-year war and a two-year siege, they destroyed the city, tore down the Temple so that there was not one stone standing on top of the other, and the Jewish people were scattered and dispersed throughout the world. The last state of that generation was, indeed, worse than the first.

[§§ 64–70] — F. Revelation in View of Rejection

After the religious leaders officially rejected Yeshua on the basis of a false claim, His ministry changed radically in the following four areas: signs, miracles, message, and teaching method.

Signs. Yeshua no longer performed signs to provoke the nation to make a decision. They had already irrevocably decided to reject His Messiahship. The purpose of His signs from this point forward was to train the apostles and prepare them for their ministry, as described in the book of Acts. The only sign He would do publicly was the sign of Jonah, or the sign of resurrection. In summary, the signs went from being for the nation to being for the apostles.

Miracles. The second area of change concerned the people for whom Yeshua performed miracles. There were two facets to the change. The first facet is that up until this event, Yeshua had performed miracles for the benefit of the masses and did not require them to have faith first. An example of this was when Yeshua, on His own initiative, healed the man at the Pool of Bethesda (Jn. 5:1-15). The man did not even know who Yeshua was or what He claimed to be. At that time, faith was not essential for Yeshua to perform miracles, because He was performing them to convince people to believe. However, all of that changed. Now, He only performed miracles in response to the needs of individuals, and He required that they first had faith. To summarize, His miracles went from masses without faith to individuals with faith. The second facet is that up until this event, He would tell the people He had healed to go and proclaim what God had done for them. An example of this is Luke 17:14, where He sent the Jewish lepers He had healed to the priesthood. Now, every time He healed someone, He forbade them to tell anyone what God had done. As will be seen, He did not apply that rule to the Gentiles, but only to Jews. Yeshua initiated a policy of silence, and He forbade those who benefited from His messianic power to tell anyone about it. To summarize, He went from "tell all" to "tell no one."

Message. Until the events described in Matthew 12, both Yeshua and the apostles traveled all over Israel, from city to city and synagogue to synagogue, proclaiming Him to be the Messiah. Now, He forbade His disciples to tell anyone that He was the Messiah. When Peter made his statement of confession, *You are the Messiah, the Son of the living God,* Yeshua told him and the other disciples not to tell anyone (Mt. 16:16-20). This policy of silence was rescinded in Matthew 28 with the Great Commission. To summarize, the policy changed from proclaiming His Messiahship to concealing it.

Method of teaching. Prior to His rejection, whenever Yeshua taught the people publicly, He spoke in terms they could and did understand, as demonstrated by their response to the Sermon on the Mount. At the end of the sermon, Matthew stated that the people clearly understood what He had said and, more importantly, they knew exactly where He differed from the scribes and Pharisees (Mt. 7:28-29). Now, whenever He taught the people publicly, He spoke to them only in parables. To summarize, His teaching went from being very clear to being parabolic. This fourth change set the stage for the next section.

It is impossible to understand why His ministry changed so radically in these four areas without understanding the unpardonable sin. It was a critical and pivotal event that set the stage for the second half of Yeshua's ministry, for the events described in the book of Acts, even for a new entity that would come into existence, the *kehillah* (Hebrew), the *ekklesia* (Greek), the church, the body of the Messiah. Finally, the unpardonable sin set the stage for the course of Jewish history for the next two thousand years. It was a crucial turning point.

[§ 64] — 1. The Course of the Kingdom Program in the Present Age

— Public Parables —

a. Introduction

Matthew 13:1-3a, Mark 4:1-2, Luke 8:4

On that day . . . he spoke to them many things in parables (Mt. 13:1, 3). Yeshua's parabolic method of teaching began on the same day that the national rejection occurred and the unpardonable sin was committed. After His first parable, *the disciples came, and said unto him, Why do you speak to them in parables?* (Mt. 13:10). The fact that they raised the question at this point indicates that He had not been speaking in parables before. Yeshua responded by saying there were three reasons for using this method of teaching.

(1) The Purpose of Parables

The first purpose of teaching in parables was for the disciples' benefit: *And he answered and said unto them, Unto you it is given to know the mysteries of the kingdom of heaven* (Mt. 13:11a). For the disciples, the purpose of these parables was to illustrate the truth.

The second purpose concerned the masses. The truth was to be hidden from them, and they were to be taught in terms they could not and would not understand:

> *11b but to them* [the multitudes] *it is not given. 12 For whosoever has, to him shall be given, and he shall have abundance: but whosoever has not, from him shall be taken away even that which he has. 13 Therefore speak I to them in parables; because seeing they see not, and hearing they hear not, neither do they understand.*

All three Gospel writers stated that the multitudes were present when Yeshua spoke and that He addressed them directly; but He spoke in a way they did not understand. By this time, they had received sufficient light to respond correctly; however, they responded incorrectly by committing the unpardonable sin. Consequently, no further light would be given to them. The sin remained unpardonable.

The third purpose of teaching in parables was to fulfill Old Testament prophecy. We see this in Matthew 13:14-17:

> *14 And unto them is fulfilled the prophecy of Isaiah, which says, By hearing ye shall hear, and shall in no wise understand; And seeing ye shall see, and shall in no wise perceive: 15 For this people's heart is waxed gross, And their ears are dull of hearing, And their eyes they have closed; Lest haply they should perceive with their eyes, And hear with their ears, And understand with their heart, And should turn again, And I should heal them. 16 But blessed are your eyes, for they see; and your ears, for they hear. 17 For verily I say unto you, that many prophets and righteous men desired to see the things which ye see, and saw them not; and to hear the things which ye hear, and heard them not.*

In these verses, Yeshua quoted Isaiah 6:9-10, which prophesied a judgment upon Israel that included parabolic speaking so they could not comprehend.

The key element of this new policy is, *without a parable spoke he nothing unto them* (Mt. 13:34). This was not true before the rejection, but it was true after the rejection. Every time Yeshua taught publicly, it was in parables using terms His audience could not understand. Yeshua explained it as follows: *that it might be fulfilled which was spoken through the prophet, saying, I will open my mouth in parables; I will utter things hidden from the foundation of the world* (Mt. 13:35). The quotation is from Psalm 78:2.[4] The point is that the change to a parabolic teaching style was in fulfillment of God's word. This in turn proved the very Messiahship that had been rejected.

Mark added a detail that Matthew left out: *And with many such parables spoke he the word unto them, as they were able to hear it; and without a parable spoke he not unto them* [this much we knew from Matthew, but then Mark added]: *but privately to his own disciples he expounded all things* (Mk. 4:33-34). After the rejection, this was Yeshua's consistent pattern. When He spoke publicly, He always used parables so that no one understood, including His own disciples. Then, when He was alone with the apostles, He explained the meaning of these parables in order to illustrate the truth.

Both Matthew and Mark emphasized that Yeshua still taught in a sitting position (Mt. 13:2; Mk. 4:1), thus still assuming the position of a rabbi.

(2) The Definition of Parables

By definition, a parable is a figure of speech which uses something common and familiar from everyday life and experience and compares it to a moral, ethical, or spiritual truth. A parable is based on reality, unlike an allegory, which is entirely figurative. The New Testament parables are quite varied in their styles. There are basic similes, which make a comparison between two things by using the words "like" and "as." One example is Matthew 10:16, where Yeshua said, *I send you forth as sheep in the midst of wolves.* Then there are basic metaphors. In a metaphor, the comparison is implied by the figurative terms used, as in John 10:7, where Yeshua stated, *I am the door of the sheep,* and John 15:1, where He said, *I am the true vine.* A metaphor does not use the words "as" and "like," yet it is obvious the statement is not meant to be taken literally. Yeshua clearly did not mean to teach that He was actually a door or a grapevine. Other parables begin with a basic simile, and then the parable expands upon the simile. An example is Matthew 13:33: *The kingdom of heaven is like unto leaven which a woman took,*

---

[4] It is a prophecy which falls in the category of literal plus application.

and hid in three measures of meal, till it was all leavened. This type of parable is based on something women normally did in those days; leavening bread was a common activity. The kingdom of heaven is compared to the leaven, the leaven is used as it normally would be, and the parable expands upon the comparison. Another form of parable is the story-type parable, a short narrative that makes a point, as in the story of the good Samaritan (Lk. 10:30-35).

Parables are designed to either answer a question or to solve a problem. In order to interpret a parable, one must investigate the immediate context to determine the question that is being answered or the problem that is being solved. The context of Yeshua's parables concerns God's kingdom program, and the question He answered is: In light of Israel's rejection of the Messiahship of Yeshua, what is the course of God's kingdom program in the period between the two comings? The problem Yeshua solved is: Why was the messianic kingdom not set up?

Not every detail of a parable necessarily needs to be interpreted, but only those parts that deal with the question or problem. A parable may make one main point or several points. When looking at a specific parable, one needs to discover the point(s) at issue. Before concluding what the spiritual lesson of a parable is, one must first know the reality behind the parable. One must fully understand the literal sense before determining the spiritual sense. In keeping with a Jewish method of teaching, a parable may go from the known to the unknown.

(3) God's Kingdom Program

The purpose of Yeshua's parables in § 64 was to explain the course of God's kingdom program in light of Israel's rejection of the messianic kingdom. A concise but good definition of the kingdom of God is that it is God's rule. It is the sphere over which the sovereign God rules. There may be degrees of authority in different aspects of His kingdom program, but the basic meaning is that God rules.

God's kingdom program has five facets, and each facet relates to a different extension of His rule. Historically, one way theologians have tried to explain God's kingdom program is by saying that the terms "kingdom of God" and "kingdom of heaven," as used in the Gospels, refer to two different kingdoms. This is the result of their not understanding the Jewish frame of reference of the Scriptures. In reality, these terms are synonymous. Only one Gospel writer used the term "kingdom of heaven," and that was Matthew. He also used "kingdom of God," but only four times. When he used these two terms, he meant the very same thing. This is obvious from the passage quoted in this section. While Matthew wrote, *Unto you it is given to know the mysteries of the kingdom of heaven* (Mt. 13:11), Mark stated, *Unto you is given the mystery of the kingdom of God* (Mk. 4:11). Luke, too, used the phrase "kingdom of God" (Lk. 8:10). So, where Mark and Luke wrote about the kingdom of God, Matthew used "kingdom of heaven." These parallel passages prove that the terms are synonymous. The reason Matthew used "heaven" in place of "God" was that he was writing to a Jewish audience. Jews then, as Orthodox Jews today, avoid using the term *God*. They never pronounce God's real name (*YHWH*), but instead substitute the word *Adonai*, meaning "Lord," *AdoShem*, "the Lord of the Name," or simply *HaShem*, meaning "The Name." The same sensitivity was applied to another Hebrew word for God, *Elohim*. One substitute was *Elokim*, changing the middle consonant. Even when writing in English, Orthodox Jews will not write out the word "God," but will always drop the middle letter and spell it as "G-d." Another substitute for *Elohim* was *HaShamayim*, "The Heaven." Matthew knew about this Jewish sensitivity, and because he was writing to Jews, he used the synonymous term "heaven," in keeping with the Jewish frame of reference. There are, indeed, different facets of God's kingdom program, but they cannot be distinguished on the basis of these two terms.

Yeshua's parables deal with the fifth facet of God's kingdom program. The following is a summary of these five facets.

(a) The Universal or Eternal Kingdom

The first facet of the kingdom program is called the universal kingdom or the eternal kingdom. This refers to God's rule, His providence and His sovereignty in that He is always in control. Nothing ever happens outside His will; every event is a result of His directive, decretive, or permissive will. The point is: God is always in control.

The two names of this facet of the kingdom program emphasize two different aspects. The term *universal* emphasizes the sphere and the scope; no matter where things exist, everything is within the sovereign will and control of God. This includes the angelic realm. The term *eternal* emphasizes the timeless aspect, the fact that God is *always* in control; He is eternally in control.

In summary, we can say that this facet of God's kingdom program is timeless, universal, providential, and miraculous. It emphasizes His eternal, sovereign rule everywhere over His entire creation and is spoken of in passages like I Chronicles 29:11-12, Psalms 10:16, 29:10, 74:12, 90:1-6, 93:1-5, 103:19-22, 145:1-21, 148:8, Proverbs 21:11, Jeremiah 10:10, Lamentations 5:19, Daniel 4:17, 6:27, Acts 17:24, *et al.* This is the kingdom that the believer enters upon death (I Cor. 15:50; II Tim. 4:18). The dispensations are the outworking of this kingdom in human history.[5]

(b) The Spiritual Kingdom

The second facet of God's kingdom program is called the spiritual kingdom. It is God's rule in the heart of the believer. The spiritual kingdom is comprised of all who have experienced the new birth by the Holy Spirit. From Adam until the end of the millennial kingdom, as long as men continue to be born on this earth, the spiritual kingdom will exist. Since the creation of man, every individual who has been born again by faith through the regenerating work of the Holy Spirit is a member of this kingdom. This is the kingdom of God of which Yeshua spoke to Nicodemus when He said that unless one is born again, he cannot see, he cannot enter into the kingdom of God (Jn. 3). This is God's rule in the heart of the believer.

So, from Adam onward, the spiritual kingdom has existed. In this present age, the spiritual kingdom and the church are synonymous. However, the spiritual kingdom existed before the church was born in Acts 2, and it will continue to exist in the hearts of believers after the church is removed in the rapture.

---

[5] For further study of the dispensations, see Arnold G. Fruchtenbaum, *The Word of God: Its Nature and Content* (San Antonio, TX: Ariel Ministries, 2014).

This facet is found in passages like Matthew 6:33, 19:16, John 3:3-5, Acts 8:12, 14:22, 19:8, 20:25, 28:23, I Corinthians 4:20, 6:9-10, Galatians 5:21, Ephesians 5:5, Colossians 1:13-14, 4:11, I Thessalonians 2:12, and II Thessalonians 1:5.

(c) The Theocratic Kingdom

The third facet of God's kingdom program is called the theocratic kingdom. It refers to God's rule by means of a theocracy over one nation, Israel. The foundations of Israel as a theocratic kingdom were laid when the Mosaic Law was given, and the law served as the constitution of this kingdom.

Over the course of history, the theocratic kingdom changed from being mediatorial to being monarchial. From Moses to Samuel, God ruled Israel through mediators, comprised of Moses, Joshua, and then the judges, with Samuel being the last judge. Then, God ruled through the monarchs of the house of David until Zedekiah, the last king. Samuel marked the transition between the two forms of this kingdom, because not only was he the last judge, but he also anointed David. David, in turn, began a dynasty, which continued to occupy the throne until Zedekiah. It was during the latter stages of the monarchial form that the theocratic kingdom went into a decline in quality. With the decline, the prophets began to announce a future, better form of God's kingdom program, the messianic kingdom. Finally, the theocratic kingdom came to an end in 586 B.C. with the destruction of Jerusalem by Babylon, and the times of the Gentiles began, which has continued until this day. Old Testament history from Exodus 19 to II Chronicles 36 is a history of the theocratic kingdom.

(d) The Messianic Kingdom or the Millennial Kingdom

The fourth facet of God's kingdom program also has two names. It is called the messianic kingdom or the millennial kingdom. The first name emphasizes that the Messiah Himself will directly rule over this kingdom. The second name emphasizes how long the kingdom will last: one thousand years. This will be an earthly, literal kingdom, during which Yeshua will rule from the throne of David and from Jerusalem over a saved Israel (Jer. 31:34a) and the Gentile nations. The kingdom is rooted in the Davidic Covenant. When God made this covenant, He promised that David would have an eternal house, an eternal kingdom, an eternal throne, and an eternal descendant.

This fourth facet of the kingdom program, the messianic kingdom, was a major topic of Old Testament prophecy. This was the kingdom Yochanan proclaimed to be *at hand* (Mt. 3:2). It was the kingdom Yeshua offered to the Jewish people. It is this kingdom that the Jewish leaders rejected, and as a result, the offer was rescinded and taken from that generation. From a human perspective, the messianic kingdom was postponed, since it was not set up at that time. From the divine perspective, the rejection was part of God's plan and the means by which the Messiah would die to provide the atonement and extend the gospel to the Gentiles (Is. 49:1-13). The messianic kingdom will be reoffered to the Jewish generation of the tribulation, who will accept it.

Some have incorrectly assumed that if Israel had accepted Yeshua as the Messiah, He would not have had to die. However, the Messiah's death was inevitable because it was essential for the atonement, which had to be by the shedding of blood, not by kingly rule. If Israel had proclaimed Yeshua king, the Romans would have seen it as an act of rebellion and treason against the empire. Yeshua would have been arrested by Roman authorities (as He was), tried by a Roman judge (as He was), died a Roman death (as He did), and then be buried (as He was). After His resurrection, He would have dispensed with the Roman Empire and established the messianic kingdom. The issue was not whether or not He would die; the issue was whether or not the kingdom would be established at that point in time. Israel's rejection was the means God ordained for Him to die.

Some of the passages on the messianic kingdom that relate to the Davidic Covenant are Psalms 2 and 72, Isaiah 9:6-7, 11:1-16, Jeremiah 23:5-6, Ezekiel 34:23, 37:24, Hosea 3:4-5, Micah 4:6-8, 5:2, and Malachi 3:1-4.

(e) The Mystery Kingdom

The fifth facet of the kingdom program is the mystery kingdom. The name is derived from Matthew 13, where, following the rejection of His Messiahship, Yeshua introduced this facet of God's kingdom program by mentioning of *the mysteries of the kingdom of heaven* (Mt. 13:11). He stated: *I will utter things hidden from the foundation of the world* (Mt. 13:35). The mystery of the kingdom had been *hidden from the foundation of the world* and was only then being revealed. Paul defines what a divine mystery is in Ephesians 3:3-5, 9, and Colossians 1:26-27. It is a divine truth that was not revealed in the Old Testament but is revealed in the New. In Paul's words, it was *not made known unto the sons of men* (Eph. 3:5) in the Hebrew Scriptures because it *has been hid in God* (Eph. 3:9) and *has been hid for ages and generations* (Col. 1:26). In New Testament times, it *has now been revealed unto his holy apostles and prophets* (Eph. 3:5) in order to *make all men see what is . . . the mystery which for ages has been hid in God* (Eph. 3:9). It has now been *manifested to his saints* (Col. 1:26). Therefore, the mystery kingdom is the one facet of the kingdom program that was not revealed in the Old Testament. Paul writes: *according to the revelation of the mystery which has been kept in silence through times eternal, but now is manifested* (Rom. 16:25-26). The mystery had been kept in silence through all eternity past, but was then being revealed: *but we speak God's wisdom in a mystery, even the wisdom that has been hidden, which God foreordained before the worlds unto our glory* (I Cor. 2:7). The mystery has been hidden, but God has preordained this mystery, and the goal is *our glory*.

The revelation of the mystery happened in two stages: Yeshua was the first one to unveil a facet of the mystery, and He did so by revealing the mystery kingdom in the parables to the apostles. In the second stage, the apostles and New Testament prophets revealed the mystery to the saints (Rom. 16:25). It was made known to Paul by revelation (Eph. 3:3); it was given to the apostles and prophets (Eph. 3:5); and it is now being revealed to the saints (Col. 1:26). While it took 1,500 years to write the Old Testament, it only took one generation to complete the New. With the death of the last apostle, the New Testament was complete, and with it, the revelation of all the mysteries.

Paul felt a unique burden as a servant entrusted with the mysteries to proclaim them: *Let a man so account of us, as of ministers of Messiah, and stewards of the mysteries of God* (I Cor. 4:1); *how that by revelation was made known unto me the mystery* (Eph. 3:3); *ye can perceive my understanding in the mystery of Messiah* (Eph. 3:4). *Unto me, who am less than the least of all saints, was this grace given, . . . to make all men see what is the dispensation of the mystery* (Eph. 3:8-9); *to make known with boldness the mystery of the gospel, for which I am an ambassador in chains; that in it I may speak boldly, as I ought to speak* (Eph. 6:19-20); *praying for us also, that God may open unto us a door for the word, to speak the mystery of Messiah, for which I am also in bonds; that I may make it manifest, as I ought to speak* (Col. 4:3-4).

When Israel rejected the Messiahship of Yeshua, the offer of the messianic kingdom was rescinded and the fifth facet of the kingdom program, the mystery kingdom, was initiated. The parables of Matthew 13 describe this mystery kingdom. It covers the age between the first and second comings of the Messiah. More specifically, it began in Matthew 12-13 with the rejection of Yeshua and will continue until Israel accepts His Messiahship just before the second coming (Mt. 23:37-39). Perhaps the best single word to define the mystery kingdom is the term "Christendom." This term includes all who claim loyalty to Yeshua anywhere in the world. The claim may be true or false, orthodox or heretical, but if anyone claims to be a "Christian," he is part of Christendom. The term describes conditions on this earth while the king is absent from the earth.

In summary, the mystery kingdom is not the same as the universal kingdom because it will exist for a limited time. It began when the Jewish people rejected Yeshua as Messiah and will end when they acknowledge their mistake and ask for Him to return and save them. The mystery kingdom is distinct from the spiritual kingdom because it includes believers and non-believers. It includes within its scope both "the wheat" and "the tares." The mystery kingdom is distinct from the theocratic kingdom; it is not God's theocratic rule over Israel, for within the mystery kingdom, there are both Jews and Gentiles. By the same token, it is not the same as the church. The church is only a part of the mystery kingdom, not the totality of it. It is not the same as the messianic kingdom either, because it is not ruled by the Messiah personally from David's throne in Jerusalem. Furthermore, the messianic kingdom was anything but a mystery in the Hebrew Scriptures, and most of what we know about it comes from these texts.

The parables of the mystery kingdom relay truths about the eternal purpose of God in relation to His eternal kingdom program. The nine parables of Matthew 13:1-53 (including the parallel accounts in Mark 4:1-34 and Luke 8:4-18) describe the outworking of the mystery kingdom in the present age.

b. The Parable of the Sower

Matthew 13:3b-23, Mark 4:3-25, Luke 8:5-18

The first parable is the Parable of the Sower. This parable is given in Matthew 13:3-9 and interpreted in 13:18-23. According to Mark 4:13, the understanding of the first parable is the key to understanding all subsequent parables, because the motifs laid down in the first parable—which Yeshua Himself interprets—become the key to understanding the others.

The parable makes four points. First, the age of the mystery kingdom will be characterized by the sowing of the gospel seed (Mt. 13:3). Second, it will receive opposition from the devil (Mt. 13:19), the world (Mt. 13:21), and the flesh (Mt. 13:22). Third, it will be marked by different preparations of the soil, which means some hearts and some parts of the world will be more responsive to the gospel than others (Mt. 13:5, 7, 8). Fourth, it is marked by different responses to the seed sown. There is the *by the way side* response (Mt. 13:19), which is the response of unbelief. These hear the gospel but never believe. Then there is the *rocky places* response (Mt. 13:20-22). These hear the gospel, believe it, and are saved. However, they are never rooted in the Word of God, so they are never stabilized in their spiritual life. They are the ones who are tossed to and fro by every wind of doctrine. They also tend to rely heavily on their experiences. This makes their spiritual life volatile. Because they are never rooted in the Word, they are never stabilized in their faith and do not produce the kind of fruit that believers need to produce. They never leave the milk stage. Then there is the *thorny ground* response (Mt. 13:22). These also believe. However, they never seem to be able to overcome the cares of this world. They are choked by the world. While those where the seed falls on rocky places are not stabilized because they were never rooted in the Word of God, these may be theologically sound and have a good knowledge of the Scriptures. They may not be experience-centered; however, they still seem to have difficulty living consistent spiritual lives because they are involved in the cares of the world. These may be family, financial, or social cares. As a result, they, too, are not stable and also do not produce the kind of fruit they should. These also never leave the milk stage. Finally, there is the *good ground* response (Mt. 13:23). These are people who believe and are rooted in the Word of God. They overcome the world, and as a result, they are productive in the spiritual life. These are the ones who progress from milk to meat.

c. The Parable of the Seed

Mark 4:26-29

The second parable is the Parable of the Seed, and it makes two points. First, the seed sown will spring to life of its own accord; the seed has an inner energy, so that it will inexplicably produce regeneration. Second, the springing to life does not depend on the sower; once he has sown the seed, there is nothing more that he can do. The gospel itself is the power of God that produces regeneration.

d. The Parable of the Tares

Matthew 13:24-30

The third parable is the Parable of the Tares, in which the *kingdom of heaven is likened unto a man that sowed good seed in his field: but while men slept, his enemy came and sowed tares⁶ also among the wheat . . .* [and] *when the blade sprang up and brought forth fruit, then appeared the tares also* (Mt. 13:24b-26). The parable is explained in Matthew 13:36-43 (see § 66).

---

⁶ Or, *darnel.*

e. The Parable of the Mustard Seed

Matthew 13:31-32, Mark 4:30-32

The fourth parable is the Parable of the Mustard Seed. It makes three points: First, the mystery kingdom will assume huge outer proportions. Second, it will have an abnormal external growth until it becomes a monstrosity. Third, this monstrosity will become a resting place for birds. In the first parable, the birds were agents of Satan (Mt. 13:4, 19). So, within this monstrosity of Christendom, under the umbrella of "Christianity," there will be various satanic elements, cultic groups that claim to believe in Yeshua but deny something essential, such as His deity.

f. The Parable of the Leaven

Matthew 13:33-35, Mark 4:33-34

The fifth parable is the Parable of the Leaven, which uses three elements that need some explanation: the woman, the leaven, and the three measures of meal. When used symbolically in the Scriptures, a woman often represents a spiritual or religious entity. This could be positive or negative. On the positive side, there are the wife of Jehovah (Israel) and the bride of Messiah (the church). On the negative side, there are the Jezebel of Revelation 2:20 and the great harlot of Revelation 17:1-8. These women refer to a false religious system. The woman in Matthew 13:33 represents false religious elements that will be introduced into the mystery kingdom, resulting in spiritual fornication.

Leaven is the symbol of sin (I Cor. 5:6-8) and, particularly in Matthew, the sin of false teaching (Mt. 16:6, 11-12). Thus, false teaching is introduced into the mystery kingdom.

The three measures of meal depict the fact that Christendom eventually breaks up into three divisions: Roman Catholicism, Eastern Orthodoxy, and Protestantism. All of these religious systems have a greater or lesser measure of false teaching. The Parable of the Leaven, then, teaches that the mystery kingdom will be marked by inward doctrinal corruption in all three divisions.

[§ 65] — 2. The Repudiation of all Earthly Relations

Matthew 12:46-50, Mark 3:31-35, Luke 8:19-21

Luke, who ordered his material chronologically, notes that members of Yeshua's family interrupted His teaching. Apparently, they had accepted the idea that *He is beside himself* (Mk. 3:21). The crowds were so thick that His mother, Miriam, and His half-brothers could not get to Him; He was informed by a voice from the crowd that they were outside wanting to see Him (Lk. 8:19-20). Matthew revealed Yeshua's answer: *Who is my mother? And who are my brethren? And he stretched forth his hand towards his disciples, and said, Behold, my mother and my brethren! For whosoever shall do the will of my Father who is in heaven, he is my brother, and sister, and mother* (Mt. 12:48-50). In His response, the Messiah repudiated all earthly blood relations and accepted only spiritual relationships. The Pharisees claimed the right of entry into the kingdom by virtue of their biological, physical ties to Abraham, but Yeshua indicated that only those who are of the spiritual seed of Abraham are going to enter into the kingdom. Physical connection by itself is insufficient. Only those who are believers are His true spiritual brothers, mothers, sisters, etc.

There is also an application to the nation of Israel. Hosea 1-3 declares that the Jewish people were *Ammi*, which is Hebrew for "my people." Covenantally and positionally, the Jews are always God's people; however, they do not experience the benefits of this when they are in unbelief. Hosea prophesied that for a period of time, the Jews would be *lo Ammi*, "not my people," insofar as they would not experience the blessings involved in being the people of God. Hosea also promised that eventually, they would become His people again when they repent. Then they will not be lo Ammi, "not my people," but Ammi, "my people." With the rejection of the Messiahship of Yeshua, Israel moved from the position of Ammi to lo Ammi.

[§ 66] — 3. The Course of the Kingdom Program in the Present Age

— Private Parables —

a. Explanation of the Parable of the Tares

Matthew 13:36-43

After retreating from the multitudes into the privacy of a house (Mt. 13:36), Yeshua revisited a parable He had previously given without further explanation.[7] This was the Parable of the Tares, which makes three points: True sowing will be imitated by a false counter-sowing; there will be a side-by-side development as a result of the two sowings; the judgment at the end of the mystery kingdom will separate the two, with the good brought into the messianic kingdom and the bad excluded. This is the same as the judgment of the sheep and the goats in Matthew 25:31-46. The essential character of each type of sowing can be known only by fruitfulness or fruitlessness.

After explaining the Parable of the Tares, Yeshua proceeded to give four additional parables.

b. The Parable of the Hidden Treasure

Matthew 13:44

The sixth parable is the Parable of the Hidden Treasure. From verses such as Exodus 19:5, Deuteronomy 14:2, and Psalm 135:4, where Israel is called God's *treasured possession*, we know that the treasure is a symbol of Israel. The point of this parable is that although most of the nation rejected the Messiah, God will gain a remnant from Israel. The treasure, thus, is the remnant of Israel today (Rom. 11:5) and *the Israel of God* (Gal. 6:16).

---

[7] See § 64.

c. The Parable of the Pearl of Great Price

Matthew 13:45-46

The seventh parable is the Parable of the Pearl of Great Price. While the Bible reveals that the treasure represents Israel, it does not state anywhere exactly what the pearl represents when it is used symbolically. Knowing that Christendom includes both Jews and Gentiles, very likely, the Parable of the Pearl of Great Price is "the other side of the coin" of the previous parable. The treasure represents the Jews, so it is natural that the pearl would represent the Gentiles. Furthermore, the pearl comes from the sea, and the sea symbolizes the Gentile world (Dan. 7:2-3; Rev. 17:1, 15). Finally, the pearl comes from the oyster, which itself was unclean in the Law of Moses but made clean by the law of Messiah. Taking all these arguments into consideration, we can deduct that the pearl represents Gentile believers.

The first point made in the Parable of the Pearl of Great Price, then, is that there will also be salvation among the Gentiles. The second point made is that the Gentiles in the mystery kingdom are added by gradual accretion, like a pearl develops when a speck of dirt falls into the oyster. The oyster begins covering this speck with calcium carbonate and continues to add small amounts of this chemical compound until, by gradual accretion, it becomes a pearl. This teaches the concept that the Gentiles in the church are added to the mystery kingdom by gradual accretion. One of the primary purposes of the church age is *to take out of them a people for his name* (Acts 15:14), and this is to continue *until the fulness of the Gentiles be come in* (Rom. 11:25). This is indeed pictured by this parable.

d. The Parable of the Net

Matthew 13:47-50

The eighth parable is the Parable of the Net. As mentioned in the commentary on the previous parable, the sea represents the Gentiles. The point of the net is that the mystery kingdom will end with the judgment of the Gentiles, with the righteous brought into the messianic kingdom, and with the unrighteous excluded. This is the same as the judgment of the Gentiles in Matthew 25:31-46.

e. The Parable of the Householder

Matthew 13:51-53

The ninth parable is the Parable of the Householder, which teaches that some aspects of the mystery kingdom have similarities with the other facets of God's kingdom program; other aspects are brand new, never found before.

f. The Progression of the Mystery Kingdom — A Summary

A summary of the nine parables allows one to see the movement of the mystery kingdom from start to finish:

- ✡ **Sower:** Throughout the mystery kingdom age, the gospel seed will be sown.

- ✡ **Seed Growing of Itself:** The seed sown will spring to life inexplicably by its own power.

- ✡ **Tares:** The true sowing will be imitated by a false counter-sowing.

The next two parables are a result of the Parable of the Tares:

- ✡ **Mustard Seed:** The mystery kingdom will assume huge outer proportions.

- ✡ **Leaven:** It will be marked by inward corruption of doctrine.

The next two parables are the result of the parables of the Sower and the Seed Growing of Itself:

- ✡ **Hidden Treasure:** Nevertheless, God will gain a remnant from Israel.

- ✡ **Pearl of Great Price:** He will also gain believers from among the Gentiles.

- ✡ **Net:** The judgment at the end of the mystery kingdom age will bring the righteous into the messianic kingdom while the unrighteous will be excluded.

✿ **Householder:** The mystery kingdom has both similarities and dissimilarities with the other four facets of God's kingdom program.

[§ 67] — 4. Power over Nature

Matthew 8:18, 23-27, Mark 4:35-41, Luke 8:22-25

Following the revelation of the new facet of God's kingdom program, a whole new set of miracles occurred, the purpose of which was to train Yeshua's disciples.

Mark stated: *And on that day, when even was come* (Mk. 4:35). This was the same day the rejection had occurred, but night finally arrived and ended that fateful day. On this day, He was officially rejected; on this day, He pronounced the judgment for the unpardonable sin on that specific generation; and on this day, He introduced the new facet of the kingdom program. As evening came on this fateful day for Israel, He ordered the apostles to get into the boat to cross over to the other side of the Sea of Galilee. His decision resulted from seeing *great multitudes about him* (Mt. 8:18). The purpose was to leave the multitude (Mk. 4:36).

Luke, who emphasized the humanity of the Messiah, stated: *But as they sailed he fell asleep* (Lk. 8:23); He fell asleep within the confines of the boat. Suddenly, a severe storm hit, which Mark described with these words: *And there arose a great storm of wind, and the waves beat into the boat* (Mk. 4:37). Matthew stated: *And behold, there arose a great tempest in the sea* (Mt. 8:24), and Luke observed: *and there came down a storm of wind on the lake* (Lk. 8:23). The Sea of Galilee is surrounded on the east and west sides by mountains, hills, and sheer cliffs. On the west side are the hills of Lower Galilee, and on the east side are the Golan Heights, or ancient Bashan. To this day, periodically, the winds come rushing down both sides of these mountains, causing a tempest to hit suddenly. Just as suddenly, the winds stop and the sea slowly calms down. These sudden storms are unpredictable,[8] and in the situation described in this passage, the winds hit while Yeshua and the apostles were crossing the sea, a fitting conclusion to what had been a stormy day of a different kind.

All three Gospels emphasize the extremity of the situation. Mark stated: *insomuch that the boat was now filling* (Mk. 4:37); the boat was filling with water faster than they could bail it out. Matthew added: *insomuch that the boat was covered with the waves* (Mt. 8:24); not only was the water going into the boat, but huge waves were also buffeting the vessel, and as they hit, more water came in. Luke concluded: *they were filling <with water>, and were in jeopardy* (Lk. 8:23), meaning there was a real danger of loss of life. These expert fishermen had been in stormy seas before, but this was obviously a very unusual storm.

Yet, Yeshua's sleep was undisturbed. Matthew stated: *but he was asleep* (Mt. 8:24). Mark was a bit more detailed: *And he himself was in the stern, asleep on the cushion* (Mk. 4:38). Finally, the apostles had to awaken Him and cried for help: *Save, Lord; we perish* (Mt. 8:25); *Master, master, we perish* (Lk. 8:24). Mark noted that the cry for help was emotionally accusatory: *Teacher, care you not that we perish?* (Mk. 4:38).

The divine purpose of this first lesson since Israel's national rejection was to teach the disciples dependence on the Messiah in every situation. In response to their request, Yeshua verbally addressed the wind and the sea (Mk. 4:39). First, *he awoke, and rebuked the wind.* The Greek word for *rebuke* means "to muzzle." It was as if the prince of the powers of the air had sent the wind, and Yeshua muzzled it.

Second, He *said unto the sea, Peace, be still* (Mk. 4:39a). Two things immediately happened: *And the wind ceased,* and *there was a great calm* (Mk 4:39b)—not merely a natural calm, but a great calm; not a slow calm, but a sudden one. The raging suddenly and totally ceased (Lk. 8:24).

Then came the lesson to be learned. The disciples had already been rebuked for their lack of faith before the miracle (Mt. 8:26). They were further rebuked by the question, *Why are ye fearful? Have ye not yet*

---

[8] The author has witnessed these sudden storms on several separate occasions.

faith? (Mk. 4:40). The Greek word for *fearful* is *deilos,* which describes a cowardly fear; they showed cowardly fear during the storm. Mark added, *And they feared exceedingly* (Mk. 4:41). The Greek verb here is *phobeó,* the root of which is the noun *phobos,* meaning fear in the sense of awe and reverence; the disciples were awestruck. Matthew described the content of the reverence: *What manner of man is this, that even the winds and the sea obey him?* (Mt. 8:27). Luke's description is: *Who then is this, that he commands even the winds and the water, and they obey him?* (Lk. 8:25). The miracle they had just observed was a visible repudiation of the Pharisaic explanation of His person. The lesson they are to learn is that He is more than a man; He is the Messianic God-Man. He was never in subjection to the prince of the powers of the air; rather, He was able to muzzle him and muzzle his winds.

[§ 68] — 5. Power over Demons

Matthew 8:28-34, Mark 5:1-20, Luke 8:26-39

For the first time, the Gospels provide a detailed description of a demonized person, and especially Mark 5:1-4 sheds light on what it is like to be possessed.[9] It is noteworthy that the event took place right after the Messiah Himself was accused of being demonized, as it disproves the allegation and verifies the truth of Yeshua's claims: He was stronger than and not subservient to Satan. He now faced a man in the most extreme degree of the demonized state described in Scripture. The possessed dwelled *in the tombs* and showed superhuman strength (Mk. 5:3); he wailed constantly and was self-destructive (Mk. 5:3-5); he was excessively aggressive (Mt. 8:28) and approached Yeshua stark naked (Lk. 8:27).

Mark stated that they crossed over *to the other side of the sea* (Mk. 5:1), the Gentile side of the Sea of Galilee. Both he and Luke noted that this event occurred in the *country of the Gerasenes* (Mk. 5:1; Lk. 8:26);

---

[9] The Greek word for "possession" is never actually used in the Scriptures mentioned here. Matthew 8:28 has the Greek verb *daimonizomai,* which means "to be controlled by a demon from within." Otherwise, the Greek texts use a phrase stating that the person has a demon.

Matthew, on the other hand, stated *it was the country of the Gadarenes* (Mt. 8:28). Critics of the New Testament have claimed that this is an obvious contradiction, but such claims show ignorance of the political lines of the first century. Gadara was both a city and a region, in the same way that New York is both a city and a state. New York City is in the state of New York, just as the city of Gadara was in the region of Gadara. Albany is also in the state of New York. Likewise, the city of Gerasa was also in the region of Gadara. Matthew focuses on the region, while the other Gospel writers emphasize the city within the region. The Sea of Galilee had both a Jewish side (from Migdol to Bethsaida) and a Gentile side (from Tiberias to Gerasa). This was Gentile territory and part of the Decapolis.

In a commonly accepted manner of reporting at that time, Mark and Luke mentioned one demoniac, emphasizing the more prominent individual, whereas Matthew noted two, providing the larger context. This type of reporting will appear again later in the Gospels.

Matthew stated that the demons recognized two things. First, they understood who Yeshua was: *What have we to do with you, you Son of God?* (Mt. 8:29). Their recognition included worship (Mk. 5:7), for demons perceive the deity of the Son. Second, they acknowledged their ultimate doom; they knew they were destined for the lake of fire, which was prepared for the devil and his angels: *Are you come hither to torment us before the time?* (Mt. 8:29).

In this incident, Yeshua used the standard Jewish approach to exorcism[10] and asked: *What is your name?* (Mk. 5:9). The answer was: *My name is Legion; for we are many* (Mk. 5:9b). A legion consists of six thousand soldiers, so these two men were possessed by that many demons. This demonstrates clearly how much stronger Yeshua is than Satan and his kingdom.

The demons knew very well that they were about to be cast out, but they made a request: *And they entreated him that he would not command them to depart into the abyss* (Lk. 8:31). The abyss is a segment of a larger place in the center of the earth called *Sheol* in Hebrew and

---

[10] Please refer to § 62 for a detailed description.

Hades in Greek.[11] As previously mentioned, the demons in this passage specifically requested that Yeshua not send them to the abyss (Lk. 8:31), but rather that they might be allowed to enter a herd of swine that was feeding nearby (Lk. 8:32). For unexplained reasons, Yeshua granted their request. The explanation frequently given is that under the Law of Moses, eating pigs was forbidden. However, this was Gentile territory, not Jewish territory, so Jewish law did not apply in this case. Thus, the reason He allowed it is unknown. Mark specified that the swine numbered about two thousand (Mk. 5:13). When these demons entered the herd, the pigs rushed into the Sea of Galilee and drowned themselves. Those in charge of feeding the swine fled from the scene and informed both the city and the country what had happened to the pigs and to the demoniacs (Mk. 5:14). The result was that *all the city* came out to see what had occurred and who was responsible (Mt. 8:34). They saw the demoniac now sitting instead of raging, clothed instead of naked, and in his right mind rather than wailing uncontrollably (Mk. 5:15).

One of the two men *that had been possessed with demons besought him that he might be with him* (Mk. 5:18). He wanted to become a disciple of Yeshua. However, he was a Gentile, and at that point in time, Yeshua was not accepting Gentile disciples. Instead, He instructed him, *Go to your house unto your friends, and tell them how great things the Lord has done for you, and <how> he had mercy on you* (Mk. 5:19). Yeshua did not apply the prohibition against telling others who He was to Gentiles. Rather, He encouraged the man to proclaim the message, which, according to Mark 5:20a, he did among the cities of the Decapolis. He had a rather extensive ministry, *and all men marveled* (Mk. 5:20b). The result of his work will be seen later in the feeding of the four thousand, when the people welcomed Yeshua instead of asking Him to leave (Mk. 7:31-8:10).

---

[11] For a detailed analysis of *Sheol*, see § 118, point 3.

[§ 69] — 6. Power over Disease and Death

Matthew 9:18-26, Mark 5:21-43, Luke 8:40-56

For the disciples, this was a lesson in Yeshua's power over the realm of both disease and death. For the two individuals who benefitted from His miracles, this was a lesson in faith.

After having cast out the demons in Gerasa, Yeshua crossed the lake and returned to Jewish territory. The multitudes from which He had escaped earlier were waiting for Him (Mk. 5:21). On His return, one man in particular approached Him: *And there comes one of the rulers of the synagogue, Yair by name* (Mk. 5:22a). *Yair*, or Jairus as he is called in English, was an elder of the synagogue. His daughter was deathly ill; in fact, she died before Yeshua got to the house.

Since the rejection by the leaders, Yeshua only performed miracles in response to personal need and on the basis of faith. Mark described the issue of personal need: *and seeing him, he falls at his feet, and beseeches him much, saying, My little daughter is at the point of death* (Mk. 5:22b-23a). Matthew showed that there was faith: Jairus *worshipped* Yeshua (Mt. 9:18a)—an obvious act of faith—and said, *but come and lay your hand upon her, and she shall live* (Mt. 9:18b). The man showed no doubt in Messiah's ability to heal.

Both Mark and Luke mention that as Yeshua moved with the elder of the synagogue, a multitude followed Him and *thronged* Him (Mk. 5:24; Lk. 8:42). The Greek word Luke uses is *sumpnigó*, which means "to choke utterly, as weeds do plants," "to press upon someone almost to a point of suffocation." In light of what was about to happen, it is therefore important to keep in mind that the multitude surrounding Yeshua was tightly compacted.

Before Yeshua and Jairus could get to the house, they encountered a woman: *And behold, a woman, who had an issue of blood twelve years, came behind Him* (Mt. 9:20). She had suffered from this condition for as long as Jairus' daughter had been alive: twelve years (Lk. 8:43). Her illness rendered her perpetually, ceremonially unclean (Lev. 15:19-30). Therefore, she had been untouchable for twelve years, and she herself was not permitted to touch anyone during that period of time.

Matthew did not mention that the woman had ever sought medical help, but Mark and Luke did. Mark stated that she *had suffered many things of many physicians, and had spent all that she had, and was nothing bettered, but rather grew worse* (Mk. 5:26). Luke added that *she had spent all her living upon physicians, and could not be healed of any* (Lk. 8:43). Both Gospel writers mention that, despite having exhausted all of her resources seeking medical treatment, the woman's condition had only further deteriorated. Luke, however, leaves out the fact that she *suffered many things of many physicians* (Mk. 5:26). This might be an example of ancient professional courtesy.

Having given up on doctors, the woman now came to Yeshua. She tried to be inconspicuous by melting into the crowd (Mk. 5:27). Matthew and Mark mentioned that she touched Yeshua's garments, but Luke was more specific: She *came behind him, and touched the border of his garment* (Lk. 8:44a). The *border* was the *tzitzit*, or tassels, that Jews were required to wear under the Mosaic Law. Since Yeshua kept the law perfectly, these tassels hung at the corners of His garments. The woman was careful to touch only the tassels, that part of His garments furthest from His body. She had been taught that her touch would render Him unclean (Lev. 15:19-24, 28-30). Her personal need was obvious. Her faith was expressed in what she believed to be true: *If I do but touch his garment, I shall be made whole* (Mt. 9:21). Indeed, her faith was instantly rewarded. Luke stated: *and immediately the issue of her blood stanched* (Lk. 8:44b). Mark added: *And straightway the fountain of her blood was dried up; and she felt in her body that she was healed of her plague* (Mk. 5:29). The healing occurred instantaneously.

As Jairus' daughter was on the verge of death, time was precious, yet Yeshua stopped the procession to raise a question: *Who touched my garments?* (Mk. 5:30), and *he looked round about to see her who had done this thing* (Mk. 5:32). Obviously, He knew who had done the touching, because He turned around and looked directly at the woman (Mt. 9:22). The purpose of the question was to get the attention of the disciples. His miracles at this point were primarily for them. Frustrated, the disciples responded: *You see the multitude thronging you, and you say, Who touched me?* (Mk. 5:31). Peter said: *Master, the multitudes press you and crush <you>* (Lk. 8:45), meaning "What do you mean, who touched you? Many people are touching you!" Once Yeshua had

His disciples' attention, they could learn the lesson. When He looked at the woman, she recognized that He knew it was she who had touched Him and came forward to confess (Mk. 5:33; Lk. 8:47). In Matthew 9:21, she said to herself: *If I do but touch his garment, I shall be made whole.* Yeshua corrected her theology: *Daughter, be of good cheer; your faith has made you whole* (Mt. 9:22). In other words, touching His tassels had not healed her; without faith, she could have touched all she wanted without results. Furthermore, the power issued from Him, not from His clothing. Her faith was the means of her healing; her touch was the visible evidence of her faith, but her invisible faith had made her whole.

This delay was just long enough for Jairus' daughter to die. A message to that effect arrived: *Your daughter is dead: why trouble you the Teacher any further?* (Mk. 5:35). However, Jairus had witnessed the woman's faith and heard Yeshua's statement. He had learned the lesson of faith! Yeshua admonished him: *Fear not: only believe, and she shall be made whole* (Lk. 8:50).

Since Yeshua no longer performed miracles for the sake of the public, *he suffered no man to follow with him, save Peter, and Yaakov and Yochanan the brother of Yaakov* (Mk. 5:37). Yeshua permitted only three of the apostles to continue the rest of the way to the house. Upon arrival, the mourning for the dead had already begun with weeping, wailing (Mk. 5:38), and flute playing (Mt. 9:23). When Yeshua announced, *The child is not dead, but sleeps* (Mk. 5:39), the people *laughed him to scorn, knowing that she was dead* (Lk. 8:53). The fact that she actually was dead had become common knowledge. In the New Testament, only believers, not unbelievers, are said to sleep when, in fact, they are dead. This emphasizes God's view that the death of believers is only a temporary suspension of physical activity.

Forcing everyone else out of the house except the three apostles with Him, Yeshua allowed the parents to enter the inner chamber where the body lay (Mk. 5:40; Lk. 8:51). While the disciples were to learn the lesson of Yeshua's power over death, the parents were to understand that He would perform miracles in response to personal need on the basis of faith. He then declared: *Talyeta* (Talitha) *kumi* (Mk. 5:41). *Talitha* is

Aramaic for "damsel," and *kumi* is the feminine imperative of "to rise." He ordered the girl to rise from the dead.

Her immediate resurrection caused great amazement on the part of the five witnesses (Mk. 5:42; Lk. 8:56). Yeshua continued His policy of silence: *And he charged them much that no man should know this* (Mk. 5:43); *he charged them to tell no man what had been done* (Lk. 8:56). However, since the daughter's death was already public knowledge, the news spread: *And the fame hereof went forth into all that land* (Mt. 9:26).

[§ 70] — 7. Power over Blindness

Matthew 9:27-34

Several harmonies, including *A Harmony of the Gospels* by A. T. Robertson, agree that this passage in Matthew 9 chronologically follows the events of Matthew 12. So, after the religious leaders of Israel and this generation had rejected Yeshua on the basis of demon possession, *two blind men followed him, crying out, and saying, Have mercy on us, You son of David* (Mt. 9:27). Expressing their personal need by crying out, *Have mercy on us,* they addressed Yeshua as the *son of David,* thereby asking for a miracle on the basis of His messianic character, which Israel had already rejected. On that basis, Yeshua could not help them; therefore, He did not respond immediately. However, *when He was come into the house, the blind men came to him* (Mt. 9:28a). They met privately. Yeshua would respond to their personal needs as requested, but only on the basis of faith. So He asked them, *Believe ye that I am able to do this? They say unto him, Yea, Lord* (Mt. 9:28b). He responded, *According to your faith be it done unto you. And their eyes were opened* (Mt. 9:29-30a). Their healing was immediate.

The new policy of silence continued: *And Yeshua strictly charged them, saying, See that no man know it* (Mt. 9:30b). However, they jointly disobeyed the command (Mt. 9:31).

Then Yeshua again cast out a demon that caused dumbness (Mt. 9:32). The uniqueness of this miracle was discussed in § 68, and the multitudes once more agreed that it was extraordinary, for they *marveled, saying, It was never so seen in Yisrael* (Mt. 9:33). Since exorcising demons was not something new, the reaction of the multitudes here again shows that Yeshua was the first in Jewish history to cast out demons that caused dumbness.

The Pharisees continued to voice their own explanation: *By the prince of demons casts he out demons* (Mt. 9:34), showing the Pharisaic basis for rejecting His Messiahship.

[§ 71] — G. The Final Rejection in Nazareth

Matthew 13:54-58, Mark 6:1-6a

As stated earlier, Nazareth was a microcosm of the nation of Israel as a whole.[12] What happened locally in Nazareth ultimately happened nationally in Israel. In Luke 4:16-30, an initial rejection occurred in Nazareth; now, a final rejection occurs in Nazareth. Earlier an initial rejection by the nation occurred;[13] later, a final rejection by the nation will occur.

Yeshua returned to Nazareth and, during the Sabbath, took the opportunity to expound upon the Scriptures in the synagogue among the very people with whom He had grown up. Hearing Him teach and expound the Word, they *were astonished, saying, Whence has this man these things? And, What is the wisdom that is given unto this man?* (Mk. 6:2). They, of all people, knew that He could not have learned all this in the Nazareth school system. They also knew that Yeshua did not attend any specific rabbinic school, and so *they were offended in him* (Mt. 13:57) because He had the arrogance to teach them. For this reason, Yeshua declared, *A prophet is not without honor, save in his own country, and among his own kin, and in his own house* (Mk. 6:4), a proven proverb.

---

[12] See § 40.

[13] See §§ 62-63.

Because of the people's unbelief, with a few exceptions (Mk. 6:5), the supernatural was withheld from them: *And he did not many mighty works there because of their unbelief* (Mt. 13:58).

This section provides details about Yeshua's family. Matthew revealed that His stepfather, Joseph, was a carpenter (Mt. 13:55). Mark stated that Yeshua was also a carpenter apprenticed to His stepfather's profession (Mk. 6:3), and both Gospel writers elaborated on the fact that the Messiah had four half-brothers: James (*Yaakov* in Hebrew), Joseph (whom Matthew called *Yoseph* and Mark called *Yosei*), Jude (*Yehudah*), and Simon (*Shimon*). James and Jude later wrote the epistles that bear their names. Furthermore, Yeshua had at least two half-sisters who are unnamed. So Miriam produced at least six more children after Yeshua. Minimally, she was the mother of seven. This disproves the teaching of the Catholic Church that Miriam's virginity was perpetual. The claim that the word *brother* here means "cousin" is wishful thinking, since in the context, the mention of father and mother emphasizes not distant, but immediate family. The text provides no indication that these brothers were sons of Joseph by a previous marriage.

[§ 72] — H. Witness in View of Rejection

Following the final rejection in Nazareth, Yeshua again sent His disciples out on a preaching and teaching tour, but with a difference this time. As they went, they were still to proclaim *the kingdom of heaven is at hand* (Mt. 10:7), but no longer were they to call the nation to repent (Mt. 3:2; 4:17). At this point, the focus was on the individual— those who believed, the remnant of that day. Yeshua warned the disciples that, as He was rejected by the nation as a whole, they too would be rejected, and for the same reason.

1. Introduction

Matthew 9:35-10:4, Mark 6:6b-7, Luke 9:1-2

Matthew reiterated Yeshua's threefold ministry as He passed through cities and villages in a summary statement of the Messiah's activities until the rejection occurred (Mt. 9:35). As to location, He had taught *in their synagogues*. As to content, He had preached *the gospel of the kingdom*. As to authentication, He had healed *all manner of disease and all manner of sickness*. In his summary, Matthew repeated what he had said in 4:23. However, back in Matthew 4:23, it was an introduction to the national ministry of Yeshua. Now, the statement was to explain the reason for the situation: *But when he saw the multitudes, he was moved with compassion for them, because they were distressed and scattered, as sheep not having a shepherd* (Mt. 9:36). The leadership had already rejected Yeshua, but the people at this point were not yet following their leaders. The debate among the masses was, "Should we follow the new shepherd or should we follow the old ones?" Their confusion and indecisiveness rendered them *as sheep not having a shepherd*, and they were *distressed*. Within the masses, however, were individuals who already believed. Therefore, the ministry had to continue for that segment, the remnant of Israel. Hence the commission: *Then said he unto his disciples, The harvest indeed is plenteous, but the laborers are few. Pray ye therefore the Lord of the harvest, that he send forth laborers into his harvest* (Mt. 9:37-38). Yeshua was teaching the principle that those who pray for laborers should also be willing to become laborers, and those who pray for the harvest can also at times reap the harvest.

Three things should be noted about the commission Yeshua now gave His disciples. First, He sent them out two by two, thus providing mutual encouragement (Mk. 6:7). Second, He sent them forth to proclaim the message of the kingdom (Lk. 9:2). As the context will later show, Yeshua specifically sent them out to the believing remnant who needed to be informed about the new facet of the kingdom program: the mystery kingdom. At this point, the disciples were unclear about all the facets of that program, thinking they were still dealing with the messianic kingdom. As the Gospels make clear, they did not yet fully comprehend all that they needed to know about this new situation;

however, they proclaimed what they understood. Third, Yeshua delegated to the disciples the authority to authenticate their message by performing miracles and to have a ministry of encouragement and healing among the remnant (Mt. 10:1).

Note the distinction Matthew made between unclean spirits and physical diseases: He *gave them authority over unclean spirits, to cast them out, and to heal all manner of disease and all manner of sickness.* It is not true that if one has a disease it is always the result of one being afflicted by a demon, as has been taught by some. Note also that the authority of exorcism and healing was given only to the twelve apostles; it was a unique power that came with apostolic authority and was not given to believers in general. Matthew's listing of the twelve apostles, the details of which were discussed earlier, immediately follows this statement of authority. Never in Scripture are believers in general given this authority. The pronoun *them* only refers to the apostles.

2. Practical Instructions for the Mission

Matthew 10:5-15, Mark 6:8-11, Luke 9:3-5

Yeshua began the commission by giving the apostles practical instructions for the ministry He was sending them out to do. He instructed them in five specific areas.

First, He gave them territorial and national limitations. They were to go only to Jews: *Go not into <any> way of the Gentiles, and enter not into any city of the Samaritans: but go rather to the lost sheep of the house of Yisrael* (Mt. 10:5b-6). This exemplifies the principle that not all of Yeshua's commandments were intended for all people for all time. Obviously, this commission was intended only for the apostles and only for a limited period of time. Later in the same Gospel (chapter 28), after His death and resurrection, Yeshua will newly commission the apostles to make disciples of all nations. Now, they were to go only to *the lost sheep of the house of Yisrael.*

Second, the practical instruction was twofold and dealt with the nature of the apostles' work (Mt. 10:7-8). They were to declare the kingdom message insofar as they understood it at that time, telling the believing remnant that the messianic program was still very much part of God's plan. The basic facts about the kingdom were still true, although it would not occur at that time. Furthermore, they were to authenticate their message by performing miracles: *Heal the sick, raise the dead, cleanse the lepers, cast out demons: freely ye received, freely give* (Mt. 10:8). However, the miracles were for the remnant only, and the apostles were to share what they were given with their fellow believers.

Third, the apostles were not to be concerned about the necessities of life. They must trust God to provide for them as they went out to minister (Mt. 10:9-10). Yeshua forbade them to take gold, silver, brass, wallet, coats, shoes, and staff. Gold, silver, and brass refer to coins made of these elements. One coat was sufficient because God would meet their minimal needs. Mark explained Yeshua's reference to shoes. They were to go *shod with sandals* (Mk. 6:9). In other words, instead of wearing shoes, they must be willing to walk with cheaper sandals. An apparent discrepancy regarding the staff appears between the Gospels. Matthew quoted Yeshua as saying not to take a staff (Mt. 10:10a), and Luke agreed with Matthew (Lk. 9:3), but Mark stated to take nothing but *a staff only* (Mk. 6:8). At least eight possible solutions address this problem, but none have won general acceptance, and the disagreement remains unresolved. It is therefore best to take Mark's version as teaching that the apostles were not to take an extra staff.

The principle behind Yeshua's instruction was: *the laborer is worthy of his food* (Mt. 10:10b). As the disciples went out, their needs would be provided. Again, this was not intended as a principle for all believers for all time, but rather for the apostles for a limited period of time. At the end of His public ministry, Yeshua told them to take the very things He had just told them not to take, illustrating that certain things were true only while the Messiah was physically present on earth. Things would change when He ascended into heaven, and it is important to distinguish between His presence and His absence from earth.

The fourth practical instruction for the mission was that the apostles' focus should be on the individual, not the nation. The term *worthy* refers to believers. When the apostles entered a city, they were to *search out who in it is worthy* (Mt. 10:11). They were instructed to preach only to the *worthy*, the individual believers, the remnant of that town. Upon finding a worthy one, they were to reside with that person. As they entered his (or her) house, they were to salute it (Mt. 10:12), meaning they were to give it an apostolic blessing, *if the house be worthy* (Mt. 10:13). In other words, if the people who lived in this house were truly believers, the apostles were to give the house their peace. However, if the house proved not to be what it claimed to be, a believing house, then they were not to give it their peace, withdrawing whatever blessing they had extended.

Fifth, if the apostles were met by unbelievers, the non-worthy, they were to shake the dust off their shoes as a sign of witness and impending judgment against the unbelievers. If the disciples entered a house that proved to be unworthy, they were to shake the dust of the house off their feet. The same applied to the city (Mt. 10:14), because eventually judgment would come upon that city. Note that while the blessing was on the individual, the judgment moved to the national element and, in this case, focused on the city: *It shall be more tolerable for the land of Sedom and Gomorrah in the day of judgment, than for that city* (Mt. 10:15). Judgment will be against *that city*. The phrase *more tolerable* indicates that there will be degrees of punishment in the final judgment.

3. Instruction in View of the Coming Persecution

Matthew 10:16-23

Because the nation as a whole rejected His Messiahship, Yeshua instructs His apostles in view of the coming persecution. Two main things may be noted here.

First, Yeshua instructed the apostles as to how they should respond to persecution (Mt. 10:16-20). In regard to wisdom, they were to be like serpents, but in regard to actions, they were to be like doves. Against the backdrop of the rejection Yeshua had already experienced, their being sent *as sheep in the midst of wolves* (Mt. 10:16a) has a negative connotation. Therefore, the apostles were to use the wisdom and cunningness of a serpent to avoid being hurt if possible. However, if it were not possible, they should be harmless as doves, willing to be hurt and yet remain harmless themselves.

Yeshua warned the apostles of coming trials and told them to expect widespread rejection: *But beware of men: for they will deliver you up to councils, and in their synagogues they will scourge you; yea and before governors and kings shall ye be brought for my sake, for a testimony to them and to the Gentiles* (Mt. 10:17-18). With the mention of Gentiles, Yeshua moved from the immediate future to the more distant future, after His resurrection, when they would have a major testimony to Gentiles. The rejection they would experience in the immediate future would continue into the distant future, providing the opportunities for witnessing and exercising faith. Indeed, they would be a testimony to the Gentiles. Yeshua concluded His instructions regarding persecution by telling the apostles not to be concerned about what to say when they suffered mistreatment, because they would receive the right words from heaven (Mt. 10:19-20).

Second, Yeshua instructed His apostles about the scope of persecution (Mt. 10:21-23). It would grow in intensity on three levels: Their family members would persecute them, all people would hate them, and the cities would reject them.

Verse 21 elaborates on the persecution through family members. A switch from the second to the third person should be noted here: *brother shall deliver up brother to death*, etc. It indicates that the prophecy of immediate divisions and family members persecuting believers to death did not apply to the apostles, but to those who believed through them.

Verse 22 elaborates on the hatred the apostles would encounter. While they would be *hated of all men*, this, of course, excluded the believing remnant. Another subtle switch occurs in this verse from the second person (*ye shall be hated*) to the third person (*but he that endures to the end, the same shall be saved*). Those who remain faithful to the end will not die in the A.D. 70 judgment, a point which will be further developed later in this study.

Verse 23 elaborates on the rejection through the cities. When persecuted in one city, the apostles must flee to another, being wise as serpents while harmless as doves. Then Yeshua stated, *Ye shall not have gone through the cities of Yisrael, till the Son of man be come.* On one hand, this might be a reference to Yeshua's second coming, since Israel will not be fully evangelized until shortly before His return. On the other hand, this may be referring to the triumphal entry. Since Yeshua specifically addressed all these admonitions to the apostles, the latter is probably the better option. He meant that the apostles would not succeed in getting through all the cities of Israel in fulfillment of this commission before He would ride into Jerusalem on the donkey in fulfillment of Zechariah 9:9.

4. Instruction in View of Rejection

Matthew 10:24-33

Yeshua next provided instruction in view of rejection, making four points. First, He warned the apostles to expect rejection on the same basis on which He was rejected (Mt. 10:24-25). He was rejected on the basis of demon possession, and they must anticipate being rejected on the same basis: *If they have called the master of the house Beelzebub, how much more them of his household!* (Mt. 10:25). This is another *kal v'chomer*, or argument from the light to the heavy, from the lesser to the greater, reversed. If the religious leaders charged Him—the greater—with being demonized, then they would certainly refer to His followers—the lesser—as being demonized.

Second, in spite of all this persecution, they were to boldly proclaim the message: *Fear them not* (Mt. 10:26). They were to proclaim the message loud and clear from the housetops everywhere. Being wise as serpents did not include hiding the gospel.

Third, the apostles were not to fear men, but God (Mt. 10:28-31). They were not to fear those who could *kill the body, but are not able to kill the soul: but rather fear him who is able to destroy both soul and body in hell* (Mt. 10:28). Only God has that authority; therefore, they should fear Him. They were in His care, and He is in control. Whatever bad things might happen to them would happen within the will of God. They were under His watchful protection, and they needed to be conscious of this whenever they were suffering persecution.

Fourth, Yeshua spelled out an issue pertaining to that generation: *Every one therefore who shall confess me before men, him will I also confess before my Father who is in heaven. But whosoever shall deny me before men, him will I also deny before my Father who is in heaven* (Mt. 10:32-33*)*. The issue for individuals of that generation was that those who denied Yeshua before men would be denied by Yeshua in heaven; but if they affirmed Him, they would be affirmed by Yeshua in heaven. These verses are not dealing with the potential loss of salvation, but with losing one's physical life during the A.D. 70 judgment. This explains Matthew's comment: *he that endures to the end, the same shall be saved* (Mt. 10:22). Those who affirmed Yeshua until the end would survive the A.D. 70 judgment. Those who did not would die in that judgment. Furthermore, this would have ramifications later concerning rewards in the messianic kingdom.

5. The Results of the Rejection

Matthew 10:34-39

In dealing with the results of the rejection, Yeshua focused on three specific issues. First, He would become the point of division in the Jewish home and the Jewish community (Mt. 10:34-36). Had the nation accepted Him, He would have established the messianic kingdom and Israel would have experienced peace; but the kingdom could not be established until they first accepted Him as their Messianic King. Instead of bringing the peace of Jewish unity, Yeshua sent a sword of division (Mt. 10:34). Throughout Jewish history, this has proven to be true. The Jewish family unit has characteristically been close-knit, but it is instantly shattered when one member becomes a believer in Yeshua. Therefore, as a result of the nation's rejection of the Messiah, division has replaced unity and the sword has replaced peace. Malachi 4:5 prophesies that Elijah will come to heal the Jewish family unit *before the great and terrible day of Jehovah*, and then the name of Yeshua will no longer be a point of division within Israel. Matthew 10:34-39 also records the fulfillment of what was prophesied in Isaiah 8:9-15, that when *Immanuel* finally arrived, He would be the point of division between the remnant and the non-remnant. For the remnant, the

Messiah would prove to be *a sanctuary,* but for the non-remnant, He is a *stone of stumbling and a rock of offense* (Is. 8:14).

Second, Yeshua became the symbol of acceptance or rejection (Mt. 10:37-38). To take up the cross meant to identify with His rejection. The individual believer must be fully committed to discipleship, so that if forced to choose between the Messiah and the family, the apostles must reject the family for the sake of following Yeshua. This truth extends past the special commission to the apostles. While salvation is based upon pure faith and trust in the substitutionary death of the Messiah, discipleship requires a much greater commitment. This commitment must be carefully considered, but it must be made.

Third, Yeshua taught the necessity of losing one's life for Him: *He that finds his life shall lose it; and he that loses his life for my sake shall find it* (Mt. 10:39). The context of this verse is important to consider. It dealt with the consequences of the unpardonable sin. If a person tried to save his life and escape persecution by denying Yeshua, he would end up losing his life in the A.D. 70 judgment. However, if he died as a martyr, he would find true life and will be especially rewarded during the messianic kingdom.

6. Rewards for Individuals Who Accept

Matthew 10:40-42

Yeshua concluded His instructions to the apostles by discussing rewards for individuals who accepted their teaching. The principle is that those who received the apostles were viewed as having received Him, because if one receives an emissary, it is the same as if he were receiving the sender himself. To receive the ambassador is to receive the one who sent the ambassador. Even giving a follower of the Messiah a cup of water for the sake of the Messiah will bring its reward. The task, however menial it may appear, will be rewarded.

7. The Fulfillment

Matthew 11:1, Mark 6:12-13, Luke 9:6

With these words, Yeshua *had finished commanding his twelve disciples* (Mt. 11:1). Matthew emphasized again that Yeshua addressed these instructions specifically to the apostles. Having received this lengthy commission, they now went out to fulfill it. Part of their message was repentance: *And they went out, and preached that <men> should repent* (Mk. 6:12). The word *repent* means "to change one's mind." The people needed to change their minds about Yeshua; He was the Messiah and was not demon possessed. Those individuals who repented received salvation and became members of the believing remnant of that day.

[§ 73] — I. The Death of the Herald

Matthew 14:1-12, Mark 6:14-29, Luke 9:7-9

Yochanan had an active ministry of about 12 to 14 months followed by an inactive ministry in prison of less than two years. The total time of his ministry, therefore, was roughly three years, during which he was free for approximately one year.

Only at this point did Herod the tetrarch start hearing about Yeshua's miracles (Mt. 14:1). This was Herod Antipas, a nominal convert to Judaism and the son of Herod the Great, who had tried to kill Yeshua in Bethlehem when He was two years old. From what the Gospel writers say, we know that by the time Antipas heard of Yeshua, Yochanan had already been executed: *This is Yochanan the Baptist; he is risen from the dead* (Mt. 14:2). Now Antipas wanted to see the man he assumed was the risen baptizer who had performed all these miracles (Lk. 9:9). His assumption that Yeshua was really Yochanan provided the Gospel writers the opportunity to report on the baptizer's execution.

Antipas had Yochanan incarcerated, but the arrest was instigated by his wife Herodias (Mt. 14:3). This woman had a rather illustrious history. She was the granddaughter of Herod the Great, who had a number of sons by a number of different wives. His favorite wife was Mariamne, and with her, he had a son named Aristobulus. Aristobulus was Herodias' father. Eventually, Herod the Great, in his paranoia, imagined his family members were all conspiring against him, so he had several of them executed, including Mariamne and Aristobulus.

Herodias first married Philip, who himself was a son of Herod, so he was her half-uncle. She later left Philip, became the mistress of a step-uncle, and finally married Herod Antipas, another son of Herod the Great. Meanwhile, Philip, her first husband, was still alive. Furthermore, Antipas married her while his former wife was still living. So all together, Herodias was guilty of triple adultery and two counts of incest. It was her lifestyle and her marriage to Antipas that Yochanan denounced (Mk. 6:18). By marrying his brother's wife, Antipas violated Leviticus 18:16 and 20:21. By marrying her uncle, Herodias violated Leviticus 18:12-14 and 20:19-20. However, she did not want to be reprimanded for her sins and instigated Yochanan's arrest. While her husband granted the arrest, he was reluctant to have the baptizer killed, because he *feared Yochanan, knowing that he was a righteous and holy man* (Mk. 6:20a). Antipas willingly and gladly listened to the baptizer, for he recognized the truth, but *he was much perplexed* (Mk. 6:20b), because he was unwilling to rectify his sin.

When Antipas' birthday came, all the high military and civil officials of Galilee attended the celebration. Herodias' daughter, Salome, whose name in Hebrew was *Shulamit*, was at the party, and she danced to the pleasure of Antipas (Mt. 14:6). He made a foolish oath that she could have anything she wanted, up to half his kingdom (Mk. 6:22-23). Not knowing what to ask for, Salome sought her mother's advice (Mk. 6:24). And *being put forward by her mother* (Mt. 14:8), she requested the head of Yochanan the Baptizer. There was no reluctance on the daughter's part to ask for such a gift: *And she came in straightway with haste unto the king* (Mk. 6:25). She was eager to witness the beheading. Although Antipas was grieved (Mt. 14:9) and exceedingly sorry (Mk. 6:26), he kept his oath, and Yochanan was beheaded at his command (Mt. 14:10-11; Mk. 6:27-28). Yochanan's head was placed on a platter and handed to Salome who, in turn, gave it to Herodias. Yochanan's disciples were permitted to fetch the body and bury it in a tomb (Mk. 6:29), and then they informed Yeshua (Mt. 14:12).

As for Salome, she later married her uncle, Philip II. Shortly thereafter, she became a widow. She died young of a rather hideous disease and did not escape divine justice for her role in the beheading of the baptizer. The Gospels clearly show that Yochanan was arrested and killed for personal reasons, but the actual charge was political, and for the last time we can note that what happens to the herald will happen to the King. From this point on, Yeshua moved toward His own coming death.

IV. The Training of the Twelve by the King
— §§ 74–98 —

Yochanan placed the next event, the feeding of the five thousand, near Passover, stating: *Now the Passover, the feast of the Jews, was at hand* (Jn. 6:4). This was the third Passover of Yeshua's public ministry. His ministry was now two years old, and He would die in a year's time.

This period of Yeshua's life lasted until the Feast of Tabernacles, a stretch of about six months. During this time, He made four separate journeys to Gentile territory where the Jewish population was a minority. These retirements put Him outside the jurisdiction of Herod Antipas, who was trying to see Him, and in the territory of Herod Philip II, better known as Philip the Tetrarch. Philip, also a son of Herod the Great, and thus Antipas' half-brother, inherited the north-east part of his father's kingdom, including Iturea and Trachonitis.

Yeshua's withdrawals into Gentile territory also took Him to less populated, mountainous areas. The primary purpose of the sojourns was to instruct the apostles. The special instructions delivered in this section were a direct result of the rejection of the Messiahship of Yeshua and the unpardonable sin.

[§ 74] — A. The Feeding of the Five Thousand

Matthew 14:13-21, Mark 6:30-44, Luke 9:10-17, John 6:1-13

The feeding of the five thousand is unique, as it is the only miracle recorded in all four Gospels. It is the fourth of Yochanan's seven signs. Since Yeshua's purpose was to train the twelve, He used this incident to teach them the nature of the ministry with which they were to be entrusted and to instruct them in His ability to provide for their needs. The situation that brought this miracle about is found in the Gospel of Mark (Mk. 6:30-31). The apostles were reporting to Yeshua concerning the mission He had sent them on, two by two. Their success was obvious, and Yeshua invited them to rest for a while: *For there were many coming and going, and they had no leisure so much as to eat* (Mk. 6:31). The *many coming and going* created this particular situation. Mark and Matthew described the location to which Yeshua and the apostles withdrew as *a desert place* (Mk. 6:32; Mt. 14:13). Yochanan stated that they crossed *to the other side of the sea of Galil* (Jn. 6:1). Luke specified it was to a city called Bethsaida (Lk. 9:10), in Herod Philip's territory. By water, this was a four or five mile journey, and by land, it was about ten miles. This was the first of Yeshua's withdrawals into Gentile territory, and in spite of the religious leaders' explanation that His power was from Beelzebub, interest in His person was still strong among the masses. They followed Him by foot, gathering from all the nearby cities, and waited for Him to arrive (Mt. 14:13-14; Mk. 6:33-34; Lk. 9:11). Yochanan specified their motivation: They *followed him, because they beheld the signs which he did on them that were sick* (Jn. 6:2). The interest of the masses was still strong because of the miracles they had seen Him perform. However, the focus was on the physical benefits, not on spiritual appropriation.

While five thousand were fed, the actual purpose of this event was the training of the twelve apostles. Yeshua's original purpose had been to get away from the multitudes, but they followed, and since they did, He was going to use them as a backdrop to teach His disciples. The miracles they witnessed were intended to instruct, even though He taught and healed the masses. This can be seen in the text itself as the focus moves from the masses to the individual apostles with whom Yeshua spoke.

Yeshua continued to respond to specific personal needs. Mark described His view of the people: *And he came forth and saw a great multitude, and he had compassion on them, because they were as sheep not having a shepherd* (Mk. 6:34). The question the multitude still contended with was, "Shall we follow the old shepherds, or the new one?" Their indecision made them as sheep without a shepherd. Yeshua had compassion on them and continued His ministry of healing (Mt. 14:14) and teaching (Mk. 6:34; Lk. 9:11) due to the personal needs of the multitude. Modeling the nature of the work of a spiritual shepherd, He engaged in the ministry of a pastor-teacher, instructing the flock in the truth and attending to them by healing and feeding them, thus meeting a specific physical need. It is not the job of the sheep to look for food; rather, it is the job of the shepherd to feed the flock.

Toward the end of the day, Yeshua taught the last lesson (Mk. 6:35). The context of His continual conversation with the apostles demonstrates His intention to teach them specifically. The disciples suggested that He send the masses away to find food for themselves (Mt. 14:15; Mk. 6:35-36; Lk. 9:12). They complained that since they were in a desert area, food would be scarce. Yeshua responded by saying: *Give ye them to eat* (Mt. 14:16; Mk. 6:37; Lk. 9:13). However, during part of the conversation, He focused on one specific apostle: *Yeshua therefore lifting up his eyes, and seeing that a great multitude comes unto him, said unto Philip, Whence are we to buy bread, that these may eat?* (Jn. 6:5). Yeshua already knew what He was going to do, so why did He ask Philip this question? Yochanan specified that He did so in order *to prove* (Jn. 6:6) or test the apostle. This was Philip's home territory (Jn. 1:44), and he would know there was not enough food available in the area for such a large crowd, nor would they have the money to buy it. Not even *two hundred shillings' worth of bread* would be sufficient (Jn. 6:7a). The Greek term here is *denarion*, which is a loan word from the Latin *denarius*. One denarius was equal to one day's wages (Mt. 20:2). Even two hundred days' salary would not have been sufficient, *that everyone may take a little* (Jn. 6:7b). In the first century, one denarius bought ten quarts of wheat or thirty quarts of barley. Therefore, two hundred denarii would have bought two thousand quarts of wheat or six thousand quarts of barley. Even this was not enough to feed the multitude of people who were present.

Philip was already involved in the conversation when another apostle, Peter's brother Andrew, joined them. Yeshua asked how much food was available (Mk. 6:38); after some checking, Andrew answered: *There is a lad here, who has five barley loaves, and two fishes: but what are these among so many?* (Jn. 6:9). Obviously, five loaves and two fish would not be sufficient to feed all those people. Yeshua instructed them to separate the multitudes into groups. *And they sat down in ranks, by hundreds, and by fifties* (Mk. 6:40). Yochanan observed that *there was much grass in the place* (Jn. 6:10). This would be true around Passover (early spring), even in desert areas.

At that point, the miracle occurred. In keeping with Jewish practice, Yeshua first recited the special blessing over the bread[1] (Mt. 14:19; Mk. 6:41; Lk. 9:16; Jn. 6:11) and had the disciples distribute the bread and then the fish. All four Gospels testify that enough food came from those five loaves and two fish to feed everyone present, and all were filled. Furthermore, there were twelve baskets of leftovers of both bread and fish (Mk. 6:43). Yeshua personally instructed the apostles to gather the leftovers *that nothing be lost* (Jn. 6:12).

All four Gospels emphasize that a total of five thousand attended this special meal (Mt. 14:21; Mk. 6:44; Lk. 9:14; Jn. 6:10). Matthew, however, specified that this number only included the men. Many women and children were also present, so the actual figure was considerably higher.

As previously mentioned, this miracle was intended as a teaching tool for the disciples, and Yeshua reminded them of the incident later. It introduced His teaching about the nature of the ministry entrusted to them. At that time, theirs was a physical ministry, but later it would be a spiritual one. The apostles learned at least three lessons. First, they were responsible for feeding the people: *Give ye them to eat* (Lk. 9:13).

---

[1] *Blessed be You, O Lord our God, who brings forth bread from the earth.*

At this point, it was a physical feeding; later it would be a spiritual feeding. Second, they had to realize that they were incapable of feeding the multitudes by themselves (Jn. 6:5-9). Third, they were to distribute that which the Messiah provided: *he . . . gave the loaves to the disciples, and the disciples to the multitudes* (Mt. 14:19).

[§ 75] — B. Messiah's Rejection of the Galileans' Offer to Make Him King

Matthew 14:22-23, Mark 6:45-46, John 6:14-15

The event described in these verses was a direct result of the miracle just performed by Yeshua, the feeding of the five thousand Galileans. After the feeding, Yeshua sent His disciples by boat to western Bethsaida (Mk. 6:45). He intended to dismiss the multitudes and send them home (Mt. 14:22), but they had just seen the sign He had done and declared Him to be the prophet of Deuteronomy 18:15-18 (Jn. 6:14). Now, because they were all fed and full, they wanted to make Him king of Galilee (Jn. 6:15). Their motive was to continue to be fed physically. When Yeshua perceived that they were forcibly going to make Him king of Galilee, He separated from them and *withdrew again into the mountain himself alone* (Jn. 6:15). He succeeded in being there alone (Mt. 14:23) and began praying (Mk. 6:46).

Yeshua rejected the people's offer of kingship over Galilee for three reasons. First, the leadership of Israel had already rejected Him, thus committing the unpardonable sin. They had irrevocably reached the point of no return. It was too late for them to crown Him king. Second, they were trying to make Him king of Galilee; however, Old Testament prophecies, such as Psalm 2, declared that Jerusalem, not Galilee, was to be the place of Messiah's enthronement. Third, their motive was wrong. They wanted to make Him king only because He had met their physical need, and they liked the idea of being fed without working. Yeshua commented on wrong motives when He met these Galileans at a later time (see § 78).

[§ 76] — C. The Training through the Storm

Matthew 14:24-33, Mark 6:47-52, John 6:16-21

The event described in these verses marks the fifth of Yochanan's seven signs. The lesson for the apostles was dependence on the Messiah in any and every situation. Yeshua sent them by way of the sea to Capernaum (Jn. 6:17), and He went to the mountain to pray. While separated from Him, the apostles again found themselves in a desperate situation.

As described by three Gospel accounts, their predicament in the storm involved four specific elements. First, the storm occurred at sunset: *And when even was come* (Mk. 6:47). Yochanan added that *it was now dark* (Jn. 6:17). Second, they were in the middle of the lake: *But the boat was now in the midst of the sea* (Mt. 14:24). For the second time in the Gospel records, the sudden winds came down, causing a storm to rage across the lake. Third, they were in the storm for about nine hours. Mark stated that they began to sail when the sun was setting and further specified that it was *about the fourth watch of the night*, which falls between 3:00 and 6:00 a.m., thus making it about nine hours that they had spent on the lake already (Mk. 6:47-48). Fourth, it was a totally hopeless situation; they were *distressed in rowing, for the wind was contrary unto them* (Mk. 6:48a). Matthew added that they were *distressed by the waves; for the wind was contrary* (Mt. 14:24). Yochanan described the situation with the following words: *And the sea was rising by reason of a great wind that blew* (Jn. 6:18). He furthermore revealed how much they had to struggle during this nine-hour period: *they had rowed about five and twenty or thirty furlongs* (Jn. 6:19), which is about three-and-a-half miles. They covered that distance in nine hours because the storm was contrary to them. They were still in the middle of the lake, not making any sig-nificant progress.

They were in the boat by themselves, because Yeshua had sent them ahead. He was conscious of their situation, however. From the land, He saw their distress (Mk. 6:47-48). In all this time, Yeshua *had not yet come to them* (Jn. 6:17). At that point, they saw Him walking on the water. Even then, He was not walking toward the boat, but in a direction in which *he would have passed by them* (Mk. 6:48). The lesson they had to learn as He appeared to be passing by was that they must call on Him for help.

Seeing Him approach the boat was not comforting, but frightening to them (Jn. 6:19). They believed they were looking at an apparition: *but they, when they saw him walking on the sea, supposed that it was a ghost, and cried out; for they all saw him, and were troubled* (Mk. 6:49-50). Matthew added: *they were troubled, saying, It is a ghost; and they cried out for fear* (Mt. 14:26). Perhaps they were fearful because they thought this approaching figure was the angel of death.

At this point, Yeshua comforted them: *Be of good cheer: it is I; be not afraid* (Mk. 6:50). In the New Testament, the Greek word for "to be of good cheer," *tharseó*, is only used in relation to Yeshua. Once the apostles realized it was Yeshua walking on the water towards them, their fear subsided: *They were willing therefore to receive him into the boat* (Jn. 6:21).

Matthew added the account of Peter, who requested that he be allowed to step out and walk on the water toward Yeshua (Mt. 14:28). Yeshua called upon him to do so and said, *Come* (Mt. 14:29). Indeed, Peter, in faith, *went down from the boat* and walked on the water to go to his Messiah. Yeshua permitted this miracle to occur for Peter's benefit, and as long as the apostle kept his eyes on Him, he was able to walk on water. However, at some point the disciple turned his eyes away from the Lord and looked upon the wind: *But when he saw the wind, he was afraid; and beginning to sink, he cried out, saying, Lord, save me* (Mt. 14:30a). Peter did not wait until he sank before crying out for help, and Yeshua rescued him by grabbing his hand (Mt. 14:31a). The lesson Peter had to learn from this was that not only must he begin in faith, he must continue to walk in faith. Yeshua emphasized the point when He said, *O you of little faith, wherefore did you doubt?* (Mt. 14:31b). Furthermore, the lesson included the principle that obedience to Yeshua's command does not automatically remove all obstacles. Yeshua commanded Peter to come, but that did not guarantee that the wind would cease. The wind was still blowing, which is what caused Peter to become so fearful. When a person experiences obstacles, he is not necessarily outside of God's will or has misinterpreted His command. Despite obstacles, he must continue to exercise obedience and allow God to remove the obstacles in His time. Only when Yeshua got into the boat did the winds cease (Mt. 14:32; Mk. 6:51). Yochanan added: *and straightway the boat was at the land whither they were going* (Jn. 6:21). They had been struggling in the middle of the lake, and suddenly they were at the shore; Yeshua got them to safety. They would not need to do any more rowing that day.

They had to learn dependence on the Messiah in any and all situations. They should already have learned this lesson from the feeding of the five thousand, a point made by Mark: *and they were sore amazed in themselves; for they understood not concerning the loaves, but their heart was hardened* (Mk. 6:51-52). Their failure to learn that lesson explained why they were so fearful. Matthew stated: *And they that were in the boat worshipped him, saying, Of a truth you are the Son of God* (Mt. 14:33). Here is an example of good theology, but bad application. The disciples clearly knew He was *the Son of God* (good theology), but they had not learned to depend on Him (bad application). They became fearful in a situation in which they should have trusted the Lord. A spiritual life without good theology is impossible. On the other hand, good theology without good application will result in spiritual deadness. The believer must apply good theology to daily life.

[§ 77] — D. The Reception in Gennesaret

Matthew 14:34-36, Mark 6:53-56

Yeshua and the apostles again crossed by boat to the other side of the Sea of Galilee. They came *to the land, unto Ginosar* (Mt. 14:34), which meant they were back in Jewish territory.[2]

Word of Yeshua's presence spread quickly, causing multitudes to come to Him, primarily for healing (Mk. 6:54-56). Yeshua was still responding to personal needs: *and they besought him that they might only*

---

[2] In the Plain of Ginosar or Gennesaret.

touch the border of his garment: and as many as touched were made whole (Mt. 14:36). They came to Him, besieging Him, because they had personal needs. Just like the woman afflicted with the bleeding disorder in Luke 8:44, they dared to *touch the border of His garment* (Mt. 14:36; Mk. 6:56b). Again, the *border* refers to the tassels, the *tzitzit*, which Yeshua wore in obedience to the Mosaic Law. They touched the tassels of His garment, an act of faith. Furthermore, the fact that they came to Yeshua in the first place showed that these particular ones had faith. Therefore, based on their personal needs and their faith, they were healed. The majority of the people, however, did not believe, as the next section will reveal.

[§ 78] — E. Instruction
Concerning the Bread of Life

John 6:22-71

This section contains the third of Yochanan's seven discourses, the discourse on the bread of life. During this speech, Yeshua made the first of the seven "I Am" statements recorded by Yochanan, saying, *I am the bread of life* (Jn. 6:35, 48), and, *I am the living bread* (Jn. 6:51). He offered the people who surrounded Him a new kind of life, but in keeping with His policy since the rejection in Matthew 12, He spoke in terms they could not and did not understand, as their responses constantly showed.

Yochanan begins the account with the historical background (Jn. 6:22-25). The following day, the same multitudes whom Yeshua had freely fed and who had wanted to make Him king searched for Him again. They knew He had not sailed away with His disciples, so they returned to the place where the miracle had occurred, but He was not there. They found Him in Capernaum teaching in the synagogue (Jn. 6:59). When they asked Yeshua how He got to Capernaum (they had not seen Him miraculously walking on water), He took the opportunity to reveal their true motives behind wanting to make Him king: *Ye seek me, not because ye saw signs, but because ye ate of the loaves, and were filled* (Jn. 6:26). Having rejected His Messiahship, they wanted the physical, not the spiritual benefits. Note that this was a widespread expectation of the time, as the Babylonian Talmud shows: "The Jews are destined to eat [their fill] in the days of the Messiah."[3] Yeshua, however, offered them something much better than the temporary satisfaction of physical needs. He offered them a new kind of life described in four ways:

1. This new life is eternal: *Work not for the food which perishes, but for the food which abides unto eternal life, which the Son of man shall give unto you* (Jn. 6:27).

2. It is a heavenly life because it originates with the Father: *It was not Mosheh that gave you the bread out of heaven; but my Father gives you the true bread out of heaven. For the bread of God is that which comes down out of heaven, and gives life unto the world* (Jn. 6:32-33).

3. It is a satisfying life: *I am the bread of life: he that comes to me shall not hunger, and he that believes on me shall never thirst* (Jn. 6:35). This life leads to spiritual fullness, where there is no longer spiritual hunger or spiritual thirst.

4. It will lead to resurrection life: *And this is the will of him that sent me, that of all that which he has given me I should lose nothing, but should raise it up at the last day. For this is the will of my Father, that everyone that beholds the Son, and believes on him, should have eternal life; and I will raise him up at the last day* (Jn. 6:39-40). The physical body may die. However, because the new life is eternal and heavenly, eventually it will produce resurrection life, and the body will be raised.

This new kind of life is available to all, but it must be found in the person of Yeshua the Messiah.

Yeshua described the four facets of the new kind of life He was offering them, but the people's response indicates that He stated it in terms they could not understand (Jn. 6:41-42, 52):

---

[3] *b. Sanhedrin* 98b.

⁴¹ The Jews therefore murmured concerning him, because he said, I am the bread which came down out of heaven. ⁴² And they said, Is not this Yeshua, the son of Yoseph, whose father and mother we know? How does he now say, I am come down out of heaven? . . . ⁵² The Jews therefore strove one with another, saying, How can this man give us his flesh to eat?

Their response shows their inability to distinguish between the physical and the spiritual. They understood the physical, but they failed to understand the spiritual appropriation because Yeshua had deliberately spoken in parables.

Yeshua went on to admonish His audience, *Work not for the food which perishes, but for the food which abides unto eternal life, which the Son of man shall give unto you* (Jn. 6:27). They needed to work for eternal life, and not for physical food. In answer to their question, *What must we do, that we may work the works of God?* (Jn. 6:28), Yeshua responded, *This is the work of God, that ye believe on him whom he has sent* (Jn. 6:29). Salvation is by the work of God, and the work of God that saves is to believe that Yeshua is the Messiah. Thus, the work of God that saves is to believe on the One whom He has sent.

However, the people still wanted physical food and requested an authenticating sign (Jn. 6:30), something He would no longer provide. By referring to *the manna in the wilderness* (Jn. 6:31), they were very specific as to the kind of sign they wanted to see, saying in effect, "Moses brought manna from heaven. What are you going to do?" Again, the focus was on the material. Yeshua reminded His listeners that it was not Moses who brought down the manna, but God Himself (Jn. 6:32-33). Moses only told the Israelites about it and provided the rules for gathering, but it was God's provision. Now, God was again providing for them by offering *the true bread out of heaven* and the bread that *gives life unto the world* (Jn. 6:32-33). While Yeshua was speaking of spiritual life, the audience understood only at the physical level and said: *Lord, evermore give us this bread* (Jn. 6:34). To this Yeshua responded, again speaking in parables, *I am the bread of life* (Jn. 6:35), furthering their misunderstanding. They sought physical food, but, obviously, they could not eat Him!

In spite of all the unbelief, Yeshua declared He would still accomplish the mission for which He had been sent (Jn. 6:36-40). His ministry would not end in failure. All whom the Father had chosen to give Him would come to Him, and those who did come would never be cast out. He would not lose a single one who believed on Him, and to those who believed, He promised resurrection from the dead.

The people's reaction was widespread unbelief and murmuring (Jn. 6:41-42). The context of their response needs to be kept in mind. The people compared Yeshua to Moses, so it is with deliberateness that Yochanan used the word *murmur*. In spite of the manna that God had provided for the Israelites in the wilderness, they still murmured against Him (Ex. 16-17). Now God provided for them a heavenly bread, the bread of life, and they still murmured. They knew Yeshua's parents personally and so they questioned His claim that He came *down out of heaven* (Jn. 6:42). The content of their grumbling again shows that Yeshua spoke in parables. He taught in ways they did not understand, and while they may have known about His human origin, they did not know of His divine origin.

Yeshua explained the reason for their unbelief: *No man can come to me, except the Father that sent me draw him: and I will raise him up in the last day. . . . Every one that has heard from the Father, and has learned, comes unto me* (Jn. 6:44-45). They were unable to come to Him on their own; but those whom God drew would come to Him without fail.

Yeshua continues to explain that if they wished to have eternal life, they must eat His flesh and drink His blood (Jn. 6:46-51). He was not referring to communion in this context. In fact, Yochanan's Gospel is the only one that gives no account of the bread and cup ceremony. Rather, as Yeshua defined it in this context, to eat His flesh and drink His blood meant to believe that He is the Messiah sent by God. Communion does not produce eternal life. Yeshua declared what would produce eternal life: *He that believes has eternal life* (Jn. 6:47). This kind of life is found only in the person of the Messiah, and they must believe that He was that Messianic Person.

He taught all this in parables, so they could not understand (Jn. 6:52). He answered their question, but continued to speak in terms that made no sense to them (Jn. 6:53b-57):

> *53b I say unto you, Except ye eat the flesh of the Son of man and drink his blood, ye have not life in yourselves. 54 He that eats my flesh and drinks my blood has eternal life: 55 and I will raise him up at the last day. For my flesh is meat indeed, and my blood is drink indeed. 56 He that eats my flesh and drinks my blood abides in me, and I in him. 57 As the living Father sent me, and I live because of the Father; so he that eats me, he also shall live because of me.*

Just as food taken into the body becomes part of the body, the Messiah becomes part of the person who puts his faith in Him. He will live in that person, and that person, in turn, will live in the Messiah. Yeshua reiterated that He is the bread that came down from heaven and will produce eternal life (Jn. 6:58). Manna sustained the physical life in the wilderness, but it did not provide eternal life.

It was impossible for the multitudes to understand what Yeshua was saying, but it was also difficult for many of His disciples outside the apostolic group of twelve: *Many therefore of his disciples, when they heard <this>, said, This is a hard saying; who can hear it?* (Jn. 6:60). Many of these disciples joined in the murmuring (Jn. 6:61). If they stumbled over the teaching that He came down from heaven, how would they respond to His ascension into heaven? Here, Yeshua restated a previous teaching, but this time directed it toward these disciples and not the multitude: *It is the spirit that gives life; the flesh profits nothing: the words that I have spoken unto you are spirit, and are life* (Jn. 6:63). His words were hard to understand and accept, and yet to understand and believe is what produces eternal life. Yochanan added an editorial comment, saying that Yeshua always knew who among His followers believed and who did not; and He knew from the beginning who would betray Him (Jn. 6:64). Yeshua repeated what He had said earlier: *For this cause have I said unto you, that no man can come unto me, except it be given unto him of the Father* (Jn. 6:65), thus explaining their unbelief.

The bread of life discourse led to three specific results (Jn. 6:66-71). First, many disciples outside the apostolic group left Yeshua: *Upon this many of His disciples went back, and walked no more with him* (Jn. 6:66). Second, eleven of the twelve apostles reaffirmed their belief. When He asked them, *Would ye also go away?* Peter answered Him, *Lord, to whom shall we go? You have the words of eternal life. And we have believed and know that you are the Holy One of God* (Jn. 6:67-69). Third, for Judas, this discourse began the road to his apostasy. For the first time, the Gospel accounts identify him as the coming traitor, indicating that his apostasy began here (Jn. 6:70-71).

[§ 79] — F. Instruction Concerning Defilement

Matthew 15:1-20, Mark 7:1-23, John 7:1

So far in the study of the conflict between Yeshua and the Pharisees, two major issues concerning Mishnaic Law were discussed: the issue of fasting (§ 49) and the proper way to keep the Sabbath (§§ 50-52). Here, a third issue arose: the ritual washing of hands before eating. Because Matthew was writing to Jews, he did not need to provide any background information about the Pharisaic tradition that was at issue here. Mark, on the other hand, wrote his Gospel account for Gentiles. Since they might not have known about such issues, he provided more details (Mk. 7:3-4).

By Yeshua's day, the Mishnah had become of equal authority with Scripture, sometimes even surpassing God's Word. If someone were to contradict only Scripture, he was not seen as a rebel, but if he contradicted the rabbis, he was considered a rebel. Mark explained their extreme caution about one of the major areas of their law: They were forbidden to partake of even the smallest seed until they first washed their hands (Mk. 7:1-4). The Greek term used here, *niptó,* suggests that they washed up to the elbow. Moses never commanded such extremism in washing hands before eating, and Mark stated that this was all based on *the tradition of the elders* (Mk. 7:3), the New Testament term for the Mishnah. Yeshua obviously did not follow this tradition. The incident described in Matthew 15 and Mark 7 occurred in Galilee (Jn. 7:1). For the time being, Yeshua would avoid Judea because He knew of the conspiracy to kill Him. Therefore, the scribes and Pharisees traveled from Jerusalem to Galilee to instigate the controversy (Mt. 15:1; Mk. 7:1). This was a rather long, three-day journey to stir up something that was not an issue according to the Mosaic Law, but which was a major issue for the Pharisees and the scribes. They launched their attack, asking Yeshua: *Why walk not your disciples according to the tradition of the elders, but eat their bread with defiled hands?* (Mk. 7:5). They never had a single opportunity to accuse Yeshua of violating the Mosaic Law, because He kept it perfectly, down to every jot and tittle. They could only accuse Him of breaking the Mishnaic Law, but without much of an impression upon Him. He readily admitted breaking Mishnaic Law and sometimes went well out of His way to do so.

In His response, Yeshua pointed out three things about Pharisaic traditionalism: First, He applied Isaiah 29:13 to the Pharisees and scribes, stating that the true nature of their traditionalism was hypocrisy, because *in vain do they worship me, Teaching <as their> doctrines the precepts of men* (Mk. 7:6-7). Legalism outwardly mimics spirituality, so these people looked religious and spiritual because they lived a legalistic lifestyle. They believed they were honoring and worshipping God by keeping this set of man-made rules and regulations. In truth, it was an empty, vain worship, because they made the precepts of men their doctrine rather than what Scripture spelled out. Indeed, obedience to divine commands is an act of worship. Israel was to show their love for God by obeying His laws (Deut. 6:4-9). Later, Yeshua will say that to love Him is to keep His commandments (Jn. 14:15, 21). Keeping God's commandments is a means of worshipping Him; keeping those made by man is not. If the focus is on man-made traditions and not on God's law, it is no longer worship but hypocrisy. Second, *Ye leave the commandment of God, and hold fast the tradition of men* (Mk. 7:8). Sometimes, keeping a tradition may mean passively ignoring a divine commandment. Third, *Full well do ye reject the commandment of God, that ye may keep your tradition* (Mk. 7:9). Sometimes, to keep a tradition involves rejecting a divine commandment, and this is what the Pharisees and scribes did. Matthew stated it more emphatically: *Why do ye also transgress the commandment of God because of your tradition?* (Mt. 15:3).

Yeshua gave an example of their behavior by elaborating on the principle of the *corban* (Mk. 7:10-13).[4] This Hebrew word means "dedicated" and describes anything that has been set aside. At any time, a Pharisee could raise his hand and say *corban*, meaning that everything he owned at that moment, materially speaking, had been dedicated.[5] Therefore, he could do one of two things with his assets. He could give all or part of it to the Temple treasury, or he could keep it for his own private use. What he could *not* do was donate it for somebody else's private use. The Law of Moses said, *Honor your father and your mother* (Ex. 20:12). The development of this Mosaic commandment included the fact that children were responsible for the welfare of their older parents if they became physically or mentally too infirm to take care of themselves. That was the Law of Moses. Many Pharisees were converts to Pharisaism, while their parents were not. Pharisees were reluctant to share their material possessions with non-Pharisees, even if they were related. To get around this issue and using a form of pilpulistic logic, the son would declare his present possessions as corban. Legally, he then could do nothing on behalf of his parents. This did not necessitate his intention to donate his material goods to the Temple treasury; he could opt to keep it for his own private use. By means of this tradition, Pharisees actively broke the Mosaic commandment to honor one's father and mother. In the words of Matthew: *And ye have made void the word of God because of your tradition* (Mt. 15:6).

Mark added, *and many such like things ye do* (Mk. 7:13). The examples from the Mishnah and other rabbinic writings are numerous.

The interaction with the Pharisees is followed by yet another example of Yeshua's new procedures since the rejection: *And he called to him the multitude again, and said unto them, Hear me all of you, and understand* (Mk. 7:14). He spoke to the multitudes in parables so that no one, not even His own disciples, understood: *And when he was entered into the house from the multitude, his disciples asked of him the parable* (Mk. 7:17). His procedure remained consistent after the rejection. Publicly, He taught in parables so that no one understood, because for the

---

[4] Another term used in place of *corban* is *konam* or *qonam*.

[5] The fuller form was *korban she-ani nehene lecha*, "a gift by whatever thing I may be profitable to you."

masses, the purpose was to hide the truth. Once He was alone with the apostles, He explained the meaning of the parables, for the purpose of illustrating the truth.

Matthew added a detail that preceded the apostles' request for an interpretation of the parable: *Then came the disciples, and said unto him, Do you know that the Pharisees were offended, when they heard this saying?* (Mt. 15:12). Yeshua responded that sometimes giving offense is necessary for the sake of the truth (Mt. 15:13-14) and stated three things about the Pharisees: First, *Every plant which my heavenly Father planted not, shall be rooted up.* The Pharisees were plants not planted by God and, therefore, must be uprooted. Second, *Let them alone: they are blind guides.* They were blind guides leading the blind and should be ignored. Third, *And if the blind guide the blind, both shall fall into a pit.* Both the blind guides and those led by them would fall into the pit of destruction in A.D. 70.

After this short interruption, the apostles asked Yeshua to explain the parable. Mark mentioned that it was the disciples in general who made the request (Mk. 7:17). Matthew, on the other hand, pointed out that Peter, as their spokesman (Mt. 15:15), was the one who raised the question.

In His explanation, Yeshua first expressed disappointment that the disciples did not yet understand the issue of where defilement really begins (Mt. 15:16-20). In the Pharisaic interpretation, defilement was only external. A person was not defiled until he did the external thing, e.g., until he actually ate forbidden meat, like pork. However, the true righteousness of the law focused on the matters of the heart. Before a Jew actually ate the pork, he first made a decision in his heart to do so. Once he made that decision, he was already defiled inwardly, and the internal defilement led to the external defilement: *For out of the heart come forth evil thoughts, murders, adulteries, fornications, thefts, false witness, railings: these are the things which defile the man; but to eat with unwashen hands defiles not the man* (Mt. 15:19-20), since this was Pharisaic, not Mosaic Law.

Mark added a detail: *<This he said>, making all meats clean* (Mk. 7:19). Part of the messianic mission was to remove the distinction between the clean and the unclean in the realm of food. With His death,

Yeshua rendered the Mosaic Law inoperative, and all meats became clean. This point is reaffirmed in the subsequent writings of the apostles, such as Romans 14:14. Although Peter had raised the question, he did not learn the lesson himself. In Acts 10, God had to teach it to him all over again.

[§ 80] — G. The Reception in Tyre and Sidon

Matthew 15:21-28, Mark 7:24-30

The event described in these verses marks Yeshua's second withdrawal into Gentile territory, specifically the areas of Tyre and Sidon. God sent Elijah to this same region, known then as Phoenicia and the home of Jezebel (I Kgs. 18). By New Testament times, the same area was known as Syro-Phoenicia, since Phoenicia had become a part of the Roman province of Syria. Today, the region is called Lebanon. Although it was always part of the Promised Land, Israel never obtained it. In Yeshua's day, His reputation had spread into this largely Greek-speaking, Gentile area of Phoenicia.

Yeshua intended to have a private time with His disciples: *And he entered into a house, and would have no man know it* (Mk. 7:24a). However, His fame was spreading ahead of Him, *and he could not be hid* (Mk. 7:24b). A persistent woman soon interrupted Him. Mark called her *a Greek, a Syro-Phoenician by race* (Mk. 7:26). Matthew wrote that she was *a Canaanitish woman* (Mt. 15:22). *Canaanite* was a generic term for a combined number of specific Canaanite tribes, such as the Perezites, the Hivites, the Jebusites, etc.; the Phoenicians were also a branch of the Canaanites. Therefore, this woman was a descendant of the ancient Canaanites through the Phoenician tribe. She was a Syro-Phoenician, since she was a resident of this Roman, Greek-speaking province. She was a Gentile, and that is the key to what happened here.

Hearing of His presence, she came to Yeshua and cried, *Have mercy on me, O Lord, you son of David, my daughter is grievously vexed with a demon* (Mt. 15:22). By calling Him *son of David*, she was asking for a miracle based on His messianic character, the very attribute rejected by the Jewish leaders. However, His Messiahship was intended for Israel, not for the Gentiles, and on that basis, He would not respond: *But he answered her not a word* (Mt. 15:23). When she kept pressing the issue, Yeshua explained the problem to her: *I was not sent but unto the lost sheep of the house of Yisrael* (Mt. 15:24). So the woman changed the basis of her plea: *But she came and worshipped him, saying, Lord, help me* (Mt. 15:25). Now she approached Yeshua not on the basis of His Messiahship, which was intended for Israel, but on the basis of her own personal need: *Lord, help me.* However, she needed faith. To make sure she understood the lesson, *he answered and said, It is not meet to take the children's bread and cast it to the dogs* (Mt. 15:26). The point was that it was improper to take that which was promised to the Jewish people and give it to the Gentiles. The portion of food intended for the children's sustenance should not be given to pets, leaving the children hungry. Mark's version quotes Yeshua as saying: *Let the children first be filled* (Mk. 7:27).

Both Gospel accounts quote Yeshua using the term *dogs* in reference to Gentiles. However, this should not be understood as negatively as the English might imply. The Greek word used here is *kynaria*, meaning "puppies." So it is not a reference to mangy street dogs, but rather household pets, fed from the table, but not from the children's portion.

The woman's response shows that she had learned the lesson He intended to teach: *But she said, Yea, Lord: for even the dogs eat of the crumbs which fall from their masters' table* (Mt. 15:27). This comment primarily displayed faith rather than cleverness. She was not asking for that which belonged to the children, i.e., for that which was intended for Israel. She asked only for that which was extended to the Gentiles, understanding that the Jewish covenants promised certain benefits would even be extended to the Gentiles (Gen. 12:3).

She came on the basis of personal need, and Yeshua's answer revealed her faith: *O woman, great is your faith: be it done unto you even as you will* (Mt. 15:28b). On that basis, the answer was "Yes." *And her daughter was healed from that hour* (Mt. 15:28c). *And she went away unto her house, and found the child laid upon the bed, and the demon gone out* (Mk. 7:30).

[§ 81] — H. The Reception in Decapolis

Matthew 15:29-38, Mark 7:31-8:9

This section marks Yeshua's third withdrawal into Gentile territory: *And again he went out from the borders of Tzor, and came through Tzidon unto the sea of Galil, through the midst of the borders of Decapolis* (Mk. 7:31). As previously mentioned, Decapolis was a union of ten Gentile-Greek cities, of which only one, Scythopolis,[6] was west of the Jordan River. The other nine were east of the Jordan in a primarily Greek-speaking, Gentile region with a minority population of Jewish residents. During Yeshua's last visit, He healed the men possessed by a legion of demons (see § 68). After having witnessed the miracle, the inhabitants asked Him to leave the territory, which He did. One of the men Yeshua healed asked to become His disciple, but at that point, He was not accepting Gentile disciples. Instead, He sent the man back to proclaim what God had done for him, which he did in the cities of the Decapolis. As a result of his ministry, this time, the inhabitants welcomed Yeshua (Mt. 15:30).

Mark alone recorded the incident of the healing of a deaf man who also *had an impediment in his speech* (Mk. 7:32). The nature and style of the healing shows that the individual was a member of one of these small Jewish communities within the Greek cities of the Decapolis (Mk. 7:33-37. For that reason, Yeshua used the same procedure that had been in force since the rejection. The incident began when *they bring unto him one that was deaf* (Mk. 7:32a). Apparently, several friends brought this man to Yeshua, because Mark stated: *and they beseech him to lay his hand upon him* (Mk. 7:32b). Interestingly, these men suggested what method of healing Yeshua should use: the laying on of hands. As it turned out, Messiah decided to do this. Notably, He did not always use the same approach in His healing ministry. The main problem was twofold: The man was deaf, and he had a speech impediment. However, besides the friends, a multitude of people were present, and Yeshua was no longer performing miracles on behalf of the masses.

---

[6] In the Hebrew Scriptures, Scythopolis is called Beth-Shean.

Therefore, *he took him aside from the multitude privately* (Mk. 7:33). This was His new policy: no more signs for the general population.

Mark observed carefully how Yeshua proceeded: He put His fingers in the man's ears in order to deal with his deafness (Mk. 7:33b). Then He spat and placed His own saliva on the man's tongue in order to deal with his impediment of speech (Mk. 7:33c). Next, He looked up to heaven for the Father's help (Mk. 7:34a). He sighed, and then He commanded the healing (Mk. 7:34b). The result was that both problems disappeared: *And his ears were opened, and the bond of his tongue was loosed, and he spoke plain* (Mk. 7:35).

Yeshua also continued His policy of silence, charging *them that they should tell no man* (Mk. 7:36a). However, they published it all over (Mk. 7:36b-37), resulting in a great multitude coming for healing (Mt. 15:30-31a). This time, the Gentiles of the Decapolis did not ask Him to leave, but welcomed Him and His ministry among them, *and they glorified the God of Yisrael* (Mt. 15:31b). Gentiles were responding to Yeshua while Jews were rejecting Him.

Both Matthew and Mark recorded the miracle of the feeding of the four thousand. While there are many similarities between this event and the feeding of the five thousand described in § 74, the situation was also quite different. This time, Yeshua's audience was almost exclusively Gentile, the result of the ministry of the demonized man.

Again, Yeshua's focus was on teaching the disciples, and He *called unto him his disciples* (Mt. 15:32). He wanted to ensure they understood the situation in order to learn the lesson correctly, and so He said: *I have compassion on the multitude, because they continue with me now three days, and have nothing to eat: and if I send them away fasting to their home, they will faint on the way; and some of them are come from far* (Mk. 8:2-3). To this, the apostles inquired: *Whence shall one be able to fill these men with bread here in a desert place?* (Mk. 8:4b). Their response reveals their failure to learn the lesson of the previous feeding—that Yeshua can provide in these situations. Focusing on the disciples, He asked them, *How many loaves have ye?* (Mt. 15:34a), and they answered: *Seven, and a few small fishes* (Mt. 15:34b). The numbers and figures differ from the feeding of the five thousand. However, as in the previous situation, Yeshua commanded the multitude to sit down. He blessed the bread and continued to break up the food, giving it to His disciples to distribute, starting with the bread and then the fish (Mk. 8:6-7). Again there was enough for everybody to eat until they were full: *And they ate, and were filled* (Mk. 8:8). Again there were leftovers, this time seven baskets full.

Mark specified that there *were about four thousand* (Mk. 8:9). Matthew noted that the figure only included the men and not the women and children (Mt. 15:38), and so the actual total figure was much higher.

The lesson for the apostles was that Yeshua can provide in any situation and that the Gentiles would benefit from His ministry. Until after the resurrection, their ministry was limited to the Jewish people; nevertheless, there were already indications from these situations that the Gentiles would profit from Messiah's coming as well.

[§ 82] — I. The Rejection in Magadan

Matthew 15:39-16:4, Mark 8:10-12

After having fed the four thousand, Yeshua sailed back into Jewish territory. Matthew stated that He *came into the borders of Magadan* (Mt. 15:39). This was Old Testament Migdol, the home of Miriam Magdalene. Mark specified that He and the apostles arrived *into the parts of Dalmanuta* (Mk. 8:10), the harbor of Magadan.

Upon His arrival, He was soon confronted again: *And the Pharisees and Sadducees came, and trying him asked him to show them a sign from heaven* (Mt. 16:1). Despite differences in their theologies, the Pharisees and Sadducees united in this one goal and came to demand an authenticating sign, specifically a sign from heaven. If Yeshua gave them a sign, they could repeat that it came from hell. However, since the rejection, He would give them no more signs, and He reiterated His new policy by saying: *Why does this generation seek a sign? Verily I say unto you, There shall no sign be given unto this generation* (Mk. 8:12). The emphasis is on this generation, the one guilty of the unpardonable sin.

Matthew provided more detail about Yeshua's answer. He noted that the religious leaders could read nature's signs and predict the weather, but they could not discern the signs of the times (Mt. 16:2-3). They were well versed in the physical, but not the spiritual. They should have discerned that messianic times had arrived, and that the signs of His Messiahship had already been given. Often the expression *the signs of the times* (Mt. 16:3) is pulled out of context to try to determine the timing of the rapture or the second coming. However, in this context, it refers to Messiah's first coming, which was carefully timed by Daniel (Dan. 9:24-27).

Like Mark, Matthew recorded Yeshua's answer to the request for a sign, but he repeated a key detail he had already mentioned in chapter 12: *and there shall no sign be given unto it, but the sign of Yonah. And he left them, and departed* (Mt. 16:4). The nation would see no other sign than the sign of Jonah, the sign of resurrection.

[§ 83] — J. The Warning against Rejection

Matthew 16:5-12, Mark 8:13-21

In preparation for the fourth departure into Gentile territory, Yeshua set sail once again. Mark noted that the disciples forgot to stock up on bread and had one loaf for all of them (Mk. 8:14). In this context, Yeshua warned them against three types of leaven: *the leaven of the Pharisees and Sadducees* (Mt. 16:6) and *the leaven of Herod* (Mk. 8:15). The word *leaven*, when used symbolically, always stands for sin. Within the Gospels, it is specifically the sin of false doctrine. The Pharisees, the Sadducees, and the Herodians were spreading lies about Yeshua. He warned the apostles not to allow themselves to be permeated by this leaven or to believe any of the false teaching they were hearing.

Each of the three leavens had a different content. The leaven of the Pharisees was that Yeshua was demonized. The Sadducees did not believe in demons, so their leaven was that He opposed the Temple ministry. They controlled the money changers and the sellers of sacrifices in the Temple compound. Yeshua accused them of turning His

Father's house into a house of merchandise and overthrew their businesses at the first Passover of His public ministry. This provided the background for the false teaching that He was against the Temple ministry. The leaven of the Herodians was that He opposed Roman rule through the house of Herod. On the contrary, Yeshua accepted the providence of God in world governmental affairs and taught that people should render to Caesar that which was Caesar's (Mt. 22:21; Mk. 12:17; Lk. 20:25).

Although Yeshua warned them against accepting these three kinds of leaven, His disciples misinterpreted what He said and assumed He was scolding them for not taking enough physical bread on this journey (Mk. 8:16). Instead, He scolded them for not understanding what He was saying: *O ye of little faith* (Mt. 16:8). *Why reason ye, because ye have no bread? Do ye not yet perceive, neither understand? Have ye your heart hardened? Having eyes see ye not? And having ears, hear ye not? And do ye not remember?* (Mk. 8:17-18). He reminded them of the two major feedings and the twelve and seven baskets full of leftovers (Mk. 8:19-20). They should have learned from the miracles that Yeshua could provide in any and all circumstances. If He could provide bread for two groups of multitudes, He could certainly provide for a group of twelve. The point was that they should be concerned about the false teaching regarding His person and His word rather than the lack of physical bread. They finally comprehended what He was saying: *Then understood they that he bade them not beware of the leaven of bread, but of the teaching of the Pharisees and Sadducees* (Mt. 16:12).

[§ 84] — K. The Healing of the Blind Man

Mark 8:22-26

Yeshua and His disciples arrived at Bethsaida, still in Jewish territory (Mk. 8:22a). The procedure which Yeshua had implemented after the rejection becomes evident once again. A group of people brought a blind man to Him (Mk. 8:22b). Since His miracles were not for the public eye, *he took hold of the blind man by the hand, and brought him out of the village* (Mk. 8:23a), away from the crowd to provide a measure of privacy.

In the past, Yeshua had healed blind people instantaneously. However, this time He removed the blindness in two stages, which makes this event unique as the only recorded miracle He performed in two phases. His procedure involved five steps:

1. He spat on the man's eyes (Mk. 8:23b).

2. He laid His hands on the man (Mk. 8:23c).

3. The man had partial, but blurred sight, and people appeared to him as trees walking (Mk. 8:24).

4. He laid His hands upon the man's eyes (Mk. 8:25a).

5. The man then received full sight and could see all things clearly (Mk. 8:25b).

Again, this was the only miracle where the healing came in two stages. Recalling the thematic development and timing of this event, its application becomes apparent in the next two sections, §§ 85 and 86. What Peter says in § 85 will show that the apostles had partial sight, in that they clearly understood who Yeshua was. However, § 86 will show that their sight was blurred, because they did not yet fully comprehend God's program of His Son's death and resurrection. At the time of Pentecost, the apostles would finally come to a full understanding through the enlightenment of the Holy Spirit.

However, there is also a wider application of this miracle for the nation. They had rejected Yeshua as their promised Messiah, and as a result, a partial blindness has befallen the Jews. It is partial, because there is always a remnant, Jewish people who come to faith, in accordance with the election of grace. When *the fulness of the Gentiles be come in* (Rom. 11:25), the blindness will be completely removed from Israel, and they will fully see, resulting in all Israel being saved.[7]

---

[7] According to Acts 15:14, one of the key purposes of the church age is to call out from among the Gentiles a people for God's name. This calling will continue until *the fulness of the Gentiles* (Rom. 11:25) is reached. The Greek word translated as *fulness* means "a full number" or "a complete number." In other words, God has a set number of Gentiles that He has destined for salvation. Once the number is reached, the church

The last verse of this section shows that Yeshua continued His policy of silence: *And he sent him away to his home, saying, Do not even enter into the village* (Mk. 8:26).

[§ 85] — L. The Confession of Peter

Matthew 16:13-20, Mark 8:27-30, Luke 9:18-21

1. The Confession

The exchange between Yeshua and His disciples illustrates the issue of partial sight. It records the fourth withdrawal into Gentile territory, specifically *into the parts of Caesarea Philippi* (Mt. 16:13). Since geography played a role in what Yeshua had to say, a few observations about the location are in order. Caesarea Philippi is at the foot of Mount Hermon, the highest mountain peak in the Holy Land, rising over nine thousand feet above sea level. A massive cliff with a cave at its base overshadows the city. In Yeshua's day, a river flowed forth from this cave. Today, the river is called Banyas, one of the four sources of the Jordan River. About a century ago, a major earthquake struck the area, causing the river to shift so that now it flows out from the base of the cliff to the right of the cave. In Yeshua's day, as the stream emerged from the cave, it broke off small stones and pebbles that filled the riverbed. The Greek word for the pebbles and small stones is *petros*, while the cliff itself is called *petra*.

Shortly before this event, Yeshua warned the disciples about three types of leaven (Mt. 16:6; Mk. 8:15). In this particular examination, He tested them to see if they had learned the lesson, asking two questions. First, *Who do men say that the Son of man is?* (Mt. 16:13); *Who do men say that I am?* (Mk. 8:27). The apostles responded that there were four

---

will be complete and will be removed at the rapture. Then God will turn His eschatological attention back to the nation of Israel. Concerning her salvation, He will deal with Israel on a national basis and not only on an individual one. This national dealing, at the end of the tribulation, will lead to the salvation of all of Israel.

different views: *Some <say> Yochanan the Baptist; some, Eliyahu; and others, Yirmeyahu, or one of the prophets* (Mt. 16:14). The masses recognized Yeshua's supernatural authority, but they failed to conclude accurately that He was the Messianic Person.

Second, *He said unto them, But who say ye that I am?* (Mt. 16:15). In the Greek text, it is more emphatic: But *ye*, who do *ye* say that I am? In contrast to what everybody else was saying, what did the apostles believe? Peter, speaking on behalf of the others, answered: *You are the Messiah, the Son of the living God* (Mt. 16:16). Again, the Greek is more emphatic: You are *the* Messiah, *the* Son of *the* God, *the* living one. Very emphatically stated, it showed they had learned the lesson and passed the test.

2. Five Statements about Peter

In response to Peter's declaration, Yeshua tells him several things, five of which require careful examination. Matthew alone records these additional statements since he is writing to Jews, and he, in particular, traces the consequences of the unpardonable sin.

a. The Source of Peter's Knowledge

Yeshua first declared: *Blessed are you Shimon Bar-Yonah: for flesh and blood has not revealed it unto you, but my Father who is in heaven* (Mt. 16:17). Peter's conclusion was not deduced from human logic; it was the result of divine illumination by God the Father.

b. The Foundation of the Church

Yeshua's second declaration was: *And I also say unto you, that you are Peter, and upon this rock I will build my church* (Mt. 16:18a). For centuries, Roman Catholics have used this verse to teach that the church was built upon Peter. They claim that he was the first pope, and by means of papal succession, all of the popes were the true representatives of God, from whom they received their authority. As a result, they claim that the Roman Catholic Church is the one and only true church.

However, this interpretation of the verse suggests that Matthew was ignorant of some very simple rules of Greek grammar: A masculine modifies a masculine, a feminine modifies a feminine, and a neuter modifies a neuter. It is a contradiction of Greek grammar for a feminine to modify a masculine or vice versa. When Yeshua said, *you are Peter*, He used the Greek word *petros*, a masculine noun meaning "small stone," "pebble." His point was, "Peter, you are a small stone, just like these pebbles in this stream of Banyas." When Yeshua said, *upon this rock I will build my church*, He used a different Greek word, *petra*, a feminine noun, meaning "cliff," just like the massive rock formation overshadowing Caesarea Philippi, which is where they were standing. Grammatically, it could not possibly mean that the church would be built upon Peter. Quite the contrary, Yeshua was contrasting Peter with the massive cliff. He was also presupposing that the disciples were familiar with an important Old Testament symbol. Whenever the word *rock* is used symbolically in Scripture, it always symbolizes the Messiah. So the church would be built not upon Peter, but upon the Messiah; more specifically, upon what Peter had just said about the Messiah: You are *the* Messiah, *the* Son, of *the* God, *the* living one. Upon that confession by Peter Yeshua would build the church.

Of course, Yeshua and the apostles were speaking in Hebrew, not in Greek. However, the Hebrew equivalent for *petros* is *even*, and for *petra*, it is *sela*, two very different words. Another point to note is the future tense: *I **will** build my church*. This is the first time the term *church* is used in the New Testament. In Greek, the word is *ekklesia*, and in Hebrew, it is *kehillah*, and it is only used in Matthew 16 and 18. Mark, Luke, and Yochanan did not speak of the church at all. As previously stated, Matthew was the one Gospel writer who traced the results of the unpardonable sin, one of which was this new entity called the church. As of Matthew 16, it was still future. This contradicts the common teaching of replacement theologians that the church existed since the beginning of time. Yeshua did not view the church as already being in existence, but rather that He would build it at a future time.

c. The Gates of Hades

Yeshua's third declaration to Peter was: *and the gates of Hades shall not prevail against it* (Mt. 16:18b). In the Hebrew Scriptures, the term *"the gates of Hades"* was an idiom for physical death (Job 38:17; Ps. 9:13; 107:18; Is. 38:10). Upon this rock Yeshua would build His church, and physical death could not destroy it—neither His death, nor the deaths of the apostles, nor the deaths of countless martyrs throughout the history of the church. According to Ephesians 2:20, the church was *built upon the foundation of the apostles and prophets, Messiah Yeshua himself being the chief corner stone.* Therefore, neither His death nor their deaths would destroy what was to be built.

d. The Keys of the Kingdom

Yeshua's fourth declaration was: *I will give unto you the keys of the kingdom of heaven* (Mt. 16:19a). Again, He referred to an Old Testament concept. When used symbolically in the Hebrew Scriptures, the word *key* represents authority (Is. 22:20-24), including the authority to open and close doors. In the context of Matthew 16, Yeshua was dealing with the church facet of God's kingdom program, and Peter would be authorized to open the door of the church. The church is part of the spiritual kingdom, as noted in the discussion on the five facets of the kingdom of heaven. This statement predicts Peter's special role in the book of Acts. In Old Testament times, humanity was divided into two groups: Jews and Gentiles. In the Gospel period, there were three groups: Jews, Samaritans, and Gentiles. Matthew gave an example of the three groups: *Go not into <any> way of the Gentiles, and enter not into any city of the Samaritans: but go rather to the lost sheep of the house of Ysrael* (Mt. 10:5-6). Peter would be responsible for opening the doors of the church facet of the kingdom program for all three groups. Once he opened the door for one group, it stayed open for that group. The church is the body of the Messiah (Col. 1:18), and the means of entering the church is Spirit baptism (I Cor. 12:13). There is an inseparable connection between this baptism and the existence of the church; one cannot exist without the other. Peter, the keys, and Spirit baptism would all come together for each of the three groups.

In Acts 2, Peter opened the door for the Jews. Once he opened the door for the Jews, it stayed open. From then on, the moment a Jew believed, the Spirit baptized them into the body.

In Acts 8, Philip entered Samaria and preached the gospel to the Samaritans, and many Samaritans believed, were regenerated by the Holy Spirit, and received salvation. However, the Spirit did not baptize them into the body, because while Philip had the gospel, he did not have the keys. So, the church of Jerusalem sent Peter to Samaria, and by the laying on of hands, the Spirit baptized the Samaritans into the body (Acts 8:17). Once Peter opened the door for the Samaritans, it stayed open. From then on, every time a Samaritan believed, the Spirit baptized him into the body.

In Acts 9, Paul was saved and God commissioned him to be the apostle to the Gentiles. However, he did not have the keys, either. So before Paul could start his missionary work, God had to send Peter to the house of Cornelius. By his preaching, the Gentiles believed and the Spirit baptized them into the body (Acts 10:44-48). Once the door opened for the Gentiles, it stayed open. From then on, the Spirit baptized every Gentile who believed into the body. Once Peter opened all three doors, I Corinthians 12:13 became the doctrinal point: *For in one Spirit were we all baptized into one body, whether Jews or Greeks, whether bond or free, and were all made to drink of one Spirit.* Now, the Spirit baptizes all who believe into the body.

e. Binding and Loosing

Yeshua's fifth declaration to Peter was: *whatsoever you shall bind on earth shall be bound in heaven; and whatsoever you shall loose on earth shall be loosed in heaven* (Mt. 16:19b). Yeshua gave this special authority only to Peter at this time. After the resurrection, He extended and limited this authority to the other apostles exclusively. In modern days, this verse has been pulled out of context to signify something other than what it meant in the Jewish frame of reference. It has often been applied to spiritual warfare and the binding and loosing of Satan and his demons. However, neither Satan nor demons are found in this context. Rather, the context is the establishment of the church, and the issue at hand is apostolic authority. The terms "binding" and "loosing" were commonly used in rabbinic writings. In fact, binding and loosing was authority the Pharisees claimed for themselves, but which God never gave them. He did, however, give it to the apostles.

There were two basic concepts of binding and loosing in rabbinic thinking. One was called the *asur*, and the other one was called the *mutar*. *Asur* means "to bind," and *mutar* means "to loose," and the terms were used in two different senses: Legislatively, *to bind* meant "to forbid," and *to loose* meant "to permit." Judicially, *to bind* meant "to punish," and *to loose* meant "not to punish," or "to set free from punishment." That was how the rabbis used binding and loosing in the context of the Second Temple period, and the usage of these terms in the Gospels must be interpreted in the light of first-century Israel.

Thus, the Messiah gave to Peter, and later to all the apostles, the authority to bind and loose both legislatively and judicially. Since there is no such thing as apostolic succession, the authority was not passed on beyond the apostles. Later, in the Epistles, the apostles exercised binding and loosing, meaning they permitted things that were formerly forbidden, and they forbade things that were formerly permitted. Legislatively, this authority was limited to the apostles only. The church has no authority to bind and loose legislatively. It has no authority to bind, meaning to issue further rules and regulations for believers to follow. Likewise, it has no authority to loose, meaning to release believers from the rules of Scripture.

One example of how the apostles practiced their authority in the judicial sense is found in Acts 5 when Peter passed the death sentence upon Ananias and Sapphira. Because they had lied to the Holy Spirit, he bound them for punishment, and they each dropped dead at his feet. The church has a limited authority to bind and loose in a judicial sense, but not to the same degree as the apostles. The apostles could impose a death sentence, while the church can only excommunicate the sinner, a point made later, in Matthew 18.

3. Yeshua's Closing Statement

Following Peter's great confession, Yeshua reaffirmed the continuation of His policy of silence: *Then charged he the disciples that they should tell no man that he was the Messiah* (Mt. 16:20). Even the apostles were forbidden to continue proclaiming His Messiahship.

[§ 86] — M. Instruction
Concerning the Death of the King

Matthew 16:21-26, Mark 8:31-37, Luke 9:22-25

While the previous event surrounding Peter's confession showed that the disciples had partial sight, this one shows that they still had partial blindness; their vision was blurry.

The apostolic confession marks the beginning of Yeshua's instruction concerning His death and resurrection. Only after Peter's proclamation of His Messiahship did Yeshua, in the last year of His life, begin to spell out His program: *From that time began Yeshua to show unto his disciples* (Mt. 16:21). As His ministry with the disciples continued and the time of His death drew closer, He provided more and more detail of the upcoming events. However, as often as He told them, and as much detail as He gave them, they never understood what He was saying. Therefore, His crucifixion and resurrection caught them by surprise.

Yeshua kept this first disclosure of the plan simple, listing four steps (Mt. 16:21). First, He must go to Jerusalem. Second, in Jerusalem, He must suffer many things at the hands *of the elders and chief priests and scribes*, including both Pharisees and Sadducees. Mark and Luke explained that this meant Yeshua would be rejected by the leadership of Israel (Mk. 8:31a; Lk. 9:22). Third, He would *be killed*. In the Greek, this phrase is in the third person passive voice, which means that it is unclear who would be doing the killing. Fourth, He would rise again. Matthew and Luke wrote that Yeshua's resurrection would happen on *the third day* (Mt. 16:21b; Lk. 9:22b), while Mark stated that He would rise *after three days* (Mk. 8:31), which may seem to imply a fourth day. However, according to the Jewish reckoning of time, these terms are synonymous: He will rise *on* the third day, and He will rise *after* three days. This will be discussed in greater depth in §§ 176–197 when we study Yeshua's death and resurrection.

Now, for the first time, Yeshua spelled out the program of His death and resurrection. Peter, the one who so gloriously passed the test in the previous section, failed here: *And Peter took him, and began to rebuke him* (Mt. 16:22a). The Greek word for *rebuke, epitiman,* means "to reprove" or "to censure," describing someone who tries to prevent an action from happening and is using physical restraint to do so. Indeed, Peter took Yeshua, using physical restraint, and rebuked Him, saying, *Be it far from you, Lord: this shall never be unto you* (Mt. 16:22b). "This is never going to happen to you." Do not miss the paradox. It was Peter who confessed, *You are the Messiah, the Son of the living God* (Mt. 16:16). Yet Peter was also the one who rebuked the Messiah, the Son of the living God.

In response, Yeshua said, *Get you behind me, Satan* (Mt. 16:23a). He had not experienced a sudden loss of memory which caused Him to forget Peter's name. At that moment, Peter was influenced by Satan and joined in the devil's goal to keep the Messiah from the cross. While Satan wanted to see Yeshua dead, he did not want Him to die at the proper time (Passover) or in the proper way (by crucifixion). His constant attempts to keep Yeshua from the cross made him *a stumbling-block* (Mt. 16:23b). Satan is not aligned with the will of God, but with the sinful desires of man.

This incident provided Yeshua an opportunity to teach three lessons in discipleship. Luke stated, *he said unto all* (Lk. 9:23). Mark clarified who the *all* were: *And he called unto him the multitude with his disciples* (Mk. 8:34). Since the masses were also included, Yeshua spoke in parables so that only the apostles would understand Him. Matthew specified: *Then said Yeshua unto his disciples* (Mt. 16:24a).

Yeshua's first lesson pertained to the differences between salvation and discipleship. The Bible draws a clear distinction between the two. Salvation is, and has always been, an act of faith, and the content of faith in this age is believing that Yeshua died for our sins, was buried, and rose again. A person trusts the Messiah, and Him alone, for salvation. That is the only prerequisite for salvation given in Scripture, and it is by grace through faith. Discipleship, on the other hand, involves much more: *If any man would come after me, let him deny himself, and take up his cross, and follow me* (Mt. 16:24). A person must be willing to identify fully with the rejection Yeshua experienced. The apostles had to make this decision in light of the Pharisaic rejection of Yeshua. Luke specified that this must be a *daily* commitment (Lk. 9:23).

The second lesson in discipleship pertained to the physical consequences of not properly following Yeshua: *For whosoever would save his life shall lose it* (Mt. 16:25a). Failure to take up one's cross for the sake of saving self meant self would be lost. If the apostles tried to save their physical lives by avoiding discipleship, they would end up losing their lives anyway. This was uniquely applicable to that generation and the destruction of A.D. 70. The writer of Hebrews warns Jewish believers against returning to the Judaism that rejected the Messiah. To do so would mean physical death.

The third lesson in discipleship pertained to the promises Yeshua made to those who properly followed Him: *and whosoever shall lose his life for my sake shall find it* (Mt. 16:25b). To those who take up their cross, Yeshua promised to provide life. The Jewish believers of that generation who chose discipleship would escape the judgment of A.D. 70; if they died, it would be at the hand of men and not as a consequence of God's judgment. In the end, they would find a better life and a greater reward in the kingdom.

Every believer today should pursue discipleship for two reasons: for true spiritual safety and for true riches, *For what is a man profited, if he gain the whole world, and lose or forfeit his own self?* (Lk. 9:25). In the context of the passage studied here, the disciples had to make a decision in light of the Pharisaic rejection.

[§§ 87–88] — N. Instruction Concerning the Kingdom

The events recorded in §§ 87 and 88 form a unit. The first contains a promise and the second the fulfillment of the promise.

[§ 87] — 1. The Promise of Revelation

Matthew 16:27-28, Mark 8:38-9:1, Luke 9:26-27

Once again, Yeshua placed a special emphasis on that particular generation when He said, *For whosoever shall be ashamed of me and of my words in this adulterous and sinful generation, the Son of man also shall be ashamed of him, when he comes in the glory of his Father with the holy angels* (Mk. 8:38). This statement is the continuation of the previous discussion about true discipleship. At the second coming, the Messiah would be ashamed of those among His believers who became ashamed of Him before that particular generation. This is not dealing with losing salvation, but losing status in the second coming and rewards in the messianic kingdom, when Yeshua will return with His angels and render unto every man according to his deeds (Mt. 16:27). This is the time when the believers' rewards will place them in a position of privilege in the messianic kingdom. However, the Jewish believers who became ashamed of Him and of His words *in this adulterous and sinful generation* will not have any such position of privilege.

At His return, Yeshua will not only come with His angels, He will also come *in his own glory, and <the glory> of the Father* (Lk. 9:26). In other words, He will come in the fullness of His unveiled Shechinah glory. This led to a promise which must be understood within this context. Yeshua promised that some of those listening would not die until they witnessed something. Luke wrote: *till they see the kingdom of God* (Lk. 9:27). Mark stated: *till they see the kingdom of God come with power* (Mk. 9:1). The focus is not on the kingdom per se, but on the power of the kingdom. Then Matthew stated: *till they see the Son of man coming in his kingdom* (Mt. 16:28). Now the focus is on the person of the

Messiah. Putting all this together, the promise, specifically, was that some of Yeshua's disciples would not die until they saw the power of the messianic kingdom and the glory Yeshua will have in this kingdom. Yeshua did not promise that some would survive until the messianic kingdom was established; rather, He promised that some would not die until they saw the glory Yeshua will have at the second coming and in the messianic kingdom. This promise was fulfilled in the next event, the transfiguration.

[§ 88] — 2. The Transfiguration: The Revelation of the Kingdom

Matthew 17:1-8, Mark 9:2-8, Luke 9:28-36a

The promise Yeshua made in the previous section was fulfilled when the three apostles Peter, James, and Yochanan witnessed the revelation of the kingdom in the transfiguration (Mt. 17:1). They did not die until they had seen the glory Yeshua will have in the kingdom.

Both Matthew and Mark mentioned that the transfiguration occurred *after six days* (Mt. 17:1; Mk. 9:2). Luke wrote that it was *about eight days after* (Lk. 9:28). Matthew and Mark may have counted only the full days, while Luke added the day of departure and the day of return. Another option is that Luke counted the time from Messiah's promise (*after these sayings*, Lk. 9:28) to the transfiguration.

The Gospels do not name the mountain, but Mark stated that Yeshua and the three apostles went to *a high mountain apart by themselves* (Mk. 9:2), emphasizing two things: the mountain was high, and it was secluded, so the four men could be by themselves. Based upon the geography of Caesarea Philippi, their most recent location before this event, this would be Mount Hermon, the highest mountain in the Promised Land. The Catholic site of this event is Mount Tabor, where the Church of the Transfiguration was built. However, Mount Tabor sits well inside Galilee. Yeshua and the apostles left that region for Gentile territory in Mark 8:27 and did not return to Galilee until Mark 9:30. This event occurred during the fourth withdrawal. Furthermore,

Mount Tabor is not significantly higher than the connecting mountains, nor was it a secluded place. It was always well fortified and inhabited, because it guarded one of the seven key entrances into the Jezreel Valley, the pass from the lake. Mount Hermon, on the other hand, meets all requirements geographically and contextually as a place where they would be alone.

At that point, Yeshua underwent a change which is now called the transfiguration. To get a complete picture of what happened, all three accounts must be considered:

✣ *and he was transfigured before them; and his face did shine as the sun, and his garments became white as the light* (Mt. 17:2).

✣ *and he was transfigured before them; and his garments became glistering, exceeding white; so as no fuller on earth can whiten them* (Mk. 9:2-3).

✣ *And as he was praying, the fashion of his countenance was altered, and his raiment <became> white <and> dazzling* (Lk. 9:29).

To summarize the accounts, Yeshua was transfigured; the fashion of His countenance changed, and His face shone with the brightness of the sun. His clothes were as white as light itself: glistening, shining, dazzling, and reflecting light, so that nothing could make them whiter.

As Messiah promised in the preceding section, the three apostles saw the glory the Son of Man will have in the kingdom. Luke affirmed: *they saw his glory* (Lk. 9:32). As discussed in § 2, Yeshua was the visible manifestation of the glory of God, the Shechinah glory. Since His birth, the brightness of this glory had always been veiled by the physical body of His flesh; here it was allowed to shine through. His garments became exceedingly white—so white that they became shiny, dazzling, radiating light of their own. Furthermore, His face shone with the brightness of the sun. These three apostles saw the brightness of His glory; they saw Him as He will be at His second coming and in His kingdom. This is similar to Moses' experience on Mount Sinai where he saw a new manifestation of the Shechinah glory and his face began to shine. The difference is that Moses' face merely reflected the glory, just as the light of the moon reflects the light of the sun, because the moon has no light of its own. Yeshua is the Shechinah glory; therefore, His face shone much brighter than the face of Moses.

Suddenly, two men from the Old Testament appeared with Yeshua: Moses and Elijah. According to Matthew and Mark, they were talking with Him (Mt. 17:3; Mk. 9:4). Luke revealed the content of their discussion: They *spoke of his decease which he was about to accomplish at Yerushalayim* (Lk. 9:31). The Greek word for *decease* is *exodos*, which literally means "departure." In the Septuagint, the same word is used for Israel's exodus from Egypt. Just as Israel's departure from Egypt meant liberation and freedom from slavery, Yeshua's departure by means of His death would mean liberation. Yeshua would be liberated from all the limitations of His humanity, such as the veiling of His glory, and the believer would be liberated from enslavement to sin.

Luke specified that Moses and Elijah *appeared in glory* (Lk. 9:31). In the case of Moses, this glory only pertained to his soul, because only the souls of believers are glorified at death, while their bodies must wait for the resurrection to be glorified. Elijah, on the other hand, never died, but was raptured to heaven, so the glory in which he appeared pertained to both his body and his soul. When he *went up by a whirlwind into heaven* (II Kgs. 2:11), his body changed from mortality to immortality, as will the bodies of all living believers at the rapture (I Cor. 15:50-58). This means that Elijah is no longer subject to death, and he cannot be one of the two witnesses of Revelation 11. As § 89 will demonstrate, Elijah will indeed return someday, but he will not be one of the two witnesses.

Moses' appearance at Yeshua's transfiguration has caused some to conclude that he finally entered the Promised Land, although only in his spirit. However, Mt. Hermon is outside the borders of Israel, as is Mount Nebo.[8] Thus, even here, Moses could see the Promised Land, but did not enter it. He will, however, be there in the messianic kingdom.

Luke alone mentioned that *Peter and they that were with him were heavy with sleep* when Yeshua was talking with Moses and Elijah (Lk.

---

[8] The place from which Moses saw the Land and where he died (Deut. 32:48-52; 34:1-6).

9:32). They became fully awake just as Moses and Elijah were depart-
ing. At that point, Peter spoke up and made a suggestion: *Lord, it is
good for us to be here: if you will, I will make here three tabernacles; one
for you, and one for Mosheh, and one for Eliyahu* (Mt. 17:4b). Luke observed that Peter spoke rashly, *not knowing what he said* (Lk. 9:33).
Mark explained why: *For he knew not what to answer; for they became
sore afraid* (Mk. 9:6). Peter's spontaneous emotional response was generated by fear. Various commentaries castigate the apostle for offering
to build three tabernacles and not just one. They claim that Peter was
either demoting Yeshua to the level of Moses and Elijah or elevating
the two men to His level. That appears to be a common Gentile percep-
tion of the passage. However, from a Jewish perspective, the response
was proper, based upon what Peter knew and understood, although his
timing was wrong because of what he did not yet understand—that the
Passover must be fulfilled before the Feast of Tabernacles is fulfilled.
From the events of Matthew 16, three things are to be noted. First, Peter
clearly understood who Yeshua was: the Messiah, the Son of the living
God, and the Messianic King. Second, he did not yet know and understand the program of death and resurrection, and hence the program
of two comings. Third, he had seen the glory the Son of Man will have
in the messianic kingdom. Peter would also know from a passage like
Zechariah 14:16-21 that the messianic kingdom is the fulfillment of the
Feast of Tabernacles. Seeing the glory Yeshua will have in the kingdom,
and not yet knowing the program of two comings, Peter assumed that
the kingdom was about to be set up, and he wanted to build three tabernacles in honor of that fact. However, the timing was wrong, because
he did not yet understand that Passover must be fulfilled before the
Feast of Tabernacles could be fulfilled, and Passover was fulfilled by
Messiah's death.

Before Peter could continue, the cloud of the Shechinah glory, which
was once on Mount Sinai, came upon this mount, overshadowing all
six men (Mk. 9:7). Apparently, the cloud initially enveloped only
Yeshua, Moses, and Elijah, and later the apostles *feared as they entered
into the cloud* (Lk. 9:34). Then God the Father spoke audibly out of
heaven for the second time. The first time His voice, the Bat Kol, was
heard was at the baptism of the Messiah (Mt. 3:17). Now, at His transfiguration, the voice came out of the cloud, uttering the same words:

This is my beloved Son in whom I am well pleased, except this time the Father added one small phrase: *hear ye him* (Mt. 17:5). They had heard the Law and the Prophets; now, they must hear Yeshua because, in keeping with Hebrews 1:1-3, the Son was the final revelation of the Father. The voice caused the apostles to be filled with fear and fall *on their face* (Mt. 17:6). Only the comforting touch of Yeshua could remove their fear (Mt. 17:7). As if to emphasize what the voice had said, *And lifting up their eyes, they saw no one, save Yeshua only* (Mt. 17:8). Moses was gone; Elijah was gone. *And when the voice came, Yeshua was found alone* (Lk. 9:36a). Mark was more emphatic: *And suddenly looking round about, they saw no one any more, save Yeshua only with themselves* (Mk. 9:8).

All of the major events in the life of the Messiah have theological implications, and the same is true of the transfiguration. Five such implications are apparent. First, the transfiguration authenticated the Messiahship of Yeshua, who was rejected by men, but accepted by God the Father. When God the Father spoke audibly, He said: *This is my beloved Son in whom I am well pleased; hear ye him* (Mt. 17:5b).

Second, the transfiguration anticipated the earthly kingdom of the Messiah. Before the transfiguration, Yeshua promised His disciples that some of them—Peter, James, and Yochanan—would not die until they had seen the glory that the Son of Man would have in the kingdom. This occurred when they witnessed the transfiguration. After the transfiguration, one of these apostles, Peter, wrote in II Peter 1:16-18:

[16] For we did not follow cunningly devised fables, when we made known unto you the power and coming of our Lord Yeshua Messiah, but we were eyewitnesses of his majesty. [17] For he received from God the Father honor and glory, when there was borne such a voice to him by the Majestic Glory, This is my beloved Son, in whom I am well pleased: [18] and this voice we ourselves heard borne out of heaven, when we were with him in the holy mount.

Reflecting upon the experience, Peter noted that the transfiguration anticipated the future power and return of the Messiah, the coming of Yeshua in His kingdom.

Third, the transfiguration guaranteed the fulfillment of all Scripture. According to Luke 9:31, Yeshua's discussion with Moses and Elijah concerned His coming *exodos*, His coming death, which would fulfill the Law and the Prophets. Moses represented the Law, and Elijah represented the Prophets. Yeshua came to fulfill all that Moses and the prophets said, and Peter reflects on this in II Peter 1:19-21:

> [19] *And we have the word of prophecy made more sure; whereunto ye do well that ye take heed, as unto a lamp shining in a dark place, until the day dawn, and the day-star arise in your hearts:* [20] *knowing this first, that no prophecy of scripture is of private interpretation.* [21] *For no prophecy ever came by the will of man: but men spoke from God, being moved by the Holy Spirit.*

Fourth, the transfiguration was a pledge of life beyond the grave. Moses, who did die, was there, representing the resurrected saints. Elijah, who never died, was there, representing the translated saints. Church saints will be translated at the rapture, and millennial saints will be translated sometime during or at the end of the Millennium. The fact that these two men exist—one in spirit form only, and the other in a glorified, translated body—shows the continuation of life beyond death. So whether by resurrection or translation, there is, and will be, life beyond death.

Fifth, the transfiguration is a measure of God's love for humanity, revealing the cost Yeshua paid to come to earth. He had to veil His glory twice: first, at the incarnation, and second, after the transfiguration. Only at His ascension was His glory unveiled forever. When Yochanan saw Him again in the vision of Revelation 1:12-16, He was in the fullness of His Shechinah glory, no longer veiled. When the Messiah returns at His second coming, it will be with unveiled glory. He will come with power and great glory in the clouds of heaven, the clouds representing the Shechinah glory.

[§ 89] — O. Instruction Concerning Elijah

Matthew 17:9-13, Mark 9:9-13, Luke 9:36b

Now the correlation between Yochanan the Baptizer and Elijah the prophet will become evident. Before Yochanan was even born, the angel Gabriel had declared that he would come in the spirit and power of Elijah (Lk. 1:17). When Yochanan was asked if he was Elijah, he decisively said, "No, I am not" (Jn. 1:21). In the verses studied in this section, Yeshua stated that, had the kingdom offer been accepted, Yochanan would have fulfilled Elijah's function, which was "to restore all things" (Mt. 17:11; Mk. 9:12). However, since Yeshua was rejected, Yochanan did not fulfill Elijah's function, and consequently, the prophet himself must come to do so.

As the Messiah and His three apostles were going down the mountain, Yeshua again reinforced the policy of silence, commanding them, *Tell the vision to no man, until the Son of man be risen from the dead* (Mt. 17:9b), something they clearly obeyed (Lk. 9:36b). They understood the matter of not telling anyone about the transfiguration, but they did not understand what He meant by *rising again from the dead*: *And they kept the saying, questioning among themselves what the rising again from the dead should mean* (Mk. 9:10). This shows that they did not yet understand the program of death and resurrection, or the program of two comings. This lack of understanding caused them to raise the next question: *And they asked him, saying, <How is it> that the scribes say that Eliyahu must first come?* (Mk. 9:11). The scribes and Pharisees had correctly deduced from Malachi 4:5-6 that the Prophet Elijah would be the forerunner of the Messiah and must come first. However, the promise of Malachi was that Elijah would appear before the second coming; it did not promise he would come before the first coming. In fact, in Malachi 3:1, the prophet said that an unnamed forerunner would arrive before the first coming:

¹ Behold, I send my messenger, and he shall prepare the way before me: and the Lord, whom ye seek, will suddenly come to his temple; and the messenger of the covenant, whom ye desire, behold, he comes, says Jehovah of hosts.

In Malachi 4:5-6, the prophet then said that Elijah would come before the second coming:

> [5] Behold, I will send you Eliyahu the prophet before the great and terrible day of Jehovah come. [6] And he shall turn the heart of the fathers to the children, and the heart of the children to their fathers; lest I come and smite the earth with a curse.

The question in Mark 9:11—<How is it> that the scribes say that Eliyahu must first come?—originated from the fact that the apostles did not yet understand the program of the Messiah's two comings. Yeshua affirmed that this scribal teaching was correct: And he said unto them, Eliyahu indeed comes first, and restores all things (Mk. 9:12a). Yes, Elijah will indeed come first and restore all things; however, in keeping with Malachi's prophecy, he precedes the Messiah's second coming, not His first. Therefore, Yeshua added: and how is it written of the Son of man, that he should suffer many things and be set at nought? (Mk. 9:12b). In other words, if Elijah came before the first coming and did the work of restoration, it would mean that the prophecies about Messiah's suffering would not be fulfilled. So, the order of events is this: Messiah comes the first time to suffer many things and be set at nought. Sometime later, Elijah will arrive to restore all things. This precedes the second coming of the Messiah, at which time He will set up the kingdom.

Mark added: But I say unto you, that Eliyahu is come, and they have also done unto him whatsoever they would, even as it is written of him (Mk. 9:13). Matthew clarified: Then understood the disciples that he spoke unto them of Yochanan the Baptist (Mt. 17:13). By combining these two statements, we can conclude that Yeshua was saying there is a sense in which Elijah has already come: he came by his type, which was Yochanan the Baptizer. We have to keep in mind that Malachi promised two forerunners, not one. Yochanan was a type of Elijah by preparing the way of the Lord before His first coming when He came to suffer and die. The Baptizer came in the spirit and power of the prophet, though he denied actually being Elijah. Elijah himself will come in future times and restore all things, but this restoration precedes and is in preparation for the second coming. The Son must suffer and die before the final restoration, before Elijah comes. So Yochanan was Elijah typologically. He was the forerunner of the Messiah when He came to suffer and die.

[§ 90] — P. Instruction Concerning Faith

Matthew 17:14-20, Mark 9:14-29, Luke 9:37-42

The four men returned to where the other nine apostles had remained and found them in a dispute. It is important to note the subject and instigators of the dispute: *And when they came to the disciples, they saw a great multitude about them, and scribes questioning with them* (Mk. 9:14). Some scribes, while questioning the apostles, had instigated the dispute which stirred up *a great multitude*. The apostles had failed to cast out a demon from a boy, and the scribes were using their failure to negate Yeshua's Messiahship. This demon was violent. The boy's father explained, *he is epileptic, and suffers grievously; for oft-times he falls in to the fire, and oft-times into the water* (Mt. 17:15). Luke added that a *spirit takes him, and he suddenly cries out; and it tears him that he foams, and it hardly departs from him, bruising him sorely* (Lk. 9:39). This extreme case of demonic control included epilepsy and suicidal tendencies. Despite their experience in exorcisms, the disciples were unable to cast out this demon.

Responding to the situation, Yeshua again emphasized that genera-tion: *O faithless generation, how long shall I be with you? how long shall I bear with you?* (Mk. 9:19). Then He said: *Bring here your son* (Lk. 9:41), *and they brought him unto him* (Mk. 9:20a), meaning away from the multitude. The demon made one last effort to cause pain: *straight-way the spirit tare him grievously; and he fell on the ground, and wallowed foaming* (Mk. 9:20b). Luke added: *And as He was yet a com-ing, the demon dashed him down, and tare <him> grievously* (Lk. 9:42).

By this time, Yeshua performed miracles on two grounds only: upon an expression of personal need and on the basis of faith. Both elements were present on this occasion. Yeshua asked the boy's father: *How long time is it since this has come unto him?* (Mk. 9:21a). He answered, *From a child* (Mk. 9:21b). This condition was prolonged; the demon had attempted to kill the child previously, sometimes by trying to cast him into the fire and sometimes into the water (Mk. 9:22a). Then the father expressed his personal need: *if you can do anything, have compassion on us, and help us* (Mk. 9:22b). However, the phrase *if you can* was not a confession of faith, but of doubt that had to be removed before Yeshua performed the miracle. So the Messiah responded: *If you can! All things are possible to him that believes* (Mk. 9:23). The father quickly got the point: *Straightway the father of the child cried out, and said, I believe; help you mine unbelief* (Mk. 9:24), and he exercised his faith.

Yeshua had removed the father and his son from the multitude, but quickly cast out the demon when He *saw that a multitude came running together* (Mk. 9:25) towards them. Miracles were no longer to benefit the masses, but only individuals in response to personal need on the basis of faith. The demon was exorcised with a painful exit (Mk. 9:26-27). Although the miracle was not intended for the masses, they could not fail to see the result: *And they were all astonished at the majesty of God* (Lk. 9:43a).

The issue was not settled for the perplexed disciples: Why had they been unable to cast out this demon despite their many successful exorcisms? *And when he was come into the house, his disciples asked him privately, <How is it> that we could not cast it out?* (Mk. 9:28).

Yeshua gave two reasons. First, *This kind can come out by nothing, save by prayer* (Mk. 9:29). They had used the wrong method. Most commentaries and sermons on this passage focus only on the last phrase, *save by prayer*, failing to recognize that it is *this kind* that can only come out by prayer. The question is, to what kind of demon did Yeshua refer? According to Mark 9:17, this was a dumb spirit. Casting out a demon that caused the possessed to become mute is one of the three miracles that this author calls messianic. In this verse, Yeshua verified the Pharisaic observation that dumb demons are different. The Pharisees could cast out all kinds of demons, but they could not cast out a demon that caused muteness. Previously, the disciples had only dealt with demons they could exorcise in Yeshua's name. However, dumb demons had to be prayed out.

Second, the apostles lacked faith: *Because of your little faith* (Mt. 17:20a). When the normal procedure failed, they should have immediately resorted to prayer. Their improper methodology revealed their lack of faith. Yeshua applied this lesson to the disciples: *If ye have faith as a grain of mustard seed, ye shall say unto this mountain, Remove hence to yonder place; and it shall remove; and nothing shall be impossible unto you* (Mt. 17:20b). Yeshua was referring to a specific mountain. If He meant a literal mountain, He was probably referring to Mount Hermon, from which He had just descended, fitting the wider context. The immediate context, however, might indicate a consistent symbolic reference to a king, a kingdom, or a throne. Yeshua had just clashed with the kingdom of Satan. In the immediate context, *this mountain* most likely refers to the satanic kingdom. Faith, coupled with the proper method, would have enabled the apostles to handle the situation.

[§ 91] — Q. Instruction
Concerning the Death of the King

Matthew 17:22-23, Mark 9:30-32, Luke 9:43-45

This was Yeshua's second announcement of His coming death and resurrection, and it came at a time when He was teaching His apostles alone: *And they went forth from thence, and passed through Galil; and he would not that any man should know it. For he taught his disciples* (Mk. 9:30-31a). Yeshua intended this to be a period of training for His disciples. Although He introduced this declaration by saying, *Let these words sink into your ears* (Lk. 9:44), for the second time, they did not understand. They *were exceeding sorry* (Mt. 17:23) because they *understood not the saying, and were afraid to ask him* (Mk. 9:32). Luke added: *But they understood not this saying, and it was concealed from them, that they should not perceive it; and they were afraid to ask him about this saying* (Lk. 9:45). When the crucifixion and the resurrection finally occurred, it took them by surprise.

[§ 92] — R. Instruction Concerning Sonship

Matthew 17:24-27

After the incident with the demon that caused dumbness and Yeshua's second announcement of future events, He and the apostles returned to His headquarters in Capernaum (Mt. 17:24a). Again, they were in Jewish territory and, therefore, under Jewish jurisdiction. This situation provided the circumstance for the event that was about to occur: *They that received the half-shekel came to Peter and said, Does not your teacher pay the half-shekel?* (Mt. 17:24b). The half-shekel was known as the Temple tax, and it was a required offering (Ex. 30:11-16). Each male in Israel had to pay the half-shekel yearly to help maintain the tabernacle and, in Yeshua's day, pay for the Temple ministry. The tax was due around March/April every year at Passover time.

However, this incident took place close to the Feast of Tabernacles, meaning that Yeshua's payment of the Temple tax was about six months overdue. The tax collectors came and asked Peter, *Does not your master pay the half-shekel?* (Mt. 17:24). Without checking with Yeshua first, Peter gave his own answer: *He said, Yea* (Mt. 17:25a) and let it go at that. Yeshua knew what had taken place, and when Peter came into the house, He had a special, private lesson for the apostle. He asked: *What do you think, Shimon? The kings of the earth, from whom do they receive toll or tribute? From their sons, or from strangers? And when he said, From strangers, Yeshua said unto him, Therefore the sons are free* (Mt. 17:25b-26). Yeshua's point was that Roman citizens—the *sons*—did not pay taxes, and because they did not have to pay taxes, the Roman government had to be financed by tribute, tolls, and taxes collected from subjugated peoples—the *strangers*. This procedure was not exclusive to the Roman Empire. In some countries, the citizens had to pay tribute, but the sons of the king were exempt from paying taxes. In Israel, the half-shekel was to be paid as a Temple tax, and as the Messiah, Yeshua was Lord of the Temple. The believers were His sons and therefore were exempt from having to pay the Temple tax. The reason Yeshua did not bother to pay this Temple tax six months earlier was that, as Lord of the Temple, He was exempt. Furthermore, His apostles, being the sons of the king, spiritually speaking, were also exempt from paying the Temple tax. Therefore, Yeshua did not tell them to go and pay it. *But, lest we cause them to stumble* (Mt. 17:27), Yeshua ordered Peter to pay this tax. There was no need to cause the religious rulers to stumble unnecessarily since this was a Mosaic issue, not a Mishnaic issue. So Yeshua provided for a miracle. He told Peter to temporarily return to fishing, and when he caught a fish, he would find a full shekel in its mouth (Mt. 17:27). This would pay for both Yeshua's and his own Temple tax.

The disciples learned that they are the sons of the King, and He is Lord of the Temple. Paying the Temple tax was not required, but for the sake of avoiding unnecessary stumbling, they were to pay it anyway, as there were more important concerns to be turned into principles.

[§ 93] — S. Instruction Concerning Humility

Matthew 18:1-5, Mark 9:33-37, Luke 9:46-48

The next two sections, § 93 and §94, belong together, as there is a correlation between them. The first teaches to "be childlike," and the second teaches to "receive those who are childlike."

The background to the lesson in these verses concerned a dispute among the disciples: *And there arose a reasoning among them, which of them was the greatest* (Lk. 9:46). Matthew provided the timing of this dispute: *In that hour came the disciples unto Yeshua, saying, Who then is greatest in the kingdom of heaven?* (Mt. 18:1). The dispute immediately followed Peter's lesson (*in that hour*) whereby Yeshua arranged for Peter's tax to be paid along with His own. As a result, the apostle might have felt that he stood in a privileged position. This event also followed the experience of the transfiguration, in which Yeshua chose only three of the 12 apostles to be witnesses. Thus, Peter, James, and Yochanan may have felt privileged. Now, the disciples not only debated over their present status, but also their status in the messianic kingdom. They still believed that Yeshua would soon establish that kingdom and debated who among them would hold the highest position.

The dispute occurred along the way. After they entered the house, Yeshua asked them: *What were ye reasoning on the way?* (Mk. 9:33). He knew, but wanted to drive home the point that the problem was the superiority felt among the apostolic group. From a sitting position (Mk. 9:35a), Yeshua *called to him a little child, and set him in the midst of them, and said, Verily I say unto you, Except ye turn, and become as little children, ye shall in no wise enter into the kingdom of heaven* (Mt. 18:2-3). The lesson was that they had to be as children, with childlike faith, in order to enter the kingdom. Children are dependent on their fathers, and so believers must demonstrate a childlike dependence on their heavenly Father. Matthew added: *Whosoever therefore shall humble himself as this little child, the same is the greatest in the kingdom of heaven* (Mt. 18:4). While only faith and trust in Yeshua are required to enter the kingdom, a believer's position in the kingdom will be determined by how he lived out his faith during his lifetime. A small child recognizes he has no authority in the home, but is in subjection to the will of the father. Consequently, to receive a great position in the kingdom, one must recognize that like a child, he has no authority of his own and is in subjection to God.

Yeshua stated: *If any man would be first, he shall be last of all, and servant of all* (Mk. 9:35b). A person desiring a superior place in the kingdom must not struggle in this life to achieve the highest position, but the lowest, while ministering to all people. To become a master in the kingdom, one must be a servant now. Luke added: *For he that is least among you all, the same is great* (Lk. 9:48). Greatness is attained by means of childlike humility.

To summarize, children have no concern for status within the home, for they know who rules the house. No debate occurs about social status between the child and the parents. Likewise, it is necessary to turn with childlike faith and humility. One must have a spirit of receptiveness to the insignificant and be willing to receive a child: *And whoso shall receive one such little child in my name receives me* (Mt. 18:5). This point will be elaborated on in the next section.

In summary, we can say that as a child is dependent upon his father, a believer must be dependent upon God. The means of attaining greatness in the kingdom involves becoming the least and becoming a servant.

[§ 94] — T. Instruction Concerning Exclusiveness and Pride

Matthew 18:6-14, Mark 9:38-50, Luke 9:49-50

While the previous lesson was to "be childlike," the next lesson was to "receive those who are childlike."

Having been rebuked by the Messiah, the apostles tried to change the subject to the problem of status. Previously, it was the status within the apostolic group; now it is the status of the apostles against non-apostles. Yochanan described the circumstances, saying, *Master, we saw one casting out demons in your name; and we forbade him, because he followed not with us* (Lk. 9:49). This is a clear expression of exclusiveness. When the disciple said, *because he followed not with us,* he did not mean that the man in question was not a follower of Yeshua per se, but rather that he was not a part of the apostolic group of twelve. Therefore, they felt superior and exclusive in regard to exorcising demons; other followers of Yeshua should not have that authority or privilege.

Yeshua rebuked them again, saying, *Forbid <him> not: for he that is not against you is for you* (Lk. 9:50). Mark's account is more elaborate: *Forbid him not: for there is no man who shall do a mighty work in my name, and be able quickly to speak evil of me. For he that is not against us is for us* (Mk. 9:39-40). Yeshua taught that a person could accomplish great things for Him without belonging to this inner circle of apostles.

Yeshua then taught a lesson regarding exclusiveness and pride: *For whosoever shall give you a cup of water to drink, because ye are Messiah's, verily I say unto you, he shall in no wise lose his reward* (Mk. 9:41). Even the most humble work of a disciple of Yeshua, like giving a cup of water to someone, will be rewarded.

Then Yeshua warned: *And whosoever shall cause one of these little ones that believe on me to stumble, it were better for him if a great millstone were hanged about his neck, and he were cast into the sea* (Mk. 9:42). The apostles had offended the man by forbidding him to cast out demons in Yeshua's name without authority to do so. All causes of stumbling will be justly punished, especially against those children who believe.

Another warning followed: *Woe unto the world because of occasions of stumbling! For it must needs be that the occasions come; but woe to that man through whom the occasion comes!* (Mt. 18:7). Unbelievers who cause little children to stumble, and invariably, there are always people who do, will someday be judged. Believers must also take great care not to cause unnecessary stumbling. Yeshua added: *And if your hand or your foot causes you to stumble, cut it off, and cast it from you* (Mt. 18:8). All matters of stumbling should be put away; even members intended for useful work may at times need to be put away to avoid the greater loss. Yeshua was not teaching self-mutilation, though throughout church history some have mutilated and even castrated themselves. The issue is not self-mutilation, but rather the need to deal with the root of the problem: Whatever causes a person to stumble or causes others to stumble must be put away.

In the case of the unbeliever, he will be cast *into the unquenchable fire* and *cast into hell* (Mk. 9:43-44). Matthew called it *the eternal fire* (Mt. 18:8). Unbelievers who cause the stumbling of believers, especially believing children, will suffer greater judgment in the lake of fire, *where their worm dies not, and the fire is not quenched* (Mk. 9:48). Believers, on the other hand, will not end up in the lake of fire. However, they will suffer greater discipline in this life and loss of rewards in the next if they cause others to stumble

After explaining the severity of the offense, Yeshua applied His teaching to the disciples: *See that ye despise not one of these little ones; for I say unto you, that in heaven their angels do always behold the face of my Father who is in heaven* (Mt. 18:10). This verse teaches that all children have guardian angels who report how people cause them to stumble.

Matthew mentioned the Father's underlying principle: *Even so it is not the will of your Father who is in heaven, that one of these little ones should perish* (Mt. 18:14). Again, the emphasis is on children, and both believers and unbelievers will suffer greater punishment if they cause one of them to stumble.

Yeshua added to this the principle of salt: *For every one shall be salted with fire. Salt is good: but if salt have lost its saltiness, wherewith will ye season it? Have salt in yourselves, and be at peace one with another* (Mk. 9:49-50). He made two points in these verses. He first mentioned the judgment all believers will undergo (Rom. 14:10-12; II Cor. 5:10). Their works will *be salted with fire* at the judgment seat of the Messiah, meaning they will be tested by fire (I Cor. 3:12-15). While the good and faithful deeds will be purified, just as precious metals are purified by fire, the bad deeds will be burnt up like wood, hay, and straw. Yeshua's second point pertains to the positive attributes of salt. In its Talmudic usage, the phrase, "Salt is good, but if the salt has lost its saltiness wherewith will you season it?", is an expression of the impossible. In Judaism, salt was added to every sacrifice to symbolize the incorruptible, the higher, and the acuteness of the intellect. Salt was compared to the soul and to Scripture, and it was a symbol of God's covenant relationship with Israel. The Talmud teaches that the world cannot survive without salt. Salt was a necessity of life in the ancient world; it was used to preserve food. Salt generally does not lose its saltiness; therefore, many people have had a problem with the statement, *if the salt loses its saltiness.* However, the salt used for the sacrifices at the Second Temple was taken from the Dead Sea. Salt from the Dead Sea can lose its savory quality and become insipid.

By way of application, salt typifies that quality which is the distinctive mark of a disciple, the loss of which will make him useless for the Lord. Thus, the disciples were to retain their salt-like quality and be at peace among themselves. When Yeshua said, *Have salt in yourselves* (Mk. 9:50), He meant they should attract others by their saltiness, being at peace with and showing love for one another. Salt causes thirst. Their saltiness should make others thirst for what they have, namely, the water of life.

[§ 95] — U. Instruction Concerning Forgiveness

Matthew 18:15-35

This is the second time the church is mentioned in the Gospel of Matthew. Previously, the term referred to the universal church (Mt. 16:18).[9] Here it refers to the local church, since the passage deals with church discipline. Yeshua naturally moved from a discussion on causing offense to a discussion on how the church is to proceed when an offense has occurred.

In such cases, church discipline should follow four steps. First, *if your brother sins against you, go, show him his fault between you and him alone: if he hear you, you have gained your brother* (Mt. 18:15). The offended brother is responsible for approaching the offender, one on one, privately, to point out his sin. Talking with anyone else in advance violates the principle. This passage does not concern moral sin, as is the case in I Corinthians 5:1-5, where Paul tells the elders to immediately remove the immoral member from the congregation. This passage addresses a personal issue where one member has offended another.

Second, if the offender does not respond, he must once again be confronted, this time by one or two additional people. The underlying principle is *that at the mouth of two or three every word may be established* (Mt. 18:16). If the offender responds positively to this confrontation, then fellowship should be restored.

Third, if the offender still fails to respond, *tell it unto the church* (Mt. 18:17a).

Fourth, if, after having been admonished by the brethren, he still refuses to repent, the principle is: *let him be unto you as the Gentile and the publican* (Mt. 18:17b). In the Jewish context, this means the person is untouchable, excommunicated, and banned from the fellowship.

---

[9] The universal church is that spiritual organism of which the Messiah is the head. It is composed of all believers from Pentecost (Acts 2) until the rapture. The universal church is also called "the invisible church" or "the body of Messiah." In the local (or visible) church, there are both believers and unbelievers as members, but that is not true of the universal church.

Excommunication means that the sinning brother is placed back under Satan's authority for the destruction of the flesh, but not his spirit, so his salvation is not affected (I Cor. 5:1-5). Normally, Satan has no authority over the death of a believer, as it is Yeshua who puts him to sleep (I Thess. 4:13-15). The one exception to this rule is the case of an excommunicated believer; Satan has the authority to put that believer to death. He can choose the moment of the believer's passing, but his authority is only over physical, not spiritual life: *If any man see his brother sinning a sin not unto death, he shall ask, and God will give him life for them that sin not unto death. There is a sin unto death: not concerning this do I say that he should make request* (I Jn. 5:16). The believer who has committed the *sin unto death* is facing physical extinction because he was excommunicated. For such a person, intercessory prayer ceases; he is not only outside the fellowship of the local church, but also outside the prayers of the saints.

The next three verses are a continuation of the teaching on church discipline, but they are frequently taken out of context and misapplied. In verse 18, Yeshua explained, *Verily I say unto you, what things so ever ye shall bind on earth shall be bound in heaven; and what things so ever ye shall loose on earth shall be loosed in heaven.* The terms "binding" and "loosing" have already been defined in the Jewish context,[10] and it was stated that they were used legislatively and judicially. Legislatively, "to bind" meant to forbid, and "to loose" meant to permit. Judicially, "to bind" meant to punish, and "to loose" meant not to punish. This authority was given to the apostles alone, and they kept it until the end of their lives. The church also has the authority to bind and to loose in a judicial sense, but not to the same degree as the apostles, who could issue a death sentence. The church can bind and loose to the point of breaking or not breaking fellowship with a sinning believer. It can excommunicate or not excommunicate. Notice, therefore, that this verse does not refer to binding Satan or his demons, so the context is not spiritual warfare, but church discipline.

Yeshua continued: *Again I say unto you, that if two of you shall agree on earth as touching anything that they shall ask, it shall be done for them of my Father who is in heaven* (Mt. 18:19). This verse, too, has

---

[10] See § 84.

been taken out of context, and many use it as a prayer promise, that if two believers agree on anything on earth, it will definitely be done, and the prayer will definitely be answered in the affirmative. This misconception has led to many disappointments. The context is not prayer, but church discipline. The two people who agree are the witnesses who confront the brother with his sin and who witness to the local church that the sinning brother had not responded appropriately (Mt. 18:15-17). Therefore, the actions of the church are based upon the testimony of the two witnesses. In turn, the decision of the church is recognized by heaven, and heaven allows Satan to take that believer's life.

Yeshua concluded: *For where two or three are gathered together in my name, there am I in the midst of them* (Mt. 18:20). This verse is also frequently taken out of context and understood to mean that this gathering of believers is a local church. However, two or three believers gathered together does not define the local church. In the New Testament, a local church is an organized entity under the authority of elders and deacons; i.e., a structured body with a chain of authority. The verse needs to be viewed in the context of church discipline. The *two or three* are the witnesses who testify to the church that the sinning brother has not repented (Mt. 18:15-17). If their testimony is valid, then Yeshua is among them, authenticating their deposition. Since Yeshua is authenticating their statement, heaven removes the protection from the sinning brother, who can then be put to death by Satan.

At this point, Peter raised a question: *Lord, how oft shall my brother sin against me, and I forgive him? Until seven times?* (Mt. 18:21). Compared to the Pharisees, the apostle was being quite generous. By Pharisaic Law, a person was only bound to forgive three times and after that was not obligated to forgive again. Peter generously doubled what the Pharisees offered and added one more for good measure. Yeshua, however, answered: *I say not unto you, Until seven times; but, Until seventy times seven* (Mt. 18:22). Yeshua's use of this figure of speech did not mean that we need to forgive exactly 490 times. In the Scriptures, the number seven often emphasizes completeness, totality, and perfection, so Yeshua's statement implies unlimited forgiveness. As often as the brother asks, just as often he is to be forgiven. The very act of counting offenses only shows external, not internal, forgiveness.

To illustrate the point further, Yeshua told the Parable of the Unmerciful Servant (Mt. 18:23-35). In this parable, a king forgave a servant a staggering amount of debt. However, the servant was unwilling to forgive someone else who owed him only a pittance. He even had the debtor sent to prison. When the king found out about it, he punished the wicked servant.

This parable teaches three things. First, having received forgiveness from God, we should develop a forgiving spirit. Realizing that we have been forgiven much should make us willing to forgive much. Obviously, we cannot extend forgiveness until the other person asks for it; nevertheless, the willingness to forgive should always be there. Second, God's children should imitate their Father's forgiveness. Third, an unforgiving person cannot, and should not, expect to be forgiven: *So shall also my heavenly Father do unto you, if ye forgive not every one his brother from your hearts* (Mt. 18:35). This is not speaking about salvation forgiveness, but fellowship and family forgiveness. Concerning salvation, our sins have been forgiven forever. However, believers still sin, and when they confess their trespasses, they receive family forgiveness from God. If a person is unwilling to forgive a brother who has sinned against him, then he has no basis for seeking forgiveness from God for his own sins. God will withhold familial forgiveness from an unforgiving believer.

[§ 96] — V. The Challenge by the Brothers

John 7:2-9

Now the feast of the Jews, the feast of tabernacles, was at hand (Jn. 7:2). This occasion raised an issue. From Zechariah 14:16-21, the Jewish people knew that the Feast of Tabernacles was to be fulfilled by the messianic kingdom. Therefore, Yeshua's four half-brothers challenged Him to go to Jerusalem and make Himself king in fulfillment of these verses, saying, *Depart hence, and go into Yehudah, that your disciples also may behold your works which you do. For no man does anything in secret, and himself seeks to be known openly. If you do these things, manifest yourself to the world* (Jn. 7:3-4). This challenge arose out of unbelief: *For even His brethren did not believe on him* (Jn. 7:5). They were saying, "If you really are the Messiah, go to the Feast of Tabernacles and make yourself king, as Zechariah 14 predicted."

Yeshua answered: *My time is not yet come; but your time is always ready* (Jn. 7:6). The appointed time for Yeshua to fulfill Zechariah 14 had not yet arrived. However, their appointed time of death was unknown to them; therefore, just in case they were in the final days, they should always be ready and walk worthily.

The world cannot hate you; but me it hates, because I testify of it, that its works are evil (Jn. 7:7). The world hated Yeshua because He testified of its sins. He recognized the danger He would face in Jerusalem. The works of His half-brothers were evil in that they were already trying to have Him killed. So He said to them: *Go ye up unto the feast: I go not up unto this feast; because my time is not yet fulfilled* (Jn. 7:8). Yeshua would not die at this Feast of Tabernacles. When He said, *I go not up unto this feast*, it did not mean He would not go there at all. It meant that He was not going in response to their challenge. Yeshua did go to Jerusalem to attend the Feast of Tabernacles, but not in response to the brothers' challenge to make Himself king. That could not happen because His time was not yet fulfilled. In light of the fact that the nation had rejected Him, this was not the time to set up the kingdom.

Thus, *having said these things unto them, he abode <still> in Galil* (Jn. 7:9). The brothers left, and Yeshua stayed in Galilee a while longer. Only in the next section do we see how He began to move toward Jerusalem for the observance of the Feast of Tabernacles.

[§ 97] — W. The Journey to Jerusalem

Luke 9:51-56, John 7:10

Yochanan's account records Yeshua's departure for Jerusalem, after waiting until His brothers had left: *But when his brethren were gone up unto the feast, then went he also up, not publicly, but as it were in secret*

(Jn. 7:10). The Messiah left for Jerusalem, but not in response to the challenge of His brothers. He went on the basis of His own motivation, His own program, His own plan: *And it came to pass, when the days were well-near come that he should be received up, he steadfastly set his face to go to Yerushalayim* (Lk. 9:51). Yeshua knew that this would be the last Feast of Tabernacles before He would be received up into heaven. This celebration marked the beginning of the last six months of His life. To ensure preparations were made, He *sent messengers before his face* (Lk. 9:52a) to prepare places along the way where He could stay.

Yeshua wanted to go up to Jerusalem by way of Samaria. As stated earlier, the Samaritans did not trouble Jews who came down from Jerusalem and passed through their territory, but they did not want Samaria to be used as a thoroughfare for Jews going up to Jerusalem, the rival city of Mount Gerizim. So while Yeshua had not been harassed when He passed through Samaria on the way from Jerusalem, He now encountered problems: *and they went, and entered into a village*[11] *of the Samaritans, to make ready for him. And they did not receive him, because his face was <as though he were> going to Yerushalayim* (Lk. 9:52b-53). The messengers sent in advance were rejected and were not allowed passage through Samaria for the specific reason that Yeshua was heading toward Jerusalem. This was a display of Samaritan animosity toward the city. According to Josephus, Samaritans were even known to kill Jews passing through Samaria on the way to Jerusalem. Here, they merely refused to give Yeshua passage through their country.

The disciples responded very negatively to this. While the Samaritan reaction was based upon anti-Judaism, the reaction of the disciples was based upon anti-Samaritanism: *And when His disciples Yaakov and Yochanan saw <this>, they said, Lord, will you that we bid fire to come down from heaven, and consume them?* (Lk. 9:54). This response came from the two brothers James and Yochanan. They wanted to destroy the Samaritans out of vengeance and personal hurt. Yochanan will later become known as the apostle of love, but that was not the attribute he displayed here. Here he is portrayed with a very different attitude which

---

[11] This was probably Ein Ganim, modern-day Jenin.

shows just how much his life changed as a result of the death and resurrection of the Messiah. Yeshua's response to the brothers' question was negative: *But he turned, and rebuked them. And they went to another village* (Lk. 9:55-56). He bypassed Samaria, taking the longer route via Perea, east of the Jordan River.

[§ 98] — X. Instruction Concerning Discipleship

Matthew 8:19-22, Luke 9:57-62

And as they went on the way (Lk. 9:57) and made their way to Jerusalem, Yeshua taught three lessons on discipleship. At this point, it is once again important to distinguish between discipleship and salvation. Salvation requires only belief in the gospel message that the Messiah died as our substitute (Jn. 1:12). Discipleship, however, requires a lot more. Previously, Yeshua had taught three lessons on discipleship: that a man must deny himself, take up his cross (identify with the Messiah's rejection), and follow Him. In this section, Yeshua elaborated, teaching a lesson on each of the three points.

Matthew provided the occasion for the first lesson: *And there came a scribe, and said unto him, Teacher, I will follow you whithersoever you go. And* Yeshua *said unto him, The foxes have holes, and the birds of the heaven <have> nests; but the Son of man has not where to lay his head* (Mt. 8:19-20). The first lesson is to count the cost before becoming a disciple. Yeshua pointed out to the scribe that He Himself lived in poverty; therefore, He could promise to provide for his needs, but He could not provide any assurance of comfort. The scribe is portrayed as being too hasty. By not counting the cost, he broke the first rule of discipleship: *let him deny himself* (Mt. 16:24; Mk. 8:34; Lk. 9:23).

The second lesson is that once committed, do not delay: *And he said unto another, Follow me. But he said, Lord, suffer me first to go and bury my father. But he said unto him, Leave the dead to bury their own dead; but go you and publish abroad the kingdom of God* (Lk. 9:59-60). This time, Yeshua initiated the call. The potential disciple requested that he first be allowed to bury his father before becoming a disciple. Yeshua has been criticized for lacking love in this situation. After all, how long would it take to bury a body? However, this criticism ignores the Jewish context from which this statement was made. The point is that the father was not yet dead. In common rabbinic teaching, the firstborn son, which presumably this man was, must stay with his father until he dies. After his father's death, the son is to stay close to where his father was buried and say the special *Kaddish*[12] for him. Then, he is free to go wherever he wants. So, the issue was not that his father had died and he was only staying to bury the body. He was saying, "I want to wait until my father dies, wait another year to say Kaddish, and then I will follow you." While the first disciple reacted too quickly and with haste, this disciple was too slow and hesitant. Discipleship requires immediate self-surrender after counting the cost. The principle is this: Once committed, do not delay. This man failed in the second principle of discipleship, to *take up his cross* (Mt. 16:24; Mk. 8:34; Lk. 9:23). Yeshua's response was to let those who are spiritually dead bury the ones who are physically dead.

The third lesson is that there must be no division of loyalty: *And another also said, I will follow you, Lord; but first suffer me to bid farewell to them that are at my house. But* Yeshua *said unto him, No man, having put his hand to the plow, and looking back, is fit for the kingdom of God* (Lk. 9:61-62). As in the first case, an individual offered himself to discipleship, but laid down a condition. He asked for permission to bid farewell to his family first. Yeshua's response has also been criticized as being unloving, but the problem was not that the man merely wanted to say farewell. Rather, members of his family were not only keeping him from fulfilling a commitment he had made, they were keeping him from fully committing in the first place. This man did not make the proper choice when he had to decide between his family or the Messiah. The principle here is: Once a person makes a commitment, there must be no division of loyalty. One must not go back, but must sever all ties that could hold him back. If the family fully encouraged discipleship, there would be no problem; but often families discourage a full commitment because it would mean the loss of a child. This disciple is

---

[12] Often called a prayer for the dead, the content does not request any benefit for the dead one, but recognizes the sovereignty of God in the matter.

characterized by being undecided. He broke the third key principle of discipleship: *Follow me* (Mt. 16:24; Mk. 8:34; Lk. 9:23).

ABOVE: Built and renovated over the course of four hundred years, the grandeur and beauty of the Second Temple in Jerusalem inspired awe and deep respect among Jews and Gentiles alike. The building was of shining white marble and gold, and the entrance doors were made of bronze. It was said that one could not look at the Temple in daylight without running the risk of getting blinded by its brilliance (3D-illustration by Jesse and Josh Gonzales).

V. THE OPPOSITION
TO THE KING
— §§ 99–112 —

The fifth division of Yeshua's life covers a three-month period during His last year, beginning with the Feast of Tabernacles in October and ending with the Feast of the Dedication (or *Chanukah*) in December. Only two of the four Gospel writers, Luke and Yochanan, covered this three-month period. Luke emphasized Yeshua's ministry in the general area of Judea, while Yochanan focused on Yeshua's ministry specifically in the city of Jerusalem.

Three observations can be made about this section. First, the masses now began to accept the explanation of the Pharisees that Yeshua was demon possessed. Up to this point, opposition had only come from the leaders. The people were not sure whom to follow; therefore, they were described as sheep without a shepherd. However, the sheep now began to follow their false shepherds, accepting the explanation of the Pharisees concerning the charge that He cast out demons by Beelzebub. Second, the key phrase in this section is, *there arose a division* (Jn. 7:43).

Third, this section contains the fourth of Yochanan's seven discourses, the discourse on the water of life (Jn. 7:25-44).

[§ 99] — A. The Conflict
at the Feast of Tabernacles

The conflict at the Feast of Tabernacles is described in John 7:11-52 and a few introductory statements are in order before examining several points.

During the Second Temple period (515 B.C.-A.D. 70), two key ceremonies were conducted during the Feast of Tabernacles. Yeshua responded to those two ceremonies in words and actions. The first ceremony, called the "Outpouring of the Water," or *Nisuch Ha-Mayim* in Hebrew, was also referred to as the "Rejoicing of the House of the Drawing," or *Simchat Bet Ha-Shoeivah*. Every day for seven days, the priests marched down the steep hill from the Temple compound to the bottom south end of the City of David. When they reached the Pool of Siloam, they filled jugs and pitchers with water and returned to the Temple through the Water Gate. They were now in the outer court of the Temple. To enter the inner court, they ascended 15 steps. On the first step, they sang Psalm 120; on the second step, Psalm 121, continuing until they had sung psalms 120 through 134. Each of these Psalms is subtitled *A Song (or Psalm) of Ascents* because the priests sang them as they ascended from the outer to the inner court.

Upon entering the inner court, they poured out the water at the base of the altar. Tremendous rejoicing followed. As the Mishnah states: "He who has not seen the rejoicing at the place of the water-drawing has never seen rejoicing in his life."[1] The Pharisaic-rabbinic interpretation of the ceremony was that this symbolized the outpouring of the Holy Spirit upon Israel in the last days. Five times in the Hebrew Scriptures, the prophets spoke of the outpouring of the Spirit on all Israel in the last days, and the ceremony of the outpouring of the water symbolized

---

[1] Tractate *Sukkah*, 5.1.

that future outpouring. The Pharisees themselves connected this with the work of the Holy Spirit. In Judaism, however, the Holy Spirit was not a personality of the Godhead, but a divine force or influence of the one God.

The second important ceremony was the "Kindling of the Lamp-stands." Throughout the entire Temple compound, in both the outer and inner courts, huge lampstands were erected, each containing four lamps. At dusk, the junior priests, or apprentices who were training for the priesthood, kindled these lampstands. The Mishnah states that so much light emanated from the Temple compound, that every private courtyard in Jerusalem received the benefit of that light. The rabbinic interpretation of the kindling of the lampstands was that it represented the Shechinah glory, the visible manifestation of God's presence.

1. Messiah's Authority Questioned

John 7:11-15

The Jews therefore sought him at [the Feast of Tabernacles], *and said, Where is he?* (Jn. 7:11). It is wise to note how Yochanan used the term "Jews" throughout his Gospel. He employed the word 71 times in three different ways. Sometimes he referred to Jews in general, meaning all the descendants of Abraham, Isaac, and Jacob, as was the case when Yeshua said to the Samaritan woman, *salvation is from the Jews* (Jn. 4:22). A second way was to distinguish Jews as Judeans from Galileans, which is the case in this chapter. Finally, Yochanan used the term in reference to the Jewish leaders, as when he wrote, *for fear of the Jews* (Jn. 7:13).

The Jews sought Yeshua because of the significance of the Feast of Tabernacles. From Zechariah 14:16-21, they knew that this feast was to be fulfilled by the messianic kingdom,[2] which is why they were now expecting Him to set up that kingdom. The theme of division in this section is evident: *And there was much murmuring among the multitudes concerning him: some said, He is a good man; others said, Not so,*

---

[2] As mentioned in § 96.

but he leads the multitude astray (Jn. 7:12). The multitudes were divided in their opinion of Yeshua. However, the discussion was carried out quietly: *Yet no man spoke openly of him for fear of the Jews* (Jn. 7:13). In this verse, the speakers were Jews (Jn. 7:11), and Yochanan used the term in reference to Judeans. These Jews did not speak openly of Yeshua for fear of other Jews, the religious leaders.

For three days, they sought Him without success: *But when it was now the midst of the feast Yeshua went up into the temple, and taught* (Jn. 7:14). The wording means that Yeshua suddenly went public in the middle of the feast, which would make it the fourth day. The content of His teaching led to this response: *The Jews therefore marveled, saying, How knows this man letters, having never learned?* (Jn. 7:15). The question challenged Yeshua's authority: How was this man able to speak with authority, since He had never attended nor received ordination from any of the rabbinical schools? The multitudes knew that the leaders had rejected Him.

2. Messiah's Answer

John 7:16-24

In answer to the multitudes' question, Yeshua made a twofold claim: He had received His teaching from God, and He was sent by God to teach it: *My teaching is not mine, but his that sent me* (Jn. 7:16). Those who truly desire to do the will of God would recognize that His teaching was from God (Jn. 7:17). Furthermore, the person who is sent seeks the glory of the sender (Jn. 7:18). Yeshua sought the glory of the Father, so there was no unrighteousness in Him. The real problem was their own failure to keep the law, as evident in their desire to kill Him: *Did not Mosheh give you the law, and <yet> none of you does the law? Why seek ye to kill me?* (Jn. 7:19). Their failure to keep the Mosaic Law was also the reason they failed to recognize who He was.

The people answered, *You have a demon: who seeks to kill you?* (Jn. 7:20). The charge of demonism now came from the multitudes, providing Yeshua with another opportunity to expose their misunderstanding of the law, such as their misinterpretation of what it meant to keep the Sabbath (Jn. 7:21-23). They accused Him of violating the Sabbath by healing someone on that day, yet the rabbis themselves said that the law of circumcision superseded the law of the Sabbath. If, for example, the eighth day of a boy's life happened to fall on a Sabbath, the rabbis were required to circumcise the child, though it was considered a "work." Yeshua reasoned that if it is permissible to mutilate on the Sabbath day, how much more is it permissible to make whole on the Sabbath day? According to the Law of Moses, Sabbath rest included the possibility of healing.

3. Messiah's Person Questioned

John 7:25-27

Some local Jerusalemites raised the next issue (Jn. 7:25). As citizens of Jerusalem, they were closest to the schools of the Pharisees and other leaders and, therefore, would first hear what the religious elite said and thought. They asked, *Is not this he whom they seek to kill? And lo, he speaks openly, and they say nothing unto him* (Jn. 7:25b-26a). The leaders' unwillingness to stop Yeshua puzzled them: *Can it be that the rulers indeed know that this is the Messiah?* (Jn. 7:26b). Did the leaders let Yeshua teach in the Temple because they knew He was the Messiah? If this were the case, the question is: *Howbeit we know this man where he is: but when the Messiah comes, no one knows from where he is* (Jn. 7:27). They questioned Yeshua's person because no one was supposed to know from where the Messiah will come, but they all knew Yeshua's origin.

4. Messiah's Explanation

John 7:28-30

In His response to the objection, Yeshua stated that while they knew His human origin, they did not know His divine origin. However, because He spoke in parables, they could not understand Him: *Yeshua therefore cried in the temple, teaching and saying, Ye both know me, and know from where I am; and I am not come of myself, but he that sent me is true, whom ye know not. I know him; because I am from him, and he sent me* (Jn. 7:28).

Some tried to take hold of Him unsuccessfully because this was not the divinely appointed time of His death: *his hour was not yet come* (Jn. 7:30).

5. The People's Response

John 7:31-36

Again, the multitude was divided. Some rejected Him, but others believed on Him (Jn. 7:30-31). They were convinced by the signs they had seen and wondered if anyone else could have performed more miracles than Yeshua had already done. The obvious answer was "no."

The antagonism of the religious leaders becomes evident in the next verse: *The Pharisees heard the multitude murmuring these things concerning him* (Jn. 7:32). Hearing the debate among the multitude concerning the person of Yeshua particularly exasperated them. With the agreement of the high priest, himself a Sadducee, they sent officers of the temple police to arrest Him.

In response to their attack, Yeshua declared His coming departure: *Yet a little while I am with you, and I go unto him that sent me. Ye shall seek me, and shall not find me: and where I am, ye cannot come* (Jn. 7:33-34). The people's response shows they did not understand what He was saying since He continued to speak in parables: *The Jews therefore said among themselves, Whither will this man go that we shall not find him? Will he go unto the Dispersion among the Greeks, and teach the Greeks?* (Jn. 7:35). The word *Dispersion* was a technical Jewish term referring to Jews living outside the land. The point of their question was this: "Will He leave the country and teach the Greek-speaking Jews?" And they tried to make sense of what He said: *What is this word that he said, Ye shall seek me, and shall not find me; and where I am, ye cannot come?* (Jn. 7:36).

6. Messiah's Invitation

John 7:37-44

This passage begins with the words, *Now on the last day, the great <day> of the feast* (Jn. 7:37a). Of the seven days of the Feast of Tabernacles, the seventh was by far the most important. During the first six days, the priests circled the altar only once; but on the last day, they circled the altar seven times and continued to recite from Psalm 118: *Hoshanah Rabbah, save us in the highest* (v. 25). The priests held an additional willow branch during their circuits around the altar, and water was especially emphasized.

As noted previously, the rabbis interpreted the outpouring of the water as the outpouring of the Holy Spirit, and so, in response to the first ceremony, Yeshua declared: *If any man thirst, let him come unto me and drink. He that believes on me, as the scripture has said, from within him shall flow rivers of living water* (Jn. 7:37b-38). Yochanan interpreted this to refer specifically to the Holy Spirit, saying that *this spoke he of the Spirit* (Jn. 7:39a). Like the rabbis, Yeshua also identified the outpouring of the water with the Holy Spirit. However, by saying that if anyone believes, *from within him shall flow rivers of living water*, He applied the ceremony individually rather than nationally. Those who accept His Messiahship will be indwelled by the Holy Spirit, and rivers of living water will flow from within.

At this point, many people already believed in Him, but had not yet received the indwelling of the Holy Spirit, *because Yeshua was not yet glorified* (Jn. 7:39b). The permanent, universal indwelling of the Spirit among all believers would only occur after His ascension. Old Testament saints experienced the regenerating work of the Holy Spirit, which was different from His indwelling work. Only some of them, especially the prophets, were indwelled by the Holy Spirit, but not on a permanent basis. David's prayer, *take not your holy Spirit from me* (Ps. 51:11), was a valid Old Testament prayer, but it is not a valid New Testament prayer because now the Holy Spirit indwells all believers forever.

Yeshua's call to salvation led to a three-way division. First, *Some of the multitude therefore, when they heard these words, said, This is of a truth the prophet* (Jn. 7:40). They viewed Yeshua as being the prophet of Deuteronomy 18. Second, *Others said, This is the Messiah* (Jn. 7:41a). Third, *But some said, What, does the Messiah come out of Galil?* (Jn. 7:41b). They did not know that Yeshua was born in Bethlehem and assumed He was born in Nazareth, which was not the prophesied birthplace of the Messiah. This leads to the motif of this section: *So there arose a division in the multitude because of him* (Jn. 7:43).

The officers sent to arrest Yeshua tried to take hold of Him but failed because no man could lay hands on Him (Jn. 7:44).

7. The Pharisaic Response

John 7:45-52

When the officers returned to the Pharisees and the Sadducean chief priests empty-handed (Jn. 7:45), they explained, *Never man so spoke* (Jn. 7:46). They were so enthralled by Yeshua's words that they did not complete the arrest. The Pharisees retorted, saying, *Are ye also led astray? Has any of the rulers believed on him, or of the Pharisees? But this multitude that knows not the law are accursed* (Jn. 7:47-49). They responded that Yeshua had not persuaded any of the Pharisees who knew the Scriptures and the law. He had only persuaded common people who did not know the law. The rabbis referred to these people in the Talmud as the *am ha-aretz*, "the people of the land," a derogatory term for those ignorant of Rabbinic Judaism.

The problem with their assessment was that one among them had begun to move towards faith: Nicodemus. Nicodemus made a half-hearted attempt to defend Yeshua: *Does our law judge a man, except it first hear from himself and know what he does?* (Jn. 7:51). Nicodemus reminded the Pharisees that their law required an open hearing before any word of condemnation could be spoken. His fellow Pharisees attacked him, saying: *Are you also of Galil?* (Jn. 7:52a). Calling a Judean a Galilean negatively implied, "Are you also as stupid as they are?" They overstated their case, however, when they demanded: *Search, and see that out of Galil arises no prophet* (Jn. 7:52b). At least three prophets came from Galilee: Hosea, Jonah, and Elisha.

[§ 100] — B. The Conflict over the Law

John 7:53-8:11[3]

Up to this point, the Pharisees had no opportunity to accuse Yeshua of breaking the Law of Moses, because He kept every jot and tittle of it perfectly. This event is their only attempt to get Him to verbally contradict that law. If they could achieve that, it would render His claim of keeping the law perfectly null and void. They chose to bring up the situation while Yeshua was teaching in the Temple (Jn. 7:53-8:2) to discredit Him publicly, especially over an issue for which the punishment was not debatable, the issue of adultery. That is the presumed case here: *And the scribes and Pharisees bring a woman taken in adultery; and having set her in the midst, they say unto him, Teacher, this woman has been taken in adultery, in the very act* (Jn. 8:3-4). To assure Yeshua that the woman had been caught in the very act of adultery and was undoubtedly guilty, they implied eyewitnesses were involved.

Yochanan pointed out that this was an obvious attempt to entrap Yeshua: *And this they said, trying him, that they might have <whereof> to accuse him* (Jn. 8:6a). The Law of Moses was very clear: A man and a woman caught in the act of adultery were to be put to death (Lev. 20:10; Deut. 22:22). So, the concern of the scribes and Pharisees was the Mosaic Law: *Now in the law Mosheh commanded us to stone such: what then do you say of her?* (Jn. 8:5). The religious leaders wanted Yeshua to contradict this law. The Greek is more emphatic: "Now Moses said to stone such, but you, what do you say?" However, to be caught in the act of adultery requires that two people be brought before the judges. So, where was the male counterpart of this relationship?

---

[3] Most of the ancient authorities omit John 7:53-8:11. Those which contain it vary from each other.

Initially, Yeshua simply refused to answer, but instead performed a specific act: He *stooped down, and with his finger wrote on the ground* (Jn. 8:6b). When the Pharisees pressed Him for an answer, Yeshua finally gave them one: *And again he stooped down, and with his finger wrote on the ground* (Jn. 8:8). Amazingly, many commentaries try to determine what Yeshua wrote on the ground, as if after two thousand years something would be left in the dust to decipher. However, in the Greek text, the emphasis is not on the writing, but on the finger. In the Greek language, the same thing can be said in different ways, but the point the author wants to emphasize is usually placed at the start of the sentence; this is called the "emphatic position" or the "emphatic state." The finger, not the writing, is in the emphatic position in this verse: *and with his finger wrote on the ground*. Why would the emphasis be on the finger? Of the 613 commandments God gave to Moses, 603 were written on parchment with the pen of a man. The other ten were inscribed onto tablets of stone, and one of the ten was the law against adultery. Furthermore, the ten inscribed onto stone were not carved with the chisel of a man, but twice it is explicitly stated that they were inscribed with the very finger of God (Ex. 31:18; Deut. 9:10). Again, the emphasis is on the finger, showing that Yeshua, as the author of this commandment, knew exactly all that the Mosaic Law said about this sin and its punishment.

The specific answer Yeshua gave them was, *He that is without sin among you, let him first cast a stone at her* (Jn. 8:7). This is often pulled out of context to mean something not intended: that one should not judge others. However, the Bible requires believers to pass judgment at times. Confronting a brother who has sinned is a matter of judgment. Church discipline leading to excommunication is a matter of judgment. Furthermore, if He were saying, "Only if you are without sin yourself should you cast the first stone," He would be contradicting the Law of Moses, which did not require the sinlessness of a witness before the accused could be executed as a criminal. Under these conditions, no one could be executed under the law, and yet the law required execution for certain sins, one of which was the sin of adultery. Therefore, if Yeshua said they should cast the first stone only if they were sinless, He would have broken the Mosaic Law, and they would have had a basis for accusing Him.

Yeshua was making the point that if this woman is judged on the basis of the Mosaic Law, they would have to judge her on all that Moses said about this sin and its punishment. Yes, Moses said anyone guilty of adultery must be stoned to death, but that was not all. Moses also said that no one could be stoned to death except at the testimony of two or three witnesses. This much they had, since they claimed she was caught in the very act. Moses also said that the two or three witnesses whose testimony condemned the guilty one to death must be the ones to cast the first stone. Furthermore, they had to be faithful and true (Deut. 13:9; 17:2-7), which indicated to some that the two or three witnesses whose testimony condemned an adulteress to death and who were responsible for casting the first stone must not be guilty of the same sin as the accused. Therefore, in the context of their own theology, Yeshua said that if the two or three witnesses were innocent of the same sin, they should cast the first stone, just as Moses had commanded. However, one by one, the men walked away, implying that, at least among the accusers, not one person was innocent of this sin. Perhaps the one with whom she had been caught in the very act was standing among the accusers.

Finally, the woman accused of adultery stood alone. Yeshua asked her: *Woman, where are they? Did no man condemn you? And she said, No man, Lord. And Yeshua said, Neither do I condemn you* (Jn. 8:10-11a). He was not excusing her sin, for He added: *go your way; from henceforth sin no more* (Jn. 8:11b). The Law of Moses required a legal condemnation, but because the two or three witnesses were unwilling to cast the first stone, there was no legal ground to condemn her.

It is worth repeating that this was the Pharisees' only attempt to get Yeshua to contradict a point of the Mosaic Law, and it failed miserably. They never tried this ploy again, but continued to accuse the Messiah of violating the Mishnaic-Pharisaic Law.

[§ 101] — C. The Conflict over the Light

John 8:12-20

Before addressing the details of these verses, two general observations can be made. First, this section contains the second of Yeshua's seven "I Am" statements as recorded in the Gospel of Yochanan: *I am the light of the world* (Jn. 8:12a). This is Yeshua's response to the second key ceremony of the Feast of Tabernacles, the kindling of the lampstands, which, in Judaism, symbolizes the presence of the Shechinah glory. Yeshua claimed to be that Shechinah glory, the visible manifestation of the presence of God. He followed this statement with one that was related to Yochanan's sub-theme of the conflict of light and darkness: *He that follows me shall not walk in the darkness, but shall have the light of life* (Jn. 8:12b). Second, this section and the next comprise the fifth of Yochanan's seven discourses, the discourse on the light of the world.

The conflict began when the Pharisees emphasized that Yeshua alone bore witness to Himself (Jn. 8:13). Therefore, because He was the only witness, His testimony could not be true. Yeshua's response was threefold. First, even if it were true that He alone bore witness of Himself, His testimony was true because of His divine and heavenly origin, something they did not understand (Jn. 8:14). Second, their judgment, based on the flesh, was wrong. But His judgment was true and valid because it was backed by the One who sent Him, God the Father (Jn. 8:15-16). Third, He was not the only witness to Himself. An additional witness fulfilled the law's requirement that for any matter to be established (Deut. 19:15), there had to be at least two witnesses (Jn. 8:17-18). The first witness was Yeshua Himself. He made verbal professions, but He also authenticated these with miracles, signs, and wonders, including unique miracles that caused the multitudes to ask if He could be the Son of David. The second witness was God the Father, who bore witness of Him at His baptism with the voice from heaven, which was heard publicly. So, to know Yeshua was to know the Father. The real problem was not a lack of witnesses and their testimonies, but the lack of knowledge of the Father (Jn. 8:19). To know Yeshua was to know the

Father, and because they did not recognize Him, they did not recognize God the Father either.

Yochanan noted that this discussion occurred in the treasury section of the Temple compound (Jn. 8:20a) and that once again Satan had failed to prematurely bring about Yeshua's death: *and no man took him; because his hour was not yet come* (Jn. 8:20b).

[§ 102] — D. The Conflict over His Person

1. Messiah the True Object of Faith

John 8:21-30

Yeshua continued teaching the public in parables, as He had since His rejection, and the people's response clearly indicates that He used terms they could not understand: *The Jews therefore said, Will he kill himself, that he says, Whither I go, you cannot come? . . . They said therefore unto him, Who are you?* (Jn. 8:22, 25). In response, Yeshua made seven specific points:

1. He would depart to a place where they could not follow: *I go away;* and *whither I go, ye cannot come.* (Jn. 8:21a and c).

2. They would die in their sins: *and shall die in your sin.* (Jn. 8:21b).

3. He distinguished between the One He represented and the one they represented: *Ye are from beneath; I am from above* (Jn. 8:23).

4. They had to accept Him as the Messiah to have eternal life and must see Him as the true object of faith: *for except ye believe that I am <he>, ye shall die in your sins* (Jn. 8:24).

5. He will ultimately be the one to judge them: *I have many things to speak and to judge concerning you* (Jn. 8:26a).

6. He was sent from the Father and was the Father's agent: *howbeit he that sent me is true; and the things which I heard from him, these speak I unto the world* (Jn. 8:26b); therefore, He was the

Father's ambassador and said what God the Father wanted Him to say.

7. They would eventually crucify Him. He stated this in a way they did not understand: *When ye have lifted up the Son of man, then shall ye know that I am <he>, and <that> I do nothing of myself, but as the Father taught me, I speak these things* (Jn. 8:28). They would realize too late that He really was the Messiah whom the Father had sent and that the Father never left the Son alone, since all Yeshua did was pleasing to Him (Jn. 8:29).

Since most of the people did not understand His parables, *They perceived not that he spoke to them of the Father* (Jn. 8:27). However, for some, the light did break through: *As he spoke these things, many believed on him* (Jn. 8:30).

2. Messiah the True Deliverer

a. From Sin

John 8:31-40

Yeshua said to those Jews who believed: *If ye abide in my word, <then> are ye truly my disciples; and ye shall know the truth, and the truth shall make you free* (Jn. 8:31-32). While their belief saved them, abiding in His word would make them true disciples. As they came to know the truth, it would set them free. However, as new believers, they were not yet free from Pharisaic teaching, as their response indicates: *We are Avraham's seed, and have never yet been in bondage to any man: how say you, Ye shall be made free?* (Jn. 8:33).[4] This reflects their adherence to the fundamental Pharisaic belief that all Israel will have a share in the age to come. Addressing the wider audience, Yeshua said that if the doctrine were true, they would not be enslaved as they were because the principle is, *Every one that commits sin is the bondservant of sin* (Jn. 8:34). They needed to be freed by exercising faith in the Messiah (Jn. 8:35). If they believed, the result would be freedom: *If therefore the Son*

---

[4] It is also possible that this response came from those who had not believed.

shall make you free, ye shall be free indeed (Jn. 8:36). They were of the physical seed of Abraham, not his spiritual seed, as demonstrated by their desire to kill Yeshua (Jn. 8:37) and their failure to recognize that He spoke the words of His Father, while they spoke the words of their father, Satan (Jn. 8:38).

When Yeshua said *your father*, it led to this response: *Our father is Avraham* (Jn. 8:39a), to which Yeshua rebutted, *If ye were Avraham's children, ye would do the works of Avraham* (Jn. 8:39b). What was Abraham's key work? He put his faith in God: *And he believed in Jehovah; and he reckoned it to him for righteousness* (Gen. 15:6). True children of Abraham seek their salvation the same way Abraham did: by grace through faith, apart from works. Abraham did not assume that by virtue of his birth he automatically had righteousness. They failed to do the works of Abraham, as evident in their desire to kill Him: *But now ye seek to kill me, a man that has told you the truth, which I heard from God; this did not Avraham* (Jn. 8:40). Their desire to kill Yeshua proved their bondage to sin. If they believed, they would have discovered that Yeshua is the true deliverer from sin: *If therefore the Son shall make you free, ye shall be free indeed* (Jn. 8:36).

b. From Satan

John 8:41-50

This section covers six specific points Yeshua made while addressing the unbelieving elements in the crowd. Two verbal reactions of the audience to His words are also included. First, Yeshua declared, *Ye do the works of your father* (Jn. 8:41a), to which the audience responded, *We were not born of fornication; we have one Father, <even> God* (Jn. 8:41b). They claimed they were not born illegitimately and that God was their Father, a valid conclusion based upon Exodus 4:22-23, which teaches that Israel is the national son of God. However, if they were the true sons of God in a spiritual sense, and not merely physical members of Israel, they would have recognized that God the Father loved the Son and that Yeshua was that Son who came forth from the Father (Jn. 8:42).

Second, Yeshua added that their father had blinded them so they could not understand: *Why do ye not understand my speech?* (Jn. 8:43a). He then answered His own rhetorical question: *<Even> because ye cannot hear my word* (Jn. 8:43b). A partial blindness had befallen Israel as a result of the judicial judgment of their rejection of Yeshua. Additionally, Satan had also blinded them so that they could not understand what Yeshua was saying.

Third, He finally identified their father: *You are of <your> father the devil, and the lusts of your father it is your will to do. He was a murderer from the beginning, and stands not in the truth, because there is no truth in him* (Jn. 8:44). Their father was Satan, who is also the father of murder and lies. He is the author of lies, because he told the first lie. He is also the author of murder, because he caused death to come upon all humanity. Yeshua's next three points elaborate upon this statement.

Fourth, in contrast to Satan, Yeshua was characterized by pure truth (Jn. 8:45-46). The people refused to believe Him, yet, when challenged and given an opportunity to identify one sin He had committed, they could not do so because He kept the Mosaic Law perfectly.

Fifth, the corollary to being of Satan was being *not of God* (Jn. 8:47). If they had been of God, they would have heard the words of God. Their deafness showed they were really Satan's children.

Sixth, Yeshua sought not His own glory, but was committed totally to God the Father. He was the one who deserves all glory, as He was the *one that seeks and judges* (Jn. 8:50).

During this discourse, Yeshua was interrupted: *The Jews answered and said unto him, Say we not well that you are a Samaritan, and have a demon?* (Jn. 8:48). Again, the masses accused Yeshua of being demonized, indicating that they had begun to accept the Pharisaic explanation and reaffirming Yeshua's accusation that they were liars and murderers because they claimed He was demonized and sought to kill Him. They knew He was a Jew and not a Samaritan, so what was the connection between the word *Samaritan* and having a demon? The connection was based on the Jewish demonology of that day. In Hebrew, the word for "Samaritan" is *Shomroni*. The root of this word, *Shomron*, also referred to a specific demon. This demon was the father of Ashmedai, who was the prince of demons in Jewish demonology. Shomron was therefore the same as Sammael, or Satan. So, the people were saying to Yeshua, "You are a child of the devil, and you have a demon." Their accusation specifically reflected the Pharisees' explanation.

c. From Death

John 8:51-59

This section also begins with a declaration: *Verily, verily, I say unto you, If a man keep my word, he shall never see death* (Jn. 8:51). This is a parabolic statement; the people listening to Yeshua assumed He meant that if they believed in Him, they would never die physically. Their response demonstrates that they failed to comprehend that He was in fact speaking of spiritual death. This led to a new accusation: *The Jews said unto him, Now we know that you have a demon* (Jn. 8:52a). The evidence they gave was as follows: *Avraham died, and the prophets; and you say, If a man keep my word, he shall never taste of death.* They asked, *Are you greater than our father Avraham, who died? And the prophets died: Whom make you yourself to be?* (Jn. 8:52b-53). Yeshua, still speaking parabolically, used terms they could not and would not comprehend. The people were angry at Him because they did not understand He was speaking about spiritual life and death, not physical life and death. They challenged Him, saying, "Who do you make yourself out to be?" By now, they should have known that He proclaimed Himself to be the Messiah. Nevertheless, Yeshua answered and stated three things. First, He was one who did not seek to glorify Himself; rather, He was the One whom the Father glorified (Jn. 8:54). Second, while they claimed God as their own, they did not know Him; but Yeshua knew Him, and to claim otherwise would make Him a liar (Jn. 8:55). Third, He was the One whom Abraham sought: *Your father Avraham rejoiced to see my day; and he saw it, and was glad* (Jn. 8:56).

Yeshua still spoke parabolically, so His audience completely misunderstood His words: *The Jews therefore said unto him, You are not yet fifty years old, and have you seen Avraham?* (Jn. 8:57). How could Yeshua, who was about 36 years old at this time, have seen Abraham, who had lived centuries earlier? Their question led Yeshua to make a clear declaration of divinity: *Verily, verily, I say unto you, Before*

Avraham was born, I am (Jn. 8:58). He did not say, "Before Abraham was, I was," as if He merely taught His own pre-existence. He was proclaiming His own deity. He used the present tense, saying, "Before Abraham was, I am," thus clearly identifying Himself as Jehovah, the *I AM* of the Old Testament, the One who revealed Himself to Moses as *I AM THAT I AM* (Ex. 3:14).

Today, not every reader of the Scriptures might immediately recognize this statement as a declaration of deity. However, if one carefully studies the reaction of the Jewish audience to whom He spoke that day, they obviously knew exactly what He was saying, as they *took up stones therefore to cast at him: but Yeshua hid himself, and went out of the temple* (Jn. 8:59). The fact that these people picked up rocks to stone Him to death is evidence that they recognized His words as a clear proclamation of deity. In the Jewish frame of reference, Yeshua clearly professed to be the Messianic God-Man. Again, the people's attempt to kill Him was premature and so failed because His hour had not yet come.

[§ 103] — E. The Conflict over the Healing of a Man Born Blind

This section contains the sixth of Yochanan's seven signs, the healing of a man born blind.

1. Physical Healing

John 9:1-12

This incident occurred on a Sabbath day as Yeshua and His apostles walked in the streets of Jerusalem and passed by a man who was born blind (Jn. 9:1). This Sabbath was also still the time of the Feast of Tabernacles, making it an especially holy or high Sabbath.

On the surface, the apostles appear to ask a very strange question: *Rabbi, who sinned, this man, or his parents, that he should be born blind?*

(Jn. 9:2). However, in the context of the Mosaic Law, their question was not that strange. The law contains the principle that God visits *the iniquity of the fathers upon the children, and upon the children's children, upon the third and upon the fourth generation* (Ex. 34:7). Conceivably, the parents in this passage had committed a specific sin, and God had visited that sin upon their son, causing him to be born blind. The strange part of the question was when the apostles wondered if the man himself had sinned. How could the man have sinned in the womb before being born? First-century Jews did not believe in reincarnation. The apostles' question reflects the Pharisaic Judaism in which they were raised. According to this doctrine, a birth defect resulted from a specific sin committed either by the parents or by the baby. At the point of conception, the fetus was thought to have two inclinations. In Hebrew, these are called the *yetzer hara* and the *yetzer hatov*, "the evil inclination" and "the good inclination." During the nine-month development period within the mother's womb, a struggle for control between the two inclinations occurs. For most people, the good inclination prevails with a few exceptions. Over the course of the pregnancy, the evil inclination may dominate the fetus, so that in a state of animosity, he kicks his mother in the womb and dishonors her with the result that he is born with a birth defect, which in the case of the man in this passage was blindness.

The Pharisaic doctrine incorporated an important implication for Yeshua's person: To heal someone who went blind was not an exclusively messianic miracle, and the Pharisees would have been able to perform it. Jewish writings give examples of this miracle coming to pass. However, being born blind was considered to be the result of divine judgment. The rabbis believed that no one born with this birth defect would see until the Messiah comes and the blind receive their sight. This seems to be based on Isaiah 35:5. The healing of the infirm is one of the signs of the Messiah, thus explaining why things occurred as they did in the passage. Yeshua performed a unique—a messianic—miracle.

Prior to healing the blind man, He corrected the apostles' theology, as they were guilty of two fallacies: First, they accepted the Pharisaic teaching that the child could have sinned in his mother's womb and therefore been born blind; second, they accepted the Pharisaic teaching that a birth defect must be due to some specific, terrible sin. Yeshua dispelled the teaching very quickly: *Neither did this man sin, nor his parents: but that the works of God should be made manifest in him* (Jn. 9:3). This man was not born with a disability because of a specific sin he or his parents had committed. All physical problems are due to Adam's fall and a result of the general problem of sin. Men die because they are descendants of Adam. However, to say that a specific birth defect, sickness, illness, or injury is always caused by a particular sin or a particular demon is a fallacious teaching. Yeshua clearly dispelled the doctrine by saying that neither this man nor his parents had sinned. God had arranged for this man to be born blind so that His works *should be made manifest in him* (Jn. 9:3). The Father could gain the greater glory by accomplishing a great work.

This incident provided another example of Yochanan's sub-theme of the conflict of light and darkness: *We must work the works of him that sent me, while it is day: the night comes, when no man can work. When I am in the world, I am the light of the world* (Jn. 9:4-5). Yeshua said this in response to the second key ceremony of the Feast of Tabernacles, the lighting of the candles. He is the true light, the light of the world, sent by the Father to give light to those who are blind.

Having dispelled and corrected the false theology of His own disciples on this point, Yeshua proceeded with the healing. He chose to remove the blindness in steps, which is why the man could not see his healer immediately. Yeshua spat on the ground. Mixing the spit with the dirt, He made a substance of mud or clay, which He smeared on the man's eyes (Jn. 9:6). He told the man to go to the Pool of Siloam and wash the clay from his eyes, and then he would be able to see: *Go, wash in the pool of Shiloach (which is by interpretation, Sent)* (Jn. 9:7). This is a play on words. Yochanan had stated that the light of the world was sent by God the Father (Jn. 9:4). Here, the light of the world sent the one in darkness to a pool named *Sent* to heal his darkness. For him to obey Yeshua and go to the pool was an act of faith.

The procedure the Messiah used to heal this man raises a question: Why would Yeshua go through all this trouble of spitting, making mud, smearing the man's eyes, and sending him to the pool? After all, He had instantly healed blind people before, so why not this time? The miracle happened on a Sabbath day. Pharisaic Judaism forbade healing on a Sabbath unless a life was at stake. Furthermore, the Talmud specifically listed the methods that could not be used in order to heal blindness on a Sabbath day, and it forbade using the very method Yeshua had chosen. By healing the man on a Sabbath day and in a manner that presented a clear provocation to Pharisaic Judaism, Yeshua once again went out of His way to break Mishnaic Law while faithfully keeping the Law of Moses.

The Pool of Siloam was not easily accessible from the main part of Jerusalem. The man had to walk down a steep hill to the lowest part of the City of David, a difficult task for those with sight, but even more difficult for those who were blind. Why did He send him to that pool and not another? The healing occurred within the context of the Feast of Tabernacles. Yeshua responded to the kindling of the lampstands by saying: *I am the light of the world* (Jn. 9:5). Now He responded to the outpouring of the water, and the Pool of Siloam was the most crowded water source in Jerusalem during this occasion. A special ceremony of drawing water from the pool for a ritual inside the Temple compound was conducted each day during the Feast of Tabernacles, and so word would spread very quickly that another messianic miracle had been performed. Nevertheless, in keeping with His policy of demanding personal faith and only responding to personal need, Yeshua removed Himself from the public eye when the miracle took place, while the man *went away . . . and washed, and came seeing* (Jn. 9:7b). When he opened his eyes, he could see for the first time in his entire life.

Since so many of the witnesses to the miracle knew this man and knew he had been born blind, it created a tremendous stir, as anticipated: *The neighbors therefore, and they that saw him aforetime, that he was a beggar, said, Is not this he that sat and begged? Others said, It is he: others said, No, but he is like him* (Jn. 9:8-9a). Confusion arose because many people recognized him as that same blind beggar; but others had difficulty believing that a man born blind was healed and said, "No, he just looks like him." Finally, the man said, *I am <he>* (Jn. 9:9b), which led them to ask the crucial question: *How then were your eyes opened?* (Jn. 9:10). "How are you now able to see?" *He answered: The man that is called Yeshua made clay, and anointed mine eyes, and said unto me, Go to Shiloach, and wash: so I went away and washed, and*

I received sight (Jn. 9:11). When they asked him, *Where is he?*, he answered, *I know not* (Jn. 9:12). He had still been in a blind state when Yeshua sent him to the pool, and therefore, he had never seen Him. Even now, when he could see, he did not know who Yeshua was or what He looked like.

Theologically, the people could not reconcile what had just happened. Something good, a miracle, which only the Messiah could perform, had occurred. He had healed a man born blind. However, He had healed the man on the Sabbath day in a way that Pharisaic Judaism forbade. So, they decided to take the man to the Pharisees for an explanation.

2. The First Interrogation

John 9:13-17

These verses describe the first interrogation of the man by the Pharisees. Since this was a messianic miracle, it required investigation and explanation (Jn. 9:13). Yeshua chose to heal the man on a Sabbath, creating a stir among the masses (Jn. 9:14). The Pharisees knew very well that they must act on this issue. As they began the interrogation to discover how he received his sight after being born blind (Jn. 9:15), a division developed among them: *Some therefore of the Pharisees said, This man is not from God, because he keeps not the Sabbath* (Jn. 9:16a). They believed healing on the Sabbath violated the Sabbath law, so they did not believe Yeshua could be a man of God, let alone *the* man of God, the Messiah Himself. Others said, however, *How can a man that is a sinner do such signs?* (Jn. 9:16b). This led to the motif of this section: *And there was a division among them* (Jn. 9:16c). Notice that the emphasis was not only upon signs. False prophets could also perform miracles. The emphasis was upon *such signs*, meaning these particular signs that were unprecedented.

When the religious leaders asked the man for his opinion regarding the one who had healed him, he simply concluded that Yeshua must be a prophet (Jn. 9:17). However, though a prophet might be able to perform miracles (as Elijah and Elisha certainly did), to perform a messianic miracle was not the Pharisaic prerogative of a prophet, but rather the prerogative of the Messiah alone. So the first interrogation of the man did not lead to any specific conclusions.

3. The Interrogation of the Parents

John 9:18-23

Since the result of the first interrogation of the man was inconclusive, the Pharisees, doubting he was really born blind, asked his parents (Jn. 9:18). Responding to their questions (Jn. 9:19), the parents confirmed two things: This man was definitely their son, and he really was born blind (Jn. 9:20-21). They eliminated any possibility that this man was a fake or that anyone was trying to deceive the Pharisees.

When the Pharisees asked the parents whether their son had really been born blind, and if so, how he was now able to see, the parents said nothing more and allowed their son to speak for himself (Jn. 9:21). The reason for their reluctance is given: *These things said his parents, because they feared the Jews: for the Jews had agreed already, that if any man should confess him <to be> Messiah, he should be put out of the synagogue* (Jn. 9:22). Here Yochanan used the term *Jews* to refer to the religious leaders. The Pharisees had already decreed that anyone who owned Yeshua as Messiah would be excommunicated from the synagogue.

The parents knew the Pharisees had made this decree, so they chose not to comment any further, except to affirm two things: that the man was their son and that he had been born blind. To avoid their own excommunication, they went no further, but told them, "Our son is a grown man; ask him!" (Jn. 9:23). Therefore, the interrogation of the parents also ended inconclusively.

4. The Second Interrogation

John 9:24-34

During the second interrogation of the man born blind, the Pharisees began to lose their sense of logic. They summoned him and said, *Give glory to God: we know that this man is a sinner* (Jn. 9:24). Knowing that someone is a sinner is not a reason to praise God, but the Pharisees were so beside themselves over Yeshua that they were no longer able to think clearly or in a logical manner.

At this point, the man healed of his blindness said tactfully: *Whether he is a sinner, I know not: one thing I know, that, whereas I was blind, now I see* (Jn. 9:25). The man's response was not simply a statement of fact; it was also a challenge to the Pharisees, one that they had to answer. He was born blind, not merely gone blind later in life. The Pharisees had taught him that only the Messiah could heal someone blind from birth. According to their theology, Yeshua should be declared Israel's Messiah. Instead, they called Him a sinner. So, could they please explain why?

The Pharisees took up the challenge and asked the question, *What did he to you? How opened he your eyes?* (Jn. 9:26). The man had already explained how the healing had occurred, so he responded, *I told you even now* [I already told you!], *and ye did not hear* [you did not listen]; *wherefore would ye hear it again? Would ye also become his disciples?* (Jn. 9:27). At this point, the man was no longer being tactful.

They replied in like manner: *And they reviled him, and said, You are his disciple; but we are disciples of Mosheh. We know that God has spoken unto Mosheh: but as for this man, we know not from where he is* (Jn. 9:28-29). The Pharisees vilified the man and accused him of being a disciple of Yeshua. They realized they had not persuaded him to accept their verdict that Yeshua was a sinner, so they gave up on him. Implying that God did not speak to *this man*, they concluded that being a disciple of Moses was superior to being a disciple of Yeshua.

But the man born blind lost all tact and said: *Why, herein is the marvel, that ye know not from where he is, and <yet> he opened mine eyes* (Jn. 9:30). The religious leadership of Israel should have been able to explain the special miracle that had occurred. The man reminded them of their own theology: *We know that God hears not sinners: but if any man be a worshipper of God, and do his will, him he hears. Since the world began it was never heard that anyone opened the eyes of a man born blind* (Jn. 9:31-32). Records of healings of people who had gone blind existed, but not one of a person born blind. For the first time in human history, this messianic miracle was performed, and the Pharisees had no grounds for rejecting Yeshua as the Messiah.

The Pharisees responded: *You were altogether born in sins, and do you teach us?* (Jn. 9:34a). According to their theology, he had been born with a disability because of a specific sin. As someone *altogether born in sins*, he could never teach them anything. Their final act was to *cast him out* (Jn. 9:34b). This "casting out" is the same as being *put out of the synagogue* (Jn. 9:22). The man was excommunicated.

5. Spiritual Healing

John 9:35-41

Until this point in the narrative, the man had never actually seen Yeshua, for when he had walked away from Him, he was still physically blind. When Yeshua heard that the man had been cast out of the synagogue, He found him and said: *Do you believe on the Son of God?* (Jn. 9:35). The man asked, *And who is he, Lord, that I may believe on him?* (Jn. 9:36), and Yeshua answered, *You have both seen him, and he it is that speaks with you* (Jn. 9:37). This led to the man's statement and act of faith: *And he said, Lord, I believe. And he worshipped him* (Jn. 9:38). For one Jew to worship another meant he understood him to be the Messiah.

The text ends with another example of Yochanan's sub-theme of the conflict of light and darkness (Jn. 9:39-41):

> [39] *And Yeshua said, For judgment came I into this world, that they that see not may see; and that they that see may become blind.* [40] *Those of the Pharisees who were with him heard these things, and said unto him, Are we also blind?* [41] *Yeshua said unto them, If ye were blind, ye would have no sin: but now ye say, We see: your sin remains.*

Yeshua contrasted the man born blind with the Pharisees. The man went from physical darkness and blindness to physical light and sight. He also passed from spiritual darkness and blindness to spiritual light and sight. The Pharisees, on the other hand, had physical light and sight, but because of their unbelief, they remained in spiritual darkness and blindness. Had they acknowledged Yeshua as the Messiah, they would have escaped their spiritual darkness and blindness. If they had accepted Him as the light of the world, Yeshua would have forgiven their sins, and they would be sinless. Instead, they claimed to see, but remained in spiritual blindness; therefore, their sin remained.

The Pharisees responded specifically to each of the three messianic miracles. When Yeshua healed the Jewish leper, they began an intense investigation of His assertions. When He cast out the dumb demon, they rejected Him on the basis of demon possession. In response to the healing of the man born blind, they rejected His followers: Any Jew who accepted Yeshua as Messiah was to be excommunicated from the synagogue, a policy that has been maintained to this day.

[§ 104] — F. The Conflict over the Shepherd

This section contains the sixth of Yeshua's seven discourses recorded in the Gospel of Yochanan, the discourse on the good shepherd, the background of which is Isaiah 40:10-11 and Zechariah 11:4-14. In these verses, the Messiah is pictured as a shepherd. This section also includes the third and fourth of Yeshua's seven "I Am" statements in this Gospel:: *I am the door of the sheep* (Jn. 10:7), and *I am the good shepherd* (Jn. 10:11, 14).

1. Messiah the True Shepherd

John 10:1-6

Referring to His conflict with their form of Judaism, Yeshua accused the Pharisees of having gained their rule by *some other way* than the one laid out by God the Father (Jn. 10:1). They claimed authority through the Mishnah. In contrast, Yeshua entered the right way, the way the Hebrew Bible had revealed; therefore, He was indeed the true shepherd (Jn. 10:2), and His sheep hear His voice: *he calls his own sheep by name, and leads them out* (Jn. 10:3). *His own sheep* is equivalent to *the poor of the flock* in Zechariah 11:4-14, where the prophet pictured the messianic shepherd as coming to feed the flock as a whole, but eventually focusing on the poor of the flock, the believing remnant of Israel. The believing remnant recognized Yeshua to be the true messianic shepherd (Jn. 10:4-5).

They did not understand because Yeshua taught in parables: *This parable spoke Yeshua unto them: but they understood not what things they were which he spoke unto them* (Jn. 10:6).

2. Messiah the Door

John 10:7-10

Having established that He was the true shepherd of Zechariah 11, Yeshua again contrasted Himself with the Pharisees, saying: *Verily, verily, I say unto you, I am the door of the sheep. All that came before me are thieves and robbers* (Jn. 10:7-8). The Pharisees usurped authority through the Mishnah; they were the *thieves and robbers*. Yeshua is the true door in which pasture, or salvation, is to be found (Jn. 10:9). The Messiah came to provide salvation and daily sustenance. Indeed, He came to provide abundant life for His sheep (Jn. 10:10).

3. Messiah the Good Shepherd

John 10:11-18

After establishing Himself as the true shepherd and the true door, Yeshua made three points. First, as the good shepherd, He would willingly lay down His life for His sheep (Jn. 10:11-15).

Second, He would unite both Jewish and Gentile sheep into one flock: *And other sheep I have, which are not of this fold* (Jn. 10:16a). *This fold* refers to Israel, because Israel is the flock of God (Zech. 11:4-14);

but Yeshua also has sheep from another fold. Subsequent revelation in the Epistles shows that these sheep are Gentiles, of whom He stated: *them also I must bring, and they shall hear my voice: and they shall become one flock, one shepherd* (Jn. 10:16b). This is the first hint that the church would be one body comprised of Jewish and Gentile believers, or one flock comprised of Jewish and Gentile sheep (Eph. 2:11-3:12).

Third, while the hireling normally does not care for the sheep (Jn. 10:12-13), the true shepherd cares. He will even give His life for the sheep: *Therefore does the Father love me, because I lay down my life, that I may take it again. No one takes it away from me, but I lay it down of myself. I have power to lay it down, and I have power to take it again* (Jn. 10:17-18). Note that Yeshua would decide the moment of His death. He had the power to lay down His life and to restore it; ultimately, He alone would decide the moment of His death.

4. Division

John 10:19-21

The motif of this section becomes evident again: *There arose a division again among the Jews because of these words* (Jn. 10:19). The masses began to accept the teaching of the Pharisees: *And many of them said, He has a demon, and is mad* (Jn. 10:20). Others were not ready to follow the Pharisees and viewed the healing of the man born blind as evidence that there was something unique about Yeshua (Jn. 10:21).

[§ 105] — G. The Witness of the Seventy

At this point in His ministry, Yeshua had many more disciples than just the twelve apostles. Admittedly, the twelve were a closed group with the Messiah constantly, and they had the title of apostles. However, another category of disciples was also present, and in this instance, He sent out seventy of them on a special mission.

1. The Seventy Sent

Luke 10:1-16

Yeshua sent the seventy disciples out two by two (Lk. 10:1) on a short-term mission with only one purpose: to prepare for the coming of the King. They were to go to those towns, villages, and cities where He would go, and to prepare places for Him to stay along the way. They needed to prepare a minimum of 35 places for Him.

Yeshua taught them to pray and be willing to answer their own prayers: *pray ye therefore the Lord of the harvest, that he send forth laborers into his harvest* (Lk. 10:2). Since many individual Jews would accept their message, not only should they be praying for the harvest, they should also be sowing and preparing to reap the harvest as well.

He also warned them to prepare for widespread rejection: *Go your ways; behold, I send you forth as lambs in the midst of wolves* (Lk. 10:3). However, they should be unconcerned with the essentials of life: *Carry no purse, no wallet, no shoes; and salute no man on the way* (Lk. 10:4). All of this emphasized a sense of urgency. A job needed to be done without delay. The seventy must get to those cities and prepare places for Yeshua to stay before He began His final journey towards Jerusalem for His approaching death. They were not to be concerned about the essentials because those would be provided; nor should they waste time conversing with people along the way.

Upon finding acceptance in one place, they should remain (Lk. 10:5-7). What Yeshua instructed the twelve apostles (Mt. 10), He also taught these seventy: When they went into a town, they should emphasize the individual. Where they found a worthy house, they were to give their peace. If the house proved to be unworthy or unbelieving, they should withdraw their peace. However, if the house proved to be worthy and comprised of believers, *in that same house remain, eating and drinking such things as they give: for the laborer is worthy of his hire. Go not from house to house* (Lk. 10:7). In other words, once they had found a house that would be willing to accept Yeshua when He came, they were not to look for better accommodations. The mission was limited to finding a place for Him to stay on the principle of first come, first served. When they found such a home, they would also be fed, so they did not have to worry about the essentials.

The disciples were to eat what was set before them without being particular (Lk. 10:8). Furthermore, they were to do good to those cities or individuals that accepted them, meaning they were to *heal the sick* (Lk. 10:9a) and proclaim that they were experiencing kingdom life, for *the kingdom of God is come near unto you* (Lk. 10:9b). When the King was present, they would experience kingdom blessings, such as immediate healing of those who come to Him. That would not be true when the King was absent.

Another part of the disciples' mission was to declare judgment on those who rejected them. After all, the kingdom had drawn near to Israel. Therefore, when rejected, the disciples were to shake the dust off their shoes, which was a sign of judgment (Lk. 10:10-11). Yeshua warned: *I say unto you, it shall be more tolerable in that day for Sedom, than for that city* (Lk. 10:12). This verse shows different degrees of judgment for the unsaved. Those who rejected the seventy disciples would suffer a greater judgment than the inhabitants of Sodom. In verses 13-15, Yeshua pronounced a curse against the three cities of Chorazin, Bethsaida, and Capernaum because they experienced the majority of His miracles and signs and still rejected Him. This is in retrospect, for as Yeshua pronounced a curse upon those cities that would reject the seventy, Bethsaida, Capernaum, and Chorazin were already cursed. Other cities that rejected the disciples' message would suffer the kind of curse these three cities had suffered.

The principle of this mission was that acceptance or rejection of the seventy was the same as accepting or rejecting Messiah Himself (Lk. 10:16). To reject the disciples was to reject the sender, the Messiah, and to reject the Messiah also meant rejecting God the Father who sent Him.

2. The Seventy Return

Luke 10:17-20

When the seventy returned, they rejoiced over the fact that even demons were subject to them (Lk. 10:17). Their happy arrival also
indicated that at least 35 places had been prepared. Yeshua responded:
I beheld Satan fallen as lightning from heaven (Lk. 10:18), signaling
Satan's coming doom. Yes, Yeshua had given them authority over serpents, scorpions, and all the powers of the enemy, and nothing could
hurt them (Lk. 10:19). However, they should really have rejoiced that
their names were written in heaven (Lk. 10:20), and not that demons
were subject to them. The focus of their excitement should have been
their salvation, not their authority over demons.

3. Messiah's Prayer

Luke 10:21-24

In that same hour he rejoiced in [or by] *the Holy Spirit* (Lk. 10:21a) and
started praying. Yeshua pointed out three things in His prayer. First,
He explained why some believed and others did not (Lk. 10:21b). Any
unbelief was because *these things* had been hidden from them due to
their sin. Though they were *wise and understanding*, they rejected the
Messiah. Conversely, the reason for belief was because these things had
been revealed to those who were considered spiritual babes. Second,
Yeshua revealed everything believers know about God the Father (Lk.
10:22). Third, these disciples had a unique advantage (Lk. 10:23-24).
Many kings and prophets of the Old Testament desired to see the fulfillment of these messianic days, but they died before Yeshua had come
on the scene. These disciples, however, saw the Messianic King. They
were given a unique advantage and were blessed in a special way, as
they saw the prophecies and the desires of prophets and kings fulfilled.

[§ 106] — H. The Conflict
over the Question of Eternal Life

Luke 10:25-37

The event described in these verses began with a trick question: *And behold, a certain lawyer stood up and made trial of him* (Lk. 10:25a). The question the lawyer was about to raise was another attempt to entrap Yeshua. The term *lawyer* indicates he was an expert on the Mosaic Law. He addressed Yeshua as a teacher, indicating he viewed Him as also being an expert on the law. The lawyer asked Yeshua a specific question: *Teacher, what shall I do to inherit eternal life?* (Lk. 10:25b). In the Greek text, the word *do* is in the aorist tense, emphasizing a completed act. In other words, he asked, "What once-and-for-all work must I do to have eternal life?" The emphasis is on doing some kind of work in order to gain eternal life.

In a typically Jewish teaching style, Yeshua answered his question by asking another question: *What is written in the law? How read you?* (Lk. 10:26). Since the lawyer's question was based upon what work he must do to gain eternal life, Yeshua directed him to the Mosaic Law. The lawyer answered by quoting the first and second most important commandments: *you shall love Jehovah your God with all your heart, and with all your soul, and with all your might* (Deut. 6:5) and *you shall love your neighbor as yourself* (Lev. 19:18). The first command controls man's relationship to God. It requires faith. The second one controls man's relationship to other human beings, and it is the practical outworking of that faith.

Then Yeshua said to the lawyer: *You have answered right: this do, and you shall live* (Lk. 10:28). In the Greek text, the verb *do* is in the present tense, emphasizing continuous action. If the man wanted to know the one work he must do to have eternal life, if he wanted to base his salvation on works, then he must continually love God and love his neighbor. If he could keep on doing this perfectly, then he would live. Obviously, the lawyer knew he could not consistently keep the two most important commandments without fail. Furthermore, in order to fulfill the second commandment, he must initially fulfill the first, which is accomplished only by grace through faith, apart from works.

Desiring to justify himself, the lawyer responded: *And who is my neighbor?* (Lk. 10:29). He realized he had lost the argument and could not entrap Yeshua. So he did what any good defender of a certain doctrine would do and argued a point of theology. His focus was not on loving God, but on loving his neighbor. If he must love his neighbor as himself, how does he determine who this neighbor is?

Yeshua responded with a story about a priest, a Levite, and a Samaritan (Lk. 10:30-35). The background to this story was the idea that the Jewish people were divided into three classes: the priests, the Levites, and the whole house of Israel. Contrary to Jewish expectation, however, Yeshua mentioned a priest, a Levite, and a Samaritan. This was strange to Jewish ears, but that was the whole point. So a certain Jew *was going down from Yerushalayim to Yericho* (Lk. 10:30). In the Jewish mindset, a person always goes *down* from Jerusalem regardless of the direction he is travelling—north, south, east, or west—and Luke wrote from a Jewish perspective. On the way to Jericho, robbers attacked and beat this man, and left him for dead. Both a priest and a Levite came by, but neither did anything to help. When a Samaritan arrived, he helped this Jew, bound up his wounds, took him to an inn, stayed with him through the night, and paid the innkeeper to watch over him until he was well. The story speaks out against the strict Pharisaic interpretation that defines a neighbor as only a fellow Jew. While the religious leaders did nothing for the Jew, a stranger—Samaritan of all people—helped him.

After finishing the story, Yeshua asked the lawyer: *Which of these three, do you think, proved neighbor unto him that fell among robbers?* (Lk. 10:36). The lawyer, unwilling to say the word "Samaritan," answered the question indirectly: *And he said, He that showed mercy on him* (Lk. 10:37), indirectly admitting that the Samaritan was the neighbor. Therefore, a neighbor is anyone with a need that can be met. The attempt to entrap Yeshua failed.

[§ 107] — I. The Example of Fellowship

Luke 10:38-42

These verses describe Yeshua's first contact with a family who would play a key role in His life from this point forward. The family included Lazarus and his two sisters, Miriam and Martha. Their home was among the 35 or more places prepared by the seventy disciples for Yeshua: *Now as they went on their way, he entered a certain village: and a certain woman named Marta received him into her house* (Lk. 10:38). The village is not named here, but later is identified as Bethany (Jn. 11:1), located on the lower eastern slopes of the Mount of Olives, about two or three miles from Jerusalem.

Martha was obviously the matriarch and the older of the two sisters. Luke distinguished between her and Miriam: *And she had a sister called Miriam, who also sat at the Lord's feet, and heard his word. But Marta was cumbered about much serving* (Lk. 10:39-40). Martha was primarily concerned with meeting the physical need of Yeshua, while Miriam was concerned with providing the spiritual need of fellowship. She took on the posture of a disciple by sitting at the Lord's feet, and because she sat and learned, she was the one who understood something that not even Yeshua's disciples understood: that He would die and rise again. Later, what Miriam learned from Yeshua would be uniquely praised (see § 148.).

When Martha complained to Yeshua about her sister's apparent laziness, He answered: *Marta, Marta, you are anxious and troubled about many things: but one thing is needful: for Miriam has chosen the good part, which shall not be taken away from her* (Lk. 10:41-42). Although it seems that Miriam should have been helping Martha (and in different circumstances, that might have been the case), in this situation, she met Yeshua's spiritual need of fellowship while learning spiritual truth.

Two lessons can be learned from this passage. First, to be occupied with the Messiah is better than to be occupied for the Messiah. Second, to be taught by the Messiah is far more important than to be busy for the Messiah.

[§ 108] — J. Instruction in Prayer

Luke 11:1-13

The circumstance that gave rise to the apostles' request to be taught how to pray was their observation that Yeshua prayed extemporaneously. The apostles, raised in Judaism, were taught prescribed prayer through prayer books. By the first century, Jews no longer prayed freely, and the apostles did not know how to pray, hence their request: *Lord, teach us to pray* (Lk. 11:1).

As discussed earlier, the Sermon on the Mount was the Messiah's interpretation of the true righteousness of the law, in contradistinction to the Pharisaic interpretation. As a unit, it was not intended to be church ethics, though certain areas of the sermon became church ethics as determined by studying what the Gospels repeated and what the apostles wrote in the Epistles. In the verses above, we find one such example. After finishing the sermon, Yeshua gave the model prayer (Mt. 6:5-15), repeated here in verses 2-4. This portion of the sermon became church ethics for this age, and it still applies today. As a model, it is intended as an outline of how to organize one's prayer life and not intended to be recited week after week. To summarize: we should address the prayer to God the Father, sanctifying Him; we should pray for the kingdom program and for our daily needs; we should confess our sins and pray about spiritual warfare.[5]

Yeshua demonstrated the significance of incessant prayer through the Parable of the Persistent Friend (Lk. 11:5-13). The parable teaches two lessons, using the *kal v'chomer* approach. First, if an unwilling person finally concedes because of persistence, how much more is it true of God, who is willing to give? The application is: *Ask, and it shall be given you; seek, and ye shall find; knock and it shall be opened unto you. For every one that asks receives; and he that seeks finds; and to him that knocks it shall be opened* (Lk. 11:9-10). Second, if an evil father gives good gifts, how much more will God the Father, who is the epitome of good, give? The application is: *If ye then, being evil, know how to give*

---

[5] For further details, see § 55.

good gifts unto your children, how much more shall <your> heavenly Father give the Holy Spirit to them that ask him? (Lk. 11:13). The promise to the apostles was that a believer who truly wished to be indwelled by the Spirit could seek God in prayer, and God would honor that prayer by giving him the Holy Spirit. This prayer was valid for believers before Acts 2, when not all were necessarily indwelled by the Spirit. Since the events of Acts 2, however, the moment a person believes, he is automatically indwelled by the Holy Spirit. Therefore, the prayer that the Father would send the Spirit is obsolete. Persistent prayer, on the other hand, is still relevant.

This parable involved three people: the host (Lk. 11:5), the friend (Lk. 11:6), and the neighbor (Lk. 11:5) who was able to provide. The host was the mediator between the one in need and the one who could meet that need. Thus, in their prayer lives, believers function as mediators between God who can provide and those who have a need that God can meet. Besides teaching persistent prayer, Yeshua also taught intercessory prayer for the needs of others. Persistent intercession is not the same as vain repetition.

[§ 109] — K. The Conflict over the Healing of the Dumb Man

The situation described in this section is similar to the one in Matthew 12:22-24 (§ 62). Once again, a demon rendered the possessed speechless, and once again, Yeshua cast the demon out. However, crucial differences indicate that these were two separate events. The previous event occurred in Galilee, whereas this one happened in Judea about a year later. Other differences are noted throughout this section.

1. The Charge

Luke 11:14-16

Yeshua cast out a demon that caused the possessed to be mute, and the exorcism amazed the multitudes (Lk. 11:14). After all, this was a miracle no one could copy. However, *some of them said, By Beelzebub the prince of demons casts he out demons. And others, trying <him>, sought of him a sign from heaven* (Lk. 11:15-16). The personal pronoun *them* refers to the multitudes, indicating that the masses were beginning to accept the Pharisaic explanation and to mimic their leaders. Ignoring the miracle Yeshua had just performed, they demanded a sign from heaven, just as their leaders had done before. In the previous incident, Yeshua's response preceded the request for a sign, whereas in this instance, it came after.

2. The Defense

Luke 11:17-23

In His defense, Yeshua made five points that are similar to the points He made in the previous event. Since the charge was the same, the answers would also be the same. First, the accusation that He cast out the demon by the prince of demons, Beelzebub, simply could not be true, because it would mean a division in Satan's kingdom (Lk. 11:17-18). Second, the people recognized that the gift of exorcism is from God, and to accuse Him of this was inconsistent with their own theology (Lk. 11:19). Third, this miracle authenticated Yeshua's message (Lk. 11:20). Fourth, it showed that He was stronger than and not subservient to Satan (Lk. 11:21-22). Fifth, there was a call to individual decision: *He that is not with me is against me; and he that gathers not with me scatters* (Lk. 11:23). Every person of that generation had to decide whether or not to follow Yeshua.

3. The Condition of the Nation

Luke 11:24-28

As Yeshua described the condition of the nation, He pointed out two things. First, He repeated the story about the unclean spirit who left and came back, emphasizing that the last state of that generation would be worse than the first (Lk. 11:24-26). Second, He repudiated all earthly ties in favor of spiritual ties (Lk. 11:27-28).

Up to this point, the two events were similar, and the only noticeable differences were the location (Galilee versus Judea) and the audience (religious leaders versus multitudes). Now, another difference emerges. In the previous account, Yeshua's mother and brothers came to Him, and Yeshua stated that only those who kept His commandments were His true family. In this instance, a different situation caused Him to repudiate earthly ties in favor of spiritual ties: *And it came to pass, as he said these things, a certain woman out of the multitude lifted up her voice, and said unto him, Blessed is the womb that bore you, and the breasts which you did suck. But he said, Yea rather, blessed are they that hear the word of God, and keep it* (Lk. 11:27-28).

4. The Sign to that Generation

Luke 11:29-32

In the previous account, Yeshua addressed the leadership; in this account, He addressed the masses: *And when the multitudes were gathering together unto him* (Lk. 11:29a). Again, the emphasis is on that particular generation: *he began to say, This generation is an evil generation: it seeks after a sign* (Lk. 11:29b). The common people began to accept the Pharisaic explanation and demanded a sign. However, *there shall no sign be given to it but the sign of Yonah,* which is the sign of resurrection (Lk. 11:29-30).

Furthermore, Yeshua condemned *this generation,* and on the day of judgment, *the queen of the south* (Lk. 11:31) and the *men of Nineveh*

(Lk. 11:32), meaning the Gentiles, will condemn this particular Jewish generation.

5. The Call to the Nation

Luke 11:33-36

Using a picture of light and darkness, Yeshua taught that to accept Him is to walk in the light and to reject Him is to be in darkness. This can be summarized in seven points:

1. The word of the Messiah is light.
2. The light that the Messiah brought was the knowledge of the Father.
3. Yeshua openly taught the revelation of the Father in public before the whole nation.
4. The nation was spiritually blinded and rejected the light.
5. The reason for the rejection was in the eye of the beholder.
6. Israel remained in darkness because the nation rejected the revelation of the Father. This was not the revealer's fault.
7. If they would receive the revelation through the Messiah, then they would have light.

[§ 110] — L. The Conflict
over Pharisaic Ritualism

Luke 11:37-54

Another Pharisee invited Yeshua *to dine with him* (Lk. 11:37). Subterfuge was still evident, as the religious leader seems to have asked Yeshua to dine with him only to find fault in Him regarding some point of their laws. He quickly noticed that Yeshua did not participate in the traditional ritual of washing His hands before sitting down to eat (Lk. 11:38). Yeshua knew the Pharisee looked upon Him with condemnation, so

He launched a reprobation of His own (Lk. 11:39-41), condemning the Pharisees for being more concerned with the external than the internal demands of the law. Their warped perspective became the basis for the woes Yeshua pronounced in the following verses and later repeated in a series of woes He uttered at the end of His public ministry (Mt. 23:13-36). They will be examined in more detail in § 143. However, we will now look at some points Yeshua summarized here in addition to a few others that do not appear in the later passage.

He began by pronouncing three specific woes on the Pharisees. The first woe criticized their concern for the lesser issues of the law, rather than concentrating on the greater demands (Lk. 11:42). The background is the Pharisaic teaching that a person should not partake of something without first tithing from it. The second woe criticized their self-glorification, as they always sought the best seats in the synagogue and looked for salutations in the market place (Lk. 11:43). The third woe criticized their hypocrisy. Yeshua pictured the Pharisees as *tombs which appear not, and the men that walk over <them> know it not* (Lk. 11:44). The Pharisees are not viewed here as whitewashed sepulchres that can be spotted without difficulty (Mt. 23:27), but as tombs, or graves, which are easily missed. Anyone touching such graves becomes ceremonially unclean and in turn inadvertently defiles others. The hypocrisy of the Pharisees caused corruption, uncleanness, and impurity in others without warning.

After pronouncing these three woes on the Pharisees, Yeshua was interrupted: *And one of the lawyers answering said unto him, Teacher, in saying this you reproach us also* (Lk. 11:45). These lawyers did not deal with civil law, but religious law. They were the experts on the Mosaic Law, and especially on the Mishnaic Law, and they were the real thinkers, the intellectual force, behind the Pharisees. They pointed out that if Yeshua condemned Pharisees in general, then He also condemned the lawyers in particular. Yeshua was not intimidated, however, and pronounced three additional woes upon the lawyers. The first woe was for making traditions mandatory: *For ye load men with burdens grievous to be borne, and ye yourselves touch not the burdens with one of your fingers* (Lk. 11:46).

The second woe was for rejecting the prophets, which had led to the rejection of the Messiah, which, in turn, would lead to the coming destruction of A.D. 70 (Lk. 11:48-51). Keep in mind that Yeshua's emphasis was still upon the generation that was guilty of the unpardonable sin. *This generation* would be held accountable for all of the blood of the prophets that has been shed from the foundation of the world. The judgment was required of this one particular generation, because the prophets had said everything that needed to be said about the coming of the Messiah. By rejecting Yeshua's Messiahship, they automatically rejected the prophets.

The third woe was for hiding the truth from the masses by means of their traditions (Lk. 11:52). They *took away the key of knowledge* by claiming that the Written Law could only be understood by the Oral Law, thereby hindering individual Jews from recognizing the Messiahship of Yeshua.

The three woes upon the Pharisees in general and the three additional woes upon the lawyers in particular led to a violent reaction by the religious leaders: *And when he was come out from thence, the scribes and the Pharisees began to press upon <him> vehemently, and to provoke him to speak of many things; laying wait for him, to catch something out of his mouth* (Lk. 11:53-54). While trying to get Yeshua to say something that would bring legal condemnation against Himself, the religious leaders lost control of themselves emotionally.

[§ 111] — M. Instruction of the Disciples

In this section, Luke provides a lengthy discourse by which Yeshua taught the apostles nine specific lessons.

1. Hypocrisy

Luke 12:1-12

Luke contrasted the approach Yeshua used to teach the multitudes with the way He taught the apostles: *In the meantime, when the many thousands of the multitude were gathered together, insomuch that they trod one upon another, he began to say unto his disciples first of all* (Lk. 12:1a). Although thousands of people surrounded Yeshua, He specifically addressed His disciples. This was during their special training in light of the rejection. The fact that Yeshua focused on the disciples and not on the multitudes is clarified by these words: *and I say unto you my friends* (Lk. 12:4); *and I say unto you* (Lk. 12:8).

The first lesson targeted hypocrisy: *Beware ye of the leaven of the Pharisees, which is hypocrisy* (Lk. 12:1b). It was based on the incident that had just occurred and consisted of six points. First, the disciples should be totally honest. There is never any need to hide anything. Eventually, all hidden sins will be revealed (Lk. 12:2-3).

Second, *Fear him, who after he has killed has power to cast into hell; yea, I say unto you, Fear him* (Lk. 12:5). God is the proper object of fear; therefore, He alone is to be feared, and not man. While man may cause damage in this life, only God controls the afterlife and determines the eternal destiny of every individual (Lk. 12:4-5).

Third, God is also the proper object of faith (Lk. 12:6-7). Their faith should be in Him alone and no one or nothing else, for two reasons: He will take care of their physical needs, and He is in control. Since they *are of more value than many sparrows*, even the very hairs of their heads are all numbered (Lk. 12:7). Nothing can possibly happen to a believer outside of the will of God.

Fourth, it is important to confess Yeshua as the Messiah and not deny Him because of intimidation by society (Lk. 12:8-9). The content of the disciples' faith was Yeshua the Messianic King, and that is what saved them. Now they must not deny Him before that generation. If they publicly confessed Yeshua before men, Yeshua would *also confess [them] before the angels of God* (Lk. 12:8). However, if they denied Him in the presence of men, Yeshua would deny them *in the presence of the angels of God* (Lk. 12:9). This speaks of a confession or denial in a public forum that will happen at the judgment seat of the Messiah (I Cor. 3:10-15). At that time, affirmation will result in reward, and denial will result in a loss of reward. While faith alone saves, there will be consequences if we deny before others what we really believe.

Fifth, Yeshua warned that no one of that generation should join the majority in committing the unpardonable sin, because *unto him that blasphemes against the Holy Spirit it shall not be forgiven* (Lk. 12:10). The blasphemy against the Holy Spirit was the rejection of Yeshua as the Messiah by claiming that the mighty works He did and the miraculous signs He performed were done by demonic power. This is the unpardonable sin, the sin that *shall not be forgiven*.

Sixth, when persecuted because they had confessed the Messiahship of Yeshua (Lk. 12:11), the disciples were not to be concerned about preparing a legal brief before a court of law: *for the Holy Spirit shall teach you in that very hour what ye ought to say* (Lk. 12:12). If they were brought before a court of law because of their faith, whether a religious court (*synagogues*) or a civil court (*rulers* or *authorities*), they had no reason to worry about what they would say. At the proper time, God would provide them with the right words to speak.

2. Covetousness

a. Occasion

Luke 12:13-15

The occasion for the lesson on covetousness was a family dispute over inheritance. The request came from *one out of the multitude* who asked Yeshua to tell his brother to share the estate (Lk. 12:13). The basis upon which this member of the multitude felt free to ask Yeshua to do this is not clear—except perhaps that, according to Psalm 72:2, the Messiah would have the privilege of arbitrating disputes. Therefore, the thought process could have been that Yeshua should arbitrate between this man and his brother over the inheritance since He claimed to be the Messiah. However, Yeshua responded: *Man, who made me a judge or a divider over you?* (Lk. 12:14). A similar statement was made to Moses in Exodus 2:14: One day, after he had killed the Egyptian overseer who was beating a Jew, Moses saw two Hebrews fighting with each other and asked why this was happening. The response was, *Who made you a prince and a judge over us?* (Ex. 2:14). That statement was the rejection of Moses by the Jewish people when he first came to them. It was the reason he departed from them, and they did not see him again for forty years. Just as Moses was initially rejected by his own people, even so, Yeshua was initially rejected by Israel, and because He was rejected, He could not be the one to arbitrate these decisions. Therefore, this was not the time to fulfill Psalm 72. Just as Moses had to come a second time before he could redeem Israel, Yeshua must come again for the final redemption to occur.

The Messiah used the interaction with this man to give a lesson on covetousness: *Take heed, and keep yourselves from all covetousness: for a man's life consists not in the abundance of the things which he possesses* (Lk. 12:15).

b. Instruction

Luke 12:16-21

The lesson on covetousness was followed by the Parable of the Rich Fool (Lk. 12:16-20), and it becomes clear that Yeshua now addressed *them*, the multitudes. The story concerns a rich man who used his wealth to store up an abundance of goods for himself in order to have a future life of ease. He did not consider sharing his surplus with his less fortunate neighbors, and therefore, he failed to fulfill the second most important commandment, recorded in Mark 12:31: *You shall love your neighbor as yourself.* This, in turn, was due to his failure to obey the first and more important commandment: *love the Lord your God with all your heart, and with all your soul, and with all your mind, and with all your strength* (Mk. 12:30). As a result, he would never enjoy the surplus he had stored up, because God decreed that he would die that very night. He would never enjoy the things he had hoarded, so God called him the *foolish one* (Lk. 12:20). The Hebrew Scriptures describe a fool as an unbeliever who denies the existence of God: *The fool has said in his heart, There is no God* (Ps. 14:1).

The lesson of the parable is this: *he that lays up treasure for himself, and is not rich toward God* is a fool (Lk. 12:21). Caring about what is beyond one's present need is dangerous. In fact, if hoarding becomes the focus of one's life, it is foolishness, even sin. However, the rich man did not sin by planning for the future. In a later situation, Yeshua taught the principle of being prepared for what lies ahead. Leaving God out of his plans was his specific sin, which demonstrated he had no love for God, so God called him the *foolish one.*

c. Application

Luke 12:22-34

Yeshua followed His new pattern in that, having spoken to the multitude, He now made the application and explained the meaning of the parable to His disciples (Lk. 12:22a). The principle behind the story is this: *Be not anxious for <your> life, what ye shall eat; nor yet for your body, what ye shall put on. For the life is more than the food, and the body more than the raiment* (Lk. 12:22b-23).

Then Yeshua presented three specific applications: First, God would feed them (Lk. 12:24-26). Second, He would also clothe them (Lk. 12:27-28). If they sought God's kingdom and desired to carry out His program in this life, He promised to supply all basic needs of food and clothing, for the *Father knows that* [they] *have need of these things* (Lk. 12:29-31). Third, God promised that He had already provided for their future: *Fear not, little flock; for it is your Father's good pleasure to give you the kingdom* (Lk. 12:32-33). Since the disciples would inherit the kingdom, they should store up treasure in heaven, not on earth, because of another principle: *For where your treasure is, there will your heart be also* (Lk. 12:34). In the meantime, they should focus on their love of God by setting their heart on heavenly things and fulfilling their love of neighbor by sharing materially with those in need.

3. Watchfulness

Luke 12:35-40

The principle of watchfulness is that the disciples were to view themselves as servants in the absence of their Lord (Lk. 12:35-36). They had a duty to be vigilant, and that meant more than looking for the King's return. They were also to occupy themselves in the work of servanthood during the King's absence. Not knowing exactly when the Lord would return, they should always be ready, day or night.

Two specific time periods are mentioned: *in the second watch* and *in the third* (Lk. 12:38). The second watch was from nine p.m. to midnight, and the third watch was from midnight to three a.m. If they fulfilled their duty, they would receive a twofold prize: a faithful servant would be ministered to by the master himself (Lk. 12:37), and their faithfulness would be the basis for their reward (Lk. 12:38).

Yeshua concluded this lesson by pointing out that watchfulness is especially important when the exact timing of an event is not known. On one hand, a lack of vigilance gives a thief an opportunity to steal (Lk. 12:39); on the other hand, it would result in Yeshua coming unexpectedly (Lk. 12:40).

4. Faithfulness

Luke 12:41-48

Peter's question prompted Yeshua's next lesson: *Lord, do you speak this parable unto us, or even unto all?* (Lk. 12:41). Yeshua answered that the application of His teaching about watchfulness is for anyone who knows the truth (Lk. 12:42-44). For believers, obedience leads to reward and greater responsibility. The servant's responsibility is to safeguard what has been entrusted to him. If a steward is faithful in performing his duties, he will be given even greater responsibility. There is never a legitimate reason to neglect duty. Those who are faithful in little will be entrusted with much more, and the reward will be greater. The principle is: *to whomsoever much is given, of him shall much be required:*

and to whom they commit much, of him will they ask the more (Lk. 12:48). For the believer, this means different degrees of reward.

The reverse is also true. For the unbeliever, it means lesser or greater degrees of punishment: *that servant, who knew his lord's will, and made not ready, nor did according to his will, shall be beaten with many <stripes>; but he that knew not, and did things worthy of stripes, shall be beaten with few <stripes>* (Lk. 12:47-48). Throughout Scripture, God repeatedly teaches that the degree of punishment will be based upon the degree of sinfulness. These verses also show that the amount of knowledge will also be taken into consideration: Those to whom much knowledge about the gospel was given will receive a greater punishment than those who heard little. A common question derived from this teaching is if those who never heard about Yeshua will end up in hell. The Bible's answer is "yes." A lack of knowledge does not save, because sin condemns one to eternal punishment. However, those who were blessed with several opportunities to obey the gospel and still rejected it will suffer greater condemnation than those who had little or no occasion to believe in the Messiah. The punishment is proportionate to the opportunities missed, and in the verses above, both the servant who knew and the servant who did not know were beaten.

5. The Effects of His Coming

Luke 12:49-53

Yeshua taught three things concerning the effects of His coming. First, He came to send judgment: *I came to cast fire upon the earth; and what do I desire, if it is already kindled?* (Lk. 12:49). The judgment is a result of His rejection. If Israel had accepted Him as the Messianic King, He would have brought peace. Since they rejected Him, He brought them judgment.

Second, He came to die: *But I have a baptism to be baptized with; and how am I straitened till it be accomplished!* (Lk. 12:50). Here, the term *baptism* refers to the baptism of suffering that would lead to His death.

Third, the family unit will be divided: *Think ye that I am come to give peace in the earth? I tell you, Nay; but rather division* (Lk. 12:51). As a consequence of the rejection, world peace will not be the result of the first coming, but of the second coming. Furthermore, the rejection of the Messiah will affect the Jewish family structure. While this structure is generally known for its unity, the one thing that will always create immediate division is when a member becomes a believer in Yeshua. This fulfills Isaiah's prophecy of Immanuel, whose arrival would become the new point of division between the remnant and the non-remnant within the Jewish world (Isa. 8:11-22). For the remnant, the Messiah would prove to be a sanctuary; but for the non-remnant, He would prove to be a *stone of stumbling* and a *rock of offense* (Rom. 9:30-33; I Pet. 2:8).

6. The Signs of the Times

Luke 12:54-59

Again turning toward the multitudes (Lk. 12:54), Yeshua addressed the topic of the signs of the times by using words of judgment. He declared that the people should have known that messianic times had arrived: *Ye hypocrites, ye know how to interpret the face of the earth and the heaven; but how is it that ye know not how to interpret this time?* (Lk. 12:56). While prophecy teachers often use the phrase "signs of the times" to refer to Yeshua's second coming, the Gospels always use it in the context of His first coming. So the people should have known from Old Testament prophecy that messianic times had arrived.

Furthermore, common sense should have told them they needed to make their peace before it was too late (Lk. 12:57-59). The way that members of this generation could have made peace was by breaking away from the majority and accepting Yeshua as the Messiah. By so doing, they would not have suffered the judgment of A.D. 70. That judgment was inevitable and deadly, but it was caused by the national sin, not an individual sin. Individual members could still escape this judgment, but they had to make their peace beforehand, reconciling the differences that separated them from God, that is, their lack of belief in the Messiahship of Yeshua. Repentance would reconcile them, meaning they had to change their mind about Yeshua and accept Him as the Messiah.

7. Concerning Repentance

Luke 13:1-9

The incident behind Yeshua's next lesson on repentance was that *there were some present at that very season who told him of the Galileans, whose blood Pilate had mingled with their sacrifices* (Lk. 13:1). Two tragedies had actually happened. Some Galileans had come to Jerusalem to offer sacrifices in the Temple. For an unknown reason, Pilate took them to be members of a rebel band and released the soldiers. The people were killed, and their blood was mingled with the blood of the sacrifices. In a second incident, the tower over the Pool of Siloam collapsed, killing 18 people (Lk. 13:4). Those who approached Yeshua to discuss these incidents assumed that this kind of violent, inexplicable death proved the victims' guilt of some secret, specific sin. Yeshua discounted that theology (Lk. 13:2-5):

> *² And he answered and said unto them, Think ye that these Galileans were sinners above all the Galileans, because they have suffered these things? ³ I tell you, Nay: but, except ye repent, ye shall all in like manner perish. ⁴ Or those eighteen, upon whom the tower in Shiloach fell, and killed them, think ye that they were offenders above all the men that dwell in Yerushalayim? ⁵ I tell you, Nay: but, except ye repent, ye shall all likewise perish.*

In other words, the violent deaths did not mean that the victims were greater sinners than others or that they were guilty of any special sin that caused a particular tragedy to fall upon them.

Yeshua explained the application: *except ye repent, ye shall all in like manner perish* (Lk. 13:3b); *except ye repent, ye shall all likewise perish* (Lk. 13:5b). The key phrases in these two verses are *in like manner* and *likewise*. The word *repent* means "to change one's mind." They needed to change their minds about Yeshua. He was the Messianic Person and not demonized. If they did not change their minds about Yeshua and repent, they would suffer and perish in like manner and likewise. Indeed, that is what happened in the year A.D. 70. As the Romans breached the walls of Jerusalem, they undermined the foundations upon which the defensive towers were built. When the towers collapsed, many died in like manner. The battle for the Temple was one of the last battles. The fight occurred at the time of the sacrifice; Jewish blood was again mingled with the blood of the sacrifices, and the people perished in like manner.

Speaking to the multitudes, Yeshua concluded with the Parable of the Barren Fig Tree to demonstrate why judgment would be delayed by forty years (Lk. 13:6-9), showing that even after a whole generation had passed, Israel still had not produced any fruit. As a nation, the Jewish people did not come to the Messiah and repent of the national rejection, so the tree had to be cut.

8. Concerning Israel's Need

Luke 13:10-17

The background to the lesson concerning Israel's need is that Yeshua *was teaching in one of the synagogues on the Sabbath day* (Lk. 13:10). This is the last recorded incident that occurred in a synagogue. A woman suffering from permanent curvature of the spine was at the synagogue service. In accordance with the medical community, Luke pointed out that she was *bowed together* and incapable of lifting herself up (Lk. 13:11). What had befallen her was *a spirit of infirmity* (Lk. 13:12).

Although it was the Sabbath day, Yeshua proceeded to heal her (Lk. 13:12-13) and was publicly rebuked by *the ruler of the synagogue* (Lk. 13:14). He responded by pointing out their hypocrisy (Lk. 13:15-16). The Pharisees recognized that works of necessity and mercy were allowed on the Sabbath. If animals could be made more comfortable on that day, how much more should that be true for a person?

Yeshua called the suffering woman a *daughter of Avraham* (Lk. 13:16), emphasizing her individual Jewishness and demonstrating again that He no longer dealt with the nation as a whole. He would, however, deal with individual members of the nation, and this was a daughter of Abraham with an obvious personal need. Since she was part of Israel and since Israel was His possession, Yeshua could care for individual sheep within the flock. In keeping with Zechariah 11:4-14, the Messiah emphasized His ministry to *the poor of the flock*, the individual believing members. Here, He cared for one *whom Satan had bound* for 18 years, and He *loosed* her from this bond (Lk. 13:16). The words *bound* and *loosed* are used here not in the sense of binding or loosing Satan, but rather that Satan had bound the woman, and Yeshua loosed her from Satan's control. The woman, not Satan, was bound. That clear distinction should not be missed or misapplied.

The incident led to two results: *all his adversaries were put to shame*, and *all the multitude rejoiced* (Lk. 13:17).

9. Concerning the Kingdom Program

Luke 13:18-21

Yeshua repeated two parables that dealt with His kingdom program, which were previously detailed in § 64. *He said therefore* (Lk. 13:18), in light of the national rejection and in favor of the individual, Yeshua provided two parables describing the new nature of the mystery kingdom. In the first, the Parable of the Mustard Seed, He taught that outwardly, the mystery kingdom will grow unnaturally large. In the second, the Parable of the Leaven, He taught that inwardly, it would also contain false doctrine. Thus, He emphasized the two facets of the mystery kingdom program: the external development and the internal corruption of doctrine.

[§ 112] — N. The Conflict
at the Feast of Dedication

John 10:22-39

And it was the feast of dedication at Yerushalayim: it was winter (Jn. 10:22-23). The Feast of Dedication, or *Chanukah*,[6] is also known as the Feast of Lights, because the manner of observing the feast is by lighting lamps or candles. The feast commemorates the rededication of the Temple after the Maccabees had recaptured it on the 25th day of *Kislev*[7] in the year 165 B.C. Although Moses did not inaugurate this feast, its observance is valid for two reasons. First, Daniel prophesied the events that brought about this holy day (chapters 8 and 11). Second, Yeshua authenticated the feast by going to Jerusalem to observe it. Yochanan mentioned that *it was winter*, for the end of the month of Kislev is usually in December.

At the time of the encounter, Yeshua was walking in a part of the Temple compound known as Solomon's Porch. The Jewish people came to Him and charged Him with obscurity: *How long do you hold us in suspense? If you are the Messiah, tell us plainly* (Jn. 10:24). The charge was false because Yeshua had clearly stated more than once in the past that He was the Messiah, and they had no trouble then in understanding what He had said (Lk. 4:21; Jn. 5:10-18).

Yeshua denied the charge and reminded them that He had made His claim clear in two ways: by His words (*I told you, and ye believe not*; Jn. 10:25a) and by His works (*the works that I do in my Father's name, these bear witness of me*; Jn. 10:25b). The real problem was not that He had been cryptic; rather, they were not His sheep and did not recognize Him (Jn. 10:26). In contrast, His sheep recognize and follow Him, so they have eternal life (Jn. 10:7-29). Finally, He said, *no one shall snatch them out of my hand ... no one is able to snatch <them> out of the*

---

[6] *Chanukah* is the Hebrew word for "dedication."

[7] Kislev is the ninth month of the Jewish year. It corresponds to November or December on the Gregorian calendar.

Father's hand (Jn. 10:28b, 29b). This teaches double eternal security. The believer is both in the hand of the Messiah and in the hand of God the Father; believers can neither be snatched out of the Father's hand, nor the Son's hand.

Yeshua answered the charge of obscurity by saying, *I and the Father are one* (Jn. 10:30). With these words, He proclaimed a unique, divine oneness with God the Father, the oneness of the *Shema: Hear, O Yisrael, the Lord our God, the Lord is one* (Deut. 6:4). If God is one, and Yeshua is one with God, He is, therefore, God Himself. The Jewish audience, understanding His words, *took up stones again to stone him* (Jn. 10:31). There was no doubt in their minds who He was proclaiming to be: the Messianic God-Man, who enjoyed a unique oneness with the Father.

As if to clarify further, Yeshua asked a question: *Many good works have I showed you from the Father; for which of those works do ye stone me?* (Jn. 10:32). Their answer proves that the multitudes understood His meaning exactly: *For a good work we stone you not, but for blasphemy; and because that you, being a man, make yourself God* (Jn. 10:33b). They understood He proclaimed to be God Himself when He claimed oneness with the Father.

In response, Yeshua spoke in parables again (Jn. 10:34-38). He based His words upon the context of Psalm 82:6: *I said, Ye are gods, And all of you sons of the Most High.* In this verse, God addressed the judges of Israel, who were His representatives with His delegated authority. By personal direct mission, they did the works of God. As His representatives acting in His name, they were called *elohim* or "gods." If these representatives were referred to as *elohim,* how could His claim to be the individual Son of God be blasphemous when He had received not merely transmitted authority, but the direct and personal command to do the Father's work? He asked them: "How could you say of me, whom the Father sanctified and sent into the world, 'You blaspheme'? Is it because I said, I am the Son of God?" (Jn. 10:36). Moses was also called "god" in the Hebrew Scriptures. In Exodus 4:16, he was a god to Aaron, and in Exodus 7:1, he was a god to Pharaoh. Moses did not become a god, but he bore God's message. If Moses, who was a man, could be as a god to Aaron and to Pharaoh, why could not Yeshua be the Son of God? He, like Moses, was God's messenger, bringing His message. The children of Israel listened to Moses, so why should they not listen to Him? Yeshua professed to be the Messiah, and His works proved Him right, showing that He was more than just God's representative. He was one with the Father.

The people's response again showed that they knew who He claimed to be: They *sought again to take him: and he went forth out of their hand* (Jn. 10:39).

VI. The Preparation of the Disciples by the King
— §§ 113–131 —

Yeshua now began to prepare the disciples for His coming death. Two phrases indicate the basic motif of this phase of His life: *And behold, there are last who shall be first, and there are first who shall be last* (Lk. 13:30), and, *For every one that exalts himself shall be humbled; and he that humbles himself shall be exalted* (Lk. 14:11).

This section of Yeshua's life covers a three-to-four-month period, from the Feast of Dedication in December A.D. 29 until the beginning of His journey to Jerusalem at Passover.

[§ 113] — A. The Withdrawal from Judah

John 10:40-42

Yeshua went beyond the Jordan to the area known as Perea, outside the jurisdiction of the Sanhedrin (Jn. 10:40). This was also the area where Yochanan the Baptizer primarily conducted his ministry to prepare a people to accept the Messiah once He became known. Indeed, his mission did not fail, because *many came unto him; and they said, Yochanan indeed did no sign: but all things whatsoever Yochanan spoke of this man were true. And many believed on him there* (Jn. 10:41). Having heard and believed the baptizer's message, these people, at their baptism, accepted the Messiah once Yochanan pointed Him out, and now they were fulfilling that commitment.

[§ 114] — B. Instruction Concerning Entrance into the Kingdom

Luke 13:22-35

And he went on his way through cities and villages, teaching, and journeying on unto Yerushalayim (Lk. 13:22). Yeshua moved toward His final journey into Jerusalem, where He would begin the last week of His life. On His way, He stayed in those places that the seventy disciples had prepared for Him.

Somewhere along the way, one of Yeshua's disciples asked: *Lord, are they few that are saved?* (Lk. 13:23). The question arose from the mass rejection in the previous section, where it was evident that the people followed their leaders' condemnation of the Messiah. The context indicates that the question actually concerned entrance into the kingdom and, therefore, more likely pertained to Israel's national salvation than to individual salvation.

Yeshua answered: *Strive to enter in by the narrow door: for many, I say unto you, shall seek to enter in, and shall not be able* (Lk. 13:24). As previously noted, the Pharisaic way into the kingdom was the wide road, and Yeshua dismissed this doctrine in the Sermon on the Mount. According to Pharisaism, all Israel would take the wide road and have a share in the age to come. However, Yeshua pointed out that there is only a *narrow door*, through Him alone, and they must strive to enter into the kingdom only by Him.

He told them this: *When once the master of the house is risen up, and has shut the door, and ye begin to stand without, and to knock at the door, saying, Lord, open to us; and he shall answer and say to you, I know you not where ye are* (Lk. 13:25). A time will come when the opportunity to enter the kingdom will be withdrawn. Once an individual dies in unbelief, he will never enter the kingdom. Therefore, they must come to Yeshua in this lifetime. The individuals of that generation must come to Him before the year A.D. 70. When the kingdom is finally established at Yeshua's second coming, the people who tried to enter by way of Pharisaism will find themselves excluded. He told them, there *shall be the weeping and the gnashing of teeth, when ye shall see Avraham, and Yitzchak, and Yaakov, and all the prophets, in the kingdom of God, and yourselves cast forth without* (Lk. 13:28). The patriarchs and prophets will all enter the kingdom, but those who chose the wide road of Pharisaism will be excluded. Those, on the other hand, who chose the narrow door through Yeshua are the ones who *shall come from the east and west, and from the north and south, and shall sit down in the kingdom of God* (Lk. 13:29). The implication is clear: Many Jewish people will fail to enter into the kingdom, while many Gentiles will enter with the patriarchs and the prophets. The motif for this section is: *there are last who shall be first, and there are first who shall be last* (Lk. 13:30).

In that very hour (Lk. 13:31a), as Yeshua was saying these things and speaking out against the false doctrine, *there came certain Pharisees, saying to him, Get you out, and go hence: for Herod would fain kill you* (Lk. 13:31b). The religious leaders appeared to be so kind as to warn Yeshua that Herod Antipas was out to kill Him, just as he had previously killed Yochanan the Baptizer. As always, they had an ulterior motive. While in Perea, on the east side of the Jordan, Yeshua was under the jurisdiction of Herod Antipas and outside the jurisdiction of the Sanhedrin. The Pharisees were trying to get Yeshua to cross over to the west side of the Jordan to have Him arrested and expedite His execution. Yeshua gave a cryptic answer (Lk. 13:32-33):

> *32 And he said unto them, Go and say to that fox, Behold, I cast out demons and perform cures today and tomorrow, and the third <day> I am perfected. 33 Nevertheless I must go on my way today and tomorrow and the <day> following: for it cannot be that a prophet perish out of Yerushalayim.*

Speaking parabolically, Yeshua hinted at His resurrection. He told them not to worry, for He would eventually cross to the west side of the Jordan. Those in Jerusalem would kill Him, not Herod Antipas, for it was not possible that the Messianic Prophet should perish outside of Jerusalem.

Yeshua closed with a lament (Lk. 13:34-35) that indicated He would not return until Israel asks Him to and said, *Blessed is he that comes in the name of the Lord* (Lk. 13:35). He used the same words to close His public ministry, and they will be detailed in § 143.

[§ 115] — C. Instruction in a Pharisee's House

1. True Sabbath Rest

Luke 14:1-6

Another incident occurred when the Pharisees invited Yeshua over for dinner. This time it was *one of the rulers of the Pharisees* who asked Him *to eat bread* with them (Lk. 14:1). He was a "high Pharisee," the head of a rabbinic school. He and his fellow conspirators were again trying to entrap Yeshua in some way. The text states that *they were watching him* (Lk. 14:1), hoping to catch Him transgressing another rule.

They also invited someone else, *a certain man* who had *the dropsy* (Lk. 14:2). This medical condition is now called edema, and it means that this person suffered from an abnormal accumulation of fluid in one part of his body. Yeshua asked the Pharisees a question: *Is it lawful to heal on the Sabbath, or not?* (Lk. 14:3). They *held their peace* (Lk.

14:4) and deliberately avoided answering His question. According to Pharisaism, healing on the Sabbath was permissible if the illness endangered the person's life. If the person's life was not endangered, then healing on the Sabbath day was not allowed. The point of Yeshua's question, however, was that Sabbath rest naturally included being healed.

When the Pharisees did not answer, Yeshua asked them another question: *Which of you shall have an ass or an ox fallen into a well, and will not straightway draw him up on a Sabbath day?* (Lk. 14:5). The obvious answer was that, indeed, they would do so. If doing good to animals on the Sabbath is appropriate, then doing good to fellow Israelites on the Sabbath is even more proper. Therefore, Yeshua took the man, healed him, and sent him on his way (Lk. 14:4). The result was that *they could not answer again unto these things* (Lk. 14:6). In other words, ultimately, nothing Yeshua said could really be used to entrap Him.

2. Humility

Luke 14:7-11

Yeshua addressed a parable to those who had also been *bidden* to the dinner (Lk. 14:7), though not for ulterior motives, as was He. He presented the parable when He noticed that the Pharisees deliberately sought out the chief seats, wanting to be noticed for their high status. Yeshua taught that a person should not elevate himself to a position of status. Rather, he should wait for others to recognize him. Those who elevate themselves to a higher position may be humiliated. The principle for this section is: *For every one that exalts himself shall be humbled; and he that humbles himself shall be exalted* (Lk. 14:11).

3. Respect of Persons

Luke 14:12-14

Yeshua next addressed the host: *And he said to him also that had bidden him* (Lk. 14:12). The principle lesson is that hospitality demonstrates one's love for fellow men, so is the means of fulfilling the righteousness of the Mosaic Law. However, a person who invites guests only to accumulate honor for himself cannot expect to be rewarded.

The hospitality of the Pharisees was self-seeking, self-glorifying, and self-righteous. They only invited people who could repay the compliment. The righteousness of the law, however, demands that hospitality be extended to those who may never have the means to return the favor. So we, too, should give to those who cannot repay: *But when you make a feast, bid the poor, the maimed, the lame, the blind: and you shall be blessed; because they have not <wherewith> to recompense you: for you shall be recompensed in the resurrection of the just* (Lk. 14:13-14).

4. The Rejection of the Invitation

Luke 14:15-24

The occasion of this section is spelled out in the following verse: *And when one of them that sat at meat with him heard these things, he said unto him, Blessed is he that shall eat bread in the kingdom of God* (Lk. 14:15). The man who made this comment had just heard Yeshua's teaching that those who served others *shall be recompensed in the resurrection of the just* (Lk. 14:14). At the mention of the resurrection, he said, *Blessed is he that shall eat bread in the kingdom of God.* This led Yeshua to tell the Parable of the Rejected Invitation, also known as the Parable of the Great Banquet.

Yeshua mentioned a certain man who had *made a great supper* (Lk. 14:16). Those people bidden had accepted the invitation, but when the dinner was ready and the servant bid them come (Lk. 14:17), each excused themselves (Lk. 14:18a), giving three different reasons. One man was too occupied with his material possessions (Lk. 14:18b); the second man was too occupied with his business (Lk. 14:19); and the third man was too occupied with his own personal pleasure (Lk. 14:20).

The shallow excuses incensed the master of the house (Lk. 14:21), and he said to his servant, *Go out quickly into the streets and lanes of the city, and bring in here the poor and maimed and blind and lame* (Lk. 14:21). Since the higher class invitees would not come when bidden, the invitation was extended to others who were needy. When they came, there was still room for more: *And the lord said unto the servant, Go out into the highways and hedges, and constrain <them> to come in, that my house may be filled* (Lk. 14:23). Yeshua concluded: *For I say unto you, that none of those men that were bidden shall taste of my supper* (Lk. 14:24).

The beginning statement of this incident is key to understanding the parable. The man who, in verse 15, said, *Blessed is he that shall eat bread in the kingdom of God,* probably believed the Pharisaic teaching that all Israel will automatically have a share in the age to come. Significantly, the host of the feast in the parable was God Himself. Those who prepared the feast were the prophets. The first servant sent out to declare that the supper was ready was Yochanan the Baptizer, and after him came Yeshua. Those originally bidden but who ultimately declined the invitation were the Jewish leaders of that generation. The invitation was then extended to those in need, and the servant found people both in *the city* (Lk. 14:21) and *the highways and hedges* (Lk. 14:23), meaning the country. Those from the city represent the Jews who would come to believe and enjoy this feast, and those from the country represent the Gentiles who would also come and enjoy the feast. When Yeshua said that *none of those men that were bidden shall taste of my supper* (Lk. 14:24), He was pointing out that the generation which rejected the invitation would fail to see the kingdom at that time or in the age to come.

[§ 116] — D. Instruction Concerning Discipleship

Luke 14:25-35

This section addresses the *great multitudes* (Lk. 14:25), among whom were believers. The emphasis in this lesson on discipleship deals with things that prevent a man from becoming a full-time follower of the Messiah. Distinguishing between salvation and discipleship is important. Salvation requires faith alone; but discipleship requires a much stronger commitment. Three lessons about discipleship are presented in this section.

The first lesson is that the disciple must be willing to leave all, even his own family members if they try to hinder him from entering a full-time commitment to discipleship (Lk. 14:26). The terms *love* and *hate* in this context are not dealing with emotions, but rather with the issue of choosing or not choosing. To love means "to choose," and to hate means "not to choose" or "to reject." This meaning is found in Malachi: *yet I loved Yaakov; but Esau I hated,* meaning that Jacob was chosen to be the covenantal son, but Esau was not chosen (Mal. 1:2-3; see also Rom. 9:13). In that sense, Esau was hated and Jacob was loved. Therefore, if family members force a person to make a choice between following them or following Yeshua, they must love Yeshua in the sense of choosing Him and hate their relatives in the sense of not choosing to follow them.

The second lesson on discipleship is that a commitment to follow Yeshua is equivalent to bearing one's *own cross,* identifying with Yeshua's rejection and being willing to suffer rejection as well (Lk. 14:27).

The third lesson is that anyone considering discipleship must count the cost (Lk. 14:28-32). The question raised is, "How much of my resources am I willing to commit to being a disciple?" The Messiah demands total commitment: So *therefore whosoever he be of you that renounces not all that he has, he cannot be my disciple* (Lk. 14:33).

The lesson closes with the concept of salt: *Salt therefore is good: but if even the salt have lost its savor, wherewith shall it be seasoned? It is fit* *neither for the land nor for the dunghill: <men> cast it out* (Lk. 14:34-35). Salt derived from the Dead Sea loses its savoriness over the course of time and is eventually discarded. If a believer never becomes a disciple, or if a disciple turns away from their commitment, then they lose their saltiness and are useless to God. To press on toward spiritual maturity, they must make the commitment Paul writes of in Romans 12:1-2:

> *¹ I beseech you therefore, brethren, by the mercies of God, to present your bodies a living sacrifice, holy, acceptable to God, which is your spiritual service. ² And be not fashioned according to this world: but be ye transformed by the renewing of your mind, and ye may prove what is the good and acceptable and perfect will of God.*

This is the way to become a full-time disciple who is salty and useful for God's work.

[§ 117] — E. Instruction Concerning God's Attitude towards Sinners

1. The Occasion

Luke 15:1-2

The occasion for this lesson was the criticism by the Pharisees that Yeshua associated with publicans and prostitutes who *were drawing near unto him to hear him* (Lk. 15:1). The incident led Yeshua to present three parables to distinguish between God's attitude towards sinners and the Pharisees' attitude towards sinners. The Pharisees had issued all kinds of rules and regulations against publicans and prostitutes, including the following examples:

- ✿ Pharisees must neither buy from nor sell to a publican or a sinner anything that is in a dry or fluid state.

- ✿ A Pharisee was not to eat at a sinner's table and thus partake of something that might not have been tithed first.

- ✿ He was not to admit a publican or sinner to his table unless they put on the clothes of a Pharisee, meaning they converted to Pharisaism.

- ✿ The Pharisee must never perform anything in the presence of a sinner that was connected with the laws of purification, lest the sinner himself should be convicted and want to be purified.

- ✿ Finally, they taught that there was joy before God when those who provoked Him perished from the earth and that God rejoiced over the death of the sinners.

Understanding this background helps grasp the religious leaders' dilemma: If Yeshua were the Messiah, He would not associate with sinners.

2. The Three Parables

a. The Parable of the Lost Sheep

Luke 15:3-7

The emphasis of the first parable is on being lost because of the sheep's tendency to stray. Although the shepherd may have 99 sheep with him and only one is lost, he would still go everywhere to find the lost one and rejoice when he found it. This emphasizes the work of God the Son, and Yeshua explained the application this way: *I say unto you, that even so there shall be joy in heaven over one sinner that repents, <more> than over ninety and nine righteous persons, who need no repentance* (Lk. 15:7).

b. The Parable of the Lost Coin

Luke 15:8-10

The emphasis of the second parable is on searching. The coin was somewhere in the house, but due to the surrounding circumstances, it was invisible. So, the woman searched every corner of the house and rejoiced when she found her lost coin. This emphasizes the work of God the Holy Spirit. Yeshua concluded by telling them the application: *Even so, I say unto you, there is joy in the presence of the angels of God over one sinner that repents* (Lk. 15:10).

c. The Parable of the Prodigal Son

Luke 15:11-32

The emphasis of the third parable is on restoration, which is the work of God the Father. The story is very well known. A man had two sons. One son asked for his inheritance early, left home, and wasted all his money with riotous living. When he was destitute, and the friends he had made deserted him, he had to become a worker. Ironically for a Jew, he was forced to work as a feeder of swine. Finally, he realized his sin against his father and returned home, hoping to become a servant. When his father saw him from afar, he ran up to him and greeted and welcomed him back. Ever since the son had left home, he had been watching for his return: *But while he was yet afar off, his father saw him* (Lk. 15:20). The emphasis in the Greek text is on the phrase *yet far off.* The father always expected the son to return home someday. He did not know when, but he lived with the expectation that his son would come back.

Although the son was willing to become a servant in his father's house without the privileges of an heir, the father would have none of it. When he restored his son, he gave him three things (Lk. 15:22): *the best robe* as a sign of his birthright, *a ring* as a sign of authority, and that demonstrated his restored position as a son in the house, and *shoes* as a sign of his sonship. He was fully restored. A great feast was given because the son had returned to the father's home.

However, the fuss over the younger son, who had wasted his inheritance, troubled the *elder son* (Lk. 15:25). He complained to his father that, though he had been faithful and obedient, he had never been treated with such honor. The father answered that the inheritance was still his and he had lost nothing. However, the prodigal son had returned to be part of the family, so joy and rejoicing should prevail in the house.

This reflects God's attitude toward sinners and the joy in heaven when one repents. The father's statement, *all that is mine is yours* (Lk. 15:31), indicates that all the privileges given to the younger brother were available to the older brother; however, the older brother refused to appropriate what was available to him. Likewise, the Pharisees failed to appropriate what was available to them.

[§ 118] — F. Instruction Concerning Wealth

The background to this section is the misconception that physical wealth is a sign of divine favor and that whomsoever the Lord loves, He makes rich. This misconception was widespread among the Pharisees.

1. The Parable of the Unjust Steward

Luke 16:1-13

In this parable, Yeshua dealt with an unrighteous steward entrusted with an important position, who made unrighteous use of it. He was unfaithful in the trust committed to him. The Pharisees had also been unfaithful in the trust given them. When the rich man discovered his steward's unfaithfulness and found that he had been *wasting his goods* (Lk. 16:1), he gave him notice of dismissal. The steward's dilemma was that he lacked training to do anything else, and he did not want to beg (Lk. 16:3). Knowing that his time was short, the steward used his position to win friends so that when he lost his job, someone would offer him another one (Lk. 16:4-7).

As a result, *his lord commended the unrighteous steward because he had done wisely* (Lk. 16:8a). He was not commending his unrighteous action or his sin, but only his wisdom in that, knowing the limited amount of time he had left, he used his position to prepare for his future. Yeshua made the application: *for the sons of this world are for their own generation wiser than the sons of light* (Lk. 16:8b). This is a basic observation that, generally, unbelievers are wiser in the realm of material things than believers. Unbelievers tend to be better prepared for the days ahead. Believers sometimes cross the line from trusting the Lord to tempting the Lord and become flippant about preparing for their future needs and security. A proper balance between giving and preparing for future retirement with things like health and life insurance without biblical compromise is one side of the coin.

The other side of the coin is this: *And I say unto you, Make to yourselves friends by means of the mammon of unrighteousness; that, when it shall fail, they may receive you into the eternal tabernacles* (Lk. 16:9). The word *mammon* was a common Jewish term used frequently in rabbinic writings to refer to everything the world offers materially. The principle is that mammon should be used for the present as well as for the future in preparation for the days ahead both in the physical realm and in the spiritual realm, without crossing the line into materialism. The statement, *Make to yourselves friends by means of the mammon of unrighteousness* (Lk. 16:9a), teaches that a way to use the material things of this world is to win friends for the Lord. That could mean monetarily supporting evangelistic efforts, missionaries, Bible distributions, etc. Yeshua added: *when it shall fail* (Lk. 16:9b). The pronoun *it* refers to the mammon. Both are in the neuter gender, meaning that when the material world fails us (i.e., when death comes), *they may receive you into the eternal tabernacles* (Lk. 16:9c). In other words, the people whom we have won to the Lord by using mammon may pass away first. When we die, those friends will greet us *into the eternal tabernacles*, that is, heaven. Therefore, mammon must also be used for the benefit of others, particularly in the spiritual realm.

To summarize, a proper balance exists for the believer to have a savings account, life insurance, and a retirement plan without losing faith in the Lord. In fact, it is evidence of faith in Him and belief in Yeshua's teaching about how to prepare for the days ahead. The believer should plan, but never hoard money so that, as a result, he never gives to the Lord's work. He should always be sensitive to and supportive of the work of God. On the other hand, believers are never told to give everything away so that their families go hungry. The Bible clearly teaches that if a believer does not provide for his own family in the material and physical realm, he is to be treated like and be considered worse than an unbeliever (I Tim. 5:8).

Having stated these principles, Yeshua taught three lessons: first, *He that is faithful in a very little is faithful also in much* (Lk. 16:10); second, *If therefore ye have not been faithful in the unrighteous mammon, who will commit to your trust the true <riches>?* (Lk. 16:11); and third, *if ye have not been faithful in that which is another's, who will give you that which is your own?* (Lk. 16:12). There are two interlinked levels: the physical (in the economic sense) and the spiritual. *A very little* refers to the unrighteous mammon, and *in much* refers to the true riches. *Your own* refers to the spiritual wealth received from Yeshua and offered to others. If unbelievers can trust believers with mammon on the economic level, they will also be willing to trust them on the spiritual level. This provides opportunity to share with unbelievers the true wealth, which only believers can share. The true wealth is the message about Yeshua, the gospel. If unbelievers accept the message of the gospel, they will have true spiritual riches: salvation. Therefore, believers need to make friends with *the mammon of unrighteousness* (Lk. 16:9), because it has the potential to lead to the exchange of spiritual wealth.

Yeshua concluded the application of the Parable of the Unjust Steward by stating, *No servant can serve two masters: for either he will hate the one, and love the other; or else he will hold to one, and despise the other. Ye cannot serve God and mammon* (Lk. 16:13). Again, the words "love" and "hate" do not refer to emotional responses to money, but indicate a choice. The principle is this: Who is the target of our service? If we, as believers, put God first and seek first His righteousness and His kingdom, then we will know how to balance the use of our material resources.

2. The Conflict with the Pharisees

Luke 16:14-18

Yeshua's teaching contradicted Pharisaic doctrine about mammon: *the Pharisees, who were lovers of money, heard all these things; and they scoffed at Him* (Lk. 16:14). In response, Yeshua accused them of four things. First, they were guilty of self-exaltation (Lk. 16:15). In keeping with the motif of this section, He warned: *that which is exalted among men is an abomination in the sight of God* and shall be humbled. Second, *The law and the prophets <were> until Yochanan: from that time the gospel of the kingdom of God is preached, and every man enters violently into it* (Lk. 16:16). The period of the Law and the Prophets culminated with Yochanan the Baptizer, the last of the Old Testament prophets. Since then, the gospel of the kingdom was offered, but was violently opposed by the Pharisees. For the individual Jew to enter the kingdom required a struggle to recognize the possibility of Yeshua being the Messiah. Third, while the Pharisees were guilty of reinterpreting the Mosaic Law by means of their traditions, Yeshua's attitude toward the law was to fulfill it: *But it is easier for heaven and earth to pass away, than for one tittle of the law to fall* (Lk. 16:17). Fourth, one example of the conflict between His interpretation of the law and their interpretation of the law was the issue of divorce (Lk. 16:18), which will be covered in a subsequent context (§ 125).

3. The Rich Man and Lazarus

Luke 16:19-31

The account of the rich man and Lazarus is sometimes referred to as a parable, but it is a true story. Jewish parables do not contain personal names; they do use figures of speech that illustrate a moral, ethical, or spiritual truth from everyday life and experience. This story deals with two men: an unnamed rich man and a beggar called Lazarus. The rich man had wealth and, based upon the common Pharisaic view of that day, was most certainly a recipient of divine favor. However, for Lazarus, a beggar, his position was unsure.

Lazarus begged as he lay at the gate of the rich man's mansion. He was always *full of sores, and desiring to be fed with the <crumbs> that fell from the rich man's table* (Lk. 16:20b-21). Only the dogs of the area cared for his wounds. Lazarus was always visible to the rich man as he went in and out of his mansion, so the rich man had sufficient opportunity to fulfill the second most important commandment of the Mosaic Law, to love his neighbor as himself (Lev. 19:18). His failure to help Lazarus showed that he also failed to keep the first and most important commandment of the Mosaic Law, to love God (Deut. 6:5).

Eventually, both men died, and what happened to them contradicted the theology of that day: The soul of Lazarus was carried by angels *into Avraham's bosom* (Lk. 16:22), while the rich man ended up in hell. Throughout the history of the Hebrew Bible, both the righteous and the unrighteous went down to *Sheol* upon death; however, they did not all go to the same place in Sheol. There were two compartments. The good side was called *paradise* and *Abraham's bosom*. The latter name is the one most frequently found in rabbinic writings, but it occurs only once in the Scriptures (Lk. 16:22). During Old Testament times, when believers died, their bodies were buried in the ground and their souls went to paradise, or Abraham's bosom. They could not directly enter God's presence because the atonement available to them with animal blood could only cover, but not remove the sins of the Old Testament saints (Heb. 10:1-4). A person's salvation was based on grace through faith, and while animal blood provided forgiveness, it did not remove sin. Therefore, until the Messiah died, a saint could not go directly into God's presence in heaven upon death. His soul went to paradise.

The second division in Sheol was reserved for the fallen angels and the souls of the unrighteous. As Luke shows, the dead on both sides of *Sheol* could see and talk to each other, but they could not cross over because *there is a great gulf fixed, that they that would pass from hence to you may not be able, and that none may cross over from thence to us* (Lk. 16:26). The bad side of Sheol had three subdivisions. One subdivision was hell, which was for unbelieving humans. Their bodies were also buried in the ground, but their souls went into hell. The second subdivision was called *Tartarus*. This was a permanent place of confinement for fallen angels, specifically for those who, in Genesis 6, had married women. The third subdivision was the abyss, which is a temporary place of confinement for fallen angels. Some are there now, and they will be released later (Rev. 9). Satan will spend the Millennium in the abyss, but then he will be released (Rev. 20:1-3). So, both the abyss and Tartarus are areas of confinement for demons; however, the abyss is temporary and Tartarus is permanent. By way of analogy, it is the difference between jail time and life in prison. The demons asked not to be sent to the abyss (Lk. 8:31).

When the Messiah died, He experienced what all other human beings experienced at the time. His body stayed in Joseph's tomb, but His soul went to Sheol. However, it is important to note that Yeshua never spent even a moment in hell. His soul went to paradise. His death accomplished all that was necessary for the atonement. He not only died for sins committed after His death, but also for all sins committed prior to His death (Rom. 3:25; Heb. 9:15). Only now were the sins of the Old Testament saints removed. While Yeshua was in Sheol, He proclaimed to those who were in paradise that the atonement had been made, and to those on the other side, His presence guaranteed their final judgment.

When Yeshua ascended into heaven, paradise was emptied and the souls of the *captives* were taken directly to heaven (Eph. 4:8-10). Today when believers die, their bodies still stay in the ground, but their souls go immediately into God's presence in heaven (Phil. 1:21-24; II Cor. 5:1-11, esp. v. 8: *to be absent from the body, and to be at home with the Lord*). However, things have not changed for unbelievers. To this day, when they die, their bodies are placed into the ground and their souls go to hell. It will stay this way until the end of the messianic kingdom. Then God will do away with this earth, and all unbelievers will be taken out of hell to stand before the Great White Throne to be judged and cast into the lake of fire for their eternal abode.

The term "Abraham's bosom" can often be found in rabbinic writings, while this is the only place in the New Testament where it appears. Abraham and the rich man saw and talked to each other, but they could not cross over the impassible gulf mentioned in this passage. A discussion ensued between Abraham, who spoke from paradise, and the rich man, who was on the hell side of Sheol. By calling Abraham *father* (Lk. 16:24, 30), the rich man emphasized the blood relationship between the two. Abraham, in turn, addressed him as *son* (Lk. 16:25). The physical relationship between Abraham and the rich man did not keep the rich man out of hell. This showed the fallacy of the Pharisaic belief that all Israel has a share in the age to come.

The rich man made it clear that he was in tremendous torment, so much so that he said if Lazarus would only dip one finger in water, bring that wet finger of water to the other side, and put it on his tongue, it would give him great relief from the *anguish in this flame* (Lk. 16:24). However, Abraham told him that was not possible, because *between us and you there is a great gulf fixed* (Lk. 16:26) which made it impossible to cross from one side to the other.

Once the rich man realized there was no relief from his agony, he became concerned about his five brothers who still lived. Knowing their spiritual state would land them in hell, the rich man asked Abraham to allow Lazarus to be resurrected from the dead, so that when his brothers saw him, they would believe. Abraham answered: *They have Mosheh and the prophets; let them hear them* (Lk. 16:29). The Scriptures were available to his five brothers. If they simply read and believed the Scriptures, that would suffice to keep them out of hell.

The rich man responded, *Nay, father Avraham: but if one go to them from the dead, they will repent* (Lk. 16:30). The rich man claimed that the Scriptures were insufficient and his brothers needed miracles, signs, and wonders. A miracle such as Lazarus raised from the dead would convince his brothers, but Scripture alone was not sufficient. Abraham responded: *If they hear not Mosheh and the prophets, neither will they be persuaded, if one rise from the dead* (Lk. 16:31). If they would not believe the Scriptures, neither would the signs convince them. After all the miracles, signs, and wonders Yeshua had performed, the people nevertheless rejected Him. They did not deny the fact of His miracles, but they ascribed them to the power of Beelzebub.

In conclusion, two observations should be made from this passage. First, the story of the rich man and Lazarus illustrates the proper use of mammon. The rich man is not named, but according to the theology of that day, the fact that he was wealthy certainly meant that he was the recipient of divine favor. Hence, there was no way he could lose out on heaven. Lazarus, on the other hand, was a poor man and, even worse, a beggar without a job. In keeping with Pharisaic Judaism, his salvation was uncertain. However, when the two men died, their positions were reversed: The rich man went to hell, and Lazarus enjoyed paradise. The point of this story is that wealth is not a sign of divine favor, nor does it guarantee heaven for anyone. Lest the meaning of this passage be misunderstood, please note that wealth is not sinful. The problem is with one's attitude toward material possessions. If a person looks upon riches as a sign of God's grace and favor, he is serving materialism and has become the slave of *the mammon of unrighteousness*. Indeed, God has blessed many believers with wealth. These believers are responsible for developing a proper attitude toward their possessions. They are not to trust in their riches or let them become a substitute for trusting in God's provision for every need. Wealthy believers should use their mammon to win friends for the Lord.

Second, what this passage teaches about the state of the lost should not be missed: Unbelievers are eternally separated from God, and they are conscious of being lost—they are not "soul-sleeping" or unconscious. The state of being lost is unchangeable and cannot be altered. They are in tremendous torment, and they remember opportunities they had in life to believe in Yeshua. This should be strong motivation for sharing the gospel.

[§ 119] — G. Instruction Concerning Forgiveness

Luke 17:1-4

After His discussion with the Pharisees about the topic of mammon, Yeshua turned away from the multitude and spoke *unto his disciples* (Lk. 17:1). The lesson He was about to teach still pertained to the previous conflict. It is one thing to despise what Pharisaism teaches, but it is another thing to despise the Pharisees as individuals. Yeshua taught three lessons on the issue of offending and forgiving.

First, the apostles must be careful not to give offense (Lk. 17:1-2). Second, they should be careful not to take offense (Lk. 17:3a). Some people are easily offended and even seek to be offended. Although sometimes offending people is unavoidable, the disciples should not be easily offended themselves. Third, as He had previously done in Matthew 18:15-35, He again taught the principle of unlimited forgiveness (Lk. 17:3b-4).

[§ 120] — H. Instruction Concerning Service

Luke 17:5-10

The occasion for this instruction was the apostles' request: *Lord, Increase our faith* (Lk. 17:5). They wanted to know how they could strengthen and deepen their faith. Yeshua responded by teaching that faith can accomplish great and useful things (Lk. 17:6).

He told a story that emphasized the position of a servant: *But who is there of you, having a servant plowing or keeping sheep, that will say unto him, when he is come in from the field, Come straightway and sit down to meat* (Lk. 17:7). After the servant had finished all the things he was asked to do, did the master *thank the servant because he did the things that were commanded?* (Lk. 17:9). Obviously not, because what he accomplished was part of the job expected of him. Therefore, the servant had not done anything out of the ordinary that required special thanks.

Yeshua then made the application: *Even so ye also, when ye shall have done all the things that are commanded you, say, We are unprofitable servants; we have done that which it was our duty to do* (Lk. 17:10). Believers must remember that whatever they do for the Lord, they do as His servants. Instead of seeking commendation, they should be satisfied to have accomplished their work as *unprofitable servants* for the Lord, fulfilling their duty.

The question arises of how Yeshua's response could have possibly answered the issue of increasing faith. Three points can be derived. First, Yeshua taught that His disciples should be simple and earnest in their faith and trust in its power to accomplish useful works for Him. Second, they must remember their relationship to their Master; all that they do for Him is a necessary part of a servant's job. Third, the disciples' faith increases when they go about Yeshua's business. Indeed, the servants' work is to involve themselves in the Lord's work. Involvement allows the disciples to see Yeshua working and answering prayer. Witnessing these things will naturally increase the servants' faith. Therefore, faith is increased by exercising the faith that is already present and by getting involved in the work of the Lord.

[§§ 121–123] — I. The Resurrection of Lazarus: The First Sign of Jonah

Before we study this miracle, a few introductory words are in order. This section contains the last of Yochanan's seven signs, the resurrection of Lazarus. It also contains the fifth of Yeshua's seven "I Am" statements recorded by Yochanan: *I am the resurrection and the life* (Jn. 11:25).

Lazarus was not the first person Yeshua raised from the dead. However, all the other resurrection accounts were covered in just a few verses and witnessed by only a few people who were then forbidden to tell anyone about what they had seen. In sharp contrast to all the other reports, Yochanan devoted 44 verses to the resurrection of Lazarus, going into great detail. Instead of being witnessed only by a few, this resurrection was witnessed by multitudes of people.

Furthermore, this resurrection differed from all the others because it was the one last sign Yeshua promised to give to Israel: the sign of Jonah, the sign of resurrection. Once Yeshua gave this sign, the people would have to respond. If one properly understands the role this resurrection played in Yeshua's relationship to Israel as her Messiah, it becomes clear why things happened the way they did.

Finally, one of the key differences between Pharisaic Judaism and Sadducean Judaism was the doctrine of the resurrection. The Sadducees denied that the resurrection was taught in the Torah.

[§ 121] — 1. The Sign of Resurrection

a. The Death of Lazarus

John 11:1-16

The event began when Martha and Miriam sent a message to Yeshua that their brother Lazarus was fatally ill (Jn. 11:1-3). Their intention was to persuade the Messiah to come quickly before Lazarus died and heal him of his illness. Since it was only a one-day walk to the town of Bethany from where Yeshua was at that point, He could have arrived in plenty of time.

Yeshua's initial response was to state that Lazarus' sickness had a divine purpose: *But when Yeshua heard it, he said, This sickness is not unto death, but for the glory of God, that the Son of God may be glorified thereby* (Jn. 11:4). Lazarus would die, not for the sake—or the honor—of death, but *for the glory of God.* This was followed by the declaration: *Now Yeshua loved Marta, and her sister, and Elazar* (Jn. 11:5). Because of His love for this family, one would expect that Yeshua would depart for Bethany as soon as He heard about Lazarus' illness, but He did not. Instead, verse 6a begins with the words: *When therefore.* The word *therefore* logically connects the statement of verse 4 with verse 6. *When therefore* (meaning "for the very specific reason") *he heard that he was sick, he abode at that time two days in the place where he was* (Jn. 11:6). Yeshua deliberately waited for Lazarus to die so that God would be glorified with his resurrection, the first sign of Jonah.

After two days, Yeshua declared that He would again enter Judea (Jn. 11:7). The disciples objected, because they knew that many in that region desired to kill Him (Jn. 11:8).

This led to another example of Yochanan's sub-theme of the conflict of light and darkness: *Yeshua answered, Are there not twelve hours in the day? If a man walk in the day, he stumbles not, because he sees the light of this world. But if a man walk in the night, he stumbles, because the light is not in him* (Jn. 11:9-10).

Finally, Yeshua told His disciples that Lazarus had died (Jn. 11:11-14), first indirectly and then plainly, saying, *Elazar is dead* (Jn. 11:14), even though no one had come to inform Him that Lazarus had finally succumbed to his illness. After waiting two days, Yeshua knew that His friend had died, and He was ready to depart for Judea and Bethany. This troubled His disciples because they knew the Sanhedrin was looking for Him. It confused them that Yeshua did not go to Bethany while Lazarus was still alive, and yet He insisted on going, at the risk of His life, after Lazarus had died. To this, Thomas responded: *Let us also go, that we may die with Him* (Jn. 11:16). This is one of several times the

Gospel of John portrays Thomas as having had a negative outlook on life.

b. Yeshua and Marta

John 11:17-27

Yeshua approached Bethany, and when Martha heard He was coming, she went out to meet Him before He arrived at the tomb (Jn. 11:17-20). She scolded Yeshua for not taking action when they first called Him: *Lord, if you had been here, my brother had not died* (Jn. 11:21). If Yeshua had come when they had first called Him, He could have healed Lazarus. Had He come earlier, her brother would still be alive. She did, however, affirm her faith in Him (Jn. 11:22).

Yeshua responded to her rebuke by saying, *Your brother shall rise again* (Jn. 11:23). Martha assumed He spoke of the prophetic future and final resurrection *at the last day* (Jn. 11:24), a fundamental belief of Judaism. She clearly affirmed her faith in His Messiahship, and she clearly recognized His power before death, but she did not recognize His power over death. This gave Yeshua the opportunity to make His fifth "I Am" statement recorded by Yochanan: *I am the resurrection, and the life: he that believes on me, though he die, yet shall he live: and whosoever lives and believes on me shall never die* (Jn. 11:25-26). Those who believe on the Messiahship of Yeshua may die physically, but they will never again die spiritually; and even though they die physically, their bodies will someday be raised from the dead.

Once more, Martha responded by affirming her faith in His declaration: *Yea, Lord: I have believed that you are the Messiah, the Son of God, <even> he that comes into the world* (Jn. 11:27).

c. Yeshua and Miriam

John 11:28-32

Martha informed her sister, Miriam, that Yeshua wanted to see her (Jn. 11:28-31). When *she came where Yeshua was* (Jn. 11:32), Miriam also scolded Him for not taking action when He was first called. Like her sister, she recognized His power before death, but not over death.

d. Yeshua and Lazarus

John 11:33-44

Yeshua observed the scene, and when He saw Miriam *weeping, and the Jews <also> weeping who came with her, he groaned in the spirit* (Jn. 11:33). The Greek word for weeping, *klaiousan*, means "wailing." Miriam and the other Jewish people were wailing. When Yochanan stated that Yeshua *groaned in the spirit*, the Greek literally reads, "He was moved with indignation in the spirit." He was angry! On one hand, He was angry at their unbelief, but in context He was also angry at what sin has cost humanity—physical death—and death's impact on the human race and His friend Lazarus in particular. In this spirit, Yeshua arrived at the location of the tomb. This is followed by the shortest verse in most English Bibles: *Yeshua wept* (Jn. 11:35). The Greek verb used here differs from the one used for the sisters' wailing. It is *edakrysen* and comes from the root *dakruó*, meaning "to shed tears." It refers to a silent weeping, unlike the wailing of the others.

Yeshua overheard the multitudes commenting on His love for Lazarus (Jn. 11:36) and asking, *Could not this man, who opened the eyes of him that was blind, have caused that this man also should not die?* (Jn. 11:37). From their perspective, healing a man born blind was unique; it was a messianic miracle. Using the *kal v'chomer* argument, they reasoned that Yeshua could also do a lesser miracle and heal Lazarus. This led Yeshua to once again "groan in Himself" (Jn. 11:38); He was angry that they failed to understand the purpose of His mission.

Having arrived at the tomb, Yeshua commanded that the stone be rolled away (Jn. 11:39a). Martha, the one who was careful about these things, objected to His instruction because her brother had been dead for four days and *by this time the body stinks* (Jn. 11:39b). Within a Jewish frame of reference, the fact that Lazarus had been dead for four days is significant. Yeshua deliberately waited for him to die and specifically waited to arrive on the fourth day. The reason for this relates to the common rabbinic teaching of that day that when a person died, their spirit hovered over the body for three days, and during those three days, there was always a small possibility of resuscitation. At the end of the third day, the spirit descended into Sheol, so resuscitation was impossible. Only by miracle of resurrection would the man live again, and resurrection, as we pointed out earlier, was believed to happen in the last days when Messiah comes. Because this was a sign Yeshua promised to give to the nation, He deliberately set the stage in such a way that they could not explain it away by claiming that Lazarus had been resuscitated. They would have to come to an understanding that the miracle supported Yeshua's assertions of being the Messiah. Lazarus had been dead for one day too many.

In response to Martha's objection, Yeshua reminded her that if she believed, she would see the glory of God (Jn. 11:40). At that point, the stone was rolled away (Jn. 11:41a).

Many commentators claim that Yeshua's love for these particular siblings motivated Him to raise Lazarus, and this was true in part (v. 5). However, discovering the textual reason for why things happen in Scripture is always wise: *And Yeshua lifted up His eyes, and said, Father, I thank you that you heard me. And I knew that you hear me always: but because of the multitude that stands around I said it, that they* [meaning the multitude] *may believe that you did send me* (Jn. 11:41b-42). Clearly, this miracle was intended for the people. As He promised, this was the one time Yeshua publicly presented a miracle to which they needed to respond.

Then Yeshua cried with a loud voice: *Elazar, come forth!* (Jn. 11:43). Lazarus was resurrected: *He that was dead came forth, bound hand and foot with grave-clothes; and his face was bound about with a napkin* (Jn. 11:44a). Yeshua had to tell them to unbind him and let him go (Jn. 11:44b). A miracle within the miracle took place. Lazarus was bound hand, foot, and face; he was blinded, yet came out of the tomb into the open. With the resurrection of Lazarus, the first sign of Jonah was given.

[§ 122] — 2. The Rejection of the First Sign of Jonah

John 11:45-54

The sign of Jonah evoked two reactions. The first response was the correct one: Many individual Jews believed and accepted His Messiahship (Jn. 11:45). The second response was that others, still driven by their leadership complex, reported the occurrence to the Pharisees (Jn. 11:46).

The Pharisees, in particular, knew that this was the sign Yeshua promised to give to the nation,[1] so they had to respond: *The chief priests* [who were Sadducees] *therefore and the Pharisees gathered a council* [meaning the Sanhedrin] (Jn. 11:47). In their deliberations, they did not deny that Yeshua had performed the miracle they heard about. There were too many witnesses to deny it. However, they feared losing their position of privilege and their prominence. They were afraid that Yeshua would be declared the Messiah and that the Romans would view this as an act of rebellion, invade the country, and destroy it. As a result, these members of the Sanhedrin would lose their place of status and privilege (Jn. 11:48).

Caiaphas, the high priest and leader of the Sanhedrin, took the lead: *Ye know nothing at all, nor do ye take account that it is expedient for you that one man should die for the people, and that the whole nation perish not* (Jn. 11:49-50). Yochanan noted an ironic point: *Now this he said not of himself: but, being high priest that year, he prophesied that Yeshua should die for the nation; and not for the nation only, but that he might also gather together into one the children of God that are scattered abroad* (Jn. 11:51-52). Caiaphas meant one thing—that they had to get rid of this man to save the nation from Roman destruction. However, Yochanan pointed out that, ironically, the high priest spoke the truth: Yeshua would die on behalf of the nation. Because of His death, the nation would not be utterly destroyed, but will someday be regathered and experience their final restoration. Caiaphas meant it one way, but God fulfilled it in another, which allows us to draw a parallel to what

---

[1] See Matthew 12:39.

Joseph said to his brothers: *Ye meant evil against me; but God meant it for good* (Gen. 50:20).

From that day forth, the Sanhedrin *took counsel that they might put him to death* (Jn. 11:53). They officially rejected the first sign of Jonah, the resurrection of Lazarus. As a result of their decision to kill Him, Yeshua left Judea for the last time (Jn. 11:54). The next time He returned to Judea would be for the purpose of dying.

[§ 123] — 3. Instruction in Light of Rejection

a. The Personal Witness to Caiaphas

Luke 17:11-19

For the final time, Yeshua traveled to Jerusalem, *passing along the borders of Shomron and Galil* (Lk. 17:11). The order indicates He first went north from Ephraim (Jn. 11:54), through Samaria, and into Galilee. He stayed near the border, just outside the jurisdiction of the Sanhedrin.

Ten men that were lepers met Him (Lk. 17:12a). Nine of them were Jewish, and one was a Samaritan. Yeshua was travelling along the borders of Galilee and Samaria when this took place, which explains why one of them was a Samaritan. The men stood a distance away because they were lepers (Lk. 17:12b). For the same reason, *they lifted up their voices* in order to be heard (Lk. 17:13a). They asked for healing based on their personal need: *Yeshua, Master, have mercy on us* (Lk. 17:13b). The fact that they came to Yeshua demonstrated their personal faith. Earlier, the Messiah healed only one Jewish leper, which led to an intensive investigation by the Sanhedrin, since this was one of the special messianic miracles (discussed in § 46). Now, Yeshua healed not one, but ten lepers, nine of whom were Jewish. According to the Law of Moses, they must go to the priesthood for the cleansing process. So Yeshua told them: *Go and show yourselves unto the priests* (Lk. 17:14a). In faith, the lepers went as they were bidden, and as they went, they were healed (Lk. 17:14b).

Caiaphas, the leader of the official rejection of the sign of Jonah, was suddenly faced with a tenfold witness of Yeshua's Messiahship as ten lepers were standing before him who claimed to have been healed of their disease. On that day, Caiaphas and his priests had to offer two birds for each leper. For the next seven days, ten times over, they had to investigate the situation and answer three questions. Ten times over, they had to declare that these men had indeed been lepers; ten times over, they had to conclude that all ten had been healed of their leprosy; ten times over, they were forced to admit that Yeshua of Nazareth did the healing. Caiaphas got a personal, tenfold witness of Yeshua's Messiahship, and this contradicted his own conclusion in the Sanhedrin hearing.

Of the ten men, only the Samaritan returned to thank Yeshua for the healing (Lk. 17:15-19), and he was healed based on his faith (v. 19). He too went to the Jewish priesthood, revealing that he no longer adhered to Samaritanism as a religion.

b. The New Form of the Kingdom Program

Luke 17:20-21

Next, the Pharisees asked Yeshua when the kingdom of God was coming. As previously noted, Yeshua's teaching method changed after Israel committed the unpardonable sin. In the parables, which replaced His clear teaching, Yeshua defined the new form of God's kingdom program, the mystery kingdom, as referenced in His response in Luke 17:20-21. This kingdom is *within* them, He told the Pharisees. However, the Greek term translated as *within* actually means "among." This kingdom was among or in the midst of the Pharisees. As a result of His rejection, the messianic kingdom would not be set up at that time, but was replaced temporarily with the mystery kingdom, which is invisible. The mystery kingdom was among them, but not visibly observable like the messianic kingdom will be.

Amillennialists, who do not believe that the Bible teaches that there will be an earthly kingdom and a final restoration of the Jewish people, use this verse to support their view. They claim that since Yeshua said *the kingdom of God is within you* (Lk. 17:21), the kingdom is only spiritual and indwells the believer. However, Yeshua used a parable to address unbelieving Pharisees, and the spiritual kingdom could not be within unbelievers. Yeshua never negated the belief in an earthly kingdom; however, since the messianic kingdom offer was withdrawn, the mystery kingdom temporarily replaced it.

c. Instruction Concerning the Second Coming

Luke 17:22-37

After responding to the Pharisees in parables, Yeshua spoke clearly to His disciples in terms they could easily understand (Lk. 17:22). Later, in the Olivet Discourse, He delivered a detailed sermon on eschatology, to be discussed in that context rather than in this particular passage.[2] However, six things should be noted.

First, when the Messiah returns, all will see Him. The second coming will not be like the first: *for as the lightning, when it lightens out of the one part under the heaven, shines unto the other part under heaven; so shall the Son of man be in his day* (Lk. 17:24). This will be preceded by a period of time when the Messiah will not be present: *The days will come, when ye shall desire to see one of the days of the Son of man, and ye shall not see it* (Lk. 17:22).

Second, before Yeshua can return, *first must he suffer many things and be rejected of this generation* (Lk. 17:25). The emphasis is on the generation that rejected Him. Hence, before the glorious appearance of the second coming, by which the messianic kingdom will be established, Yeshua will be rejected by the nation and suffer many things. At this point, the disciples did not understand the program of His return.

Third, also before the second coming, a period of tribulation will follow a time of normal activity on the earth (Lk. 17:26-30). People will be eating, drinking, marrying, buying, selling, planting, and building.[3] While men are saying, "peace and safety," suddenly the day of the Lord, the tribulation, will hit, occurring unexpectedly while life is going on normally.

---

[2] See § 145.

[3] Also see I Thess. 5:1-11, which makes the same point.

Fourth, once the tribulation begins, people must choose to believe or not to believe, to accept or to reject (Lk. 17:31-33). The moment one believes, there is no looking back, as did Lot's wife.

Fifth, the second coming will occur only after the tribulation and the judgment (Lk. 17:34-36).

Sixth, having heard all these details about Yeshua's second coming, the disciples questioned where He would appear: *And they answering say unto him, Where, Lord?* (Lk. 17:37a). Yeshua's cryptic response presupposes Old Testament knowledge: *And he said unto them, Where the body <is>, thither will the eagles also be gathered together* (Lk. 17:37b). In Greek, the word translated as *eagles* is *aetoi*, which can also mean "vultures." When animals are used symbolically in the Hebrew Scriptures, they often refer to nations (e.g., Is. 34:1-7), and so it is fair to deduce that in this verse, the vultures represent Gentiles who gathered together to devour the body. From nations gathering together in order to perform an act of aggression, one can deduce that the passage is speaking of a military act. Furthermore, Ezekiel's vision of the valley of dry bones (Ez. 37:1-14) allows a correlation of the body with Israel. The answer to the question then is: Wherever the body of Israel is, that is where the Gentile armies will gather together, and where the Gentile armies are gathered together, that will be the place of the second coming. According to Micah 2:12-13, the remnant of Israel will be in a place called *Bozrah* in Hebrew, but better known today by the Greek name *Petra*. Jeremiah 49:13-14 states that this is where the Gentile armies will come against Israel, and Isaiah 34:1-7 and 63:1-6 confirm that this is also the place of the second coming.[4]

---

[4] For additional study of eschatology and of these specific issues, see: Arnold G. Fruchtenbaum, *The Footsteps of the Messiah: A Study of the Sequence of Prophetic Events* (San Antonio, TX: Ariel Ministries, 2003); Arnold G. Fruchtenbaum, *Israelology: The Missing Link in Systematic Theology* (San Antonio, TX: Ariel Ministries Press, 1992).

[§ 124] — J. Instruction in Prayer

Luke 18:1-14

After instructing His disciples about eschatological issues, Yeshua taught two principles concerning prayer. The first principle is that of persistence (Lk. 18:1-8): *And he spoke a parable unto them to the end that they ought always to pray, and not to faint* (Lk. 18:1). Perpetual prayer was especially necessary in relation to the second coming. Since the kingdom would not be set up at this point in time, the disciples should pray as He had taught them earlier: *Your kingdom come* (Mt. 6:10). To encourage that type of prayer, Yeshua told the Parable of the Importunate Widow (Lk. 18:2-5), in which a woman came to a judge, demanding: *Avenge me of mine adversary* (Lk. 18:3). The judge was not too concerned about justice, but because the widow kept returning, he finally gave in and granted her request. Her persistence, not the righteousness of the judge (Lk. 18:6), accomplished her goal.

The application is this: *And shall not God avenge his elect, that cry to him day and night, and <yet> he is longsuffering over them? I say unto you, that he will avenge them speedily. Nevertheless, when the Son of man comes, shall he find faith on the earth?* (Lk. 18:7-8). The phrase, *when the Son of man comes*, indicates that this prayer pertains to the second coming. If an unrighteous judge responds because of persistence, how much more will God, being righteous, respond to perpetual prayer? Although the verse implies that the second coming is some years away, it also clarifies that it will certainly come. The principle regarding prayers for the second coming is this: The certainty of that which is asked should lead us to constancy in prayer. Thus, the believer should persistently pray, *Your kingdom come.*

The second principle concerns humility in prayer (Lk. 18:9-14). The stated purpose of this lesson deals with those *who trusted in themselves that they were righteous, and set all others at nought* (Lk. 18:9). To illustrate His point, Yeshua presented a second parable, the Parable of the Pharisee and the Publican (Lk. 18:10-14). Two men went to the Temple to pray at the regular prayer time, one a Pharisee and the other a publican (Lk. 18:10). Yeshua first described the Pharisee's prayer (Lk.

18:11-12). The Pharisee let God know what a righteous man he was. He was not guilty of the grave sins that some others were and was probably correct in saying that he was *not as the rest of men, extortioners, unjust, adulterers, or even as this publican.* Instead, he followed Pharisaic tradition, fasting twice a week (Mondays and Thursdays). Furthermore, he gave tithes of all that he received (Lk. 18:12). Indeed, the Pharisees were careful to tithe of even the smallest seed (Mt. 23:23).

The Pharisee's prayer was one of self-righteousness. For him, prayer was an opportunity to display his piety. He approached God based on his own good works, his fasting twice a week, and his carefulness to tithe of everything.

Next, Yeshua described the prayer of the publican (Lk. 18:13-14). The publican approached God based on his personal need and God's mercy. The humility of the publican's prayer is evident in four ways. First, he stood *afar off* (Lk. 18:13a); he did not think himself worthy to get too close to the presence of God in the Holy of Holies. Second, he *would not lift up so much as his eyes unto heaven* (Lk. 18:13b); he kept his eyes downcast because he felt truly burdened by his sins. Third, he *smote his breast*; he was so very grieved by his sin that he afflicted his body, thus displaying a physical response to his sin before God (Lk. 18:13c). Fourth, he pleaded, *God be merciful to me a sinner* (Lk. 18:13d). The Greek word for *be merciful* really means "be propitious" or "make propitiation for." To propitiate means to satisfy the wrath of God, and the proper place of propitiation was the mercy seat in the Holy of Holies. So when the publican prayed, *be merciful to me a sinner,* he was basically asking, "Look upon me as you look upon the mercy seat and atone for my sins."

While the Pharisee approached God based on his self-righteousness and his own good works, the publican approached God based on his spiritual needs and God's mercy. The result was: This *man went down to his house justified rather than the other* (Lk. 18:14a). The principle for this section is stated again: *for everyone that exalts himself shall be humbled; but he that humbles himself shall be exalted* (Lk. 18:14b).

[§ 125] — K. Instruction on Divorce

Matthew 19:1-12, Mark 10:1-12

On the question of divorce and remarriage, the Pharisees were divided between two schools: the school of Shammai and the school of Hillel. The issue was the correct interpretation of Deuteronomy 24:1, which granted divorce on the basis of *ervat davar*, meaning "a matter of uncleanness." Hillel chose a wide interpretation, according to which a husband could divorce his wife for any reason, including over-cooking or over-salting his food. Shammai, on the other hand, took the very narrow view that the only basis for divorce was fornication. The Pharisees presented the issue to Yeshua as He departed from Galilee and came near the border of Judea; He was still on the east side of the Jordan in what was then known as Perea. The multitudes were following Him (Mt. 19:2). This set the stage for the Pharisaic encounter (Mt. 19:3; Mk. 10:2).

When the religious leaders questioned the legality of divorce, they were not honestly seeking an answer, but were tempting Yeshua. Reading the account, one must ask how this served as a temptation, since however He answered, at least one school of Pharisees would support His position. The answer lies in the fact that Yeshua was in Perea under the jurisdiction of Herod Antipas, the same person who ordered Yochanan the Baptizer's beheading due to his preaching against the illegal divorce of Herodias and her remarriage to Antipas. The Pharisees asked Yeshua the question while He was in Antipas' territory, hoping His answer would offend Herodias so that her husband would do to Yeshua what he had done to Yochanan. It should be noted that the way they phrased the question about divorcing for every cause reflected Hillel's view.

Yeshua responded with five points. First, God's original intent and ideal for marriage was that it be permanent (Mt. 19:4-6). When the Pharisees asked a follow-up question, *Why then did Mosheh command to give a bill of divorcement and to put <her> away?* (Mt. 19:7), Yeshua made His second point: Moses did not command divorce, he only permitted divorce because of the hardness of their hearts (Mt. 19:8; Mk.

10:4-6). The biblical ideal is always forgiveness, restoration, and reunion.

Yeshua made the two declarations publicly, but privately He taught three additional lessons to His disciples when they asked for clarification. In making His third point, Yeshua opposed the one-sidedness of Jewish divorce law, which stipulated that adultery could only be committed against the husband, not against the wife. So when a married woman has relations with another man, she commits adultery against her husband. When a man has relations with a married woman, he also commits adultery against her husband. Yeshua declared that adultery goes both ways. Matthew, writing to Jews, only mentioned divorcing the wife (Mt. 19:9), because under Jewish law a wife can never divorce her husband. Currently, a woman in Israel cannot legally divorce her husband, according to the religious law that governs family matters, and no civil divorce law exists. Mark, writing to Romans, who practiced divorce both ways, mentioned both options (Mk. 10:11-12).

In His fourth point, Yeshua identified fornication as the only basis for divorce (Mt. 19:9). The term "fornication" generally describes immorality, including adultery, pre-marital sex, homosexuality, incest, and bestiality. Under the Mosaic Law, adultery was not grounds for divorce, because a person guilty of adultery would be stoned to death, making the partner a widow or widower, free to remarry. However, the Hebrew Bible stipulated two other grounds for divorce. The first was sexual incompatibility (Deut. 24:1-3). The second was religious incompatibility (Ezra 10:10-11; Neh. 10:30). The husband of a Gentile who worshipped pagan gods was commanded to divorce her. In both cases, divorce automatically severed the marriage and permitted remarriage. Clearly, the Hebrew Scriptures always permitted remarriage, following a proper divorce. The New Testament rescinded both of these two Old Testament grounds for divorce. Sexual incompatibility is rescinded by Yeshua in this particular section in the Gospels, and religious incompatibility is rescinded in I Corinthians 7:12-13, where Paul teaches that a believer cannot divorce a mate because he or she is an unbeliever. At the same time, the New Testament lays down two new grounds for divorce. The first is fornication, discussed in the verses above. The second is when two unbelievers marry and one of them becomes a believer during the marriage (I Cor. 7:12-16). If the unbelieving spouse wants a divorce on those grounds, Paul instructs the believer not to fight it, but to grant that divorce. The remarriage principle remains the same: A valid, biblical divorce automatically allows for a remarriage.

While in the Gospels, fornication is the only God-given basis for divorce, divorce is not commanded, but only permitted. The biblical ideal always was and will always be forgiveness and reconciliation. Yeshua sided with the school of Shammai in this position and against the school of Hillel, although it is not apparent from these verses if the innocent party in a divorce is allowed to remarry. Clearly the guilty party cannot remarry, but Yeshua stayed silent about the innocent party, causing the church to take two different views about this issue. Some extend the prohibition to both parties and do not believe in remarriage for either the guilty or the innocent. Others limit it to the guilty party, but allow the innocent one to remarry. Either way, the basis for divorce and remarriage is limited, and a valid, biblical divorce automatically allows for a remarriage.

The disciples responded to Yeshua's narrow position by saying: *If the case of the man is so with his wife, it is not expedient to marry* (Mt. 19:10). In other words, if they could not divorce their wives for any reason they wanted, then it was better not to marry. This response, reflecting a low view of marriage, led to Yeshua's fifth point: *Not all men can receive this saying, but they to whom it is given* (Mt. 19:11). One of the nineteen gifts of the Holy Spirit is the gift of singleness (I Cor. 7:1-7). Only those *to whom it is given* should choose this option. While marriage is the norm, it is ideal for a person to remain single, because their status allows them to devote all of their time to the Lord's work, while a married person cannot.

Yeshua went on to say that there are three categories of eunuchs: *For there are eunuchs, that were so born from their mother's womb: and there are eunuchs, that were made eunuchs by men: and there are eunuchs, that made themselves eunuchs for the kingdom of heaven's sake. He that is able to receive it, let him receive it* (Mt. 19:12). Some are born eunuchs due to a birth defect. Others are forced to become eunuchs because they were castrated for one reason or another. However, some become eunuchs voluntarily by making *themselves eunuchs for the kingdom of heaven's sake*. These have the gift of singleness, choosing to stay unmarried for the kingdom of heaven. The gift of singleness is a choice for these people: *He that is able to receive it, let him receive it* (Mt. 19:12b).

[§ 126] — L. Instruction on Entrance into the Kingdom

Matthew 19:13-15, Mark 10:13-16, Luke 18:15-17

This teaching arose out of an incident where little children tried to approach Yeshua. The disciples stopped them, assuming that the Messiah was too important to be bothered by children (Mt. 19:13; Mk. 10:13; Lk. 18:15). *But when Yeshua saw it, he was moved with indignation* (Mk. 10:14). He was angry with them because they would stop the children from coming to Him just because they were children. The lesson the disciples had to learn was this: *Suffer the little children, and forbid them not, to come unto me: for to such belongs the kingdom of heaven* (Mt. 19:14). *Verily I say unto you, Whosoever shall not receive the kingdom of God as a little child, he shall in no wise enter therein* (Mk. 10:15). Childlike faith is the basis of entering the kingdom.

[§ 127] — M. Instruction on Eternal Life

Matthew 19:16-20:16, Mark 10:17-31, Luke 18:18-30

This incident began when a man approached Yeshua with a question about eternal life. Matthew (Mt. 19:16) and Mark (Mk. 10:17) only identified him as *one*, but Luke (Lk. 18:18) specified he was *a certain ruler*. This may imply he was a member of the Sanhedrin, but, more likely, he was a synagogue leader. Mark detailed his approach: He *ran* to Yeshua, demonstrating a sense of urgency; he *kneeled* before Yeshua, a posture of respect; and, contrary to the custom of that day, he addressed Yeshua as *Good Teacher* (Mk. 10:17). Virtually not a single example of a rabbi being addressed as "good" appears in any Jewish writing. When the religious community spoke of someone as being good, it was always in the third person, not in the second person, and it was always used of speaking about, not to someone. On the other hand, one of the names the rabbis used to speak of God was "the Good One."

Furthermore, there are two Greek words for "good," *kalos* and *agathos*. *Kalos* means "externally pleasing," but the word used by the ruler is *agathos*, which means "intrinsically good," therefore referring to Yeshua's very character. Since Yeshua claimed to be the Messiah, the Son of God, it meant that He claimed to be intrinsically good.

The ruler's specific question was: *Teacher, what good thing shall I do, that I may have eternal life?* (Mt. 19:16). He was a wealthy man, and by the common theology of that day, he should have concluded that he was already a recipient of divine favor. Evidently, he realized something was lacking in his life. In the typical Jewish way of teaching, Yeshua answered this question by asking one of His own: *Why do you call me good? None is good save one, <even> God* (Mk. 10:18). Cults who deny the deity of the Messiah use this passage to show that Yeshua never claimed to be God and that He denied being God. However, they miss the point of the methodology Yeshua used when He answered the question by asking another question. The ruler called Him *Good Teacher*, using the word *agathos*. Yeshua answered the ruler's question with a question of His own: "Why do you call me *agathos* if only God is intrinsically good?" Yeshua declared Himself to be the Messianic King; hence, He claimed to be intrinsically good. Now the question was: Does this ruler agree or disagree? The ruler should have responded, "I call you good because you are God." Had he answered Yeshua that way, he would have answered his own question, for the one thing he had to do to receive eternal life was to accept Him as the Messianic God-Man. However, the ruler remained silent.

So, Yeshua cited several commandments from the Mosaic Law in the order in which they were given in Exodus 20:1-17 and Deuteronomy 5:4-21, but reversing the sixth and the seventh commandments. Both orders are known in Jewish tradition. Yeshua was also selective as to which of the commandments He mentioned, only quoting those that

413

control a man's relationship to other men and not any that control a man's relationship to God. Furthermore, He added Leviticus 19:18: *You shall love your neighbor as yourself* (Mt. 19:19).

The ruler answered: *Teacher, all these things have I observed from my youth* (Mk. 10:20). In other words, insofar as those commandments dealing with human relationships were concerned, the ruler had kept them well; however, he added, *what lack I yet?* (Mt. 19:20). He recognized that something was still missing.

This gave Yeshua the opportunity to drive the point home: *If you would be perfect, go, sell that which you have, and give to the poor, and you shall have treasure in heaven: and come, follow me* (Mt. 19:21). Yeshua revealed the real issue. While the ruler may have kept the commandments that control human relationships, he had not kept the commandments that control man's relationship to God, such as having faith and loving God with all his heart, mind, soul, and whole being. His wealth had kept him from fulfilling these commandments. The tendency of the rich was to trust their wealth as a sign of divine favor. Therefore, the ruler's love of wealth kept him from obeying the commandment to love God, and his trust in his wealth kept him from trusting God. Therefore, Yeshua told him to do three things. First, he should sell everything and get rid of his wealth to show his love for God, since that kept him from trusting God. Second, *give to the poor,* to show love for his neighbor. Third, *come follow me,* to show he accepted Yeshua as the Messiah.

Yeshua gave him the answer, but obviously it was not what the ruler wanted to hear, and he walked away in sorrow: *for he was one that had great possessions* (Mk. 10:22) and *he was very rich* (Lk. 18:23).

After the ruler left, Yeshua applied the lesson to His apostles: *How hardly shall they that have riches enter into the kingdom of God!* (Mk. 10:23), causing the disciples to be *amazed at his words* (Mk. 10:24a). Was the problem with wealth? The answer is no, and Yeshua clarified what He meant: *Children, how hard is it for them that trust in riches to enter into the kingdom of God!* (Mk. 10:24b). This was the real root of the problem. Mammon in itself is neutral. The problem was the tendency to trust the wealth. The rich looked upon their wealth as a sign that they had eternal life because of the Pharisaic teaching, and so it was more difficult for them to trust God for their salvation. Yeshua then added: *It is easier for a camel to go through a needle's eye, than for a rich man to enter into the kingdom of God* (Mk. 10:25). This was a common rabbinic saying. Unfortunately, many travelers return from Israel believing a myth that they heard from a tourist guide regarding a small gate in the walls of Jerusalem called "the eye of the needle." Supposedly, at this gate, a camel had to go down on its knees to squeeze through. All the other gates in Jerusalem are quite large, so why would anyone even bother? Such a gate in the walls of Jerusalem never existed, and Yeshua really did mean the eye of a needle. This is obvious in the Greek text. Mark and Matthew used the Greek word *rapsidos*, which refers to a sewing needle. Luke, who was a medical doctor by profession, used a different Greek word, *balogeis*, which means a surgeon's needle. The point is, it is easier for the camel to go through the little eye of a sewing needle or a surgeon's needle than for a rich man to trust God instead of his wealth.

Exceedingly astonished, the disciples responded: *Who then can be saved?* (Mt. 19:25b). This shows how ingrained the rabbinic theology on wealth was: "If the rich cannot make it, what chance do we have?" Yeshua responded: *With men this is impossible; but with God all things are possible* (Mt. 19:26). God can save all people in any circumstance. This includes the rich.

Having heard that news, Peter raised the question: *Lo, we have left all, and have followed you; what then shall we have?* (Mt. 19:27). Yeshua responded with three promises. The first promise was applicable to the apostles only. The second and third promises are applicable to believers in general.

The first promise was: *Verily I say unto you, that ye who have followed me, in the regeneration when the Son of man shall sit on the throne of his glory, ye also shall sit upon twelve thrones, judging the twelve tribes of Yisrael* (Mt. 19:28). The apostles will have a special role in the messianic kingdom. They will sit on twelve thrones, and each one will be given authority over a specific tribe of Israel.

The second promise is a measure of restoration in this life (Mk. 10:29-30a). It may not necessarily be material or physical, but there will be a measure of restoration in this life. Yeshua promised to give mothers, fathers, brothers, and sisters to those who believe. Obviously, these are not going to be new biological relatives. Yeshua was referring to the spiritual realm, meaning He was going to provide spiritual parents and siblings to those who lost their families because of their faith. This promise of restoration does not mean the believer will then be free from persecution.[5]

The third promise is this: *in the world to come eternal life* (Mk. 10:30b). In the age to come, believers will enjoy everlasting life in the presence of God.

The promises were followed by the motif of this section: *But many shall be last <that are> first; and first <that are> last* (Mt. 19:30). To illustrate this central theme, Yeshua told the Parable of the Workers in the Vineyard (Mt. 20:1-16), the point of which is that rewards for the believer will not be based upon seniority. Three lessons apply: Believers should work in God's vineyard and leave the rewards to Him (Mt. 20:14a); God will be just, fair, and gracious (Mt. 20:15b); He has the absolute right to dispense His rewards as He chooses (Mt. 20:15a).

Yeshua concluded His teaching on eternal life by restating the motif: *So the last shall be first, and the first last* (Mt. 20:16).

---

[5] As an example, this author was expelled from home because of his beliefs. When he finished high school, he had to move out and lost his father and his mother, his two brothers and four sisters. However, by the time he had graduated from college, his key ring held keys to three different homes: one in Long Island, NY; one in Ringwood, NJ; and one in Maryland. He was free to come and go, whether anyone was home or not. Although he was never legally adopted, he was spiritually adopted, and to this day he calls these people "mom and pop" and their children "brother and sister," and they refer to him as their son and brother. In fact, when he graduated from college, his New Jersey family took out an ad in the local paper announcing the graduation of their son. In this life, the author has received a measure of restoration where parents and siblings are concerned.

[§ 128] — N. Instruction Concerning His Death

Matthew 20:17-28, Mark 10:32-45, Luke 18:31-34

For the third time, Yeshua spelled out His program of death and resurrection, providing the most detail so far. The circumstance was that He and His apostles *were on the way, going up to Yerushalayim* (Mk. 10:32a). Yeshua was on His final journey to Jerusalem, still on the east side of the Jordan, outside the jurisdiction of the Sanhedrin. Mark continued: *And Yeshua was going before them: and they were amazed; and they that followed were afraid* (Mk. 10:32b). They feared crossing the river, knowing very well that the Sanhedrin wanted to lay hold of Him.

At that point, Yeshua spelled out the details of His death and resurrection, telling the disciples that it was the time of fulfillment: *And he took unto him the twelve, and said unto them, Behold, we go up to Yerushalayim, and all the things that are written through the prophets shall be accomplished unto the Son of man* (Lk. 18:31). All that was about to happen fulfilled prophecy, so Yeshua gave His apostles the most detailed description of the future events (Mk. 10:33-34):

1. He must go up to Jerusalem.
2. He would fall into the hands of *chief priests* (Sadducees) and *scribes* (Pharisees).
3. The Jewish people would *condemn him to death*.
4. The Jewish people would turn Him over to the Gentiles.
5. The Gentiles would *mock him*.
6. The Gentiles would *spit upon him*.
7. The Gentiles would *scourge him*.
8. The Gentiles would *kill him*.
9. He would then be resurrected after three days (also Mt. 20:19; Lk. 18:33).

Luke added that Yeshua would be shamefully treated (Lk. 18:32).

Although the disciples had just received the most detailed account of Yeshua's coming death and resurrection, they still did not understand what He was saying: *they understood none of these things; and this saying was hid from them, and they perceived not the things that were said* (Lk. 18:34).

Their lack of understanding is demonstrated by the next incident: *Then came to him the mother of the sons of Zavdi with her sons, worshipping <him>, and asking a certain thing of him* (Mt. 20:20). The mother of the sons of Zebedee was Salome. Salome is the Greek version of the Hebrew name *Shulamit*. She was the sister of Miriam, which made Yeshua and the sons of Zebedee first cousins. She requested: *Command that these my two sons may sit, one on your right hand, and one on your left hand, in your kingdom* (Mt. 20:21). Obviously, James and Yochanan did not understand what Yeshua had taught them. Salome's request indicates that they only understood the fact that Yeshua was going up to Jerusalem, assuming it was to set up His kingdom. They did not understand He was going to die. While Matthew emphasized the kingdom itself, Mark accentuated its glory: *And they said unto him, Grant unto us that we may sit, one on your right hand, and one on <your> left hand, in your glory* (Mk. 10:37). Also, Mark stated that the two brothers themselves made the request, thus giving the actual source. Matthew clarified that the mother did the asking on their behalf.

Yeshua responded with a question: *Are ye able to drink the cup that I drink? Or to be baptized with the baptism that I am baptized with?* (Mk. 10:38). The cup was the cup of suffering, and the baptism was the baptism of suffering. James and Yochanan answered: *We are able* (Mk. 10:39a). Yeshua responded: *The cup that I drink, ye shall drink; and with the baptism that I am baptized withal shall ye be baptized* (Mk. 10:39b), and indeed, they suffered as He did. James was the first apostle to be martyred. Yochanan was the only apostle to die of old age, but he suffered exile on the island of Patmos. Yeshua added: *but to sit on my right hand or on <my> left hand is not mine to give; but <it is for them> for whom it has been prepared* (Mk. 10:40). Ultimately, the final decision will not be for the Son to make, but it is in the hand of God the Father, as Matthew pointed out: *but <it is for them> for whom it has been prepared of my Father* (Mt. 20:23). The teaching was that those closest to the King must reach the position in the same way He did—

by means of suffering. Only God the Father can appoint those who will sit next to the King.

James and Yochanan's request created a problem within the apostolic group: *And when the ten heard it, they began to be moved with indignation concerning Yaakov and Yochanan* (Mk. 10:41). This gave Yeshua an opportunity to teach them yet another lesson (Mk. 10:42b-44):

> [42b] *Ye know that they who are accounted to rule over the Gentiles lord it over them; and their great ones exercise authority over them.* [43] *But it is not so among you: but whosoever would become great among you, shall be your minister;* [44] *and whosoever would be first among you, shall be the servant of all.*

Position in the kingdom will not be granted based on personal ambition or on private requests. Rather, position will be assigned as a reward for faithful service. The best example of faithful service was their own King: *For the Son of man also came not to be ministered unto, but to minister, and to give his life a ransom for many* (Mk. 10:45). Yeshua, as King, gained His kingship because He was the Servant of Jehovah.

[§ 129] — O. The Healing of the Blind Men

Matthew 20:29-34, Mark 10:46-52, Luke 18:35-43

Critics of the New Testament identify an alleged discrepancy between these three reports, because Mark wrote: *And they came to Yericho: and as he went out from Yericho, with His disciples and a great multitude* (Mk. 10:46). Matthew confirmed this by saying: *And as they went out from Yericho, a great multitude followed him* (Mt. 20:29). However, Luke stated: *And it came to pass, as he drew near unto Yericho* (Lk. 18:35). According to Mark and Matthew, this incident occurred while He went out from Jericho, whereas Luke reported that it happened while He was approaching Jericho. However, the historical geography of Israel dispels the apparent discrepancy. In the first century, two Jerichos existed: the Old Testament Jericho and the New Testament

Jericho, built by Herod the Great and also where he died. Separated by about three miles, one had to first go through Old Testament Jericho to reach New Testament Jericho when approaching Jerusalem from the north. This incident occurred between the two Jerichos, as Yeshua went out of Old Testament Jericho and approached New Testament Jericho.

Another alleged discrepancy is the number of blind men. Matthew mentioned two (Mt. 20:30), while Luke recorded only one: *a certain blind man sat by the way side begging* (Lk. 18:35). Mark was even more specific and gave the beggar's name: *the son of Timai, Bartimai,*[6] *a blind beggar, was sitting by the way side* (Mk. 10:46). Of the two blind men, Bartimaeus was the prominent one, indicated by the fact that his name was mentioned. So while two men were involved in this miracle, Luke and Mark focused their attention on only one of them because, for an unknown reason, he was the more conspicuous. Often one Gospel writer provided a full account, while another focused on a particular detail of the same incident. Furthermore, neither Mark nor Luke stated that there was only one blind man; they simply reported only on one.

Yeshua was in Jericho, which shows that He had crossed the Jordan River and was, therefore, back under the jurisdiction of the Sanhedrin. As He walked out of Old Testament Jericho and arrived in New Testament Jericho, a great multitude followed Him. The blind men inquired about the excitement (Lk. 18:36) and discovered that Yeshua of Nazareth was passing by (Lk. 18:37). They petitioned for the Messiah to have mercy upon them, but Yeshua did not immediately respond to their plea. They continued to beseech Him as He walked through the city, and the multitude rebuked them for doing so (Mk. 10:47-48), causing the men to cry out *the more*, with Bartimaeus acting as the main spokesman. The basis of his plea was Yeshua's position: *you son of David, have mercy on me* (Mk. 10:47, 48). Since the rejection, Yeshua healed only on the basis of personal need, which they expressed: *Lord, have mercy on us, you son of David* (Mt. 20:31). They knew from Isaiah 35:5 that when Messiah came, He would heal the blind, so they asked Him to heal their blindness. However, they based their pleading on

---

[6] The Hebrew name *Bartimai* eventually became the English name Bartimaeus, which is really the hellenized form of *bar Timai,* meaning "the son of Timai."

Yeshua's messianic title, the *son of David*, so He could do nothing for them, because His messianic character had already been rejected.

Finally, Yeshua *stood still, and said, Call ye him* (Mk. 10:49), making it more private. The blind man, *casting away his garment, sprang up, and came to Yeshua* (Mk. 10:50). When the blind man left his clothes behind, he demonstrated faith by believing he would see and find his garment later. The issue of personal need came up again when Yeshua asked him specifically: *What will you that I should do unto you?* (Mk. 10:51). Their request was obvious, but Yeshua required them to state their personal need clearly, and they did: *They say unto him, Lord, that our eyes may be opened* (Mt. 20:33), using the most honorable of all titles, *Rabboni* (Mk. 10:51), meaning "my great master." Yeshua responded positively, and Matthew emphasized His motivation: *And Yeshua, being moved with compassion, touched their eyes; and straightway they received their sight, and followed Him* (Mt. 20:34). Mark accentuated their faith: *Go your way; your faith has made you whole* (Mk. 10:52). The basic procedure remained the same. Yeshua called them aside to state their personal need; they demonstrated their faith; and, based on their faith, He healed them.

[§§ 130–131] — P. Instruction Concerning the Kingdom Program

[§ 130] — 1. Personal Faith

Luke 19:1-10

Having healed the two blind men, Yeshua entered New Testament Jericho, where He met a man about whom Luke revealed three things (Lk. 19:1-2). First, his name was Zacchaeus, which is the Hellenized form of *Zakkai*. Second, he was a chief publican, meaning he was in charge of other tax collectors. In Jewish literature, he would be known as a *moches gadol*, or "a great publican," rather than a *moches katan*, which is "a little publican." Third, he was rich, and publicans only became wealthy by extorting from their own people. Being a chief publican meant he was also collecting funds from other tax collectors who reported to him.

As noted earlier, a great multitude followed Yeshua. Zacchaeus wanted to see Him as well, but being of short stature, he was unable to see over the crowd (Lk. 19:3). So he climbed into a sycamore tree (Lk. 19:4), where Yeshua found him and said: *Zakkai, make haste, and come down; for today I must abide at your house* (Lk. 19:5). Indeed, Zacchaeus welcomed Yeshua gladly (Lk. 19:6), because other Jews would not associate with publicans.

Yeshua's willingness to enter Zacchaeus' house created quite a stir: *And when they saw it, they all murmured, saying, He is gone in to lodge with a man that is a sinner* (Lk. 19:7). While this was contrary to the Pharisaic practice of that day, it was typical of Yeshua's practice.

The encounter with Yeshua led to Zacchaeus' salvation, and his works revealed his salvation: *And Zakkai stood, and said unto the Lord, Behold, Lord, the half of my goods I give to the poor; and if I have wrongfully exacted anything of any man, I restore fourfold* (Lk. 19:8). In other words, he was quite willing to let go of his wealth and to do what the rich young ruler would not do. Under the Mosaic Law, a person was required to return twenty percent to those he had wronged (Lev. 5:16; Num. 5:7); however, this man offered to return four times the amount, to express his sincere thankfulness for the grace bestowed upon him.

Yeshua then declared: *Today is salvation come to this house, forasmuch as he also is a son of Avraham* (Lk. 19:9). Just as was the case with the woman in Luke 13:16 whom He had called *a daughter of Avraham*, Yeshua emphasized Zacchaeus' individual Jewishness as a son of Abraham. As a result of the national rejection, Yeshua focused on the individual rather than on Israel as a whole. Salvation came to the Jews individually and not nationally. Yeshua emphatically called Zacchaeus *a son of Avraham*. The lesson was on individual, personal faith and ended with the purpose of the first coming: *For the Son of man came to seek and to save that which was lost* (Lk. 19:10). Zacchaeus, a son of Abraham, was lost but now was found; his personal faith in the Messiah saved him.

[§ 131] — 2. Postponed Kingdom

Luke 19:11-28

The people heard all that Yeshua spoke to Zacchaeus about personal salvation and the purpose of His first coming. Now, the Messiah added the Parable of the Talents to address their misconception that when He arrived in Jerusalem He would establish the messianic kingdom (Lk. 19:11). They still failed to understand His program of death and resurrection and His second coming, even though, according to the Gospel record, He had told them about it at least three times (see §§ 86, 91, and 128). Yeshua was going to Jerusalem, but not to set up the messianic kingdom, a privilege rescinded because of the unpardonable sin. Yeshua told this parable to show the people what was to happen. He explained to His disciples the meaning of the parable, as He normally did, but this time even they did not comprehend.

The parable concerned a nobleman who had to leave for *a far country, to receive for himself a kingdom and to return* (Lk. 19:12). Prior to leaving, *he called ten servants of his, and gave them ten pounds* (Lk. 19:13). The Greek word is *mina*, which was equal to three months' wages. He gave them all an equal amount of money *and said unto them, Trade ye <herewith> till I come* (Lk. 19:13). Although he left the servants behind with sufficient funding to use for trade, *his citizens hated him, and sent an ambassage after him, saying, We will not that this man reign over us* (Lk. 19:14), showing the element of rejection. When the nobleman returned, he asked each of the servants for an accounting. All but one servant had been productive for their lord. As a reward, they were given authority over cities in the nobleman's kingdom. However, the one servant merely hid the money and did nothing with it, and he stood condemned: *He said unto him, Out of your own mouth will I judge you, you wicked servant* (Lk. 19:22). The servant knew the lord was *austere* and expected a return (Lk. 19:21). If he had just put his money in the bank, he at least would have gained some interest. Even if that was less than he could have made by trading, it was better than nothing. So the pound that had been given to him was taken away: *Take away from him the pound, and give it unto him that has the ten pounds* (Lk. 19:24).

Yeshua stated the principle: *I say unto you, that unto every one that has shall be given; but from him that has not, even that which he has shall be taken away from him* (Lk. 19:26). If a person does not use what is given to him, then even that which had been given will be taken away. As for those citizens who did not want the master to rule over them, they were brought before him and slain (Lk. 19:27).

The basic meaning of the parable can be summarized in six points:

1. The Messiah will leave.
2. The servants will be left behind to carry on the ministry.
3. The citizens will reject Him as King.
4. Eventually, He will return.
5. The servants will be judged; those who are rewarded will be given authority in the kingdom, but those who are not rewarded will lose what they have, and they will have no authority in the kingdom.
6. The citizens will be judged.

After teaching the parable, Yeshua departed: *And when he had thus spoken, he went on before, going up to Yerushalayim* (Lk. 19:28). He was finally on the last leg of His journey to Jerusalem.

VII. THE OFFICIAL PRESENTATION OF THE KING

— §§ 132–144 —

[§ 132] — A. The Arrival in Bethany

John 11:55–12:1, 9–11

Bethany, located on the lower eastern slopes of the Mount of Olives, is a convenient place to stay outside the city walls, as it is within easy walking distance of Jerusalem. During His last weeks, Yeshua stayed overnight in Bethany and traveled to and from Jerusalem until His last Passover, and now, the feast *was at hand* (Jn. 11:55). This was the fourth Passover of His public ministry. Yochanan baptized Him four to six months before Passover (§ 24), and so His public ministry spanned about three-and-a-half years. However, since His ministry began the Passover after His baptism (Jn. 2:13), it technically lasted only three years, starting and ending at the feast.

Yeshua therefore six days before the Passover came to Beit Anyah (Jn. 12:1), which, by the Jewish calendar, was the eighth of the month of Nisan. This corresponds to the modern western calendar date of March 31, A.D. 30.[1]

The first sign of Jonah was the resurrection of Lazarus (§§ 121–123), and the Sanhedrin responded to this sign by meeting and officially rejecting it and decreeing a sentence of death against Yeshua *in absentia.* This decision filtered down to the masses: *Now the chief priests and the Pharisees had given commandment, that, if any man knew where he was, he should show it, that they might take him* (Jn. 11:57). While this verse reconfirms the official rejection of the first sign of Jonah, the uniqueness of the miracle still attracted the multitudes: *The common people therefore of the Jews learned that he was there: and they came, not for Yeshua's sake only, but that they might see Elazar also, whom he had raised from the dead* (Jn. 12:9). The uniqueness of the resurrection of Lazarus—apart from being the most recent resurrection Yeshua had performed—was that Lazarus had been dead for four days. According to Jewish theology, it was impossible to dismiss the miracle by claiming that he had simply been resuscitated. Many people desired to visit Lazarus when they received word that he was raised after being dead for four days.

At the time of the resurrection, many Jews reported the event to the Pharisees, but many other Jews believed in Yeshua as a result of that miracle. This point is reiterated in the next verses: *But the chief priests took counsel that they might put Elazar also to death; because that by reason of him* [Lazarus] *many of the Jews went away, and believed on Yeshua* (Jn. 12:10-11). Many believed on Yeshua when He first performed the miracle, and many more believed when they saw Lazarus. The Sanhedrin's illogical conclusions are apparent. The chief priests not only conspired to kill Yeshua, they also wanted to kill Lazarus because he had the audacity to allow himself to be resurrected, causing many Jewish people to believe Yeshua was the Messiah. Did the chief priests think they could keep Lazarus dead this time?

---

[1] If the crucifixion occurred in A.D. 33, that date then was March 29, A.D. 33. This is based on when the Passover occurred during those years.

[§ 133] — B. The Triumphal Entry:
The Setting Aside of the Passover Lamb

Matthew 21:1-11, 14-17, Mark 11:1-11, Luke 19:29-44, John 12:12-19

The day of the triumphal entry came to be referred to as Palm Sunday. It was on the tenth of Nisan, or the second of April, A.D. 30.[2]

1. The Significance of the Triumphal Entry

Often, the triumphal entry is interpreted as being the time when Yeshua formally offered Himself to the Jews as their King and Messiah. Another common interpretation is that it was the final offer of the kingdom to Israel. However, neither view represents the actual significance of the event. Yeshua offered Himself as the Messiah, the King of the Jews, during the previous three years. Israel rejected His Messiahship about one-and-a-half years earlier (Mt. 12:22-45). Yeshua declared that the generation of His day was guilty of committing the unpardonable sin and rescinded the offer of the kingdom to that generation. They were now under the judgment of A.D. 70. Hence, the purpose of this ride into Jerusalem was not to officially present Himself as the King, something He had done all along. Nothing He said during the ride hinted at a re-offer of the kingdom. On the contrary, when Yeshua spoke, He spoke words of judgment, proclaiming again the coming destruction of Jerusalem. Hence, the theological significance of this event lies elsewhere.

The Jewish calendar date was the tenth of Nisan, the day of the month on which the Jewish people were to set aside the Passover lamb, according to Exodus 12:3-6. From the tenth until the fourteenth day of Nisan, the lamb was tested to ensure it was spotless and without blemish. Yeshua's ride into Jerusalem occurred on the same day that the Passover lamb was set aside. Herein lies the theological significance of

---

[2] Or March 29, A.D. 33.

this event. When Yochanan the Baptizer first introduced Yeshua as the Messiah, the title he used (and there were many from which he could have chosen) was: *the Lamb of God that takes away the sin of the world* (Jn. 1:29). Just as on the tenth day of Nisan, the Jews set aside the literal lamb, on this same day, Yeshua rode into Jerusalem and was set aside as the Passover Lamb of God.

2. In Fulfillment of Passover

The town of Bethphage was located on the slopes of the Mount of Olives between Bethany and Jerusalem. As they passed by Bethphage, Yeshua sent His disciples to fetch a donkey: *ye shall find an ass tied, and a colt with her: loose <them>, and bring <them> unto me* (Mt. 21:2). While the mother had been gentled, the colt had never yet been sat upon: *ye shall find a colt tied, whereon no man ever yet sat* (Mk. 11:2). Nevertheless, this colt did not buck when Yeshua rode it, showing His lordship over the animal kingdom. Yeshua further instructed the disciples that if anyone asked them what they were doing, they were to simply answer: *The Lord has need of them* (Mt. 21:3). The word *need* indicates necessity. To what necessity was He referring? Zechariah 9:9 reads: *Rejoice greatly, O daughter of Zion; shout, O daughter of Yerushalayim: behold, your king comes unto you; he is just, and having salvation; lowly, and riding upon an ass, even upon a colt the foal of an ass.* Yeshua had need of the animals because He was about to fulfill the messianic prophecy of Zechariah. As He rode the colt into Jerusalem, the rumors quickly spread that He was coming, just as Zechariah had prophesied.

The way the Jewish people responded is significant, and taken together, the four Gospel accounts fully describe their reactions: they cut palm branches and laid them before the feet of the colt upon which Yeshua rode; they cried out, *Hosanna*; and they said, *Blessed is he that comes in the name of the Lord.* These are actions performed during the Feast of Tabernacles, and not Passover, so the response of the multitude showed that they expected Tabernacles to be fulfilled on this occasion. This they did in accordance with Zechariah 14:16-21, which prophesies that the Feast of Tabernacles will be fulfilled by the messianic kingdom.

The declaration and actions of the multitude showed that they expected the messianic kingdom to be set up. However, they failed to realize that Yeshua had come to fulfill the Passover, not the Feast of Tabernacles, and the Passover would be fulfilled by His death, not the establishment of His kingdom. So, clearly, the multitude misinterpreted the purpose of His riding into Jerusalem. They made the same mistake that Peter made during the transfiguration.

The disciples did not understand either, as John 12:16 indicates: *These things understood not his disciples at the first: but when Yeshua was glorified.* Only after the ascension and the coming of the Holy Spirit would they finally realize the significance of it all.

3. The Palm Branches

A few additional notes help to clarify the mindset of the multitudes who witnessed Yeshua riding into the royal city of Jerusalem on the back of a donkey. In Leviticus 23:40, Moses commanded the gathering of palm branches for the Feast of Tabernacles, but not for Passover. However, their action demonstrates that the multitudes thought in terms of a military establishment, and history tells us other events triggered a similar response from the people of Jerusalem. On two previous occasions, palm branches were broken off in preparation for the arrival of a victorious Jewish military leader. The first instance occurred in the second century B.C., when Judah Maccabee entered Jerusalem:

> Therefore bearing ivy-wreathed wands and beautiful branches and also fronds of palm, they offered hymns of thanksgiving to him who had given success to the purifying of his own holy place.[3]

The Jews repeated this celebratory recognition of military success for Simon, the last of the Maccabees, when he entered Jerusalem:

> On the twenty-third day of the second month, in the one hundred and seventy-first year, the Jews entered it [Jerusalem] with praise and palm branches, and with harps and cymbals and stringed instruments, and

---

[3] Second Maccabees 10:7 (RSV).

with hymns and songs, because a great enemy had been crushed and removed from Israel.[4]

Both Judah and Simon Maccabee brought a military victory to the Jewish people, cleansed the Temple, and expelled the Gentile authorities who were the Syrian Greeks. When Yeshua entered Jerusalem, the Jewish people once again brought branches, expecting Him to set up the messianic kingdom and expel the Gentile overlords, in this case, the Romans.

Furthermore, one of the statements they applied to Yeshua was *baruch haba b'shem Adonai, Blessed is he that comes in the name of the Lord.* From a Jewish perspective, that phrase is an official messianic greeting. The rabbis taught that when the Messiah comes, He must be greeted with these words, which come from a messianic psalm in the Hebrew Bible (Ps. 118:26). The myriads of people applied these words to Yeshua, thus proclaiming Him to be the Messiah of Israel.

4. The Response of the Pharisees

While the masses proclaimed Yeshua to be the Messiah, the Pharisees responded differently, saying *among themselves, Behold how ye prevail nothing: lo, the world is gone after him* (Jn. 12:19). Luke added: *And some of the Pharisees from the multitude said unto him, Teacher, rebuke your disciples* (Lk. 19:39). To the objections of the Pharisees, Yeshua responded that there must be a testimony to the fact that the Messiah had come: *And he answered and said, I tell you that, if these shall hold their peace, the stones will cry out* (Lk. 19:40). If the multitudes had been silent, the stones would have cried out the very same words.

The fact that Yeshua was not riding into Jerusalem to establish His kingdom is made clear by what happened next. In spite of the many *Hosannas*, the greetings of *Blessed is he that comes in the name of the Lord,* and the proclamations of His Messiahship, Yeshua's words remained those of judgment (Lk. 19:41-44):

---

[4] First Maccabees 13:51 (RSV).

41 And when he drew near, he saw the city and wept over it, 42 saying, If you had known in this day, even you, the things which belong unto peace! But now they are hid from your eyes. 43 For the days shall come upon you, when your enemies shall cast up a bank about you, 44 and compass you round, and keep you in on every side, and shall dash you to the ground, and your children within you; and they shall not leave in you one stone upon another; because you knew not the time of your visitation.

If Yeshua had offered to restore the kingdom as He rode into Jerusalem on the day of the triumphal entry, the multitudes would have accepted Him as the Messiah. Thousands upon thousands of Jews proclaimed Him as the Messiah because Matthew mentioned that it was true for *the most part of the multitude* (Mt. 21:8). The leaders objected, but the masses proclaimed His Messiahship. If it was true that Yeshua was again offering Himself as the King and re-offering the kingdom, then the masses were definitely accepting it. However, that was not the purpose of the triumphal entry. One-and-a-half years earlier Yeshua had pronounced that the sin of rejecting Him as Messiah on the grounds of demon possession committed by this generation was irrevocably unpardonable. So, in spite of the many hosannas and many messianic proclamations, Yeshua's words were words of judgment. He reiterated that Jerusalem was destined for destruction. The Temple would be torn down until not one stone would stand upon another because they knew not the time of their visitation (Lk. 19:44). The time of visitation that they did not know came to a climax in Matthew 12. After Yeshua authenticated the validity of His claims by performing many miracles, signs, and wonders, and after the people heard Him teach, preach, and proclaim His Messiahship, they rejected Him. Therefore, they did not know the time of their visitation, and they remained under judgment.

5. Yeshua's Acceptance

As stated, the purpose of the triumphal entry was to set aside the Lamb of God in preparation for the Passover sacrifice. Mark reported that Yeshua continued on and entered Jerusalem (Mk. 11:11). Matthew elaborated on what happened once He arrived: *And when he was come into Yerushalayim, all the city was stirred, saying, Who is this? And the multitudes said, This is the prophet, Yeshua, from Natzeret of Galil* (Mt. 21:10-11). The whole city understood the significance of what was happening but, once again, the priests and the scribes objected (Mt. 21:15-16):

> *[15] But when the chief priests* [Sadducees] *and the scribes* [Pharisees] *saw the wonderful things that he did, and the children that were crying in the temple and saying, Hoshannah to the son of David; they were moved with indignation, and said unto him, Hear you what these are saying? [16] And Yeshua said unto them, Yea: did ye never read, Out of the mouth of babes and sucklings you have perfected praise?*

When the Pharisees objected to the worship He received, Yeshua informed them that the Messiah deserved their worship. His acceptance of their praise and worship showed that He honored the people's assertions that He was the Messiah. Then Yeshua left Jerusalem and, *it being now eventide, he went out unto Beit Anyah with the twelve* (Mk. 11:11b).

On that day, the tenth of Nisan, the Passover Lamb of God was set aside. From the tenth until the fourteenth, this Lamb was tested to show that He was spotless and without blemish.

[§§ 134–135] — C. The Authority of the King

The Monday of Yeshua's final week was the eleventh of Nisan on the Jewish calendar, or April 3, A.D. 30.[5]

[§ 134] — 1. The Cursing of the Fig Tree

Matthew 21:18-19a, Mark 11:12-14

Mark introduced the incident by noting that it was now *the morrow* (Mk. 11:12a), the day after Yeshua's triumphal entry. The occasion was that *he hungered* (Mk. 11:12b), emphasizing His humanity. *And seeing*

---

[5] Or March 30, A.D. 33.

a fig tree afar off having leaves, he came, if haply he might find anything thereon: and when he came to it, he found nothing but leaves; for it was not the season of figs (Mk. 11:13). The question this incident raises is why Yeshua cursed the fig tree, since it was not the season for figs. His action appears unjust, but it is understandable considering the nature of fig trees in Israel. Normally, when a fig tree in Israel first gives forth its leaves, edible knobs or nodules appear. These are the *paggim*, so-called "green figs" (Song 2:13), that are really tiny flowers covered with a soft skin. The figs themselves grow about six weeks later. Although it was not fig season and Yeshua could not expect to see any fruit, the tree was giving forth leaves, and hence, the edible knobs should have been present but were not. The tree was professing to have something it did not have. Therefore, Yeshua cursed the fig tree, thus emphasizing His deity.

Likewise, Israel had no fruit due to the people's rejection of the Messiah. By adhering to Pharisaic Judaism, they professed righteousness based on a reality they simply did not have, so Yeshua cursed that generation, just as He cursed the fig tree, declaring, *Let there be no fruit from you henceforward forever* (Mt. 21:19). The Greek term used here and translated as *forever* does not mean "eternity," but "for an age." For the period of "an age," Israel would be fruitless, but not forever, because she is destined for restoration.

Mark added: *And his disciples heard it* (Mk. 11:14), meaning that they noted what Yeshua said about the fig tree. The relevance of this incident became obvious to them the next day.

[§ 135] — 2. The Second Possession of the Temple

Matthew 21:12-13, Mark 11:15-18, Luke 19:45-48

In John 2:13-16, Yeshua began His public ministry by cleansing the Temple at the Passover, thus exercising His possession of His Father's house. At the last Passover of His public ministry, He again exercised possession of the Temple: *And they come to Yerushalayim: and he entered into the temple, and began to cast out them that sold and them that bought in the temple, and overthrew the tables of the money-changers, and the seats of them that sold the doves* (Mk. 11:15). As the Messiah, He is the lord of the Temple. It belongs to Him.

Although Yeshua had cleansed the Temple before, things returned to business as usual. He dealt with the disarray largely in the same manner as previously, casting out the money-changers and merchants, overturning their tables and seats, and accusing them of turning the house of God into a business venture and *a den of robbers* (Lk. 19:46). However, this time He did one new thing: *and he would not suffer that any man should carry a vessel through the temple* (Mk. 11:16). He forbade any merchandise to be carried through the Temple compound, demonstrating a threefold messianic authority over the Temple: His authority to cleanse, His authority to possess, and His authority to safeguard the Temple.

Yeshua's actions did not please the rulers: *And the chief priests and the scribes heard it, and sought how they might destroy him: for they feared him, for all the multitude was astonished at his teaching* (Mk. 11:18). Fear of His influence on the masses prevented them from killing Him right away.

The situation repeated itself over the course of a few days, as *he was teaching daily in the temple. But the chief priests and the scribes and the principal men of the people sought to destroy him: and they could not find what they might do; for the people all hung upon him, listening* (Lk. 19:47-48). While their fear of Yeshua's influence kept them from destroying Him immediately, their antagonism was unbroken: Throughout His last week, from Monday through Thursday, the religious leaders kept looking for opportunities to arrest and kill Him. However, the ever-present crowd forced them to wait for a moment when He was alone. Judas would provide them with that opportunity.

[§ 136] — D. The Invitations by the King

1. The Two Invitations

John 12:20-36

The historical background that led to the invitations by the King was the desire of some *Greeks* to see Yeshua (Jn. 12:20). It took several steps to pass the news on to Him, as the Greeks first told Philip, Philip then told Andrew, and both Andrew and Philip finally told Yeshua. This was complicated because these men were Gentiles, as the term *Greeks* indicates. The fact that they went up to worship at the feast, however, indicates that they were also converts to Judaism. Because they were Gentile converts to Judaism, the disciples did not know what to do with their request to come and see the Messiah.

It appears from Yeshua's response that He never really answered their question, but that is not the case. He responded to them, albeit indirectly, by spelling out His program of death and resurrection: By His death He would produce life (Jn. 12:23-24); His death would judge the world (Jn. 12:31); by His death He would defeat Satan (Jn. 12:31b); and only after His death would Gentiles be free to come to Him: *And I, if I be lifted up from the earth, will draw all men to myself. But this he said, signifying by what manner of death he should die* (Jn. 12:32-33). By saying that after His death, He would draw *all men* to Himself, He included both Jews and Gentiles. However, it also meant that at this point in time, Yeshua was only ministering to the lost sheep of the house of Israel. The hour had not yet come for Gentiles to freely approach Him. Only after His death would they be permitted to come to Him, but for now, these Greeks were not free to see Yeshua.

After this instruction, Yeshua repeated His invitation to salvation and discipleship, emphasizing the individuality of a decision to follow Him: *He that loves his life loses it; and he that hates his life in this world shall keep it unto life eternal. If any man serve me, let him follow me; and where I am, there shall also my servant be: if any man serve me, him will the Father honor* (Jn. 12:25-26). An important point to note in this section is Yeshua's statement: *Now is my soul troubled; and what shall I say? Father, save me from this hour. But for this cause came I unto this hour. Father, glorify your name* (Jn. 12:27-28a). With these words, Yeshua clearly expressed that He would not ask the Father to prevent His death, nor would He ask the Father to save Him *from this hour*, because He had come for the specific purpose of this hour. This point will come up again in the discussion on Gethsemane (§ 164).

At that point came another Bat Kol, and God the Father spoke audibly out of heaven for the third time in Messiah's public ministry. He said, *I have both glorified it* [meaning His name], *and will glorify it again* (Jn. 12:28b). The multitude close by heard something. A few thought *that it had thundered* (Jn. 12:29a), but this was not the season for thunderstorms in Israel, and so others recognized that something supernatural had occurred. They said, *An angel has spoken to him* (Jn. 12:29b). Yeshua responded: *This voice has not come for my sake, but for your sakes* (Jn. 12:30). For the third time, God the Father spoke audibly from heaven. They should have recognized that Yeshua was the Son of God.

Since He was addressing the multitude, Yeshua again spoke in parables, and the people failed to understand: *The multitude therefore answered him, We have heard out of the law that the Messiah abides forever: and how say you, The Son of man must be lifted up? Who is this Son of man?* (Jn. 12:34). From the Hebrew Scriptures, they understood that the Messiah is eternal, so how could He die? They did not comprehend the God-Man concept; they also failed to understand the messianic program. Yeshua answered by saying: *Yet a little while is the light among you. Walk while ye have the light, that darkness overtake you not: and he that walks in darkness knows not whither he goes. While ye have the light, believe on the light, that ye may become sons of light* (Jn. 12:35-36). This again exemplifies the conflict of light and darkness that spans Yochanan's Gospel. Earlier, Yeshua gave an invitation to salvation with the emphasis on individuality. His second invitation was that the people should walk in the light while it was still available to them.

2. Yochanan's Summary of Messiah's Ministry

a. Summary of Israel

John 12:37-43

The generation of Israel that denied Yeshua's Messiahship could be described as "willfully disobedient," as the following verse shows: *But though he had done so many signs before them, yet they believed not on him* (Jn. 12:37). The Greek reads, "they kept on not believing." Their unbelief was confirmed by the fact that they did not even believe the signs they had witnessed. Yeshua pointed out that their unbelief was predicted by Isaiah 53:1, and that their blindness was judicially imposed upon them by God, as predicted in Isaiah 6:1-10.

However, some did understand: *Nevertheless even of the rulers many believed on him* (Jn. 12:42a). Unfortunately, fear intimidated them: *but because of the Pharisees they did not confess <it>, lest they should be put out of the synagogue* (Jn. 12:42b). Many individual Jews had come to believe in Yeshua's Messiahship, but did not let it be known publicly because they feared the Pharisees, who had already decreed that any Jew proclaiming Yeshua to be the Messiah would be excommunicated from the synagogue. These secret believers feared excommunication, and furthermore, *they loved the glory <that is> of men more than the glory <that is> of God* (Jn. 12:43).

b. Summary of Yeshua

John 12:44-50

While Israel could be described as willfully disobedient, Yeshua could be characterized as willfully obedient. His ministry can be summarized in five points: The Father had testified of Yeshua three times already; He sent His Son (Jn. 12:49); Yeshua is the light (Jn. 12:46a); accepting Him will result in salvation (Jn. 12:46b); and, conversely, rejecting Him will result in judgment by the Father (Jn. 12:48).

Notably, this is yet another example of Yochanan's sub-theme of the conflict of light and darkness: *I am come a light into the world, that whosoever believes on me may not abide in the darkness* (Jn. 12:46).

[§ 137] — E. The Proof of Authority

Matthew 21:19b-22, Mark 11:19-26[6]

It was Tuesday of the last week of Yeshua's life, the 12th of Nisan on the Jewish calendar, which would have been April 4th, A.D. 30 by the Gregorian calendar.[7] Mark described Yeshua's daily routine during that week. In the mornings, He went from Bethany to Jerusalem in order to teach, and *every evening he went forth out of the city* (Mk. 11:19) and returned to Bethany.

On Monday, Yeshua had cursed the fig tree (Mk. 11:12-14). Tuesday morning (Mk. 11:20), as He and His disciples were heading for Jerusalem, they passed it again: *And immediately the fig tree withered away. And when the disciples saw it, they marveled, saying, How did the fig tree immediately wither away?* (Mt. 21:19b-20). Yeshua's hunger had attested to His humanity; the fact that His curse had withered the tree in one day proved His deity.

Mark, who often recounted events from Peter's perspective, revealed the apostle's comment on the phenomenon: *And Peter calling to remembrance said unto Him, Rabbi, behold the fig tree which you cursed is withered away* (Mk. 11:21).

Yeshua taught the disciples an important principle of prayer. Two conditions must be met in order to receive an answer to one's prayer. The first condition is faith: *Have faith in God* (Mk. 11:22); *If ye have faith, and doubt not . . . even if ye shall say unto this mountain, Be you taken up and cast in the sea, it shall be done* (Mt. 21:21). This may refer to the fact that the Jews used to call their greatest teachers "removers of

---

[6] Luke 21:37-38 is to be found at the end of § 145.

[7] Or March 31, A.D. 33.

mountains." When they solved problems of the law, they "uprooted mountains." When they took care of "apparently impossible things, such as those which a heathen government may order a man to do,"[8] they "pulverized" them. Their faith in God gave them knowledge of how to solve difficult issues of everyday life, theology, and Scripture. However, this is taken, the first condition concerning answered prayer is faith: *And all things, whatsoever ye shall ask in prayer, believing, ye shall receive* (Mt. 21:22). However, Yeshua did not hand out a blank check here, for elsewhere, Scripture teaches that one must ask according to God's will. True faith recognizes the Lord's will; asking in His will and believing go hand in hand and will result in receiving.

The second condition concerning answered prayer is: *whensoever ye stand praying, forgive, if ye have anything against anyone; that your Father also who is in heaven may forgive you your trespasses* (Mk. 11:25). If we are not willing to forgive our brethren, our prayers will remain unanswered.

[§§ 138–141] —
F. The Authority of the King Challenged:
The Testing of the Lamb

In § 133, the motif of Yeshua as the Passover Lamb of God was introduced. His triumphal entry into the royal city of Jerusalem coincided with the setting aside of the sacrificial animals for the feast. From the tenth of Nisan, the lambs were to be tested for four days to ensure they were without spot or blemish. This motif is repeated in this section. Just as the sacrificial animals were tested, Yeshua, the Lamb of God, was also tested. Four times a specific group in isolation or a combination of groups examined Him. There were two basic purposes for this period of testing. The first purpose was to incite the people against Him. The

---

[8] Edersheim, *The Life and Times of Jesus the Messiah*, 2 volumes (London, England: Longmans, Green, and Co., 1883), 2:109.

religious leaders feared arresting Yeshua because they feared the multitudes, so they tried to incite the crowd against Him. The second purpose was to find a way of charging Him with breaking a law, particularly a point of Roman law.

[§ 138] — 1. By Priests and Elders

The first attack came from the combined group of priests and elders. The priests were Sadducees, and the elders were Pharisees. The specific issue was the question of authority.

a. The Attack

Matthew 21:23, Mark 11:27-28, Luke 20:1-2

Trying to turn the multitudes against Him, the Pharisees and Sadducees asked Yeshua, *By what authority do you these things? Or who gave you this authority to do these things?* (Mk. 11:28). Luke gave the occasion: *as he was teaching the people in the temple* (Lk. 20:1). The religious leaders waited for a time when Yeshua was in the public eye, because their purpose was to discredit Him publicly. In this public situation, they questioned Yeshua's authority and its source.

Luke specified that Yeshua was *preaching the gospel* (Lk. 20:1). The term "gospel" simply means "good news," but the content of the good news can only be determined by the context. In this context, the content of the gospel could not be as Paul defined it in I Corinthians 15:1-4 since Messiah's death, burial, and resurrection had not yet occurred. In this context, the good news was simply that Yeshua was the Messianic King.

The Jewish frame of reference provides some validity to the question. According to the rabbis, authoritative teaching required previous rabbinic authorization, so they questioned who had authorized Yeshua to teach. Furthermore, in their theology, a teacher should only teach what was handed down to him by his own teacher.

b. The Answer

Matthew 21:24-27, Mark 11:29-33, Luke 20:3-8

Using Jewish custom, Yeshua answered the religious leaders with a question of His own: *The baptism of Yochanan, was it from heaven, or from men?* (Lk. 20:4). In other words, "By what authority was Yochanan baptizing? Through human authority or through divine authority?" The Pharisees and Sadducees were caught on the horns of a dilemma. Yochanan's martyrdom caused people to consider him a true prophet. If the religious leaders answered that Yochanan was baptizing on the basis of human authority, the masses would turn against them. So, while they rejected the baptism of Yochanan, they were unwilling to say anything against him at this point. If they stated that the baptism of Yochanan was from heaven, Yeshua could simply answer, "I received my authority from Yochanan," since it was Yochanan who said of Him, *Behold, the Lamb of God, that takes away the sin of the world* (Jn. 1:29). Either answer would discredit or humiliate them. So they simply responded, *We know not* (Mt. 21:27; Mk. 11:33). Since they would not answer His question, Yeshua was not obligated to answer their question. However, He went on to give three parables.

(1) The Parable of the Two Sons
Matthew 21:28-32

The main point of the Parable of the Two Sons was that sinners will enter the kingdom, while the religious leaders will not.

The basic story is of a father who asked his two sons to work in the vineyard. The first son refused, but later obeyed and did the work. The second son initially declared he would do what his father had asked of him, but later disobeyed and refused to work in the vineyard. Sonship is proven by obedience. Obviously, the first son actually obeyed his father. Therefore, Yeshua likened him to publicans and prostitutes. Initially, they did not obey, but later they accepted Yeshua as their Messiah. The Pharisees, in contrast, expressed obedience like the second son, but ended up refusing to work.

Yeshua made the following application (Mt. 21:31b-32):

31b Verily I say unto you, that the publicans and the harlots go into the kingdom of God before you. 32 For Yochanan came unto you in the way of righteousness, and ye believed him not; but the publicans and the harlots believed him: and ye, when ye saw it, did not even repent yourselves afterward, that ye might believe him.

While the Pharisees and Sadducees would not say where Yochanan received his authority to baptize, Yeshua willingly validated it as being from heaven. Yochanan's divine authority was recognized by publicans and prostitutes, two totally ostracized classes of people by Pharisaic Law. Yet, those who outwardly claimed a high level of spirituality would be excluded from the kingdom.

(2) The Parable of the Householder
Matthew 21:33-46, Mark 12:1-12, Luke 20:9-19

The Parable of the Householder, also called the Parable of the Vineyard, emphasized that just as the Jewish leaders had killed the prophets, they would also kill the Son.

Yeshua had just accused the Pharisees and Sadducees of being outwardly pious and obedient to God. Internally, they failed miserably because God knows the heart. As a result, they would be excluded from the kingdom. Yeshua added a second parable, the Parable of the Householder, based on a similar story found in Isaiah 5:1-7, whereby God was the householder and Israel the vineyard. The Jewish leaders were the husbandmen responsible for stewarding the vineyard and giving God His due. The landowner sent three sets of servants to collect his portion, and all three were rejected in one form or another. Some were even killed. The three sets of servants were the pre-exilic prophets (those who preceded the Babylonian Captivity), the post-exilic prophets, and Yochanan the Baptizer and his disciples.

After having been rejected repeatedly, the householder finally sent his beloved son, hoping that the husbandmen would respect him (Mt. 21:37). However, they conspired and had him killed as well. How would the householder respond to this terrible sin (Lk. 20:15)? *He will come and destroy these husbandmen, and will give the vineyard unto others* (Lk. 20:16). And so it was. The punishment for the unpardonable sin came in A.D. 70 with the destruction of Jerusalem and the Temple.

As stated earlier, the messianic greeting, *Blessed is he that comes in the name of the Lord,* comes from Psalm 118:26. This messianic psalm also declared: *The stone which the builders rejected is become the head of the corner* (Ps. 118:22). This verse prophesied that the Messiah would be rejected, but would become the head of the corner when they finally cry: *Blessed is he that comes in the name of the Lord.* Yeshua pointed out that the rejected Son had yet to become the head of the corner, in keeping with that messianic prophecy (Lk. 20:17; Mt. 21:42a; Mk. 12:10).

Concerning the concept of the Messiah as the stone, Yeshua made both a national and an individual application. Nationally, *The kingdom of God shall be taken away from you, and shall be given to a nation bringing forth the fruits thereof* (Mt. 21:43). Replacement theologians commonly teach that God took the kingdom away from the Jews and gave it to the church. The problem with this interpretation is that the church is never referred to as a nation; rather, Romans 9 teaches that the church is comprised of believers from all nations. Hence, the *nation bringing forth the fruits* refers to future Israel. The kingdom was withheld from the generation of Jews who rejected Yeshua's Messiahship, and specifically the leadership of this generation would not see the kingdom. However, in later times, it will be offered to the leadership of a future generation that will accept it and produce its fruits. That will be the Jewish generation living in the tribulation.

The messianic stone of Psalm 118 entailed another concept, to which Yeshua referred when He made an individual application of the parable: *Everyone that falls on that stone shall be broken to pieces; but on whomsoever it shall fall, it will scatter him as dust* (Lk. 20:18). In Isaiah 8, the prophet predicted that the Messiah would become a point of division between the remnant and the non-remnant of Israel, between believing Jews and unbelieving Jews. Yeshua would be a sanctuary for Jewish believers, but He would be *a stone of stumbling* and *a rock of offense* for unbelieving Jews (Is. 8:14). Using this imagery, Yeshua made two points. First, the religious leaders stumbled over the stone of His Messiahship; a person who stumbles over a stone will bruise himself. Second, when a large stone falls on a person, it will crush him. Because this generation stumbled over His Messiahship, they bruised themselves; eventually, the stone would become the smiting stone that will crush them. The smiting came in A.D. 70 when Jerusalem and the Temple were destroyed. Yeshua is the smiting stone of Daniel 2:34-35, 44-45.

The leadership then understood that Yeshua applied this parable to them: *And when the chief priests and the Pharisees heard his parables, they perceived that he spoke of them* (Mt. 21:45). The kingdom is not taken away from Israel, but only from that generation and especially its leaders. *And they sought to lay hold on him; and they feared the multitude; for they perceived that he spoke the parable against them: and they left him, and went away* (Mk. 12:12).

(3) The Parable of the Wedding
Matthew 22:1-14

The main point of the Parable of the Wedding Feast is that those bidden, like the Pharisees, will not participate in the marriage feast, while others will. The marriage feast in this and other parables symbolizes the messianic kingdom. Those originally invited will fail to enter the messianic kingdom, while others will enter in.

The context of this parable is Yochanan's ministry. The baptizer made an initial invitation when he told Israel to repent and be prepared, *for the kingdom of heaven is at hand* (Mt. 3:2). Two sets of servants, Yochanan's servants and Yeshua's servants, specifically the twelve apostles, continued with the baptizer's work. However, those bidden always had excuses for not accepting the invitation. Consequently, *the king was angry; and he sent his armies and destroyed those murderers, and burned their city* (Mt. 22:7). Their rejection of the kingdom offer resulted in the destruction of the murderers (the leadership of Israel) and their city (Jerusalem) because *they that were bidden* [the generation to whom Yeshua came] *were not worthy* (Mt. 22:8).

After those who had rejected the invitation were properly punished, the king declared: *Go ye therefore unto the partings of the highways, and as many as ye shall find, bid to the marriage feast* (Mt. 22:9). So some-time after the city was destroyed and the murderers were killed, the king issued a new invitation. This invitation will be extended to the Jewish generation of the great tribulation, and the wedding feast will be *filled with guests* (Mt. 22:10) when the kingdom is established.

Among those who attended the feast was a man dressed inappropri-ately (Mt. 22:11-12). Because he was improperly attired, the host declared, *Bind him hand and foot, and cast him out into the outer dark-ness; there shall be the weeping and gnashing of teeth* (Mt. 22:13). In the parable, the wedding garment symbolizes righteousness through salva-tion. From the beginning, God provided a covering for our sin. Adam and Eve used fig leaves to cover their shame, but God provided the skins of animals (Gen. 3:7, 21). God decided what was the appropriate attire and how one could approach Him. In Revelation 7:9, believers are depicted in heaven as wearing white robes. The brilliance of these robes is being achieved by washing them in the blood of the Lamb (Rev. 7:14). Therefore, anyone who wants to approach God and participate in the wedding feast must rely on God's provision of righteousness and not on his own. In the case of the man who attended the wedding feast improperly attired, he had rejected the king's offer of the wedding gar-ment, which symbolized righteousness through salvation. Therefore, he was expelled and cast *into the outer darkness; there shall be the weep-ing and the gnashing of teeth* (Mt. 22:13). Yeshua later repeated what He taught in this parable when He spoke about the judgment of the sheep and the goats (Mt. 25:31-46). We will study this passage carefully in § 145. Notably, expressions like *outer darkness* and *gnashing of teeth* are descriptive terms used of the lake of fire.

[§ 139] — 2. By Pharisees and Herodians

The second attack came from the Pharisees and the Herodians, a strange alliance, since they were on opposing sides of the political spec-trum. The Pharisees opposed Roman rule under any circumstances, while the Herodians favored Roman rule initiated through the house of Herod, hence the term "Herodians." However, these two groups found common ground in their antagonism to Yeshua. The Pharisees attacked His Messiahship because He did not fit the mold of their expectations for the Messiah. The Herodians opposed Yeshua because, as the Messiah, He competed with Caesar and would dishonor the house of Herod, as did Yochanan the Baptizer. Politics fueled their joint attack on Yeshua, and the Pharisees hoped to either anger Roman authorities so that they would execute Yeshua or to anger the Jewish masses.

a. The Attack

Matthew 22:15-17, Mark 12:13-15a, Luke 20:20-22

The Herodians and the Pharisees attempted to provoke Yeshua into doing or saying something that would then allow them to charge Him with sedition against Rome. Their specific question was: *Is it lawful to give tribute unto Caesar or not?* (Mk. 12:14). A positive response would anger the people, and a negative response could result in the charge of sedition.

The Pharisees believed that to give tribute to Caesar was to accept him as king and, therefore, disown Jehovah as King. To pay taxes to Rome was to recognize Rome's authority over Israel. Of course, they had no choice but to pay their taxes, but they did so only under compulsion without recognizing its legality.

b. The Answer

Matthew 22:18-22, Mark 12:15b-17, Luke 20:23-26

Yeshua knew His attackers' purpose was to trap Him, so before answering, He asked for a coin: *Show me the tribute money* (Mt. 22:19). He did not ask for a Jewish shekel, but for the Roman tribute coin. Tribute money had an image of Caesar, and that type of coin could not be used to pay the Temple tax that was due at Passover time. In fact, the people had to bring it to Him because they were reluctant even to carry coins with the image of Caesar.

When Yeshua received the coin, He asked: *Whose is this image and superscription? And they said unto him, Caesar's* (Mk. 12:16). Then Yeshua made His point: *Render therefore unto Caesar the things that are Caesar's; and unto God the things that are God's* (Mt. 22:21). In other words, because the coin had the image of Caesar, they could not use it to pay the Temple tax anyway. According to their law, they could only return it to Rome.

The principle Yeshua established, already found in the Hebrew Bible, was that two authorities existed, not one. The first is divine authority exercised by God, and that which is God's must be given to God. Second, ever since Genesis 9, delegated authority by means of human government has existed.[9] At this point in history, Caesar ran the government. It is not "either/or," but "both/and;" i.e., both divine authority and delegated governmental authority. Paying taxes to Caesar did not nullify or reject God's rule over Israel.

Yeshua's answer left the Herodians and Pharisees without religious or political grounds for accusation: *And they were not able to take hold of the saying before the people* (Lk. 20:26).

[§ 140] — 3. By Sadducees

The third attack was launched by the aristocratic Sadducees who came from a few rich families. Usually, the high priests and the common priests, as members of this sect, were the more religiously conservative of the two factions of Judaism in that they rejected the Oral Law of the Pharisees. They were also more Hellenized than the Pharisees. They strictly based their theology on the literal interpretation of the Mosaic Law. Topics like the afterlife are not mentioned in the books of Moses, so they did not believe in the resurrection of the dead. The focus of their religious life was the scrupulous upholding of the sacrificial system and the Temple traditions. In contrast to the Pharisees, they supported Rome since the protection of their wealth and status depended on the Caesar. In an uprising against Rome, they could lose everything, which,

---

[9] For details, see Arnold G. Fruchtenbaum, *The Book of Genesis* (San Antonio, TX: Ariel Ministries, 2009).

indeed, they did in the war of A.D. 66. When, in 70, the Temple was destroyed, they disappeared from history. Since none of their writings were passed on to the following generations, all we know about them comes from Pharisaic literature. The specific issue they raised against Yeshua was theological, pertaining to the question of the resurrection, with the intention of making Yeshua look ignorant.

a. The Attack

Matthew 22:23-28, Mark 12:18-23, Luke 20:27-33

While the Pharisees believed in a future resurrection, the Sadducees did not. They taught that the soul dies with the body. The Sadducees liked to ask the Pharisees tricky questions to make them look ignorant, and often they succeeded. So they tried one of their questions on Yeshua. The background was the contrived example of a childless widow who, over the course of time, married one after the other of seven brothers. Eventually, she also died. The theological trick question was: In the resurrection, whose wife would she be, since all seven brothers had been married to her?

b. The Answer

Matthew 22:29-33, Mark 12:24-27, Luke 20:34-40

Yeshua pointed out that the Sadducees' lack of understanding was based upon two problems: *Ye do err, not knowing the scriptures, nor the power of God* (Mt. 22:29). He answered their question by pointing out three things.

First, Yeshua made an appeal to the power of God: *but they that are accounted worthy to attain to that world, and the resurrection from the dead, neither marry, nor are given in marriage: for neither can they die any more: for they are equal unto the angels; and are sons of God, being sons of the resurrection* (Lk. 20:35-36). Those who are believers are as angels in heaven (Mt. 22:30). The resurrection will not merely be a re-awakening or a restoration back to natural life, but will be a transformation of the physical body where corruption puts on incorruption and mortality puts on immortality (I Cor. 15:53). These glorified bodies will no longer be subject to death, nor can such bodies be reproduced through natural generation. Therefore, marriage will be unnecessary. So Yeshua's first response dealt with the Sadducees' ignorance in respect to the power of God. The answer is that in heaven, the widow will be like the angels and will not be married to anyone. The mention of angels must have peeved the Sadducees since they did not believe in angels or demons.

This passage is sometimes used to show why the sons of God of Genesis 6 could not have been angels. The argument goes that angels are sexless, so could not have sired the Nephilim; but this passage doesn't say that. Throughout the Hebrew Scriptures, angels are always described in the masculine gender. When they become visible, it is always in the form of young men. Yeshua specified that believers are like the good angels in heaven, not fallen angels on earth. In heaven, the holy angels do not marry, but Genesis 6 was about fallen angels on earth. Humans on earth, but not in heaven, marry and are given in marriage.

Second, Yeshua answered their question by referring to the Abrahamic Covenant: *I am the God of Avraham, and the God of Yitzchak, and the God of Yaakov* (Mt. 22:32). This is the biblical formula for the covenant God made with Abraham in Genesis. Yeshua had a good reason for not quoting the three classic Old Testament passages on the resurrection: Daniel 12:2, Isaiah 26:19, and Job 19:25-26. As already noted, one of the doctrinal differences between Pharisees and Sadducees was the resurrection. Another major difference was that the Pharisees believed that doctrine could be derived from all parts of Scripture, but the Sadducees believed that all doctrine was derived only from the five books of Moses. While it was permissible to use the Prophets and the Writings to illustrate doctrine, every doctrine had to originate from Moses. If Yeshua had quoted Daniel, Job, or Isaiah, it would have been authoritative for the Pharisees, but it would not have been acceptable for the Sadducees. Therefore, He quoted the law from Exodus, one part of the Bible that both factions fully accepted, where God said to Moses, *I am the God of thy father, the God of Avraham, the God of Yitzchak, and the God of Yaakov* (Ex. 3:6-7), the formula for the Abrahamic Covenant.

The question arises where in that covenant God promised a resurrection. It is found in this principle: If God makes a promise to an individual, and that individual dies before the promise is fulfilled, God obligates Himself to raise that person back to life in order to fulfill the promise. Every promise of God must be fulfilled, specifically to the person to whom it was made. That principle was in Abraham's mind when God asked him to sacrifice Isaac (Heb. 11:17-19). Abraham, based on that principle, did not hesitate to obey God, knowing that if he had to kill Isaac, God would raise him back to life. How did he know? Abraham knew God to be a covenant keeper. God, having made certain promises concerning Isaac which as yet were unfulfilled, was obligated to raise Isaac from the dead.

Furthermore, regarding the Abrahamic Covenant, God said at different times to all three men, Abraham, Isaac, and Jacob, "To you and to your seed I will give this land." God not only promised the land to the descendants of Abraham, Isaac, and Jacob, but also to the patriarchs themselves. All three men died, yet the extent of their combined real estate holdings in the Promised Land was one burial cave purchased at a heavily inflated price, some wells, and a plot of land near Shechem for which they paid good money. How will God fulfill His promise to Abraham, Isaac, and Jacob? He must first raise them from the dead, and then restore them to the land. Thus, the resurrection is found in the Abrahamic Covenant by virtue of unfulfilled promises.

Third, Yeshua answered the Sadducees' question by stating, *God is not <the God> of the dead, but of the living* (Mt. 22:32). God has a living relationship with the patriarchs; therefore, He cannot leave them dead.

His answers resulted in three reactions: When *the multitudes heard it, they were astonished at his teaching* (Mt. 22:33), for this was an entirely new way of looking at Exodus 3:6. Saying, *Teacher, you have well said* (Lk. 20:39), the Pharisees were impressed; Yeshua had provided them with new evidential support for the resurrection. The Sadducees were silenced, and *they dared not any more ask him any question* (Lk. 20:40). Although He impressed them, the Pharisees were not yet silenced.

[§ 141] — 4. By Pharisees

The fourth attack came from the Pharisees, and it, too, was a question of theology.

a. The Attack

Matthew 22:34-36, Mark 12:28

The man who launched the attack was a lawyer with expertise in the details of the Law of Moses. The specific question was: *Teacher, which is the great commandment in the law?* (Mt. 22:36). *What commandment is the first of all?* (Mk. 12:28).

b. The Answer

Matthew 22:37-40, Mark 12:29-34

Yeshua's answer surpassed the lawyer's question. He replied by saying that the most important commandment is found in Deuteronomy 6:4-5, which says: *Hear, O Yisrael: The Lord our God, the Lord is one. You shall love the Lord your God with all your heart and with all your soul and with all your might.*[10] The first part, verse 4, is the famous *Sh'ma*, which Jews recite twice a day, in the morning and evening, and they are also taught to recite it just prior to their death: *Hear O Yisrael; the Lord our God, the Lord is one.* The second part, verse 5, contains the most important of the 613 commandments of the Mosaic Law: one must love the Lord God with every aspect of his being. Although in Rabbinic Judaism verse 4 is used to teach the absolute oneness of God, even the rabbis understood that at times the Hebrew word for *one* used in this verse can mean a plurality.[11]

Yeshua continued, giving the second most important commandment: *You shall love your neighbor as yourself* (Mk. 12:31, quoting Lev.

---

[10] This was taken from the English Standard Version.

[11] An example of this would be Genesis 2:24.

451

19:18). Then He concluded: *On these two commandments the whole law hangs, and the prophets* (Mt. 22:40). These two commandments summarize the Law and the Prophets. Every one of the commandments either concerns a person's relationship to God or their relationship to men. If they love God with their entire being, they will naturally keep the commandments that control their relationship to Him. If they love their neighbor as themselves, they will keep the commandments that control human relationships. This was in keeping with Pharisaic doctrine, and they could not accuse Him of anything. In fact, the lawyer who had questioned Yeshua complimented Him (Mk. 12:32-33).

From then on, the Pharisees were also silenced and did not ask Yeshua any further questions (Mk. 12:34b).

[§ 142] — G. The Challenge by the King

Matthew 22:41-46, Mark 12:35-37, Luke 20:41-44

After the different groups had challenged Him four times, Yeshua challenged them with this question: *What think ye of the Messiah? Whose son is he?* (Mt. 22:42). They answered correctly, *<The son> of David.* The thrust of the Old Testament prophecies was that the Messiah would be the Son of David.

Then came a follow-up question: *How then did David in the Spirit call him Lord, saying, The Lord said unto my Lord, Sit you on my right hand, Till I put your enemies underneath your feet? If David then called him Lord, how is he his son?* (Mt. 22:43-45). This question was based on Psalm 110:1. Normally, a father does not call his own son "lord." The religious leaders were unable to answer Yeshua's question. Despite all they knew and taught about the Messiah, one messianic concept was missing in rabbinic theology: the concept of the God-Man. That was where the answer lay. The Messiah is the God-Man. As to His humanity, He is David's Son. As to His deity, He is David's Lord.

Thus, the Lamb of God had been tested and shown to be without spot or blemish. The attempts to discredit Him or base an accusation against Him, either before the Romans or the Jewish population, had ended in failure.

[§ 143] — H. The Judgment by the King

With a lengthy denunciation, which will be discussed in this section, Yeshua closed His public ministry three years after it had begun. Having commenced at Passover, it ended at Passover. This was His final public proclamation. Until His arrest, Yeshua mostly remained alone with the apostles and other believers.

Yeshua's severe accusations raised against the leadership of Israel in this section of the New Testament are often denounced as being anti-Semitic, ignoring the specifics and the context of the passage. Yeshua did not say terrible things about the Jews as a people; He focused specifically on the Jewish leadership of that day. Furthermore, He followed the tradition of the prophets, like Isaiah, Jeremiah, Ezekiel, and several of the minor prophets, who condemned the Jewish leadership over and over again for leading the nation of Israel astray and bringing divine judgment upon them. So what Yeshua said in Matthew 23 was very much a part of the tradition of the prophets of the Hebrew Bible. While the specific sins were different, the principle remained the same: The leadership of Israel was guilty of leading the nation astray, and they were therefore responsible for bringing judgment upon the people. Furthermore, judgment came upon the nation because the people blindly followed their leaders. This was equally true in the Hebrew Bible and in the New Testament.

1. To the Disciples and Multitudes

Matthew 23:1-12, Mark 12:38-40, Luke 20:45-47

Yeshua initially spoke to the disciples and multitudes about the Pharisees, proclaiming five things about them.

First, the true nature of Pharisaism was hypocrisy: *but do not ye after their works; for they say, and do not* (Mt. 23:3b). Yeshua's prior statement has often been misunderstood: *The scribes and the Pharisees sit on Mosheh's seat: all things whatsoever they bid you, <these> do and observe* (Mt. 23:2-3a). Some interpret this passage to mean that believers ought to obey whatever the rabbis say. However, as this study has shown numerous times, Yeshua frequently disobeyed Pharisaic Law, going out of His way to break it. If He intended believers today to obey rabbinic law, then He Himself could be accused of hypocrisy because of the many examples where He did not do so.

In this verse, Yeshua's statement must be understood in the phraseology of the writings of that day. The seat of Moses was a literal seat. Also called "the throne of the Torah," it was made of wood or stone and placed at the entrance of the town synagogue.[12] Just as Moses sat when judging Israel (Ex. 18:13-26), the local judge sat upon this seat as litigants stated their cases before him, much like today's judges in civil courts of law decide civil suits. After the litigants presented their cases, the judge sitting on Moses' seat decided the verdict based upon case law. These judges had the authority to apply case law in specific civil situations. However, they did not have the authority to issue new religious laws that had to be obeyed. Yeshua simply recognized their authority to decide the application of case law in specific civil situations, and on these issues their decisions were considered final. Just as a judge or jury's decision in a civil suit is final and is to be obeyed by both parties, when the Pharisees sat as judges on Moses' seat and issued a verdict based upon case law, both parties had to obey whether they agreed with the verdict or not. This differs greatly from having to obey the religious law of the Pharisees, their extra-biblical rules and regulations. This passage cannot be used to teach that believers today must observe Orthodox Judaic rules since Yeshua neither obeyed nor obligated believers to obey these laws.

Second, the Pharisees were guilty of burdening others with the Mishnah while they themselves circumvented it: *Yea, they bind heavy*

---

[12] Such a seat has been uncovered in Chorazin at the ancient black basalt synagogue. It is made of the same kind of volcanic stone common in that area. A Hebrew inscription identifies it as Moses' seat.

burdens and grievous to be borne, and lay them on men's shoulders (Mt. 23:4a). The discussion of the concepts of binding and loosing in rabbinic theology in § 85 established that the term "bind" means "forbid." The many religious prohibitions they added to the Mosaic Law turned it into a burden rather than a joy: *but they themselves will not move them with their finger* (Mt. 23:4b).

Third, the Pharisees were guilty of self-righteousness because when they obeyed points of the Mosaic Law, it was with wrong motives. Yeshua gave two examples: *they make broad their phylacteries, and enlarge the borders <of their garments>* (Mt. 23:5). Phylacteries, also known as *tefillin*, are the little boxes that Orthodox Jews bind to their foreheads and left arms in obedience to Deuteronomy 6:8. Inside the box is a parchment on which are written three passages of the Mosaic Law: Exodus 13:3-16, Deuteronomy 6:5-9, and Deuteronomy 11:13-21. While wearing phylacteries was biblical and in accordance with the Mosaic Law, the Pharisees made *broad their phylacteries*, meaning they made them unusually large just *to be seen of men*. They went beyond the requirement of the law out of their own self-righteousness. The Pharisees also enlarged *the borders <of their garments>* (Mt. 23:5b). These are known as the *tzitzit* or *tzitziot*, and they are the tassels that Orthodox Jews still wear on the corners of their garments. This, too, complied with the command of the Mosaic Law in Deuteronomy 22:12. However, the Pharisees made the tassels unusually long, only *to be seen of men*. Thus, they obeyed the Mosaic Law with wrong motives. The proper motivation for obeying the commandments is to show love for God. Yeshua said: *If ye love me, ye will keep my commandments* (Jn. 14:15). The Pharisees followed these commandments just to be seen of men, with self-seeking and self-righteous motives.

Luke added a few additional details about the hypocrisy of the Pharisees. They desired *to walk in long robes* (Lk. 20:46a), reaching down to the feet and decorated with long tzitziot. They were part of a collection of expensive clothes. They also loved *salutations in the marketplaces* (Lk. 20:46b). According to the Talmud, such greetings were required for teachers of the law. Furthermore, they sought the *chief seats in the synagogues* (Lk. 20:46c). These were places of honor, the *prótokathedria* in Greek, and this likely refers to the rows of seats in the synagogues closest to the ark. The ark (*Aron Kodesh*) where the Torah scrolls are kept is considered the holiest place in the synagogue. Finally, the Pharisees were eager to sit in the *chief places at feasts* (Lk. 20:46d), the *prótoklisia* in Greek. To sit next to the host during a banquet was an honor.

Fourth, the Pharisees loved man-exalting titles and wanted to be *called rabbi, teacher, father and master* (Mt. 23:7-10). These four titles were used in teacher-pupil relationships, and so the term "father" refers to a religious rather than a familial relationship. The Pharisees coveted these titles for the accompanying status and the extreme authority they exercised over the decision-making processes of their pupils in matters totally unrelated to discipleship. The titles did much more than merely describe an office, a position, or a job function. For example, the rabbi was considered as the most important person in a disciple's life, surpassing even the father. Yet, not all rabbis considered this exalted position the highest good, as a statement from the Talmud proves: "He who humbles himself for the sake of the Torah in this world is magnified in the next; and he who makes himself a servant to the [study of the] Torah in this world becomes free in the next."[13] This statement by Rabbi Jeremiah expresses the proper motivation and resonates with Yeshua's view of leadership and discipleship: *And whosoever shall exalt himself shall be humbled; and whosoever shall humble himself shall be exalted* (Mt. 23:12). This was not the prevalent view in first-century Judaism.

Fifth, the Pharisees prostituted their religion by using their prayers to hide their covetousness, which was demonstrated in the way they foreclosed on the homes of widows: *they that devour widows' houses, and for a pretence make long prayers; these shall receive greater condemnation* (Mk. 12:40). Under the Mosaic Law, they were to provide special protection for those who had lost their husbands (Ex. 22:22-23). In deference to this commandment, a Pharisee would foreclose on the home of a widow only after he prayed about it, thus prostituting their religious requirement. When James defined pure religion in 1:26-27, he included taking care of widows; mere prayer could not acquit the Pharisees for their failure.

---

[13] *b. Baba Meẓi'a* 85b.

2. To the Pharisees

Matthew 23:13-36

Yeshua directly pronounced seven woes upon the Pharisees for a variety of sins, forming a circle beginning and ending with the same sin.

The first woe condemned the Pharisees for two reasons: *Because ye shut the kingdom of heaven against men: for ye enter not in yourselves, neither suffer ye them that are entering in to enter* (Mt. 23:13). Yeshua condemned the Pharisees because they rejected His Messiahship and because they led the nation in rejecting Him.

The second woe condemned them, *For ye compass sea and land to make one proselyte; and when he is become so, ye make him twofold more a son of hell than yourselves* (Mt. 23:15). They went everywhere to convert people to Pharisaic Judaism, but often the converts became even more zealous legalists than the Pharisees themselves.

The third woe condemned the Pharisees for switching priorities by focusing on the consecrated and not the Consecrator (Mt. 23:16-22). Yeshua provided two examples from rabbinic theology. The first example was the rabbis' claim that swearing an oath on the basis of the Temple did not obligate the person to keep it; however, making an oath on the basis of the gold of the Temple required the person to keep it (Mt. 23:16). This gold was no different than gold anywhere else in the world, so what made this gold special was its location in the Jewish Temple. The Temple sanctified the gold; the gold did not sanctify the Temple, so the rabbis' priority was misdirected. The second example was that making an oath on the basis of the altar did not obligate the person to keep it; however, swearing on the basis of the sacrifice on the altar obligated one to keep the oath (Mt. 23:18). The dead body of the animal sacrifice was no different from any other animal's dead body found anywhere else in the world. What made it special was its placement on the holy altar. The altar sanctified the sacrifice; the sacrifice did not sanctify the altar. The Pharisees were again guilty of giving priority to the consecrated and not the Consecrator.

The fourth woe condemned the Pharisees for focusing on the minors and ignoring the majors (Mt. 23:23-24). Yeshua stated: *For ye tithe mint and anise and cumin* (Mt. 23:23a), referring to the three smallest seeds known in Israel in the first century. The Mosaic Law required tithing of the harvest, but not necessarily tithing of the smallest herbs. In fact, the Talmud states that tithing of herbs is from the rabbis, an Oral Law, rather than a specific Mosaic commandment. Tithing herbs by itself was not wrong, because Yeshua goes on to say, *but these ye ought to have done* (Mt. 23:23c). The problem was what they left undone: *justice, and mercy, and faith* (Mt. 23:23b). These three elements were far more important than tithing even the smallest seed, so the Pharisees were guilty of focusing on the minors and ignoring the majors.

The fifth woe condemned the Pharisees for being far more concerned with the external demands of the law than the internal demands of the law (Mt. 23:25-26). Yeshua compared them with those who wash the outside of the cup and the platter after eating, but not the inside where the food was found, leaving the dishes dirty with spoiling food. They will eat again from the inside of the cup, so the old will corrupt the new. The Mosaic Law required a balance between both external and internal conformity.

In the last three woes, Yeshua called the Pharisees blind five times: *ye blind guides* (Mt. 23:16); *Ye fools and blind* (Mt. 23:17); *Ye blind* (Mt. 23:19); *Ye blind guides* (Mt. 23:24); and *You blind Pharisee* (Mt. 23:26).

The sixth woe condemned the Pharisees for their hypocrisy and compared them to *whited sepulchres* (Mt. 23:27-28). To this day, tombstones throughout Israel are given a fresh coat of white paint once a year. Members of the tribe of Levi, especially the Cohens, the priestly line within the tribe of Levi, were forbidden to come in contact with tombs because it rendered them ceremonially unclean. The sepulchres are given a coat of white paint every year to ensure their visibility. On the outside, they look nice and clean, but inside nothing has changed. They still contain corrupt dead men's bones. Such is the nature of legalism. Obedience to man-made rules and regulations, whether they are Mishnaic rules or church rules, might make a person look religious and spiritual on the outside, but changes nothing on the inside.

The seventh woe elaborates upon the first woe, condemning the Pharisees for rejecting the prophets' testimony of the Messiah (Mt. 23:29-36). Yeshua's point is that they will be held accountable for all of the blood of the Old Testament prophets in addition to the rejection of His Messiahship. The prophets had said everything they were going to say about the coming of the Messiah, and the Old Testament canon had been closed for well over four-and-a-half centuries. To reject Yeshua as the Messiah automatically included the rejection of the testimony of the prophets. No one claiming to believe the prophets can reject Yeshua as the Messiah. Furthermore, the Pharisees heard Yochanan's proclamation of the arrival of the King. Finally, during His own public ministry, Yeshua authenticated His claim to be the Messiah with signs and wonders, including the miracles the Pharisees themselves had labeled as uniquely messianic. They still rejected Him; consequently, they will be held accountable for the written truth revealed to them. In this context, Yeshua referred to two men, Abel and Zechariah (Mt. 23:35), following the order of the Hebrew Bible. The number of books is the same in the Hebrew and Christian Old Testaments, but the order is different. Genesis is first in both; however, the last book in the Jewish Scriptures is II Chronicles, not Malachi. Abel is found in Genesis 4:8, the first book, and Zechariah is found in II Chronicles 24:20-21, the last book in the Jewish order. By naming these two men, Yeshua declared that the Pharisees would be held accountable for everything from Genesis to II Chronicles. This Jewish figure of speech indicated the whole body of revealed written truth, much as people today use a similar figure of speech when they say "from Genesis to Revelation."

Yeshua concluded His condemnation of the Pharisees by declaring, *Verily I say unto you, All these things shall come upon this generation* (Mt. 23:36). The emphasis is again on the guilt of this generation, which was held accountable for committing the unpardonable sin of rejecting the whole body of revealed written truth.

3. The Lament

Matthew 23:37-39

Yeshua's denunciation of the leaders of Israel ended with a lament and marks the official closing of His public ministry three years after it had started.

Yeshua began His lament by summarizing His ministry to Israel (Mt. 23:37): How often He had longed to spread out His hands and give the holy city the messianic protection predicted by the prophets of old! But the verse ends, *and ye would not!* Literally, in Greek, they *willed it not* when they rejected Him.

Yeshua then stated, *Behold, your house* (Mt. 23:38), that is, the Temple, and prophesied that it was destined to lie desolate. It was destroyed forty years later in A.D. 70.

Still speaking to the leadership of Israel, Yeshua continued, *Ye shall not see me henceforth till ye shall say, Blessed <is> he that comes in the name of the Lord* (Mt. 23:39). With this official messianic greeting based upon Psalm 118:26, Yeshua established the precondition for the second coming: He will not return until the Jewish leaders ask Him to come back. Just as the Jewish leaders once led the nation to reject Him, a day must come when they will lead the nation to accept Him.

This, in turn, provides the theological foundation for anti-Semitism. Satan has led, is leading, and will lead a special war against the Jews in general, but in particular against Messianic Jews. Satan knows that his career will be over when the Messiah returns at the request of the Jewish people. If he could succeed in destroying the Jews before they plead for His return, then Yeshua will not come back, and Satan's career will be eternally safe. This explains the motivation for Satan's relentless war against the Jews, the Crusades, the Russian pogroms, the Nazi Holocaust, etc. Once Satan is confined to the earth in the tribulation (Rev. 12:7-17), knowing his time is short, he will expend all of his energies trying to destroy the Jews once and for all. Anti-Semitism in any form, active or passive, whether it is political, national, racial, ethnic, social, religious, theological, or otherwise, is part of the satanic strategy to prevent the second coming.

After establishing the precondition to His return, Israel's national regeneration headed by the leadership of Israel, Yeshua closed His public ministry, ending where it began, in the Temple compound.

[§ 144] — I. Instruction at the Treasury

Mark 12:41-44, Luke 21:1-4

As Yeshua left the Temple compound for the last time, He passed the treasury area, where 13 large boxes, known as corban chests, were kept. He *sat down over against the treasury* (Mk. 12:41), by the 13 chests, and gave His disciples a vivid picture of the distinction He had made between the external and the internal. Mark pointed out that many wealthy people cast in a lot of money (Mk. 12:41). However, a poor widow only cast in *two mites* (Mk. 12:42; Lk. 21:2). During the first-century, Jewish, Greek, and Roman coins circulated in Israel, and the Jewish coins included shekels, half shekels, quarter shekels, and leptons. Luke and Mark called these last coins "mites." Made of copper, they had the least value of all the coins, much like the U.S. penny today. The text does not state the age of the widow, only that she was poor. Incidentally, her contribution was the legal minimum; putting in less than two mites was prohibited. The observers might have disdained the widow for her two mites compared with the myriad of money cast in by the wealthy. Yeshua, however, distinguished between the two types of gifts, noting that the wealthy *did cast in of their superfluity* (Mk. 12:44). They were so wealthy that what they gave neither hurt them, nor did it affect their lifestyle or indicate that they trusted the Lord. In contrast, the widow essentially gave all that she had, indicating that she had to trust God to provide for her basic needs. Her offering was acceptable to the Lord and provided an object lesson of what Yeshua had just taught His disciples (§ 143): that true conformity to the law must be both internal and external, not merely the latter.

VIII. The Preparation for the Death of the King
— §§ 145–164 —

The eighth division of the life of Messiah begins with a major prophetic discourse from the King and ends with the agony of Gethsemane.

[§ 145] — A. The Olivet Discourse: The Prophecies of the King

When Yeshua closed His public ministry, He clearly proclaimed that His return depended upon Israel's specific belief and request (Mt. 23:37-39). Previously, when He rescinded the offer of the messianic kingdom, He promised to offer it again to a future generation (Mt. 12-13). In Jericho, Yeshua told His disciples that the kingdom would not immediately appear (Lk. 19:11-28). In the following section, the Olivet Discourse, Yeshua answers the question: What will be the circumstances that will cause Israel to call Him back?

This section also marks the end of Yeshua's prophetic ministry. Theologians have observed that the Messiah holds three offices—those of prophet, priest, and king. However, He does not function in all three offices simultaneously, but sequentially. During His first coming, He held the position of a prophet. A prophet receives direct revelation from God, proclaims God's will for his own generation, and predicts future events, both near and far. In the Sermon on the Mount, Yeshua proclaimed God's will for His own generation as He expounded on the righteousness of the law. In this section, Yeshua predicts future events, both near and far, and presents these events in basic chronological sequence, with the exception of two times, clearly indicating when He does so.

With His ascension, Yeshua's function as a prophet changed to that of a priest. He is presently the high priest in heaven, ever making intercession for believers. So Yeshua was a prophet, He is a priest, but He will be a king, specifically the King of the Jews and of the world, beginning at His second coming. The Olivet Discourse deals with the circumstances that will bring about Yeshua's functioning in this third office, the office of king.

This book surveys the life of the Messiah presented in the four Gospels, so this section only deals with the basics of the Olivet Discourse, or the prophecies of the King, rather than every detail, as would a book on eschatology.

1. The Historical Setting

Matthew 24:1-2, Mark 13:1-2, Luke 21:5-6

It was still Tuesday. Yeshua, having publicly denounced the scribes and the Pharisees for leading the nation in rejecting Him, spelled out the precondition for His second coming. As He left the Temple compound for the last time, His disciples pointed out the buildings: *and his disciples came to him to show him the buildings of the temple* (Mt. 24:1), emphasizing the structures themselves. Evidently, they were particularly focused upon the stones: *Teacher, behold, what manner of stones and what manner of buildings!* (Mk. 13:1). Luke wrote: *And as some spoke of the temple, how it was adorned with goodly stones and offerings* (Lk. 21:5).

Herod had begun restoring the Temple and enlarging the compound in the year 20 B.C. While the building was completed in a matter of months, the outer courts and structures were still under construction when this event took place in A.D. 30 and would not be completed until A.D. 64. Six years later, in A.D. 70, the whole Temple compound was totally destroyed.

The stones the disciples pointed out are called "Herodian blocks" and were the largest stones used in construction in Israel in those days. They averaged about ten to twelve feet in length and weighed eight to ten tons, but many were much larger and much heavier, up to four hundred tons. Today in Jerusalem, many of these impressive stones are visible, especially on the south and west walls.

When the disciples pointed out the buildings, Yeshua prophesied: *There shall not be left here one stone upon another, that shall not be thrown down* (Mt. 24:2). This prophecy was fulfilled literally in A.D. 70, and to this day, the Temple sits in ruins so that there is not one stone upon another.

2. The Three Questions

Matthew 24:3, Mark 13:3-4, Luke 21:7

Yeshua's prophecy regarding the coming destruction of Jerusalem and especially the Temple compound caused the apostles to pose three questions, each asking Yeshua for the sign which would forewarn them of these things about to happen. To understand Yeshua's answer, both Matthew and Luke must be consulted. Matthew observed: *And as he sat on the mount of Olives* (Mt. 24:3a). Yeshua sat, the posture from which a rabbi would teach, and presented the message often referred to as the Olivet Discourse. Matthew stated that the disciples asked Yeshua the question. Mark specifically stated that four disciples approached Him: the brothers Peter and Andrew, and the brothers James and Yochanan.

Matthew worded the three questions this way: *Tell us, when shall these things be? And what <shall be> the sign of your coming, and of the end of the world?* (Mt. 24:3b). Luke, however, provided more detail about the nature of the first question concerning signs: *Teacher, when therefore shall these things be? And what <shall be> the sign when these things are about to come to pass?* (Lk. 21:7).

In an attempt to systematize the questions, we can note the following:

✡ Question 1: What is the sign of the coming destruction of Jerusalem and the Temple?

✡ Question 2: What is the sign of your coming, or what is the sign that the second coming is about to occur?

✡ Question 3: What is the sign of the end of the age? The Jews spoke of two ages: this age, meaning the present age, and the age to come, which is the messianic age. So, what is the sign that this age is about to end and the age to come, the messianic kingdom, is about to be established?

Keep in mind that the apostles still did not understand the program of death and resurrection, nor the program of two comings. Hence, they asked the questions based on their perspective at that time, which was shaped by the Jewish eschatology that speaks of the present age as *this age* and the messianic age as *the age to come*. They wished to know when the current age would end and the new messianic age begin, anticipating that it would happen at this Passover. While the apostles asked their questions based on what they understood, Yeshua answered them based on what would actually occur. It should also be noted that Yeshua did not answer the questions in the order in which they were asked. He answered the third question first, the first question second, and the second question last. Furthermore, not all three Gospel writers recorded all of His answers to all three of the questions. Mark and Matthew both ignored Yeshua's answer to the first question, while Luke chose to record it.

3. The General Characteristics of the Age
Between the Two Comings

Matthew 24:4-6, Mark 13:5-7, Luke 21:8-9

Yeshua answered the third question first, both negatively and positively. In this section, He answered the question negatively, citing two elements which in no way indicate that the last days have begun. They are not signs of the last days.

He told them the first general characteristic of the present age: *many shall come in my name, saying, I am the Messiah* (Mt. 24:5).[1] The first element that will define the entire period is the rise of false messiahs. This alone is not prophetically significant and is not a sign of the last days. In Jewish history, Yeshua was the first to claim to be the Messiah, followed by a long line of false messiahs, beginning with a man named Simon Bar Cochba, the leader of the second Jewish revolt against Rome, in A.D. 132-135. More recent false messiahs were Jacob Frank of Poland (1726-1791) and Menachem Schneerson (1902-1994).[2] Some of these men had a large worldwide following, such as Shabbetai Tzvi in the seventeenth century. Among the Gentiles, false messiahs arose throughout history as well, yet none were prophetically significant or a sign of the last days.

Yeshua said the second general characteristic of this age is: *ye shall hear of wars and rumors of wars* (Mt. 24:6a). This refers to local wars; but again, by itself, it is not prophetically significant. The entire church age will be characterized by local wars. Nevertheless, the verse has led some to assume that the many conflicts in the Middle East must be prophetically significant. Americans often suspect that a war affecting the United States must be prophetically significant, yet careful study of the Scriptures shows that America is not mentioned in any of the prophetic passages. Local wars in the Middle East or those in which the United States is engaged are not signs of the end.

---

[1] The present age can also be called church age, which means it began with Acts 2.

[2] While many of his followers declared him to be the Messiah, there is no record that he himself made that claim.

In summary, local wars and the rise of false messiahs are character-istics of the entire church age, not signs of the last days, and Yeshua said that *<these things> must needs come to pass; but the end is not yet* (Mt. 24:6b).

4. The Sign of the End of the Age

Matthew 24:7-8, Mark 13:8, Luke 21:10-11

After answering the apostles' question negatively, Yeshua answered positively, providing the specific sign of the end of the age. Matthew recorded it as follows: *For nation shall rise against nation, and kingdom against kingdom; and there shall be famines and earthquakes in divers places. But all these things are the beginning of travail* (Mt. 24:7-8). The term *travail* means "birth pang," referring to the series of contractions a woman undergoes before giving birth to a baby. This term is used in many Old Testament prophecies that pictured the last days as a series of contractions before the birth of the new—the messianic—age. Yeshua was specifically referring to the birth pang at the beginning of contractions, the first birth pang. This first birth pang is the rise of na-tion against nation, kingdom against kingdom. While the *wars and rumors of wars* were not a sign of the last days, this event is the first sign of the end, the very first birth pang. The rise of nation against nation and kingdom against kingdom was a rabbinic idiom for a world war. Yeshua's point was that a world war, in contrast to local wars, would signal the beginning of the last days.

The rabbinic understanding of the phrase *nation against nation and kingdom against kingdom* was based upon the Hebrew Scriptures, where it was an idiom for a total conflict within the area of the context. For example, the context of Isaiah 19:1-2 is Egypt, and the idiom de-scribes total conflict throughout the land of Egypt. Also, in II Chronicles 15:3-6, the context is the nations of the Middle East, de-scribing total conflict throughout this area. In the context of Yeshua's discourse, the world (or earth) is mentioned several times (Mt. 24:14, 21, 30, 35; Mk. 13:27, 31; Lk. 21:26, 33, 35). In this context, the idiom would refer to a worldwide conflict. So, when they saw a world war, in contrast to local wars, that would be a sign that the last days had begun.

The last days did not begin in 1948, when Israel became a state, but with World War I (1914-1918). For all practical purposes, the Second World War (1939-1945) was a continuation of the first, and both wars had a decisive impact on Jewish history. As far as the prophetic timetable is concerned, the issue is how world events affect the Jewish people and Israel. The events of World War I were the impetus for a massive growth of the Zionist movement, and the events of World War II and the Holocaust set the stage for the establishment of the state of Israel. These two world wars constitute the first birth pang,-and according to Yeshua, it would be coupled with famines and earthquakes. Beginning with an estimated 19 million people who starved to death in India in 1900, several major famines occurred in Russia, Ukraine, and China between the two world wars.[3] There is a general consensus that a tremendous rise in earthquakes has occurred.[4] No doubt, this is influenced by the improved ability to detect earthquakes, but that does not suffice to explain the increase since the time in which the first sign, the first birth pang, was given. Several other birth pangs have occurred since World War I, such as Israel becoming a state in 1948 and Jerusalem falling under Jewish control in 1967. These things are prophetically significant.

---

[3] See Cormac Ó Gráda, *Famine: A Short History* (Princeton, Ny. Princeton University Press, 2009), pp. 23-24.

[4] In connection with World War I, a partial list of victims of earthquakes includes the following: 1905, India, 19,000 killed; 1908, Italy, 70,000 killed; 1915, Italy, 32,600 killed; 1920, China, 200,000 killed; 1923, Japan, 143,000 killed. (Source: "Historic World Earthquakes." USGS. December 1, 2012. Accessed November 20, 2015. http://earthquake.usgs.gov/earthquakes/world/historical.php). Since then, there have been many more earthquakes.

5. The Personal Experiences of the Apostles

Mark 13:9-13, Luke 21:12-19

Generally, the Olivet Discourse provides a chronological sequence of events. However, twice the text offers a clue when Yeshua broke with the chronological order, as is the case in the verses above. Luke added a detail that puts the prophecies in chronological order: *But before all these things* (Lk. 21:12a). Before what things? Before the first birth pang signaling the beginning of the last days happens (Lk. 21:10b-11), the apostles will have nine specific experiences.

First, the Jewish community would reject them (Mk. 13:9a; Lk. 21:12b). Yeshua mentioned that they would be delivered to councils and synagogues, Jewish establishments, where they would suffer rejection.

Second, forced to stand *before governors and kings*, Gentiles would also reject them (Mk. 13:9b; Lk. 21:12c). In those days, governors and kings were all Gentiles, and so the statement shows they should be ready for widespread rejection by the Gentile community as well.

Third, these persecutions would provide opportunities for a testimony: *It shall turn out unto you for a testimony* (Lk. 21:13). As the Jewish and Gentile communities persecuted them, they would have the chance to testify to their faith.

Fourth, in spite of opposition, they would preach the gospel everywhere: *And the gospel must first be preached unto all the nations* (Mk. 13:10). Unfortunately, no records show how this was fulfilled in the apostolic period. By the time Paul wrote Colossians, he affirmed that the gospel had been proclaimed to *all creation under heaven* (Col. 1:5-6, 23).

Fifth, Yeshua promised that the apostles would receive divine utterance when taken before a court of law: *be not anxious beforehand what ye shall speak: but whatsoever shall be given you in that hour, that speak ye: for it is not ye that speak, but the Holy Spirit* (Mk. 13:11). Luke noted: *Settle it therefore in your hearts, not to meditate beforehand how to answer: for I will give you a mouth and wisdom, which all your adversaries shall not be able to withstand or to gainsay* (Lk. 21:14-15). The specific promise here is to the apostles. They had no need to prepare a legal brief to defend themselves when taken before a judge in a court of law because they would be given divine utterance. The book of Acts records that when the apostles were brought before either a Jewish or a Gentile court of law, they were given *a mouth and wisdom*, which their enemies could not *withstand* or *gainsay*. Some take these verses out of context as an excuse not to prepare for a Sunday school lesson or a sermon. The speaker claims the promise that when he opens his mouth, the Holy Spirit will fill it. Any person with discernment realizes that the message from the preacher's mouth is not from the Holy Spirit and results from the lack of study. Yeshua's promise was specifically for the apostles and limited to cases where they were involved in legal court cases.

Sixth, family members would also reject the apostles (Mk. 13:12; Lk. 21:16), making it more personal. They knew they would be widely rejected by the Jewish and Gentile communities, but now they heard their own family members would also personally reject them.

Seventh, all men would hate them. Mark stated: *And ye shall be hated of all men for my name's sake* (Mk. 13:13a). Luke recorded: *and <some> of you shall they cause to be put to death. And ye shall be hated of all men for my name's sake* (Lk. 21:16-17). The apostles would be hated so much that some would die as martyrs. In fact, ten of Yeshua's eleven faithful apostles were killed for their faith. Only Yochanan died of old age. Thus, they were told that some of them would die before the beginning of the birth pangs, before the last days ever came.

Eighth, Yeshua promised: *And not a hair of your head shall perish* (Lk. 21:18). Some have pulled this promise out of context to teach a false application of physical security. Contextually, that interpretation is impossible because earlier Yeshua said that *<some> of you shall they cause to be put to death* (Lk. 21:16). The solution to this alleged contradiction is that Yeshua's promise refers to spiritual, not physical security. While the apostles' lives were indeed threatened, their salvation was not.

Ninth, in spite of all the opposition from the Jewish and Gentile communities and their own families, the apostles would win souls. Yeshua stated: *In your patience ye shall win your souls* (Lk. 21:19). By the time the last apostle died, churches were established throughout the world, both inside and outside the Roman Empire.

6. The Sign of the Fall of Jerusalem

Luke 21:20-24

In this section, Yeshua answered the apostles' first question, What would be the sign that Jerusalem and the Temple were about to be destroyed? Only Luke recorded the Messiah's answer, which again shows his special concern for the city of Jerusalem in his Gospel. The sign was: *But when ye see Yerushalayim compassed with armies, then know that her desolation is at hand* (Lk. 21:20). When the first Jewish revolt against Rome broke out in the year A.D. 66, the Roman General Cestius Gallus brought his legions out of Caesarea in order to besiege and surround the city. The messianic church of Jerusalem took that to be the sign Yeshua had given and, in obedience to His instructions, left the city before it was destroyed: *Then let them that are in Yehudah flee unto the mountains; and let them that are in the midst of her depart out; and let not them that are in the country enter therein* (Lk. 21:21). With these words, the Messiah instructed the Jewish believers to leave Jerusalem. If they were in the city, they were to get out. If they were out in the country, they were not to go into the city.

This was exactly what the Jewish believers intended to do when they saw the Roman armies surrounding Jerusalem. However, as long as the soldiers besieged the city, they could not flee. A misjudgment by Cestius Gallus provided the opportunity to flee. The general mistakenly assumed that he was facing a regional uprising around Jerusalem. He soon discovered that it was a widespread, grassroots revolt, with Jewish guerilla forces cutting his supply lines. As a result, he was forced to lift the siege and retreat to Caesarea. Jerusalem would not be besieged again for two years.

The messianic community took the opportunity to abandon the city. Over twenty thousand believers from Jerusalem joined by thousands of believers from other parts of the country, such as Judea, Galilee, and even the Golan Heights, fled to Pella, where they waited out the war.

Pella, one of the Greek cities of the Decapolis, was located outside of the war zone, south of the Sea of Galilee and east of the Jordan River. As a result, Jewish believers survived that conflict.

Luke described the A.D. 70 judgment as *days of vengeance* and as *wrath unto this people* (Lk. 21:22-23). The *vengeance* and the *wrath* were prophesied judgments for the unpardonable sin. Indeed, 1,100,000 Jews were killed in the first Jewish revolt, and 97,000 were taken into slavery. Because the messianic believers were obedient to Yeshua's command to abandon the area, not one lost his life.

Luke concluded: *And they shall fall by the edge of the sword, and shall be led captive into all the nations: and Yerushalayim shall be trodden down of the Gentiles, until the times of the Gentiles be fulfilled* (Lk. 21:24). We now live in "the times of the Gentiles," the era of Gentile domination of Jerusalem and the Jewish people. According to the book of Daniel, this period spans from the destruction of Jerusalem and the Babylonian Captivity in 586 B.C. to the second coming of the Messiah—from the dethronement of the last Davidic king (Zedekiah) until the enthronement of the Messianic Davidic King. Four Gentile empires will rise and fall during the times of the Gentiles, with the Antichrist as the last ruler until his reign is terminated by the second coming.

The book of Daniel provides the background necessary for proper understanding of the verses above. Unfortunately, some people, ignoring Daniel, wrongly assume that the times of the Gentiles ended in the year 1967 with the Six Day War, when Israel conquered east Jerusalem. They assume that not even a temporary Jewish control of the city can occur during the times of the Gentiles. However, the Six Day War in 1967 was the fourth temporary takeover of Jerusalem by Jewish forces. They lost the previous three, and they will lose this one too, as will be shown below. The first takeover occurred during the Maccabean period (165-63 B.C.) and lasted slightly over a century. During this time, the Jews dominated Jerusalem, but they lost control to the Romans. The second time they had full control of the city was during the first Jewish revolt (A.D. 66-70), and they lost it again. The third time was during the second Jewish revolt, also called the Bar Cochba revolt (A.D. 132-135), but again, they lost the control. 1967 was the fourth

Jewish takeover of Jerusalem. However, they will lose their control in the middle of the tribulation. The book of Revelation points this out and states specifically that the city of Jerusalem and the Temple compound will be trodden down by the Gentiles for a period of 42 months (Rev. 11:1-2). Thus, the times of the Gentiles have not ended. Even at the present time, the majority of the population of the Old City of Jerusalem is Gentile. Current political events have also shown that Israel is not yet exercising full sovereignty over the Old City or the Temple area. Even in the Olivet Discourse, Yeshua talked about the future loss of the city of Jerusalem.

7. The Great Tribulation

a. The First Half

Matthew 24:9-14

Giving a brief account of the first half of the tribulation, Yeshua mentioned five specific things. First, the saints will be persecuted (Mt. 24:9). People will be saved after the rapture, so there will be saints in the first half of the tribulation. However, many of these will undergo tremendous persecution. These are the same as the fifth-seal saints described in Revelation 6:9-11.

Second, many false prophets will arise. They will *lead many astray* (Mt. 24:11).

Third, sin will increase because the restraint of lawlessness will be removed (Mt. 24:12; II Thess. 2:6-7).

Fourth, Yeshua promised that those Jews who endure to the end of the tribulation will be saved (Mt. 24:13). This does not teach that unless believers today endure to the end, they will not be saved, or that they will lose their salvation. Rather, the context deals with Jews during the tribulation who endure to the end, survive physically, and will be alive when Yeshua returns. They will also be part of Israel's national salvation, so they will be saved spiritually. Therefore, the main point of this verse is that the Jews who survive to the end of the tribulation will be saved physically and spiritually.

Fifth, the gospel will be proclaimed throughout the world. The statement is very explicit: *And this gospel of the kingdom shall be preached in the whole world for a testimony unto all the nations; and then shall the end come* (Mt. 24:14). The phrase *in the whole world* could be taken as a general term, not necessarily including every specific country. However, Yeshua went on to say that the gospel will be preached *for a testimony unto all the nations*, indicating a totality. Some have interpreted this as prophecy for the church, saying that Yeshua will return after the church evangelizes the whole world. However, the context focuses on Israel, and the prophecy will be accomplished by 144,000 Jews proclaiming the gospel throughout the world (Rev. 7:1-8). Myriads of Gentiles from every nation, every tribe, and every language group will emerge from the tribulation as believers due to the ministry of the 144,000 Jews (Rev. 7:9-17), having *washed their robes . . . in the blood of the Lamb* (Rev. 7:14). The gospel will indeed go out to all nations, not by the church, but by the 144,000 Jews of the book of Revelation.

b. The Second Half

Matthew 24:15-28, Mark 13:14-23

Concerning the second half of the tribulation, Yeshua mentioned eight specific things.

(1) The Abomination of Desolation

Yeshua identified the sign that will begin this time period: *When therefore ye see the abomination of desolation, which was spoken of through Daniel the prophet, standing in the holy place* (Mt. 24:15). In 167 B.C., the Greek king Antiochus Epiphanes profaned the Temple in Jerusalem by setting up an altar to Zeus. He "also brought into the temple things that were forbidden, so that the altar was covered with abominable offerings prohibited by the laws" (II Maccabees 6:4b-5), including a pig. This event has become known as the abomination of desolation. However, Yeshua mentioned the abomination of desolation roughly two hundred years after this incident, adding that it *was spoken of through Daniel the prophet.* Obviously, He expected the apostles to know this specific prophecy. While Daniel's prophecy in chapter eight speaks of the events fulfilled in 167 B.C. by Antiochus Epiphanes, chapters nine and ten clearly predict an incident that will occur during the tribulation. The prophecy states that the abomination of desolation will occur exactly in the middle of the tribulation: *and in the midst of the week he shall cause the sacrifice and the oblation to cease; and upon the wing of abominations shall come one that makes desolate* (Dan. 9:27b). This means that the middle of the tribulation will begin with a specific event occurring in two stages: The first stage will occur when the Antichrist *sits in the temple of God, setting himself forth as God* (II Thess. 2:4). The second stage will occur when the false prophet makes an image of the Antichrist and sets it within the Holy of Holies of the Jewish Temple (Mt. 24:15; Rev. 13:11-15). This image will be allowed to stand there continually for 1,290 days, which is thirty days beyond the end of the tribulation (Dan. 12:11). Thus, the apostles knew from the book of Daniel that the abomination of desolation will signal the breaking of the seven-year covenant between Israel and the Antichrist, the beginning of the second half of the tribulation, and from that point to the second coming will be exactly 1,260 days. It also signals the beginning of the final war against the Jews, as Satan will seek to destroy them in order to prevent the second coming.

(2) Israel's Flight from the Land

Yeshua then prophesied Israel's flight from the land. The abomination of desolation will signal the Jews that it is time to leave: *then let them that are in Yehudah flee unto the mountains* (Mt. 24:16). Urgency is emphasized. Anyone on the housetop for any reason must not collect their possessions from the chambers within (Mt. 24:17), but instead must immediately make their way out of the country. If anyone plowing in the field hears of this event taking place, they must not waste the few precious moments to go back to the *kibbutz* living quarters to take so much as a coat (Mt. 24:18). They must leave the field and escape out of the country.

Matthew listed three possible difficulties for a quick escape. The first obstacle is for pregnant women in the last stages of pregnancy or mothers with small babes in arms; women in these conditions cannot flee as quickly as necessary (Mt. 24:19). The second adversity is if the abomination of desolation is set up in the winter months (Mt. 24:20a). Israel's fixed rainy season extends from mid-October to early May. Rainfall peaks from December through February. During the winter months, when the rain falls on the mountain ranges of Israel, water floods normally dry riverbeds (known as *wadis*) with tremendous force, carrying tons of rock and debris. Israelis enjoy hiking through these picturesque riverbeds, many of which resemble miniature Grand Canyons. Often in the winter months, the waters flow suddenly and heavily down the wadis from distant rainfall. Almost every year, Israeli hikers are reportedly killed that way. If the Jews will have to flee the land by means of these wadis during the winter months, their escape would be much more difficult and dangerous. The third difficulty is if the abomination of desolation is set up on a Sabbath day (Mt. 24:20b). Public life, corporate dealings, and public transportation largely halt in Israel from sundown Friday until sundown Saturday, and this will make fleeing Jews dependent on cars or other means of private transportation.

(3) Unparalleled Global Anti-Semitism

The second half of the tribulation will be a time of unparalleled anti-Semitism: *for then shall be great tribulation, such as has not been from the beginning of the world until now, no, nor ever shall be* (Mt. 24:21). The Jewish people have frequently endured local, regional, national, and even continental anti-Semitism. However, under the Antichrist's leadership, the whole globe will turn against the Jews, and they will face worldwide persecution. Using the Antichrist and the false prophet, Satan will inaugurate his last Nazi-like attempt to annihilate the Jewish people once and for all. It is described as the worst period of persecution that the Jews have ever suffered; however, they will never suffer anything like this ever again (Jer. 30:4-7; Dan. 12:1).

Satan's zeal to annihilate the Jewish people seems random unless one understands God's prophetic timeline. If we keep in mind that the precondition to the second coming of the Messiah is Israel's national salvation, Satan's actions become more understandable. Satan knows that Yeshua's return will end his domination of the earth. He also knows that the second coming depends on the Jewish people pleading for Yeshua to come back. So if he were to succeed in annihilating the Jews before they have a chance to ask the Messiah to return, his career would be safe for all eternity. Once Satan is confined to the earth in the second half of the tribulation, knowing his time is short, he will inaugurate one last effort to try to destroy the Jews once and for all (Rev. 12:6-17). For this reason, the Jews will flee the land.

(4) The Survival of the Jewish People

In spite of this worldwide attempt to annihilate the Jewish people, they will survive: *And except those days had been shortened, no flesh would have been saved: but for the elect's sake those days shall be shortened* (Mt. 24:22). Some assume that the word *elect* always refers to the elect of the church, but that is simply not the case. The Bible uses the word *elect* in three senses:

- ✿ Elect angels (angels elected not to fall),
- ✿ Individual election (saints who are elected for salvation on an individual basis),
- ✿ The elect nation (the nation of Israel).

The context of this statement is Jerusalem, Judea, and the Jewish Temple. Hence, in this verse, Yeshua referred to the elect nation, Israel. The promise is that the Jewish people will survive despite Satan's attempts to annihilate them.

The phrase *those days had been shortened* has also been erroneously taken to mean that the tribulation will not last a full seven years. However, that contradicts many other passages of Scripture. The tribulation will be seven years, with each half enumerated by Daniel and Yochanan in terms like "a time and times and half a time" (Dan. 7:25; 12:7; Rev. 12:14), or "42 months" (Rev. 11:2; 13:5), as well as "1,260 days" (Rev. 12:6). These prophetic passages confirm that the tribulation will be a full seven years or two periods of three-and-a-half full years. The word *shortened* infers the sense of "being cut short," meaning that this time will not be allowed to continue for one second beyond 1,260 days. The period of Jewish persecution allotted by God will last exactly three-and-a-half years, and then will suddenly be cut short. The purpose of cutting it short is, for the sake of the elect Israel, to ensure that Jewish people survive. According to Zechariah 13:8-9, two-thirds of the Jewish population will die in the tribulation. God will end the period of persecution to ensure the survival of the remaining one-third.

(5) False Messiahs

The great tribulation will be a time of the rise of many false messiahs (Mt. 24:23-24), including one claiming to be God Himself (II Thess. 2:3-4).

(6) The Rise of False Prophets

During the great tribulation, many false prophets will emerge (Mt. 24:24). Yeshua already mentioned in Matthew 24:11 that *many false prophets shall arise*. However, there is a difference between the two occurrences. The false prophets described in the first half of the tribulation give false prophecies to lead many astray. The false prophets of the second half of the tribulation will perform great signs and wonders; because of their satanic power, they will deceive many. These points are also affirmed in passages such as Zechariah 13:2-6, II Thessalonians 2:8-10, and Revelation 13:11-15.

(7) Rumors of Yeshua's Return

Yeshua warned not to believe any rumor that the second coming has already taken place. The second coming differs from the first because when it occurs, all will see it: *For as the lightning comes forth from the east, and is seen even unto the west; so shall be the coming of the Son of man* (Mt. 24:27). The second coming will be visible to all, and therefore, those fleeing from persecution are to remain hidden.

(8) The Place of the Second Coming

Yeshua mentioned the place of the second coming in cryptic terms: *Wheresoever the carcase is, there will the eagles be gathered together* (Mt. 24:28). The *eagles* (or better, the vultures) will be gathered together at the site of the body. Yeshua made a similar statement in Luke 17:37b: *Where the body <is>, thither will the eagles also be gathered together.* § 123 shows the meaning of the verse. Wherever the body of Israel hides during the second half of the tribulation, the Gentile armies will come against them, and there the second coming will occur. Matthew stated that the Jews will flee to the mountains (Mt. 24:16) without specifying the exact location of these mountains. The book of Revelation also states that Israel will flee into the wilderness without specifying which wilderness (Rev. 12:6, 13-15). The prophets Micah and Jeremiah provided these details centuries before Yeshua's prophecy. The remnant of Israel will hide in the city of Bozrah, the Hebrew name for the place known today by its Greek name, Petra. The Gentile armies will gather together at Bozrah to finally annihilate the Jewish people (Jer. 49:12-14). Bozrah is the place of the second coming, a fact which is further confirmed by Micah 2:12-13, Habakkuk 3:3, and Isaiah 34:1-7 and 63:1-6.

8. The Second Coming

Matthew 24:29-30, Mark 13:24-26, Luke 21:25-27

Yeshua finally answered the apostles' second question, "What is the sign that the second coming is about to occur?" He pointed out four specific things. First, a massive blackout will occur immediately after the tribulation: *But immediately after the tribulation of those days the sun shall be darkened, and the moon shall not give her light, and the stars shall fall from heaven* (Mt. 24:29). No light from the sun, moon, or stars will reach the earth. This will signal the end of the allotted 1,260 days of Jewish persecution.

Second, tremendous perplexity will be upon the earth: *and upon the earth distress of nations, in perplexity for the roaring of the sea and the billows; men fainting for fear, and for expectation of the things which are coming on the world: for the powers of the heavens shall be shaken* (Lk. 21:25-26). Colossal tidal waves of all kinds will rock the globe, resulting in anarchy and confusion. Throughout the world, mankind will tremble over the events that will occur at that point in time.

Third, *then shall appear the sign of the Son of man in heaven* (Mt. 24:30a). This verse has various interpretations. Some claim that the sign must be a star, since a star announced Yeshua's birth, and others say it will be the sound of a great trumpet. Many believe the sign will be the cross, but given the context of the Gospel accounts, a more conclusive deduction is that the sign of the Son of man will be the Shechinah glory. In Matthew 16:27, we read: *For the Son of man shall come in the glory of his Father with his angels; and then shall he render unto every man according to his deeds.* So, at His second coming, the Messiah will appear *in the glory of His Father.* Matthew 24:30a elaborates, stating that just prior to the second coming, the sign of the Son of man will appear in the heavens, and that sign will be the Shechinah glory. Suddenly, the darkness enveloping the world will be dispersed by the light of the Shechinah. The Bible says the whole world will see the second coming; they will see the brightness of Yeshua's glory dispersing the worldwide darkness. Thus, the answer to the second question, "What is the sign of the second coming?" is that the earth will be enveloped by blackness, and suddenly this darkness is dispersed by the light of the Shechinah glory.

Fourth, the second coming will occur, *and then shall all the tribes of the earth mourn, and they shall see the Son of man coming on the clouds of heaven with power and great glory* (Mt. 24:30b). The mention of tribes rather than nations indicates Yeshua's reference to the twelve tribes of Israel, showing them to be saved, and because of their salvation, the second coming will occur. The mourning of these tribes is the same as that of Zechariah 12:10-13:1.

With this statement, Yeshua answered all three questions, but He chose to continue giving more details regarding the last days.

9. The Regathering of Israel

Matthew 24:31, Mark 13:27

In one sentence, Yeshua summarized many prophecies from the Hebrew Bible detailing the final regathering of Israel. A small sampling includes Isaiah 11:11-12:6, 43:5-7, Jeremiah 23:5-8, 31:7-14, Ezekiel

11:16-21, 20:40-42, and 36:22-31. Repeating all of the specific aspects was unnecessary since they were already familiar with the details in the Hebrew Bible. The prophets spoke of two regatherings: one in unbelief in preparation for the judgment of the tribulation and one in faith in preparation for the blessings of the kingdom. This passage clarifies that the latter will only occur after the second coming.

While the statements in the two Gospel accounts are similar, they originate from two different Old Testament backgrounds. Matthew noted: *And he shall send forth his angels with a great sound of a trumpet, and they shall gather together his elect from the four winds, from one end of heaven to the other* (Mt. 24:31). The background to this statement is found in Isaiah, who, in 27:12-13, prophesied about the final regathering of the Jewish people. He also mentioned that the sound of a great trumpet would be the signal:

> *12 And it shall come to pass in that day, that Jehovah will beat off his fruit from the flood of the River unto the brook of Egypt; and ye shall be gathered one by one, O ye children of Yisrael. 13 And it shall come to pass in that day, that a great trumpet shall be blown; and they shall come that were ready to perish in the land of Assyria, and they that were outcasts in the land of Egypt; and they shall worship Jehovah in the holy mountain at Yerushalayim.*

Mark's statement differs slightly: *And then shall he send forth the angels, and shall gather together his elect from the four winds, from the uttermost part of the earth to the uttermost part of heaven* (Mk. 13:27). The Old Testament background to this verse is found in Deuteronomy 30:4:

> *If any of your outcasts be in the uttermost parts of heaven, from thence will Jehovah your God gather you, and from thence will he fetch you.*

Both Gospel passages speak about the Jews' regathering from two localities: from the four corners of the earth and the four corners of heaven. Why these two localities? The final restoration will include both the living Israel and the resurrected Israel. The Old Testament saints are destined to participate in the messianic kingdom. They are those to whom the Abrahamic Covenant promised the inherited land, beginning with men such as Abraham, Isaac, and Jacob, to whom God said, "To you as well as to your seed I will give this land" (Gen. 35:9-

15). They will be resurrected and regathered from the four corners of heaven along with the surviving third of tribulation Jews regathered from the four corners of the world. Together, they will enjoy the messianic kingdom.

10. The Exhortation

Luke 21:28

After outlining the things to come from their own day until the beginning of the kingdom, the Messiah presented an exhortation, saying that when believers see *these things begin to come to pass*, then they are to look up—raise their heads—because it will mark their imminent redemption from this world. The question arises: What is the antecedent to the phrase *these things*? The context of the verse begins in Luke 21:20 with the phrase: *But when ye see Yerushalayim compassed with armies.* This happened in A.D. 66, and subsequently, the Temple was destroyed four years later. Luke specified that when they see Jerusalem destroyed, which is the beginning of these things (Lk. 21:20-27), they should look up, for their *redemption draws near* (Lk. 21:28). Once Jerusalem was destroyed in A.D. 70 and the judgment for the unpardonable sin finally came, every prophecy that must precede the rapture of the church was fulfilled. Since A.D. 70, the rapture has been imminent.[5] Imminence does not mean that the rapture must happen soon, but that as of A.D. 70 there is nothing left to precede it. The events prophesied in the Olivet Discourse lead up to the tribulation. Obviously, the closer the tribulation, the closer the rapture must also be. Since A.D. 70, the rapture has been imminent; therefore, the exhortation applies to all generations since A.D. 70. The Olivet Discourse will shortly contain a clear promise of a pre-tribulation rapture.

---

[5] However, the expectation that the rapture was about to occur may have set in earlier, since in both rapture passages (I Cor. 15:50-58; I Thess. 4:13-18), Paul anticipated being alive when it happened.

11. The Parable of the Fig Tree

Matthew 24:32-35, Mark 13:28-32, Luke 21:29-33

These passages have been taken out of context repeatedly to identify the date for the rapture and/or the second coming, totally ignoring Yeshua's words in the Olivet Discourse. In Matthew 24:33, Mark 13:29, and Luke 21:31, He clearly stated that no one will ever know the day or the hour of the rapture. The Parable of the Fig Tree must be interpreted by its own context.

During the twentieth century, the logic used in interpreting the parable to identify the date went something like this: The fig tree represents Israel becoming a state in 1948. Furthermore, the term *generation* must mean forty years. Yeshua said, *This generation shall not pass away, until all these things be accomplished* (Mt. 24:34; Mk. 13:30; Lk. 21:32), so according to this theory, the second coming would be in 1988. By subtracting seven years for the tribulation, the rapture would occur in 1981. Obviously, such logic failed.

The purpose of the Parable of the Fig Tree was never to predict the date of the rapture. Those who use it to predict the future make two interpretive mistakes. The first mistake is to assume that the fig tree represents Israel. The Bible uses objects in three ways: literal as literal, literal as an illustration, or symbolic. This particular passage fits into the second category: Yeshua used the fig tree literally as an illustration, the point of which will become evident from Luke's account.

Those using the parable to identify a date for the rapture consider Matthew's and Mark's accounts while ignoring Luke's. Luke, however, wrote: *And he spoke to them a parable: Behold the fig tree, and all the trees* (Lk. 21:29). Luke not only mentioned the fig tree, but *all the trees*. What was true of the fig tree was also true of all the other trees. If the fig tree represents Israel, what do the other trees represent? Other new nations? With the breakup of the Soviet Union and Yugoslavia, several nations formed. When does the forty-year countdown begin in light of this? Assuming that the fig tree here is a symbol of Israel is the first mistake. The more common symbol of Israel in the Scriptures is the vine. So, the fig tree is definitely being used literally as an illustration in the Olivet Discourse.

The second interpretive mistake is to assume that the word *generation* always equals forty years. The Bible never makes that limitation upon the term. In one passage in Scripture *generation* correlates to one hundred years: *Know of a surety that your seed shall be sojourners in a land that is not theirs, and shall serve them; and they shall afflict them four hundred years ... And in the fourth generation they shall come hither again* (Gen. 15:13, 16). In scriptural terminology, *generation* refers to a span of time of some duration, sometimes forty years, other times twenty, sixty, eighty, or even one hundred years. In most cases, it is used in the same sense as in modern English, in the sense of being "contemporaries." When a person refers to their generation in contrast to their father's generation, people do not automatically assume the gap is forty years between themselves and their father. Generally, people understand that the speaker is referring to their contemporaries in contrast to their fathers' contemporaries. The term *generation* must be understood this way here. Yeshua referred to the contemporaries of a specific generation or time period. The question is, which generation and what time span was He speaking about?

Matthew introduced the illustration: *Now from the fig tree learn her parable: when her branch is now become tender, and puts forth its leaves, ye know that the summer is near* (Mt. 24:32). According to Luke, when the fig tree and all the other trees leaf out, it signifies that summer is coming. That is the literal meaning of this illustration. Yeshua then gave the application: *even so ye also, when ye see all these things, know ye that he is near, <even> at the doors* (Mt. 24:33). When they saw *all these things*, they would know that the second coming was near. While Matthew and Mark focused on the second coming, Luke stated: *know ye that the kingdom of God is near* (Lk. 21:31). He emphasized the establishment of the messianic kingdom, which occurs at the second coming.

What is the antecedent to *these things*? In the context of Matthew's Gospel, the antecedent is the abomination of desolation: *When therefore you see the abomination of desolation* (Mt. 24:15) and *even so, ye also, when ye see all these things, know ye that he is near, <even> at the* *doors* (Mt. 24:33). The illustration is that the blossoming fig tree and all the other trees signify that summer is coming. The application of the illustration is that when they see *these things*, they will know the second coming and the kingdom are near at hand. How would they know? From Daniel, they knew that the period of time from the abomination until the second coming will be exactly 1,260 days. So when they see these things, i.e., the abomination of desolation, they will know that Messiah's coming is exactly 1,260 days away.

Matthew continued: *This generation shall not pass away, till all these things be accomplished* (Mt. 24:34). Which generation did Yeshua speak about in this context? Was it the generation of 1948 who witnessed the reestablishment of Israel? Or was it the generation that witnessed the Six Day War of 1967 which brought Jerusalem under Jewish control? Neither event was discussed anywhere in the context of the Olivet Discourse. A text apart from its context is a pretext, so this verse must be interpreted within its own context. The Jews living in the second half of the tribulation are the generation in this context that will see the abomination of desolation, and to them, He extended a word of comfort. The abomination of desolation signals Satan's final attempt to annihilate all Jews living at that time. Yeshua shows that the satanic goal, initiated by the abomination of desolation, will fail. The Jewish generation that sees the abomination of desolation will survive until Yeshua's return 1,260 days later.

The section ends with, *Heaven and earth shall pass away, but my words shall not pass away* (Mt. 24:35), emphasizing the fact that every prophecy that Yeshua gave in this discourse will be fulfilled. What has not yet been fulfilled will certainly be fulfilled in the future.

The Parable of the Fig Tree can be summarized in two points: when the abomination of desolation occurs, it will signal that the return of the Messiah is three-and-a-half years away and that the Jewish generation that sees the abomination of desolation will survive to see the second coming. These are comforting words in light of the worldwide attempt to destroy the Jewish people.

12. The Rapture

Matthew 24:36-42, Luke 21:34-36

In the past, the majority view among pre-tribulational, pre-millennial dispensationalists was that this section deals with the rapture. However, today the majority believes this section refers to the second coming, and the proponents of this view support their interpretation for two reasons. The first is that the verses follow Yeshua's discussion on the second coming in the previous sections, so it seems logical that He would detail the events following the second coming, since He is dealing with events chronologically. The second reason is based upon Matthew's use of the words *taken away*. When the flood came, it took away the unbelievers in judgment (Mt. 24:39). Just so, those people taken away in Matthew 24:40 must be removed in judgment, not in the rapture.

In response, two points counter these assumptions: The phrase translated as *taken away* is not a technical term and could be used in more than one way in the same context. Furthermore, while the same word is used in the English translation, it is not in Greek. Verse 39 contains the verb *airó* ("to raise," "take up," "to lift") and verse 40 the verb *paralambanó* ("to receive from"), suggesting that the verses might be dealing with two separate concepts.

The reasons for subscribing to the initial view that the passage is speaking of the rapture will be presented in the exposition below, appropriately noted in five specific points. First, Matthew began the passage with the word *but* (Mt. 24:36). There is more than one way of saying *but* in the Greek language. Here, the English word is a translation of two Greek words, *peri de*, meaning "now concerning." As Greek grammar books show, this construction denotes a contrast and often introduces a new subject. Paul used the formula frequently in his writings when presenting a new topic (e.g., I Cor. 7:1, 25; 8:1; 12:1; 16:1, 12; I Thess. 4:9; 5:1; etc.). In the context of Matthew 24, Yeshua had been talking about one topic (the second coming), then introduced a new subject (the rapture). Although Yeshua generally developed the Olivet Discourse in chronological sequence, He had already disrupted this approach once before, in Luke 21:12, with the phrase, *But before all these things.* In the passage above, He introduced the new topic by using the *peri de* construction.

Second, no one will ever know the timing of the rapture. Yeshua noted that *the angels of heaven* do not know when it will occur (Mt. 24:36). Not even the Son in His humanity knew the timing. Only God the Father knows when the believers will be taken up to meet their Messiah in the air. This will always be true of the rapture. The second coming, on the other hand, will occur exactly seven years after the signing of the seven-year covenant and 42 months, or 1,260 days, after the abomination of desolation. Once the tribulation begins, the second coming can be accurately calculated, so the passage above must be dealing with the rapture and not the second coming. Those who are still attempting to determine the date of the rapture use the phrase *neither the day nor the hour* (Mt. 24:36) to claim that while one cannot know the exact day and hour, it is possible to know the week, month, or year of the rapture. This only shows their ignorance of the Jewish idiom meaning "the impossible." English speakers understand that the expression "not an inch" does not mean that while it is prohibited to take an inch, it is permissible to take a foot or a yard. Rather, they know that it means "not at all." The same thing is true of the phrase *neither day nor hour*; it means "not at all."

Third, the rapture will occur when conditions on earth are normal and people are *eating and drinking, marrying and giving in marriage* (Mt. 24:38). These are common activities in human society. Marrying and giving in marriage are necessary to propagate life; eating and drinking are essential to sustain it. During the time of Noah, life was normal when suddenly the flood came and took the people away. The rapture will occur in the same manner: *so shall be the coming of the Son of man* (Mt. 24:39). Nothing spectacular will forewarn people that the believers are about to be taken up. However, things will be very abnormal at the time of the second coming. Nearly three-quarters of the earth will be destroyed in seven long years of tribulation. A blackness paired with tremendous tidal waves, anarchy, confusion, and perplexity will envelop the world. The Olivet Discourse shows that conditions will be abnormal at the time of the second coming, and so it is better to interpret this passage as referring to the rapture.

Fourth, when the rapture occurs, believers will be separated from unbelievers. Yeshua illustrated this as two men being in a field; one is taken, and one is left behind (Mt. 24:40). Two women will be grinding at the mill; one is taken, and one is left (Mt. 24:41). The fact that believers and unbelievers are working side by side again refers to a time before the tribulation when that will still be the case, but in the second half of the tribulation and even more so at the second coming, this will not be the case (Rev. 13:1-18). Other passages on the rapture also show that this event will separate believers from unbelievers (Jn. 14:1-3; I Cor. 15:50-58; I Thess. 4:13-18). Yeshua concluded, *Watch therefore: for ye know not on what day your Lord comes* (Mt. 24:42). With these words, He reiterated that no special sign will precede the rapture. It is imminent and can happen anytime, so believers must live with the awareness of that possibility.

Fifth, Luke recorded Yeshua's warning to be watchful in order to escape the tribulation by means of salvation. This is the first indication in the New Testament that the rapture will be pre-tribulational. Yeshua clearly stated that the tribulation is going to affect all the people in this world: *for <so> shall it come upon all them that dwell upon the face of all the earth* (Lk. 21:35). Everyone living on the earth will be affected by the tribulation, unable to escape the judgments. Notice Yeshua's statement: *But watch ye at every season, making supplication, that ye may prevail to escape all these things that shall come to pass, and to stand before the Son of man* (Lk. 21:36). Here and in the next section of the Olivet Discourse, the word *watch* emphasizes readiness equal to salvation. Those who are watchful are saved.

Yeshua gave two reasons for being watchful, or in the context of the Olivet Discourse, for salvation. First, *that ye may prevail to escape all these things that shall come to pass* (Lk. 21:36a). The tribulation judgments of *all these things* described in Matthew 24:9-28 will fall upon all who dwell on the earth. However, the way to escape these judgments is by being watchful, or having salvation. Second, the means of escape will be *to stand before the Son of man* (Lk. 21:36b) as a result of the rapture. These statements clearly present a pre-tribulational promise of a way to escape the judgments of the tribulation that will fall upon the face of the world. The means of escape is by standing before the Son of man, which results from the rapture of the church.

At this point, Luke's account of the Olivet Discourse ends, and all additional information is found only in Matthew and Mark.

13. Parables Urging Watchfulness, Readiness, and Diligence

This section contains a series of five parables, all of which urge one of the following three characteristics: watchfulness, readiness, and diligence in laboring. By way of introduction, two observations should be made.

First, when a rabbi used the parabolic teaching method, he told one parable or several parables in succession and then made the application. In this section, Yeshua used the parabolic teaching method, telling a series of parables and making the application at the end with the the judgment of the sheep and the goats.

Second, it is important to remember the purpose of these parables and to whom they apply. The distinction made in these parables is not between Jews and Gentiles or between Israel and the church or even between spiritual and carnal believers. The distinction is between believers and unbelievers, the saved and the unsaved. The point is that the saved who live during the tribulation will be characterized by watchfulness, readiness, and diligence. The unsaved will not be characterized by these three qualities.

a. The Parable of the Porter

Mark 13:33-37

The emphasis of the first parable is watchfulness. That word occurs four times: *Take ye heed, watch* (Mk. 13:33), *to watch* (Mk. 13:34), *Watch therefore* (Mk. 13:35), and *Watch* (Mk. 13:37).

At this point, Mark's version of the Olivet Discourse ends, and all that follows is found only in Matthew's account.

b. The Parable of the Master of the House

Matthew 24:43-44

The emphasis of the second parable is on readiness: *Therefore be ye also ready* (Mt. 24:44).

c. The Parable of the Faithful Servant and the Evil Servant

Matthew 24:45-51

When the owner of a house plans for his absence, he delegates the care for his household and his other responsibilities to his servants. He expects them to faithfully perform their duties. Hence, the emphasis of the third parable is on laboring diligently while vigilantly awaiting the master's return: *Blessed is that servant, whom his lord when he comes shall find so doing* (Mt. 24:46).

d. Application

Each of the three short parables just studied emphasize either watchfulness, readiness, or diligence. Concerning the unbeliever, who is characterized by his failure to watch, be ready, or labor diligently, Yeshua declared that they shall be put in the place where *there shall be weeping and gnashing of teeth* (Mt. 24:51). This is one of several descriptive terms for the lake of fire, where the unbelievers will be weeping for their lost condition and gnashing their teeth because of the torment they experience.

e. The Parable of the Ten Virgins

Matthew 25:1-13

Following the three short parables, Yeshua told two longer ones, reemphasizing the same points of watchfulness, readiness, and diligence. The Parable of the Ten Virgins reemphasizes the first two points. The facet of being ready is evident in verse 10: *And they that were ready went in with him to the marriage feast.* The facet of watchfulness appears in verse 13: *Watch therefore, for ye know not the day nor the hour.*

This parable presupposes a familiarity with first-century Jewish marriage customs. There were four stages to a wedding. The first stage was called "the arrangement," where the father of the groom came to an understanding with the father of the bride and paid the bride price. This often occurred when the bride and groom were children. The second stage of the wedding was called "the fetching of the bride." At least a year after the fathers arranged the marriage, the groom went to the home of the bride to fetch her. The waiting period could be much longer, and many years could transpire between the arrangement and the fetching of the bride. After picking up his bride, the groom returned to his hometown. The bride was led to the *mikvah*, the immersion pool for ritual cleansing. Once she achieved ritual purity, the wedding ceremony could take place, making this the third stage of a traditional Jewish wedding. Only a few people were invited to the ceremony, usually the close friends and relatives of the bride and the groom. The fourth stage was the wedding feast, usually lasting seven days. Many more people were invited to the feast than to the ceremony.

In reference to Messiah and the church, the first stage was fulfilled when God, the Father of the groom, made the arrangement and paid the bride price, which was the blood of His Son (Eph. 5:22-33). The second stage, the fetching of the bride, will be fulfilled by the rapture, when Messiah comes to pick up the church saints (His bride) to bring them to His home (Jn. 14:1-3). The third stage, the wedding ceremony, will occur in heaven before the second coming (Rev. 19:6-8), while the fourth stage, the wedding feast, will take place on earth, at the beginning of the messianic kingdom, and may last for seven days or seven years.

In the Parable of the Ten Virgins, the groom, accompanied by the bride, came to celebrate the wedding feast, showing that the fetching of the bride, the rapture, had already occurred. The parable focuses on the second coming, when the Messiah returns with His bride, the church, to celebrate the wedding feast, and deals with those who will be part of the wedding feast and those who will not: *And they that were ready went in with him to the marriage feast* (Mt. 25:10).

To fully understand the implications of the Jewish wedding system in the Parable of the Ten Virgins, more detail is needed concerning the role of the virgins. The term *virgins* does not describe their spiritual condition, only their status in the community. They could not be sure whether the groom would return in the daytime or at night to celebrate the wedding, so they brought their lamps with them to be ready in either case. The virgins of this parable must be viewed in this particular facet of the Jewish wedding system as symbols of the Gentiles in the tribulation. Some, but not all, will be watching in readiness for the Messiah's return, and He will come back with His bride, the church, at the second coming.

Many assume that the ten virgins of this parable represent different categories of believers within the church. However, the Scriptures never use the word "virgin" symbolically of saints. Another misconception is that the foolish virgins represent believers who lost their salvation because they ran out of oil. That is not what the text says: *For the foolish, when they took their lamps, took no oil with them, but the wise took oil in their vessels with their lamps* (Mt. 25:3-4). As Zechariah 4:1-14 shows, oil is a symbol of the Holy Spirit. All ten virgins had lamps, and they all had heard the same message. Five had oil with their lamps, meaning they had the Holy Spirit; they had salvation. The other five did not have oil and, therefore, did not have salvation. Yeshua used the terms *foolish* and *wise* the way they are used in the Hebrew Scriptures, where we read in Psalm 14:1: *The fool has said in his heart, there is no God.*[6] So the distinction between the wise and the foolish is the distinction between believers and unbelievers. Those with the oil were saved, and those without the oil were unsaved.

The issue of the lamps and the oil shows that in this context, the time of day is significant. Would the groom return by day or by night? The emphasis is clearly on watchfulness and readiness. When, at the second coming, Yeshua finally arrives with His bride to celebrate the wedding feast, the foolish ones will be excluded from the messianic kingdom because they do not have salvation. The wise ones will be brought into the marriage feast because they did have oil; they did have salvation, which

---

[6] Especially in the book of Proverbs, the terms "wisdom" and "faith" are often interchangeable. See also Job 28:28 and James 3:17.

493

led them to be watchful and ready. The foolish ones, on the other hand, failed at these things because they were not saved, and Yeshua confirmed this when He said: *Verily I say unto you, I know you not* (Mt. 25:12). He will not say this to believers, even carnal believers. He will, however, say this to those who are unbelievers.

To summarize, the distinction in these parables is between believers and unbelievers. The believers are characterized by watchfulness and readiness, and the unbelievers are not. The Parable of the Ten Virgins simply reemphasizes the points of the first and second parables, watchfulness and readiness.

f. The Parable of the Talents

Matthew 25:14-30

The fifth parable emphasizes diligent laboring, the point of the third parable. Again, the distinction is made between believers and unbelievers. The believers were laboring, and the unbelievers were not laboring: *But his lord answered and said unto him, You wicked and slothful servant* (Mt. 25:26). The servant is called *wicked*, showing he was unsaved, and he is called *slothful*, indicating he was not laboring.

The servant is unsaved, so he is cast *into the outer darkness: there shall be the weeping and the gnashing of teeth* (Mt. 25:30). In this statement, Yeshua used two descriptive terms for the lake of fire. The first one repeats a statement He made in Matthew 8:12 and 22:13. The lake of fire is the place of weeping and gnashing of teeth. The second term is *the outer darkness*. In the physical world, fire produces light as well as heat, but in the spiritual realm, the lake of fire is unique in that the fire will not produce light, only torment. Everyone in the lake of fire will live in total outer darkness, feeling very much alone. They will see no one, but will hear the others in their weeping and gnashing of teeth.

14. The Judgment of the Gentiles

Matthew 25:31-46

The final segment of the Olivet Discourse contains the application of the five parables to the judgment of the Gentiles. With this, the Olivet Discourse ends.

In verse 31a, Yeshua gave the timing of the judgment: *But when the Son of man shall come in his glory, and all the angels with him.* Daniel points out that there will be a 75-day interval between the end of the tribulation and the beginning of the messianic kingdom (Dan. 12:11-13). During this interval, a number of things will occur, one of which will be the judgment of the Gentiles.

While Yeshua omitted the place of the judgment, Joel 3:1-3 states that it will occur in the Valley of Jehoshaphat, that part of the Valley of Kidron separating the Old City and the Temple Mount from the Mount of Olives:

> *¹ For, behold, in those days, and in that time, when I shall bring back the captivity of Yehudah and Yerushalayim, ² I will gather all nations, and will bring them down into the valley of Jehoshaphat; and I will execute judgment upon them there for my people and for my heritage Yisrael, whom they have scattered among the nations: and they have parted my land, ³ and have cast lots for my people, and have given a boy for a harlot, and sold a girl for wine, that they may drink.*

The Gentiles who survive the tribulation will be judged: *then shall he sit on the throne of his glory: and before him shall be gathered all the nations* (Mt. 25:31b-32). The term *nations* is a translation of the Greek word for Gentiles, *ethnos*, and that is the way it should be translated here. The final issue here concerns eternal life and eternal damnation for individuals who are either believers or unbelievers. Nations are not judged in their entirety on whether they are saved or not; therefore, the verse should read like this: "Then he shall sit on the throne of his glory, and before him shall be gathered all the Gentiles." All the Gentiles who survive the tribulation will be gathered into the Valley of Jehoshaphat for this judgment, which Yeshua illustrated as a separation between the subjects of the judgment, the sheep on His right hand and the goats on His left hand (Mt. 25:33).

The judgment will be based on the Gentiles' treatment of the Jews during the tribulation, revealing either anti-Semitism or pro-Semitism (Mt. 25:34-45). The Joel passage identifies the same basis. The Messiah will deal with the sheep and the goat Gentiles separately, beginning with the sheep (Mt. 25:34-40). He will say to them: *Then shall the King say unto them on his right hand, Come, ye blessed of my Father, inherit the kingdom prepared for you from the foundation of the world* (Mt. 25:34). He invites them to enter the messianic kingdom because they fed Him food and water, provided Him with clothing and shelter, and visited Him when He was sick and in prison. The sheep Gentiles, whom Yeshua called *the righteous* ones (Mt. 25:37), the believers, will respond by saying that they do not remember seeing Him in any of these conditions, nor do they remember doing any of these things for Him. Yeshua will answer: *Verily I say unto you, Inasmuch as ye did it unto one of these my brethren, <even> these least, ye did it unto me* (Mt. 25:40b). *My brethren* have to be distinguished from the sheep and the goats. The sheep and the goats comprise all Gentiles, believers and un-believers. Therefore, the brethren cannot be another category of Gentile believers, but are Yeshua's brethren according to the flesh. The Joel passage clearly states that the judgment of the Gentiles is based on their treatment of the Jews in the tribulation. Furthermore, only Matthew records this segment of the Olivet Discourse, and he focused on what was particularly relevant to the Jewish audience for whom the Gospel was written. Yeshua will say to these sheep Gentiles that what-ever they did for the Jewish people during the tribulation will be reckoned as having been done unto Him. For that reason, they will en-ter the messianic kingdom.

Then Yeshua turned to the goat Gentiles, declaring: *Depart from me, ye cursed, into the eternal fire which is prepared for the devil and his angels* (Mt. 25:41b). These goat Gentiles, initially destined for hell, are ultimately destined for the lake of fire, because they are cursed before Him. Yeshua then explained the reasons why, repeating what He said to the sheep Gentiles in a negative manner, identifying what they failed to do for Him. The goat Gentiles will also respond that they do not re-member seeing Him in any of those conditions. However, because they failed to do these things for Him, Yeshua will say to them: *Inasmuch as ye did it not unto one of these least, ye did it not unto me* (Mt. 25:45b). At this point, the goat Gentiles will be killed and the sheep will enter into the messianic kingdom, where they will populate the Gentile nations. The Messiah and the church saints together with the tribulation saints will rule over these Gentile nations for a thousand years (Rev. 20:4-6).

Finally, Yeshua summarized the result for each group: *And these* [meaning the goat Gentiles] *shall go away into eternal punishment: but the righteous into eternal life* (Mt. 25:46). The goat Gentiles will begin eternal punishment without entering the messianic kingdom. The righteous, on the other hand, who received eternal life because of their faith, will first enter the messianic kingdom and then into the eternal order of the New Jerusalem. Some might question whether or not these people are saved because of their pro-Semitic stand during the tribulation. The answer is no, as this would be salvation by works. Rather, this exemplifies the principle found in James 2:14-26: that faith is evidenced by works. The sheep Gentiles are the believers of the tribulation period who showed their faith by their pro-Semitic works. The goat Gentiles are the unbelievers of the tribulation period whose lack of faith is evident by their anti-Semitic works.

In summary and in keeping with the application of these five parables, the sheep Gentiles are characterized by watchfulness, readiness, and diligent laboring, specifically laboring on behalf of the Jews. The goat Gentiles lack these attributes and will reveal their lack of faith by their anti-Semitic acts. With this, Yeshua concluded the longest prophetic discourse of His public ministry.[7]

---

[7] There is, of course, a lot more to the prophetic word, but this must be limited to what is found in the life of the Messiah within the Gospels. For more details, see this author's book, *The Footsteps of the Messiah: A Study of the Sequence of Prophetic Events* (San Antonio, TX: Ariel Ministries, 1982, revised ed. 2003).

15. Luke's Summary

Luke 21:37-38

In these verses, Luke summarized Yeshua's daily activities from Sunday until Tuesday, when He delivered the Olivet Discourse. The Messiah left the town of Bethany near the Mount of Olives daily to teach at the Temple, and then returned to Bethany to spend the night. *And all the people came early in the morning to him in the temple, to hear him* (Lk. 21:38).

[§§ 146–160] —
B. The Preparation for Messiah's Death

[§ 146] — 1. The Prediction of His Death

Matthew 26:1-2

This was the fourth time Yeshua announced His coming death. In two days, during the Passover feast, He would be delivered up. He stated this on a Tuesday; Passover would fall on Thursday. Yeshua again specified the manner of His death: crucifixion. Since crucifixion was a Roman, not a Jewish method of execution, the law code under which He would die was clear.

[§ 147] — 2. The Conspiracy of the Rulers

Matthew 26:3-5, Mark 14:1-2, Luke 22:1-2

Two days after Yeshua predicted His death, it was time to celebrate *<the feast of> the Passover and the unleavened bread* (Mk. 14:1a). During that specific year, the traditional Passover celebration would be held at sundown Thursday evening. During the day, a conspiracy was launched by the chief priests and the scribes (Mk. 14:1b), including both Pharisees and Sadducees.

Matthew added: *Then were gathered together the chief priests, and the elders of the people, unto the court of the high priest, who was called Kayapha* (Mt. 26:3). Other translations render *the court of the high priest* as "his palace." However, the Greek word used is *aulé*, which indicates that this was an atrium, or courtyard, and not a palace. Neither was it the place where the Sanhedrin gathered together. While Mark 14:1 makes it sound as if this was an informal meeting, Matthew's rendering suggests the gathering turned into a formal, yet secret, session of the court. The high priest, Caiaphas, a Sadducee, headed up the conspiracy. His given name was Joseph, and he was appointed high priest by Valerius Gratus in A.D. 18. Deposed by the procurator Vitellius in A.D. 36/37, he was the longest serving high priest. This indicates that Caiaphas had the support of the Roman authorities. The Sadducees and Pharisees gathered together at Caiaphas' house to conspire against Yeshua. Matthew added a third group: *the elders of the people* (Mt. 26:3).

The conspiracy of these men included two elements. The first was to find a way to arrest Yeshua apart from the multitude: *and they took counsel together that they might take Yeshua by subtlety, and kill him* (Mt. 26:4). Shortly, Judas would provide this opportunity. The second part of the conspiracy was not to do it during Passover: *Not during the feast, lest haply there shall be a tumult of the people* (Mk. 14:2). This was the satanic element of the conspiracy. While Satan certainly wanted to see Yeshua dead, he did not want Him to die at this Passover. If Yeshua had died at any time other than the Jewish Passover and in any other way than by crucifixion, there would have been no atonement. The death of Yeshua alone was essential for the atonement, but He had to die at the proper time and in the proper way. The Gospels record how throughout Yeshua's life, several attempts were made to kill Him at the wrong time (before or after Passover) and in the wrong manner (by sword or stoning). Yet all such attempts failed because *His hour was not yet come* (Jn. 7:30; 8:20). The conspiracy was to wait until after Passover and the multitudes of pilgrims to leave the city before they carried out their plot. However, God was in control, and they were forced to act precisely during Passover.

[§ 148] — 3. The Pouring of Ointment

Matthew 26:6-13, Mark 14:3-9, John 12:2-8

Yeshua was a guest in Bethany at the house of Simon, the former leper Yeshua had healed. Furthermore, a woman whose name was not mentioned by Mark or Matthew was present. Yochanan the apostle specified that it was Miriam, the sister of Martha and Lazarus (Jn. 12:3a). They, too, were guests at the house of Simon the leper, and they both lived in Bethany.

Miriam brought a pound of spikenard, broke the cruse, and poured it over Yeshua's head (Mk. 14:3) and feet, then wiped them with her hair (Jn. 12:3b). Spikenard, a perfume for royalty and commoners alike, was so expensive that a woman would have to save her money and use it only on her wedding night, as did Shulamit, the bride in the Song of Solomon. Yet Miriam willingly used all of hers on Yeshua. How expensive was it? *For this ointment might have been sold for above three hundred shillings* (Mk. 14:5), meaning denarii. In that day, one denarius was equal to one day's wages. This means the spikenard Miriam used was worth almost one year's wages.

The disciples thought this was a waste, since the ointment could have been sold in the market and the funds given to the poor. Judas initiated their complaint and verbalized his objection to using the spikenard in this manner: *But Judas Iscariot, one of his disciples, that should betray Him, said, Why was not this ointment sold for three hundred shillings, and given to the poor?* (Jn. 12:4-5). The other disciples joined in agreement and were probably genuinely concerned for the poor. Judas, however, had a different motive: *Now this he said, not because he cared for the poor; but because he was a thief, and having the bag took away what was put therein* (Jn. 12:6). Judas' ulterior motive was greed, and he was guilty of embezzlement. He was the group treasurer, but would often take the money for his own private use.

Yeshua Himself explained why Miriam was willing to use her precious ointment on Him: *Suffer her to keep it against the day of my burying* (Jn. 12:7b). *For in that she poured this ointment upon my body, she did it to prepare me for burial* (Mt. 26:12). *She has done what she could: she has anointed my body beforehand for the burying* (Mk. 14:8). Miriam understood something that Yeshua's own apostles did not yet comprehend: The Messiah was going to die. She also knew that He would be raised from the dead. Thus, Miriam did not accompany the women who went to the tomb in the resurrection account. The others were not expecting a resurrection, but she was. While Martha was busy meeting Yeshua's physical needs, Miriam met His spiritual needs by listening to Him, fellowshipping with Him, and learning from Him while sitting at His feet. Her understanding resulted from paying attention to His teaching more carefully than the disciples themselves.

This event had two results. The first concerns Miriam: *Wheresoever this gospel shall be preached in the whole world, that also which this woman has done shall be spoken of for a memorial of her* (Mt. 26:13). Miriam's act of love and obedience was rewarded with being honored. The mention of her deeds in this book is an example of the fulfillment of this prophecy. The second result is Judas' decision to betray Yeshua.

[§ 149] — 4. The Promise to Betray

Matthew 26:14-16, Mark 14:10-11, Luke 22:3-6

Luke stated that *Satan entered into Yehudah* (Lk. 22:3), which means that the devil now controlled him. Judas had already exposed himself to this possibility. As the group treasurer, he was entrusted with an important job; however, he was guilty of embezzlement. There is a spiritual principle that one sin can lead to another until finally the person falls under demonic control. Due to the nature of this spiritual conflict, Satan took control of Judas rather than sending one of his demons. The result of this satanic control was that Judas approached the chief priests and the captains, or temple police (Lk. 22:4). He conspired with their leaders to provide the opportunity they desired to have Yeshua arrested apart from the multitude.

Judas was needed to fulfill three things, but only accomplished two of these. First, while the Jewish leaders knew Yeshua and could identify Him, the Roman soldiers needed Judas to show them where to arrest the Messiah apart from the multitude. Judas succeeded in fulfilling this function. Second, by Roman law, someone needed to appear before the governor to accuse Yeshua of a crime punishable under Roman law before a cohort could be released to arrest Him. At some point, Judas appeared before Pontius Pilate to accuse Yeshua of a crime, and only then was a cohort released to find and arrest Him. Judas also fulfilled this function. Third, he needed to serve as the prosecuting witness at the Roman trial. Judas was not needed for the Jewish trial, but was absolutely needed for the Roman or civil trial. He failed to fulfill this third function.

The specific price of betrayal was *thirty pieces of silver* (Mt. 26:15). This was not an arbitrary price. According to Exodus 21:32, if an ox gored a neighbor's slave to death, the owner was obligated to pay the neighbor thirty pieces of silver, the price at which a dead slave was valued. Thereafter, it became symbolic of contempt. At one point in his ministry, Zechariah the prophet was asked to play a messianic role (Zech. 11:4-14), meaning a role the Messiah Himself would play in the future, the role of the good shepherd. For a period of time, Zechariah was to feed a flock destined for slaughter. He then was to approach the Jewish leaders and say that since they did not agree to a price in advance, they should pay him what they thought his labor was worth. If it was worth something, they should pay him accordingly; if it was worthless to them, it was acceptable to pay him nothing. To show their contempt for the prophet, the leaders deliberately chose to pay him thirty pieces of silver, conveying to Zechariah that his work among them was not only worthless, but more insultingly, was worth only the price of a dead slave. Then God told Zechariah two things. First, take the thirty pieces of silver and cast it in the Temple compound, just as Judas would do centuries later. Second, this was *the goodly price that I was prized at by them* (Zech. 11:13). The prophecy declared that someday the Jewish leaders would sell out God Himself for the price of a dead slave. These Jewish leaders deliberately chose thirty pieces of silver to show their contempt for Yeshua; thus, they sold out the Messianic God-Man for the price of a dead slave.

As tragic as this is, ironically, the thirty pieces of silver came from the chief priests, so the money ultimately came from the Temple treasury. One major purpose of the Temple treasury was to purchase sacrifices.

Though it was not their intent, the chief priests purchased a sacrifice, specifically, the final sacrifice for sin.

When the price of betrayal was agreed upon, Judas actively looked for the opportunity the Jewish leaders sought: *And he consented, and sought opportunity to deliver him unto them in the absence of the multitude* (Lk. 22:6).

[§§ 150–160] — 5. The Last Passover and the First Lord's Supper

[§ 150] — a. The Preparation for the Seder

Matthew 26:17-19, Mark 14:12-16, Luke 22:7-13

It was now Thursday, the 14th of Nisan, or April 6, A.D. 30. At sundown, the Passover began, ending 24 hours later, on the evening of the 15th. At that point, the first of the seven days of the Feast of Unleavened Bread began (Ex. 12:1-20; Deut. 16:1-8).

Often, these two festivals are mistaken as being one, and when one is referred to, both are meant. However, while God commanded that both feasts should be observed by the Jewish people, they commemorate different events.

In the Scriptures, the Feast of Passover is mentioned more than any other feast of Israel, over fifty times in the Hebrew Scriptures and 27 times in the New Testament. Within the framework of Judaism, this is the most important festival of the entire Jewish religious calendar.

Two different names are given for this feast. The first name, *Pesach*, is the Hebrew word meaning "Passover," originating with the angel of death motif found in Exodus 12.[8] The Jews were commanded to take a lamb, slay it, and sprinkle its blood upon the lintel and doorposts of each home. That night the angel of death passed through the land of Egypt. When he came to a Jewish home and saw the blood upon the

---

[8] Biblically, it was the Lord Himself who passed through the land of Egypt (Ex. 12:23). In rabbinic tradition, it was the angel of death.

lintel and doorposts, he passed over that home. But when he came to an Egyptian home and did not see the blood upon the lintel and doorposts, instead of "passing over," he would "pass through" and slay the firstborn son of that Egyptian family. This is the origin of the name for this feast: the passing-over of the Jewish homes by the angel of death.

The second Hebrew name for this festival is *zman cheruteinu*, which means the "season of our emancipation." This name emphasizes the result of the first Passover: freedom from Egyptian slavery.

As soon as Passover ends at sundown on the 15th of Nisan, the Feast of Unleavened Bread begins. Moses described its observance in Leviticus 23:6-8. The main component of this seven-day festival is God's commandment to not eat any leavened bread. The Hebrew name for this feast is *Hag haMatzot*, which simply means "the feast of unleavened bread."

Leaven is a symbol of sin when used symbolically in the Scriptures. The Feast of Unleavened Bread is fulfilled by the offering of the sinless, unleavened blood of the Messiah (Heb. 9:11-10:18). While the actual death of Yeshua fulfilled the Passover, the offering of His sinless blood fulfilled the Feast of Unleavened Bread.

During Passover, Jewish pilgrims from all over the region and the Roman Empire flocked into Jerusalem for this national celebration. The main part of the Feast of Passover was the *Seder*, a meal whose Hebrew name means "order." When the disciples asked Yeshua, *Where will you that we make ready for you to eat the Passover?* (Mt. 26:17), they were referring to the Passover meal. Luke added: *And he sent Peter and Yochanan, saying, Go and make ready for us the Passover, that we may eat* (Lk. 22:8). Peter and Yochanan were assigned to prepare the meal. Before they performed their duties, they had to first deliver the Passover lamb to the Temple compound. The lamb was killed, and its blood was poured into a bowl, carried to the altar, and poured out at the base of the altar. During the process, they sang Psalms 113-118, known as the *Hallel* (praise) psalms. The lamb was then cleaned, meaning it was skinned and the entrails removed. Parts of the lamb were burned on the altar; the rest was taken home and roasted. Then, additional Passover items were prepared: unleavened bread; wine; bitter herbs; and a concoction called *charoset,* a combination of apples, nuts, honey, cinnamon, lemon juice, and wine, chopped and mixed together until it turned a deep brown color. This is what was involved in making ready the Passover.

It was impossible to house the hundreds of thousands of pilgrims who came to Jerusalem to observe the Passover within the city walls. Therefore, huge tent cities were erected around the walls where the people ate the Seder meal with their families and others. Some residents of Jerusalem were asked to arrange special accommodations for other people, and this year, Yeshua was one of them: *Behold, when ye are entered into the city, there shall meet you a man bearing a pitcher of water* (Lk. 22:10a). Yeshua had made previous arrangements for the place where He and His disciples would observe the Passover within the city walls. Peter and Yochanan were to go into Jerusalem and look for a man carrying a pitcher of water, a notable detail because in the Middle East, even to this day, only women, not men, carry the water. To see a man carrying water would be unusual and therefore a sign. Upon seeing this, they were to *follow him into the house whereinto he goes* (Lk. 22:10b). Then, upon arrival, *ye shall say unto the master of the house, The Teacher said unto you, Where is the guestchamber, where I shall eat the Passover with my disciples?* (Lk. 22:11). The Matthew account shows the significance of this Passover: *The Teacher said, My time is at hand; I keep the Passover at your house with my disciples* (Mt. 26:18). Yeshua had observed the Passover with His disciples before, but this was to be the Passover of fulfillment, the Passover of His coming death. The result would be this: *Now before the feast of the Passover, Yeshua knowing that his hour was come that he should depart out of this world unto his Father, having loved his own that were in the world, he loved them unto the end* (Jn. 13:1). The awareness of this last Passover came before the feast, so Yeshua knew this was to be the special Passover of fulfillment.

And he will show you a large upper room furnished: there make ready (Lk. 22:12). A large upper room like this was called the *Aliyah*, the best room in the house, located on the second level, with an outdoor stairwell leading up to it, making it unnecessary to enter the first floor. While the disciples had to prepare the meal, everything else had been prearranged by Yeshua: *And he will himself show you a large upper room furnished <and> ready* (Mk. 14:15). The room was already furnished with a low table and pillows for reclining and was ready for the

505

Passover with all the other necessary provisions, such as the water to wash the hands, etc.

The church tradition that this upper room was in the home of John Mark, the author of the Gospel of Mark, and that in this same room the church was born (Acts 1:13), is unsubstantiated.

Not every detail of the Passover is actually mentioned in the Gospels, but those that are will be noted here.

[§ 151] — b. The Start of the Passover Observance

Matthew 26:20, Mark 14:17, Luke 22:14-16

Yeshua made the point that He had been looking forward to this particular Passover because He would now fulfill the Passover by His death. He said: *I shall not eat it, until it be fulfilled in the kingdom of God* (Lk. 22:16), meaning this was the last Passover He would observe until the kingdom is established. Ezekiel prophesied that the Passover observance will be reinstituted when the messianic kingdom is established (Ez. 45:21). The basis of the kingdom is the New Covenant, and on this Passover, the New Covenant would be ratified by His blood. We will now explore the world's best known Passover celebration.

[§ 152] — c. The First Cup

Luke 22:17-18

During the Jewish Passover, four cups of wine are drunk. According to rabbinic law, even the poor had to purchase wine to partake of these four cups. The wine is consumed at specific points of the Seder, so the names of the cups reflect the part of the celebration during which they are drunk. The first cup is called "the cup of blessing" because it is for the *Kiddush*, a prayer of blessing said at the beginning of the Seder. The Hebrew term *Kiddush* means "sanctification." Therefore, the cup is also called "the cup of sanctification." The second cup is called "the cup of plagues" or "the cup of deliverance." The third is "the cup of redemption," and the last is "the cup of *Hallel*," or "the cup of praise." The

Hallel is a prayer during which the Jewish people recite Psalms 113-118. The Gospels deal only with the first and third cups. The second cup is not mentioned at all, and there is only an indirect reference to the fourth cup. Over each cup, a special prayer is recited.

The Passover begins with the kindling of lights, after which Yeshua *received a cup, and when he had given thanks, he said, Take this, and divide it among yourselves* (Lk. 22:17). This was the first of the four cups of the Jewish Passover Seder. While all cups are preceded by a blessing, the first cup receives the longest of the blessings, called "the Kiddush." Because of the nature and content of the prayer, this cup is also called "the cup of blessing." Its beginning stanza says, *Baruch atah Adonai, Eloheinu melech ha-olam, borei peri hagafen*, which means, "Blessed are you, Lord, our God, King of the universe, Creator of the fruit of the vine." The phrase *fruit of the vine* is a technical Jewish term for Passover wine. Passover wine must be fermented naturally, without any additives that would speed up the fermentation process. To this day, Passover wine is still referred to as *the fruit of the vine*.

Yeshua then repeated that this was the last time He would observe the Passover until the kingdom is established: *for I say unto you, I shall not drink from henceforth of the fruit of the vine, until the kingdom of God shall come* (Lk. 22:18).

[§ 153] — d. The Washing of the Feet and the First Prediction of Betrayal by Judas

John 13:1-20

Following the first cup of the Passover observance is the washing of hands, called *Ur'chatz*. Before reporting on this part of the Seder, Yochanan repeated a point of crucial importance: *And during supper, the devil having already put into the heart of Yehudah Ish Kriyot, Shimon's <son>, to betray him* (Jn. 13:2).[9] This verse reiterates the fact that Satan had entered Judas.

---

[9] For John 13:1, see § 150.

Yeshua had come from God, and as a result of the events of this Passover season, He would soon return to God, emphasizing His divine origin (Jn. 13:3). In Philippians 2:6-8, Paul teaches that although Yeshua was in the form of God, He did not consider existing only in the form of God a thing to be grasped, but emptied Himself into the role of a servant. He did not cease to be God, but added human nature to His divine nature, taking on the role of a servant. What happened during the Passover Seder and especially during this stage, the washing of hands, exemplifies what Paul taught in the Philippians passage. During the hand washing ceremony, the one who takes the servant role (usually the mother or daughter) goes from person to person with a pitcher of water, a bowl, and a towel. The participants would place their fingers over the bowl, the mother or daughter would pour water over them, and then they would dry their hands with the towel. Yeshua followed this Jewish procedure during certain portions of the ceremony at the proper time. However, He did two things differently: He took the servant's role by performing the washing, and He washed the disciples' feet instead of their hands.

Laying aside His garments, Yeshua took a towel and girded Himself. *Then he poured water into the basin, and began to wash the disciples' feet, and to wipe them with the towel wherewith he was girded* (Jn. 13:5). Although normally performed by the woman in the household following the first cup, the Messiah Himself took on the role of a servant. The second departure from the norm was His going from person to person to wash their feet, not their hands. While they might have felt uneasy about their Messiah washing their feet, nobody verbally objected until Yeshua came to Simon Peter, who said, *Lord, do you wash my feet?* (Jn. 13:6). The Greek is emphatic, reading, "Is such a one as you going to wash the feet of such a one as I?" It was beyond Peter's comprehension that the Messiah would take on this kind of role.

Yeshua initially explained: *What I do you know not now; but you shall understand hereafter* (Jn. 13:7). A time would come when Peter would fully understand Yeshua's motive behind this act of service. Now, however, he still objected: *You shall never wash my feet* (Jn. 13:8a). Peter's logic was contradictory. He called Yeshua *Lord*, then he told Him what He could or could not do by saying, "You will never wash my feet!" Yeshua did not try to explain His motive at that point, but He told Peter, *If I wash you not, you have no part with me* (Jn. 13:8b). The disciple did not yet understand that Yeshua was to die and be resurrected. He assumed that the Messiah would soon be setting up His kingdom, so he believed that he was being threatened with loss of position in the kingdom. So he changed his mind and said, *Lord, not my feet only, but also my hands and my head* (Jn. 13:9). In other words, "If that is the case, then go ahead and give me a bath!"

Then Yeshua made the application: *He that is bathed needs not save to wash his feet, but is clean every whit: and ye are clean* (Jn. 13:10). During the Second Temple period, only the wealthy class had a private bath house. Most people went to a public bath house to wash themselves. On the way home, because the streets of Israel were dusty, one's feet would be dirty by the time they arrived home. So, a small bowl or pitcher of water for washing the feet was always at the entry of the door to the home. Since one was already bathed and clean, only their dirty feet needed to be cleaned again. The contrast was between the body and the feet. By way of application, the washing of the body happens at salvation, when the believer is thoroughly washed clean. Because believers still sin in this life (i.e., their feet still get dirty), they must continue to have their feet washed. This happens by means of I John 1:9: *If we confess our sins, he is faithful and righteous to forgive us our sins, and to cleanse us from all unrighteousness.* The body is washed and saved by salvation, but our dirty feet, our daily sins, are cleansed by confessing those sins to God.

After declaring in verse 10 that they were all clean, Yeshua made one exception: *For he knew him that should betray him; therefore said he, Ye are not all clean* (Jn. 13:11). Although Yeshua did not name anyone at this stage, this was the first implication of a betrayal. Later in the Passover observance, Yeshua gave two clues that showed Judas was not saved.

The lesson the apostles were to learn from this was the principle of servanthood. They recognized Yeshua to be Master and Lord, and that was a correct conclusion: *For so I am* (Jn. 13:13). If their Master and Lord willingly took on the role of a servant and washed their feet, then they should do the same: *For I have given you an example* (Jn. 13:15). The principle is this: If the Lord was willing to take on the role of a servant, how much more should those who are His servants take on the role of servanthood (Jn. 13:16)? Yeshua promised that their obedience would bring a reward: *If ye know these things, blessed are ye if ye do them* (Jn. 13:17).

Finally, Yeshua repeated that He would be betrayed: *I speak not of you all: I know whom I have chosen: but that the scripture may be fulfilled: He that eats my bread lifted up his heel against me* (Jn. 13:18). He still did not clearly identify His betrayer, but when He said, *He that eats my bread*, He implied it would be someone within His close circle of companions.

[§ 154] — e. *Karpas*:
The Second Prediction of the Betrayal by Judas

Matthew 26:21-25, Mark 14:18-21, Luke 22:21-23

The ceremony that follows the washing of hands is called *karpas*. This Hebrew term comes from the Greek *"karpos,"* which refers to a fresh, raw vegetable. The ceremony consists of everyone dipping a piece of green vegetable (usually parsley or celery) into salt water and then eating it. Green is a symbol of spring, the symbol of youth, reminding the Jewish people that when Israel was young, in the springtime of her nationhood, God saved her by means of salt water when God divided the Red Sea, allowing the Jews to cross on dry land, but drowning the Egyptian army.

Mark mentioned the timing: *And as they sat and were eating* (Mk. 14:18). The Greek word for *sat* is *anakeimai*, which means "to be laid up," "to recline." At certain intervals during Passover, one reclines towards the left when eating. One such time for reclining is during the ceremony of the karpas, and so, as Yeshua and His disciples observed the Passover, reclining, the Messiah made a prediction: *Verily I say unto you, that one of you shall betray me* (Mt. 26:21). This was more specific than His previous statement. Luke's account points out that this was already determined through the counsel of God and had been prophesied: *For the Son of man indeed goes, as it has been determined: but woe unto that man through whom he is betrayed!* (Lk. 22:22). Yeshua clearly stated that one of the twelve men would betray Him. When they all wanted to know who it was, He named no one, but gave a clue: *He that dipped his hand with me in the dish, the same shall betray me* (Mt. 26:23). With at least 13 people present, this was a rather large Passover. Therefore, several salt water dishes were placed upon the table so that at least one dish would be within easy reach of three or four people. The answer to the question was that whoever dipped his vegetable in the same dish as Yeshua was the betrayer. This was the second prediction, but the first clear identification of the traitor. The context shows that the disciples missed the clue. However, Judas knew, because he had already made the bargain: *And Yehuda, who betrayed Him, answered and said, Is it I, Rabbi? He said unto him, You have said* (Mt. 26:25), a Greek idiom meaning, "Yes, indeed."

[§ 155] — f. The Breaking of the Middle *Matzah*

Matthew 26:26, Mark 14:22, Luke 22:19, I Corinthians 11:23-24

On the Passover table lies a linen bag with three compartments called the *matzah tosh*. If no such bag is available, a linen cloth is folded into quarters to create the three compartments. Three loaves of *matzah*, or unleavened bread, are placed into each one of the compartments. The *matzot*[10] are the focus of a special ritual known as the *afikomen* ceremony, which occurs in two stages. The middle matzah is taken out and broken in half. The larger of the two pieces is wrapped in a linen cloth and hidden. This is done before the main course. After the main course, the hidden matzah, or the *afikomen*, is retrieved, unwrapped, broken into smaller pieces, and distributed among the Seder guests as their "desserts."

By Jewish law, the Passover bread must meet three requirements. It must be unleavened, striped, and pierced so that when held up against a candle or a lamp, the light can be seen through the holes. The holes are poked into the bread in rows, so when it is baked it comes out striped. The rabbinic reason given for the striping and piercing was to impede leavening. However, Yeshua identified His body specifically

---

[10] Plural for *matzah*.

with the Passover matzah: *And he took bread, and when he had given thanks, he broke it, and gave to them, saying, This is my body which is given for you* (Lk. 22:19); *Take, eat; this is my body* (Mt. 26:26). It is important to remember that when Yeshua said, *this is my body*, He specifically referred to the Jewish Passover bread, and no other bread. The Passover bread was a fitting symbol of His body for three reasons. First, it is unleavened. Leaven is the symbol of sin. Since Yeshua was the only Jew who ever kept the Mosaic Law perfectly, down to every jot and tittle (Mt. 5:17-18), His body was unleavened, or sinless. If He had committed even one sin, it would have disqualified Him from being the Passover sacrifice. Second, the matzah bread had to be striped. The body of Yeshua was also striped by way of the Roman whip during the time of His scourging. Third, the bread had to be pierced, and the body of Yeshua was pierced twice, by the nails at the crucifixion, and by the spear thrust into His side.

Another element of the afikomen ceremony also has messianic relevance. The three compartments of the matzah tosh are a picture of one God who exists in three persons: the Father, the Son, and the Holy Spirit. The middle matzah is the only one removed during the ceremony,[11] a picture of the incarnation, when the second person of the Trinity became man and took upon Himself the likeness of sinful flesh. The breaking of the bread is a picture of His death. When Yeshua reached this part of the ceremony, He said, *This is my body which is given for you* (Lk. 22:19). The matzah is then wrapped in a linen cloth. When the body of Yeshua was taken from the cross, it was also wrapped in a linen cloth (Jn. 19:40). Hiding the matzah is a picture of the burial. The removal and unwrapping is a picture of the resurrection. This is done in connection with the third cup, the cup of redemption, because after dying for the sins of the world, Yeshua rose again on the third day. The distribution of the pieces of matzah is a picture of what Yeshua taught in the discourse on the bread of life: One must eat His flesh and drink His blood to have eternal life (Jn. 6:53). As § 78 explained, that meant believing He is the Messiah. Notably, Judas was only present during the first part of the afikomen ceremony, until the matzah was

---

[11] The other two loaves can be eaten during the meal, but they do not have a ceremonial purpose.

hidden. He was not present during the unwrapping and the distribution.

The key symbolic meaning of this whole ritual is remembrance: *This do in remembrance of me* (Lk. 22:19; I Cor. 11:24). In fact, remembrance is the key word for the entire Passover ceremony.

[§ 156] — g. The Sop:
The Third Prediction of Judas' Betrayal

John 13:21-30

One of the ceremonial items prepared for the Passover is called *charoset*, a mixture of apples, nuts, honey, cinnamon, lemon juice, and wine. It is prepared the day before Passover so that by Passover night, it has a deep brown color, symbolizing brick mortar as a reminder that when the Jews were slaves in Egypt, they had to make bricks and mortar to build the cities of Pharaoh. The officiator of the Seder dips a piece of unleavened bread first into the charoset and then into bitter herbs, such as horseradish. He then passes the sop on to one of the guests and repeats this procedure until he and all the participants received their portion.[12]

For the third time during the Passover observance, Yeshua announced that one of the men sitting with Him would betray Him (Jn. 13:21). Again, the disciples wanted to know who it was: *The disciples looked one on another, doubting of whom he spoke* (Jn. 13:22).

This occurred during a part of the Seder when the guests again were reclining at the table (Jn. 13:23a). They leaned to the left against pillows

---

[12] Before the dipping of the sop, the second cup, called the cup of plagues, is drunk. Although not mentioned in the Gospels, it symbolizes the ten plagues that fell upon Egypt. Before anyone can drink the second cup, they must first spill out ten drops of wine. As the ten drops fall, the guests call out the names of the ten plagues. They can only drink the second cup after all ten drops are spilled and the names are called. Drinking wine symbolizes joy, but Jewish law forbade rejoicing over the misfortunes of others, even if they happened to be one's worst enemies. Therefore, the ten drops are spilled as a sign of mourning.

as they partook of certain ceremonial items, and *in Yeshua's bosom* [reclined] *one of his disciples, whom Yeshua loved* (Jn. 13:23b). Typically, ancient biographers showed the reader that they were eyewitnesses of a certain event by writing themselves into the story without actually identifying themselves. Here, Yochanan the apostle identified himself as the disciple whom Yeshua loved by stating that he was reclining against the Messiah's chest. However, some artists have inaccurately portrayed this scene, showing Yochanan's head on the bosom of Yeshua who Himself sits up straight. Since Yeshua was officiating, He would have been sitting at the head of the table, reclining to the left. The apostle, therefore, was at His right side, also reclining towards the left. Peter, who was too far away to ask Yeshua himself, signaled to Yochanan to raise the question, *Tell <us> who it is of whom he speaks* (Jn. 13:24b). Yochanan, already reclining left towards Yeshua, had only to recline a bit further to question Yeshua: *He leaning back, as he was, on Yeshua's breast said unto him, Lord, who is it?* (Jn. 13:25).

Again, Yeshua named no one, but provided a second clue: *He it is, for whom I shall dip the sop, and give it him. So when he had dipped the sop he took and gave it to Yehudah, <the son> of Shimon Ish Kriyot* (Jn. 13:26). The answer to Yochanan's question was that the first person to receive the sop was the betrayer, and so it went. Yeshua dipped the unleavened bread into the charoset and the bitter herbs and gave it to Judas. The disciples did not understand Yeshua's clue; yet, *after the sop, then entered Satan into him* (Jn. 13:27a). The devil first entered into Judas when he made the commitment to betray the Messiah and bargained with the chief priests about the price. Here, Satan entered Judas a second time so that he would follow through with the act of betrayal. Yeshua said, *What you do, do quickly* (Jn. 13:27b).

The disciples completely misunderstood the scene (Jn. 13:29), assuming that because Judas had the moneybag, he either had to buy some missing items or give to the poor.[13]

Now, Judas left the feast: *He then having received the sop went out straightway: and it was night* (Jn. 13:30). Normally, the phrase *and it was night* would be irrelevant because Passover is only observed at

---

[13] To this day, it is a Jewish practice to give alms to the poor at Passover time.

night, never in the daytime. However, Yochanan recorded this, and it supports his sub-theme of the conflict of light and darkness. Obviously, it was nighttime, but Judas himself was of the night and of the darkness, and the deed he was about to perform was one of the night and of the darkness.

Remembering that a part of the original conspiracy was to prevent Yeshua's crucifixion on Passover, this was the chief satanic element of the plot. When Yeshua identified Judas as the betrayer, He forced the conspirators' hands; they had to act on the very night they were trying to avoid, resulting in confusion and disorganization during the initial stages of the Jewish trial. The elders and chief priests did not have the false witnesses lined up, so they were delayed and subsequently disorganized in getting everything together. Yeshua forced their hand, showing that even in the death of the Messiah, God was in full control.

[§ 157] — h. The Third Cup

Matthew 26:27-29, Mark 14:23-25, Luke 22:20, I Corinthians 11:25-26

Following the dipping of the sop, the Seder guests enjoy the main course, which consists of roasted lamb, unleavened bread, and bitter herbs. Then the second part of the afikomen ceremony occurs, with the unwrapping, breaking, and distribution of the hidden matzah, followed by the third of the four cups of wine, called "the cup of the redemption." In Judaism, this cup symbolizes the blood of the lamb that saved the Jewish firstborns from the last plague in Egypt. Yeshua identified His blood with this cup. Luke made that clear when he specified: *And the cup in like manner after supper* (Lk. 22:20a). The first two cups are drunk before supper. The cup of redemption comes after the meal: *This cup is the new covenant in my blood, <even> that which is poured out for you* (Lk. 22:20b). Matthew stated: *for this is my blood of the covenant, which is poured out for many unto remission of sins* (Mt. 26:28). The third cup, which reminds the Seder guests of the shed blood of the innocent lamb that brought redemption from Egypt, now becomes the symbol of the blood of the Lamb of God that takes away the sins of the world. When Yeshua handed out the cup to His disciples, He repeated what He had said about the first cup: *Verily I say unto you, I shall no more drink of the fruit of the vine, until that day when I drink it new in the kingdom of God* (Mk. 14:25). This was the last Passover He would celebrate and the last time He would drink Passover wine until His return. Matthew added a special emphasis: *I shall not drink henceforth of this fruit of the vine, until that day when I drink it new with you in my Father's kingdom* (Mt. 26:29). Yeshua addressed the eleven disciples who remained with Him; Judas had left. The first Passover Yeshua will observe in the messianic kingdom will be in the presence of these apostles.

Paul explains the basic meaning of the ceremony: *For as often as ye eat this bread, and drink the cup, ye proclaim the Lord's death till he come* (I Cor. 11:26). Israel once had a sacrificial system and will again have a sacrificial system in the messianic kingdom.[14] Meanwhile, one of the ways the church must *proclaim the Lord's death till he come* is by partaking of the bread and the cup. The ceremony, an abridged version of the Jewish Passover, is known by different names. Some churches call it "communion," others call it "the Lord's Supper," and others simply call it "the breaking of bread." The phrase *till he come* indicates that this ceremony will terminate with the second coming. The bread of which the church partakes is the middle of the three matzah loaves. The cup of which the church partakes is the third of the four cups of the Passover. This is done to proclaim Yeshua's death, because by that death came the remission of sins. Once the Messiah returns, the ceremony will be replaced by the sacrificial system described in Ezekiel.

The phrase *this do in remembrance of me* is key. When believers in Yeshua share the bread and the cup, they are to remember the Messiah's death and resurrection and to look for His glorious return in the future. It is not transubstantiation, as taught in Catholicism. The elements do not turn into the actual body and blood of Messiah. Nor is it consubstantiation, as taught in Lutheranism. The elements do not contain the actual body and blood of Messiah. The ceremony is simply commemorative, in keeping with the Jewish Passover motif. Every part of the Passover Feast is to remind the participants of something. This remembrance motif is ascribed to the elements of the Lord's Supper,

---

[14] This sacrificial system is described in Ezekiel 40-48.

and those who partake of the bread and the cup are to do it in remembrance of Him. That is the meaning of communion from its Jewish frame of reference, and it is to be done until He returns.

Yeshua also stated, *as often as ye eat this bread and drink the cup* (I Cor. 11:26), which raises the question: How often is "often"? Passover was celebrated once a year, which establishes that minimally, every church should observe communion once a year. Beyond that, the frequency is a question of preference. Some churches observe communion weekly; some monthly; and others observe it periodically, three or four times a year. Biblically, all are equal options.

[§ 158] — i. A Lesson in Greatness

Luke 22:24-30

During the Passover Seder, the third cup initiates a second ceremony, which tends to be less formal and can include readings and recitations as well as singing and discussions. This was the setting for the lesson of this passage, which was brought about by a dispute among the disciples: *And there arose a contention among them, which of them was accounted to be greatest* (Lk. 22:24). The rivalry is ironic in light of the fact that earlier the same evening, Yeshua taught His disciples the principle of servanthood (Jn. 13:1-20). The lesson was that there must be a distinction between the world and the body of believers. The world exercises lordship by man-made authority and/or position; but for the body of believers, greatness is to be shown by serving. Yeshua's life exemplified this kind of greatness (Lk. 22:25-27).

After admonishing His disciples with these words and reminding them of the lesson they had already been taught, Yeshua repeated an earlier promise: that in the messianic kingdom twelve thrones will be set up, and the apostles will sit upon those thrones and rule the twelve tribes of Israel (Lk. 22:28-30). An absolute monarchy will administer the kingdom. The king will be Yeshua the Messiah (e.g., Ps. 2:6-8; Is. 9:6-7; Jer. 23:5-6; Zech. 14:9). His government will consist of two branches, one Jewish and one Gentile. The church and tribulation saints will co-rule with Yeshua over the Gentile branch of government (e.g., Rev. 20:4-6). Under them will be earthly kings in natural bodies, and below them will be the Gentile nations. Co-ruling with Yeshua over the Jewish branch of government will be the resurrected King David (Jer. 30:9; Ez. 34:23-24, 37:24-25; Hos. 3:5). Under David will be the twelve apostles, ruling the twelve tribes of Israel (Mt. 19:28).[15]

[§ 159] — j. The Prediction of Peter's Denial

Matthew 26:31-35, Mark 14:27-31, Luke 22:31-38, John 13:31-38

The Passover observance continued, and Yochanan noted the departure of Judas from the scene: *When therefore he was gone out* (Jn. 13:31a). Judas' departure guaranteed the betrayal, and the betrayal, in turn, assured the coming death of Yeshua. By His death, both the Father and the Son would be glorified (Jn. 13:31b-32). His death also guaranteed that He would soon leave this world: *Little children, yet a little while I am with you. Ye shall seek me: and as I said unto the Jews, Whither I go, ye cannot come* (Jn. 13:33a).

In light of His imminent departure, Yeshua gave a commandment, which in one sense was new, but in another sense it was not: *love one another* (Jn. 13:34a). This was a well-established rule insofar as the second most important commandment of the Mosaic Law was to *love your neighbor as yourself* (Lev. 19:18). So, the standard for loving one's neighbor was love of self. The new facet of this commandment was: *love one another; even as I have loved you* (Jn. 13:34b). The standard was no longer an individual's love for himself, but Yeshua's love for him, and He loved us perfectly and unconditionally—enough to die for us. The way the world will know whether someone is a disciple of Yeshua is if he has the same kind of unconditional love for others (Jn. 13:35).

Having said this, Yeshua announced that after His arrest, the disciples would soon scatter (Mt. 26:31, quoting Zech. 13:7). Knowing that they would forsake Him, He left them clear instructions to leave Jerusalem immediately and go to Galilee (Mt. 26:32). This was the first of three such commands; however, as often as He had taught them the

---

[15] For details on these prophetic themes, see the author's book *The Footsteps of the Messiah: A Study of the Sequence of Prophetic Events* (San Antonio, TX: Ariel Ministries, 2003); chapter 18 details the governments of the messianic kingdom.

whole program of death and resurrection, the disciples never understood it, so they never obeyed this order.

Hearing Yeshua's words, Peter asked: *Lord, whither go you?* (Jn. 13:36). Yeshua answered: *Whither I go, you cannot follow now; but you shall follow afterwards* (Jn. 13:36). He referred to His return to heaven after His death, something Peter did not yet understand: *Lord, why cannot I follow you even now? I will lay down my life for you* (Jn. 13:37). Maybe all the other disciples would fall away from Yeshua, but Peter was sure that he would not. He was confident that he would follow Yeshua to the point of laying down his life.

Yeshua informed Peter that unbeknownst to him, a spiritual war was underway. Just as he had once requested regarding Job, Satan had asked God to let him have Peter, that he might sift him as wheat (Lk. 22:31). However, Yeshua interceded on the apostle's behalf that his *faith fail not* (Lk. 22:32a). Due to this satanic sifting, Peter would stumble, but would not permanently fall from the faith. Yeshua instructed him that *once you have turned again,* meaning once he had repented, *establish your brethren* (Lk. 22:32b). Peter's response was self-assured: *If all shall be offended in you, I will never be offended* (Mt. 26:33). Even if all the other disciples deserted Yeshua, he would never do so!

In response to Peter's adamant proclamation of allegiance, Yeshua uttered yet another prophecy: *Verily I say unto you, that you today, <even> this night, before the cock crow twice, shall deny me thrice* (Mk. 14:30). This is not to be taken as an actual rooster crowing, because roosters are unreliable timepieces. The term *the cock crow* referred to specific times of day. There were four watches of the night. The first watch began at midnight, and the second watch began at 3:00 a.m. So by the second cock crow, or between the first watch at midnight and the second watch at 3:00 a.m., Peter would have denied Yeshua three times.

Peter was not the only one who swore allegiance to Yeshua: *Likewise said all the disciples* (Mt. 26:35b), promising not to deny nor betray Him, nor would they scatter from Him. Yeshua chose not to argue the point, and that night He saw His prophecies fulfilled.

The repeal of a previous commission followed next (Lk. 22:35). Twice before, Yeshua commanded the apostles not to take a purse, a wallet, or shoes. As long as He was visibly and physically present on earth, all these things were automatically provided for them. However, certain things that were true when the Messiah was present are not true now that He is in heaven. Yeshua would soon leave the apostles, so He repealed the previous commission, and gave them a new one: *And he said unto them, When I sent you forth without purse, and wallet, and shoes, lacked ye anything? And they said, Nothing. And he said unto them, But now, he that has a purse, let him take it, and likewise a wallet; and he that has none, let him sell his cloak, and buy a sword* (Lk. 22:35-36). Now that Yeshua was going to depart from them, the disciples must even buy a sword for personal protection rather than to defend the faith.

This is a good example of why careful study of the context of each passage is important to determine if personal application is appropriate. People have claimed for themselves the previous admonitions, but ignored this one, although it negates Yeshua's previous orders. The previous commissions were intended only for the apostles and only while the Messiah was with them. Others incorrectly teach that Yeshua's supernatural acts on earth—such as healing all who came to Him—automatically transferred to His followers. Certain conditions existed and were true while He was on earth, but they are not true in His absence. When He returns, He might reestablish certain commissions, and He will reinstate certain conditions, such as physically healing all who come to Him. However, as long as He is in heaven, we must carefully study the verses to discern correct application for believers today.

[§ 160] — k. The *Hallel*

Matthew 26:30, Mark 14:26

To bring the Passover observance to a close, the Seder guests sing Psalms 113-118, especially focusing on Psalms 117 and 118. While singing, they drink the fourth cup, called *hallel*, or "the cup of praise," which gives this last part of the Passover observance its name.

Matthew and Mark did not specifically mention the fourth cup, but they hinted at it: *And when they had sung a hymn, they went out unto the mount of Olives* (Mt. 26:30). As this passage reads in English, the word *hymn* appears as a noun. Yeshua and the disciples sang a single hymn. In the Greek, it is a verb: They "hymned." They hymned the Psalms in connection with the fourth cup, the cup of praise, with Psalm 118 holding great messianic significance.

[§§ 161–162] —
C. The Promises and Admonitions by the King

The lengthy Upper Room Discourse falls into two geographical divisions. Yeshua spoke the first part while in the upper room during the Passover observance and the second part on the way to Gethsemane. The discourse contains 25 promises and 13 admonitions. Before dealing with the specifics, some introductory observations need to be made.

This is the last of Yeshua's seven discourses recorded in the Gospel of John (Jn. 13:31-15:26), and Yeshua made two major points: First, "I am going away, but it is to my Father's house, and I will come back to take you there in the future." Second, "I am going away, but I will send you a Comforter to be with you until the day that I come for you."

The Upper Room Discourse contains the last two of Yeshua's seven "I Am" statements, in John 14:6 (*I am the way, and the truth, and the life*) and John 15:1 (*I am the true vine*).

The Passover observance, during which the discourse occurred, allowed ample time for conversation. Yochanan recorded parts of the dialogue between Yeshua and the apostles. The following shows the conversation from the disciples' point of view:

Toma said unto him, Lord, we know not whither you go, how know we the way? (Jn. 14:5)

Philip said to him, Lord, show us the Father, and it suffices us. (Jn. 14:8)

Yehudah (not Ish Kriyot) said unto him, Lord, what is come to pass that you will manifest yourself unto us, and not unto the world? (Jn. 14:22)

<Some> of his disciples therefore said one to another, What is this that he said unto us, A little while, and ye behold me not; and again a little while, and ye shall see me: and, Because I go to the Father? They said therefore, What is this that he said, A little while? We know not what he said. (Jn. 16:17-18)

His disciples say, Lo, now you speak plainly, and speak no dark saying. Now know we that you know all things, and need not that any man should ask you: by this we believe that you came forth from God. (Jn. 16:29-30)

Their comments show that the disciples still did not comprehend the program of death and resurrection, and it took Yeshua's forty-day ministry between the resurrection and the ascension for them to finally grasp the significance of what happened. By the time they preached the gospel in the book of Acts, they finally fully understood.

Four observations can be made concerning the significance of the Upper Room Discourse. First, it marks a transition from Yeshua's office of prophet to the office of priest. As previously mentioned, the Messiah holds three offices: prophet, priest, and king. He does not function in all three offices simultaneously, but chronologically. During His first coming, Yeshua functioned in the role of prophet. He currently functions as priest. In the future, He will be king. The Upper Room Discourse is the transition from the office of prophet to the office of priest.

The second significance of the Upper Room Discourse is that it marks the beginning point of the transition from the dispensation of law to the dispensation of grace. Technically, the dispensation of law ended with the death of the Messiah, and the dispensation of grace began with the birth of the church and the coming of the Holy Spirit's ministry of Spirit baptism in Acts 2. Between the two dispensations was a transitional period, during which the dispensation of law was slowly phased out and the dispensation of grace began to be phased in. By the time of Acts 2:1-4, the dispensation of law had finally ended, and the dispensation of grace had been established. The Upper Room Discourse began this transitional period.

The third significance of the discourse is that Yeshua planted many seeds of New Testament doctrine. In the Epistles, the apostles exposited, elaborated upon, and formed doctrine from many of the things Yeshua taught in seed form in the Upper Room Discourse.

The fourth significance is that the discourse began to describe the new relationship believers would have with Yeshua following His death and resurrection. The apostles' relationship with the Messiah was unique and available only during the Messiah's earthly ministry when He had a mortal body. Believers today can never have the same kind of relationship the apostles enjoyed with Yeshua before His death. Following His resurrection, the disciples entered into a new relationship with Him, the same type of relationship that all believers have with Yeshua today. The Apostle Paul later elaborated upon what this relationship means for the believer. It entails the concept of being "in Christ" and the positional truths that come with being part of the body of Messiah.

It is beyond the scope of this harmonized study of the life of the Messiah to give a detailed exposition of the Upper Room Discourse, so the commentary will focus on delineating the specific promises and admonitions found in the discourse.

[§ 161] — 1. In the Upper Room

John 14

First Promise: He Is Preparing a Place for Us

The first promise Yeshua made during the Upper Room Discourse is that He would leave the earth for the purpose of preparing a place for the believers: *for I go to prepare a place for you* (Jn. 14:2). This was not a promise to the disciples only; it is for all believers. Everyone who becomes a believer will have a place prepared for them in the New Jerusalem, which presently is in heaven.

Second Promise: He will Come for the Believers

Once the preparations are complete and every believer has his own place in the Father's house, Yeshua will fulfill His second promise: *And* *if I go and prepare a place for you, I come again, and will receive you unto myself; that where I am, <there> ye may be also* (Jn. 14:3). This special coming to take believers to the place He has prepared is the promise of the rapture, not the second coming. The purpose of the second coming is for Yeshua to judge the living and the dead and to set up His kingdom. He will come to earth and reign from Jerusalem for a thousand years. In contrast, the promise in John 14:3 is that when He comes for the saints, He will take them to the place where He is going to be, which is heaven (Mk. 16:19; Acts 1:9, 7:55; I Pet. 3:22). So, when Yeshua returns at the second coming, He will stay on earth; but at the rapture, He will take the saints into heaven. It is important that the rapture is distinguished from the second coming because post-tribulationalism teaches that believers will meet Yeshua in the air only to turn around and immediately come back to the earth. That is not the promise Yeshua made. He promised to take the believers to heaven, where He was then going. This is the pre-tribulational view of the rapture: Yeshua will take believers into heaven after they meet Him in the air (I Thess. 4:17).

Third Promise: Believers Will Do Greater Works

The third promise is that believers will do greater works than Yeshua: *Verily, verily, I say unto you, he that believes on me, the works that I do shall he do also; and greater <works> than these shall he do; because I go unto the Father* (Jn. 14:12). Unfortunately, based on this verse, some teach that believers will be able to accomplish works of greater quality than Yeshua; however, no one will ever be able to surpass the quality of Yeshua's works. After all, He was the perfect God-Man. The term *greater* can be understood in two ways: greater in quality or greater in number. The second option is the correct way to understand this promise. Believers will not perform works of greater quality, but of greater quantity. The history of the church has extended over nearly two millennia; Yeshua's ministry covered three-and-one-half years. If the works of the church throughout the centuries are considered, they are greater in quantity, but certainly not in quality.

Fourth Promise: Answered Prayers

The fourth promise is that Yeshua will answer prayers: *And whatsoever ye shall ask in my name, that will I do, that the Father may be glorified in the Son* (Jn. 14:13). With these words, Yeshua established a new basis of prayer: to pray and ask in His name. Asking in Yeshua's name means to ask based on His authority, for His sake, and because of the believer's relationship with Him. What a believer asks in His name, this Yeshua will do. Ignoring all the other verses concerning prayer, it is easy to take this verse and teach that if a believer asks anything in Yeshua's name, his prayer will automatically be answered. However, it is important to remember the totality of the biblical teaching on prayer. One of these teachings is that God will answer every prayer in the name of Yeshua that is exercised by faith in accordance with His will. Sometimes prayers are not answered, not because of a lack of faith or for praying the wrong way, but because it was not in accordance with the Father's will. After all, the Father knows best. He can see the end from the beginning. He knows the future consequences of the request, and He knows whether such a prayer should be answered or not. Yeshua promised to answer all prayers in His name that are in accordance with the will of the Father (I Jn. 5:14). The divine motive for answering prayer is *that the Father may be glorified in the Son* (Jn. 14:13); hence, it must be in accordance with His will.

Fifth Promise: The Coming of the Holy Spirit

The fifth promise is that the Holy Spirit will come and abide with the believers forever (Jn. 14:16-18):

> [16] *And I will pray the Father, and he shall give you another Comforter, that he may be with you for ever,* [17] *<even> the Spirit of truth: whom the world cannot receive; for it beholds him not, neither knows him: ye know him; for he abides with you, and shall be in you.* [18] *I will not leave you desolate: I come unto you.*

Three things should be noted about this promise: First, the Holy Spirit is referred to in Greek as *allon Parakleton*, meaning *another Comforter*. Just as Yeshua is our *Paraclete*, the Holy Spirit is also called to our side to console, comfort, encourage, and intercede on our behalf as an advocate in court. Of the two Greek terms that are translated by the

English word "another," *allon* means "another of the same kind," rather than "another of a different kind." Thus, the Holy Spirit is another Comforter of the same kind. Yeshua and the Holy Spirit are both God; they are both members of the Trinity; and they both are divine. The disciples experienced one divine comforter, the Son. Upon His departure, they would be given another divine comforter, the Holy Spirit.

Second, the apostles would have a new relationship to the Holy Spirit. The Holy Spirit was no stranger to them, which is why Yeshua said, *ye know him* (Jn. 14:17). The Holy Spirit had already been active in the disciples' lives and was a well-known entity in the Hebrew Bible. However, they were to enter into a new relationship with Him that they had not heretofore experienced. The distinction is clear: *for he abides with you, and shall be in you* (Jn. 14:17). This is the dispensational distinctive in that during the dispensation of law, the Holy Spirit was **with** the saints but only indwelled a few. Yeshua's death and resurrection would initiate a new relationship. The Holy Spirit would not only abide with all believers, but would also be **in** all believers.

The third point is that the Holy Spirit will never leave the believer. The few people in the Old Testament who were indwelled by the Holy Spirit were not necessarily indwelled permanently. Now this would change, as Yeshua promised, *I will not leave you desolate* (Jn. 14:18). The Greek word for *desolate* is *orphanous*, an adjective meaning "as orphans." He would not leave them orphaned, but through the Spirit, they would be the adopted sons of God.

Sixth Promise: Loved by the Father and the Son

The sixth promise is that both the Father and the Son would love them: *He that has my commandments, and keeps them, he it is that loves me: and he that loves me shall be loved by my Father, and I will love him, and will manifest myself to him* (Jn. 14:21). The whole Trinity plays a role in the relationship with believers. The Holy Spirit will be another Comforter of the same kind who will indwell the believers, but the Father and the Son will have a special love for them. Believers show their love for God by keeping His commandments. God the Father and God the Son will show their love for the believers by rewarding them for keeping His commandments.

Seventh Promise: Indwelled by the Father and the Son

The seventh promise is that the believer will be indwelled by both the Father and the Son (Jn. 14:23-24):

> *23 Yeshua answered and said unto him, If a man love me, he will keep my word: and my Father will love him, and we will come unto him, and make our abode with him. 24 He that loves me not keeps not my words; and the word which ye hear is not mine, but the Father's who sent me.*

Eighth Promise: Taught by the Holy Spirit

The eighth promise was that the Holy Spirit will teach the apostles and bring to remembrance all that Yeshua had taught them: *But the Comforter, <even> the Holy Spirit, whom the Father shall send in my name, he shall teach you all things, and bring to your remembrance all that I said unto you* (Jn. 14:26). Some have wondered how the disciples could remember all of Yeshua's words and correctly record them as late as A.D. 90, approximately sixty years after Yeshua made the statements. The answer is found in this verse. One of the special ministries of the Holy Spirit to the apostles was to bring to remembrance all that Yeshua had taught them so they could record His teachings accurately. The Gospels of the New Testament exist because the Holy Spirit brought to remembrance all that Yeshua taught.

Ninth Promise: Divine Peace

The ninth promise is peace: *Peace I leave with you; my peace I give unto you: not as the world gives, give I unto you* (Jn. 14:27). Yeshua promised that there would be peace in the heart of the apostles, but not in the world, for that will only come during the millennial kingdom. They could experience peace knowing that God was in control, regardless of what happened to them. If they accepted and believed this promise, they would have the peace of Yeshua reigning in their hearts.

[§ 162] — 2. On the Way to Gethsemane

John 15 & 16

Tenth Promise: A New Relationship with the Messiah

Yeshua's tenth promise is that believers, being the branches, would have a new relationship to the vine: *I am the vine, ye are the branches. He that abides in me, and I in him, the same bears much fruit: for apart from me ye can do nothing* (Jn. 15:5). This is the relationship of being in Messiah (in Christ), a concept that the Apostle Paul spells out later in detail.

Eleventh Promise: Yeshua's Friends

The eleventh promise is that believers are to be Yeshua's friends (Jn. 15:14-15):

> *14 Ye are my friends, if ye do the things which I command you. 15 No longer do I call you servants; for the servant knows not what his lord does: but I have called you friends; for all things that I heard from my Father, I have made known unto you.*

This is not friendship in place of servanthood, but friendship in addition to servanthood. Throughout the Epistles, even the apostles refer to themselves as servants. The difference between servanthood and friendship is that a servant simply obeys the master's orders without being told in advance or in detail what the master's plans are. He knows the plans only insofar as the master chooses to reveal them and only as much as he needs to know to participate in those plans. He does not know the goal nor see the bigger picture. Just so, Yeshua had been teaching the disciples piecemeal. Only now would they begin to receive the comprehensive truth of God's plan regarding things to come. This greater knowledge of His plans elevates them to the position of friendship.

Twelfth Promise: Chosen for Good Works

The twelfth promise is that believers are chosen for good works: *Ye did not choose me, but I chose you, and appointed you, that ye should go and* *bear fruit, and <that> your fruit should abide: that whatsoever ye shall ask of the Father in my name, he may give it you* (Jn. 15:16). Every believer is chosen for the purpose of bearing fruit. When they fulfill their purpose, their prayers will be answered, presuming that they ask in His will.

Thirteenth Promise: Hated by the World

The thirteenth promise is found in John 15:19-22:

> *¹⁹ If ye were of the world, the world would love its own: but because ye are not of the world, but I chose you out of the world, therefore the world hates you. ²⁰ Remember the word that I said unto you, A servant is not greater than his lord. If they persecuted me, they will also persecute you; if they kept my word, they will keep yours also. ²¹ But all these things will they do unto you for my name's sake, because they know not him that sent me. ²² If I had not come and spoken unto them, they had not had sin: but now they have no excuse for their sin.*

The promise is that the world will hate His disciples for four reasons. First, as believers, they are no longer part of the world system (Jn. 15:19). Yeshua draws a clear distinction between being *of the world* and being *in the world*. As long as believers and unbelievers are alive, both are in the world. The difference is that unbelievers are in and of the world, whereas believers are in the world but no longer of the world, meaning they are no longer part of the world system. They no longer think the way the world thinks, set the same worldly goals, or subscribe to the same programming that the world produces. For this reason, believers will be hated by the world.

The second reason believers will be hated is because it is easier to direct anger toward Yeshua's followers than toward the Messiah because He has left (Jn. 15:20). Now that He is gone, the world can no longer vent its anger and hatred upon Yeshua personally as when He was present, although they continue to attack Him verbally. Instead, they direct their hatred toward His followers.

The third reason believers will be hated is that the world does not know the Father (Jn. 15:21). Had they known the Father, they would have known the Son and not persecuted Him. They refused to recognize the Son, so they never came to know the Father either, which then causes them to hate those who do have this knowledge. While the believers' knowledge of the Father makes them friends of the Son, the unbelievers' lack of knowledge causes them to hate the ones who are the friends of God.

The fourth reason believers will be hated is that they operate by a new, divine standard (Jn. 15:22). Believers living consistently in accordance with a divine standard will cause conviction to come upon unbelievers. Their lives render the unbelievers' sins inexcusable. With their backs against the wall, unbelievers try to retaliate, and since they cannot vent their wrath upon the Son, they hate believers instead.

Fourteenth Promise: The Holy Spirit's Witness

The fourteenth promise is that the Holy Spirit will bear witness of the Messiah: *But when the Comforter is come, whom I will send unto you from the Father, <even> the Spirit of truth, which proceeds from the Father, he shall bear witness of me* (Jn. 15:26). Earlier Yeshua talked about the Holy Spirit as Comforter, who will indwell believers. Another reason for the coming of the Holy Spirit is now revealed: He will bear witness to the Messiahship of Yeshua. Whoever responds to His witness will become a child of God, and those who reject His witness will come to hate the saints.

Fifteenth Promise: The Believer's Witness

The fifteenth promise was that the apostles will also bear witness to the Messiahship of Yeshua: *and ye also bear witness, because ye have been with me from the beginning* (Jn. 15:27). Just like the Holy Spirit, the believers will testify to Yeshua's Messiahship, and their ministries go hand in hand: While the believers explain the content of the gospel to others, the Holy Spirit authenticates their testimony by convicting the listeners to see the truth of what the believers are saying.

Sixteenth Promise: Excommunication from the Synagogue

The sixteenth promise was that the believers would be excommunicated from the synagogue: *These things have I spoken unto you, that ye should not be caused to stumble. They shall put you out of the synagogues* (Jn. 16:1-2a). In the beginning, the Jewish believers were looked upon as simply another sect within Judaism. However, over the course of time, they were no longer recognized as such, which led to their excommunication from the synagogue.

Seventeenth Promise: Martyr's Death

The seventeenth promise was that many of the apostles would be killed: *the hour comes, that whosoever kills you shall think that he offers service unto God* (Jn. 16:2b). Of the eleven disciples whom Yeshua addressed in these verses, ten died martyrs' deaths. While the Jews excommunicated them, primarily the Gentiles killed them. Over the course of history, many other believers were also martyred. Those who killed them believed they were doing a service for God. Perhaps the best example is the Apostle Paul, who at one time was a persecutor of the church. He killed Jewish believers, convinced that by so doing, he was serving God, until he learned otherwise on the Damascus road.

Eighteenth Promise: The Spirit's Work of Conviction

The eighteenth promise is that the Holy Spirit will convict the world (Jn. 16:7-11):

> *⁷ Nevertheless I tell you the truth: It is expedient for you that I go away; for if I go not away, the Comforter will not come unto you; but if I go, I will send him unto you. ⁸ And he, when he is come, will convict the world in respect of sin, and of righteousness, and of judgment: ⁹ of sin, because they believe not on me; ¹⁰ of righteousness, because I go to the Father, and ye behold me no more; ¹¹ of judgment, because the prince of this world has been judged.*

The work of conviction is to clarify the gospel in the minds of unbelievers so that they acknowledge it is true. This work does not presuppose that those who are convicted will accept the good news. The Spirit's conviction will cause the unregenerate mind to understand and acknowledge the truth of the issues at stake. Whether the hearers accept it or not is another issue.

When the Holy Spirit performs this work, He convicts the world of three things: *of sin, and of righteousness, and of judgment* (Jn. 16:8). He convicts the world specifically of the sin of unbelief, as demonstrated by their failure to believe in the Messiahship of Yeshua (Jn. 16:9). He convicts the world of righteousness, specifically the righteousness of Yeshua, as proven by His ascension to the Father (Jn. 16:10). If Yeshua had been unrighteous, He would not have ascended into heaven, where He took His place at the right hand of God the Father. Lastly, the Holy Spirit will convict the world of God's final judgment, as demonstrated by the fact that *the prince of this world has been judged* (Jn. 16:11). If the prince of this world has been judged, then the followers of the prince of this world will also be judged at the Great White Throne Judgment.

Nineteenth Promise: Revealing the Truth

The nineteenth promise was that the Holy Spirit will reveal the truth to the disciples (Jn. 16:13):

> *13 Howbeit when he, the Spirit of truth, is come, he shall guide you into all the truth: for he shall not speak from himself; but what things soever he shall hear, <these> shall he speak: and he shall declare unto you the things that are to come.*

The Holy Spirit's revelations originate from the Father and the Son. Those things He has heard from the Father and the Son, He will reveal to the believers. For this reason, the inspired New Testament record exists. The Holy Spirit inspired the apostles to write the Gospels and the Epistles, and He showed Yochanan things that are to come so that he could write the book of Revelation.

Twentieth Promise: The Holy Spirit Will Glorify the Messiah

The twentieth promise is that the Holy Spirit will glorify the Messiah: *He shall glorify me: for he shall take of mine, and shall declare <it> unto you* (Jn. 16:14). The purpose of the coming of the Holy Spirit is to glorify the Son. Any movement that centers around the Holy Spirit rather than the Son violates this specific principle and does not have God's blessing. In fact, even a movement that is Father-, rather than Son-centered, is not ordained by the Word of God.

Twenty-first Promise: The Apostles Will See Yeshua Again

The twenty-first promise was that the apostles would see Yeshua again: *A little while, and ye behold me no more; and again a little while, and ye shall see me* (Jn. 16:16). While most of these promises are for believers in general, a few are limited to the disciples. Here is one such promise: The apostles will see Him again after the resurrection. When Yeshua said, *A little while, and ye behold me no more*, He meant His coming death and burial. When He said, *and again a little while, and ye shall see me*, He meant that they would see Him again after His resurrection. By saying *a little while*, Yeshua referred to the short interval of three days between His death and resurrection.

Twenty-second Promise: New Method of Teaching

The twenty-second promise was a new teaching method: *These things have I spoken to you in dark sayings: the hour comes, when I shall no more speak unto you in dark sayings, but shall tell you plainly of the Father* (Jn. 16:25). In the Greek, the phrase *dark sayings* consists of one word, *paroimia*, meaning "allegory" and "proverb." However, it differs from the proverbs of the book of Proverbs containing pithy sayings and teachings. Rather, here it refers to parabolic teaching. Yeshua had taught His disciples many things in parables, but that would change. The promise is that of a new teaching method: He would teach them in plain language. Of course, Yeshua had been teaching them plainly before this, but He also taught them parabolically, and from that point on, Yeshua did not use any more *dark sayings*.

Twenty-third Promise: The Scattering of the Apostles

The twenty-third promise was that the disciples would be scattered and desert Him: *Yeshua answered them, Do ye now believe? Behold the hour comes, yea, is come, that ye shall be scattered, every man to his own, and shall leave me alone: and <yet> I am not alone, because the Father is with me* (Jn. 16:31-32). This was fulfilled that very night. After finishing the discourse, Yeshua went to the garden of Gethsemane and experienced great agony. When He returned to where His disciples were waiting, a horde came to take Him into custody. During the arrest, the disciples forsook Yeshua, fled, and scattered. This fulfilled the promise the Messiah made in this passage.

Twenty-fourth Promise: Persecution

The twenty-fourth promise is that believers will be persecuted in the world: *These things have I spoken unto you, that in me ye may have peace. In the world ye have tribulation* (Jn. 16:33a). For ten of the eleven disciples, the persecution meant martyrdom. The only one who did not die for his faith was this Gospel's author, the Apostle Yochanan. However, he suffered persecution and in his old age was exiled to Patmos, a desert island off the west coast of present-day Turkey to which people were sent to die. Since then, many believers have been martyred or have suffered some form of persecution for their faith. The degree of suffering varies and may be as mild as being ostracized by friends and neighbors, or heavier, such as experiencing divorce or the loss of home, job, or position in society. One thing is certain: All believers will suffer some degree of persecution because of their faith in Messiah.

Twenty-fifth Promise: Victory

The twenty-fifth promise is one of final victory: *but be of good cheer; I have overcome the world* (Jn. 16:33b). After warning His disciples and believers in general of many things—persecution, martyrdom, hatred by the world, excommunication from the synagogue, and persecution by the religious people who believed they were serving God—Yeshua promised the final victory would be theirs because He has overcome the world.

3. Admonitions by the King

Just as with the promises, some of Yeshua's admonitions were especially for the apostles, while others are for believers in general.

First Admonition: Do not Be Troubled

The first admonition specifically addressed the apostles: *Let not your heart be troubled: believe in God, believe also in me* (Jn. 14:1). Yeshua had told His disciples that He would depart from them physically—

first for a short period of time, and then return to them for a much longer duration. They were not to be troubled or disturbed by His absence. Rather, they were to believe that His departure was a necessary part of God's divine plan.

Second Admonition: No One Comes to the Father apart from Yeshua

The second admonition concerns the way into heaven: *Yeshua said unto him, I am the way, and the truth, and the life: no one comes unto the Father, but by me. If ye had known me, ye would have known my Father also: from henceforth ye know him, and have seen him* (Jn. 14:6-7). The way into heaven is by Yeshua the Messiah, because no one comes unto the Father but by Him. Anyone claiming that God can be known apart from Yeshua is a false teacher. Of course, all the world's religions outside the Scriptures claim that people are able to come directly to God apart from Yeshua. However, Yeshua taught that no one comes unto the Father, but by the Son of God.

Third Admonition: The Content of Faith

The third admonition concerned the content of faith: *Believe you not that I am in the Father, and the Father in me? The words that I say unto you I speak not from myself: but the Father abiding in me does his works. Believe me that I am in the Father, and the Father in me: or else believe me for the very works' sake* (Jn. 14:10-11). To believe on Yeshua meant three things:

1. He is the one who knows the Father.
2. To know Him is to know the Father.
3. His words prove His origin, while His works authenticate His words. In light of these works, which authenticated His words, the admonition is to believe that Yeshua is the Messiah.

Fourth Admonition: Keep the Law of Messiah

The fourth admonition is to keep Messiah's commandments: *If ye love me, ye will keep my commandments* (Jn. 14:15). The way a believer shows love for Messiah is by keeping His commandments. The verse does not say, "Keep the commandments in order to love Him," for that would mean salvation is by works. Salvation is by grace through faith plus nothing. If a believer seriously loves Yeshua, he will show it by keeping the commandments which are part of the law of Messiah. Although believers are not obligated to keep the commandments of the Law of Moses, they are obligated to keep the commandments of the law of Messiah, and thus show their love for Yeshua. Any person who claims to love the Son but does not keep His commandments is making a false profession.

Fifth Admonition: Love the Messiah

The fifth admonition relates to the fourth (Jn. 14:23-24):

> *²³ Yeshua answered and said unto him, If a man love me, he will keep my word: and my Father will love him, and we will come unto him, and make our abode with him. ²⁴ He that loves me not keeps not my words: and the word which ye hear is not mine, but the Father's who sent me.*

This admonition is to love the Messiah. Again, the way to prove love for the Lord is to keep His word.

Sixth Admonition: Rejoice

The sixth admonition was to rejoice that Yeshua was going to the Father: *Ye heard how I said to you, I go away, and I come unto you. If ye loved me, ye would have rejoiced, because I go unto the Father: for the Father is greater than I* (Jn. 14:28). The apostles should rejoice that Yeshua was going to leave them to return to the Father. Their failure to rejoice would show that their love for Him was selfish. If they loved Him unselfishly, they would be neither troubled nor disturbed about His departure; they would rejoice in it, because He would be with the Father.

Seventh Admonition: Abide in the Messiah

The seventh admonition concerned the relationship the believers are to have with Yeshua: *Abide in me, and I in you. As the branch cannot bear fruit of itself, except it abide in the vine; so neither can ye, except ye abide in me. I am the vine, ye are the branches: He that abides in me, and I in him, the same bears much fruit: for apart from me ye can do nothing* (Jn. 15:4-5). To abide in Yeshua means to be in a continuous, living relationship with Him.

John 15:1-2 and 6 explain what this relationship entails:

> *¹ I am the true vine, and my Father is the husbandman. ² Every branch in me that bears not fruit, he takes it away: and every branch that bears fruit, he cleanses it, that it may bear more fruit. . . . ⁶ If a man abide not in me, he is cast forth as a branch, and is withered; and they gather them, and cast them into the fire, and they are burned.*

A vineyard in biblical times did not bear much resemblance to its modern counterpart. The vines grew upon the ground instead of being tied to some sort of support, yet as long as the vine lay on the soil, it could not bear fruit. Therefore, the winegrower placed a rock underneath the vine to lift it off the ground, enabling it to bear fruit. That is the point of this passage. The Greek word *airó* in John 15:2, translated here as *takes it away*, can also mean "to lift up." If the intent was "take away," it would refer to fruitless believers who are disciplined by death, as in I Corinthians 5:1-5, 11:28-30, and I John 5:16. However, another way to understand the term is "to lift up," as is intended here. The Messiah lifts up every fruitless branch so that it can bear fruit.

The second step is: *every <branch> that bears fruit, he cleanses it, that it may bear more fruit* (Jn. 15:2b). Cleansing here means pruning. The Messiah prunes the branch so that it can bear even more fruit.

Some believers never seem to produce fruit, and then comes the third step: *If a man abide not in me, he is cast forth as a branch, and is withered; and they gather them, and cast them into the fire, and they are burned* (Jn. 15:6). This is not the fire of hell, but the fire of the judgment seat of Messiah; if the believer proves to be fruitless, then that which will burn is the fruitless branches they have produced—the wood, hay, and stubble of I Corinthians 3:10-15. The result is not the loss of salvation, but rather the loss of rewards.

In summary, the believer's relationship with the Messiah entails those who abide in Him being lifted up by Him and bearing fruit. He will prune them by way of discipline so they can bear even more fruit. If they fail to produce fruit, then their barren branches will be judged by fire.

Eighth Admonition: Bear Fruit

The eighth admonition is to bear fruit: *Herein is my Father glorified, that ye bear much fruit; and <so> shall ye be my disciples* (Jn. 15:8). This builds upon the seventh admonition to abide in the Messiah. If believers abide in Him, they will bear fruit. So to bear fruit presupposes that believers are abiding in Messiah. This is how the Father is glorified: Believers glorify the Father by bearing fruit.

Ninth Admonition: Abide in the Messiah's Love

The ninth admonition is to abide in Yeshua's love: *If ye keep my commandments, ye shall abide in my love; even as I have kept my Father's commandments, and abide in His love* (Jn. 15:10). This is related to the fourth admonition, to keep the law of Messiah. Believers are admonished to abide in Yeshua's love. The evidence that they are doing as commanded is that they keep His law. Yeshua used Himself as an example: *I have kept my Father's commandments, and abide in His love.* The Son kept the commandments of the Father by abiding in His love, and He proved His love for the Father by keeping the Father's commandments. If believers abide in Yeshua's love, they will keep His commandments, that is, the law of Messiah. By abiding in His love, they keep His commandments; and the act of keeping His commandments is how they demonstrate their love for Him.

Keeping Yeshua's commandments shows love in two respects: It shows that believers are experiencing His love in their lives, and they are showing their love for Him. The external evidence is not emotions, but works, meaning the keeping of the commandments. We are not saved by these works; rather, these works are the evidence that we are a saved people.

Tenth Admonition: Love One Another

The tenth admonition is to love one another: *This is my commandment, that ye love one another, even as I have loved you. Greater love has no man than this, that a man lay down his life for his friends* (Jn. 15:12-13). Based upon the believer's love for God and God's love for the believer, the admonition is that they are to love one another; they are to love the brethren. They should be closer to fellow believers than to unsaved members of their own families. If believers abide in His love and show their love for Him by keeping His commandments, they will also love one another.

Eleventh Admonition: Bear Witness

The eleventh admonition was that the apostles were to bear witness concerning Yeshua: *and ye also bear witness, because ye have been with me from the beginning* (Jn. 15:27). The apostles were to testify specifically that Yeshua is Israel's Messiah because they had been with Him from the beginning of His public ministry, hearing all He said and taught, and observing His actions and the miracles He performed. Therefore, they were to testify concerning the truth of His Messiahship based on these things they had seen with their eyes, heard with their ears, and understood with their minds, and the Holy Spirit would bring to remembrance everything the Messiah had taught them.

Twelfth Admonition: Pray in the Name of Yeshua

The twelfth admonition provided the new basis for prayer. From that point on, prayer and petitions were to be made in the name of Yeshua:

> And in that day ye shall ask me no question. Verily, verily, I say unto you, if ye shall ask anything of the Father, he will give it to you in my name. Hitherto have ye asked nothing in my name; ask, and ye shall receive, that your joy may be made full. (Jn. 16:23-24)
>
> This is a dispensational distinctive. Earlier in His ministry, the disciples came to Yeshua and asked Him, Lord, teach us to pray. (Lk. 11:1)

In response, He taught them how to pray and gave them a six-fold outline. However, He did not command them to pray in His name, and up to the Upper Room Discourse, the disciples did just as He bid. They prayed and made petitions to God the Father, but not in the name of Yeshua. Now this was to change. To pray in someone's name is to pray in their authority. Believers are to pray in Yeshua's name because the Messiah has given them the authority to ask in His name. Just as an ambassador, acting as a government official on behalf of one's country, can speak in his country's name, so believers can pray in the name of

Yeshua, in His authority, because of the position believers have in the Messiah.

Thirteenth Admonition: Be of Good Cheer

The thirteenth and final admonition was to be of good cheer: *These things have I spoken unto you, that in me ye may have peace. In the world ye have tribulation: but be of good cheer; I have overcome the world* (Jn. 16:33). Yeshua had told His disciples both good and bad news, and their response was to be of good cheer. All they had heard and all that would happen was part of God's plan, and they should be cheerful; the plan of God is working its way out. He is and will always be in control.

4. Additional Observations

Yeshua warned His disciples of the coming spiritual battle: *I will no more speak much with you, for the prince of the world comes: and he has nothing in me; but that the world may know that I love the Father, and as the Father gave me commandment, even so I do* (Jn. 14:30-31). Yeshua was soon to face a very important spiritual battle, and Satan was coming against Him; but as much as Satan had tried, he had *nothing in* Yeshua, meaning he could not legitimately accuse the Messiah of a single thing.

Yeshua described the effects of His coming departure and death: *Verily, verily, I say unto you, that you shall weep and lament, but the world shall rejoice: ye shall be sorrowful, but your sorrow shall be turned into joy* (Jn. 16:20). Indeed, when Yeshua was killed, the disciples sorrowed deeply. They did not anticipate His resurrection, and their enemies, the world, rejoiced. Suddenly, by means of His resurrection, all their sorrow was turned into joy. He added, *And ye therefore now have sorrow: but I will see you again, and your heart shall rejoice, and your joy no one takes away from you* (Jn. 16:22). Once again, Yeshua prophesied His death and resurrection.

[§ 163] — D. The High Priestly Prayer

After finishing His farewell discourse to the disciples, Yeshua prayed an extended prayer known today as His "high priestly prayer." He prayed as He was walking, shortly before entering the garden of Gethsemane. Previously, He taught that prayer should not be haphazard, but organized. In keeping with this instruction, He arranged His prayer into three main divisions.

1. Concerning Himself

John 17:1-8

In the first main division, Yeshua prayed concerning Himself. He began His prayer by *lifting up his eyes to heaven* (Jn. 17:1). In dealing with the subject of prayer, the Bible speaks of various postures, but never mentions that the eyes should be closed during prayer. Praying with the eyes closed is not wrong; in fact, sometimes it sets the mind upon God without being distracted by something else. However, while the Scriptures speak of people praying while standing up, kneeling down, prostrating themselves with their faces on the ground, lifting up their heads, or directing their eyes to heaven, they never mention praying with closed eyes. On this occasion, Yeshua lifted His eyes to heaven, and with open eyes, He spoke to God the Father.

First, He specifically requested His glorification: *Father, the hour is come; glorify your Son* (Jn. 17:1b). Yeshua's first reason for His request was so that He might glorify God the Father (Jn. 17:1c). The purpose and goal of all prayer is to glorify the Father. Yeshua pointed out that the Son glorified the Father by providing eternal life (Jn. 17:2). Second, He had finished the work the Father had given Him (Jn. 17:4) and now faced His death.

Yeshua's second request was for the restoration of the glory that had been veiled since the incarnation: *And now, Father, glorify you me with your own self with the glory which I had with you before the world was* (Jn. 17:5). This was His unique Shechinah glory, the bright and shining glory that He possessed for all eternity past, but that was veiled by His physical body. Now He would leave the earth and return to heaven, and so He prayed for the restoration of His Shechinah glory. He again gave a reason for His petition: He had revealed the Father to the apostles (Jn. 17:6), one of the two sub-themes of the Gospel of John, and therefore, He requested the restoration of the Shechinah glory.

Two principles regarding the way Yeshua prayed should be noted. First, His requests were specific, and believers should make their specific requests known unto God through prayer. Second, He gave reasons for His petitions. Believers should follow Yeshua's example and do the same. The reasons might be valid or invalid. If they are invalid, God will not grant them. Believers should know and explain why they make a petition and then leave it with God. In Yeshua's case, God the Father fulfilled His two requests. The Messiah was glorified by means of His resurrection, and His previous glory was restored to Him at His ascension.

2. Concerning the Apostles

The second part of the high priestly prayer concerned the eleven apostles (Jn. 17:9a), and Yeshua prayed for three specific things.

a. Preservation

John 17:9-14

Yeshua prayed for the preservation of the apostles, presenting five reasons for His petition.

First, *for they are yours: and all things that are mine are yours, and I am glorified in them* (Jn. 17:9b-10). The apostles belonged to Yeshua, and that which belongs to the Son automatically belongs to the Father as well. God the Father should preserve the disciples because they were His, and God the Son was glorified in them.

Second, *And I am no more in the world, and these are in the world, and I come to you* (Jn. 17:11a). Yeshua was leaving this world. Since He would no longer be physically present to preserve the apostles, God the Father should take on the task of keeping them.

Third, *that they may be one, even as we <are>* (Jn. 17:11b). The Father should preserve the apostles so that they might develop a unity, the kind of oneness that God the Father has with the Son. The book of Acts and the Epistles show the fulfillment of this prayer. Although they had differences among themselves, the apostles always reconciled their disagreements, united in fellowship.

Fourth, *While I was with them, I kept them in your name which you have given me: and I guarded them, and not one of them perished, but the son of perdition; that the scripture might be fulfilled* (Jn. 17:12). While Yeshua was present on earth, He guarded the disciples, which is why they were preserved. However, since He would soon leave them, He asked the Father to take over the role of sustainer. The eleven who truly believed were kept safe. Judas, who never believed, perished.

Fifth, *I have given them your word, and the world hated them because they are not of the world, even as I am not of the world* (Jn. 17:14). The Messiah revealed to the apostles God's word, with the result that the world hated them. The reason the world hated them was that, while they were still in the world, they were not of the world, meaning they were no longer of this world's nature.

b. Protection

John 17:15-16

In His second request, Yeshua prayed for the protection of the apostles, particularly from the evil one, Satan (Jn. 17:15). His prayer for their preservation was that they would be safeguarded from the world. His prayer for their protection was that they would be protected from Satan.

Yeshua again gave a reason for His petition. The apostles needed protection because while they were no longer of the world, they were still in the world (Jn. 17:16). The world is a dangerous place for any believer, because Satan is the prince of this world (Jn. 12:31). Yeshua clarified that He was not asking God the Father to take these apostles out of the world, although that would happen someday. They needed to remain in the world to fulfill their commission in the world. However, they were no longer of the world, and that meant they were no longer of this world's system. As they were no longer of this world's system, they needed preservation because the world hated them (Jn. 17:9-14), and Satan also hated them (Jn. 17:15-16).

c. Sanctification

John 17:17-19

The third request was for the sanctification of the apostles: *Sanctify them in the truth: your word is truth* (Jn. 17:17). The word *sanctify* means "to be set apart." Yeshua asked God the Father to set the disciples apart *in the truth*, meaning by the truth, so that they could accomplish a specific mission: *As you did send me into the world, even so I sent them into the world* (Jn. 17:18). They were to be set apart for the same mission as had Yeshua. As Yeshua was sanctified or set apart by God the Father for a mission to the world, even so these eleven apostles were also to be sanctified or set apart for a mission to the world. Yeshua sanctified Himself (Jn. 17:19), so that they would also be sanctified in truth.

3. Concerning All Believers

a. Unity

John 17:20-23

In the third part of His high priestly prayer, Yeshua prayed for all believers: *Neither for these only do I pray, but for them also that believe on me through their word* (Jn. 17:20). He prayed specifically for the unity and the glorification of all believers.

Regarding unity, He prayed that the believers *may all be one* (Jn. 17:21a). While praying for the apostles, He made a similar request (Jn.

17:11b), and that prayer was answered. Unfortunately, the prayer concerning all believers has not always been answered. In one sense Yeshua's prayer that all believers are united in the body of Messiah has been answered. However, the passage goes beyond the positional unity that all believers share in the body. This prayer included unity of fellowship among all believers, and this has not always occurred, nor was this strictly a post-apostolic problem. Acts and the Epistles record disunity among believers even in the first century.

Again, Yeshua gave a reason for His request, saying that by unity among believers, the world would know that He indeed was sent by the Father: *that the world may know that you did send me* (Jn. 17:23b). Such a unity is possible because of the indwelling of the Godhead in the believer: *I in them, and you in me, that they may be perfected into one* (Jn. 17:23a). Disunity, infighting among believers, and undue and unfair criticism among believers have been major stumbling blocks that hinder people from recognizing Yeshua as their Lord, Savior, and Messiah. Some criticism is necessary, especially in the area of church discipline. However, many disagreements are petty, based on character, personality conflicts, personal preferences, or unwillingness to accept a fellow believer because of race or social status. Such disunity is a reproach to the name of Yeshua the Messiah. Where believers show a unity of fellowship, people come to the Lord because they are impressed by the love they see. Disunity, on the other hand, turns unbelievers away from facing the issue of the Messiahship of Yeshua and thus disgraces the Son of God.

b. Glorification

John 17:24-26

Yeshua's second request concerning all believers was that they would ultimately be where He is—in glory in heaven. That prayer will be answered someday, and when it happens, the believers will behold Yeshua's glory, which the Father restored to Him (Jn. 17:24).

Believers will be in glory with the Messiah, but their glory and His will differ. The believers' glory will be a reflected glory, while Yeshua's glory is an innate glory that is rightfully His. The relationship of the sun to the moon illustrates this difference. Both the sun and the moon give forth light. The sun, however, has light innately within itself. Moonlight, on the other hand, does not originate from itself; it reflects the sun's light. Yeshua is the light, and the light of believers in glory in heaven will be a reflected light. They will reflect the glory which is Yeshua's (II Cor. 3:18).

c. Conclusions

This section teaches several things about prayer:

- ✿ Prayer should be addressed to God the Father, as Yeshua did six times in this prayer.

- ✿ Prayer should be organized as Yeshua's prayer was organized.

- ✿ Prayer should contain petitions and requests.

- ✿ When making petitions, reasons for the requests should be given.

- ✿ Prayer should be for ourselves, as Yeshua prayed for Himself.

- ✿ Prayer should be for those whom we know personally, even as Yeshua prayed for the apostles.

- ✿ Prayer should be for those we do not know, such as people in the mission field whom we may never meet in this life.

Yeshua addressed God as *Father* six times in His high priestly prayer: *Father, the hour is come* (Jn. 17:1); *And now, Father, glorify you me* (Jn. 17:5); *Holy Father, keep them in your name* (Jn. 17:11); *even as you, Father, <are> in me* (Jn. 17:21); *Father, I desire that they also whom you have given me* (Jn. 17:24); and, *O righteous Father* (Jn. 17:25). This is significant in light of Yeshua's statement from the cross when He cried, *My God, my God, why have you forsaken me?* (Mt. 27:46). We note this here because it will be discussed further in the section on the crucifixion.

[§ 164] — E. The Agony of Gethsemane

Matthew 26:36-46, Mark 14:32-42, Luke 22:39-46, John 18:1

During the agony of Gethsemane, Yeshua entered one of His greatest spiritual battles as Satan made one more attempt to keep Him from the cross.

1. The Agony

After crossing the brook Kidron (Jn. 18:1), Yeshua and the eleven apostles arrived at the garden of Gethsemane on the Mount of Olives (Mt. 26:36). When they entered the garden, He left eight of His disciples near the gateway to serve as the first guard: *Sit ye here, while I pray* (Mk. 14:32). Then He took Peter, James, and Yochanan, who had also accompanied Him during the transfiguration, further up the mount to serve as the second guard (Mk. 14:33). He told them their main function: *abide ye here, and watch* (Mk. 14:34), and also, *Pray that ye enter not into temptation* (Lk. 22:40). Finally, Yeshua further separated Himself from those three, *about a stone's cast* (Lk. 22:41a). Initially, *he kneeled down and prayed* (Lk. 22:41b); but eventually, *he went forward a little, and fell on his face, and prayed* (Mt. 26:39). Then the ordeal of His agony began.

The Gospels provide a vivid description of Yeshua's agony with six statements. First, He *began to be greatly amazed* (Mk. 14:33a). In Greek, the term is expressed by the word *ekthambeó*, meaning "to be utterly surprised" or "to be stunned with astonishment." Second, He was *sore troubled* (Mk. 14:33b), meaning He was full of heaviness. Third, He said, *My soul is exceeding sorrowful* (Mk. 14:34a); He was pressed upon and engulfed by sorrow. He was suffering great pressure at that moment. Fourth, *even unto death* (Mk. 14:34b), meaning the sorrow was so great that His physical frame was in danger of collapsing. Fifth, *And being in an agony* (Lk. 22:44a) or conflict, He struggled with two things, which will be discussed shortly. Sixth, *his sweat became as it were great drops of blood falling down upon the ground* (Lk. 22:44b). He was in so much agony that He actually began sweating blood. This is a known but very rare medical condition called *hematohidrosis*. The rupture of some capillaries surrounding the sweat glands leads to blood entering the glands and oozing out of the sweat ducts.

While the Gospels emphasize the emotional and physical sides of Yeshua's agony, the Hebrew Bible provides additional insight. Isaiah 50:4-9 sheds light on His suffering, and Isaiah 49:1-13 provides a reason for His agony. This passage speaks about the Servant of Jehovah, Isaiah's favorite term for the Messiah. The Messiah is pictured as being in a state of discouragement because of Israel's rejection of His Messiahship (Is. 49:1-4). The implication is that His mission ended in failure: *But I said, I have labored in vain, I have spent my strength for naught and vanity; yet surely the justice due to me is with Jehovah, and my recompense with my God* (Is. 49:4). The Servant of Jehovah is seen as agonizing over His failure. In the midst of this agony, a message reaches Him. According to Luke, it was brought by an angel: *And there appeared unto him an angel from heaven, strengthening him* (Lk. 22:43). The message was sent by God the Father and is recorded in Isaiah 49:5-6:

> *⁵ And now says Jehovah that formed me from the womb to be his servant, to bring Yaakov again to him, and that Yisrael be gathered unto him, (for I am honorable in the eyes of Jehovah, and my God has become my strength); ⁶ yea, he says, It is too light a thing that you should be my servant to raise up the tribes of Yaakov, and to restore the preserved of Yisrael: I will also give you for a light to the Gentiles, that you may be my salvation unto the end of the earth.*

The message of comfort to the Messiah is that Israel's rejection of His Messiahship did not surprise God the Father; rather, it was a part of His divine plan. For the Messiah to be only Israel's restorer was too simple of a mission (*it is too light a thing*). The messianic mission included being the light to the Gentiles and thus becoming God's *salvation unto the end of the earth*. The term *end of the earth* is an idiom for the Gentile world: The Messiah was to be God's salvation to the entire Gentile world. In God's divine program, the Messiah would come and be rejected by His own people, making Him the light to the Gentiles for a while. Eventually, Israel too will turn to Him: *Thus says Jehovah, In an acceptable time have I answered you, and in a day of salvation have I helped you; and I will preserve you, and give you for a covenant of the people, to raise up the land, to make them inherit the desolate heritages* (Is. 49:8). Eventually, Israel will turn to the Messiah, and then He will be *a covenant of the people*, fulfilling all the covenantal promises God made to Israel. One of the covenantal promises was that He would restore the land to the people and restore the people to the land. Ultimately, Israel will indeed turn to Him. Isaiah's outline is the same used by Paul in his Israelology, found in Romans 9 – 11.

2. The Threefold Prayer

The Gospels emphasize another point of Yeshua's agony: His prayer. Three times, the Messiah prayed that a certain cup would be removed from Him. The first time, He said: *Abba, Father, all things are possible unto you; remove this cup from me: howbeit not what I will, but what you will* (Mk. 14:36). Yeshua called God *Abba*, which is a very intimate term meaning "my Father" or "Daddy." He then asked that His Father remove the cup from Him, but the content of the cup and His reason for requesting that it be removed from him was not explained. The meaning of the cup will be discussed in point 3. After making His request, He said, *not what I will, but what you will*. The best models the believer has for praying are the prayers of Yeshua. When He made His request known to God, *Remove this cup from me*, He added, *not what I will, but what you will*. Believers must always pray in the will of the Lord.

After praying for the first time, Yeshua returned to find the three apostles at the second watch sleeping. He asked them: *Could you not watch one hour?* (Mk. 14:37). Apparently, His first prayer lasted approximately one hour. He admonished them: *Watch and pray, that ye enter not into temptation: the spirit indeed is willing, but the flesh is weak* (Mk. 14:38). The disciples, failing to watch and pray, scattered, and when the temptation came, they were weak and could not resist.

Yeshua's second prayer is summarized by Matthew: *Again a second time he went away, and prayed, saying, My Father, if this cannot pass away, except I drink it, your will be done* (Mt. 26:42). This time, He focused more on accepting the fact of having to drink the cup, then returned to His disciples and again found them sleeping (Mk. 14:40).

Yeshua repeated the two previous prayers a third time: *And he left them again, and went away, and prayed a third time, saying again the same words* (Mt. 26:44). When He returned, the disciples were sleeping again, but it was inconsequential because Judas was approaching the garden (Mk. 14:41). Matthew added: *Arise, let us be going: behold, he is at hand that betrays me* (Mt. 26:46).

3. The Meaning of the Cup

Three times, Yeshua prayed that *the cup* might be removed, so the question arises: What was this cup from which He did not want to drink? Three suggestions have been made as to the meaning of this prayer.

Suggestion One: The Cup Represents Physical Death

One suggestion is that the cup represents physical death. The argument goes something like this: Yeshua, afraid of dying, asked God to spare Him from physical death. This interpretation is weak for three reasons. First, since the Messiah was *the Lamb slain from the foundation of the world* (Rev. 13:8, NKJV), it would mean that Yeshua was asking for a cancellation of God's program which He put into effect before the earth was formed. Second, it would mean that He was asking to cancel the whole purpose of the incarnation. Yeshua became human so that He could die. God as God cannot die; God had to become a man to die, so the request would render the incarnation meaningless. Furthermore, Yeshua predicted that He would die (Jn. 10:17), that He came for the purpose of dying (Lk. 19:10; Heb. 10:5-9), and that His obedience included the obedience of the cross (Phil. 2:8). Hence, it is impossible that He would ask for death to be taken away, rendering Himself a false prophet. Third, He clearly said that He would not ask the Father to spare Him from death (Jn. 12:27). Therefore, if He now asked the Father to spare Him from death, then He had lied, making Himself a sinner and disqualifying Himself from being the atonement sacrifice.

Suggestion Two: The Cup Represents Premature Death

Another suggestion is that the cup refers to premature physical death; Yeshua feared dying before He actually got to the cross. This is not a good interpretation either because there was no danger of this happening. The Messiah—not the Jewish or Roman leaders or Satan—was in total control of everything pertaining to His death. Yeshua alone controlled everything pertaining to His death. When the soldiers came to arrest Him, He said one word, and that was sufficient to force them all to the ground (Jn. 18:6), proving that He could only be arrested if He allowed it. On the cross, Yeshua dismissed His spirit from His body. If He had wanted to, He could have hung on the cross forever. He chose the moment of His own death (Lk. 23:46). John 10:18 is probably the best verse to refute the notion that Yeshua feared premature death, as it says: *No one takes* [my life] *from me, but I lay it down of myself.*

Suggestion Three: The Cup Represents Separation from God

The third suggestion is most convincing, since it views the word *cup* as it is often used symbolically in the Hebrew Scriptures: representing the wrath of God. Spiritual death accompanies this wrath and indicates separation from God. All are born spiritually dead, and only those who believe in Yeshua become spiritually alive through rebirth and regeneration by the Holy Spirit. The spiritual death Yeshua faced in the garden of Gethsemane does not result in His torture by Satan in hell for three days, as some have claimed. For a time, He would be spiritually separated from His Father, and He dreaded that experience. The spiritual separation affected His human spirit, not His divine Spirit, which could never die.

Concerning the Hebrew Bible, two observations can be made. First, while many Old Testament prophecies predicted Messiah's physical death, not one prophesied that He would die spiritually. Second, while His physical death was essential for the atonement, His spiritual death was not, because the principle was always that atonement comes by the shedding of blood (Lev. 17:11). The Old and New Testaments emphasize the shedding of His blood for the atonement, and so Yeshua could not legitimately ask to be spared from the physical death that was both predicted and necessary for the atonement. His spiritual death was neither essential for the atonement, nor prophesied in the Hebrew Scriptures; therefore, Yeshua could request to avoid spiritual death. It is difficult for those who are born spiritually dead to appreciate His agony over this. From the time of the incarnation, Yeshua had an unending, uninterrupted relationship and fellowship with God the Father. Facing a severance of this relationship was agonizing for Him.

4. Conclusions

God the Father's will was that the Messiah would partake of this cup of wrath, and during the second three hours on the cross, in the period of darkness, He indeed partook of the cup of the wrath of God. For three hours, He was spiritually dead and separated from His Father.[16] While this was not essential to the atonement, it became important and relevant to His present high priestly ministry (Heb. 4:14-16).

A common misconception about prayer is that if a person fails to receive what is requested, it is due to a lack of faith. The agony of Gethsemane disproves that teaching. Yeshua prayed that He would not have to drink the cup, and yet God the Father said, "No." Did Yeshua lack sufficient faith? If so, then He was a sinner, because the Bible teaches that *whatsoever is not of faith is sin* (Rom. 14:23b). Sometimes God does say "no" because of a lack of faith (Jam. 1:6), but sometimes He says "no" because He knows what the believer will face down the road. God knows what is important for spiritual growth and development. Therefore, a negative answer is not always due to lack of faith.

Centuries earlier, in another garden, the first Adam learned disobedience and brought death. Now, in this garden, the last Adam learned obedience and brought life.

---

[16] This will be discussed in § 178.

IX. THE TRIAL OF THE KING
— §§ 165-175 —

The Pharisees rejected Yeshua as the Messiah of Israel because He repudiated their Mishnaic Law. Ironically, the Pharisees broke 22 of their own rules and regulations concerning arrests and trials in order to expedite Yeshua's trial and death.

The following is a list of rules derived from several rabbinic sources, along with comments about many of them:

Rule 1: *There was to be no arrest by religious authorities that was effected by a bribe.*

This was based on Exodus 23:8.

Rule 2: *No steps of criminal proceedings were to occur after sunset.*

This was to avoid the possibility of conspiracy, especially one that would be carried out using the cover of night. Once the sun had officially set, the authorities were not to proceed with any form of criminal proceedings. By Jewish reckoning, the sun officially sets once three stars are visible.

Rule 3: *Judges or members of the Sanhedrin were not allowed to participate in an arrest.*

The purpose was to ensure their neutrality. If they participated in the arrest, it meant they had already taken sides.

Rule 4: *There were to be no trials before the morning sacrifice.*

All of the daily morning rituals in the Temple had to be completed before any trial could be conducted.

Rule 5: *There were to be no secret trials, only public.*

In keeping with the second rule, secret trials were forbidden in order to avoid the possibility of conspiracy.

Rule 6: *Sanhedrin trials could only be conducted in the Hall of Judgment of the Temple compound.*

Since all trials had to be public, the people would have to know where to go to observe a trial. Sanhedrin trials, therefore, had to be held only in this room, the Hall of Judgment in the Temple compound. It was known in Hebrew as the *Lishkat ha-Gazit*, the Chamber of Hewn Stones.

Rule 7: *During the trial, the defense had the first word before the prosecutors could present the accusations.*

This is the reverse of the western system. The defense provided all reasons why the accused could not be guilty of anything and presented character witnesses. Then the two or three witnesses for the prosecution officially presented the accusation.

Rule 8: *All could argue in favor of acquittal, but all could not argue in favor of conviction.*

It was permissible under Jewish criminal law to "stack the deck" in favor of the accused, but not against him. It was permissible for everyone to argue only for acquittal, but it was not permissible for everyone to argue only for conviction. The accused had to have at least one defender.

Rule 9: *There were to be two or three witnesses, and their testimony had to agree in every detail.*

This rule was based on Deuteronomy 19:15.

Rule 10: *There was to be no allowance for the accused to testify against himself.*

This was to avoid two possible situations. First, a man might be suicidal and so confess to a crime he did not commit. Second, he might be trying to protect someone else who was guilty and so confess to a crime he did not commit. Therefore, the individual himself could not be counted among the two witnesses that were minimally required for a court case to be heard.

Rule 11: *The high priest was forbidden to rend his garments.*

This rule was based on Leviticus 21:10. In a Jewish context, the tearing of garments was a sign of the emotions. For example, if a family member died, the relatives would tear their clothing. This also happened if a family member married a Gentile or became a believer in Yeshua. Because the trial had to be decided based on the facts presented by two or three witnesses, not on the basis of emotions, the high priest could not tear his clothing during the trial.

Rule 12: *Judges could not initiate the charges; they could only investigate charges brought to them.*

Like the third rule, this law was supposed to keep judges neutral. If they originated the charge, it would mean that they had already taken sides.

Rule 13: *The accusation of blasphemy was only valid if the name of God itself was pronounced.*

In Hebrew, the name of God is comprised of four letters that correspond to the Latin letters YHWH or YHVH. Unless a person actually pronounced this four-letter name of God, they could not technically be accused of blasphemy.

Rule 14: *A person could not be condemned solely on the basis of his own words.*

This rule emphasized the necessity of having two witnesses.

Rule 15: *The verdict could not be announced at night.*

This rule was to avoid a rush to judgment. It might have been a very long day with many witnesses being questioned, arguments back and forth, and people getting tired and edgy. To avoid a rush to judgment, once the night had come (meaning once three stars were visible), the judges had to wait until the next day to announce the verdict, even if they knew what it would be.

Rule 16: *In the case of capital punishment, the trial and guilty verdict could not occur at the same time, but had to be separated by at least 24 hours.*

The purpose of this law was to permit more time for information to become available which might favor the accused.

Rule 17: *Voting for the death penalty had to be done by individual count, beginning with the youngest, so the young would not be influenced by the elders.*

Rule 18: *A unanimous decision for guilt showed innocence, since it is impossible for 23 to 71 men to agree without plotting.*

The figure 71 is the full membership of the Sanhedrin. Not all the members needed to be present, but there had to be a minimum of 23. However, even with the minimum, it was inconceivable in a Jewish context that all 23 men could agree on one issue, unless there was a plot involved. This came from the observation that Jews enjoy arguing among themselves, as noted earlier in the discussion on the school of the Sopherim.

Rule 19: *The sentence could only be pronounced three days after the guilty verdict.*

The trial and the verdict had to be separated by 24 hours, but three more days had to pass before pronouncing the sentence, for the same reason: to allow more time for information to come forth that would favor the accused.

Rule 20: *Judges were to be humane and kind.*

Rule 21: *A person condemned to death was not to be scourged or beaten before his execution.*

Rule 22: *No trials were allowed on the eve of the Sabbath or on a feast day.*

Obviously, these were not all of the Sanhedrin laws; there were hundreds of them. However, these 22 were violated during either the arrest or the trial of Yeshua, and these violations will be noted as they occur in the Gospel accounts.

[§ 165] — A. The Arrest

Matthew 26:47-56, Mark 14:43-52, Luke 22:47-53, John 18:2-11

It was now the 15th of Nisan, or April 7, A.D. 30,[1] when Judas set out to betray Yeshua: *Now Yehuda also, who betrayed him, knew the place: for Yeshua oft-times resorted thither with his disciples* (Jn. 18:2).

1. Judas

When the members of the Sanhedrin bribed Judas with thirty pieces of silver to do this deed, they violated the first Mishnaic law: *There was to be no arrest by religious authorities that was effected by a bribe.*

As mentioned earlier, the religious leaders needed Judas for three reasons, and the first was to show where Yeshua could be arrested apart from the multitude. Here Judas fulfilled his first function. As Yeshua's disciple for some time, he knew the Messiah's habits when He was in Jerusalem. Although this is the only record of Him doing so, one such habit was to pray at the garden of Gethsemane, as the Gospel of John points out: *Yeshua oft-times resorted thither.* Judas knew this, so he could easily lead the soldiers to where they could arrest the Lord apart from the multitude.

After Judas procured a *band <of soldiers>, and officers from the chief priests and the Pharisees,* they came to the garden with lanterns and torches and weapons (Jn. 18:3). The Greek word for *band* is *speira,* which means "cohort." Judas had been given a Roman cohort. Per Roman law, a cohort could not be released to make an arrest until someone appeared before the governor to accuse a person of a crime punishable under that law. So, the second reason Judas was needed was to satisfy this Roman law by officially accusing Yeshua of some crime.

When Judas left the Passover Seder, he first went to the chief priests who had originally bribed him. They then took him to Pontius Pilate, where he accused Yeshua of a crime punishable under Roman law and

---

[1] Or April 3, A.D. 33.

then received this Roman cohort. Normally, the governor was stationed in his headquarters in Caesarea, which, under Rome, was the capital of Israel.[2] However, Pontius Pilate always went to Jerusalem to help maintain order during the Jewish festivals, making it convenient for Judas and the chief priests. This also explains why Pilate was already dressed and ready to conduct the trial in the early hours of the morning: He anticipated conducting a trial because he had already released a cohort to make this arrest. Again, neither Judas nor the chief priests intended to do any of this that night. However, when Yeshua identified Judas as the betrayer, He forced their hands, and thus, Judas also fulfilled his second function.

2. The Arresting Forces

The fact that the arresting soldiers came *thither with lanterns and torches* (Jn. 18:3b) shows that it was nighttime when the arrest occurred. This violated the second law: *No steps of criminal proceedings were to occur after sunset.*

A sizeable crowd of people consisting of four different groups and one specific individual went into the garden to arrest one person. The first group was the Roman cohort, which consisted of four hundred to six hundred soldiers.

Also present was an individual described as *the servant of the high priest* (Lk. 22:50). These were the crucial hours between the first night of Passover and the first day of Passover, during which the high priest was forbidden to leave his compound, lest he become ceremonially unclean and rendered unfit to offer up the special Passover sacrifice. While the high priest could not participate in the arrest, he sent his servant to make sure everything went correctly.

Luke mentioned a third party, the *captains of the temple* (Lk. 22:52a). These were the Jewish temple police. Gentile soldiers could be stationed in the outer court of the Temple to maintain order, but were not allowed to enter the inner court. A sign on the wall between the outer and inner courts announced that any Gentile entering the inner court

---

[2] During the first century, it took two days to travel from Caesarea to Jerusalem.

would be punished by execution. For that reason, an order of Jewish temple police called the *captains of the temple* were responsible for maintaining order in the inner court.

Finally, *chief priests* and *elders* (Lk. 22:52b), both including members of the Sanhedrin, were part of the multitude who accompanied Judas. Their participation in the arrest violated the third law: *Judges or members of the Sanhedrin were not allowed to participate in an arrest.* Mark observed that *a multitude with swords and staves* also came into the garden (Mk. 14:43). Such a large group of people, both Jewish and Gentile, carrying swords and clubs to arrest just one individual, revealed the high level of respect they had for this one man.

3. The Great I Am

As this large body of people surrounding Judas came into the garden, Yeshua quickly took the initiative and asked, *Whom seek ye? They answered him, Yeshua of Natzeret. Yeshua said unto them, I am <he>* (Jn. 18:4b-5). In the Greek text, this verse does not contain the personal pronoun *he*, which is why the ASV puts it in brackets. The Greek *egō eimi* simply means *I am*; the phrase can be interpreted as the great *I AM,* Jehovah of the Hebrew Bible, the one who revealed Himself to Moses as the *I AM that I AM* (Ex. 3:14), or simply as *I am He,* meaning, "I am the one for whom you are looking." Yeshua used the phrase both ways. The first time, He meant the *I AM,* Jehovah of the Hebrew Bible (Jn. 18:5), and He clearly used the phrase deliberately: *When therefore* [meaning for the very specific reason] *he said unto them, I am* (Jn. 18:6a). The result was that the crowd *went backward, and fell to the ground* (Jn. 18:6b). Yeshua's deliberate use of the phrase displayed His deity; by uttering mere words, He forced the entire group to the ground. Fully in control, they could arrest Him only when He permitted them to do so. There is a small hint of something which will occur in the future: At the second coming, the power of Rome will fall to its knees at the feet of the King of the Jews.

Yeshua asked the arresting soldiers and chief priests a second time, *Whom seek ye? And they said, Yeshua of Natzeret* (Jn. 18:7). Again Yeshua responded, *I told you that I am <he>* (Jn. 18:8). This time He meant simply, "I am that Yeshua whom you seek." He added that they should let the disciples go free since He was the one they sought: *if therefore ye seek me, let these go their way* (Jn. 18:8b). In the midst of His own endangerment, Yeshua interceded for His disciples, fulfilling one of His near prophecies: that *the word might be fulfilled which he spoke, Of those whom you have given me I lost not one* (Jn. 18:9). This was Yeshua's prayer of John 17.

By this time, Yeshua had clearly identified Himself twice to the group. However, Judas had arranged with the captain of the cohort that they should arrest no one until they saw whom he kissed: *Whomsoever I shall kiss, that is he: take him, and lead him away safely* (Mk. 14:44). The kiss would signal to the Romans the one to arrest (Mt. 26:48), and although Yeshua had identified Himself twice, Judas insisted on earning his money and *drew near unto Yeshua to kiss him* (Lk. 22:47). Before he applied the kiss, Yeshua warned him against doing so (Lk. 22:48), but Judas insisted and *came to him, saying, Rabbi; and kissed him* (Mk. 14:45). Literally, the Greek reads, *kissed him much*. He kissed Yeshua not once, but many times, profaning something that was then sacred to Jewish people. A disciple submitted himself to his teacher by kissing him to signal discipleship and as a sign of homage (Ps. 2:12). In the case of Judas, however, this was not a kiss of homage or of discipleship, and although he called Yeshua "rabbi," it was a kiss of betrayal.

4. Peter's Impetuous Swing

Peter then decided he would take action and pulled out a sword: *Shimon Peter therefore having a sword drew it, and struck the high priest's servant, and cut off his right ear* (Jn. 18:10a). There are several Greek words for *sword*, and the one used in this verse is *machaira*, which refers to a long, ceremonial knife with a single cutting edge. By this action, Peter at least temporarily proved his claim during the last Passover: that he was willing to die for his Lord. Imagine the scene: On one side were four hundred to six hundred Roman soldiers, an unknown number of Jewish temple police, and many others, all carrying swords and staves. Peter, on the other side, pulled out his one lone knife. He quickly proved that he was a fisherman and not a soldier by profession. He swung at someone's head and missed, cutting off the man's right ear. However, he demonstrated some wisdom by attacking *the high priest's servant*, who may or may not have been armed, rather than a Jewish police officer or a Roman soldier. By using the definite article, Matthew indicated it was *the* servant, this one in particular (Mt. 26:51). The Apostle Yochanan provided the most detail because his family and the high priest's family happened to be friends (Jn. 18:16), which is why he knew that *the servant's name was Melech* (Jn. 18:10).

Yeshua quickly stepped in and *touched his ear*, thus healing the servant's severed ear (Lk. 22:51). By so doing, He no doubt saved Peter's life. All four Gospel writers recorded that Peter sliced off the man's ear, but only Luke recorded the healing of the ear, showing his interest in the medical side of these things. For him, it was significant enough to mention.

Notably, this was the only miracle Yeshua performed on a fresh wound and on an enemy, though He did it to save Peter's life. This is a sign of Yeshua's victory in the spiritual warfare in the garden of Gethsemane: *the cup which the Father has given me, shall I not drink it?* (Jn. 18:11). He asked not to have to drink the cup, but realized it was God the Father's will for Him to do so. Therefore, nothing would interfere with His drinking of this cup, not even Peter. This marked Yeshua's personal victory over His agony.

Yeshua proceeded to teach Peter three lessons. First, *all they that take the sword shall perish with the sword* (Mt. 26:52). There is a proper time to use the sword, such as in personal defense and defense of the state. However, for issues of the faith, believers must turn the other cheek and be willing to become martyrs. Second, this was a spiritual conflict, and it was to be fought by spiritual means. Yeshua had at His disposal twelve legions of angels, and He could have called upon them at will (Mt. 26:53). He did not need Peter's lone, long knife. Third, all of this was necessary for the fulfillment of prophecy (Mt. 26:54-56). These things had to happen to Him because they were part of His messianic credentials.

Addressing those who came to arrest Him, Yeshua declared: *But this is your hour, and the power of darkness* (Lk. 22:53). The *hour* refers to what He anticipated in the garden of Gethsemane: He was ready to face the wrath of man and the wrath of God.

When the disciples realized that Yeshua would do nothing more to defend Himself, they *left him, and fled* (Mt. 26:56), thus fulfilling the Messiah's prophetic words that they would scatter and disperse. As previously mentioned, sometimes the author of a biography wrote himself into the account when he witnessed an event. That is why Yochanan referred to himself as "the disciple whom Yeshua loved" (Jn. 13:23; 19:26, etc.). Mark did the same thing (Mk. 14:51-52). In passing, he mentioned that *a certain young man* was present when the soldiers seized Yeshua. When they tried to also arrest the young man, they took hold of his clothing, and he fled naked, leaving a linen cloth in the hands of his would-be captors. In keeping with the way biographers wrote in those days, this young man was John Mark, the author of the Gospel.

[§§ 166–170] — B. The Religious Trial

Yeshua underwent two distinct trials: a religious, Jewish trial and a civil, Gentile trial led by the Romans. Blasphemy was the issue in the religious trial, but not in the civil trial. Both trials had three distinct stages.

[§ 166] — 1. The Trial before Annas

John 18:12-14, 19-23

This was the first stage of the religious trial, and its purpose was to establish a religious charge. If everything had gone the way the religious leaders had intended, they would have had false witnesses lined up, ready to testify. However, the events caught them by surprise; they were not organized and were still looking for specific charges to bring against Yeshua. Verse 14 makes it clear that the trial which was about to take place was a farce: *Now Kayapha was he that gave counsel to the Jews, that it was expedient that one man should die for the people* (Jn. 18:14).

The verdict had already been determined, and the sentence was decreed well before the trial.

According to the Gospel of John, the arresting forces led Yeshua to Annas first: *So the band* [the Roman cohort] *and the chief captain* [the leader of the cohort], *and the officers of the Jews* [the temple police], *seized Yeshua and bound him, and led him to Chanan first* (Jn. 18:12-13). Annas served as high priest during the years A.D. 6 or 7 to A.D. 14, then was deposed by Valerius Gratus, the Roman governor at that time. However, Annas retained control of the priesthood, because he was succeeded by four or five of his sons; his son-in-law; and, at the end of his life, his grandson. He was the head of what the Pharisees called "the Bazaar of the Sons of Annas," a private money-changing and sacrifice-selling business. Yeshua overthrew his tables twice, at the first and last Passovers of His public ministry. Therefore, Annas held a personal grudge against Yeshua.

By immediately taking Yeshua to His trial in the night, the religious leaders violated the fourth Mishnaic Law: *There were to be no trials before the morning sacrifice.* Yochanan's description of the trial implies that this trial was held in secret (Jn. 18:19-22), which broke the fifth law: *There were to be no secret trials, only public.*

Annas questioned Yeshua about two key issues: *of his disciples,* to incriminate them, *and of his teaching,* to incriminate Him (Jn. 18:19). However, Yeshua turned the tables and insisted on His rights under Jewish civil law: *I have spoken openly to the world; I ever taught in the synagogues, and in the temple, where all the Jews come together; and in secret spoke I nothing* (Jn. 18:20). He was not responsible to answer their questions, but they must produce two or three witnesses to conduct this trial. Everything He taught was in public, and so if He had truly said anything amiss, they should have no trouble finding these witnesses. Yeshua challenged them to keep their own law and support their charges by producing the proper witnesses: *Why do you ask me? Ask them that have heard <me>, what I spoke unto them: behold, these know the things which I said* (Jn. 18:21). For this response, which was His right to make, He was smitten (Jn. 18:22). This was the first of several mistreatments Yeshua suffered that night. He responded: *If I have spoken evil, bear witness of the evil: but if well, why do you smite me?* (Jn. 18:23). They were conducting an illegal proceeding.

This first stage of the religious trial concluded without the authorities establishing a specific charge. The lack of organization, the element of chaos, and the confusion which characterized the first stage were also evident at the beginning of the second stage. The religious leaders were ill-prepared to conduct the trial because none of this was supposed to occur on the night of the Passover observance. However, Yeshua had forced their hand by identifying the traitor, and so they were confused and disorganized.

[§ 167] — 2. The Trial Before Caiaphas

Matthew 26:57, 59-68, Mark 14:53, 55-65, Luke 22:54a, John 18:24

This was the second stage of the religious trial. As mentioned in § 31, Caiaphas was Annas' son-in-law, and he served as high priest during the years A.D. 18-36/37. He had led the religious leaders in rejecting the first sign of Jonah, the resurrection of Lazarus. Yeshua's trial took place in A.D. 30, a few years after the midpoint of Caiaphas' high priesthood.

Luke noted that the Sanhedrin gathered *into the high priest's house* (Lk. 22:54), thereby violating the sixth law: *Sanhedrin trials could only be conducted in the Hall of Judgment of the Temple compound.* The Sanhedrin was comprised of 71 members, carefully divided along party lines: 24 seats went to the chief priests, who were Sadducees; 24 seats went to the elders, who were Pharisees; 22 seats went to the scribes, who were also Pharisees; and the last seat went to the high priest, a Sadducee. The high priest conducted the proceedings, but the majority vote was with the Pharisees. For capital cases, not all 71 members of the Sanhedrin had to participate in the trial, but a minimum of 23 had to be present. If only the minimum attended, and 11 members voted for innocence, the accused was acquitted, since conviction required 13 votes. A vote of 11 for innocent and 12 for guilty could not convict the accused; conviction must be by a majority of two. The number of the Sanhedrin members present is unknown, but it will become evident that at least two members were missing: Nicodemus and Joseph of Arimathaea.

a. The Search for Witnesses

Matthew and Mark provided the details of the second stage of the religious trial. It began with the religious leaders seeking *false witness against Yeshua* (Mt. 26:59), thus breaking the seventh law: *During the trial, the defense had the first word before the prosecutors could present the accusations.* Mark noted that the whole council sought to act in unison against Yeshua (Mk. 14:55), breaking the eighth law: *All could argue in favor of acquittal, but all could not argue in favor of conviction.*

The religious leaders presented one false witness after another, trying to find two in agreement; but one by one, their testimonies were disqualified. This demonstrates the disorganization of the whole process. After several attempts, the prosecutors found two men who seemingly said the same thing (Mk. 14:57) and formally presented them to the court. However, when each testified individually, they ended up disagreeing: *And not even so did their witness agree together* (Mk. 14:59). A comparison of Mark and Matthew reveals the crucial point of difference that disqualified their testimonies. Mark quoted one witness as saying: *We heard him say, I will destroy this temple that is made with hands, and in three days I will build another made without hands* (Mk. 14:58). Matthew quoted the other witness as saying: *This man said, I am able to destroy the temple of God, and to build it in three days* (Mt. 26:61). The question came to this: Did Yeshua say, *I will destroy this temple*, or did He say, *I am able to destroy the temple*? The first is a statement of intent, the second a statement of ability. This discrepancy disqualified the two witnesses, so by Jewish law, Yeshua should have been released. Failure to do so broke the ninth law: *There were to be two or three witnesses, and their testimony had to agree in every detail.*

The specific charge the religious leaders desired—disrespect of the Temple—did not materialize. Only this offense would have had merit under Roman law. Generally during that time, the Sanhedrin lacked authority to put anyone to death under Roman law, with the exception of this one charge: If they proved that the person had shown disrespect toward the Temple, the ruling authorities allowed them to execute the perpetrator. However, they could not find two witnesses to establish the charge against Yeshua.

b. Caiaphas Takes Charge

This all frustrated Caiaphas: *And the high priest stood up, and said unto him, do you answer nothing? What is it which these witness against you?* (Mt. 26:62). Asking Yeshua to speak before the two witnesses broke the tenth law: *There was to be no allowance for the accused to testify against himself.* Exercising His Jewish civil rights, *Yeshua held his peace* (Mt. 26:63a). Legally, He was not obliged to respond at this point. All of this further exasperated Caiaphas, so he put Yeshua under oath: *Yeshua, I adjure you by the living God, that you tell us whether you are the Messiah, the Son of God* (Mt. 26:63b). In a Jewish court of law, the phrase *I adjure you* means to put someone under oath. Based upon his statement, Caiaphas obviously understood that Yeshua claimed to be the Messiah, and he clearly understood that the Messiah was supposed to be the Son of God. Mark quoted Caiaphas as saying, *Are you the Messiah, the Son of the Blessed?* (Mk. 14:61). In the Jewish mindset, the term *the Blessed* is a substitute for the name of God.

A person placed under oath in a Jewish civil court of law had to answer. Yeshua responded positively, saying, *I am* (Mk. 14:62), meaning, "I am the Messiah, the Son of God." He added that someday they would recognize the truth of His claims: *Henceforth ye shall see the Son of man sitting at the right hand of Power, and coming on the clouds of heaven* (Mt. 26:64). They would see Him seated at the right hand of God the Father, and they would see Him coming again in the clouds of heaven; the second coming will be visible in hell itself. Mark's Gospel records Yeshua using the same distinctive phrase, saying that the religious leaders would see Him *sitting at the right hand of Power* (Mk. 14:62). This demonstrates the Jewishness of both Gospels, since *Power* was another term for "God."

c. The Verdict and Sentence

Several things then happened in quick succession. First, *the high priest rent his garments* (Mt. 26:65a). Generally, the high priest was forbidden to rend his garments; the one exception was when he heard a blasphemy uttered. But Yeshua had not blasphemed God, so Caiaphas broke the eleventh law, which prohibited the high priest from tearing his garments.

Second, Caiaphas, the chief judge, originated the charge of blasphemy: *He has spoken blasphemy* (Mt. 26:65b), breaking the twelfth law: *Judges could not initiate the charges; they could only investigate charges brought to them.* Because the specific charge was blasphemy, Caiaphas also broke the thirteenth law: *The accusation of blasphemy was only valid if the name of God itself was pronounced.*

Third, the high priest stated, *what further need have we of witnesses?* (Mt. 26:65c). This was a magnanimous statement given that his witnesses had all been disqualified, including the two whose testimonies had originally seemed to agree. This broke the ninth law again, and requesting condemnation on the basis of what Yeshua had just said also broke the fourteenth law: *A person could not be condemned on the basis of his own words alone.* Nevertheless, the religious leaders *answered and said, He is worthy of death* (Mt. 26:66) and pronounced Him guilty while it was still nighttime, which broke the fifteenth law: *A verdict could not be announced at night, only in the daytime.* Blasphemy was a capital offense; therefore, announcing the guilty verdict on the same day as the trial broke the sixteenth law: *In the case of capital punishment, the trial and guilty verdict could not occur at the same time, but had to be separated by at least twenty-four hours.*

Furthermore, the religious leaders quickly condemned Yeshua without properly voting, thus breaking the seventeenth law: *Voting for the death penalty had to be done by individual count, beginning with the youngest, so the young would not be influenced by the elders.* Mark specified, *And they all condemned him to be worthy of death* (Mk. 14:64). The word *all* indicates a unanimous decision. By Jewish law, Yeshua should have been released, and failure to do so broke the eighteenth law: *A unanimous decision for guilt showed innocence, since it is impossible for 23 to 71 men to agree without plotting.* Furthermore, in declaring He was worthy of death—announcing the death sentence—on the same day as the guilty verdict, they broke the nineteenth law: *The sentence could only be pronounced three days after the guilty verdict.*

Next, some of those present at the trial *began to spit on him, and to cover his face, and to buffet him, and to say unto him, Prophesy: and the officers received him with blows of their hands* (Mk. 14:65). *Then did they spit in his face and buffet him: and some smote him with the palms of their hands* (Mt. 26:67). This records the violation of the twentieth and twenty-first laws, respectively: *Judges were to be humane and kind. A person condemned to death was not to be scourged or beaten beforehand.* This was the second mistreatment Yeshua suffered this night, as some men hit Him with their fists, some slapped Him with the palm of their hands, and some spit into His face. Yeshua thus suffered what are considered to be some of the highest indignities under Jewish law, and all were punishable by fines. To hit someone with the fist was punishable by a fine of four denarii. One denarius was equal to one day's salary, so four denarii equaled four days' wages. Even more insulting was to slap someone with the palm of the hand; this was punishable by a fine of two hundred denarii. Still more insulting was to spit in another's face; this was punishable by a fine of four hundred denarii, more than a year's salary. Obviously, no one was fined on this occasion.

Finally, this event took place between the first night and the first day of Passover, violating the twenty-second law: *No trials were allowed on the eve of the Sabbath or on a feast day.*

[§ 168] — 3. The Denial by Peter

Matthew 26:58, 69-75, Mark 14:54, 66-72, Luke 22:54b-62, John 18:15-18, 25-27

Peter's three denials all took place during the second stage of Yeshua's religious trial. The disciples had scattered, but Peter and Yochanan regrouped and began to follow the procession. Since Yochanan's and the high priest's families were acquainted, the apostle knew the name of the servant whose ear Peter had severed (Jn. 18:26). This relationship now worked to Yochanan's advantage: *Now that disciple was known unto the high priest, and entered in with Yeshua into the court of the high priest* (Jn. 18:15). Caiaphas' servants obviously knew Yochanan, giving him easy access to the courtyard where the trial was being conducted. He used his influence to bring Peter in as well: *but Peter was standing at the door without. So the other disciple, who was known unto the high priest, went out and spoke unto her that kept the door, and brought in Peter* (Jn. 18:16). Now Peter and Yochanan both were there. Yochanan thought he was doing Peter a favor, but instead, he unwittingly set the stage for the apostle's threefold denial. The fact that Caiaphas' home had a court big enough to contain the Sanhedrin and all the other religious leaders attending the trial as well as the soldiers and the officers shows that the high priest was wealthy.

Three times Peter was accused of being a disciple of Yeshua. Three times he denied it, with each denial becoming more intense. The first accusation came from a maid who said: *You also were with Yeshua the Galilean* (Mt. 26:69b). Peter and Yochanan were not alone when she made the statement; they were with a group of people in the courtyard. The night was chilly, so they kept a fire burning (Lk. 22:55). Peter denied the accusation (Mk. 14:68). The Greek verb used here, *ernesato*, refers to a simple denial; he simply denied that he was a disciple of Yeshua. The first cock crow came, indicating it was midnight.

A little while later, another maid saw him (Lk. 22:58) and also accused him of being with Yeshua the Nazarene (Mt. 26:71). Peter responded: *And again he denied with an oath* (Mt. 26:72). The apostle moved from a simple denial to denying with an oath that he knew Yeshua or was His disciple.

More time passed, and *after the space of about one hour* (Lk. 22:59), someone mentioned that Peter was a disciple of the Galilean: *they that stood by said to Peter, of a truth you are <one> of them; for you are a Galilean* (Mk. 14:70). The give-away was Peter's accent: *for your speech makes you known* (Mt. 26:73); *another confidently affirmed, saying, Of a truth this man was also with him: for he is a Galilean* (Lk. 22:59). Peter denied Yeshua for the third time: *But he began to curse, and to swear, I know not this man of whom ye speak* (Mk. 14:71). This time, cursing and swearing accompanied his denial. The Greek verbs used here require an object. In other words, Peter swore against and cursed Yeshua in this third denial. The progression was from a simple denial to a denial with an oath to a denial accompanied by cursing Yeshua.

Then came the second cock crow (Mk. 14:72), at three o'clock in the morning. The second stage of the religious trial apparently ended at the same time, and the door either opened or was already open: *And the Lord turned, and looked upon Peter* (Lk. 22:61). Their eyes met at the moment following the second cock crow. Instantly, Peter remembered Yeshua's prophecy at the Last Passover: *before the cock crow twice*, Peter would deny Yeshua thrice (Mk. 14:30). Peter left the scene weeping with repentance.

[§ 169] — 4. The Mockery and Beating

Luke 22:63-65

Yeshua then suffered the third mistreatment of the night. In addition to the physical abuse, He also suffered mockery: *And the men that held <Yeshua> mocked him, and beat him* (Lk. 22:63). This was the first of eight mockeries He would experience over the next several hours.

[§ 170] — 5. The Condemnation by the Sanhedrin

Matthew 27:1, Mark 15:1a, Luke 22:66-71

The only purpose of the third stage of the religious trial was to give it a semblance of legality. Apparently, some came to their senses, realizing that the entire proceedings so far were entirely illegal. So they waited for a measure of daylight; all three accounts make that point: *Now when morning was come* (Mt. 27:1); *And straightway in the morning* (Mk. 15:1a); *And as soon as it was day* (Lk. 22:66). The religious leaders deliberately waited until daylight to give the trial a measure of legality; then they quickly reconvened, and asked Yeshua two questions. First, *If you are the Messiah, tell us* (Lk. 22:67). Yeshua answered that it was useless to tell them because they had already chosen not to believe. But someday they will know His claims are true, when they see Him seated at the right hand of God the Father (Lk. 22:67-69). Second, *And they all said, Are you then the Son of God?* (Lk. 22:70). Yeshua answered: *Ye say that I am.* In Greek, this is an emphatic way of saying, "Yes, indeed, I am the Son of God."

The religious trial ended with Yeshua being condemned to death for blasphemy, a verdict unsupported by the actual evidence. The rabbinic definition of blasphemy was to expressly pronounce the four-letter name of God, and Yeshua had not done so. If the Sanhedrin had carried out the death sentence on these charges, Yeshua would have been stoned and then hanged. This would have been contrary to the prophecies concerning how the Messiah would die. Messiah was to be crucified. The plan of God could not be diverted or subverted.

[§ 171] — C. The Death of Judas

Matthew 27:3-10, Acts 1:18-19

Despite their best efforts, the religious leaders were unable to prove their accusation that Yeshua had tried to destroy the Temple, so they lacked the authority to order His execution. While the Sanhedrin found Him guilty of blasphemy and sentenced Him to death, they could not execute the death sentence, as the Roman senate had revoked the Sanhedrin's power of capital punishment. Therefore, if Yeshua was going to be executed, He had to be found guilty of committing a capital offense under Roman law. Blasphemy was punishable by death under Jewish law only. Therefore, the religious leaders needed to trump up a different charge. While Judas was not needed for the religious trial, he was needed for the civil trial.

However, between the two trials, Judas committed suicide: *Then Yehuda, who betrayed him, when he saw that he was condemned, repented himself* (Mt. 27:3). Because the word *repented* is used, the question arises as to whether or not Judas was saved. Two Greek words are translated as "repent" in English. One is *metanoia*, carrying the sense of salvation-repentance. However, in this text, a different Greek word, *metamelomai*, is used, which means, "to be filled with regret or remorse," "to experience a change of concern after a change of emotion." So, the answer to the question is: No, Judas was not saved. Being full of regret and remorse, he tried to return the money to the chief priests and admitted that he had betrayed innocent blood (Mt. 27:4). When they refused to accept the money, *he cast down the pieces of silver into the sanctuary, and departed; and he went away and hanged himself* (Mt. 27:5).

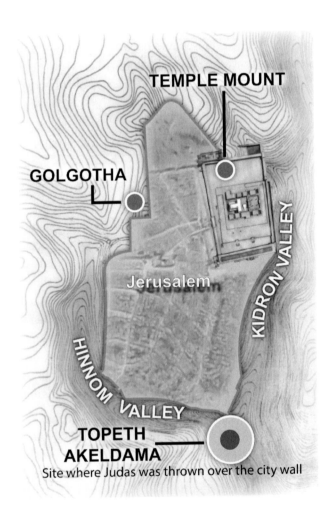

TEMPLE MOUNT

GOLGOTHA

Jerusalem

KIDRON VALLEY

HINNOM VALLEY

TOPETH
AKELDAMA
Site where Judas was thrown over the city wall

1. Resolving Two Alleged Contradictions

Critics of the New Testament have pointed out that the two accounts of Judas' suicide seem to contradict each other. The first alleged variance is the way Judas actually died. According to Matthew, he died by hanging. However, Luke stated that *falling headlong, he burst asunder in the midst, and all his bowels gushed out* (Acts 1:18). So how did Judas die? By hanging or by falling with his bowels gushing out?

A specific point of rabbinic law clarifies Luke's statement. By Jewish reckoning of time, a day begins at sundown. Therefore, the Sabbath begins at sundown Friday and ends at sundown Saturday. Once the sun has set on Saturday, the Sabbath law no longer applies. The same reckoning of time applies to any other event or day. For example, the first night of Passover always comes before the first day of Passover. Jewish families eat their Seder on the first night of Passover, as Yeshua did with His apostles. Then at nine o'clock in the morning on the first day of Passover, only the priesthood ate a special Passover sacrifice called the *chagigah*. If, between the first night and the first day of Passover, a dead body was found within the walls of Jerusalem, the city was reckoned as ceremonially unclean. As long as the body was within the walls, the priests could not proceed with the special sacrifice of the first day. If the corpse was thrown over the wall facing the Valley of Hinnom, the city would be reckoned as cleansed. The priesthood could then proceed with the morning Passover sacrifice. When Judas hanged himself, he defiled the city. As long as his body was within the walls, the priests could not proceed with the chagigah sacrifice, so they took it and threw it over the wall facing the Valley of Hinnom. In that fall, Judas' guts gushed out. Therefore, no contradiction exists; Matthew recorded how Judas died, while Luke described what happened to his body after it was found.

The second alleged contradiction critics have cited concerns who actually purchased the field. According to Matthew, it was the chief priests (Mt. 27:7-8). Yet, Luke stated: *Now this man [Judas] obtained a field with the reward of his iniquity* (Acts 1:18). From a Jewish viewpoint, both statements are true. By Jewish law, money wrongfully gained could not be put into the Temple treasury: *It is not lawful to put them into the treasury, since it is the price of blood* (Mt. 27:6). The priesthood knew this money was wrongfully gained, and they were legally obligated to return the money to the donor. However, the donor was dead. Although the money could not be placed into the Temple treasury, it could be used for purchasing something to benefit the whole community in the name of the donor. So, the religious leaders purchased the field for the public, as a place to bury strangers, and despite Judas' death, all legal documents of sale reflected his name. Matthew recorded the events as they occurred, and Luke documented the fact that legally, Judas purchased the field.

2. Jeremiah or Zechariah?

Two other verses in this context, Matthew 27:9-10, also tend to draw criticism. Matthew noted that what happened with Judas was a fulfillment of something spoken of by the Prophet Jeremiah, probably referring to Jeremiah 18:2-3 and 32:8-9, but he quoted Zechariah 11:12-13, which says:

> *12 And I said unto them, If ye think good, give me my hire; and if not, forbear. So they weighed for my hire thirty pieces of silver. 13 And Jehovah said unto me, Cast it unto the potter, the goodly price that I was prized at by them. And I took the thirty pieces of silver, and cast them unto the potter, in the house of Jehovah.*

Several answers have been suggested. One is that sometimes the divisions of the Hebrew Scriptures are referred to by the first book of the scroll. For example, the third section of the Hebrew Bible is called "The Writings," but sometimes is referred to as the book of Psalms, which is the first book contained therein. The first book of the prophetic scroll would be Joshua or, if only dealing with the latter writing prophets, Isaiah. Therefore, had Matthew mentioned Joshua or Isaiah, this answer would make sense. However, he mentioned Jeremiah, and so this explanation does not support the solution stated above.

A second answer may be that this is simply a scribal error. This is a more valid option, since scribal errors exist in the text of both testaments.

A third answer is that Matthew quoted from both Zechariah and Jeremiah, but named only one of the prophets from which he was quoting.

The fourth answer is based on the fact that only Matthew records this event. In his Gospel, he was particularly concerned with the development of the rejection of the Messianic King, the unpardonable sin, resulting in the destruction of Jerusalem in the year A.D. 70. That may account for his reference to Jeremiah while quoting Zechariah, as Jeremiah referred twice to a particular curse that has relevance to Judas' burial place, the curse of Topheth. Jerusalem is surrounded by two valleys: the Valley of Kidron on the eastern side , and the Valley of Hinnom coming around the west side down to the south side. Topheth is located where the two valleys meet. Some of the more wicked kings of Jerusalem practiced human sacrifice here. As a result, God pronounced a curse upon this section of the valley, in Jeremiah 7:31-34:

> *31 And they have built the high places of Topheth, which is in the valley of the son of Hinnom, to burn their sons and their daughters in the fire; which I commanded not, neither came it into my mind. 32 Therefore, behold, the days come, says Jehovah, that it shall no more be called Topheth, nor The valley of the son of Hinnom, but The valley of Slaughter: for they shall bury in Topheth, till there be no place to bury. 33 And the dead bodies of this people shall be food for the birds of the heavens, and for the beasts of the earth; and none shall frighten them away. 34 Then will I cause to cease from the cities of Yehudah, and from the streets of Yerushalayim, the voice of mirth and the voice of gladness, the voice of the bridegroom and the voice of the bride; for the land shall become a waste.*

In the Hebrew Scriptures, the Valley of Hinnom was known as *Gei* (or *Gai*) *Ben-Hinnom*, literally the "Valley of the son of Hinnom" (as in the verses above). In the Talmud, it was referred to as *Gehinnam* or *Gehinnom*, the place where humans were burned as sacrifices. The Hebrew words were Hellenized as *Ge'enna*, which became the term used for the lake of fire, the place of the future burning of humans. After a few additional etymological changes, the term found its way into the English dictionary as *Gehenna*.

Referring to Gehenna, Jeremiah wrote: *Thus says Jehovah of hosts: Even so will I break this people and this city, as one breaks a potter's vessel, that cannot be made whole again: and they shall bury in Topheth, till there be no place to bury* (Jer. 19:11b). To summarize, the curse of Jeremiah was that someday the people of Israel would bury in Topheth until there was no more room to bury. Matthew showed that when the religious leaders purchased this particular area of the Hinnom Valley, they also purchased the Jeremiah curse. When the unpardonable sin was judged and punished in A.D. 70, so many were slaughtered (altogether 1,100,000 Jews were killed in that war) that they buried until there was no more room in the field. One ancient writer observed:

> After Titus has taken Jerusalem, and when the country all round was filled with corpses, the neighboring races offered him a crown; but he disclaimed any such honor to himself, saying . . . that he had merely lent his arms to God, who had so manifested his wrath.[3]

Acts 1:19 notes that the field initially became known by the name *Akeldama*, Aramaic for "the field of blood," because it was bought with the purchase price of blood. However, it literally ended up being a place of slaughter. Therefore, Matthew mentioned Jeremiah to point out that the curse of Topheth would come to pass as the result of the unpardonable sin, and he quoted Zechariah to show that the actual purchase price was that of a dead slave.

Once Judas was dead, the religious leaders lost their one witness for the prosecution. For that reason, just as disorganization and confusion dominated the initial stages of the religious trial, the same was true in the civil trial.

---

[3] Flavius Philostratus, *Life of Apollonius*, 6:29. Translated by F. C. Conybeare. Online at http://www.livius.org/ap-ark/apollonius/life/va_6_26.html.

[§§ 172–175] — D. The Civil Trial

Like the religious trial, the civil trial also proceeded through three specific stages. While the issue of blasphemy in the religious trial was not punishable by death under Roman law, sedition or treason against Rome, the issue in the civil trial, was punishable by death.

Twenty-two Jewish laws were broken during Yeshua's religious trial; only two Roman laws affected His civil trial. First, all proceedings must be public. Yeshua's trial was quite public, much to Pilate's later regret. Second, a trial was to begin with the accuser(s) presenting formal charges for a crime that had to be punishable under Roman law, and for this the religious leaders would have needed Judas, as he was their sole witness.

[§ 172] — 1. The First Trial Before Pilate

Matthew 27:2, 11-14, Mark 15:1b-5, Luke 23:1-5, John 18:28-38

Pilate, born in Spain, was a Roman citizen and served as procurator during A.D. 26-36. This trial took place in A.D. 30, at the midpoint of his term. In contemporary Jewish writings, Pilate was noted as being cruel, and his career ended when, after having ordered the massacre of a group of Samaritans, he was recalled to Rome to answer for what he had done.

Although it was the early morning hours, Pilate was up and dressed. He expected the trial, since earlier he had released the Roman cohort to Judas. Yochanan noted: *They led Yeshua therefore from Kayapha into the Praetorium: and it was early; and they themselves entered not into the Praetorium, that they might not be defiled, but might eat the Passover* (Jn. 18:28). Because the Passover is mentioned, some assumed that Yeshua ate His Passover a day early. However, He observed the Mosaic Law perfectly, down to every yod and tittle, and the law specified the day of the month Passover must be observed, so undoubtedly, Yeshua obeyed that commandment. The pronoun *they* refers to the chief priests. Jewish families ate their Passover meal on the first night of Passover. At nine in the morning of the first day of Passover, the special sacrifice, the chagigah, was made, of which only the priesthood could eat. It was offered immediately after the regular morning sacrifices and was roasted and eaten later that day. If, however, the priests became ceremonially unclean before the chagigah was served, they could not eat of it. One way to become ritually defiled was to enter the home of a Gentile. That was why the chief priests did not enter the Praetorium.

a. Attempts to Find an Accusation

In keeping with the second Roman law, Pilate asked: *What accusation bring ye against this man?* (Jn. 18:29). At this point Judas should have stepped forward, but Judas was dead. Instead, the religious leaders responded: *If this man were not an evildoer, we should not have delivered him up unto you* (Jn. 18:30). Their sole accuser was conspicuously absent, so they pressured Pilate to pass the sentence without any accusation or trial. Pilate, following Roman law, refused: *Take him yourselves, and judge him according to your law* (Jn. 18:31a). With no accusation, there would be no trial; no trial, no condemnation; no condemnation, no sentence.

The religious leaders responded: *It is not lawful for us to put any man to death* (Jn. 18:31b). Since Rome had revoked the Sanhedrin's authority to impose capital punishment, it was unlawful for them to put anyone to death. The Talmud reveals the exact year the right was revoked: "Forty years before the destruction of the temple, the Sanhedrin were exiled . . . They did not try capital charges."[4] Another tractate in the Talmud states: "Forty years before the destruction of the temple the Sanhedrin went into exile and took its seat in the Trade Halls,"[5] meaning they no longer had the authority to execute criminals. Subtracting forty years from the year of the Temple's destruction results in the year A.D. 30. This was also the year of Yeshua's crucifixion and the year that the Jews lost the authority to sentence someone to death.

---

[4] *b. Sanhedrin* 41a. See also: *b. 'Abodah Zarah* 8b.

[5] *b. Shabbath* 15a.

Yochanan made an editorial comment, saying *that the word of Yeshua might be fulfilled, which he spoke, signifying by what manner of death he should die* (Jn. 18:32). Yeshua prophesied a number of times that He would die by crucifixion. However, the Jewish method of execution was stoning, not crucifixion. If Yeshua had been executed under Jewish law, He would have been stoned to death, making Him a false prophet, because He prophesied He would die by crucifixion. If the trial had occurred six months earlier, Yeshua would have been stoned to death and rendered a false prophet. In His providence, at the proper time, God moved the Roman Senate to take away the power of capital punishment from the Sanhedrin, so that Yeshua would die in accordance with His prophecies.

b. Sedition

When the religious leaders realized that Pilate required a proper accusation to proceed, they claimed Yeshua was guilty of sedition on three counts. First, *We found this man perverting our nation* (Lk. 23:2a). They accused Yeshua of perverting the nation by mixing truth with heresy and therefore fomenting a rebellion. Second, they accused Him of *forbidding to give tribute to Caesar* (Lk. 23:2b), a treasonous act. They obviously lied, because Yeshua said, *render unto Caesar the things that are Caesar's* (Mt. 22:21; Mk. 12:17; Lk. 20:25). Third, they reminded Pilate that Yeshua claimed to be Messiah, a king, and therefore a competitor to Caesar.

c. The Conversation with Pilate

Once Pilate had a specific charge, he proceeded. In a Roman trial, after the indictment was officially presented, the accused was questioned. Pilate asked Yeshua: *Are you the King of the Jews?* (Jn. 18:33). Note that he did not ask Him, "Are you the Messiah?" The question from his perspective as an official of the Roman government was, "Are you really a competitor to Caesar?"

To clarify the issue, Yeshua responded to Pilate's question with one of His own: *Do you say this of yourself, or did others tell you it concerning me?* (Jn. 18:34). In other words, did Pilate, the Roman procurator, ask Him this of his own accord or did he repeat what others—specifically the Jewish leaders—had told him? Furthermore, did he ask the question from the viewpoint of a Roman or the viewpoint of a Jew? Pilate answered: *Am I a Jew? Your own nation and the chief priests delivered you unto me: what have you done?* (Jn. 18:35). Pilate asked the question based upon what the Jewish leaders told him, but as the Roman procurator he needed to know, "Are you a competitor to Caesar?"

Once the issue was clear, Yeshua gave a specific answer: *My kingdom is not of this world: if my kingdom were of this world, then would my servants fight, that I should not be delivered to the Jews: but now is my kingdom not from hence* (Jn. 18:36). For two reasons, Yeshua was not a competitor to Caesar. First, He said, *My kingdom is not of this world*. This is a favorite passage for replacement theologians, especially those of the amillennial school, who use this verse to support their argument that when Yeshua returns, He will not set up a literal, earthly kingdom. They believe in His second coming, but not that when He returns He will set up His earthly kingdom. They instead interpret Yeshua's statement to mean that His kingdom will not be in this world. However, there is a difference between "of the world" and "in the world." Yeshua made that distinction in John 17:11, 14, 16, and 18, where He said to the Father that He and the believers are in the world, but not of the world. To be of the world means to be of this world's nature, and believers are no longer of this world's nature. As long as believers are alive, they are in this world, but no longer of this world's nature. When Yeshua returns to earth, He will not depose Caesar and sit upon his throne. He will come with His own throne, the throne of David, and with His own kingdom, the messianic kingdom. His kingdom will someday be in the world, but will never be of this world. Second, He said, *but now is my kingdom not from hence*, meaning "not from now." As a result of the rejection of His Messiahship, Yeshua's kingdom would not yet be established. For these two reasons, He was not a competitor to Caesar.

To verify that he understood Yeshua correctly, Pilate asked a follow-up question: *Are you a king then?* (Jn. 18:37a), meaning, "Are you a king in any sense of the term?" Yeshua answered, "Yes, in one sense, I am a king even now; I am the king of the truth," and *Every one that is of the truth hears my voice* (Jn. 18:37b).

This ended the interrogation, and Pilate answered with a sarcastic question, *What is truth?* (Jn. 18:38). Sadly, for Pilate, at that very moment, he was looking at the Truth and did not recognize Him.

d. Declarations of Innocence

The procurator then issued the first of several declarations of innocence (Lk. 23:4). As far as he was concerned, Yeshua was not a threat to Rome. The first declaration of innocence was rebuffed and countered with many other accusations: *And the chief priests accused him of many things* (Mk. 15:3). Yeshua responded with silence. When Pilate asked Him to defend Himself against these charges, *Yeshua no more answered anything* (Mk. 15:5); *And he gave him no answer, not even to one word* (Mt. 27:14).

As the accusations were blurted out, someone mentioned that Yeshua was from Galilee: *But they were the more urgent, saying, He stirs up the people, teaching throughout all Yehudah, and beginning from Galil even unto this place* (Lk. 23:5). The mention of Yeshua's Galilean origin gave Pilate an escape from the situation. While both Samaria and Judea were under his jurisdiction, Galilee was under the jurisdiction of Herod Antipas, who also came to Jerusalem during the festivals to help maintain order. So Pilate sent Yeshua to him.

[§ 173] — 2. The Trial before Herod Antipas

Luke 23:6-12

Herod Antipas was the son of Herod the Great. About a year earlier, he had beheaded Yochanan the Baptizer. Only then did he hear about Yeshua's miracles, and for a while thought that Yeshua was Yochanan raised from the dead. He had wanted to meet Him in person *of a long time* (Lk. 23:8). Pilate now sent Yeshua, a Galilean, to Herod Antipas because He was under Antipas' jurisdiction (Lk. 23:7). So, Antipas finally got his wish: Yeshua stood before him, and he wanted to see miracles and be entertained. The same desire had cost Yochanan his life. However, Yeshua refused to perform for Antipas, because miracles were never for the purpose of entertainment. Disappointed, Antipas mocked Yeshua by *arraying him in gorgeous apparel* (Lk. 23:11), the second mockery the Messiah suffered that night. Even Herod Antipas acknowledged that Yeshua posed no threat to Rome, regardless of the accusations brought against Him by the chief priests and scribes (Lk. 23:10), so this trial concluded with a second declaration of innocence (see § 174, Lk. 23:13-25, esp. v. 15).

Luke observed: *And Herod and Pilate became friends with each other that very day: for before they were at enmity between themselves* (Lk. 23:12). The hostility between the two rulers had started when, as the newly appointed procurator, Pilate ordered his legions to carry ensigns with Caesar's portrait into Jerusalem. This violated Jewish law, which forbade the making of images. Herod Antipas, a nominal convert to Judaism, understood these Jewish sensitivities; he knew that as long as the ensigns were within the walls of Jerusalem, a constant threat existed of Jewish agitation turning into rebellion. He asked Pilate to take them down, but Pilate refused. Then Antipas wrote a letter of complaint to the Roman Senate, who ordered Pilate to comply. Pilate and Antipas *were at enmity between themselves*, because each felt the other was not recognizing his authority. Now that the ruler of Judea had sent a Galilean to the one in charge of Galilee, they recognized their mutual authority and became friends, at Yeshua's expense.

Herod Antipas and his wife Herodias eventually paid for beheading Yochanan and mocking Yeshua. In the year A.D. 39, Herodias prompted her husband to go to Rome to request the title of king. The Senate had given that title to his father, Herod the Great, and if Rome also made Antipas king of Judea, she could be called queen. The emperor at that time was Gaius Julius Caesar Germanicus, better known by his childhood nickname Caligula, meaning "little boots." He was in power for only four years, but it was a bloody reign, for Caligula was mad. His excesses knew no bounds. Whenever he exhausted the government treasury to pay for his personal expenditures, he accused a wealthy landowner of some crime, killed the whole family, and seized their property. Eventually, the situation worsened so that the Praetorian Guard, once his protector, assassinated him. When Antipas and Herodias came before Caligula to request the title of king and queen, he banished them to Lyon, where they died in abject poverty.

[§ 174] — 3. The Second Trial before Pilate

Matthew 27:15-26, Mark 15:6-15, Luke 23:13-25, John 18:39-19:16

After Herod Antipas failed to find a charge against Yeshua, Pilate made several specific efforts to release Yeshua, in the process again declaring His innocence. He gathered the religious leaders and said, *Ye brought unto me this man, as one that perverts the people: and behold, I having examined him before you, found no fault in this man touching those things whereof ye accuse him* (Lk. 23:14). Herod could find no fault in Yeshua and determined that *nothing worthy of death has been done by him* (Lk. 23:15b). If one wanted to keep a list of these declarations of innocence, Herod's statement would be the second and Pilate's the third. However, the crowd rejected these proclamations of Yeshua's innocence.

a. Yeshua Bar Abba

In his second attempt to free Yeshua, Pilate offered the people a choice. A custom had developed that during the Passover the Roman authorities would release one Jewish prisoner as a goodwill gesture (Jn. 18:39). Besides Yeshua, another man, named Barabbas, was imprisoned, whom Yochanan referred to as a *robber* (Jn. 18:40). A better translation might be "malefactor" or "rebel," since robbery was not punishable by death. Mark clearly stated that Barabbas *had made insurrection, and in the insurrection had committed murder* (Mk. 15:7). Barabbas was actually guilty of the crime of which Yeshua was accused. This is reaffirmed by Luke 23:19.

The irony is that "Barabbas" was not a proper name, but a Greek transliteration of the Aramaic words *bar*, which means "son of," and *Abba*, which was his father's name, making him the "son of Abba." The Gospels do not give his actual name, probably to avoid confusing the reader. However, other sources reveal that his name was also Yeshua, a common first-century name.[6] So two men shared the same name; one was guilty of sedition, and the other was accused but innocent of sedition. Even more ironic is the fact that Barabbas' father's name was Abba, which in Aramaic means "the father." So, Barabbas' name and title was *Yeshua the son of the father*. One bore the name and title, but the other was the true Yeshua, the true Son of the true Father.

The two men were brought forward. Pilate tried hard to release Yeshua because *he perceived that for envy the chief priests had delivered him up* (Mk. 15:10). As it was with Yochanan the Baptizer, so it would be with the Messiah: The actual reasons were personal, but the charge was political. Pilate assumed that the people would ask for Yeshua's, not Barabbas', release.

The procedure was temporarily interrupted when Pilate received a message from his wife warning him not to get involved with the situation because of a dream she had just had (Mt. 27:19). By church tradition, her name was Claudia, and she later became a believer. The interruption was long enough so that *the chief priests and the elders persuaded the multitudes that they should ask for Bar Abba, and destroy Yeshua* (Mt. 27:20), and that is what they did: *But they cried out all together, saying, Away with this man, and release unto us Bar Abba* (Lk. 23:18), and thus, Pilate's second attempt to free Yeshua also failed.

b. The Chastisement

Pilate made a third attempt to free Yeshua by satisfying the bloodlust of the crowd in a different way: *Then Pilate therefore took Yeshua, and scourged him* (Jn. 19:1). Details are omitted from the Gospels because people would have been familiar with this type of punishment. Now,

---

[6] The name *Iesous Barabbas* appears in the 9th century Codex Koridethi and in some Syrian sources. In his commentary on Matthew, Origen refers to ancient manuscripts that had this reading.

more than two thousand years later, many do not understand what it means to be scourged, so they miss the degree of Yeshua's suffering prior to the cross. To be scourged was to be beaten or flogged with a whip with multiple lashes. The Jews had exact rules regarding this form of punishment. The actual stripes given were restricted to "forty save one," because according to the Mosaic Law, nobody could be lashed more than forty times (Deut. 25:3). The Sopherim raised the question, "Suppose the lasher was lashing, miscounted and gave the victim 41 lashes and broke the law?" Therefore, they built a fence around that law by stopping the count at 39, and called it "forty save one."[7]

The Jewish scourge was made either of leather or wood for the handle and had short leather lashes. The only part of the body beaten was the victim's back. The whipping was excruciating, but never deadly. Paul suffered this Jewish punishment five times and survived (II Cor. 11:24). However, Yeshua was flogged by Romans, not Jews, with a vastly different procedure. The number of times a person could be struck with the scourge was limitless. The Roman whip had long leather lashes which could wrap around the whole body. At the end of each lash was a piece of metal, nail, glass, or sharp lamb bone. Sometimes even small jagged iron balls were used. After only a few applications of the scourge, the skin of the victim was torn away and the muscle exposed. The entire body was affected: the front, back, sides, and face. The face was lacerated and became like pulp. Paintings of the crucifixion often reveal a faulty interpretation of this scene, portraying Yeshua's face intact except for a line of blood on the brow from the crown of thorns. In reality, His face would have been a pulpy mass. By the time a Roman flogging was over, family members no longer recognized the victim. This fulfilled the specific messianic prophecy of Isaiah 52:13-15, which said that the Messiah's face was so disfigured that He no longer resembled a man.

This was the fourth mistreatment Yeshua endured on that night, and He also suffered the third mockery (Jn. 19:2-3). The accusation was that He claimed to be a king, so the soldiers *platted a crown of thorns, and put it on his head, and arrayed him in a purple garment* (a sign of royalty), thus mocking Yeshua. The thorns of some plants in Israel come

---

[7] See: *b. Makkoth* 2a; p. 1, n. (4).

to almost razor sharp points, so that even lightly brushing against one can cause bleeding. Merely placing it on Yeshua's head after His scourging would cause pain, but they kept striking Him. If they struck Him on the head where the crown rested, the thorns would cut deeper and more painfully.

The symbolism is important. Thorns symbolize the Adamic curse (Gen. 3:18); therefore, by means of His suffering, Yeshua bore upon Himself the Adamic curse. Pilate, believing that this severe corporal punishment without a guilty verdict would satisfy the Jewish leadership, issued a fourth declaration of innocence (Jn. 19:4). However, although the crowd saw that Yeshua was beaten to a bloody mess, they still cried out for His crucifixion (Jn. 19:5-6).

c. A New Charge

Pilate made a fourth attempt to free Yeshua by again declaring Him innocent of any crime (Jn. 19:6). Without a sentence by Rome, He could not be executed. The Jewish leaders dropped the charge of sedition and returned to the real issue troubling them all along, Yeshua's claim to be the Messiah: *We have a law, and by that law he ought to die, because he made himself the Son of God* (Jn. 19:7). Since Pilate had a new charge, he had to conduct a new interrogation (Jn. 19:8-11). This time, Yeshua did not answer any of his questions, probably because Pilate had previously received sufficient light to respond correctly, but instead asked sarcastically, *What is truth?* (Jn. 18:38). Therefore, Yeshua gave him no further truth. Pilate, pressing for an answer, pointed out that he had the authority to release Yeshua or have Him crucified, but Yeshua reminded Pilate that his authority was delegated: *You would have no power against me, except it were given you from above: therefore he that delivered me unto you has greater sin* (Jn. 19:11). Final authority comes from heaven above. Furthermore, those who turned Yeshua over to Pilate were guilty of the greater transgression, proving that there are varying degrees of sin. The Great White Throne judgment will judge the works of the unbeliever and determine the appropriate degree of punishment in the lake of fire.

Pilate made a fifth attempt to have Yeshua released: *Upon this Pilate sought to release him* (Jn. 19:12a). However, his effort was spoiled when the people started crying out, *If you release this man, you are not Caesar's friend: everyone that makes himself a king speaks against Caesar* (Jn. 19:12). While sounding like an empty threat, it still intimidated Pilate: *When Pilate therefore* [for the specific reason] *heard these words* [referring to the words, *If you release this man, you are not Caesar's friend*] *he brought Yeshua out, and sat down on the judgment seat* (Jn. 19:13). Why was Pilate so intimidated by this statement? Why did he care what the Jewish people thought? If this trial occurred in A.D. 30, the cause of the intimidation is unknown. However, if these events occurred in A.D. 33, it is possible that he was intimidated because of events occurring in Rome. Pilate received his position as procurator through his close friend Lucius Aelius Sejanus. Sejanus was a soldier and a confidant of Emperor Tiberius. When he became the captain of the imperial bodyguard, known as the Praetorian Guard, he used his influence to have Pilate appointed procurator over Judea. Later, Sejanus desired the position of emperor and conspired to assassinate Tiberius. However, the plot was discovered before the machination could be carried out, and Sejanus, along with others, was executed. The Roman Senate launched an investigation of everyone in the empire who had connections to Sejanus to root out any remaining pockets of conspirators. Because of Pilate's friendship with Sejanus, he too was being investigated. The last thing he needed was for news to get back to Rome that he released someone claiming to be king and, therefore, a competitor to Caesar. Again, this would only apply if the trial took place in A.D. 33.

Nevertheless, the people's threat intimidated Pilate enough to make him immediately close the proceedings and take his place on the judgment seat, or *bema*. The bema was an elevated stand probably erected outside the Praetorium, from where public meetings were directed and courts were held. If the Jewish leaders had entered the Praetorium, they would have defiled themselves and could not have eaten the chagigah, the Paschal lamb, later that morning. Therefore, Pilate left the palace to take his seat on the bema and render the verdict. If found guilty, the accused would then be sentenced.

d. Behold Your King

Sitting on the bema, Pilate made his sixth and final attempt to release Yeshua, presenting Him to the people and saying: *Behold, your King!* (Jn. 19:14). The masses, however, countered by demanding His crucifixion. When he asked them, *Shall I crucify your King? The chief priests answered, We have no king but Caesar* (Jn. 19:15). That cry came from the chief priests, the Sadducees, who, with this statement, disowned the Messiah as their king and proclaimed their allegiance to Caesar. The Pharisees would not have made such a proclamation.

Pilate made no further attempts to free Yeshua. Instead, taking a pitcher of water, he washed his hands before the multitude (Mt. 27:24), assuming that this gesture would absolve him of guilt, but it did not. From a human perspective, the final decision as to whether Yeshua lived or died was not with the Jewish leaders, but with this one man, Pontius Pilate. He clearly knew what the right decision should be, but allowed himself to be intimidated into making the wrong one. Merely washing his hands did not absolve him from blame. Later, when Peter preached a sermon (Acts 3), he listed several people by name who were responsible for the Messiah's death, and he included Pontius Pilate (Acts 4:27). The earliest creed in church history, the Apostles' Creed, states, *He suffered under Pontius Pilate.* God did not absolve Pilate of what he did. In A.D. 36, Caligula deposed Pilate and banished him to Gaul, where he committed suicide and paid for his role in this miscarriage of justice.

Pilate then issued his fifth declaration of innocence, calling Yeshua *this righteous man* (Mt. 27:24). This was the most significant of the five attestations, because it was made from the judgment seat. Still, *all the people answered and said, His blood <be> on us, and on our children* (Mt. 27:25). They took upon themselves the curse of the blood, limiting it to themselves and their children. When the judgment for the unpardonable sin finally came in A.D. 70, it indeed fell upon them and their children, fulfilling the curse. Matthew alone recorded this response, since he carefully traced the outworking of the unpardonable sin.

Finally, Pilate issued the death sentence (Lk. 23:24), while releasing Yeshua Bar Abba, or Barabbas (Lk. 23:25). There was a symbolic substitution in that the innocent one went to His death in place of the guilty one, who was set free: *Then therefore he* [Pilate] *delivered him* [Yeshua] *unto them to be crucified* (Jn. 19:16).

[§ 175] — 4. The Mockery

Matthew 27:27-30, Mark 15:16-19

Having been turned over to Roman soldiers, Yeshua suffered the fourth mockery of the night (Mk. 15:17): *Then the soldiers of the governor took Yeshua into the Praetorium, and gathered unto him the whole band* (Mt. 27:27). In Greek, the word *band* actually means "cohort." A cohort had arrested Yeshua earlier, and now it reconvened for the crucifixion. After stripping Him of His clothes, they *put on him a scarlet robe* (Mt. 27:28), thus mocking His royalty. Instead of a crown of gold, they placed a crown of thorns on His head (Mt. 27:29a) and *a reed in his right hand* (Mt. 27:29b) to mimic a royal scepter. After spitting on Him (Mt. 27:30), they took the reed out of His hand and used it to strike Him on the head (Mk. 15:19). This was the fifth mistreatment He suffered on that night.

X. THE DEATH OF THE KING
— §§ 176–181 —

[§ 176] — A. The Procession to Calvary

Matthew 27:31-34, Mark 15:20-23, Luke 23:26-33a, John 19:17

In harmonizing the four Gospel accounts, the best way to chronologically trace the exact sequence of events surrounding Yeshua's crucifixion is to enumerate them stage by stage, commenting upon them accordingly. The hours leading up to Yeshua's death, from the time He began His procession to Calvary until the tomb was sealed, are recounted in 32 distinct stages. The procession to Calvary encompasses the first five stages.

Stage 1: The Messiah Bears the Cross

They took Yeshua therefore: and he went out, bearing the cross for himself (Jn. 19:17). Yochanan's description of the first stage of the procession corresponds to the observations of the Greek historian

Plutarch: "Every criminal who goes to execution must carry his own cross on his back, vice frames out of itself each instrument of its own punishment."[1] Thus, standard Roman procedure for the condemned was to carry his own cross to the site of his crucifixion. Generally, they were forced to carry only the cross beam, their outstretched arms tied to it. Yochanan here describes, *he went out, bearing the cross for himself.* However, the flogging left Yeshua tremendously weakened, so that He was unable to carry the cross very far.

Stage 2: Simon of Cyrene Forced to Carry the Cross

[21] And they compel one passing by, Shimon of Kirenyah, coming from the country, the father of Alexander and Rufus, to go <with them>, that he might bear his cross. (Mk. 15:21)

Kirenyah, or Cyrene in English, was located in North Africa, so Simon was a Jew from North Africa who came to Jerusalem to observe the Passover. Because hundreds of thousands of pilgrims traveled from far and near to attend the feast, it was impossible to house everyone within the city walls. Huge tent cities were erected outside the walls, and unless the pilgrims made special arrangements as Yeshua had done, they ate the Passover in these tent cities on the first night of Passover. On the first day of Passover, when the special Passover sacrifice was offered, many Jews came into the city to observe this special sacrifice. Apparently, Simon of Cyrene was doing that when he was compelled to carry Yeshua's cross the rest of the way.

Matthew and Luke also reported this incident; however, only Mark noted that Simon was the father of Alexander and Rufus, a detail he considered significant to his readership. As previously mentioned, the Gospel of Mark was written for the Romans. Later, when Paul wrote his Epistle to the Romans, he mentioned a man named Rufus (Rom. 16:13). This could have been Simon's son. If so, this event led to the salvation of Simon, his wife (mentioned in Romans), and two sons.

---

[1] M. Eugene Boring, Klaus Berger and Carsten Colpe, eds., *Hellenistic Commentary to the New Testament* (Nashville, TN: Abingdon Press, 1995), p. 180, quoting Plutarch, *Moralia*, "On the Divine Vengeance" 9.553-54 (45-125 CE).

What caused him to conclude that Yeshua was the Messiah is un-known. However, one thing is certain: Yeshua did not act like other people hanging upon their crosses. The condemned often yelled, screamed, and hurled obscenities or curses at their executioners. Some-times the invectives were so bad that soldiers cut out the victims' tongues just to silence them. Yeshua did not yell, scream, or curse. In-stead, He prayed for His executioners. As Simon observed this scene, he might have concluded that Yeshua was indeed who He professed to be, leading to his salvation and the salvation of the rest of his family.

Unlike other churches of the first century, the church of Rome was not founded by an apostle; rather, it was planted by Jewish believers who migrated to Rome (Rom. 1). That may have included the family of Simon of Cyrene. If so, the long-term consequences of this event, the second stage in Yeshua's final hours, reached all the way from Jerusalem to Rome.

Stage 3: The Lament Over Jerusalem

In first-century Israel, professional wailers and lamenters customarily followed any Jew being taken out for execution, especially at the hands of Gentile authorities. Such wailers now followed Yeshua (Lk. 23:27-31):[2]

> [27] *And there followed him a great multitude of the people, and of women who bewailed and lamented him.* [28] *But Yeshua turning unto them said, Daughters of Yerushalayim, weep not for me, but weep for yourselves, and for your children.* [29] *For behold, the days are coming, in which they shall say, Blessed are the barren, and the wombs that never bore, and the breasts that never gave suck.* [30] *Then shall they begin to say to the mountains, Fall on us; and to the hills, Cover us.* [31] *For if they do these things in the green tree, what shall be done in the dry?*

The wailers were not the women who traveled with Yeshua from Gali-lee to Jerusalem, but were "the daughters of Jerusalem," local people. At some point, Yeshua stopped the procession and said, *weep not for*

---

[2] During certain types of Jewish funerals, wailers can still be found today.

me, but weep for yourselves, and for your children (Lk. 23:28), alluding to the curse they took upon themselves at the end of the civil trial: *His blood <be> upon us, and our children* (Mt. 27:25). They were destined to suffer severe judgment for the unpardonable sin. The A.D. 70 judgment was severe for the country as a whole, and was especially severe for the city of Jerusalem.

Yeshua then made a statement understandable only from a Jewish perspective: *For if they do these things in the green tree, what shall be done in the dry?* (Lk. 23:31). This was a *kal v'chomer* argument which was based upon Ezekiel 20:47. It means, "If I suffer this much and I am innocent, how much more are you going to suffer who are guilty?"

Stage 4: The Arrival at Golgotha

And they bring him unto the place Golgota, which is, being interpreted, The place of a skull (Mk. 15:22). The procession now arrived at Golgotha, the place of the crucifixion. All the Gospels simply state that the site was called "Golgotha," translated as *the place of a skull*, without indicating that it actually looked like a skull. This appellation was not due to its appearance, but was due to its being a place where people were crucified. Similarly, the term Boot Hill is a common name for cemeteries where gunslingers were buried in the American West, in such places as Dodge City, Kansas, and Tombstone, Arizona. These cemeteries are not called "Boot Hill" because they are located on a hill that is shaped like a gigantic boot. Rather, the name refers to the fact that most of those buried in these cemeteries "died with their boots on," in a violent manner, either by being shot or by hanging. Similarly, *The place of a skull* simply refers to a place of execution, specifically by crucifixion.

Stage 5: Wine Mingled with Gall and Myrrh

And they offered him wine mingled with myrrh: but he received it not (Mk. 15:23). Matthew added that the drink was also mingled with gall (Mt. 27:34). Having arrived at Golgotha, the soldiers offered Yeshua this concoction, which was given to victims just before nailing them to the cross to help numb some of the pain. It also stupefied the condemned, making him lightheaded, or even unconscious, but when Yeshua *had tasted it, he would not drink* (Mt. 27:34b). He needed full control of His senses for the spiritual warfare He was about to fight on the cross, so He rejected this mixture and suffered the full effects of the pain of the crucifixion.

[§§ 177–179] — B. The Crucifixion

The date was Friday, the 15th of Nisan, or April 7, A.D. 30.[3]

[§ 177] — 1. The First Three Hours: The Wrath of Men

Matthew 27:35-44, Mark 15:24-32, Luke 23:33b-43, John 19:18-27

During the first three hours on the cross, Yeshua suffered the wrath of man. These were the hours from 9:00 a.m. until noon. The wrath of man encompasses the sixth through seventeenth stages of His suffering.

Stage 6: The Crucifixion

At nine o'clock in the morning, or *the third hour*, the Roman soldiers crucified Yeshua (Mk. 15:24-25). The time is significant, because at nine o'clock in the morning on the first day of Passover, the priests offered up the special Passover sacrifice. While the *chagigah* was sacrificed on the Temple Mount, the Lamb of God was nailed to the cross and offered up on Golgotha. All four Gospel writers kept the accounts of the crucifixion simple, as they did with the flogging, because their audience understood what these executions entailed. Two thousand years later, much of what we imagine we know about

---

[3] Or April 3, A.D. 33.

Yeshua's crucifixion comes from the many highly romanticized artistic depictions of it in paintings, frescos, and movies.

Crucifixion was the harshest form of capital punishment in the ancient world. In Greece and Rome, it was initially only used to execute slaves. The Roman Empire started to kill its own citizens this way in order to instill fear, especially in those who were scheming sedition.

THE TYPES OF CROSSES:

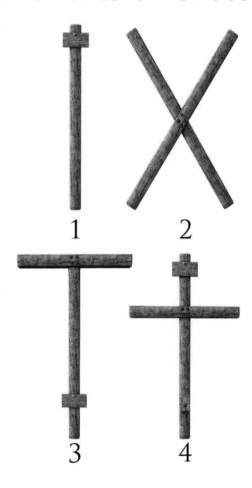

ABOVE: The Romans used four types of crosses, called *crux simplex* (1), *crux decussata* (2), *crux commissa* (3), *crux immissa* (4). By Jesse and Josh Gonzales.

The Romans used four different types of crosses. The first type was a pole, similar to a telephone pole, though not nearly as smooth (see illustration on previous page). This cross was called *crux simplex*. The hands of the victim were crisscrossed and nailed to the pole above the head. The second type was the *crux decussata*, resembling the Roman numeral X (ten), or *decussis,* from which it derived its name. According to church tradition, Peter was crucified upside down on this type of cross. The third type was called *crux commissa*, meaning "connected cross," and it was shaped like the Greek letter *tau*, "T," and was commonly referred to as a "Tau cross." The fourth type is called *crux immissa*, meaning "inserted cross." This is the type of cross traditionally seen in depictions of the crucifixion resembling a lower case "t."

The Gospels do not provide enough information to be certain about which type of cross was used; however, it is possible to make an educated guess. The first and second types of crosses were generally only used on the Italian peninsula, although there are known exceptions to the rule, and therefore, these crosses cannot be completely ruled out. If the only other options were the third and the fourth types of crosses, then the most likely choice is the fourth. During the crucifixion procedure, a piece of parchment or wood, known as *titulus*, which displayed the reason the person was being executed, would be nailed somewhere on the cross. On the Tau cross, it was placed underneath the feet, and on the lower case "t" cross, it was placed over the head. Matthew clearly stated that the sign displaying Yeshua's name and "crime" was placed over His head, so if the only choice was between the third and fourth types, then it was clearly the *crux immissa*. However, the placards were also placed over the head on the pole type, so one would have to know whether Yeshua's hands were crisscrossed over each other or stretched out, something the Gospels do not report.

Two nails fastened the hands to the pole type, and three nails were used in the other types. The paintings of many artists mistakenly portray the nails going through the palm of Yeshua's hands, yet the crucifixion accounts never specify this. They merely say, "They crucified Him." Furthermore, the bone structure in the palm is not strong enough to hold the weight of a full-grown human body, and so the nails were driven through the wrists, where the bone structure is stronger.[4] Once the convicted was nailed to the crossbeam, it was raised and affixed to the upright pole. Then the feet were placed one on top of the other, angled a certain way so that the nail would go through the back of the heel into the wood. A wooden footrest would be nailed where the feet touched the pole; the purpose of this will be explained later. The bones would get pulled out of joint when the crossbar was lifted and dropped upon the pole, because of the way the body was stretched. This fulfilled a messianic prophecy of the Hebrew Scriptures concerning the part of the Messiah's death agony that was caused by His bones being pulled out of joint: *I am poured out like water, And all my bones are out of joint: My heart is like wax; It is melted within me* (Ps. 22:14).

Once the condemned hung on his cross, the waiting began. It might take hours or even days for the victim to die, because while they were given no food, they were given all the liquid they wanted. Under biblical and Jewish law, there was a special curse for those who were executed and then hung on a tree. Once death occurred, the body had to be removed from the tree and buried by sundown (Deut. 21:22-23).

Stage 7: The First Statement from the Cross

And Yeshua said, Father, forgive them; for they know not what they do (Lk. 23:34). Yeshua spoke seven times from the cross. This was the first statement, and He prayed for the forgiveness of those who crucified Him, specifically for those who acted in ignorance, *for they know not what they do*, perhaps including the Roman soldiers assigned to perform the gruesome task of hanging the Messiah on the cross. Herod Antipas, Pontius Pilate, Annas, Caiaphas, and many of the Jewish leaders, who knew exactly what they were doing, were not included. The extension of forgiveness to those who acted out of ignorance is repeated

---

[4] Both the Greek and the Hebrew words for hand, *cheir* and *yad*, include all parts of the arm from the elbow to the fingers. Passages such as Psalm 22:16, Luke 24:39, and John 20:20 which speak of Yeshua's hands would therefore include the possibility of His wrists having been pierced.

in Peter's sermon in Acts 3:17 and is also implied by Paul in I Corinthians 2:8.

Stage 8: The Parting of the Garments of Yeshua

[23] The soldiers therefore, when they had crucified Yeshua, took his garments and made four parts, to every soldier a part; and also the coat: now the coat was without seam, woven from the top throughout. [24] They said therefore one to another, Let us not tear it, but cast lots for it, whose it shall be: that the scripture might be fulfilled, which said, They parted my garments among them, And upon my vesture did they cast lots. [25] These things therefore the soldiers did. (Jn. 19:23-25a)

Part of the Roman procedure at crucifixions was that the soldiers assigned to perform the execution were entitled to take the clothing of the victim as spoil. Psalm 22:18 predicted that those who crucified Yeshua would divide His garments. The artistic representations of the crucifixion showing Yeshua with a loincloth are misleading. He was naked and in the Jewish context, that would add to the shame.

The average Jewish male of first-century Israel wore five pieces of clothing:

- ✿ The upper garment, also called the "outer garment"
- ✿ The under garment, also called the "inner garment" or "tunic"
- ✿ Some kind of head covering
- ✿ Shoes or sandals
- ✿ The robe or outer coat, which was the largest single piece of cloth

Four soldiers were assigned to each crucifixion. The upper garment, the under garment, the head covering, and the shoes were distributed among the four. Due to its size, the robe would usually be torn into four parts, and every soldier would take one of the four pieces of cloth. However, Yeshua's coat was an expensive robe normally worn by members of the upper classes. While He lived in poverty (Mt. 8:20), several wealthy women financed His ministry (Lk. 8:1-3). One of them could have given Him this particular coat. The soldiers felt it would be a shame to tear a robe of such quality, so instead they cast lots, and one soldier won it. This fulfilled another prophecy, in Psalm 22:18, that they would gamble for the Messiah's clothing.

Stage 9: The Superscription

[19] And Pilate wrote a title also, and put it on the cross. And there was written, YESHUA OF NATZERET, THE KING OF THE JEWS. [20] This title therefore read many of the Jews, for the place where Yeshua was crucified was near to the city; and it was written in Hebrew, <and> in Latin, <and> in Greek. [21] The chief priests of the Jews therefore said to Pilate, Write not, The King of the Jews; but, that he said, I am King of the Jews. [22] Pilate answered, What I have written I have written. (Jn. 19:19-22)

As previously stated, a prisoner's crimes were publicly posted on the cross upon which he was crucified, written upon a parchment or piece of wood and nailed to the cross, either above the condemned person's head or below his feet. Matthew specified: *And they set up over his head his accusation* (Mt. 27:37). Pilate's wording of the charges read like a title, not an accusation, simply stating, *Yeshua of Nazareth, the King of the Jews.* The text was written in three languages: Hebrew for the Jews, Latin for the Romans, and Greek for everyone else. The Jewish leaders recognized that the superscription read like a title, not an accusation, and they wanted Pilate to change the wording. These leaders were the chief priests, the Sadducean members of the Sanhedrin. Pilate refused to do so and enjoyed a bit of revenge against those who had intimidated him into doing something he knew was wrong.

Stage 10: The Crucifixion of the Other Two

Then are there crucified with him two robbers, one on the right hand and one on the left (Mt. 27:38). The fact that to the left and right of Yeshua two other men were crucified fulfilled the prophecy of Isaiah 53:12 that declared the Messiah would be numbered among the transgressors. As was the case with Barabbas, "robbers" is a poor translation of the Greek word *lestai* used here by Matthew, because robbery was not punishable by crucifixion. In his writings, the historian Josephus referred to insurgents by this term, so it is safe to assume that the two men probably participated in the rebellion against Rome under Barabbas. Barabbas was released in the Passover exchange, but these two men were less fortunate and were crucified along with Yeshua.

Stage 11: The Fifth Mockery

[29] And they that passed by railed on him, wagging their heads, and saying, Ha! You that destroy the temple, and build it in three days, [30] save yourself, and come down from the cross. (Mk. 15:29-30)

Yeshua suffered four mockeries before His crucifixion. While hanging on the cross, He was sneered at four more times. Those who happened to be passing by committed the fifth mockery. The site of the crucifixion was near a main road leading into Jerusalem. On Passover morning, the city gates were open, and traffic flowed in and out. People could read the superscription above Yeshua's head. They knew the original accusation against Him was disrespect for the Temple, and they mocked Him for it.

Stage 12: The Sixth Mockery

[31] In like manner also the chief priests mocking <him> among themselves with the scribes said, He saved others; himself he cannot save. [32] Let the Messiah, the King of Yisrael, now come down from the cross, that we may see and believe. (Mk. 15:31-32)

The Jewish leaders committed the sixth mockery, and both the chief priests and scribes, meaning the Sadducees and the Pharisees, were guilty of taunting Yeshua while He was on the cross.

Stage 13: The Seventh Mockery

[36] And the soldiers also mocked him, coming to him, offering him vinegar, [37] and saying, If you are the King of the Jews, save yourself. (Lk. 23:36-37)

The seventh mockery came from the Roman soldiers, so both Jews and Gentiles were guilty of scoffing at Yeshua while He was on the cross.

Stage 14: The Eighth Mockery

And the robbers [better: "rebels"] *also that were crucified with him cast upon him the same reproach* (Mt. 27:44). The eighth mockery was committed by the two men crucified with Yeshua, and initially, both participated in ridiculing Him.

In summary, four different groups committed the four mockeries during Yeshua's crucifixion. Two common elements were in all four of these incidents. First, all scorned specific messianic claims Yeshua had made during His public ministry. Second, all four groups challenged Yeshua to prove His Messiahship by coming down from the cross. This was Satan's last attempt to keep Yeshua from the cross. The devil wanted Him to die, but not at this time and in this way. If Yeshua had died at any other time or in any other way, no atonement would have been made, and if He had used His messianic power to free Himself, He would have proven to be a false messiah, because crucifixion was how the Messiah was supposed to die. Therefore, Satan made one last attempt to keep Him from the cross.

Stage 15: The Conversion of One of the Malefactors

[39] And one of the malefactors that were hanged railed on him, saying, Are you not the Messiah? Save yourself and us. [40] But the other answered, and rebuking him said, Do you not even fear God, seeing you are in the same condemnation? [41] And we indeed justly; for we receive the due reward of our deeds: but this man has done nothing amiss.

⁴² And he said, Yeshua, remember me when you come in your kingdom. (Lk. 23:39-42)

Luke used a different Greek term than Matthew to describe the men to the left and right of Yeshua, calling them *kakourgōn*, or "criminals." While both of these malefactors initially participated in mocking Yeshua, one of them reflected on what was happening. Based on his statements to the other rebel and to Yeshua, he came to four conclusions. First, he concluded that he was a sinner. That is significant, because no one can recognize his need for a savior until he first sees himself as God sees him: a sinner. Second, he recognized that Yeshua was sinless when he said, *this man has done nothing amiss.* Third, although he saw that Yeshua was dying the same kind of death as he, he concluded that Yeshua could still save him. This is an astounding conclusion showing that the criminal believed Yeshua was indeed the Messiah. Fourth, equally incredible is the fact that although he saw that Yeshua was dying, he concluded that He would come again in His kingdom and specifically requested to be remembered when that happened.

Stage 16: The Second Statement from the Cross

And he said unto him, Verily I say unto you, Today shall you be with me in Paradise. (Lk. 23:43)

In the second statement from the cross, Yeshua told the criminal that he would not have to wait until the kingdom to be remembered; he would be remembered that same day. He would die that day, and his spirit, like Yeshua's spirit, would go down to the paradise section of Sheol.[5] The truth of this would prove that Yeshua was the Messiah, the Son of God, the point that all the others contested and mocked.

---

[5] For additional information about the place of the dead, see Arnold G. Fruchtenbaum, *The Footsteps of the Messiah: A Study of the Sequence of Prophetic Events* (San Antonio, TX: Ariel Ministries, 2003).

Stage 17: The Third Statement from the Cross

25b But there were standing by the cross of Yeshua his mother, and his mother's sister, Miriam the <wife> of Klophah, and Miriam Magdalit. 26 When Yeshua therefore saw his mother, and the disciple standing by whom he loved, he said unto his mother, Woman, behold, your son! 27 Then said he to the disciple, Behold, your mother! And from that hour the disciple took her unto his own <home>. (Jn. 19:25b-27)

Four women stood at the foot of the cross. By comparing Yochanan's account with that of Mark (15:40) and Matthew (27:56), the names of the four women can be deduced. The most prominent was Yeshua's own mother, Miriam. The second woman was also named Miriam, and she is referred to as the mother of James and Judas, two of Yeshua's disciples. She was the wife of Cleopas (Jn. 19:25), who, by church tradition, was the brother of Yeshua's stepfather Joseph. If that is true, then James and Judas were Yeshua's step-cousins. Cleopas was also one of two disciples on the Emmaus Road. The third woman was named Salome. She was the mother of the sons of Zebedee, James and Yochanan, two other members of the apostolic group. She was also the sister of Yeshua's mother (Jn. 19:25), making her His aunt, and James and Yochanan His first cousins. The fourth woman was Miriam Magdalene.

Among this group of four women stood the Apostle Yochanan, the only one to record this incident. In His third statement from the cross, Yeshua addressed His mother, saying, *Woman, behold, your son,* meaning Yochanan. Turning to the apostle, He said, *Behold, your mother,* meaning Miriam. With these words, Yeshua fulfilled a Jewish expectation, for it was the firstborn son's responsibility to care for the physical welfare of his widowed mother. Yeshua was leaving the earth and none of His four half-brothers believed in Him yet. He chose to leave the welfare of His mother in the hands of Yochanan, a believer. The apostle was to look upon Yeshua's mother as his own, caring for her physical welfare, *And from that hour the disciple took her unto his own <home>* (Jn. 19:27).

With this, the first three hours on the cross, in which Yeshua suffered the wrath of men, ended.

[§ 178] — 2. The Second Three Hours: The Wrath of God

Matthew 27:45-50, Mark 15:33-37, Luke 23:44-46, John 19:28-30

During the second three hours on the cross, Yeshua partook of the cup and suffered the wrath of God. It was Friday, from noon until three o'clock in the afternoon. The wrath of God encompasses the eighteenth through twenty-fifth stages of the passion narrative.

Stage 18: The Darkness over the Whole Land

44 And it was now about the sixth hour, and a darkness came over the whole land until the ninth hour, 45a the sun's light failing. (Lk. 23:44-45a)

Darkness covered the entire land and apparently some of the surrounding territories. It extended for three full hours, from noon until three o'clock in the afternoon, normally the brightest time of the day. The Gospel writers implied this darkness was extensive, and other records confirm their reports. Archaeologists have uncovered three writings from the same period that mention the phenomenon. Two of the records come from Egypt, south of Israel, and the other comes from Asia Minor in what is modern-day Turkey, north of Israel. The first writer was Dionysius, a Greek scientist living in Egypt, who reported experiencing this darkness while in the city of Heliopolis. The irony is that the Greek name *Heliopolis* means "The City of the Sun," and yet "Sun City" was blacked out. Diogenes, the second writer, was also a Greek scientist living in Egypt. Although a pagan, Diogenes had a measure of spiritual insight, and his reaction to this darkness was rather profound. He wrote, "Either the Deity himself suffers at this moment, or sympathizes with one that does."[6] Diogenes could not have known that both statements were true. The deity God the Son suffered in that darkness, and God the Father and God the Spirit sympathized with Him as He suffered. The third writer was Phlegon of Tralles, a Greek from Asia Minor. He was one of several educated freedmen employed by Emperor

---

[6] Fred. W. Krummacher, D.D., *The Suffering Saviour; or, Meditations on The Last Days of Christ* (Boston: Gould and Lincoln, 1859), p. 412.

Hadrian (A.D. 117-138) and was the author of various books. In his historical compendium *Olympiads*, he wrote that there was a great and remarkable eclipse of the sun above any that had happened before. He stated that the day was turned into night at the sixth hour, so that the stars were seen in heaven and that a great earthquake shook the Roman province of Bithynia, now northwest Turkey, and that many of the houses in Nicea were toppled. As we will see in the following section, the moment Yeshua gave up His spirit, a tremendous earthquake occurred, and this fact was confirmed by Phlegon.

The three hours of darkness represented the cup that Yeshua had prayed He would not have to drink, but He indeed partook of the cup of the wrath of God. This was the period of Yeshua's spiritual death. For three hours, He was separated from God the Father. This referred to His human spirit, not His divine spirit, which remains eternal and unchangeable. The theological significance of the three hours of darkness is the spiritual death of the Messiah.

Stage 19: The Fourth Statement from the Cross

[46] And about the ninth hour Yeshua cried with a loud voice saying, Eli, Eli, lama sabachthani? That is, My God, my God, why have you forsaken me? (Mt. 27:46)

Yeshua was quoting Psalm 22:1, which, along with Isaiah 53, contains the most detailed prophecy of Messiah's death. Taken in isolation, it might imply that Yeshua uttered a cry of despair and defeat. However, in the context of Psalm 22, Yeshua actually cried for help at the end of the three hours of His suffering the wrath of God.[7]

In stage 24, Yeshua's cry for help was answered. He died spiritually and was resurrected spiritually before finally dying physically on that cross. This is evident in the way He addressed God the Father. Here,

---

[7] A footnote in *The Complete Jewish Study Bible* explains: "In Judaism, when a Bible verse is cited, its entire context is implied if appropriate. Often the opening words, 'My God! My God! Why have you deserted me?' serve as the title for the passage. Thus Yeshua refers all of Ps. 22 to himself . . ." (*The Complete Jewish Study Bible*; Peabody, Massachusetts: Hendrickson Publishers; 2016; p. 1436.)

He called Him *My God*, and this was the only time in all four Gospels that He addressed Him this way. Usually, He called Him "Father" (170 times) and, more intimately, "My Father" (21 times). Now, however, their relationship became judicial, and Yeshua did not address Him as *Avi, Avi* ("My Father, My Father"), but *Eli, Eli* ("My God, My God"). In the twenty-fourth stage, His cry for help was answered as He again called God His Father.

Stage 20: The Reaction of the Bystanders

[47] And some of them that stood there, when they heard it, said, This man calls Eliyahu. [48] And straightway one of them ran, and took a sponge, and filled it with vinegar, and put it on a reed, and gave him to drink. [49] And the rest said, Let be; let us see whether Eliyahu comes to save him. (Mt. 27:47-49)

The bystanders' response was based upon a misunderstanding of what Yeshua actually cried out. The Hebrew, *Eli, Eli,* means *My God, My God,* but is also a shortened form of the name *Elijah.* Therefore, to the Hebrew ear, *Eli* could mean "My God" or "Elijah." The onlookers assumed that Yeshua called for Elijah to rescue Him.

Someone in the crowd thought Yeshua was delirious and tried to give Him some liquid, but others called him back so they could wait to see if Elijah would come to His rescue.

Stage 21: The Fifth Statement from the Cross

After this Yeshua, knowing that all things are now finished, that the scripture might be accomplished, said, I thirst. (Jn. 19:28)

The fifth statement from the cross, *I thirst,* came after Yeshua had suffered the wrath of God. In the account of the rich man and Lazarus, after the rich man suffered the wrath of God and the pains of hell, his response was that he had thirst (Lk. 16:22-24). Yeshua, having suffered the wrath of God, responded in the same way.[8]

Stage 22: The Drinking of the Vinegar

There was set there a vessel full of vinegar: so they put a sponge full of the vinegar upon hyssop, and brought it to his mouth. (Jn. 19:29)

Yeshua partook of this vinegar or sour wine because it was not the stupefying mixture which induced lightheadedness He had refused earlier. This moistened His mouth, lips, and tongue so that the last two statements Yeshua made from the cross, by far the two most important of the seven statements, could be heard clearly and distinctly.

Stage 23: The Sixth Statement from the Cross

When Yeshua therefore had received the vinegar, he said, It is finished. (Jn. 19:30)

Those three English words translate only one Greek word, *tetelestai*, an accounting term meaning "paid in full." All of the animal sacrifices made over the centuries were merely installment payments. With the Yeshua's death, the final atonement was made: It is finished; our sin is paid in full!

Stage 24: The Seventh Statement from the Cross

And Yeshua, crying with a loud voice, said, Father, into your hands I commend my spirit. (Lk. 23:46)

In His seventh statement, Yeshua emphasized the voluntary character of His death when He said, *I commend* [dismiss] *my spirit.* He chose the moment of His death and dismissed His spirit from His body.

---

[8] The Scripture that was directly fulfilled by this stage is Psalm 22:15.

He once again addressed God as "Father," showing that His cry for help in the nineteenth stage was answered, and the paternal relationship was restored. Yeshua died spiritually and was resurrected spiritually before He died physically.

Stage 25: The Death of Yeshua

Yeshua's physical death followed. Mark and Luke noted that He *gave up the ghost* (Mk. 15:37; Lk. 23:46). Matthew stated that He *yielded up his spirit* (Mt. 27:50). Normally, a man's head falls after he dies; however, Yeshua put His head down and then dismissed His spirit from His body, as can be seen in Yochanan's Gospel: *and he bowed his head, and gave up his spirit* (Jn. 19:30).

The death of Yeshua is the first of the three points of the gospel message: *that Messiah died for our sins* (I Cor. 15:3). His death specifically accomplished the atonement, which is why the New Testament writers developed in detail the theological implications and significance of His death.

[§ 179] — 3. The Accompanying Signs

Matthew 27:51-56, Mark 15:38-41, Luke 23:45b, 47-49

The moment Yeshua died, several things occurred, encompassing the twenty-sixth stage.

Stage 26: The Earth Shakes,
the Dead Are Raised, and the Veil Tears

A tremendous earthquake shook the land and split rocks, marking the moment of His death (Mt. 27:51b). Furthermore, many tombs opened, and many believers were resurrected from the dead (Mt. 27:52-53), but they came out only after Yeshua's resurrection. This explains why only those in tombs were raised and not those in graves buried below the ground. If they had remained there for three days, they would have suffocated quickly, while tombs provide enough air to breathe. After Yeshua was resurrected, the resurrected believers appeared to many people in Jerusalem. This is all the Bible says about them, and then they disappear from the records. The event, however, does portray the concept that by His death, Yeshua provided life.

Clearly this was not the resurrection of the Old Testament saints into their eternal state, because no one could be resurrected into immortality until after Yeshua's own resurrection (I Cor. 15:20-23). Since they were all raised before His resurrection, they were restored to natural life in the same way as Lazarus, Jairus' daughter, and the son of the widow of Nain; eventually, they died again. The resurrection of the Old Testament saints into their immortal state will occur after the second coming (Is. 26:19; Dan. 12:2).

In addition to the earthquake and the raising of the dead, *the veil of the temple was rent in two from the top to the bottom* (Mk. 15:38). The veil was a curtain sixty feet high and thirty feet wide, with the thickness of a palm breadth, about four inches, separating the holy place from the Holy of Holies in the Temple. It was woven in *blue, and purple, and scarlet, and fine twined linen* (Ex. 26:31b). The size and thickness of the veil alone made it impossible for man to tear the material, but if anyone had tried, they would have torn it from the bottom up, not from the top down. However, Mark pointed out that the curtain was torn from top to bottom, emphasizing that it was God who tore it.

The book of Hebrews teaches the theological significance of this event: *Having therefore, brethren, boldness to enter into the holy place by the blood of Yeshua, by the way which he dedicated for us, a new and living way, through the veil, that is to say, his flesh* (Heb. 10:19-20). As long as the Mosaic Law was in force as the rule of life, only one man of one family, of one clan, of one tribe, of one race, and of one nation—only one man out of all of humanity—had access to the presence of God, and that was the Jewish high priest. Even he had access only one day of the year: the Day of Atonement. However, the tearing of the veil signified that Yeshua's death rendered the law inoperative. The law was no longer the rule of life, and therefore, access to God's presence became freely available to all.

The rabbinic writings do not mention the rending of the veil. Since few people had access to the interior of the Temple and the curtain hung well inside the building, the religious leaders could keep the tearing a secret. While Jewish sources do not record the rending of the veil, rabbinic legends exist concerning unusual events occurring at the Temple forty years before it was destroyed, the year A.D. 30, the year of the crucifixion. We will survey only four of the many existing early non-biblical sources. The first legend is mentioned in the Jerusalem Talmud, *Tractate Yoma 6:3*: "It has been taught: Forty years before the destruction of the Temple the western light went out." The western light refers to the center lamp of the menorah standing in the first room of the Temple, the holy place. According to rabbinic tradition, it symbolized God's presence and blessing. As of the year A.D. 30, this light mysteriously kept going out, thus indicating to the Jewish mind that God had departed.

A second legend is recorded by both Josephus and the Talmud. The heavy temple doors usually took several men to open, but they swung open of their own accord in the year A.D. 30. In the Jewish mindset, this either demonstrated the departure of God's presence or the invitation to invaders. Either option had clear undertones of coming destruction.

A third legend states that the lintel of the Temple doorway, an enormous stone at least thirty feet long, cracked and fell in that year. One of the early church fathers, Jerome (347-420), connected the rending of the veil with this event and deduced that the lintel broke due to an earthquake.

The most significant of legends, however, is that of *Azazel*. The Hebrew word *azazel* means "removal," but it became the technical name for the scapegoat of the Day of Atonement (Lev. 16). On that day, two goats were presented before the high priest. By the casting of lots, one goat was chosen to die, and one was chosen to live. The goat chosen to die was killed at the base of the altar. The high priest took its blood into the Holy of Holies and sprinkled it upon the mercy seat, which was the lid of the ark of the covenant. After sprinkling the blood, the priest came out and approached the second goat, the one chosen to live, placing his hands upon its head. The laying on of hands in the Hebrew

Scriptures was the means of identification; the priest identified the goat with the people of Israel. By confessing the sins of Israel, he symbolically transferred them onto the goat, and then chased the animal with the sins of Israel into the wilderness. Based on Isaiah 1:18, which says, *though your sins be as scarlet, they shall be as white as snow; though they be red like crimson, they will be as wool,* the practice of tying a red ribbon on the horn or neck of the goat before it was chased out into the wilderness was initiated. According to the legend of Azazel, year after year the red ribbon miraculously turned white, showing God had forgiven the sins of Israel for that year. However, forty years before the Temple was destroyed, the red ribbon stopped turning white; God no longer forgave the sins of Israel by means of the two goats. How sad that the rabbis recorded these legends, but never drew the proper conclusion. Why did the red ribbon stop turning white? Because tetelestai—It is finished! *Now where remission of [sin] is, there is no more offering for sin* (Heb. 10:18).

In summary, Jewish writings never mention the tearing of the veil, but they record a number of legends connected with the Temple, all dating from the year A.D. 30, indicating that something significant happened in connection with the Temple that year.

The signs that accompanied Yeshua's death led the Roman centurion who stood by the cross to saving faith: *Truly this was the Son of God* (Mt. 27:54). They also struck fear in the Jewish multitude: *And all the multitudes that came together to this sight, when they beheld the things that were done, returned smiting their breasts* (Lk. 23:48). Standing afar off were several Galilean women who observed the whole scene in silence (Mt. 27:55).

[§ 180] — C. The Burial of the Messiah

Matthew 27:57-60, Mark 15:42-46, Luke 23:50-54, John 19:31-42

The burial of the Messiah encompassed the twenty-seventh through thirtieth stages of the passion narrative.

Stage 27: The Breaking of the Bones of the Other Two, and the Piercing of Yeshua

Yeshua died on the Day of Preparation (Mk. 15:42; Lk. 23:54; Jn. 19:31). In Judaism, the term was used to describe the sixth day of the week, Friday. As the name implies, this day was generally spent preparing what was necessary to avoid work on the Sabbath. The preparations included cooking, completing work, and spiritual purification. Less frequently, the term *Preparation* could also refer to another day of the week falling just before a festival.

The time reference in all four Gospels implies that Yeshua's corpse had to be buried before the Sabbath began: *the bodies should not remain on the cross upon the Sabbath (for the day of that Sabbath was a high <day>)* (Jn. 19:31b). In the year A.D. 30 (as well as the year 33), the Passover day fell on the day of Preparation, meaning it began on Thursday evening and lasted until Friday evening. The moment the sun set on Friday, the Sabbath and the seven days of the Feast of Unleavened Bread began. In the Mosaic Law, the first and the seventh days of this feast were holy days. Whenever a Sabbath day fell on a Jewish holy day, it became a high Sabbath. If possible, the Jews would not leave a dead body exposed and unburied over a Sabbath day. This was all the more true if the day were a high Sabbath; thus, the Jewish leaders asked Pilate to hasten the death process: *The Jews therefore . . . asked of Pilate that their legs might be broken, and <that> they might be taken away. The soldiers therefore came, and broke the legs of the first, and of the other that was crucified with him* (Jn. 19:31-32).

As mentioned earlier, where the feet touched the wood on the cross was a footrest, the *sedile*, that was nailed there for a specific reason. A person ultimately died by asphyxiation when crucified because of the way the condemned hung on the cross. The footrest was nailed onto the pole so that the victims could raise themselves, breathe, lower themselves, raise themselves again, breathe, lower themselves, and as long as they had the strength to do this, they survived for some time. In some cases, it took days for someone to die this way. As the victims moved up and down, rubbing against the rugged wood of the cross, their backs became painfully raw. Because Yeshua was flogged beforehand, He felt the pain from the time He was first placed on the cross and throughout the six-hour period during which He slid up and down against that rough wood. One way to accelerate the death process was to break the legs of the victims to prevent them from lifting themselves up to take a breath.[9] They died by suffocation shortly thereafter. For that reason, the legs of the men hanging to the left and right of Yeshua were broken (Jn. 19:32). However, by the time the soldiers came to Yeshua, He had already dismissed His spirit from His body (Jn. 19:33). Therefore, they did not bother to break His legs, thus fulfilling the Passover motif that not one bone of the Passover lamb could be broken (Ex. 12:46).

To ensure Yeshua had died, one soldier drove a spear into His side (Jn. 19:34), thus fulfilling the messianic prophecy of Zechariah 12:10 that the Messiah would be pierced. Blood and water flowed from the wound. Many have discussed the medical significance of this phenomenon. Some medical doctors believe that Yeshua's heart ruptured, and He died of a broken heart. Other doctors dispute this conclusion. However, they miss the point. The significance of the blood and the water is not medical, but theological. Yochanan alone recorded this incident, stating that he was an eyewitness to the event: *And he that had seen has borne witness, and his witness is true: and he knows that he said true, that ye also may believe* (Jn. 19:35). Later, the apostle, reflecting on the outpouring of blood and water, made a theological deduction: This was the sign that God had provided eternal life (I Jn. 5:6-12). The blood and water were evidence that Yeshua died and by His death provided eternal life.

Stage 28: The Request for the Body

And when even was now come (Mk. 15:42a), a man went boldly to Pilate to request Yeshua's body. This man was Joseph of Arimathaea, about whom the Gospel accounts report eight things:

---

[9] This procedure is known as the *crurifragium*.

1. He was *of honorable estate* (Mk. 15:43), meaning he came from a family with a good background.

2. He was *rich* (Mt. 27:57); he was a wealthy man, setting the stage for the nature of the burial.

3. He was a *good man* (Lk. 23:50), emphasizing his external conformity to the law.

4. He was *a righteous man* (Lk. 23:50), emphasizing his internal conformity.

5. He was *looking for the kingdom of God* (Mk. 15:43; Lk. 23:51); he was looking with expectation for the coming of the Messiah and the messianic kingdom and was, therefore, a member of the believing remnant of that day.

6. He was a *councilor* (Mk. 15:43; Lk. 23:50), which means he was also a member of the Sanhedrin.

7. He *had not consented to their counsel and deed* (Lk. 23:51), meaning he was not present to vote for the death penalty.

8. Up to that point, Nicodemus and Joseph were secret believers *for fear of the Jews* (Jn. 19:38). However, Joseph now came *boldly* before Pilate to ask for Yeshua's body (Mk. 15:43).

Pilate sent someone to verify whether Yeshua was really dead (Mk. 15:44). Once that was confirmed, he permitted the body to be turned over to Joseph of Arimathaea and Nicodemus (Mt. 27:58; Mk. 15:45).

Stage 29: The Removal of the Body from the Cross

At this point, Joseph was joined by Nicodemus (Jn. 19:39). The body was removed from the cross and wrapped in linen cloth (Mk. 15:46; Jn. 19:39-40). John 19:40 speaks about *cloths*, which means "strips of cloth." The common Jewish burial procedure was to wrap strips of cloth around the body. This is one reason the shroud of Turin could not be Yeshua's shroud.

Stage 30: The Burial of Yeshua

The place of burial was not a public cemetery, but a tomb in a privately-owned garden that had never been used (Jn. 19:41-42). The fact that a great stone was rolled in front of the opening reveals that this was a rich man's tomb (Mt. 27:60), and so Yeshua was buried in a rich man's unused grave, just as Isaiah 53:9 prophesied He would: *And they made his grave with the wicked, and with a rich man in his death; although he had done no violence, neither was any deceit in his mouth.* The Messiah was assigned a criminal's grave, but was to be buried in a rich man's tomb.

It was now late afternoon and early evening on Friday, *the day of the Preparation, and the Sabbath drew on* (Lk. 23:54).

Three theological implications can be deduced from Yeshua's burial. First, the burial was the last act of what theologians call Messiah's humiliation, signifying the death of the God-Man. The humiliation began with the incarnation when He took on the likeness of sinful flesh and ended with His burial. Since He was sinless, He should not have died; yet He did die, as the burial signified. For the sinless God-Man, death was a humiliation. Furthermore, none of those close to Yeshua during His life and ministry were involved in the burial—not His eleven loyal disciples following the betrayal by Judas; not any of the women who followed Him from Galilee; not Miriam and Martha, who lived nearby in Bethany; not even His mother, who was in Jerusalem on this occasion. Instead, two Pharisees who had secretly believed in Yeshua buried Him. His burial marked the end of the period of His humiliation.

Second, just as theologians speak of the humiliation of the Son, they also speak of His exaltation. Normally, they say the exaltation began with His resurrection and culminated with His ascension and enthronement at the right hand of God the Father. However, it would be better to see His exaltation as beginning with His burial. It also marked the first stage of His exaltation in several ways: He was buried in a new, unused, rich man's tomb. Furthermore, although He was buried in a tomb, that tomb was in a private garden, a significant detail. Centuries earlier, in the Garden of Eden, the first Adam brought physical and spiritual death, but in this garden, the last Adam brought blessing and new life to come.

Third, the burial is an integral part of the gospel message. According to I Corinthians 15:1-4, the gospel includes three events in the life of Messiah: His death, burial, and resurrection. He died *for our sins according to the scriptures* (I Cor. 15:3). He then *was buried* (I Cor. 15:4a). Finally, He rose *on the third day according to the scriptures* (I Cor. 15:4b). This is the full gospel message; any addition is false. The burial of Yeshua is very much part of the gospel as the evidence of His death. The burial is less important than the death and resurrection, but it marks the transition from one to the other. Out of His burial came the resurrection.

[§ 181] — D. The Sealing of the Tomb

Matthew 27:61-66, Mark 15:47, Luke 23:55-56

The sealing of the tomb contains the last two stages of the passion narrative.

Stage 31: The Preparation for the Embalming

It was now *on the morrow, which is <the day> after the Preparation* (Mt. 27:62a). This makes it Saturday, the 16th of Nisan, or April 8, A.D. 30.[10] Two women, both named Miriam, were *sitting over against the sepulchre* (Mt. 27:61). Mark noted that they knew the exact location of the tomb where Yeshua was laid (Mk. 15:47). Luke recorded that some of the women who came from Galilee to Jerusalem with Yeshua observed the location of the tomb. Intending to wash and anoint the body after the Sabbath, they returned to prepare the spices needed to complete the customary Jewish burial procedures (Lk. 23:55-56). Clearly, with all their preparations, they did not anticipate Yeshua's resurrection.

---

[10] Or April 4, A.D. 33.

Stage 32: The Sealing of the Tomb

Only Matthew records the events surrounding the sealing of the tomb. He noted that *the chief priests and the Pharisees were gathered together unto Pilate* (Mt. 27:62b) because they had another problem: *Sir, we remember that that deceiver said while he was yet alive, After three days I rise again* (Mt. 27:63). Avoiding Yeshua's name, they called Him *that deceiver*, as was typical in Pharisaic Judaism. When the rabbis had an issue with someone else, they substituted an epithet, title, or derogatory term for that person's proper name; hence, they called Yeshua *that deceiver*. Even today, He is still called *Yeshu*, which in Hebrew forms a three-letter acronym meaning "May his name and memory be blotted out." He is also referred to as *Ha-Ish Ha-Hu*, meaning "that man," and *Ha-Taloui*, meaning "the hanged one."

The men now approaching Pilate clearly recalled that Yeshua not only prophesied His death by crucifixion, but also His resurrection on the third day. They were concerned that someone might steal the body and then preach a resurrection, so that *the last error will be worse than the first* (Mt. 27:64).

THE SEALING OF THE TOMB

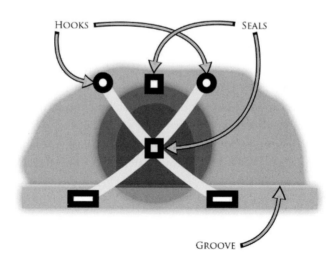

Pilate responded by ordering two things (Mt. 27:65-66). First, he released to the chief priests and Pharisees Roman guards to secure the tomb for three days. Failure on the guards' part to keep the body from being moved was punishable by death. Second, Pilate ordered the tomb to be sealed with hooks placed in the wall of the tomb and on the side of the stone, and ropes threaded through the hooks. Where the corner of the stone touched the wall of the tomb and the ropes crisscrossed to form an "X," a clay seal of the official Roman insignia would be placed, making it impossible to roll away the stone without breaking the seal. Anyone caught breaking into the tomb would be executed.

E. Additional Comments and a Map

To conclude the narrative of the death and burial of Messiah, two specific questions will be addressed. Furthermore, a map shows Yeshua's final week.

1. The Day of His Death

The first question pertains to the day on which Yeshua died. Some who do not understand the Jewish reckoning of time incorrectly conclude that the crucifixion occurred on a Tuesday, Wednesday, or Thursday. The Gospels, however, clearly indicate that Yeshua was killed on a Friday and placed in the tomb before sundown. The term *Sabbath* need not be interpreted other than normally, which is from sundown Friday until sundown Saturday. Scripture emphasizes this, and John 19:31, Mark 15:42, Luke 23:54, and Matthew 27:62 clarify that Yeshua died around three o'clock on Friday afternoon. He was then placed in the tomb before the Sabbath began, which, by Jewish reckoning, was when three stars appeared in the night sky.

Besides the Gospels, ancient Jewish records such as the Talmud confirm that the day the Messiah died was a Friday during Passover:

> On the eve of the Passover Yeshu was hanged. For forty days before the execution took place, a herald went forth and cried, 'He is going forth

to be stoned because he has practiced sorcery and enticed Israel to apostasy. Anyone who can say anything in his favor, let him come forward and plead on his behalf.' But since nothing was brought forward in his favor he was hanged on the eve of the Passover! . . . A Florentine Ms. adds: and the eve of Sabbath.[11]

This Talmudic quote refers to Yeshua's trial and execution, and the Florentine manuscript mentions twice that He was executed on the eve of the Sabbath, which is Friday. Furthermore, twice it mentions that it was at the Passover, which is why Yochanan stated that the Sabbath was a high Sabbath: *The Jews therefore, because it was the Preparation, that the bodies should not remain on the cross upon the Sabbath (for the day of that Sabbath was a high <day>), asked of Pilate that their legs might be broken, and <that> they might be taken away* (Jn. 19:31). Finally, the Talmudic quote reveals the exact charge against Yeshua, claiming that He practiced sorcery and seduced Israel and estranged them from their God. This reflects what occurred when Yeshua was officially rejected on the grounds of being demonized (Mt. 12). Interestingly, the rabbis of this period never denied that He performed real miracles. In this particular quote, they admit that He did. Still, the main import of this quote is that Yeshua died on a Friday before the Sabbath, and during the week of the Passover and the Feast of Unleavened Bread. Teaching that His death occurred on a Tuesday, Wednesday, or Thursday violates the clear statements of the Gospels and also other historical documents.

2. The Three Days in the Tomb

The second question pertains to the time Yeshua spent in the tomb. Many believe that the statement *three days and three nights* refers to three full 24-hour periods. The crucifixion would have occurred earlier in the week with Yeshua in the tomb for a period of 72 hours. However, if Yeshua had been in the tomb for three full days and was resurrected the moment the third 24-hour day had ended, it would have been the fourth day. Furthermore, He met the two disciples on the Emmaus

---

[11] *b. Sanhedrin* 43a; p. 281, n. (7).

road on Sunday afternoon, and many hours had passed since the resurrection (Lk. 24:13-32; Mk. 16:12-13). Not recognizing the Messiah, the disciples related to Yeshua the events of the arrest, trial, and crucifixion, and early reports of a resurrection, pointing out that *it is now the third day since these things came to pass* (Lk. 24:21). The only way Sunday afternoon could be the third day is if the crucifixion occurred on Friday.

In defense of those who misread the Gospels, it must be acknowledged that when considering all of Yeshua's statements, they appear contradictory. For example, sometimes He prophesied that the resurrection would occur *on the third day* (Mt. 16:21; 17:23; 20:19; 27:64; Lk. 9:22; 18:33; 24:7, 21, 46; Acts 10:40; I Cor. 15:4). Other times He said that it would happen *after three days*, meaning on the fourth day (Mt. 26:61; 27:40, 63; Mk. 8:31; 9:31; 10:34; 14:58; 15:29; Jn. 2:19-20). Then again He said He would be in the tomb *three days and three nights* (Mt. 12:39-40).

These statements are easily reconciled by looking to the Jewish context of the Gospels. The Mosaic Law stipulated that the new year began on the first of Nisan. In the Jewish mode of counting years, any part of the end of the previous year, or any part of the new year, whether it be a few months or even just days, counted as a full year. If, for example, a king took the throne on the last day of a year, he was viewed as having ruled the whole year. A day later, the new year began, but the records would read, "the second year of his reign." The second day of his reign would be considered the second year of his reign because even the first day of a year was officially considered to be one year. Likewise, even the last hour of a day or the first hour of a day counted as a full day. Yeshua was in the tomb during the waning hours of Friday, the full 24 hours of Saturday, and then in the early hours of Sunday, which in the Jewish reckoning of time counts as three days.

Accordingly, Yeshua's seemingly contradictory statements are reconciled: First, the resurrection was to be *on the third day*, and although He was in the tomb in the early hours of the third day, later on that same day, Yeshua was resurrected, so He was resurrected *on the third day*.

Second, the resurrection was to be *after three days,* and since Yeshua was in the tomb part of Sunday, it counted for all of Sunday. Therefore, from a Jewish point of view, counting one full day and the two partial days as whole days, Yeshua was not only resurrected *on the third day,* He was also resurrected *after three days.*

Third, the Jewish expression *three days and three nights* is also reconcilable, for it is a figure of speech referring to any period of time that touches three days and is used in the Hebrew Scriptures several times (Gen. 42:17-18; I Sam. 30:12-13; I Kgs. 20:29 [seven days]; II Chron. 10:5, 12; Esth. 4:16, in comparison with 5:1).

All this is to say that the Gospels were written by Jews using the Jewish frame of reference to reckon time. In keeping with their frame of reference and terminology, Yeshua was buried on Friday before sundown and before the Sabbath began. He was resurrected sometime after the Sabbath, on Sunday, the first day of the week. From a Jewish perspective, the Sabbath had already ended and the first day of the week had already begun as of sundown Saturday

3. Map of Yeshua's Final Week

The map following this list shows Yeshua's final week in and around Jerusalem.

(1) On the first day of this week, He rode into Jerusalem on a donkey. This became known as His triumphal entry. In the days to follow, Yeshua made daily trips from Bethany to the Temple area, where He taught, allowing everyone to examine His teachings.[12] At night, He returned to Bethany.

(2) On the night of the Passover, He entered Jerusalem and made His way to the Upper City, which included modern-day Mount Zion (the biblical Mount Zion was the Temple Mount). It was there that He held His last Passover in the upper room with His

---

[12] Despite what is depicted on the map, Yeshua never entered the Temple building itself. The law prohibited anyone except Levitical priests of the line of Aaron from entering the Temple proper, and Yeshua was of the tribe of Yehudah. Therefore, His activities were limited to the inner and the outer courts.

family of disciples. The map shows an approximation of where that upper room may have been, but it could have been anywhere in the Mount Zion area.

(3)   After the Passover meal, Yeshua went to the west side of the Mount of Olives at Gethsemane.

(4)   There, He was arrested and forced to walk up to the Upper City, where the homes of the high priests were located. He underwent the trial before Annas and then Caiaphas, who condemned Him to death on the basis of a charge of blasphemy.

(5)   From there, He was taken to the Antonia Fortress, where He underwent the first stage of His Roman trial before Pontius Pilate. However, Pilate, learning that He was from Galilee, sent Him to Herod Antipas, who was staying at the Hasmonean Palace. There, Yeshua underwent the second stage of the civil trial. Herod sent Him back to Pilate at the Antonia Fortress, where He was flogged and eventually condemned to death.

(6)   Then, He began His slow walk along what is known today as the Via Dolorosa from the Antonia Fortress to just outside the second wall, a place called Golgotha. Based upon Messianic Jewish history as well as archaeological evidence, the Church of the Holy Sepulchre marks the actual spot of Yeshua's death and burial.

BELOW: Map by Debra Riley depicting Yeshua's final week in and around Jerusalem.

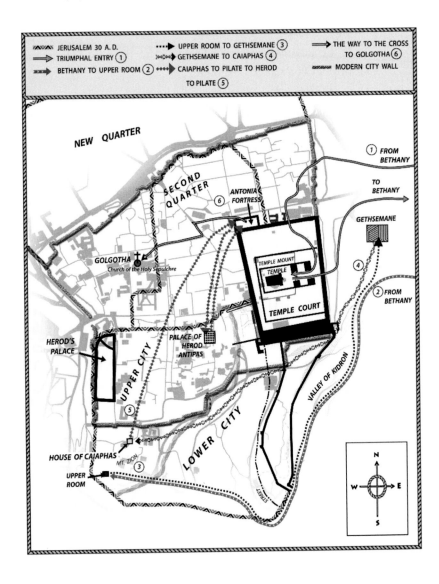

XI. THE RESURRECTION AND ASCENSION OF THE KING
— §§ 182-197 —

The resurrection of the King was the second sign of Jonah; it is also the third point of the gospel: *that he has been raised on the third day* (I Cor. 15:4).

[§ 182] — A. The Dawning of Resurrection Day

Matthew 28:1, Mark 16:1

Three women visited the tomb together: *Miriam Magdalit, and Miriam the <mother> of Yaakov, and Shulamit* (Mk. 16:1). It was now *late on the Sabbath day, as it began to dawn toward the first <day> of the week* (Mt. 28:1). In English, the word *dawn* usually refers to the early morning light, just before the sun rises above the horizon. Therefore, some assume this event occurred just before sunrise on Sunday morning. However, in a Jewish context, the word *dawn* meant the beginning of the new day, and for Jews the new day began after sunset, when three stars were visible in the night sky. Since Matthew was addressing Jews, *dawn toward the first <day> of the week* meant late Saturday afternoon, shortly before sundown. The Greek text literally reads *late [of] the Sabbath*, or *in the lighting to one of the Sabbath*. The phrase *late [of] the Sabbath* reflects the Hebrew *be-motza'ei Shabbat*, "the going out of the Sabbath;" and *to one of the Sabbath* reflects the Hebrew *le-echad ba-Shabbat*, referring to the hours of darkness preceding the coming of daylight.

Once the sun set and three stars were visible, shops often opened for business. The women could purchase spices (Mk. 16:1), intending to finish the burial procedure early Sunday morning. This indicates they did not anticipate the resurrection.

[§ 183] — B. The Opening of the Tomb

Matthew 28:2-4

On the 17th of Nisan, or April 9, A.D. 30,[1] closer to the wee hours of Sunday morning before sunrise, three things suddenly occurred. First, *behold, there was a great earthquake* (Mt. 28:2). This was the second earthquake, the first marking the moment of Yeshua's death, and the second marking the moment of His resurrection. Second, an angel descended from heaven and rolled the stone away, thus breaking the Roman seal. Third, because the angel's *appearance was as lightning, and his raiment white as snow* (Mt. 28:3), fear fell upon the Roman guard, and they *became as dead men* (Mt. 28:4), literally scared stiff!

---

[1] Or April 5, A.D. 33.

[§ 184] — C. The Visit of the Women

Matthew 28:5-8, Mark 16:2-8, Luke 24:1-8, John 20:1

At first glance, the Gospels appear to give four different accounts of the women's visits to the tomb. While differences exist, there are no discrepancies, no contradictions. Instead, each Gospel complements the information found in the other three, and by combining all four accounts, a complete picture of the events of resurrection morning emerges.

On Sunday morning (Mk. 16:2a), several women went to the tomb in two separate visits. The first to arrive was *Miriam of Migdal*, who went alone *early, while it was yet dark* (Jn. 20:1). Miriam found the stone rolled away and the tomb empty. She did not see an angel and assumed that the body had been removed. With that, she left the tomb area.

Later, after she left, a group of women arrived *when the sun was risen* (Mk. 16:2b), providing more light. They also found the stone rolled away, but unlike Miriam, they saw the angel, whose message was twofold. First, Yeshua had risen from the dead, just as He said He would (Mt. 28:6). Therefore, there was no reason to seek *the living among the dead* (Lk. 24:5). Second, the women were to go to the apostolic group and tell the disciples to leave for Galilee, where Yeshua would meet them (Mk. 16:7). This was the second time they received this command. The first time was during the last Passover, when Yeshua told them that when He was arrested, they were to immediately leave Jerusalem (Mt. 26:32; Mk. 14:28). They did not understand what He meant, so they were caught by surprise and never left the city. Therefore, the angel repeated the message, telling them clearly that Yeshua would appear to them in Galilee.

Then two specific things happened. First, the women *remembered his words* (Lk. 24:8), the prophecy about His death and resurrection. Second, they ran to tell the disciples what they had seen and what the angel had told them (Mt. 28:8). The frightened women told no one outside the apostolic group (Mk. 16:8).

[§ 185] — D. The Report to the Apostles

Luke 24:9-12, John 20:2-10

Miriam ran to tell two of the apostles, Peter and Yochanan, that the body had been removed from the tomb. She assumed this when she saw that the tomb was opened and was empty. The other women told the other nine apostles, but they did not believe the reports (Lk. 24:9-11). To them it was *idle talk*, or *lēros* in Greek. Most concordances and dictionaries translate this word simply as "that which is totally devoid of anything worthwhile, idle talk, nonsense, humbug."[2] However, Hippocrates seems to have used it to describe a certain form of delirium.[3] The fact that Luke was familiar with this is another indication of his profession.

Peter and Yochanan raced together to the tomb to investigate (Lk. 24:12; Jn. 20:2-10). Yochanan outran Peter. However, when he reached the entrance to the tomb, he stopped without entering. He stooped down, looked inside, and saw the strips of linen cloths still rolled up, indicating the resurrection had occurred right through the grave clothes, as the cloths were not unwrapped. The headpiece, however, lay by itself, separated from the cloths that had wrapped the body.[4]

Peter finally caught up and, always impetuous, ran right into the tomb, seeing the same thing as Yochanan, who now also entered in. When the two men left the area, each had come to a different conclusion. Yochanan believed that the resurrection had taken place (Jn. 20:8). Peter was perplexed, uncertain of what he should make of the evidence (Lk. 24:12).

---

[2] Frederick W. Danker, *A Greek-English Lexicon of the New Testament and Other Early Christian Literature*, Third Edition (Chicago, IL: The University of Chicago Press, 2000).

[3] See Robley Dunglison, M.D., *A New Dictionary of Medical Science*, Fourth Edition (Philadelphia, PA: Lea and Blanchard, 1844), p. 226.

[4] These details prove the shroud of Turin cannot possibly be the shroud of Yeshua.

[§ 186] — E. The First Appearance: To Miriam Magdalit

Mark 16:9-11, John 20:11-18

After the two disciples left the tomb area, Miriam returned, still assuming that the body had been removed. Mark considered it important to add that she was the one who had been plagued by seven demons and whom the Lord had freed (Mk. 16:9). When she came back to the tomb, she saw two angels, but did not recognize them as such, since they appeared as young men (Mk. 16:5; Jn. 20:11-12). When the angels asked, *Woman, why do you weep?* (Jn. 20:13a), she revealed her belief: *they have taken away my Lord, and I know not where they have laid Him* (Jn. 20:13b).

1. Yeshua's Resurrected Body

When Yeshua appeared to her, she did not recognize Him immediately (Jn. 20:14). He asked her the same question, *Woman, why do you weep? Whom are you seeking?* (Jn. 20:15a). She assumed Him to be the gardener and most likely, therefore, the one to have moved the body. She asked, *Sir, if you have borne him hence, tell me where you have laid him, and I will take him away* (Jn. 19:15b). Yeshua then called her by name, and perhaps something in His tone of voice or the way He pronounced her name was familiar, for at that point, she finally recognized Him and called to Him in Hebrew, *Rabboni* (Jn. 20:16), meaning "my rabbi," "my teacher."

This delay in recognition occurred at several of the post-resurrection appearances. One reason for this is that His resurrected body had changed to such a degree that identification was not immediate. However, enough things remained the same so that eventually those who saw Him recognized Him. Miriam identified Yeshua by the way He called her name. This may imply that the tenor of His voice remained the same. Some things changed, but others remained the same.

Note that the first appearance of the resurrected Messiah was to a woman, not a man. This was significant because by Jewish law, women could not serve as witnesses. The two or three witnesses necessary in a court of law had to be men, never women, as a woman's testimony was not considered valid. Those who do not believe that Yeshua rose from the dead often claim that the Gospels are fabricated. If that were true, then it was a Jewish fabrication, because the apostles were all Jewish. However, they would not have fabricated the story like this. They would have tried to make it as believable and acceptable to their audience as possible, making sure that all the witnesses were men, not women. But they had to report it the way it really happened, with a woman as the first witness to the resurrection. This fact is a strong argument for the authenticity of the resurrection account.

2. Cleansing the Heavenly Tabernacle

As Miriam moved toward Him, Yeshua said to her, *Touch me not* (Jn. 20:17). Many have asked why Yeshua forbade her to touch Him when later that day, He allowed other women to do so. A week later, He even commanded Thomas to put his finger on His hands and His side (Jn. 20:27). There are two possible answers. First, two different Greek words translate into English as *to touch*. One of these words has the connotation of "clinging" and is used here in John 20:17. Miriam wanted to cling to and hang onto Yeshua so that He could not leave, but He had to go. The other Greek word is used in John 20:27 in the context of Thomas touching the Lord. This word means "to feel" or "to touch," without the sense of clinging. This is a valid answer.

However, a second option as to why Yeshua told Miriam not to touch Him is directly related to the Mosaic Law. He explained: *for I am not yet ascended unto the Father* (Jn. 20:17). His statement specifically related to the high priest's activities on the Day of Atonement (Lev. 16). The high priest began the day by removing the multicolored garments he wore on a daily basis. Once undressed, he underwent a ritual immersion, then put on the white garments, symbolizing purity, that he wore only once a year, on the Day of Atonement. After this, the priest went through the whole procedure as discussed in § 179, and when he finished, he took off his white clothes, underwent a second ritual immersion, and put on his multicolored garments. If anyone touched the high priest between the first and the second immersion, it rendered him unclean, and he could not enter the Holy of Holies to sprinkle the goat's blood upon the mercy seat; he could not make the atonement with the blood. Therefore, until the ritual was completed, the high priest was untouchable.

The tabernacle Moses built on earth was merely a copy of something already existing in heaven. While the earthly tabernacle could be cleansed by animal blood (Lev. 17:11; Heb. 9:22), the heavenly tabernacle required cleansing by better blood, innocent human blood. Yeshua, in His function as the perfect high priest, ascended into heaven at some point to sprinkle His blood in the heavenly tabernacle to cleanse it (Heb. 9:11, 12, 24; 10:12). Ezekiel 28:11-19 explains why this tabernacle needed to be cleansed: Satan, a cherub, the highest order of celestial beings, had defiled it. He was the anointed cherub, and prior to his fall, Satan had some kind of priestly function. He was the angelic choir director, so to speak, and led the other angels in the worship of God in heaven. He was covered with ten special stones, the same kind of stones that were set on the breastplate of Israel's high priest. At some point, He rejected this exalted position; Isaiah 14 tells us that Satan wanted to make himself like God. This was Satan's sin, and when he sinned in heaven, he defiled the heavenly sanctuary. Ezekiel used the plural, *sanctuaries*, because both the Holy Place and the Holy of Holies were defiled. Because these are heavenly sanctuaries, they require cleansing by better blood. Yeshua had to ascend into heaven to sprinkle His blood in the heavenly sanctuary. When He encountered Miriam, His comment suggests that He had not yet cleansed the heavenly tabernacle, making Him untouchable. Once He performed His duty as the perfect high priest, He could return and people could touch Him.

After telling her this, Yeshua admonished Miriam: *go unto My brethren*, referring to His disciples (Jn. 20:17). The word reflects the new relationship He now had with the apostles as a result of His death and resurrection. However, the disciples did not believe the first report that Yeshua had been resurrected (Mk. 16:11).

[§ 187] — F. The Second Appearance: To the Women

Matthew 28:9-10

After Miriam left, the other women arrived, and Yeshua greeted them. *And they came and took hold of his feet, and worshipped him* (Mt. 28:9). This act of devotion surpassed mere touching or feeling and shows that sometime between talking to Miriam and talking to these women, Yeshua had ascended into heaven, sprinkled His blood, and became touchable. The fact that the second appearance was also to women and not to men strengthens the argument that the Gospel accounts are genuine. Any Jewish author fabricating a story would not have written it this way, but the Gospel writers reported the truth.

Yeshua told the women, *go tell my brethren that they depart into Galil* (Mt. 28:10b), where He would meet them. For the third time, the apostles received a clear message to leave Jerusalem, but they did not believe the second report of the resurrection, so they never left town.

[§ 188] — G. The Report of the Guard: The Initial Rejection of the Second Sign of Jonah

Matthew 28:11-15

In this section, the Roman guard's report to the chief priests triggers the initial rejection of the second sign of Jonah, the resurrection of Yeshua, as is evident in their collusion to explain the empty tomb by claiming the body had been stolen.

When the guards responsible for securing the tomb finally overcame their fear, they *came into the city* (Mt. 28:11). By Roman law, they would be executed for failing in their mission to guard the tomb, so they avoided Pilate knowing he would not believe their story of an angel that looked like lightning rolling away the stone. Instead, they reported to the chief priests who had arranged the guarding of the tomb.

Realizing the enormity of the events and their possible impact, the chief priests quickly assembled with the Pharisees, or *elders*, thus reconvening the Sanhedrin (Mt. 28:12). After taking counsel, they conspired to give the soldiers a large sum of money to walk through the city telling people that the apostles had stolen Yeshua's body while they were sleeping (Mt. 28:13). This was the origin of the oldest of many explanations for the empty tomb: the stolen body theory. The chief priests also told the guard that if the report reached the ears of Pontius Pilate, they promised to intervene so that the soldiers would not be executed: *And if this come to the governor's ears, we will persuade him, and rid you of care* (Mt. 28:14). After the Passover, the governor would return to Caesarea; possibly he would never hear of their failure.

The guard did as they were told, spreading the story that while they were sleeping, the disciples had stolen Yeshua's body (Mt. 28:15). If a thoughtful Jewish person heard this explanation, they should have detected the discrepancy in the testimony. If the soldiers were sleeping, how could they know who stole the body?

Only two groups had a vested interest in risking their lives to commit the crime of stealing the body: Yeshua's enemies or His friends. His enemies were those who later tried to silence the apostolic preaching of the resurrection in the book of Acts. While they tried all kinds of ploys, they could never produce the body, indicating that they did not have it. The second group with a vested interest was Yeshua's friends. These same disciples later underwent tremendous persecution for preaching the resurrection. James, for example, was beheaded. According to church tradition, Peter was crucified upside-down. Matthew was killed by the sword. Philip was hanged from a pillar. Bartholomew was flayed alive. Andrew was crucified. Thomas' body was run through with a lance. Matthias was first stoned and then beheaded. Of those outside the apostolic group and yet eyewitnesses, Mark was tortured to death. Yeshua's half-brother James was thrown down from the pinnacle of the Temple and then stoned. Jude was shot to death with arrows. They all died horrendous deaths. In almost every case, they were given the option of renouncing their faith and dying in a more humane way or being released. They refused in each case. It is difficult to believe they would all be willing to undergo such tremendous suffering for what they all knew was a lie. The only reasonable explanation for their actions in the book of Acts and beyond is that they believed Yeshua was resurrected.

[§ 189] — H. The Third Appearance: To the Two on the Emmaus Road

Mark 16:12-13, Luke 24:13-32

In addition to the inner circle of the twelve apostles, Yeshua was also close to an outer circle of disciples, such as the seventy of Luke 10:1-24. The men on the road to Emmaus belonged to this outer circle. Only one, Cleopas, is named (Lk. 24:18), probably because he was the husband of one of the Miriams of the Gospels. Furthermore, he may have been the same Cleopas who later played a significant role in the history of the church of Jerusalem. The first head of that church was James, the half-brother of Yeshua and the author of the Epistle of James. When he was executed for his faith, Cleopas assumed the headship and led the church out of the city in the first Jewish Revolt, in A.D. 66. If this was the same Cleopas, it makes sense that he alone was named in this account.

That Sunday afternoon, these two disciples were walking toward their home town, Emmaus (Lk. 24:13), discussing the things that had happened recently concerning Yeshua. Suddenly, a third figure drew near to them that they did not immediately recognize (Lk. 24:14-16). He asked what they were discussing, and their answers revealed what they did and did not believe. Up until that time, they believed that Yeshua was a prophet of God, one who received direct revelation from God (Lk. 24:19a); they believed He was authenticated by His words and His works, for He not only proclaimed He was the Messiah, His works authenticated what He said (Lk. 24:19b); they believed He was tried, condemned, and crucified by the religious leaders (Lk. 24:20); and they believed that He was the redeemer of Israel: *But we hoped that it was he who should redeem Yisrael* (Lk. 24:21). However, the recent events seemed to discredit their belief.

They then pointed out one thing they did not believe (Lk. 24:22-24). They did not believe the women's report that they had seen angels who declared that Yeshua was alive. They said: *And certain of them that were with us went to the tomb* [meaning Yochanan and Peter], *and found it even so as the women had said: but him they saw not* (Lk. 24:24). Because the apostles saw nothing, the disciples on the road to Emmaus disbelieved the reports of the resurrection from the women.

An interesting time reference occurs in these verses. When telling Yeshua about all that had happened, the disciples mentioned that *it is now the third day since these things came to pass* (Lk. 24:21). Sunday afternoon was still the third day, confirming that Yeshua died on a Friday.

In response to their report, the Messiah first scolded them for their unbelief (Lk. 24:25-26), then delivered an exposition of all the biblical prophecies pertaining to the Messiah's first coming: *And beginning from Moses and from all the prophets, he interpreted to them in all the scriptures the things concerning himself* (Lk. 24:27). The things that seemed to militate against His Messiahship actually were evidence of it. If they had possessed a better understanding of the messianic prophecies of the Hebrew Scriptures, these things would not have surprised them.

When they arrived at Emmaus, Yeshua *made as though he would go further* (Lk. 24:28). However, this was the hometown of Cleopas and the other disciple, and so they invited Him to have dinner with them. *And it came to pass, when he had sat down with them to meat, he took the bread and blessed; and breaking <it> he gave to them* (Lk. 24:30). Yeshua recited the Jewish blessing over the bread: *Baruch atah Adonai, Eloheinu melech haolam, hamotzi lechem min ha-aretz*, which means "Blessed are You, O Lord our God, King of the Universe who brings forth bread from the earth." Traditionally, during a Jewish dinner, the host, not the guest, recites the blessing over the bread. Another Jewish tradition, however, says that if two eat together, and one of them is an educated Bible scholar, or *sopher*, and the other of them is an ordinary man, the sopher gives the blessing over the food. Due to Yeshua's exposition of messianic prophecy, the disciples recognized Him as a Bible scholar and had Him give the blessing over the bread. At that moment their eyes were opened, and they suddenly recognized Him; just as suddenly, Yeshua disappeared from sight (Lk. 24:31-32).

These two disciples returned to Jerusalem to inform the apostles of what had happened, but *neither believed they them* (Mk. 16:13).

[§ 190] — I. The Fourth Appearance: To Peter

Luke 24:33-35, I Corinthians 15:5a

Peter was the first member of the apostolic group to see the resurrected Messiah. The private meeting may have comforted him after his threefold denial. When Yeshua predicted Peter's failure at the last Passover, He also said that the apostle would be re-established, and this appearance was probably necessary in order to fulfill this promise. This, in turn, set the stage for Peter to become the chief of the apostles. His leadership role developed in the book of Acts.

[§ 191] — J. The Fifth Appearance: To the Ten

Mark 16:14, Luke 24:36-43, John 20:19-25

It was Sunday evening. The apostles never went to Galilee, as instructed three times. In His grace, Yeshua finally appeared to them in Jerusalem. Ten of the eleven were present during this encounter: *When therefore it was evening, on that day, the first <day> of the week, and when the doors were shut where the disciples were, for fear of the Jews* (Jn. 20:19). Still fearful of being arrested, they hid inside a house, where suddenly, Yeshua appeared to them and said, *Peace <be> unto you* (Lk. 24:36), the customary Jewish greeting, *Shalom aleichem.*

When the apostles finally saw Him, they still did not believe they were seeing a resurrected individual. Rather, they were filled with fear, because they thought they were looking at a spirit or a ghost (Lk. 24:37). Yeshua scolded them for their unbelief (Mk. 16:14), which they demonstrated in three specific ways. First, they failed to leave for Galilee. Second, they failed to believe the first witnesses. By now, both women and men had reported that He had been raised from the dead. Third, when they finally saw Him, they thought He was a ghost. To prove He stood before them in His resurrected body, Yeshua told the apostles to touch Him, to feel His flesh and bones (Lk. 24:38-40). A spirit does not have flesh and bones, but a resurrected body is solid matter. Yeshua also showed the apostles His hands and feet, because they could see that the nail prints remained. Although Yeshua was resurrected, He was not yet glorified, for a glorified body would not have such imperfections. Yeshua would be glorified after His ascension, so during the forty-day period from the resurrection until the ascension, the wounds from His crucifixion remained visible. When Yochanan later saw Him in a vision, he provided a detailed description of His glorified body, but he did not mention these wounds (Rev. 1:12-16).

When the apostles still had trouble believing that He was resurrected, Yeshua asked them for something to eat. They handed Him a piece of broiled fish, which He ate (Lk. 24:41-43), demonstrating that He was not a ghost. This indicates that while resurrected bodies do not need food to live, they can enjoy eating.

The apostles then received the first of three final commissions, which contained two points. First, they were sent with the Son's authority: *as the Father has sent me, even so send I you* (Jn. 20:21). Just as the Son was sent with the Father's authority, they were being sent with the Son's authority. Second, He now extended to all of the apostles the commission that He previously had given solely to Peter: *Whose so ever sins ye forgive, they are forgiven unto them; whose so ever <sins> ye retain, they are retained* (Jn. 20:23). This was not forgiving sins in the sense of salvation, as only God has that authority. This concerned binding and loosing in a judicial sense, in the sense of punishing or freeing someone from punishment.[5]

---

[5] See § 85.

He also *breathed on them, and said unto them, Receive ye the Holy Spirit* (Jn. 20:22). This was not the baptism of the Spirit, which occurred later, in Acts 2. The Spirit has a number of different ministries. Some were present in the Old Testament; others began with Acts 2. One of the Spirit's ministries is His continuous work of illumination (I Cor. 2:9-3:3), with which He enlightens the mind of the believer to understand the spiritual things of God. On at least four occasions, Yeshua clearly communicated to His apostles the whole program of His coming death and resurrection, each time adding more details. Yet they simply did not understand the message, so they were surprised when it finally occurred. Between the resurrection and the ascension, Yeshua had much to teach them in preparation for their mission, described in the book of Acts, so they needed to understand all these things. When they received the Spirit, He began His work of illumination in them.

One would think that now they would rise and go to Galilee, but they did not because one disciple, Thomas, was not present at Yeshua's appearance (Jn. 20:24). When he heard the witness of the other ten, he declared, *Except I shall see in his hands the print of the nails, and put my hand into his side, I will not believe* (Jn. 20:25).

[§ 192] — K. The Sixth Appearance: To the Eleven

John 20:26-31, I Corinthians 15:5b

An eight-day period passed (Jn. 20:26), and because of Thomas, the apostles remained in Jerusalem. Once again, Yeshua graciously appeared to them and told Thomas to do what he had said he wanted to do: *Reach here your finger, and see my hands; and reach <here> your hand, and put it into my side: and be not faithless, but believing* (Jn. 20:27). Finally, Thomas was convinced and acknowledged Yeshua: *My Lord and my God* (Jn. 20:28). With these words, he affirmed the truth that the resurrection proved Yeshua to be the Son of God (Rom. 1:4).

A common misconception is that these disciples were especially blessed because they saw Yeshua resurrected, making it easier to believe. The basis for this idea is that experience is more important than the testimony of Scripture. The truth is just the opposite: *Because you have seen me, you have believed: blessed <are> they that have not seen, and <yet> have believed* (Jn. 20:29). The greater blessing belongs to those who believe in the resurrection based upon the testimony of the Word of God rather than personal experience.

Thomas' confession, *My Lord and my God*, is the theme of Yochanan's Gospel: Yeshua the Messiah, the Son of God. These words, therefore, perfectly conclude his narrative. He added an appendix (Jn. 21), but closed his Gospel with this statement: *Many other signs therefore did Yeshua in the presence of the disciples, which are not written in this book* (Jn. 20:30). Yochanan only recorded seven signs, but as far as he was concerned, those seven signs were sufficient: *that ye may believe that Yeshua is the Messiah, the Son of God; and that believing ye may have life in his name* (Jn. 20:31). With these words, the apostle revealed the purpose of his writing: The Gospel was evangelistic, so that the reader might come to faith and have eternal life.

[§ 193] — L. The Seventh Appearance: To the Seven

John 21

At long last, the apostles finally made it to Galilee. Seven of them were fishermen, and they had left their profession for approximately three years. Hearing that Yeshua would soon leave them for a lengthy time and not yet understanding their new commission, they felt compelled to return to their fishing jobs, and in doing so, caught nothing. Then Yeshua appeared to them on the shoreline and asked, *Children, have ye anything to eat? They answered him, No. And he said unto them, Cast the net on the right side of the boat, and ye shall find. They cast therefore, and now they were not able to draw it for the multitude of fishes* (Jn. 21:5-6). Under normal circumstances, a fisherman may cast his nets on either side of the boat without influencing how many fish he catches. In this case, Yeshua's instructions made a difference where they cast their nets, and the apostles caught a multitude of fish. The narrative greatly resembles their original call to be fishers of men (Lk. 5:1-11). In that instance, they caught nothing after fishing all night; Yeshua then told them to do something that normally would not make a difference, and they caught a multitude of fish. Similarly, the Messiah called them again into full-time ministry.

1. The Promise of Provision

This action caused Yochanan to recognize Yeshua, and he told Peter, *It is the Lord* (Jn. 21:7). Peter jumped overboard and waded back to shore. The others followed him, dragging all the nets. At the shoreline, they quickly realized that they did not need a single fish, because Yeshua already had a fire going, fish broiling, and bread prepared (Jn. 21:9). From this they learned they had a new commission to fulfill, and Yeshua would provide for them as they carried out their work. They need not return to their fishing business.

That day, the apostles caught a total of 153 fish (Jn. 21:11). Some have tried to find a deeper meaning to this number.[6] However, Yochanan's point was that *for all there were so many, the net was not rent* (Jn. 21:11). The remarkable thing was not some hidden meaning to the number itself, but that the large amount of fish did not cause the net to tear.

They ate only the food Yeshua provided for them: *Yeshua said unto them, Come <and> break your fast. And none of the disciples dared inquire of him, Who are you? Knowing that it was the Lord. Yeshua comes, and takes the bread, and gives them, and the fish likewise* (Jn. 21:12-13). From this experience, they learned that they only needed to fulfill their commission. Yeshua would provide for them.

---

[6] One example is the teaching that the number represents the United Nations, which at one time had 153 members. This is no longer true, and the interpretation has since fallen by the wayside.

Although this was Yeshua's seventh post-resurrection appearance, He appeared to the apostles only three times: *This is now the third time that Yeshua was manifested to the disciples, after that he was risen from the dead* (Jn. 21:14).

2. The Conversation with Peter

Yeshua then conversed privately with Peter, cancelling out the apostle's threefold denial with a threefold affirmation of love (Jn. 21:15-17). Unfortunately, the same English word, *love*, is used throughout this passage, obscuring the point. Yochanan used two different Greek words, the first being *phileó*,[7] an emotional love in response to attraction, a love of friendship. The second Greek word is *agapaó*, the verbal form of the better-known noun *agape*.[8] This is a love of the will and is considered superior because a person can will to love even the most unlovable. In the Scriptures, both words are used of God and of men, so to claim that *phileo* is human love and *agape* divine love is an oversimplification. The difference is that one is a love of the emotions and friendship, and the other is a love of the will. When the Bible commands the believer to love everyone, it does not say to phileó everyone. No one has that ability. Believers are commanded to agape everyone, exercising the will to seek the betterment of the person.

Following this introduction, the actual conversation can be divided into three parts, beginning with the following words: *So when they had broken their fast, Yeshua said to Shimon Peter, Shimon, <son> of Yochanan, do you love me more than these?* (Jn. 21:15a). Yeshua asked, "Simon, do you agapaó me?" More specifically, did Peter love Him *more than these*, meaning more than these other apostles? Yeshua asked the question this way because this was exactly what Peter claimed at the last Passover. When Yeshua prophesied that His disciples would abandon Him, Peter emphatically declared that even if all the others deserted Him, he would never leave Yeshua and was ready to die for Him. He thus claimed to have a superior agape love for Yeshua to that

---

[7] Since Yeshua and Peter spoke Hebrew with each other, the word would have been *ra'eyah*.

[8] The Hebrew word is *ahavah*.

of the other apostles (Mt. 26:33; Mk. 14:29; Lk. 22:31-34). In light of Peter's recent experience during the trial, Yeshua wanted to know if he really loved Him with this *agape* love and *more than these.* Peter answered *Yea, Lord; you know that I love you* (Jn. 21:15b), but he used the word *phileó*. Peter meant, "No, I can no longer claim that I agapaó You more than the others. The best I can do is to claim I do phileó You; I am your friend." Peter then received his first commission: *Feed my lambs* (Jn. 21:15c). Lambs are baby believers who need to be fed with the milk of the Word of God. Peter fulfilled the first commission by writing his first epistle (I Pet. 2:1-3).

In the second part of the conversation, *He said to him a second time, Shimon, <son> of Yochanan, do you love me?* (Jn. 21:16a). Yeshua asked him again, "Do you agapaó me?" This time, He dropped the phrase "more than these." If Peter could not affirm that he had more agape for Yeshua than the others, could he at least say he had an equal amount of this love? Peter answered, *Yea, Lord; you know that I love you* (Jn. 21:16b), again using the word *phileó*, meaning, "No, I cannot affirm that I agapaó you more than the others, nor can I affirm that I agapaó you at all. The best I can say for now is that I do phileó you. I am your friend." Peter then received his second commission, *Tend my sheep* (Jn. 21:16c). The Greek word for *tend* is *poimainó*, and it means "to exercise oversight and authority." Peter fulfilled this commission, as recorded in the book of Acts, which describes his activities in the early church and his authority as the chief of the apostles.

In the third part of the conversation, Yeshua *said unto him the third time, Do you love me?* (Jn. 21:17a), this time using the word Peter had used, phileó, to stress the point: "Peter, you cannot affirm that you agapaó Me more than the others; nor can you affirm that you agapaó Me at all; but can you truly affirm that you at least phileó Me?" This grieved Peter, and he responded, *Lord, you know all things; you know that I love you* (Jn. 21:17b), confirming that while he could not affirm that he agapaó Yeshua more than the others, nor that he agapaó Him at all, he could truly affirm that he really did phileó Him. He was His friend. Peter then received his third commission, *Feed my sheep* (Jn. 21:17c). The word *sheep* refers to older believers who need to be fed with the meat of the Word of God. Peter fulfilled the third commission when he wrote II Peter, dealing with meaty doctrine for the more mature believer. With this, Peter's earlier threefold denial was replaced by a threefold affirmation of love.

Yeshua continued to assure Peter that someday he would prove that he had agape love for Yeshua, not more than the other apostles, but at least equal to theirs (Jn. 21:18-19). In the future, he would give his own life on behalf of the Messiah. When Peter was martyred, he proved he had not only phileó, but also agape love.

When Peter learned that he would die for his love of Yeshua, he inquired about Yochanan's future. Yeshua responded, *If I will that he tarry till I come, what <is that> to you? Follow you me* (Jn. 21:22). Yochanan must fulfill his calling from the Lord, just as Peter would fulfill his calling. Peter's only concern should be God's will for him and not for Yochanan.

3. The Closing Words of the Gospel of John

Chapter 21 of the Gospel of John can be viewed as an appendix. After declaring that he had been an eyewitness to all he reported, Yochanan ended his Gospel by stating that *his witness is true* (Jn. 21:24). He revealed that he was selective in choosing what to report, because *there are also many other things which Yeshua did, the which if they should be written every one, I suppose that even the world itself would not contain the books that should be written* (Jn. 21:25). The truth of this is seen in the fact that Yochanan only recorded about 75-80 days of Yeshua's life.

[§ 194] — M. The Eighth Appearance: To the Five Hundred

Matthew 28:16-20, Mark 16:15-18, I Corinthians 15:6

These verses contain the second of three final commissions with which Yeshua equipped His disciples. They also encompass five statements that require careful examination, three of which are definite and two of which should be viewed with caution (for reasons to be explained below).

Yeshua's first statement was that all authority has been given to the resurrected Son (Mt. 28:18). Therefore, He had the authority to commission His apostles as He now did.

In His second statement, Yeshua ordered the apostles to make disciples (Mt. 28:19). Most English translations of this verse begin with the word *go*, which appears to be an imperative. The implication is that the word *go* is the commandment, which is probably why this is the favorite verse used in mission conferences. However, in the Greek text, the only imperative is to *make disciples*. The imperative is followed by three subordinate participial clauses: going, baptizing, and teaching. They spell out the three elements of making disciples. The first participle, *going*, means evangelizing the whole world and preaching the gospel to the whole creation (Mk. 16:15). It means going to preach, to evangelize, and to witness. In many mission conferences, this is where the Great Commission stops. However, while going fulfills the work of evangelism, it alone does not make disciples. The second participle is *baptizing*, and the formula is to baptize *into the name of the Father and of the Son and of the Holy Spirit* (Mt. 28:19). The specificity of this phrase was necessary because baptism was a common Jewish practice, and there were different kinds of baptisms, such as proselyte baptism, Yochanan's baptism, etc. To distinguish believer's baptism from other baptisms, this one had to be done *into the name of the Father and of the Son and of the Holy Spirit*, emphasizing both the unity and trinity of the Godhead. The word *name* is singular, emphasizing unity, and baptizing in the name of three persons emphasizes trinity. However, evangelizing and baptizing alone do not fulfill the Great Commission. The third participle is *teaching*, specifically *teaching them to observe all things whatsoever I commanded you* (Mt. 28:20). The mark of a disciple is obedience. Hence, the commission Yeshua gave His disciples was to go to make disciples, evangelizing, then baptizing those who became believers, and teaching them His commandments.

In His third statement, Yeshua explained, *He that believes and is baptized shall be saved; but he that disbelieves shall be condemned* (Mk. 16:16). This verse needs further exposition because some use it to teach that one must be baptized by water to be saved. However, over two hundred times in the Scriptures, faith is given as the only condition of salvation, leaving two possible responses to this teaching. The first is to note that this verse is missing from the oldest and best manuscripts of the Greek New Testament; therefore, whether Mark wrote it is questionable. Basing a major doctrine such as salvation on a verse that is missing from those manuscripts is dangerous. But let's assume that Mark wrote this verse, is he teaching that one must be water baptized to be saved? Not at all. Baptism is subordinate to believing; it is an outward sign of the inner faith that saves. Mark coupled believing and baptizing in this context because in his day, one was baptized the same day they believed, as is true in every case in the book of Acts (Acts 2:38-41; 8:12, 38; 9:17-18; 10:44-48; 16:13-15, 30-33; 18:8; 19:3-5). This was fine then, because people understood believing and baptizing occurred together. However, due to so much confusion today, it is wise to wait before baptizing a new believer to ensure that they understand what they are doing and why they are doing it. Furthermore, in the second half of the verse, Mark only identifies a failure to believe as the cause of condemnation: *he that disbelieves shall be condemned.* He did not say, "He that disbelieves and is not baptized shall be condemned," nor did he state, "He that believes but is not baptized shall be condemned." What actually condemns a person is a lack of belief, not a lack of baptism. So even if Mark did write this verse, it does not teach that baptism is essential for salvation, for this would suggest that salvation is not by faith alone but by works.

In His fourth statement, Yeshua prophesied that within the body of believers certain signs would follow (Mk. 16:17-18): They would speak with new tongues, cast out demons, heal by the laying on of hands, pick up venomous serpents, and drink poison without getting hurt. These verses also need to be viewed cautiously because certain groups use them to teach that those who are unable to perform such signs are not saved or not spiritual or not baptized by the Spirit. Again, there are two possible responses. First, the correct response is to indicate that these verses are also missing from the oldest and best manuscripts; therefore, whether Mark really wrote them is questionable. The mention of the gift of tongues here seems to be anachronistic, as the phenomenon does not appear until Acts 2. Furthermore, the other Gospels do not corroborate this statement. Second, let us assume that Mark wrote these verses. Did he mean that these things must be true of every believer? Note that Mark switched from the singular to the plural between the two verses. In verse 16, he wrote, *he that believes*, speaking about the individual, because salvation is not a corporate matter. Then he switched to the plural, stating, *And these signs shall accompany them that believe* (Mk. 16:17). The plural pronoun *them* shows that in the corporate body of believers, the five signs will be present, but not that they will be manifested by every single believer. People teaching from this passage tend to mention only tongues, healing, and casting out demons, but omit picking up serpents and drinking poison. If this passage teaches that every believer must speak in tongues, heal by the laying on of hands, and cast out demons, then every believer must also handle poisonous serpents and drink lethal potions. The point, however, is not that every believer exhibits all five signs, but that within the church, such things will happen. In fact, the book of Acts accounts for four of them; the drinking of poison is not mentioned. Furthermore, the only ones performing signs and wonders in the book of Acts are the apostles and those upon whom they lay their hands.

In His fifth and final statement, Yeshua promised to be present with them *even unto the end of the world* (Mt. 28:20).

[§ 195] — N. The Ninth Appearance: To James

I Corinthians 15:7

The ninth appearance of the risen Messiah was to James, Yeshua's half-brother. Up to this point, all four of the half-brothers were unbelievers, but Yeshua's appearance to James caused him and the others to come to faith (Acts 1). It also set the stage for James to become an apostle and the first head of the church of Jerusalem.

There were two categories of apostles. The first category was the closed apostolic group of the twelve disciples who were with Yeshua from His baptism until His ascension. When the apostles had to replace

Judas, only two men met this prerequisite, and one, Matthias, was chosen. The second category required that its members had to have seen the resurrected Son. Paul, Barnabas, and James became apostles of the second category.

[§ 196] — O. The Tenth Appearance: To the Eleven

Luke 24:44-49, Acts 1:3-8

In both his Gospel and the book of Acts, Luke provided the content of Yeshua's teaching ministry over the forty-day period between the resurrection and the ascension with two main categories of teaching.

The first category encompassed messianic prophecy from all three divisions of the Hebrew Scriptures: *And he said unto them, These are my words which I spake unto you, while I was yet with you, that all things must needs be fulfilled, which are written in the law of Mosheh* [Torah], *and the prophets* [Neviim], *and the psalms* [Ketuvim, or the Writings], *concerning me* (Lk. 24:44). The three divisions encompassed the totality of the Jewish Scriptures in the first century and beyond. Luke expounded, *Then opened he their mind, that they might understand the scriptures* (Lk. 24:45). They needed the illuminating work of the Holy Spirit: What they could not understand heretofore, they were then enabled to understand.

The second category pertained to *things concerning the kingdom of God* (Acts 1:3). The messianic kingdom was withdrawn and temporarily replaced by the mystery kingdom because Israel had rejected her King. In light of this development, Yeshua taught His apostles clearly about the kingdom program. His teaching raised the question, *Lord, do you at this time restore the kingdom to Yisrael?* (Acts 1:6). The apostles wanted to know when Yeshua would finally restore the kingdom to Israel, now that He had been resurrected. Amillennialists claim that Yeshua declared there would be no such kingdom; however, that is not what He said: *It is not for you to know times or seasons, which the Father has set within His own authority* (Acts 1:7). Someday, the kingdom will be restored to Israel, but it was not for them to know the exact timing. They had a job to fulfill.

Yeshua then gave His apostles the third and final commission. They were to remain in Jerusalem until the coming of the Holy Spirit (Acts 1:4-5). When the Spirit arrived, three things would occur. First, *the promise of the Father* would be fulfilled (Lk. 24:49a). During the Upper Room Discourse, the Father, through the Son, promised to send them another Comforter—the Holy Spirit. Second, they would receive divine power, or *power from on high* (Lk. 24:49b), to fulfill their commission (Acts 1:8). Third, a new ministry of the Spirit would begin, the work of Spirit baptism (Acts 1:5). While the Spirit had many ministries in the Hebrew Bible, He never baptized anyone. The result of Spirit baptism is membership in the body of the Messiah: *For in one Spirit were we all baptized into one body, whether Jews or Greeks, whether bond or free; and were all made to drink of one Spirit* (I Cor. 12:13). Spirit baptism caused the birth of the body, the church (Col. 1:18), and according to Acts 11:15-16, it began in Acts 2:1-4.

Upon receiving this power, they were to preach the gospel in four stages, proceeding from Jerusalem to Judea, Samaria, and then to *the uttermost part of the earth* (Lk. 24:47; Acts 1:8). *The uttermost part of the earth* was a Jewish idiom for the Gentile world (Is. 49:6).

[§ 197] — P. The Ascension of the King

Mark 16:19-20, Luke 24:50-53, Acts 1:9-12

Six key points concerning the ascension are apparent from these passages. First, it occurred on the Bethany side of the Mount of Olives: *And he led them out until <they were> over against Beit Anyah* (Lk. 24:50a). Yeshua ascended into heaven from the village of Bethany, on the lower eastern slopes of the Mount of Olives, and not from the peak of the mountain, where a church now stands to mark the spot.[9]

Second, Yeshua blessed the apostles in a typical Jewish fashion: *and he lifted up his hands, and blessed them* (Lk. 24:50b).

Third, *while he blessed them, he parted from them, and was carried up into heaven* (Lk. 24:51). Yeshua did not ascend under His own power, but was *carried up* into heaven. Luke reaffirmed this fact in the book of Acts: *And when He had said these things, as they were looking, he was taken up* (Acts 1:9a).

Fourth, Yeshua's ascension was then veiled by a cloud: *and a cloud received him out of their sight* (Acts 1:9b). When Yeshua ascended to a certain height in the air, a cloud hid the rest of the ascension. Therefore, the apostles did not actually see Him disappear into heaven itself. They could only view the ascension up to an indeterminate height before a cloud veiled it.

Fifth, there was an angelic message (Acts 1:10-11):

> [10] *And while they were looking steadfastly into heaven as he went, behold, two men stood by them in white apparel;* [11] *who also said, Ye men of Galil, why stand ye looking into heaven? This Yeshua, who was received up from you into heaven shall so come in like manner as ye beheld him going into heaven.*

The angels' message was that someday Yeshua will also return in the clouds of heaven, thus emphasizing the manner, not the place, of the second coming. He left in the clouds of heaven, and He will return in the clouds of heaven, but in a different location. His second coming will be at the city of Bozrah (Is. 34:6-7; 63:1-6; Mic. 2:12-13).

Sixth, Yeshua entered into heaven and sat down at the right hand of God the Father: *So then the Lord Yeshua, after he had spoken unto them, was received up into heaven, and sat down at the right hand of God* (Mk.

---

[9] Today on the summit, there is a Russian Orthodox church with a high steeple called the Church of the Ascension. It was primarily built there because it is the highest point of the Mount of Olives, but it ignores Luke's reference here. Another nearby chapel on the western slopes of the mountain contains a slab of stone with indentations that are supposed to be two footprints burned into the rock by Yeshua when He ascended. Both places ignore Luke's specific wording.

16:19). This fulfilled an Old Testament prophecy that for a period of time, the Messiah would be seated at the right hand of God the Father (Ps. 110:1). The prophecy of Yeshua's own words, that He would go to the Father, was also fulfilled (Jn. 14:2; 16:17, 28; reaffirmed later, in I Tim. 3:16; Heb. 1:3). There He sits to this day, waiting for Israel's call to bring Him back.

After Yeshua ascended into heaven, the apostles returned to Jerusalem to await the fulfillment of the Father's promise. Luke noted the distance between Jerusalem and the Mount of Olives as being *a Sabbath day's journey* (Acts 1:12). In rabbinic theology, a Sabbath day's journey is called a *tehum shabbat*, or "Sabbath boundary," which is approximately three-quarters of a mile.

XII. THE SEQUELS
— §§ 198-201 —

The Gospels record the life of the Messiah, but the remainder of the New Testament documents occurrences in Jerusalem, Judea, Samaria, and the surrounding Gentile world in the immediate decades after Yeshua's ascension. This concluding section will look at the New Testament development of several issues that originated in the Gospels.

[§198] — A. The Policy Concerning Signs

I Corinthians 1:21-24

When the Jewish people committed the unpardonable sin, Yeshua changed His policy concerning signs. Originally, the purpose of His signs was to get Israel to decide who He was. They rejected Him on the basis of being demonized, and their decision was irrevocable. After their rejection, Yeshua declared that there would be no more signs for Israel except one, the sign of Jonah, the sign of resurrection. This policy continues to the present day. Paul's point in I Corinthians 1:21-24 was that Jews may continue seeking after signs, just as Greeks may continue seeking after philosophical wisdom. However, neither will get what they desire, and both will receive the same message: *Messiah crucified* (I Cor. 1:23), the preaching of the cross, and with it the preaching of the resurrection. This policy is also in effect today.

[§ 199] — B. Relationship to the Book of Acts

Acts 2:38, 40-41, 22:12-16, I Peter 3:21-22

Two issues develop in the book of Acts. The first issue pertains to the sign of Jonah; the second regards the relationship of water baptism to salvation.

In John 11, the Sanhedrin rejected the first sign of Jonah, the resurrection of Lazarus. In the book of Acts, they also rejected the second sign of Jonah, the resurrection of Yeshua Himself (Acts 1-7). The stoning of Stephen by the Sanhedrin marks the official rejection (Acts 7) and the moment when the gospel message started to spread to the non-Jewish world (Acts 8).

The Jewish audience of the book of Acts was the same generation that was guilty of the unpardonable sin and faced the coming massive destruction of A.D. 70. The unpardonable sin, in its context, was a national rather than individual sin. Individuals could escape that judgment; the nation could not. The relationship of water baptism to spiritual salvation, as compared to physical salvation, must be understood in this light. Two passages in the book of Acts are used to teach that one has to be water baptized in order to be saved. They are Acts 2:38-41 and 22:16:

> *2:38 And Peter said unto them, Repent ye, and be baptized every one of you in the name of Yeshua Messiah unto the remission of your sins; and ye shall receive the gift of the Holy Spirit. 39 For to you is the promise, and to your children, and to all that are afar off, even as many as the Lord our God shall call unto him. 40 And with many other words he testified, and exhorted them, saying, Save yourselves from this crooked*

generation. [41] They then that received his word were baptized: and there were added unto them in that day about three thousand souls.

[22:16] And now why tarry you? arise, and be baptized, and wash away your sins, calling on his name.

Two observations can be made concerning these verses. The first is that both passages are addressed to a Jewish, not a Gentile, audience. The second is that the word "save" does not always pertain to spiritual salvation. Sometimes it refers to physical salvation. That is the point of both verses.

To escape the divine judgment, the individual members of that generation had to do two things (Acts 2:38a). First, they must repent. The word "repent" means "to change one's mind." They needed to change their mind about something specific, and that specific thing was Yeshua. He was not demon possessed, but He really was the Messiah. That repentance or change of mind concerning Yeshua would save them spiritually, but not physically. Second, they must be baptized (Acts 2:38b). In this Jewish context, baptism meant a new identification, which in turn meant a separation from the old one. By being immersed in water, they separated themselves from their old identification with the Judaism that rejected Yeshua and identified themselves with the new body of believers. That act of baptism would save them physically. This is the point of baptism: *Save yourselves from this crooked generation* (Acts 2:40). When Peter admonished them to save themselves, He could only mean that they were to save themselves physically, since no one can save himself spiritually. They could save themselves physically by avoiding the punishment of A.D. 70. Again, that particular generation is emphasized: *this crooked generation.* By separating themselves from this crooked generation, their physical lives would be saved, and those who *received his word were baptized* (Acts 2:41).

One other passage used to teach that baptism is necessary for salvation is I Peter 3:21: *which also after a true likeness does now save you, <even> baptism.* Peter specifically wrote to Jewish believers, not the church at large (I Pet. 1:1-2), who still needed the milk of the Word of God because they were immature (I Pet. 2:1-3). Peter emphasized one thing that kept them in a state of immaturity (I Pet. 3). Although they were believers and had received salvation, they were reluctant to under-go water baptism. Many Jewish believers in the Messiah are reluctant to undergo water baptism because they know it marks a decisive sepa-ration from the community around them. Because Peter's audience was disobedient to the command to be baptized, they felt guilty. Peter encouraged them to finally follow through and stated that baptism will save them (I Pet. 3:21). But save them how? Throughout the preceding verses and chapters, Peter said repeatedly that they had salvation, so baptism would not save them spiritually. However, water baptism would save them from their bad conscience, which troubled them due to their disobedience to that command. Also, they would be saved physically, just as Noah's obedience saved his life. Was it the ark that saved Noah spiritually? By no means. Noah was saved spiritually before he even started building the ark. However, the ark saved him and his family physically from the judgment of the flood. Baptism would phys-ically save Peter's audience from the coming judgment of A.D. 70. These verses must be interpreted in their specific Jewish context for clarity.

[§ 200] — C. Relationship to the Book of Hebrews

Luke 21:20-24, Hebrews 13:11-14

The book of Hebrews was also written to a body of Jewish believers who belonged to the generation that was guilty of the unpardonable sin. These believers were undergoing tremendous persecution and were se-riously considering returning to Judaism. They thought they could return temporarily, until the wave of persecution had subsided, and then be "saved" all over again, erasing the sin of their previous apostasy. The author of Hebrews wrote to warn them that they had two options, but this was not one of them. They had been saved to the uttermost. The work of the Messiah was finished and complete. He could not be re-crucified. Therefore, they could not forfeit their salvation and then be saved again later.

The first option was to return to Rabbinic Judaism, but this option would only place them back under the judgment of A.D. 70, when they would die a terrible physical death. The five judgment passages in Hebrews often used to teach that salvation can be lost are actually dealing with physical, not spiritual, judgment and destruction. Not once does the author of Hebrews threaten his readers with the possibility of losing their salvation. He does, however, warn them that they would lose their rewards in the next life if they returned to Judaism. The warning pertains to losing spiritual rewards, not spiritual salvation.

The second option was the only valid one. They must press on to spiritual maturity and break from Rabbinic Judaism once and for all. For Jewish believers, water baptism confirmed the break and would save the readers of Hebrews physically from the A.D. 70 judgment, because it would remove them from the community they lived in. So while they lacked the option they thought they had, they had two alternatives and were encouraged to choose pressing on to spiritual maturity rather than returning to Rabbinic Judaism.

From the book of Hebrews, the readers' response is unknown. By combining material from three other ancient writers, however, what happened can be approximately surmised. The first writer is the historian Josephus, who, while not a believer in the Messiah, was an eyewitness of the events of A.D. 70. The second writer is Hegesippus, a Jewish believer who lived in the second century. He wrote a seven-volume work on church history which is now lost; however, much of his work is quoted by Eusebius. Third is Eusebius, a Gentile-Christian writer from the fourth century. These three authors reported different aspects of the events surrounding the judgment of A.D. 70, but much can be inferred from a composite view of their writing. Upon reading the letter to the Hebrews, apparently the believers obeyed and completed their separation. When the first Jewish revolt against Rome broke out in the year A.D. 66, the entire messianic community in Jerusalem, numbering over twenty thousand believers, crossed the Jordan River and escaped to Pella, one of the ten cities of the Decapolis located south of the Sea of Galilee, but on the east side of the Jordan, and thus outside the war zone. Other Messianic Jews from Judea, Galilee, and the Golan Heights joined the Jewish believers from Jerusalem. By the war's end in A.D. 70, a total of 1,100,000 Jews were killed and 97,000 were taken into slavery. However, according to records available at the present time, not a single Jewish believer died in the revolt. Ultimately, those who were vacillating apparently heeded the warnings of the letter to the Hebrews.

[§ 201] — D. The Third Sign of Jonah

1. Zechariah 4:1-14

Twice Israel has received and rejected the promised sign of Jonah. However, she will receive the sign once more, and this time the people will accept it. The third sign of Jonah originates in this passage from the book of Zechariah.

Zechariah the prophet saw a vision, parts of which he understood because of previous revelation; but there was one key element he did not understand (Zech. 4:1-10). He saw a seven-branched lampstand, a menorah, standing in the Temple. Over the menorah was a bowl, and on each side of the bowl stood an olive tree. From each olive tree, a pipe emptied oil into the bowl. From the bowl, seven smaller ducts fed oil to each of the seven lamps, totaling 49 ducts.

Zechariah's vision showed Israel as a saved nation, filled with the Holy Spirit, and fulfilling its original calling to be the light to the Gentiles. The olive oil is the single unifying element of the whole vision. It is in the trees, which are its sources, as well as the two pipes, the bowl, the 49 ducts, and the seven lamps. Oil is a common symbol of the Holy Spirit, and this passage identifies it as such: *Not by might, nor by power, but by my Spirit, said Jehovah of hosts* (Zech. 4:6). The two olive trees are the source of the oil, or of the Spirit.

Zechariah understood most of this vision, but the olive trees, the source of the oil, were new to him. He questioned what they represented and received a rather cryptic answer: *These are the two anointed ones, that stand by the Lord of the whole earth* (Zech. 4:14). How much he understood from this is not known; by their own admission, the prophets did not always understand the visions they saw. The Scriptures eventually revealed the meaning of the angel's cryptic answer in Revelation 11:3-13.

THE THIRD SIGN OF JONAH

WITNESS · SINGLE PIPE · WITNESS

SEVEN SMALLER PIPES
FEEDING EVERY SINGLE LIGHT
(ALTOGETHER 49 SMALL PIPES)

By Jesse and Josh Gonzales

2. Revelation 11:3-13

The cryptic answer to Zechariah's vision is explained in the account of the two prophets in the book of Revelation. These prophets, or witnesses, as they are called, will have a specialized and localized ministry in the city of Jerusalem during the tribulation (Rev. 11:3-13). The speaker here is God, who identified the two witnesses as *the two olive trees* (Rev. 11:4). Note that He used a definite article. These were specific trees, *the* two olive trees. Olive trees are not mentioned in the first ten chapters of Revelation nor do the Hebrew Scriptures ever mention *two* olive trees outside of Zechariah. Hence, the two olive trees of Zechariah are the same as the two witnesses of Revelation.

How then are they the source of this oil, the source of the Spirit to Israel? After three-and-a-half years of ministry, during the first half of the tribulation, the witnesses will be killed (Rev. 11:7). Their bodies will lie exposed and unburied in the streets of Jerusalem for three-and-a-half days (Rev. 11:8-9). Everyone will celebrate their death by throwing parties and exchanging gifts (Rev. 11:10). After three-and-a-half days, however, in plain view of everyone, God will resurrect the witnesses and take them up into heaven (Rev. 11:11-12). The resurrection and ascension of the two witnesses will lead to several results: An earthquake will strike Jerusalem, destroying one-tenth of the city; seven thousand people will be killed; and *the rest were affrighted, and gave glory to God of heaven* (Rev. 11:13). The resurrection and ascension of the two witnesses will lead to the salvation of the Jews of Jerusalem in the middle of the tribulation, initiating the process for all of Israel to be saved three-and-a-half years later, in the last three days of the tribulation (Hos. 5:15-6:3). The prerequisite for the second coming is Israel's national salvation (Deut. 30:1-10; Jer. 3:11-18; Hos. 5:15; Zech. 12:10-13:1; Mt. 23:37-39, et. al). When the whole nation is saved, it will plead for Messiah's return (Is. 64; Ps. 79; 80); He will then return and set up His kingdom.

Israel rejected the first and second signs of Jonah. However, Israel will accept the third sign of Jonah, the resurrection of the two witnesses, resulting in her national salvation, the second coming, and the establishment of the messianic kingdom. Finally, the Messiah will bring to Israel the peace she has sought for so long.

CHARTS

A. 24-hour Timeline

Time	Description of Event
Sundown, Thursday	Passover Seder
After dinner	Yeshua's prayer in Gethsemane
Before midnight	Yeshua's arrest
	1st stage of religious trial before Annas
	1st mistreatment of Yeshua
	2nd stage of rel. trial before Caiaphas/Sanhedrin
Midnight (first cock crow)	Peter's 1st denial
Before 3 a.m.	2nd and 3rd mistreatments of Yeshua
	1st mockery of Yeshua
2 a.m. ("a little while" after 1st denial, Lk. 22:58; one hour before 3rd denial, Lk. 22:59)	Peter's 2nd denial
3 a.m. (second cock crow)	Peter's 3rd denial; 2nd stage of religious trial ends
Dawn	3rd stage of religious trial: Yeshua condemned to death for blasphemy by religious leaders; sending Him off to be tried before a civil court
	Judas commits suicide

Early morning hours (Jn. 18:28)	1st stage of civil trial before Pilate in the Praetorium
	1st declaration of innocence
	Pilate tries to set Yeshua free and fails, so Yeshua is led before Herod Antipas
	2nd stage of civil trial before Herod Antipas
	2nd mockery of Yeshua
	2nd declaration of innocence, so Yeshua is led back to Pilate, who again tries to set Him free
	3rd stage of civil trial before Pilate
	Temporary interruption of trial by Pilate's wife
	Religious leaders use interruption to persuade the masses to ask for Yeshua's execution (Mt. 27:20)
	Pilate again tries to set Yeshua free after flogging Him (4th mistreatment of Yeshua)
	3rd mockery
	3rd declaration of innocence
	New charge: instead of sedition, blasphemy
	Pilate again tries to release Yeshua
	4th declaration of innocence
	Crowd threatens to report Pilate to Rome
	Pilate leaves his palace, sits down on the bema, tries again to release Yeshua
	5th declaration of innocence
	Pilate finally sentences Yeshua to death
	4th mockery
	5th mistreatment
9 a.m.	Crucifixion (for stages, see p. 171)
	5th to 8th mockeries
12 p.m.	Darkness covers the whole land
3 p.m.	Yeshua gives up His spirit
Before sundown Friday	Removal from cross and burial

B. The Stages of the Trial

Major Event	Stage #	Description of Stage
Procession to Calvary	1	The Messiah Bears the Cross
	2	Simon of Cyrene Forced to Help
	3	The Lament over Jerusalem
	4	The Arrival at Golgotha
	5	Wine Mingled with Gall and Myrrh
The Wrath of Men	6	The Crucifixion
	7	The First Statement from the Cross
	8	The Parting of Yeshua's Garments
	9	The Superscription
	10	The Crucifixion of the Other Two
	11	The 5th Mockery
	12	The 6th Mockery
	13	The 7th Mockery
	14	The 8th Mockery
	15	The Conversion of One of the Malefactors
	16	The 2nd Statement from the Cross
	17	The 3rd Statement from the Cross
The Wrath of God	18	The Darkness over the Whole Land
	19	The 4th Statement from the Cross
	20	The Reaction of the Bystanders
	21	The 5th Statement from the Cross
	22	The Drinking of the Vinegar
	23	The 6th Statement from the Cross
	24	The 7th Statement from the Cross
	25	The Death of Yeshua
The Accompanying Signs	26	Accompanying Signs
The Burial	27	The Breaking of the Bones and the Piercing
	28	The Request for the Body
	29	The Removal of the Body
	30	The Burial of Yeshua
The Sealing of the Tomb	31	The Preparation for the Embalming
	32	The Sealing of the Tomb

C. The Trials

Religious Jewish Trial	Civil Roman Trial
1st Stage (§ 166)	**1st Stage (§ 172)**
Trial before Annas: Jn. 18:12-14, 19-23	**First trial before Pilate:** Mt. 27:2; Mk. 15:1b-5; Lk. 23:1-5; Jn. 18:28-38
Goal: Establish religious charges	**Goal:** Establish a case punishable by execution; try Yeshua for sedition
Outcome: Lack of organization resulted in no witnesses, no verdict	**Outcome:** Declaration of innocence
2nd Stage (§167)	**2nd Stage (§173)**
Trial before Caiaphas and Sanhedrin: Mt. 26:57, 59-68; Mk. 14:53, 56-55; Lk. 22:54a; Jn. 18:24	**Trial before Herod Antipas:** Lk. 23:6-12
Goal: Prove disrespect towards Temple; establish charge of blasphemy	**Goal:** Establish charge of sedition against Rome. Being a Galilean, Yeshua was sent to Herod Antipas who had jurisdiction over Galilee
Outcome: Witnesses' testimony did not agree; no verdict was reached	**Outcome:** Declaration of innocence
3rd Stage (§170)	**3rd Stage (§174)**
The Condemnation: Mt. 27:1; Mk. 15:1a; Lk. 22:66-71	**Second Trial before Pilate:** Mt. 27:15-26; Mk. 15:6-15; Lk. 23:13-25; Jn. 18:39-19:16
Goal: Give a sense of legality to the trial; prove the charge of blasphemy	**Goal:** Set Yeshua free. Jewish leaders then come up with charge of blasphemy
Outcome: Official condemnation for blasphemy	**Outcome:** Declaration of innocence
Verdict: Guilty, sentenced to death	**Verdict:** Innocent, yet sentenced to death
Consequence: Because Sanhedrin had no authority to execute, they had to take the case to Rome	**Consequence:** Crucifixion

D. Five Mistreatments

#	Timing	Verses	Mistreatement	Inflicted by
1	1st stage of religious trial	Jn. 18:22	Stuck in the face	Religious leaders
2	2nd stage of religious trial	Mt. 26:67; Mk. 14:65	Punched, slapped, spat upon	Religious leaders
3	2nd stage of religious trial	Lk. 22:63	Beaten	Religious leaders
4	3rd stage of civil trial	Mk. 15:15; Jn. 19:1	Flogged	Roman soldiers
5	3rd stage of civil trial	Mt. 27:29-30; Mk. 15:17, 19; Jn. 19:2-3	Thorns pressed on head; hit; spat upon; head struck with reed	Roman soldiers

E. Eight Mockeries

#	Timing	Verses	Mockers
1	2nd stage of religious trial	Lk. 22:63-65	Religious leaders
2	2nd stage of civil trial	Lk. 23:11	Herod Antipas and soldiers
3	3rd stage of civil trial	Jn. 19:2-3	Roman soldiers
4	3rd stage of civil trial	Mk. 15:17	Roman soldiers
5	During crucifixion	Mk. 15:29-30	Passersby
6	During crucifixion	Mk. 15:31-32	Jewish leaders
7	During crucifixion	Lk. 23:36-37	Roman soldiers
8	During crucifixion	Mt. 27:44	Two men crucified with Yeshua

F. Herod's Temple

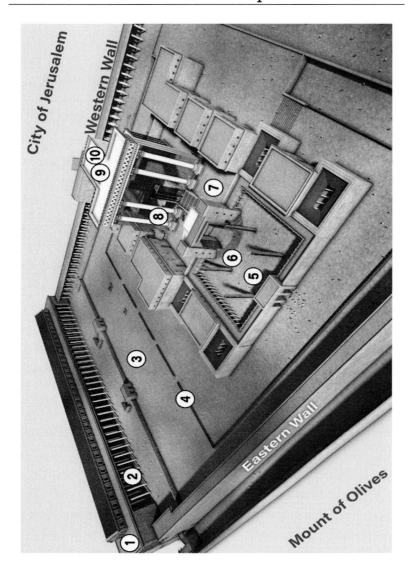

1. The pinnacle of the Temple (temptation of Yeshua); 2. the Royal Stoa (Temple market, Sanhedrin meeting place); 3. the Court of the Gentiles; 4. the Dividing Wall of Partition (only Jews permitted beyond this point); 5. the Women's Court; 6. the Levitical Choir at steps of Nicanor Door; 6. the Sanctuary Portico; 7. the Holy Place; 8. the Holy of Holies (by Jesse and Josh Gonzales).

SCRIPTURE INDEX

Numbers

Leviticus

Deuteronomy

I Samuel

I Kings

II Kings

I Chronicles

II Chronicles

Lamentations

Ezekiel

Daniel

Hosea

Joel

Mark

Luke

John

Acts

Romans

I Corinthians

II Corinthians

Galatians

Ephesians

Philippians

Colossians

Revelation